CONVERSATIONS WITH THE GREAT MOVIEMAKERS OF HOLLYWOOD'S GOLDEN AGE

CONVERSATIONS

with the GREAT
MOVIEMAKERS
of HOLLYWOOD'S
GOLDEN AGE

at the American Film Institute

Edited and with an Introduction by

George Stevens, Jr.

ALFRED A. KNOPF   NEW YORK   2006

This is a Borzoi Book
Published by Alfred A. Knopf

Library of Congress Cataloging-in-Publication Data
Conversations with the Great Moviemakers of Hollywood's Golden
Age at the American Film Institute / edited and with an
introduction by George Stevens, Jr.
p. cm.
Includes index.
ISBN 1-4000-4054-X (alk. paper)
1. Motion picture producers and directors—United States—Interviews.
2. Motion pictures—Production and direction.   I. Stevens, Jr., George,
1932–   II. American Film Institute.

PN1998.2A45 2005
791.4302'3'0922—dc22   2005044061

Manufactured in the United States of America
First Edition

To my mother

Yvonne Stevens at the
Mack Sennett Studio, 1924.

She lived Hollywood's Golden Age
As the daughter of a silent film star,
As a Mack Sennett Bathing Beauty,
As the wife and confidante of a film director,
As an inspiration to her son.
A petite beauty with Irish wit, she celebrated
her 100th birthday in Hollywood on July 31, 2005.

Contents

Introduction

This book contains the ideas and wisdom of many of the great filmmakers of what is often called the *Golden Age*—those adventurous years when a new art was flowering and when filmmakers were innovators creating from original impulses. Throughout history, art forms evolved slowly over one or two civilizations, but motion pictures grew from a crude photographic device to maturity in only a few decades. There were no models and imitation did not yet prevail.

The one thing the ideas in this book have in common is that they were discussed in seminars with young filmmakers at the American Film Institute. They are the ideas of many of cinema's most accomplished creators, and represent a summing up in which men look back over long careers—passing on knowledge gained from decades of practical experience. It is unlikely that there will ever be a comparable era in which so many films of lasting value will be produced—films that if you happen upon them late at night on television and decide to watch just a few minutes, you are drawn to stay to the final fade-out.

These films were made during the relatively short period in cinema history when the only way to see a motion picture was to gather in groups in a darkened theater to watch larger-than-life images. The movies existed *only* as a shared experience. Beginning in the 1950s people started watching films on small television screens by themselves, or with one or two others, and later video and DVDs increased private viewing. The filmmakers of the Golden Age worked for a large and vibrant communal audience that no longer exists. David Thompson, in his book *The Full Equation,* reminds us that they were making five hundred films a year, as opposed to two hundred today—"when so few films hold or entertain the 'whole' audience, let alone speak for the nation."

In his foreword to *What Is Cinema?*, Jean Renoir wrote, "Civilization is but a sieve through the holes of which there passes the discard—the good remains." The filmmakers in this volume are responsible for much of that good—the relative handful of fine films that remain popular from among the many thousands made during the twentieth century.

The first class gathered at AFI's Center for Advanced Film Studies in September of 1969. Most of the pioneers who had created the classics of American film were still alive. I grew up in Hollywood, so I knew most of the people in this book and was able to enlist them to meet with the fellows who were at AFI to study before embarking on a career.

THE ROOTS

The roots of this book and of the AFI itself go back to an occasion in 1961 that changed my life. I was twenty-nine years old and living in Hollywood, working as a television director and collaborating with my father on the preparation of *The Greatest Story Ever Told*. President Kennedy had been elected a year earlier and had asked Edward R. Murrow to come to Washington to head the United States Information Agency, the organization dedicated to telling America's story overseas. Murrow announced a visit to Los Angeles to meet with motion picture leaders at a Saturday night dinner at Chasen's, one of the film community's favorite restaurants. Invitations were prized as a symbol of who counted among the mighty of the movie world.

A few of us young turks knew we had no chance of making the cut at Chasen's, but we believed we were more in tune with the New Frontier that Kennedy had spoken of in his inaugural address than were most of the old guard who would assemble at Chasen's. So we sent a telegram to Murrow suggesting that he might be interested in hearing the ideas of some of the younger people in Hollywood. A Friday afternoon meeting was added to his schedule, and we reserved a room at the offices of the Screen Directors Guild.

It turned out to be the afternoon of the terrible Bel Air fire, when many houses burnt to the ground and one of our group, Samuel Goldwyn, Jr., missed the meeting because he was standing on his roof with a hose. But Richard Zanuck, Paul Newman, Gore Vidal, and screenwriters Stewart Stern, Leslie Stevens and Ivan Moffat were among those at the Guild that day. With JFK's call to "Ask not . . ." still ringing in our ears, we were anxious to find out what we could do for our country.

Murrow, in a chalk-striped Savile Row suit, chain-smoked and offered fascinating insights into the inner workings of the Kennedy government. People who toil in the world of make-believe, even young turks, are impressed by people who grapple with the real world. Americans had heard Murrow's voice reporting on the German air attacks on England during World War II, with his famous signature "This . . . is London." During the 1950s he was the conscience of television news at CBS, a role demonstrated most dramatically by his brave and fatal dissection of Joseph McCarthy when the junior senator from Wisconsin had the nation cowed by his smearing of citizens he accused of being communists. Murrow was relaxed and seemed genuinely pleased with our ideas and our willingness to help. At six o'clock sharp he said good-bye and rode off in a black limousine.

Early the next morning I got a call at my house in the Hollywood Hills. It was Sam Goldwyn, Jr., who was happy to have saved his home. "Ed Murrow," he said, "wonders if you could come by and spend an hour with him tomorrow." I was surprised and asked Sam if he knew why Murrow wanted to see me. "Ed's looking for someone to run the motion picture division of USIA." I caught my breath and thought for a moment. I said, "I'm afraid it's not possible." I explained that I had worked as my father's associate producer and directed the location scenes on *The Diary of Anne Frank* and now I was busy as his partner on *The Greatest Story Ever Told.* "I couldn't just walk away," I said. "I would love to spend an hour with Ed Murrow, but it wouldn't be fair to waste his time." Sam said he understood, and signed off. Ten minutes later he called back. "Ed says you won't be wasting his time. He's staying at my father's house. Come by at two tomorrow afternoon?"

I wound my way past the grand houses of Beverly Hills on a sunny California Sunday and into Samuel Goldwyn's curling driveway. As I approached the house I saw the famous Sunday croquet game in progress on the lawn, with the likes of Goldwyn, Mike Romanoff, Jean Negulesco and Louis Jourdan.

Murrow and I talked for two hours. I remember asking him what he thought of President Kennedy, his taking a long drag on a Camel and saying, "He's a very impressive young man." As a twenty-nine-year-old, I found it bizarre to hear the president of the United States referred to as a young man. Murrow, who appeared somewhat stern and forbidding on television, was warm and easy to talk with, displaying a wry and sometimes sardonic sense of humor. He listened to my ideas of how motion pictures and filmmakers might contribute to the New Frontier and then, suddenly, offered me the

USIA job. The way he put it was, "Wouldn't you like to come to Washington? I think you could make a difference." I told him that, sadly for me, it wasn't possible and offered the explanation I had given Sam. We parted with Murrow saying, "If anything changes, you know where to find me."

Two days later I was with my father at Twentieth Century Fox and Murrow's name came up. I told him about the meeting. He looked at me and said quietly, "You have to do it."

It was an act of generosity and paternal understanding that touches me to this day. Generosity because making *The Greatest Story Ever Told* was to be a backbreaking endeavor that my collaboration would have eased, and understanding because Dad recognized the importance of this opportunity—a chance for his son to see a new world and to make his own mark.

That meeting with Murrow took me to Washington, D.C., and to an exhilarating opportunity for service during what many Americans believe was the most exciting time ever to be in government. The job instilled in me an understanding of the value of public service and public institutions, and provided me a chance to run a large division of a government agency, producing and distributing overseas three hundred documentary films a year. And it led me to believe that motion pictures had a larger and different role to play on the national scene.

So when the National Endowment for the Arts, the nation's first federal institution to support the arts, was proposed in Congress two years later, I was on hand with a point of view on how film should be supported. In the film-crazed world of today, where even minor directors are celebrities, it's hard to comprehend how different the landscape was in the early 1960s. Films were considered by the elites to be an avenue of middle-class escape, a lower form of entertainment than theater, ballet and opera. Movie stars' names were household words, but few Americans knew the names of directors, with the possible exception of Cecil B. DeMille and Alfred Hitchcock, who were public personalities because they appeared on television. Most young people with a creative itch still wanted to write the great American novel; relatively few had their eyes on filmmaking.

The legislation introduced to create the National Endowment listed theater, painting, dance, music and literature, and proposed financial support for symphony orchestras, dance companies, painters and poets. Motion pictures, arguably the most dynamic and American of all the arts, was not mentioned. From my perch at USIA, I wrote to Senator Hubert Humphrey, a driving force behind the arts legislation, and made the case for including film. He responded positively, and the next draft of the bill included motion pictures. It seems the garment industry felt left out too, because fashion design was also added.

At USIA we had considerable success making documentaries by enlisting filmmakers who had never worked for the government, young directors such as Charles Guggenheim, James Blue, Ed Emshwiller, Bruce Herschensohn, William Greaves and Carroll Ballard, and veteran documentarians Leo Seltzer and Willard Van Dyke. The historian Arthur Schlesinger, Jr., observed, "There have not been so many striking films stimulated in Washington since the days of Pare Lorentz and the Department of Agriculture's film program a generation ago." Murrow built support for USIA by showing our films to opinion makers at the Motion Picture Association screening room across Lafayette Square from the White House, where they earned a cachet in the capital. *Nine from Little Rock,* our film about the first black students who entered Little Rock High School, was honored with an Academy Award, and Murrow, a man who shared credit easily, nominated me for the showcase for young Americans—the Ten Outstanding Young Men in the United States—and I was selected. Under Ed Murrow's wing I had gained a reputation of my own.

I was named to a committee to advise the National Council on the Arts, the governing board of the new Endowment, on how it might support film. The committee included the architect William Pereira, Gregory Peck and my father, who had been appointed to the Arts Council by President Johnson. The Stanford Research Institute was commissioned to conduct a planning survey, which provided a sufficient basis for the committee to recommend that an American Film Institute be created to foster the film arts, and that I be its founding director.

Lyndon Johnson signed the National Foundation on the Arts and Humanities Act into law in the White House Rose Garden on September 29, 1965, before a gathering that included members of Congress and the Arts Council, as well as leaders of arts constituencies from around the United States. I was there and was as surprised as the others present when Johnson said, "We will create an American Film Institute, bringing together leading artists of the film industry, outstanding educators, and young men and women who wish to pursue the twentieth century's art form as their life's work." What had been an idea under consideration suddenly had the mandate of a presidential declaration—words we would repeat through the years to shore up the validity of the sometimes teetering AFI.

George Stevens, Jr., right, with his boss at the USIA, Edward R. Murrow,
at the ceremony for the Ten Outstanding Young Men in Government,
Washington, D.C., 1963. At left is Secretary of Interior Stewart Udall.

I began then, while still at USIA, working with the chairman of the
National Endowment, Roger L. Stevens, to organize funding for the new
institute. Roger had been a tasteful and successful theatrical producer and a
bold businessman, famous for buying the Empire State Building within the
space of a few hours one afternoon. He had moved to public service and
became an enduring ally of mine. The NEA pledged $1.3 million on the con-
dition it be matched three times. Roger and I secured $1.3 million from the
Ford Foundation, an amount specifically tied to the conservatory for young
filmmakers we were planning. Jack Valenti, new in the job as head of the
Motion Picture Association of America, corralled the seven motion picture
studios to pledge another $1.3 million, and we promised to raise the last quar-
ter from foundations, corporations and individuals.

So, on June 6, 1967, at a press conference in Washington, Gregory Peck,
as chairman, and I, as the founding director, announced the creation of the
American Film Institute.

THE AMERICAN FILM INSTITUTE

A primary goal of the AFI was training young filmmakers, but its cornerstone was film preservation. When I was at USIA, I headed the American delegation to the 1963 Cannes Film Festival and was sought out by a man named Henri Langlois. Langlois was the pioneer who recognized that the precious legacy of motion pictures was rapidly disappearing through deterioration and neglect. He had founded the Cinémathèque Française, where he salvaged a collection of the world's great films. Langlois, a portly bohemian figure with wild hair and unpressed suits, and I met in the elegant bar on the terrace of the Carlton Hotel, where he railed passionately about America's neglect of its film heritage, then decaying in warehouses uncared for by the studios that owned the negatives. That was my awakening to the painful fact that all motion pictures made before 1950 were on nitrate-based film stock, which

Founding Trustees of the American Film Institute at the first board meeting in Washington, D.C., August 5, 1967. Seated, foreground, George Stevens, Jr., Charles Ruttenberg. Seated left to right, Gregory Peck, Daniel Taradash, Jack Valenti, Sidney Poitier, Arthur Knight, John Hall, Arnold Picker, Sherrill Corwin. Standing, Rev. John Culkin, Charles Benton, David Mallery, Bruce Herschensohn, Francis Ford Coppola, Richard Leacock, William L. Pereira, George Seaton, Arthur Schlesinger, Jr.

tends to turn to powder over time. Moreover, the nitrate content caused some reels to combust spontaneously in their vaults, incinerating other negatives stored nearby. The 1965 Stanford study reported that at least half the films made in the United States since the beginning of the century were either lost, destroyed or in advanced stages of deterioration.

Our first AFI initiative was to launch a film rescue program with the Museum of Modern Art, George Eastman House and the Library of Congress. Alan Dwan, a great director of the silent era who started his career two years after D. W. Griffith and made more than four hundred films, including *Robin Hood, Stage Struck* and *The Sands of Iwo Jima,* wrote me a letter that gave poignant insight into the problem. Dwan said that he had kept none of his films or scripts: "It never occurred to me that my work would be of interest to a later generation."

Years earlier the seed had been planted in me to become a "test of time" person. I began to appreciate films not just for the pleasure of a first viewing, but also for what their worth would be in the future. This awakening came in 1952, when as a college student I went to the Academy Awards with my father, my mother and my father's mother, Georgie Cooper Stevens, who had been a leading lady in the theater and later a film actress. It was the year of *A Place in the Sun,* my father's film based on Theodore Dreiser's *An American Tragedy* that starred Elizabeth Taylor and Montgomery Clift. I sat next to my father and watched him go to the stage to receive the Oscar for Best Director. On the way home he was driving the car with my mother and grandmother in the backseat. The Oscar was on the seat between my father and me. I guess I was excited, maybe too excited in his eyes. I remember him looking over at me with a thoughtful smile and saying, "We'll have a better idea what kind of a film this is in about twenty-five years." It was a stunning comment; cinémathèques and directors' retrospectives did not exist then, and it was two decades before home video. In those days, Hollywood films had a first run in theaters followed by a second run on double bills in smaller houses, and then were forgotten. On rare occasions a great hit like *Gone With the Wind* was rereleased. It was a very different film culture from today's.

That was the night the idea of the "test of time" took hold in me. It would be the watchword and guiding light for so much of what we undertook at AFI.

We opened the Center for Advanced Film Studies in Beverly Hills, California, in 1969. I saw it as a place for young filmmakers to learn the craft of screen storytelling, with the great filmmakers playing a tutorial role. The setting was bizarre: the city of Beverly Hills leased Greystone, the once lavish

Doheny estate, to the AFI for a dollar a year. It had been built by the oil tycoon E. L. Doheny, who had bought up much of Los Angeles in the 1920s, before he ran into trouble in the Teapot Dome scandal that plagued President Harding's administration. On September 23, we welcomed eighteen fellows who had been carefully chosen to study and make short films at AFI. I set one criterion as a priority for admission—we were less interested in what prospective fellows knew about the mechanics of filmmaking than what ideas and imagination they would bring to the film medium. Terrence Malick was a Rhodes Scholar who was teaching philosophy at MIT; Tom Rickman was a hard-living storyteller from Paducah, Kentucky; Paul Schrader was a prickly Calvinist scholar from the Midwest who was obsessed with Japanese films; David Lynch was an art student from Philadelphia who would spend his years at AFI making *Eraserhead* in the stables that Mr. Doheny's horses used to call home. Others had graduated from film schools at Columbia University, NYU, USC and UCLA.

They came together that first day and met in the afternoon with Elia Kazan and that evening with Harold Lloyd. This was the beginning of what later would be named the Harold Lloyd Master Seminar Series, which continues in much the same form thirty-six years later. It is a selection of these seminars that make up this book.

THE FILMMAKERS

The men in this book rank among the best of the Golden Age; there are no women. From AFI's earliest days, we set out to redress the gender imbalance in filmmaking, starting in 1974 with the Directing Workshop for Women. However, except for Dorothy Arzner and later Ida Lupino, women directors were sorely absent in the early days.

There are twenty-five directors, two writers, one producer and four cameramen featured in this book. Twenty of the directors are Americans who made most of their films in the United States, the exceptions being David Lean, Jean Renoir, Ingmar Bergman, Federico Fellini and Satyajit Ray. Of the twenty Americans—including Hitchcock, who never took American citizenship but lived and worked here for forty years—nine were born in Europe and immigrated to the United States. The extraordinary influence of European immigrants on American culture is vividly demonstrated in our movies. Men in this book like William Wyler, Frank Capra, Rouben Mamoulian, Fritz Lang, Billy Wilder and Fred Zinnemann, and others not included, like Ernst Lubitsch, found their voices in their adopted country and adopted language.

The reader will discover common themes and ideas that link the twenty-five directors: foremost is the universal quest to control their work. They say it in different ways, but each one believes that a single point of view is at the heart of great films. And without exception they talk about the importance of planning, structure and craft. Billy Wilder put it this way: "We have to put those pillars in, otherwise that beautiful ceiling is going to come crashing down." Fellini told the students, "Making a movie is a mathematical operation. It is like sending a missile to the moon."

I admire these directors for the films they made and for their ability to sustain careers over as many as six decades. I have special affection and respect for the ones I knew well—for the kind of men they were. I sense that we will not see their like again. William Wyler, John Huston and my father were far beyond draft age when World War II came along, yet they chose to give up brilliant careers in the prime of their lives for combat assignments in the armed forces. I saved two documents from the time that illustrate the sacrifice involved: a letter from Harry Cohn to the accounting department at Columbia Pictures instructing them to discontinue my father's $3,000 weekly salary and to keep his office suite vacant for his return; and my father's U.S. Army pay card stating his salary and benefits as an army major of $250 a month. My father would not return to that office suite at Columbia, but when he and the others came back from the war they made films of a depth and maturity they would not likely have achieved were it not for their experiences in Europe and the Pacific. These three and Fred Zinnemann, King Vidor, Frank Capra, David Lean and Alfred Hitchcock were men whose humor, dignity, style and good manners I saw firsthand. Look at the glistening black-and-white photographs of them on the set and you see they had the charisma of leading men. Each one was tough when it came to dealing with intrusions from producers or studio heads, but none felt the need to swagger or *act* tough. I remember them all as men of considerable grace.

The nature of film production meant that to one degree or another they were businessmen, required to mobilize and lead large numbers of people and to accept responsibility for great sums of money. This meant they must at once be both poet and general—the dichotomy that still today challenges men and women who want to excel as film directors.

Filmmaking is a collaborative endeavor—the greatest directors depend on the contributions of many. Today the role of some directors is exaggerated, particularly with the ubiquitous and annoying credit "a film by," which appears even on undistinguished films of novice directors. Nonetheless, I believe that with rare exceptions the great films are realized with the benefit of one guiding hand and a single point of view. This does not minimize the contributions of the many collaborators who are vital to a fine film. It simply recognizes that there is one person who is up at dawn worrying about the coming day's work, who spends the day making a couple of hundred decisions large and small, and who goes to sleep late reflecting back on the day's work, trying to keep the whole picture in his or her head. It is the director who normally invests time in shaping the screenplay, if not writing it, and spends months in the editing room weaving the film together and polishing it into final form. Are there directors who do less? Of course. But the directors in this book were almost always there at the very beginning of the process and there at the end.

At the AFI conservatory we stressed the importance of collaboration. This led us to invite producers, screenwriters, cinematographers and representatives of the other crafts to engage in seminars and tutorials with the AFI fellows. While the directors are the core of this book, I felt it important to recognize the significance of collaboration and have included seminars with Hal Wallis, perhaps the most prolific of Hollywood producers; two accomplished writers, Ernest Lehman and Ray Bradbury; and four cameramen who among them earned thirty-seven Academy Award nominations.

I rarely heard the individuals in this book refer to themselves as artists. I attribute that to the rough-and-ready atmosphere in which they operated, as well as to a certain kind of modest self-assurance. My father and I worked with Carl Sandburg, the poet and historian, in the early 1960s, and I remember him watching a new young director being interviewed on television who repeatedly referred to "my art" and to himself as an artist. Sandburg growled, "Artist is a *praise* word. You let *others* call you an artist." Kevin Brownlow, in his definitive biography of David Lean, quotes from a letter Lean sent to the playwright and screenwriter Robert Bolt. "I'm not at all sure what an artist is," Lean wrote. "I've thought about it quite a lot since your letter. I feel rather hot if someone calls me an artist. I am somewhere on the fringe and have a real feeling for things artistic—but an artist? Pasternak; of course. Chaplin; ditto. Bob Hope? Where does one draw the line?"

In writing about these men I realized that all had long careers and reached great heights, but none, with the possible exception of Ingmar Bergman, ended his career on top. Billy Wilder, who had difficulties at the box office late in his career, said, "It happens to ballplayers, film directors, even to vineyards. When you want a home run too badly you press and strike out." I believe the huge cost of motion pictures, and the consequent need for great success at the box office, placed enormous pressure on these men year in and year out—and too often their later pictures failed financially, giving a sad turn to their creative lives. Orson Welles, himself a victim of a declining career, argued that film directors should be doing their best work in their later years, citing Toscanini and Stravinsky, who did some of their finest conducting in their eighties. David Lean, at eighty-three, told his doctor that he wanted to continue making movies because he was just beginning to get the hang of it.

One reason I so admire these men is that it takes bravery and great self-confidence to set out to spend millions of dollars of investors' money and a year or two or three of your own life making a movie—often in the face of corrosive skepticism, even on the part of your backers. It brings to mind two films that were never made that might well have become classics. Fred Zinnemann had finished all preparation for his film of André Malraux's *Man's Fate,* and was rehearsing with his cast on a soundstage in London, when a management change at MGM brought James Aubrey, known as "The Smiling Cobra," over from CBS to head the studio. Aubrey abruptly cancelled *Man's Fate* and attempted to make Zinnemann personally responsible for a million dollars in costs. David Lean spent years trying to mount Robert Bolt's screenplay of *Mutiny on the Bounty* and became the butt of jokes among Hollywood agents, who referred to him as "the old man and the sea." Aubrey, disparaging another Lean epic, declared, "I would rather make twenty *Easy Rider*s for what *Ryan's Daughter* cost." Of course, if Peter Fonda and Dennis Hopper had shown up in Aubrey's office with scruffy beards and dirty blue jeans seeking money for a biker/dope road picture called *Easy Rider,* he would have had the MGM police throw them out. It's an illustration of the mentality that has held forth at studios through the years—it's much easier to back a film that's modeled on a previous success than to strike out in new directions. These directors fought fiercely for their own instincts and intuitions throughout their careers and achieved a body of highly original work.

André Bazin, the French critic, wrote: "Man's primitive need, going back to Ancient Egypt, is to have the last word in the argument with death by means of the form that endures." It is remarkable how frequently these filmmakers won that argument. So many of their films live on in the hearts and minds of new generations, and represent a worthy fulfillment of remarkable lives. I hope their ideas about how motion pictures are made will add to their legacy and inspire the filmmakers of tomorrow.

CONVERSATIONS WITH THE GREAT MOVIEMAKERS OF HOLLYWOOD'S GOLDEN AGE

It sounds like bragging, but we didn't borrow from the bank. We kept a certain amount of money aside and financed our own pictures. In a way we gambled a little heavier than some people do at Las Vegas, but we always got away with it.

HAROLD LLOYD
(Born in Burchard, Nebraska, 1893—Died 1971)

Few screen images are more fondly remembered than the young man with horn-rimmed glasses desperately clinging to the hand of a clock high over Los Angeles. That young man was seventy-six years old the night he joined twenty aspiring filmmakers who had earlier seen a thirty-five-millimeter print of *Kid Brother* in the old library of the Doheny estate in Beverly Hills. For most of them this was their first look at Harold Lloyd, a comic genius whose screen triumphs four decades earlier had made him one of the world's most famous faces, an international star who produced his films and took responsibility for every detail. He never took director credit, but he was the guiding light of his comedies.

Lloyd owned his films and preserved them, but kept such a tight grip on them that he missed the opportunity for the kind of revivals enjoyed by his contemporary rivals, Charlie Chaplin and Buster Keaton. In fact, most filmgoers remember him only for the famous clock scene in *Safety Last!* because it is seen so often in film history compilations. But in the 1920s audiences crowded into theaters and howled at Lloyd's antics in *Grandma's Boy, Girl Shy, The Freshman, The Kid Brother* and *Speedy*—which were always accompanied by a live orchestra. I remember Lloyd insisting that a piano was all right for two-reelers, but you had to have a big orchestra for features.

He was slight at five foot nine, optimistic and genial. When he arrived at AFI he seemed more like someone's happy uncle than a man whose success had enabled him to build a forty-four-room house in Beverly Hills with a hundred-foot waterfall, a nine-hole golf course and a staff of sixteen full-time gardeners.

Lloyd gave the world thrills and laughs. His era was the magical time of grand movie palaces, huge audiences and shared laughter, and his legacy includes some of the finest comedies ever made. It's just as well that Lloyd, a perfectionist who died two years after his AFI seminar, didn't live to see the postage-stamp screens of the modern shopping mall.

I invited him to be AFI's first speaker because I felt it important to establish this series with a pioneer who went back to the roots of American film-making, a pioneer who understood the importance of AFI's goal of preserving our motion picture heritage. And it is fitting that the seminar series that he inaugurated continues today as the Harold Lloyd Master Seminars.

Lloyd's friend and colleague King Vidor joined the fellows in the questioning.

Harold Lloyd (wearing glasses) on location of *Welcome Danger* in 1928. The picture began production as a silent; then Lloyd decided to reshoot scenes adding sound. Walter Lundin, seated at camera, was Lloyd's first cameraman on most of his films.

HAROLD LLOYD

September 23, 1969

May I just say that being a guest here tonight, I feel highly honored being in on the initial shove-off, as it were, of the AFI Conservatory. Certainly I'm sure that everyone here, every guest you have, is rooting that it's going to go tremendous places. I'm happy to say that I have the honor also of being one of the original men on the Academy of Motion Picture Arts and Sciences, and to tell the truth, I don't believe it was as big as this when we started. I was on the original board that elected Doug Fairbanks, Sr., president, and it has gone quite a ways, so I'd say that if your institute here gathers momentum and keeps going, you may well outdistance the Academy Awards. I hope that takes place.

This picture that you've just seen, *Kid Brother,* well, we had a little problem with that one. It is what I call a "character comedy." I made two different types of pictures. I made what we call "gag pictures," for instance *Safety Last!,* where I climbed a building and hung on a clock. But *Kid Brother* is more what I call a character comedy because we start slow, we plant the character, we very carefully try and let it grow, letting the picture gain momentum as it goes on through to the end. I think we accomplished that. Now, where we took quite a chance with *Kid Brother* was in putting a fast-moving half-hour composite at the front of it with mostly comedy business and gags. After you've gone that length of time and then stop—and start a picture from scratch to build your character—you are taking quite a chance.

I used to hear stories about how adroit you and the cameramen were at slowing down right in the middle of a scene. Did you have the same cameraman with you all the time?

Yes, Walter Lundin. He was with me for years and years.

These were all done with hand-cranked cameras?

That's right.

I was amazed at the scene with the bus running through what seemed to be normal traffic. They must have had everything else on the street move at a snail's pace.

That was done right down here in the streets. I mean, we had our own traffic. We did that in New York, too. In fact there was a picture called *Speedy* where I had two horses pulling a horse cart down the thing, and we'd block off about three blocks. We looked like we had the whole police force there with us. We had our own traffic. It wasn't cheating. Of course, we had a terrible time on that one. One of our own cars got in the way of the horses, and to keep from running into the car, the man had to pull the horse and go down the subway. It didn't hurt the horse, I'm happy to say, but we never used him again. He was a little shy after that. But these scenes you saw here were shot with our own traffic and generally with the car in front or in back with the camera. The camera was taking every bit as much of a chance.

The bus was going very much faster than anything else?

We had that bus on a cantilever and the bus tipped itself, so as we'd go around the corner we'd tip it and over you'd go. One thing you had to watch was when you're hanging over the edge—which I was—that you didn't get your leg caught in between the tip. But we actually did all that stuff. You see, you can't slow your camera down too much because the pedestrians look jerky. In fact in the film they might be jerky, but we didn't want them to look that way.

What speeds did the cameras run at?

I'd say they were down around fourteen frames per second, except in some places they might drop it even more. As you were saying, the cameramen in those days had a certain technique and an ability to really keep that crank going. The majority of the audience think we cranked that way, they think we wanted it to go exceptionally fast, and they accept that as the way we made it. Of course, everyone here knows it's not true, but no matter how many times you tell people it was cranked at a much different speed, and that you had to get a much smaller number of frames through the camera than you do now and therefore it's got to go much faster, they don't hear you at all. As much as it's been repeated, I don't think the majority of people have any idea about speed. They don't care, really. I guess if they did care, your picture wouldn't be worth a damn. But the students here would know the difference.

Now, a picture that I was always afraid of was *Safety Last!* because I had several scenes in there and they moved pretty fast. But I put it in front of an audience, and it didn't seem to spoil the laughs any. I showed it recently to a group of high school students at Hollywood High and it went as well as it ever did with the crowd I first made it for. So why am I worrying about speed?

Do you think audiences today like the film because of the fast pace?

In some cases they might, and in other places, no. But I think if your comedy is basic enough and they're with you—they're laughing with you as well as at you—I really don't think it makes too much difference.

There's a thematic element in The Kid Brother, *and I'm curious about how it evolved and how you feel about it now.*

Basically the theme is "brains over brawn." In the film I have two older brothers who are behemoths, and I'm the puny little fellow, the boy who thinks and in the end outwits those people who just use their muscles. In a lot of the pictures—especially the character comedies—we tried to have some kind of hidden theme in there. I guess if you boil it down to "be yourself" that would be about the shortest you could make it.

But when it comes to the theme of a picture, we're supposed to be comics, and the audience came to get a chuckle or two. I'd go back to another picture we made that Hal Roach and I had a little contention on, and we were both right, in a way. Hal Roach and I made *Grandma's Boy* and we previewed it, and it kind of lay there, to a certain degree. The film had a fine theme in it, that of "mind over matter." The boy's a terrific coward and his grandmother recognizes that. To help him out she gives him a talisman that she says his grandfather had owned. His grandfather had been more cowardly than he, but with this talisman the boy just can't fail, and he becomes a great hero. Of course, at the end he finds out that the talisman was just a handle to her umbrella. He finally realized he'd accomplished these things himself. But we didn't put enough comedy in it, so the audience didn't laugh as much as they should have.

In the editing room with Harley M. "Beany" Walker, who wrote
titles for Lloyd's comedies.

Did you ever preview any of your pictures?

I think we were one of the very first, even back in the old one-reel days, to start previews. We used to go out here to Glendale. I can remember the old gentleman who was manager of the theater. His name was Howard and he would always put on tails to come out to explain to the audience what was going on, that this picture had never been shown before and that we expected to do a lot more work on it. He made it clear that the audience was the judge and so forth. After the preview of *Grandma's Boy* we went back and Hal said, "Harold, you're a comic, you've got to get laughs. Let's go back to work." So we went back and worked for months putting comedy-business gags all over the place. The second time we previewed it, it blossomed. It was fine and it's been fine ever since. In fact, the picture probably did as much for us as anything because it was the first feature picture we made. We didn't intend for it to be a feature—we started it as a two-reeler. In fact, our group—Hal and myself, our staff—we were thoroughly entrenched in making two-reel pictures and doing pretty well with them. But this had such a nice theme that it just kept growing, and we let it grow. It grew into a five-reel picture. When it came to getting more money for it, the exhibitors were a little loathe to pay us more than they had been paying us for two-reelers. They were perfectly happy with the two-reelers, so we couldn't go anyplace with this longer film. Eventually they offered us a little more, but not so much. So we went down to Broadway and we took a third-run house that was showing newsreels and we put the picture in there. They thought we were off our rocker, but the picture ran nineteen weeks. It established a tremendous record, and from then on we had no trouble.

We ran into the same thing on *Safety Last!* Sometimes you had to take the film to Chicago, which was tied up with various circuits: Lubliner and Trinz, Balaban and Katz, one or the other. We felt that we had something a little out of the ordinary with *Safety Last!* because it had the thrill in it that audiences were reacting to very strongly in those days. We could get nowhere with the circuits, so we took a house on Michigan Boulevard called Orchestral Hall and established a fine record there, and had no trouble with Lubliner and Trinz, and Balaban and Katz after that.

Are you planning to rerelease Grandma's Boy?

Here's the way I look at it. If I thought there was a demand with the public for the pictures, I would love to release a great many of them, but I feel very loathe to release them unless I feel they're really wanted and desired. What I mean by that is, even though I have stayed off the screen for many years and I think I'm quite well known with the nostalgia group, I'm known very little, if at all, with a great many cinemagoers. Now, what's the use of releasing pictures in the theaters if audiences don't know who they're going to see? The general public is different today. That's my situation, and it's the reason I took it to Hollywood High down here. Somebody presented the opportunity to me, and I went down there and found that this generation is more "hip," I think, than the generation I made them for. They've seen more television. Their whole response was tremendous because they didn't miss a gag, even things that were a little subtle. They got them right away. I went around and did a symposium with about eleven universities. They had a student congress and the picture went about as well there as I've seen it.

What about showing the films on television?

I could go on television very easily if I wanted to; I've had many offers. My price is a little high. I don't mind telling you what I'm asking. They've come up close to it, but they haven't come up. I want three hundred thousand dollars for myself for two showings. That's a high price, but if I don't get it, I'm not going to show it. That's it.

How did it happen that you kept control of your films?

Well, that was kind of fortunate. I know because Buster Keaton was a very good friend of mine, and I knew Laurel very well, and Hardy, and they got into situations where they weren't able to retain control of their pictures. At first I made pictures for Roach, and Roach had complete control. Later on he came to me and said, "Harold, you don't need me anymore. I've got so many pictures of my own to do, we might as well just go our own way." Which we did, and it was I think the most amicable way that any two people could have parted.

From that time on I produced and financed my own pictures. It sounds like bragging, but we didn't borrow from the bank. We kept a certain amount of money aside and financed our own pictures. In a way we gambled a little heavier than some people do at Las Vegas, but we always got away with it. In one picture we put in close to a million dollars. No one wants to lose that much, which you can very easily in the picture business. But by doing that I was able to control my own pictures. Pathé, who owns so many of my Roach films, turned them over to me, and I bought a number of them from Roach. So I either own or control practically all of them.

Back then it seemed to be a time when the people who were making films finished a film and then forgot it, and that's why so many have been lost. You seem to have a respect for what you did.

Well, right now we're going through the throes of trying to keep a lot of one-reelers from being lost. Nitrate, as you all know, is a very dangerous form of film and very tricky. It turns into jelly. Of all the pictures ever made on nitrate negatives, more than half have been lost, including many of mine. They were stored in New Jersey, in a place called Bonbrook. Everybody stored them there, and they had a tremendous fire and all of ours were destroyed. And I had a fire at my house though, fortunately, I didn't keep the ones that I treasure the most there. Nitrate film, for no reason at all, just explodes sometimes. They're such nasty fires because of the fumes and everything. That's why a great many films have been lost, and a lot of others are gone because no one preserved them. They just didn't think they were valuable.

You once said that comedies have a better chance than dramatic pictures today. Why do you think that?

We didn't make a local type of humor. We were smart enough to realize that they had to be understood in India or Tokyo or Holland as well as here, so we tried to make what I consider to be a basic type of humor— that they would understand too. It's not local humor, so it's understood today and is fresh today, if the picture was well made. The gags that you see—the Keatons, the Chaplins, and the Laurel and Hardys—some of them are just as fresh today as you could possibly dig up to put in the modern picture.

Did you start with a story or with an idea for a gag?

We never had a script until we made a talking picture. When I say we didn't have a script, we had a script in our mind, up to a point. The first thing to find was a character. It was the thing that identified me as Harold Lloyd, the man with the glasses. This was a little contrary to what most of my contemporaries did. Most of them played exactly the same character. Chaplin played his little tramp, Keaton was the stone face, Laurel and Hardy were practically always the same. But in the pictures that I did, one character could be an introvert, a little weakling, and another could be an extrovert, the sophisticate, the hypochondriac. Each one thought differently. Well, they looked alike in appearance, with the glasses, which I guess you'd call a typical American boy. Still, the sophisticate thought entirely differently than the character in *Grandma's Boy* or the character in *The Freshman.*

How did the introduction of sound affect you?

Some of the comedians—in fact most all of them—weren't equipped for sound. Now, my going into sound was sort of like when we went into features. It was an evolutionary thing. It was difficult to keep the same kind of pace in sound pictures as you did in the silents. Another thing is that everybody went sound happy. They thought that because you were making a sound picture you had to talk all the time. It was much cheaper to go verbal. You can get verbal laughs much easier than you can get sight gags. You had to pay some nice, handsome prices for your gagmen, as they were called.

In my case it wasn't that way because I had completed a picture called *Welcome Danger.* I had finished it as a silent, and when we previewed it for about the third time, there was a one-reeler sound comedy on the bill and they howled at it. It had the punkest gags, but they were laughing at the pouring of water, the frying of eggs—it didn't matter what—the clinking of ice in a glass. We said, "My God, we worked our hearts out to get laughs with thought-out gags and look here: just because they've got some sound, they're roaring at these things." I said, "Let's get on the ball. We ought to try and make this a sound picture. Let's see how much we can keep of it and dub it"—we didn't know much about dubbing in those days either—"and we'll make the rest of it over." That was the one that cost me the most—close to a million dollars. It also made the most money. *Welcome Danger* is the one made in underground Chinatown.

So you see, for me it was a kind of natural transition because I had the silent picture to start with, so it had silent technique to it, and the dubbing was horrible. We just didn't know what we were doing. We had a screen up there and we'd run the picture with X marks on it and tried to hit those things. Cutters didn't know too much about cutting them in. I look at the film today and groan, but it worked fine back then because they liked the sound gags. It didn't turn out to be one of our best pictures, but it has its good points.

Did you ever improvise?

The way we would ad-lib was that we would have a number of gagmen in our office, as many as four to eight of them. They were very expensive—in those days you paid eight hundred dollars. That's quite a figure. I'd come in and they'd throw ideas at me. I knew what we wanted and we worked out a theme or story line which could be changed at any moment. Maybe I can explain it best with two pictures. When we made *Safety Last!*, we knew that the boy had to come to the city to make good and he was going to pretend to make good before he actually had, and that the girl was going to come on thinking he had made good, and then he would have to find some way to do it. One of the devices was climbing. He was going to get his pal—who was an iron girder worker—to climb this building. We filmed the climb first and we were very pleased with it. We thought we had something. Now, from there we went back and started the picture. But that, as I say, was a gag picture.

We tried the same thing with *The Freshman.* We went out to the Rose Bowl and for two weeks did comedy business. We tried to play a football game and got nowhere at all. All the dailies were just sad. We had to start at the beginning because it's a character comedy that needed to be built on a particular idea. We knew that the whole picture was really a boy who wanted to go to college with the idea of trying to be very popular. He goes with a completely erroneous idea of how to go about it. So he's in nothing but trouble all the time, and something pulls him out. That's the kind of story line we worked with.

In trying to be spontaneous, we'd work out a series of scenes for the day. We knew we had little islands of what we were going to do, but in between those set ideas, we'd ad-lib. By the time we had shot it four times, little islands would be left out and maybe we'd change the whole idea, we'd have all new business, things came to us that we didn't think of in the gag room. That's the reason you got adept at ad-libbing, creating as you went along, thinking of different things.

Is there anything you can tell us about the basic structure of the gags in your films?

When you study comedy, there are many times when you've got to judge things very carefully. Is it good to let the audience in on your gag, to let them enjoy knowing what's going to happen, or should you surprise them? I've had many gags that we had to shoot both ways because we weren't sure. I would say that three-fourths of the time surprise is best, but sometimes it turns out to be much funnier when the audience is in on it and enjoying what's happening to the comic.

In *The Monkey,* I'm in the hold of this ship and this big heavy who has just killed a man is trying to kill me. I try to stand up to him. I fight him, but he knocks me down very easily and finally throws me up against the bulkhead. I'm very exhausted, and he takes this iron belaying pin and hits me over the top of the head—which should have crushed my skull—but all I did was blink and, of course, he's astounded. So he looks at me with a ferocious look and takes it again and hits me much harder. The iron pin bends a little and all I do is blink. The next time he hits me so hard he bends the belaying pin and is flabbergasted. He looks at me and I run. There's an iron bracket on the ship—he didn't hit me at all—he was hitting this iron bracket that was over my head, so he could hit me all day long. Now, is it better for the audience to know he's hitting the iron bracket, or is it better for them to find out when I run away and there's the bracket? We previewed it both ways.

Which way worked?

The surprise way worked, because then we had a "topper." Another example is in *Safety Last!* where I'm caught in an office and I've rung a bell, and the office boy comes in. I'm not supposed to be there. I'm trying to show off to my girl. In order to do it, I show him this dollar bill and he sees it and he's happy to get it. So I tell him to take the wastepaper basket out and empty it, and I drop the dollar bill in it. He gives me a wink, but as he starts out, I crumble a piece of paper and say, "Oh, boy, come here. You'd better pick that up." As he picks that up, I reach in the wastepaper basket and get my dollar bill back. Now, for those kinds of things you want the audience in on it.

I don't believe you ever took credit on your pictures as a director. Were you actually in control?

Lloyd told the AFI fellows, "You had to pay some nice, handsome prices for
your gagmen." Here, during filming of *Hot Water* (1924), are some of the
beneficiaries. Left to right: Fred Newmeyer, John Grey, Thomas Gray, Sam
Taylor, Tim Whelan and Lloyd.

I think that for more than sixty percent of the pictures I could have taken
full credit on the direction. I took writers who had never been directors
out of the writing room and gave them credit for directing the pictures.
My thinking was that the audience was giving me credit I needed by
being the main comic, so why did I have to have the credit for doing the
direction? I enjoyed being the comic, and it helped the boys.

Do you have anything like a philosophy of comedy?

Gags are done from inside. You must feel them, you must know how they
are, you must time them, you must react to them. If you could get ten
comics doing the same piece of business, one will invariably do it much
funnier if it suits him, if it's his type of business. You must have that feeling of comedy within you, and my character was a funny character—
that's the reason I used him. He belied his appearance when he put on
horn-rimmed glasses for a mollycoddle type. He was a kind of weakling. I

got the idea of wearing the glasses from a picture where the minister wore glasses and he took after this girl who had been kidnapped. He got the girl and had a terrible fight with her fellow. He licked the fellow and he was very casual about the whole thing. He just belied his appearance—you didn't think he could fight, or do anything else.

One thing I had to do was to stay within the semblance of reasonability, for example, when I was on the side of the building in *Safety Last!* Lots of people would have ruined the whole thing because they'd do something impossible and then ask you to believe them from then on. But practically all the gags I did, with one or two exceptions, were things that could actually happen. Many of the others didn't do that. They got into situations where they did something that spoiled the whole thing. Bob Hope used to try and mix oil and water all the time because he'd go along with a cartoon gag and then he'd want a very serious gag. You can't make the audience go both ways. Preston Sturges used to do something very dramatic and then he'd do this other thing. The audience would get confused; they don't know where you want to go. If you want to make it a cartoon type of picture, then make it a cartoon. There's nothing wrong with that. It may be better than the other way. But stick to it. Don't try to blend the two and ask the audiences to believe both things.

Lloyd appeared in nearly two hundred short films before making feature-length films.

Silent Features

1921 *A Sailor-Made Man*	1925 *The Freshman*
1922 *Doctor Jack*	1926 *For Heaven's Sake*
Grandma's Boy	1927 *The Kid Brother*
1923 *Safety Last!*	1928 *Speedy*
Why Worry?	
1924 *Girl Shy*	
Hot Water	

Sound Feature Films

1929 *Welcome Danger*	1936 *The Milky Way*
1930 *Feet First*	1938 *Professor Beware*
1932 *Movie Crazy*	1947 *The Sin of Harold Diddlebock*
1934 *The Cat's-Paw*	

In those days we used to work until three or four in the morning. When I'd get home at daybreak there'd be a new script on my lawn, next to the *Los Angeles Times*. We went back and started work at nine o'clock.

RAOUL WALSH
(Born in New York City, 1887—Died 1980)

Raoul Walsh ran away from home to go to sea and landed in Hollywood at the beginning of the silent era, working as an actor and then as assistant to D. W. Griffith. Before long he was a director himself, completing somewhere between 130 and 200 films over six decades before he retired in 1964. The number is in doubt because, sadly, many of Walsh's early silents are lost.

Walsh, at eighty-four, was the oldest director to meet with the AFI fellows, as well as the crustiest and most garrulous. His first wife, the actress Miriam Cooper, wrote in her autobiography, "Raoul never bored you with the truth." He was raised in New York City at the end of the nineteenth century, and one day the great actor Edwin Booth came by the house. Young Raoul noticed that Booth had a sad face and asked his father why. The elder Walsh explained, "Because his brother was the man who shot President Lincoln." Neither could have foreseen that one day Walsh would portray John Wilkes Booth in Griffith's *The Birth of a Nation*.

Walsh worked on cattle drives in Texas and Montana as a young man and maintained an appetite for the adventurous life, so when he turned to moviemaking he especially enjoyed pictures that he could shoot outdoors on location, working with leading men such as Fairbanks, Flynn, Cagney, Bogart, Cooper and Gable.

His first success of the silent era was *The Thief of Bagdad* starring his good friend Douglas Fairbanks, Sr. It established Walsh as a major director and led to *What Price Glory?* as well as to *Sadie Thompson*—which he wrote, directed and starred in with Gloria Swanson—and *In Old Arizona*, the first outdoor talkie that he starred in and directed. During its production Walsh lost his right eye in a freak accident. The doctor on location told him he needed

Raoul Walsh, left, with Gloria Swanson in *Sadie Thompson* (1928). Walsh
explained his decision to play the sergeant as well as directing. "I took tests of
most every male actor for the part of the sergeant, but she didn't like them."

surgery if he wished to wear an artificial eye. "Hell no," the director told the
doctor. "Everytime I get in a fight, I'd have to put it in my pocket." Walsh
wore a black patch the rest of his life.

He had a long run at Warner Bros. in the late 1930s and the 1940s, making well-crafted studio pictures such as *The Roaring Twenties, High Sierra,
White Heat* and *They Died with Their Boots On*. You would think the interior
world of Ingmar Bergman and the rugged world of Raoul Walsh would be
poles apart, but the Swedish auteur wrote in *Bergman on Bergman* that the
film noir directors were his gods, and he singled out Walsh for his ability to
tell a story "quite clearly, simply and straightforwardly."

Walsh's reputation today rests largely on his being the director of hard-
edged crime thrillers, but when given the opportunity, he spread his wings.
His last film at Mutual, where he had gone to work with Griffith in 1913, was
an adaptation of Ibsen's *Pillars of Society.* In 1915 he directed a version of *Car-*

men with Theda Bara for Cecil B. DeMille, and what is probably the first full-length gangster feature, *The Regeneration.*

Walsh was famous for one of the legendary Hollywood stories in which he and a friend stole the body of John Barrymore from a Hollywood mortuary and seated it in Errol Flynn's living room to greet the actor when he came in from a night on the town. As Walsh says in the seminar, "There was a lot of the laughing water around in those days."

RAOUL WALSH

—◆—

February 16, 1972

Do you mind giving your age?

Not at all. I'll give you a guess.

Seventy-five?

I'm eighty-four. Born 1887. I was six months old before my father knew I was born.

We've just watched They Died with Their Boots On. *Could you tell us a little about the production?*

I think the shooting time was six weeks. In those days they gave the schedule to you by the day. For a short picture you got thirty-two days, and for an extra-long picture they gave you forty-two, maybe forty-three. They would say you'd have five days on location, so you'd go on location and it would rain for five days. They'd put the five days back again, and we'd struggle through it. It was kind of a rough picture to make with all those riders and stuff. Now, in the early days of pictures, I knew of fifty cowboys and good riders that I would request, but the Guild passed a ruling that there could be no requests and that the casting office would supply the riders. Well, half of them couldn't ride, and there were about two hundred people hurt during production. I'd go down in the morning to watch them getting on the horses and they'd be getting on from the wrong side. They didn't last long.

Walsh on location for *In Old Arizona* (1929), his first outdoor sound
film and the picture on which he lost his right eye. Asked if he wanted
an artificial eye, Walsh said, "Hell no, every time I get in a fight,
I'd have to put it in my pocket."

There was a young actor playing the part of a lieutenant. When doing
a long shot where they have swords, we would supply them with wooden
swords with a silver tint to them so it looks like the real blade. When the
property man went to take this chap's real sword away from him and give
him the phony sword, he said, "No, I'm going to use this one." The property boy argued with him a while and couldn't get anywhere, so he let him
keep the real sword. So we shot the scene and there were a couple of
explosions on either side, and he was thrown off the horse. The sword was
thrown up into the air, came down like that into the ground, and him on
top of it. I saw the whole thing and ran down and pulled the sword out of
him, called a limousine and sent him to a hospital. Unfortunately his
mother wouldn't sign to let them operate and in three days the boy died.
Another cowboy who was pretty drunk fell off a horse and broke his neck.
Another fellow was watching the scene and evidently it didn't look too
good because he had a heart attack and died.

I think we spent the better part of a week filming the battle sequences
at Little Big Horn. At one time we had seven hundred horses, and I think
we averaged three or four hundred extras each day. Most of the ones who
got hurt were fellows who had never been on horses before. We had Chi-

Mae West, left, and Marlene Dietrich with Walsh.

nese . . . everybody. We had four or five doctors going along with the troops, and we left the studio in the mornings in four or five buses, limousines and finally two ambulances, like a traveling circus. Some of the extras would look out the bus and see these ambulances, so one day somebody played a joke and had a hearse follow us. But I did have some good boys there. They did a lot of good falls. That picture was made twenty-five years ago, and I think the top price for a fall in those days was fifteen dollars. If the fall was no good you gave him five dollars. And if it was terrible you got rid of him.

Did you ever do stunts yourself?

Yes, I did in the early days. I was a better stuntman than I was an actor. That's why I quit acting. I started off sixty years ago, but I was just terrible. It's a wonder I wasn't shot. I shot Lincoln; they should've shot me.

In a film you shot Lincoln?

Yes, in Griffith's *The Birth of a Nation.*

Was it your idea to make They Died with Their Boots On?

It was partly my idea, and I had worked with Errol Flynn before and he requested me. I'd done quite a few Westerns.

Did you do most of the casting yourself?

Well, for the principals we'd interview people and try to select them for the part. The extras were all handled through the casting bureau. Most female stars don't like to play in Westerns because they have nothing to do but kiss the guy going off to kill the Indians and then sit down to knit him a sweater until he gets back—and when he gets back, the sweater doesn't fit him. So they didn't want any part of Westerns. But this was a fairly good part and Olivia de Havilland was very popular at the box office at the time. She starred alongside Errol Flynn and we didn't have any trouble getting her for the part. She's a brilliant actress—a fine lady.

When casting actresses did you work strictly with stars from Warner Brothers?

Yes. See, they had a stock company that we'd use. As I say, I did mostly action pictures, and women played very small parts, with the exception of *Strawberry Blonde,* where I had Olivia and Rita Hayworth. I did direct Dietrich and Gloria Swanson and some others I don't want to mention. The curious thing about actresses who come for an important part is that the first thing they ask is, "How many changes of wardrobe, Mr. Walsh?" The actors would say, "How many guys do I knock down, pardner?"

How many pictures had Anthony Quinn made before They Died with Their Boots On?

He had played very small parts in a number of pictures. I made a bullfight story one time at Fox and had Tony dressed as a bullfighter. He told me that he didn't know how to fight bulls, so we got two real bullfighters—at least they said they were real bullfighters—from Tijuana. We started taking this scene, and when they turned the bulls loose, the two *real* bullfighters couldn't be found anywhere, and Quinn was over in a restaurant on Pico Boulevard.

What about the casting of High Sierra?

Well, I liked the script when I first read it, and Jack Warner sent the script to Raft, and he read it and turned it down. So Warner said to me, "Raoul, you're a good friend of George's. See what the hell he turned it down for. It's a good script." So I went over to see him. George refused to play in it because he did not want to die at the end. I said, "Well, look, George, the censors will demand, after you kill a couple of people, that you pay the penalty." He said, "I don't give a damn about the censors. I don't want to do it." So I went back to Warner and told him, "I can't talk him into it, Jack." He said, "Well, we've got to get started. Who the hell can we use?" I said, "Well, you've got a guy here under contract called Bogart. I'll take a chance with him." So he said, "All right, go ahead." And Bogart got the part.

That was his first big one?

Yes. They doubled—even tripled—his salary, and also signed Ida Lupino for seven years for her performance in it.

Why did you remake High Sierra *as* Colorado Territory?

They were stuck for a release. Everybody had turned down scripts, and nothing had come up. I spoke with Warner and said, "Make this a Western." He said, "All right. Start tomorrow."

What were the circumstances surrounding Sadie Thompson, *which starred Gloria Swanson? At what stage did you decide to act in it?*

I took tests of most every male actor for the part of the sergeant, but she didn't like them. I don't know why—I worked pretty hard with these fellows, friends of mine, trying to get them the part, but Swanson turned them all down. So Joe Schenck, who was a partner with her in the project, sent for me one morning and said, "Raoul, you know you're never going to start this picture unless you play the part yourself." I said, "All right. I'll start tomorrow." That was the only reason I acted in the film and also directed it.

How did Fairbanks choose you to direct The Thief of Bagdad?

Well, he was a great fellow for athletics, and I did a little bit of that myself in the early days. He had a gym and asked me to come down and work out with him. Then he finally said, "Irish, I'm going to make a picture and I want you to direct it." That was all. Now, I'd been making gangster pictures where everybody got murdered in the first and third scenes, and all of a sudden he picked me for this fantasy. So it was a relief. Anyhow, I took a chance with it and it turned out fairly good. Fairbanks rehearsed for almost a month on his acrobatics before we started the picture. He kept in fine physical condition. He weighed a hundred fifty-two pounds and he'd mark what he weighed each day after he worked out. He had his own pool that he'd jump into after his steam bath. Charlie Chaplin used to come over every evening and the three of us would take a steam bath and talk about pictures.

What was the schedule and the budget?

They had no budget in those days. Fairbanks had his own organization, and they never set a schedule because sometimes he'd work for two or three days and then lay off to work on the script or something and then go again. I don't think it took too long, maybe two months. That was one of the longest schedules ever given out. We hired the best designer in the business at that time, a fellow named William Cameron Menzies, and told him the story. Then he went about his business and designed the sets. He'd bring them in and show them to Doug and myself.

Do you feel you learned a lot from your work with D. W. Griffith?

Oh, yes—continuity and cutting and progression.

What about setting up the shots?

Well, that's easy once you're there with the script.

But you're talking about seven hundred people. How do you just know how to set up a shot?

Well, that comes from experience. I'd always directed crowds, mostly. Big movement, you know.

So you mean it was an instinctual process?

I guess so. A lot of directors fight away from crowds. They sort of get a bit panicky, particularly young directors coming in. But they never panicked me at all. The more the merrier. I pick out how they enter the shot, then how to get rid of them. One time I made a picture in Italy with four thousand extras for four or five days. Then you get down to close-up shots and you need only two thousand.

There must be a way to train yourself to think about how to handle that many people.

Well, I come from a large family.

Do you usually work with scripts that are already finished, or do you come up with your own ideas and work with someone else?

Well, when you get the script, you know, you go over and over it. You make notes where you can boost it up.

Did you usually have a choice of scripts, or did you just take what the studio handed down?

No, the director could turn down a script if it didn't fit him. But then they'd generally plead with you. You see, most of these pictures were already sold and had to be released on January 15, and here you were in December. "How are you coming? Do you think you'll finish tomorrow?" I was under contract to Warner Bros. They were really fine people and I didn't mind working overtime. The Warner brothers were three fine gentlemen.

At the studios you get into the habit of just working, taking everything—just do it and get out of there. Once in a while you'd get a nice one, a gem, but the rank and file of the films were not too hot. I remember once I made a picture in New York with Theda Bara. It was a Spanish picture and we built a big Spanish street there. The day we started the thing a blizzard hit New York. Bill Fox, the studio executive, who was a nice fellow, said to me, "Raoul, what can we do?" I said, "Well, Mr. Fox, I think that if we put a few domes on the set, we can change it to a Russian picture." He called all the people and he said, "Get the Spanish costumes the hell out of here and bring the Russian costumes in." We made the thing in about three and a half weeks, and the salesmen came to New York for a preview. Some fellows from Cincinnati were saying, "Gee, we advertised a Spanish picture. Where the hell is it?"

When sound came in, was there much of a change in directing films? And did you find it a problem?

Of course there was a great upheaval amongst the directors when talking pictures came in, but I handled it the same way. They called me a renegade because I was one of the first ones to do an outdoor talking picture. They said that they had created this medium and now all this talking stuff was going to destroy it. I said it was going to destroy us if we didn't get along with it.

I'd like to ask you about the death of James Cagney on the steps of the cathedral in The Roaring Twenties. *He takes a long time to die and runs through most of New York.*

Well, it's pretty hard to kill an actor. In those days Cagney and Bogart were the only two stars you could kill in a picture. You couldn't kill Flynn, you couldn't kill Gable, you couldn't kill Cooper or any of those fellows. The exhibitor wouldn't even play the picture. But with Cagney and Bogart they accepted it. So I thought, as long as they accepted it, we'd give them a good load of it.

How did it happen that Flynn died at the end of They Died with Their Boots On?

Well, you couldn't change history. He didn't mind dying, as long as he got paid.

How much of real history behind the story did you change?

There are about ten different versions of Custer—what he did and what he didn't do and why he did it. You could go on and make ten pictures with different endings.

The final scene of his crossing is a very faithful reproduction of a couple of Charles Russell's paintings. Did it just sort of happen that you were on the side of a hill and they were grouped the way they were?

I'd seen all the Remingtons and I knew Russell. When I was a young boy, my father introduced me to Remington, and I knew the groupings and the different things. You see, the Sioux Indians, the Blackfoot and the Crow were a good husky bunch of horsemen with great features. Now, here we had blue-eyed Indians. They'd use Apaches dressed as women. They didn't look good at all.

You made some of the greatest gangster movies of all time. Were there specific things that you felt had to be in a gangster film for it to work?

Well, in the first place you had to keep it moving. You had to have a lot of bullets. At times, you had to have a bit of sympathy for the party who was going to get killed or wasn't going to get killed. And a fairly slight love story going through it to hold that part of it together. But there's no set rule. They're all different.

Your most notable films were from the point of view of the gangster. I was wondering if there was any conscious reason you preferred to look at it from the point of view of the gangster rather than from, say, the law enforcement angle?

Well, law enforcement would be routine, shot in a police station or something. With gangsters you portrayed their thoughts and what they want to do and how they do it. There's a slew of those police things on television now.

What is your most satisfying film?

Well, it's hard to tell. I made almost two hundred of them. In those days we used to work until three or four in the morning. When I'd get home at daybreak there'd be a new script on my lawn, next to the *Los Angeles Times*. We went back and started work at nine o'clock.

Walsh at the AFI, February 1972.

How many films did you work on without actually being credited as director?

Some twenty or thirty, probably. You know, the director gets sick, or he'd leave or do something else—have a fight with the star. Or if he's had too much of the laughing water. Of course, there was a lot of laughing water around in those days.

The last one I remember was with Bette Davis. John Huston was directing her in a picture, and they had a fight about how the picture was going to end just before the end of the shoot. She wanted it to end one way and he wanted it to end another way, so he took a walk. Warner called me up and said, "Raoul, this is one tough dame and I think you can handle her." That was the way he approached it. He said, "Will you go over to Pasadena and make this ending so we can get this thing done and get this dame out of the studio." Nice girl, but really tough. She'd demand this, that and the other thing. So I got into a car with Bette. On the way to Pasadena we stopped for dinner. While we were having a drink there the unit manager came in and handed me the script with the new ending. I said, "Bette, this will probably interest you," and passed it over. She read it and you never heard such a volley of oaths in your life. The ceiling went off from her screaming and yelling. People started to get up, but I finally talked her into it after a couple of shots of laughing water.

How do you work with your cinematographers? Is there a lot of time spent in pre-production with them?

Not too long. I'll sit down with the script and tell them, "Play this in shadow. This gal can't act very well. This guy is a dog, don't light him at all."

Do you have any particular methods for shooting a chase sequence, in particular the one in High Sierra?

No, chase scenes are very easy to shoot. Just keep going, keep going, keep going. Get on top of the mountain, turn around, bring them down again, and just hope there's nobody on the road.

What do you do with your time now?

I've just written a book. It took me two years to write. It's the longest project I was ever on. I took it over to France last June and a French publisher bought it. I submitted it to a publisher here, and he said, "It's a great story. It's a story of Americana. But you've got too much action in it for a book." So I'm trimming some the action out of it now. The original title I had was *Come Hell or High Water,* but the French didn't like that and they changed it to *Days of Wrath.* The American publisher didn't like that; they thought it sounded too much like *The Grapes of Wrath.* I'll let them fight it out.* But I've got a place up in the hills, and I still fool around with the ranch, get some exercise and stuff. But at my age you have to keep the bags packed.

———◆———

Films as Director

1915 *Regeneration* (also coadaptation)	*The Silent Lie* (also scenario)
Carmen (also scenario)	*The Innocent Sinner*
1916 *The Serpent* (also scenario)	(also scenario)
Blue Blood and Red (also	*The Conqueror* (also scenario)
scenario)	*Betrayed* (also scenario)
1917 *The Honor System* (also scenario)	*The Prussian Cur* (also scenario)

*Walsh's autobiography *Each Man in His Time* was published by Farrar, Straus and Giroux in 1974.

This Is the Life (also scenario)

1918 *The Pride of New York* (also scenario)

Woman and the Law (also scenario)

On the Jump (also scenario)

Every Mother's Son (also scenario)

I'll Say So (also scenario)

1919 *The Strongest* (also scenario)

Evangeline (also scenario)

Should a Husband Forgive? (also scenario)

1920 *The Strongest* (also scenario)

The Deep Purple (also producer and scenario)

1921 *The Oath*

Serenade (also producer)

1922 *Kindred of the Dust* (also producer)

1923 *Lost and Found on a South Sea Island*

1924 *The Thief of Bagdad*

1925 *East of Suez*

The Spaniard

1926 *The Wanderer*

The Lucky Lady

1927 *The Monkey Talks*

Loves of Carmen

What Price Glory

1928 *Sadie Thompson* (also screenplay)

Me, Gangster (also co-scenario)

1929 *In Old Arizona*

The Cock-Eyed World (also co-screenplay)

Hot for Paris (also co-screenplay)

1930 *The Big Trail* (also producer)

1931 *The Man Who Came Back*

1932 *Wild Girl*

Me and My Gal

1933 *Sailor's Luck*

The Bowery

Going Hollywood

1935 *Under Pressure*

Baby Face Harrington

Every Night at Eight

1936 *Big Brown Eyes* (also co-screenplay)

Spendthrift (also co-screenplay)

Klondike Annie

1937 *You're in the Army Now*

When Thief Meets Thief

Artists and Models

Hitting a New High

1938 *College Swing*

1939 *St. Louis Blues*

The Roaring Twenties

1940 *Dark Command*

They Drive by Night

1941 *They Died with Their Boots On*

High Sierra

The Strawberry Blonde

Manpower

1942 *Desperate Journey*

Gentleman Jim

1943 *Background to Danger*

Northern Pursuit

1944 *Uncertain Glory*

The Horn Blows at Midnight

1945 *Objective, Burma!*

Salty O'Rourke

1946 *The Man I Love*

1947 *Cheyenne*

Pursued

1948 *Silver River*

Fighter Squadron

1949 *One Sunday Afternoon*

Colorado Territory

White Heat

1951 *Along the Great Divide*

Captain Horatio Hornblower

Distant Drums

1952 *Glory Alley*

The World in His Arms
Blackbeard, the Pirate
1953 *The Lawless Breed*
Saskatchewan
Sea Devils
A Lion in the Streets
Gun Fury
1955 *Battle Cry*
The Tall Men
1956 *The Revolt of Mamie Stover*

The King and Four Queens
1957 *Band of Angels*
1958 *The Naked and the Dead*
1959 *The Sheriff of Fractured Jaw*
A Private's Affair
1960 *Esther and the King* (also producer and co-screenplay)
1961 *Marines, Let's Go* (also producer and co-screenplay)
1964 *A Distant Trumpet*

I'm a firm believer in the fact that you put your individual stamp on your work. I think the whole job is to show one's individual viewpoint.

KING VIDOR
(Born in Galveston, Texas, in 1894—Died in 1982)

King Vidor landed a job as a part-time projectionist at the Globe Theater in Galveston in 1909, when he was just a teenager. In his autobiography, *A Tree Is a Tree,* he recalled the thrill of gazing through the glass from the booth and seeing the light flickering across the darkness with images of French pantomimist Max Linder. It seems his destiny was shaped in that small Texas movie house.

Vidor learned his trade as a newsreel cameraman in Texas covering storms, elections and events of national interest, then headed to Hollywood in a Model T Ford with his young wife, Florence Vidor. She became a star and he—after working as an extra, a production assistant and a director of two-reelers—got his chance as a feature director and never looked back.

Vidor came to the AFI in three different years to meet with the fellows, and five of his films were screened before each visit: *Our Daily Bread, The Crowd, Hallelujah, Show People* and *Duel in the Sun.* Vidor was a tall, broad-shouldered man whose cordial manner concealed the determination and stubbornness that had seen him through fifty-six feature films in a career that started with two-reelers in 1915—a body of work that includes five Oscar nominations over forty-five years. Even though he had retired fifteen years before his first visit to AFI, his vitality and clarity of mind gave the impression that he was ready to climb in the saddle if the call came from a studio.

I met Vidor in the fifties and recall his warm and generous way toward young people. I knew him then for his recent pictures, which seemed to me less distinguished than the best work of his peers—but film classics were rarely shown in those days, so I had no way of appreciating his silent masterpieces of the twenties and his great successes of the early sound period. In the early days of AFI there was a restoration and a showing of *Show People,* his

1928 comedy with Marion Davies, and I remember the screening as a revelation that earned him a new generation of admirers.

Vidor described his pleasure at taking the streetcar from Hollywood to downtown Los Angeles to see *The Birth of a Nation* on the big screen of one of the movie palaces of the day. It is hard to fully comprehend the excitement that must have been generated when thousands gathered to watch Vidor's classics *The Big Parade* and *The Crowd,* accompanied by an orchestra of a hundred musicians. During the silent era, and for a while after the advent of sound, Vidor was free to design and construct his films, but later he became more a servant of the studios. His keen intellect and his appetite for personal expression shined through his best work, though he admits his "guts" weren't in some of the later studio pictures, such as *War and Peace,* even though it earned him his last Oscar nomination in 1956. "That was just a job," he said.

Vidor remained an independent spirit, always more fulfilled when he was dealing with material that was personal to him. "Artistic Freedom and the Studio System" is the title of the opening chapter of his fascinating book *Film Making*—an expression of his determination to maintain integrity in his work. When a young filmmaker asked him what was the most important thing he had learned in becoming a director, Vidor thought for a moment and said, "The most important thing was to be an individual."

King Vidor with AFI fellows at Greystone in Beverly Hills, February 1980.
Vidor lived nearby and was a frequent visitor to the AFI campus.

KING VIDOR

November 2, 1977[*]

You started making films in the silent era. What was the hardest thing about moving over to sound films?

We'd been so used to titles and trying to have as few as possible. Some of the funniest titles in *Show People* were written after the picture was finished. They had a title writer, and after he saw the picture he'd come up with the words. You had that flexibility. When we started working on dialogue we thought of it like titles. In other words, sparse, not a lot of words.

Silent picture scripts were such that you could ad-lib anywhere because nobody had to write dialogue, which took time, and nobody had to learn dialogue, which also took time. You would have a script that said "Love Scene." Just two words, and that was it. In fact, sometimes you had "Battle Scene," and you might spend a week on a battle scene. One time I remember thinking, I've run out of all the love scenes I know. And in the days of silent pictures you could go to the theater full of people and go up to the projection booth and watch the audience, and cut out three frames if you wanted to. It didn't hurt anything because you didn't have synchronized sound. I would go every night to see *The Big Parade* on Hollywood Boulevard and I kept trimming and trimming, three or four frames at a time, to get a laugh out that I didn't want because the producers were frightened of that particular laugh. Maybe it was a release of nervous ten-

*This transcript contains segments from seminars King Vidor gave at the American Film Institute on February 26, 1975 and February 20, 1980.

sion or something. The great advantage of silent films was that they didn't have words, so not everything was literal. The audience could make up its own words and dialogue, and make up its own meaning.

When sound films first came in and the audience heard a great lover, like John Gilbert, say "Darling" or something, it got a laugh. The minute you say, "I love you," it sort of gets humorous. But if it's silent it can mean a lot of other things. In silent pictures you couldn't turn away from the screen as much. When sound first came in, that's when popcorn and all the drinks started, and necking in the theater, because you could turn away and do all sorts of things and still hear. You wouldn't miss anything—the sound would take care of it. But in silent pictures you had to just sit there and try to figure it out. When silent films ended I know that most of my director friends were just horrified with the idea of being able to use words. Not musical accompaniment, not sound effects, but words. It was just a terrible idea, and I know that René Clair and Eisenstein wrote articles against it. I'm sure that people at that time felt we were being ruined by words, and it was true for a while. Why? Because we had developed a sense of pantomime. It was just like saying to Marcel Marceau, "We've had enough of your pantomime; you've got to start speaking tomorrow." You can understand how he would have felt, and that was the way we felt.

I was very aware for quite a while after the introduction of sound of the directors who had made silent films, and how much more graphic and interesting their films were. They were still thinking in terms of photography and were more articulate and dynamic than just the soundtrack coming through the loudspeakers. I was at a film conference in the Midwest and I began to hear the word *metaphor* a lot. One fellow asked me, "Do you have a lot of metaphor in your films?" And I said, "Well, I sort of know what the word means, but I never connected it up with my films exactly. How do you connect it with a film?" And he said, "Well, you have something up on the screen in front of you that means something else." I looked it up later, and the real meaning of the word is that you tell a parable or something using different symbols. It's like Santa Claus or *Alice in Wonderland* where they tell some other truth with different things on the screen. So I began to think: do I think of one thing and have someone doing something else to suggest it? Then I began to fill in some gaps in my memory. For example, there's a scene in *The Crowd* with the boy walking up a stairway. A while back I was in the house in which I was born, where I hadn't been since I was ten years old, and I walked upstairs and I was in the exact scene from *The Crowd.*

Over the years I have learned that things will be dug out of your unconscious. This is particularly true of silent films, where we didn't have all those words to explain things and we thought in terms of symbols and graphic arrangements or possibilities. We were trained in those terms. When you had to explain something, you didn't think the way you do when you're writing. You thought, "What's the picture, the symbol I'm looking for, to explain what I am trying to say?" I think with that scene in *The Crowd* I was trying to suggest a painful moment in my youth that I felt without being entirely aware of it.

What about the technical problems of shooting with synchronous sound?

For my first sound picture they told me, "We don't have any portable equipment." But I wanted to go on location in Arkansas and Tennessee, and we ended up shooting without sound recording equipment. This turned out to be the greatest blessing because at that time all the sound equipment and cameras were in booths, so you could get no low setups, no high setups, no panning, no boom shots, no perambulating shots. So we went on location and shot it just as we would a silent film, think-ing that somehow we would put the sound in, which we did when we got back to the studio. At the studio they would bring out the big booths with the camera in there at a certain height looking out through a window. What can you do looking out through a pane of glass like that? The only thing you could shoot was two people sitting on a couch like in a stage play, so it was just exactly like being in the the-ater. I was very conscious of camera movement and perambulating shots—after watching the German films like *Metropolis* and *The Last Laugh,* where I think they followed somebody through a lobby and up in an elevator—but then we were being told, "Well, you have to be in the booth" because the cameras were noisy. So I just said, "To hell with the sound," and we'd shoot the scene and then go into the editing room and try to synchronize it. But we didn't have Moviolas. The only thing we could do was go into the projection room and run the film and try to read lips. Our editor went absolutely nuts one day. He threw all the cans off the shelf, and the film was rolling out everywhere. He'd had a few drinks.

Why do you think a star like John Gilbert never made the transition to sound?

There's an interesting story about that. The general story that goes around is that his voice was too high and he had to quit pictures. Rouben Mamoulian made a picture with him called *Queen Christina* and his voice was not that high, but they didn't know what else to blame it on. So he was out, even though he was under contract for $250,000 per picture; he never made another picture and died from frustration. I knew him well because I'd made four or five films with him. What I believe happened was that he was the image of the aggressive lover, and they thought he could just speak the same words he did when doing silent scenes that nobody actually heard. He would arouse himself by saying things like "I love you, I adore you, I worship you, I can't wait to get you alone tonight," the kinds of things that were funny when you heard them. So I think it wasn't his high voice but that you couldn't just take an image and suddenly change it by putting a lot of words on the soundtrack. The words destroyed the image. You'll see that a lot in life—somebody will look like something and then they'll start to talk with maybe a deep Texas accent and it changes the image.

I thought the casting for Duel in the Sun *was fantastic, and was wondering if that was the cast you wanted from the beginning.*

Well, I'll tell you something. A lot of people ask, "What's a producer? What's his function?" I know of only two or three producers who ever actually contributed anything. David Selznick was one of the few producers who actually contributed. He was the greatest guy in supplying you with a tremendous cast. He gambled and didn't mind paying big money for actors, and he was just the fellow I was looking for when I made *Duel in the Sun.* It's pretty hard to say whether the principals were the ones I first thought of. Joe Cotten was under contract, Gregory Peck was under contract to Selznick, and Jennifer Jones was married to Selznick. Lillian Gish I had directed years before in *La Bohème,* and we were pretty good friends. I was speaking last week and someone asked me about Jackie Cooper in *The Champ.* I'm sure we saw him in another picture and thought he was promising. Very often that's the way pictures are cast. They look for the story to suit some personality that's hot at the moment. In a big studio like MGM they had talent scouts and people who were training young actors. They had a big casting department, and you had a casting director assigned to your picture. Today you have television, but we never had television to check on actors. The whole process is pretty hard to define.

What about the script of Duel in the Sun?

David Selznick originally said to me, "I don't want anything to do with this film. You take it over and be the producer. Make a wonderful little well-done classic small picture." I thought of a film like *High Noon* and that I had a chance to win the Academy Award or something. I thought it would be an intense little Western. He had a fellow named Oliver Garrett as a writer who I guess wasn't expanding and blowing it up enough, so Selznick took over the writer's job after Garrett had written a complete script. Selznick was lengthening things all the time—he wanted to make a *Gone with the Wind* of the West.

During production we had Josef von Sternberg as an assistant director for a few weeks. He had done so much toward making Dietrich's career successful that Selznick thought maybe he could do something with Jennifer Jones, some sort of light on her hair or something that would make her more interesting. He wanted to utilize any particular talents von Sternberg had. I think it was also because Selznick wanted to do something for him, an act of friendship, and von Sternberg made many of the photographic and costume tests. After that Selznick asked me if I would mind if Joe stayed on, and I said, "No." Joe told me, "Anything you want me to do I'd be glad to do." He was just glad to be on the film. In the battle scene Joe's job was to have a bucket of water and throw it over Jennifer to make her look sweaty. One afternoon I had to leave at about five o'clock, and there was a shot of the sheriff coming in and looking through the doors. It was rehearsed and I said, "Joe, you shoot that for me, will you?" A couple of days later Selznick called me in and said, "My God, you shot until nine o'clock on one scene, five thousand feet of Technicolor film for one little shot." Joe went crazy on it, shot it from different angles over and over, and Selznick raised hell with me about letting him do it.

I quit the picture two days before it was finished. I warned David that if he walked on the set and raised hell, I would quit. He blew up over that big scene with the cavalry and three hundred head of cattle and two hundred cowboys. I said, "You've been wanting to be a director for a long time. Here's your opportunity." He tried to get me back the next day and I said that I'd had it, so then he got William Dieterle. I didn't want to shoot the prologue of the film, so Dieterle did it. I was still thinking in terms of a picture like *High Noon*.

Was there talk of Dieterle receiving a directing credit?

I'd been on the picture for months and months. I don't know how long Dieterle was on it, and everyone, including the Directors Guild, was against double credits anyway.

I understand you did some work on The Wizard of Oz. *How did that come about?*

They had just taken George Cukor off *Gone with the Wind,* and Selznick gave me this stack of scripts to take home over the weekend. I spent from about Friday afternoon to Monday morning reading and studying and worrying about them. The picture had already been in production for a month or so. Monday morning I got up and I thought, "God, I don't want to take this on." I wanted about three months or six months to adapt this thing and get used to it, at least a month or so, so I went in saying I didn't think I wanted to do it. In the meantime Clark Gable had worked with Victor Fleming, who they had seen on Sunday but who was directing *The Wizard of Oz*. He said he would do *Gone with the Wind* if someone would take *The Wizard of Oz*. I was so damn glad to get out of doing *Gone with the Wind* that I said, "Sure, I'll take over *The Wizard of Oz*." I went over on Monday morning and sat on the set all day, and late that afternoon ran all the stuff that they'd shot. Next morning, I carried on with *The Wizard of Oz* for maybe two or three weeks. I shot "Over the Rainbow." Fleming had been in there on all the casting and designing sets and locations and all this sort of stuff, so I thought for somebody to come in for two weeks when most of the sets were up and the picture was all cast, he shouldn't get credit, and neither did the Directors Guild. My name isn't on *The Wizard of Oz*—I wouldn't permit it.

You see, by the time you have continuity sketches, half your work is done. After that I work on the script and with the set design and the picking of the locations and the casting. That's half of it before you ever start to shoot on the stage. You can't help but visualize as you go along if you're working on the script and the continuity. Take the actor in *The Crowd*. I had pictured the guy so often in my mind that when I saw a fellow who looked like that image I said, "That's it. He's perfect for the role." I had a vision of an ordinary average man, and saw a bunch of extras walking out of the studio one day. I saw the face of one guy, James Murray, and I chased after him.

Is it true you originally had a different ending to The Crowd?

Actually, we made seven endings and had seven previews. It was thought in that era that the film should have happy endings, so we had to shoot one. I quickly forgot it, but it's a happy ending, with them living in a nice home, children, grandchildren, Christmas, I think it was. And they insisted that the picture go out with this small reel in the can of the last reel, and the exhibitors had a note—if they thought the ending they saw was too depressing, they could paste on this other ending. And I checked for a year or so afterward, and to my knowledge no exhibitor ever put the happy ending on it, and it never was seen with the happy ending outside the studio. Which only goes to prove that the studios don't always know what the exhibitors or the public prefer. They have some sort of vague dream or fantasy about it.

Of course, you must remember that this picture was made at a big studio, MGM, which made about fifty pictures a year, and in a time when the accent was on glamour; penthouses; women stars like Norma Shearer, Gloria Swanson, Joan Crawford, Greta Garbo, and Clark Gable, Spencer Tracy, so forth. And to make a picture of this sort with more or less a realistic mood about it was a big departure on their part. Today, seen many years later, it might not look like a departure. Vittorio De Sica told me that he gives *The Crowd* credit for starting neorealism in Italy. He said he was inspired to make pictures like *Umberto D.* and *The Bicycle Thief* after he saw the film.

How did it happen that they agreed to let you make this kind of film?

Well, I had made *The Big Parade* with John Gilbert, which was a big film and put MGM on the map. After that I was sort of the fair-haired boy at the studio, so they thought I might come up with a blockbuster, and they were afraid to say no at the time of *The Crowd*.

The Big Parade was selling out at one theater in New York, where it played for around two years. I passed Irving Thalberg on the lot and he asked, "Now *The Big Parade* is a hit, what are you going to do next?" Up until then they'd never made a picture about the war with an enlisted man as the central character. They were always officers, generals planning attacks, planning battles. I saw a film as a story where the fellow walked through the war and reacted to things. He was just an average guy who enlisted or got drafted, and his attitude was just sort of go along and do what they tell you. He wasn't fighting it, he wasn't causing it. That was my whole feeling of *The Big Parade*. It wasn't written into the script, but that's the way I directed the leading character, who is in almost every shot. Nothing happens that he doesn't see—he's the observer all the time. He is experiencing this from first-person viewpoint, like a novel, and not the director or the producer's viewpoint. It's the same with *The Crowd* where the fellow is looking at life, and *Our Daily Bread* where the fellow is walking through Depression times. I believe in subjective reality, that every man makes his own universe.

So I said to Thalberg, "There must be a lot of other things that a fellow could walk through and react to." And he said, "Like what?" and I said, "Well, life." At the time, you know, I was one of the directors under salary at MGM and I could tell the head guy an idea, and he could say, "Yes, go ahead." This doesn't happen today. He didn't say, "What stars are you going to have?" I didn't have stars—I had unknowns. So he said, "It sounds good, why don't you go ahead with it." That's the way the picture was made. That's the way the best pictures that I made were made. Just saying, "Okay, go ahead." So I went home and got a writer to work with me, a fellow who had written sort of down-to-earth stuff, and we just put down a list of the things that happen to a fellow in ordinary life. So what's the first one? The first one is he's born, the first experience he has to react to is birth. I mean, that's still in it. And then, what's the last one? The last one is death. And what comes after birth? Well, when his father dies, probably, and he has to be the man of the family. We just went through things—he meets a girl and falls in love, gets married, pregnancy, has a child, so forth. One of the original ideas for the prologue was to go up the building, and go in the twentieth floor, with all these clerks and desks, and pick out one man. By sharing his life and his emotions you would then know that all the others are more or less the same. Pick out one of the mob, one of the crowd, and follow him, and he'd go through the same emotions and same experiences as other people. Now, the idea that he has to be a winner—well, that's just a fantasy. Not everybody can be winners. This is why I think the ending where the camera pulls back and he's lost in the crowd is a realistic ending. The other endings with him prosperous and happy were false.

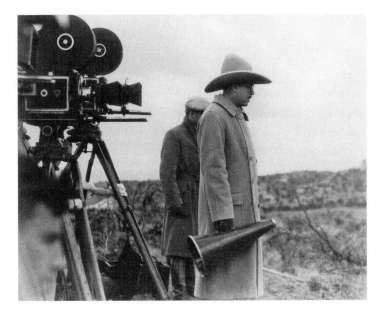

Vidor on the set of *The Texas Rangers* in 1936.

That's the way the picture was written, maybe in two or three weeks. There was no dialogue. All we had to do was have a good bunch of notes, the silent script. *Our Daily Bread* is a sequel to *The Crowd,* using the same two characters' names, John and Mary, signifying Man and Woman. It was part of a trilogy I had in mind.

Some of the shots in The Crowd *are extraordinary, for instance at Coney Island where you seem to have the camera moving on the slide, and another shot where the camera goes up the side of a building.*

I'm glad you asked that because it's interesting. For the Coney Island part the cameraman was on a slide, sliding down backward, on a piece of rug as I remember. There were no booms or zoom lenses. How easy it would be with a boom or a zoom lens! What we did was tilt up on some building in New York. The idea was to go up to the twenty-second floor and move up the building, and then go close to a window and dissolve through the window to a very long shot of a big office—I think we had two hundred desks—and move down to one man. When the camera starts to move up, the building is actually a miniature about fifteen feet high, lying flat on a sound stage. The cameraman and camera were on this bridgelike affair on wheels. It tilted up on the building and then the thing wheeled along, and they had a windlass type of deal to let it down close to the window that we'd picked out. We'd already shot the interior. We had a still, an enlargement of some sort, that you could see lit through the window. Once inside, we used the tracks on top of the stage that were used to move around these Cooper-Hewitt lamps, great big banks of these vapor lamps. We built a platform with windlasses, and it ran on those tracks, and the cameraman and his assistant got on the platform and they rolled forward and let the camera down to one man at a desk. It came down the same way a boom would. The desks were closer together at the far end of the room than in the foreground, to force perspective so as to give extra depth. You have to keep tall people in the foreground—they don't work in the upper part of the set. Or if you do have people back there, you get midgets. The whole thing is built on the idea of the camera angle. I remember I was learning about Picasso and change of perspective, and was very aware of that at the time.

Didn't anyone at the studio suggest that you just use an establishing shot with fifty desks? How did you convince them that you actually had to construct this elaborate shot?

In that period they didn't interfere. They were making too many pictures to interfere on any one of them, particularly if you had made a lot of money on previous pictures. It was the same thing with going on location, which was not done in those days. The first time I remember going across country on location was for *Wild Oranges.* I had to convince the studio to go to Florida, and with *The Crowd* we had to go to New York. It took three or four days on the train and everybody was on salary, and then three or four days coming back. They tried to talk us out of that, but we had to get a lot of shots of Wall Street and lower New York. In New York we built a thing that looked like packing boxes on a pushcart and had a cameraman inside. It had a hole in it for the lens. The other shots in New York are from a hidden camera in a truck. I think that's the first time it had been done in New York, shooting on the street with a hidden camera. In the end they appreciated it—they were aiming high, aiming for the best.

What was the public reaction to The Crowd?

It wasn't a big box office success, but it was a critical success right away. They didn't have small theaters—they had these big theaters. The Criterion, the Astor, the Capitol Theater in New York—these big, tremendous things. They were all tuned up to big names on the marquee and getting the people in quickly, but the actors in the film were unknown. By the time Federico Fellini or Ingmar Bergman came along there was a chain of small theaters, and a film could go in there and get enough critical reaction, and enough people who were interested in it would see it, and it could build slowly.

What was it like working with Irving Thalberg and Louis Mayer at MGM?

Thalberg's great ability—or perhaps I'm speaking about courage and determination—was that when he saw a first cut, if it was weak or could be better, he didn't mind having it reshot and paying for it, even when the director might think that his film was all right and let it alone. He would watch the dailies, too. If he saw some actor that wasn't as good as he felt he should be, he would say, "Hold it right there. Let's reshoot. Let's put somebody new in there." He always aimed high and never compromised. But he practically never came to the set.

Mayer held the whole thing together and persuaded stars to stay. It was like a family. His greatest talent was to keep all those stars and actors satisfied, to keep the organization going. If you started to leave he'd practically break down and cry. He would say, "You're walking out on your home." There's one actor who wanted to talk about a raise, but when he came out of Mayer's office his agents asked him, "Did you get the raise?" The actor said, "I not only didn't get the raise, but I got Louis B. Mayer for a father."

How did you come to make Hallelujah!—*the first all-black film? Did you slip that one by on them too?*

Hallelujah! is a picture made in 1929 about the rural South of the United States. My father lived near the sawmills in Texas and I worked near there, and also in Arkansas as a kid, where I saw the black people down there. I used to spend summers in a little town in Arkansas, so I knew many of the spirituals. I had met Paul Robeson and kept telling the studio—for three years—that I wanted to make a film with only blacks. They kept turning

Vidor directing Lillian Gish in *La Bohème* (1926). Next to Vidor is MGM
chief Irving Thalberg, who Vidor said practically never came on the set;
apparently there were exceptions.

me down. I was in Europe when sound come in and there was a headline
in *Variety* that said, "Hollywood Goes 100 Percent Sound." And I
thought, with the singing and dancing, this will clinch it. So I came back
by ship to New York and went to Nicholas Schenck, who was actually the
head of the studio—Mayer and Thalberg had been turning me down—
and talked to him about sound. I gave him the list of all the things that we
could have in the picture. The Jolson picture had just been a big hit, but
he still refused. I was under contract for X number of dollars per picture,
and I said I was willing not to draw any salary. That did it, and they said,
"We'll let you make a picture about whores, if that's the way you feel."
Last week I got a check for $217. I'm still getting my salary out of that one.

To finance *Our Daily Bread* I went to Goldwyn and two or three other
places and got turned down. So I went out and mortgaged everything I
had—automobiles and house and everything—and raised the rest from
the bank. It cost one hundred thousand dollars for the film and twenty-

five thousand for the music. The film didn't make a lot of money, but I paid it all back. And it's still going. Janus Films distributes it, and the last estimate was that over the next five years it will make about twenty thousand dollars.

Was the film seen back in 1929?

There was trouble making it and trouble distributing it, but today it's still running in Paris. I still get a kick out of it. I had put my salary in with the rest of the investment, and MGM didn't lose any money.

What is Our Daily Bread *about?*

It's a cooperative during the Depression, where stonemasons, plumbers and carpenters all exchange services rather than money. They don't have any money, they're all broke. One fellow, the leading character, had the use of a farm, and he doesn't know what to do with it, so he takes in all the guys that are broke, all the fellows that can do some sort of a trade, including an undertaker. I got the idea from an article in *Reader's Digest* that said, "The solution is to exchange goods and services rather than money."

Did you have any censorship problems with the film?

When we opened at the Pantages on Hollywood Boulevard, the fellows in publicity got up a full-page ad, and the day before the opening the ad was canceled. The Hearst papers wouldn't run the ad. We called them up and they said it was "pinko propaganda." Then a group came from Russia, where the film had been screened, and they said to me, "We would have given you the first prize, except your film is capitalistic propaganda." I don't know which the film is, though I think it's quite an honor to have one picture called both.

There is an incredible rhythmic feel to Our Daily Bread. *Have you ever consciously choreographed action in your films to establish a kind of rhythm?*

Yes, I started working with a thing called "silent music" that I picked up from Griffith. In the chases scene of *The Birth of a Nation,* and especially

Intolerance, I began to watch the crescendos and climaxes. I started experimenting with the first picture I made at MGM by marking up the script with a metronome, following the idea that each scene would be speedier than the one before. Why can't you carry that feel in your head? You can't because of shooting out of continuity. So I took a metronome and put down eighty, sixty, fifty-five, whatever, at the edge of each scene. We used to have music on the set so I could apply it to the movie. I would put the metronome on the portable organ and tell the fellow, "Play this fast," and hope that the actors would react to the speeding up of the music. I was always trying to get music into the pictures—music that you didn't hear—only you heard it once you got to the theater because pictures never ran without musical accompaniment.

A good example would be in *The Big Parade* with the sequence walking through the woods. Everybody was walking to a metronome because I patterned it after funeral march scenes. With *Our Daily Bread* we had a limited budget and we were shooting with sound, and I decided to let the sound go for the last week and save that money. So we did the whole thing with a metronome, picks coming down on beats one and three, shovels coming down on beats two and four. And each scene we speeded up over the previous scene, and as it got faster and faster it actually got faster than they could swing with the picks and shovels, so we started slowing down with the camera a little bit. Griffith, Chaplin, Sennett—their cameras never stayed the same speed. Chaplin once told me that nobody ever saw him walk at his normal speed. All the cameramen hand-cranked and knew how much to slow down.

How do you work with your actors?

Different actors, different ways. A psychiatrist friend of mind once spent the day on the set and said, "You're doing the same thing I am." But it was different things for different people. With Jennifer Jones you had to tell her the whole story every day from beginning to end. She does not see herself as a pro. She saw herself as a little girl and was scared to death about what she was doing. So you had to get her in the mood and tell her the story about what was going on up to that point, and then she could do it. Now, you wouldn't do that with a guy like Spencer Tracy who was a real pro. I think just to be an actor always engenders a certain amount of fear. I think all of them come on the stage every day scared to death that they won't be able to do the job. Tracy was always threatening me that he was going to quit and go home, so I figured out that we had to have some attractive woman sitting there admiring him and telling him how great he was. We employed a woman to do that—an attractive woman, a vacationer or something, who was excited by watching him.

I watched Chaplin direct Marlon Brando and Sophia Loren once, and they were having a terrible time trying to copy him because he was acting all the parts first. I saw Brando looking and sort of wondering, "Can I do that? Can I mimic him?" Naturally Brando wouldn't do it the same way that Chaplin did, so I feel that if you don't dominate the actors too much then you give them a chance to be more creative. Let them create their own parts. In other words, they're thinking about their parts exclusively, and I'm thinking about the whole overall thing. So I didn't ever try to get in there and act for them. That was their job.

How did you get along with the writer Ayn Rand when you directed The Fountainhead?

A script had been written by a husband-and-wife team by the time I arrived at the studio. I read it and then studied the book carefully. I thought they were spoiling the book. So they asked, "What do you suggest?" I said, "Why not get Ayn Rand?" They said she didn't know anything about screenplays, but I said I would work with her and take care of the screenplay continuity and technique—sort of guide her. I spent a couple of weeks going through the chapter headings and marking out what the film should keep and what it shouldn't. By the time she came in I had a pretty good skeleton of what the screenplay was. I got along great with her. They didn't even have to pay her because she was so anxious to get the book on the screen. She said she'd do it under one condition—if they changed any lines, she wanted the possibility to be telephoned and come to the studio. That was a great help to me because actors always want to change lines. So I used that as a prop. I'd say to Gary Cooper, "Okay, you'll have to phone Ayn Rand." And he'd say, "How long will it take her to get here?" "Oh, it'll be about an hour." And he'd say, "Oh, God, let's go, I'll read the line." Many actors, out of nervousness or fear, will say, "I can't read that line." But if they try hard they can.

The Fountainhead *has a look about it, for a film of its time, that no other film has for me, a very particular way of lighting the interiors.*

This was all influenced by Frank Lloyd Wright. I got all of the Frank Lloyd Wright books, the plans of houses, and I remember I would sit just absorbing these feelings. And then I got the cameraman and the art director and they'd do the same. We also looked at other modern structures of the time, buildings like the United Nations.

The philosophy espoused by Ayn Rand in The Fountainhead *might seem analogous to the film director. As a creative artist yourself, how do you feel about the fact that film is a community art form? How does an artist protect his integrity, as Howard Roark tries to protect his integrity in Rand's story?*

Well, that's something that I've spent a lot of time thinking about. You see, when a fellow writes a book, he's the sole originator. He's got to be. The difficulty with movies is that you are depending on a lot of other people. But as far as I'm concerned, even if the cameraman has a big contribution to make, the director has to be the one to say yes or no. I think the basic interest in any work of art is that you're seeing that fellow's individuality. I firmly believe that everybody has a distinct individuality. Maybe I didn't always believe this, but the whole problem is being able to express your individuality, and that is the theme of *The Fountainhead.* I miss seeing that today, the continuity of the individual. Certainly with Federico Fellini, it's a Fellini film; Ingmar Bergman, it's a Bergman film. I guess Bernardo Bertolucci is okay, too. But Sydney Pollack? I don't know. American directors have a hard time because they're jumping around in different things. But the strength of filmmaking has got to be the viewpoint of one person. If the writer doesn't want to accept that his story is going to go through the hands of a director, then he should write a book. You simply have to take that stance, and I think when you do, everybody working on the film feels a hell of a lot better for it.

For *The Fountainhead* I always thought that either Humphrey Bogart or James Cagney was the ideal casting, not Gary Cooper because he's such a nice and quiet guy. But when I saw the picture a few years later I thought Cooper was ideal *because* he's very quiet and he just says, "No, that's not the way I want it." Very quiet, like the strong guy of *High Noon,* and I thought it was much better than having a guy losing his temper and being arrogant and yelling.

How did Show People, *which starred Marion Davies, come about?*

It was inspired by Gloria Swanson and Mack Sennett. Marion Davies was a Sennett bathing beauty. William Randolph Hearst* always put her in costume dramas. Because I'd made *The Big Parade* he wanted me to direct Marion in a film. But I wouldn't do it—I wouldn't make one of those costume dramas. So a writer friend of mine and I went up to San Simeon where Hearst lived and happened to see her clowning all over the place. We realized she was a marvelous comedienne, so we wrote in the script that she gets hit in the face with a custard pie. When it got time to start, Hearst was adamant, he wouldn't give in or okay the script. We found out he refused to have Marion hit with a custard pie. I stood pat and said, "No, that's the whole point—that's the symbol." There was a standoff. Finally, wanting to move ahead, we compromised with a seltzer bottle and a hose in the face.

Did you always like to discuss things with your cameramen before starting shooting?

If I went location scouting I always wanted the cameraman there because he would then have a feeling of what time of day was the best time to do certain shots. He could think in terms of light. I was always having to go to the head of the studio, Warner Bros. and so forth, who said, "Why the hell do you need the cameraman? You just pick the location, take along the production manager, assistant director and art director. What the hell do you need the cameraman for?" It was so that he could contribute to the film properly, but there was always a fight because usually the cameramen were doing another film. They would finish one film on Saturday and start a new one on Monday, so it was always a battle to get them ahead of time.

You spoke about moving from silent films into sound films, but how was it moving from black and white into color?

When dialogue came along, the studios thought we all didn't know anything about dialogue, and in fact we didn't know too much, so they put a

---

*William Randolph Hearst (1863–1951). Publishing magnate, film producer, lover of Marion Davies and basis for the character of Charles Foster Kane in Orson Welles' *Citizen Kane* (1941).

stage actor or dialogue director to work with us. The guys who were directors were immediately clever enough to make a job out of learning what
dialogue meant. Now, I remember very specifically about the first color
film that I had to do, *Northwest Passage*. We'd been thinking in terms of
black and white and gray, and that I'd better get busy and find out what
color meant—what reds and greens meant, and things about hot colors
and cool colors—and I'd better learn that fast. So the quickest way was to
lay off—I probably skipped a picture or so—and study painting. I didn't
take any lessons, I just started painting to find out.

*Are you able to think back on your past and pinpoint what motivated you to want
to tell certain stories or why you chose a certain type of material?*

Yes, I've thought of it from time to time. The first year I made silent films
we didn't have any budget to buy stories. You'd just write your own, and I
made four pictures that first year and they were all out of my past. But you
can't keep doing that. *Hallelujah!* was just a bunch of things that I'd seen
happening in my boyhood in Texas and Arkansas. I just made a list of all
the stuff that I'd seen, and we connected it up with some sort of story
thread. Fellini's still doing that with a film like *Amarcord*. He's psychoana-
lyzing himself with practically every picture he does. I think part of your
career is very much pulling from your own life, and when I saw *Amarcord*
I said that I could write a whole picture based around scenes in my early
life. I have enough material from remembering things that happen in this
small Texas town which has stayed just the same; it hasn't changed at all.
In fact, there was nothing in *Hallelujah!* that I didn't see myself.

I'm a firm believer in the fact that you put your individual stamp on
your work. I think the whole job is to show one's individual viewpoint.
One day I had the advantage of seeing *The Crowd* in the afternoon and
Our Daily Bread that night, and I could see connections between them. I
could see something maturing on my part, an attitude about life, about
people. I don't know if all my films have that touch—I think the most
important ones do have the continuity of an individual. But how many
directors today achieve that? I went into a projection room at MGM one
time and sat down waiting for some dailies to end, and said, "Oh, that's
George Stevens." I spotted his style in that footage. Another time I went
in and—with no name on it or anything—knew it was von Sternberg. I
spotted that because of the photography. It's what I look for in the new

American directors. How many of them are doing that? How many films have an individuality or personality within them?

Do you think it's fair to say that nowadays the system doesn't really promote or encourage that kind of individuality in filmmakers?

I think that's exactly right. I know I stopped making pictures long before I wanted to. The number one reason was that I didn't feel like being a promoter, a businessman. Today you have to have a terrific feeling for packaging and wooing stars and putting the whole thing together. Pictures cost so damn much today, and that takes away from individuality.

What are some of the things that prevent a director from putting his individual stamp on a picture?

My ideal way in the days when I made my best films—and to me it is still the best way—was to tell somebody the type of story I'd like to do and then they'd finance it. They'd give you a writer and assist you in getting your ideas into script form. Both *The Crowd* and *Hallelujah!* were done that way: just built up from an idea with a studio backing me up. Then when the studios broke up and the conglomerates took over there was nobody you could go to and say, "This is an idea I have to make into a film." They'll say, "What stars have you got?" Immediately they start to think about bankability and financial insurance, and you'll have to say, "This is a best seller," or "Two stars have seen it and they're going to go for it." I would never have made *The Crowd* like that. I made *War and Peace* based on a book that's out of Tolstoy's guts, I guess. I agree with the leading character, the search for truth and meaning. But for me, it was just a job. The producer called me up and asked if I wanted to direct it. But that film isn't out of *my* guts.

I haven't made a picture for the past ten or fifteen years. I worked on a picture about Cervantes, the fellow who wrote *Don Quixote,* but the people who financed the script and developed the story from the book ran into an impossible problem of getting stars and finding the money. I thought it was a marvelous script, but they couldn't complete it because in order to get the stars you have to show them a script and give them a starting date. In order to get a starting date you have to have a star. It's kind of a vicious circle—one defeats the other.

Child star Jackie Cooper relaxes with his director on the set of *The Champ* in 1931. Wallace Beery, who was cast by Vidor as the ex-heavyweight champion Andy "Champ" Purcell, won the Academy Award in a tie with Fredric March.

Do you often look back at your old films? And do you ever go to the movies today?

Well, I was told that good wine gets better with age, and that bad wine gets worse with age. I think that pictures are the same: bad pictures get worse and good pictures get better. I remember years ago when I saw *The Birth of a Nation.* They had a two-reel Mack Sennett comedy, then the big film with a one-hundred-piece orchestra, and I think a newsreel too. I remember I would take a streetcar from Hollywood all the way downtown. It was an exciting evening—you got your money's worth. It was a big picture show.

Is there any advice you can give to students wanting to become directors?

It sometimes takes years to find out who you are and what you are because we don't accept ourselves as distinct individuals. We're not trained that way. When you're very young your parents always want you to pattern yourself after them. There's a great resistance to saying, "What do I believe in? What do I feel?" and not being ashamed of it. This is the number one thing I've learned: to find out who you are and respect yourself, the divinity of yourself. If God isn't expressed by the individual, where the hell is he expressed? You have to respect yourself first and you have to find out who you are and have the courage and guts by any means in the world to put yourself into whatever you're doing. Remember that, will you?

———————

Films as Director

1919 *The Turn in the Road* (also scenario)
Better Times (also scenario)
The Other (also story)
Poor Relations (also scenario)

1920 *The Family Honor* (also producer)
The Jack-Knife Man (also producer)

1921 *The Sky Pilot* (also producer)
Love Never Dies (also producer)

1922 *The Read Adventure*
Dusk to Dawn
Conquering the Woman (also producer)
Peg O' My Heart

1923 *The Woman of Bronze*
Three Wise Fools

1924 *Wild Oranges* (also adaptation)
Happiness
Wine of Youth (also producer)
Wife of the Centaur

His Hour (also co-scenario)

1925 *Proud Flesh*
The Big Parade

1926 *La Bohème*
Bardelys the Magnificent

1928 *The Crowd* (also co-scenario and story)
The Patsy
Show People

1929 *Hallelujah!* (also story)

1930 *Not So Dumb*
Billy the Kid

1931 *Street Scene*
The Champ

1932 *Cynara*
Bird of Paradise

1933 *Stranger's Return*

1934 *Our Daily Bread* (also story)

1935 *So Red the Rose*
The Wedding Night

1936 *The Texas Rangers* (also co-story)

1937 *Stella Dallas*

1938 *The Citadel*

1940 *Northwest Passage*

       Comrade X

1941 *H. M. Pulham, Esq.* (also co-screenplay)

1944 *An American Romance* (also producer and story)

1946 *Duel in the Sun*

1948 *A Miracle Can Happen*

1949 *The Fountainhead*

       Beyond the Forest

1951 *Lightening Strikes Twice*

1952 *Japanese War Bride*

       Ruby Gentry (also coproducer)

1955 *Man without a Star*

1956 *War and Peace* (also coadaptation)

1959 *Solomon and Sheba*

A director is one who has not just to study people but in a certain way he has to love them. And when I say love them, I mean understand them, understand why they do certain things.

FRITZ LANG
(Born in Vienna, 1890—Died 1976)

When Fritz Lang died in Beverly Hills at the age of eighty-five, *The New York Times* offered an obituary that would have pleased the great man: "The film world of Lang, whose innovative craftsmanship influenced hundreds of younger directors and put an indelible stamp on the art of cinema, was populated largely by psychopaths, master criminals, prostitutes, child murderers, sadists and the insane."

Lang was one of the most colorful and sardonic figures in film history. For much of his life he wore a monocle and was by turns autocratic, charming, abusive, romantic and vain. He saw himself as a visual person, saying, "I experience with my eyes and rarely, if ever, with my ears"—an observation that is fulfilled in the striking expressionist imagery of his films.

Lang had a brilliant career in Germany before fleeing Europe for the United States when Hitler came on the stage. He became an American citizen and sustained his career despite the disparity between his creative impulses and the commercial demands of Hollywood. He first wanted to be an architect, like his successful father in Vienna, but ran away to Paris to study art. "Anyone who wants to be something should run away from home," he advised the AFI fellows. His adventure in Paris ended with the outbreak of the First World War, when he was called into service in the Austrian army and wounded four times in combat. While recovering in a hospital in Vienna, he appeared in stage productions that led to his first opportunity as a screenwriter. The German films he directed were groundbreaking and stand today as classics, notably *Metropolis, M,* his first sound film, and *The Last Will of Dr. Mabuse.* As the Nazis were tightening their hold on German society, Joseph Goebbels, Hitler's propaganda minister,

Fritz Lang reviews the script of *You and Me* on a soundstage at Paramount
in 1939. The picture starred Sylvia Sidney and George Raft.

offered the young director a job making films for the party. Lang made the
sudden decision to take the night train to Paris, leaving Germany and all his
belongings behind.

Lang led an active professional life in Hollywood, making twenty-four
films between 1936 and 1956. He had creative control of his films in Germany,
but never mastered that game in Hollywood, ending his life blind and bitter
about his career in America. Nonetheless, *Fury, Manhunt, You Only Live
Once, Scarlet Street* and *The Big Heat* are considered noir classics. Other pictures didn't live up to his standards. He explained one failure to Peter Bogdanovich, saying, "I did it because I had to eat." It is ironic that this
American immigrant is most admired in the United States for the work he
did in Germany and is most admired in Europe for the films he made in
America.

FRITZ LANG

—▬—

June 13, 1973

How do you like your coffee, Mr. Lang?

Black . . . as my soul.

You said you often learned more from bad films than good films. Why was that so?

I learned only from bad films. When a young actor or a writer came to me and asked, "What can I do to learn to make films?" I was always in a mess because I didn't know what to tell them. So I asked myself how I learned. Now, when I looked at the good films, I always was a very good audience. I was never interested in who the actor was, who the director was or where the cameraman was. I lived with the film. I enjoyed it. It was an adventure. When I saw a lousy film there was something which made me say, "Wait a moment, this is not good, this I would have done differently." In my opinion, this is the only way I learned anything. I don't know if another person could do the same thing. You talk to me about myself, you know.

In the very beginning there was nobody to learn from, was there?

No. You see, I lived in Paris before the First World War started and I wanted to become a painter. And then I went to a movie and this whole thing started to interest me because they were not static pictures which I made when I was painting the canvas, they were moving pictures, and I looked at quite a lot of them. Mostly they were adventure pictures. Do you know *Arsène Lupin?** That kind of film. Not that I had the slightest idea to become a motion picture man—but this interested me and probably there something was created in me. I don't know. I am asked, "How did you make the first films which you made in Berlin?" I can only give one honest answer: I made them almost sleepwalking. I had nobody whom I admired so much that I said, "I would like to make a film like this director or like this director." In those days I wrote the stories myself. I used four days and four nights to write a story. I remember one day Erich Pommer[†] was asking me for something, and I hadn't written anything and I said, "Take my word of honor that I'll give it to you in five days." So he asked me for my word of honor, and I sat down with a bottle of French red wine and started that night. In those days you had one page for each scene, so you could interchange whenever you wanted. When you suddenly said, "I need something before," you just put another number on a scene; so you could write a film in four days.

When you were in Paris before World War I, studying to be a painter, was it then that you decided you wanted to make motion pictures?

No, I never decided. That came much, much later. When the First World War broke out, I left Paris with the fast train and was captured on the borderline in Belgium. Then, the same night, we escaped. Probably they were very happy to get rid of us, and it was very stupid. Anyway, I was captured because a lady who also was in the last train had forgotten her handbag and I went back to get her handbag with her, and they caught me. And probably they were very happy to say, "Leave the door open and let the son of a bitch go." I'd had a hernia. I wouldn't serve as a soldier before I went to Paris and I had the hernia operated on because nobody was thinking about a war at the time, and now, with an operated hernia, I was absolutely fit to go to war. In the meantime I worked in a cabaret. It was 1913 or 1914 when I fled from Paris. I had no money. I left everything and took the train to Vienna, where my parents lived, and there I went, not immediately, to the military. I think they called me three or four months later. But anyway, I made a little money in a cabaret. I had a stupid comedy act. I met a young man who was a bank clerk, and he wrote songs for

Arsène Lupin, directed by Jack Conway in 1932, tells the story of a Parisian gentleman thief.
[†]Erich Pommer (1889–1966), German producer, was active in the production company UFA.

the same cabaret, and he came to me and said, "Why don't we write a film script together?" and I said, "Fine." I had already written one about the railroads because for me it was so interesting to see the steps of the man in the snow slowly dissolving into the paw of the wolf, you know. And so we decided we wanted to write films together, but I didn't like very much what he wrote. He was a very nice man, so I said to him, "Let me write the scripts and you sell them." So we sold one, and then I had to go to war. I came back, I think it was the third time I was wounded, and I had a sweetheart who was working in a cabaret, and I had only 120 kroner. I was sitting in a cafe, these kind of Viennese cafes that don't exist anymore.

Not even in Vienna?

Not even in Vienna, not in this way. You came there and you ordered a coffee and with the coffee came two glasses of water and with this you could sit the whole day. You could read all the papers, you could play billiards, and you didn't pay for anything. I see it as if it were yesterday, sitting there on the corner of the billiard table. And I had some decorations—I'd been wounded—and was thinking what you do if you have a very, very nice sweetheart and you need money. A man came to me and said in an East Prussian dialect, "Excuse me, Herr Lieutenant, would you be interested to play in a stage play?" I looked at him very odd and said, "Who are you?" And he said, "Oh forgive me, I am the director of a play." And I said, "So what do you want?" He said, "Well, Mr. Lieutenant, we would like to know if you'd try to play a part in the patriotic Red Cross play?" It was a play for the Red Cross, the story of an Austrian lieutenant. And sometimes, very seldom, I am at the right place at the right moment, and I said, "How much do you pay? I'm a wounded lieutenant living in a hospital with . . ." and he said 750 kroner. My heart fell from here into my shoes, so I said, "That's not very much." And he said, "Well, Mr. Lieutenant, more than a thousand we could not give you." So I made a deal for a thousand. Now I was out of trouble. I had a thousand kroner and a sweetheart. I didn't give a damn about this play. I'd never been onstage. What they wanted from me was to play a Prussian officer. It was in the last year of the war. So we made the first rehearsals, and Mr. Olstermeyer said, "Impossible. This man can never play the part we've written." But I had a contract, so they gave me the main part, the Austrian officer, who was wounded.

During this time I met Erich Pommer, who looked at me. I wore a monocle, and he said, "This monocle, son of a bitch, I don't want anything to do with it." But we came together after a performance, sat together until four or five o'clock in the morning, and then I had a job—in German you call it a dramaturge. You would call it here a script doctor. Now don't forget I was an Austrian officer, and Pommer belonged to the German army, and they could do whatever they wanted. He promised me that I wouldn't have any trouble. I couldn't go into the war anymore with the wounds and my bad eyes, so he would give me a vacation for two months. The German government would see to it that I would get out of the army and work as a script editor. So after the play was over, I went to Berlin.

Let's go back to the years prior to the war, when you were in Paris and you saw your first motion pictures. Were you more interested in cinema as a technological phenomenon or an aesthetic one?

Take what I'm telling you now with a grain of salt. I ran away from home when I was eighteen or nineteen. Anybody who wants to be somebody should run away from home. I could tell you funny adventures which I had which take hours and hours, but what is important is I lived in Brussels and then I went to Paris and then the whole Mediterranean. And I went up to Bali and then I came back on a ship. I would have to lie if I told you what I did on the ship.

You mean you went to Bali in the South Seas?

Yes, from Paris through the whole Adriatic Sea over from Cairo and then to Bali and then back. I lived from making postcards and selling them. When I came back, I lived in Paris. I didn't have much money, just to buy the most necessary things, and I always liked martinis. I went to a bar and said, "Give me a dry martini," and I drank half of it and it wasn't so dry. So he changed it to a little less dry. I had at least one and a half martinis for the price of one. But I'm looking around, and there was a very nice girl sitting with an elderly man. I went over to them and said, "Would you mind if I make a sketch?" When it was finished, I showed it to her. "Oh, it's wonderful," she said. I said, "It is a present for you." She said, "Thank you." Do you know what she did? [*Folds a piece of paper*] . . . and put it in her bosom. Then the man with her usually said, "How much do I owe you?" and I said, "It's up to you." I usually got ten or twenty francs.

Anyway, I'll tell you something that is important for somebody who wants to become a director. I was interested in people. Look, a director should know how prostitutes behave but he should also know how a queen behaves, a cook behaves. He should also know, which is practically the same, how a high financier behaves. Like a housewife behaves. A director is one who has not just to study people but in a certain way he has to love them. And when I say love them, I mean understand them, understand why they do certain things. And naturally, when I went on all these big travels—speaking with sailors and speaking with rich girls, and poor people and poor girls—I learned a lot of things.

Do you find that contemporary films lack that kind of deep understanding of the people they portray?

I don't see very many films nowadays. From time to time I look at films. I saw *The Getaway,* a film which preaches: commit murder, commit crime, and we'll have a happy life ever after.*

A happy life and lots of money, too.

You have no happy life without money, unfortunately. Have you seen *Deep Throat?* Look, let me for a moment be very Catholic. I'm a born Catholic and am very puritan, and so I am opposed to this film for a very simple reason. First of all, it is not film as art. But there's something else. If two young people, a boy and a girl, watch the film, they may find out there's another way to make love to each other. I go down on you, and you go down on me, whatever you want, right? Something that is very beautiful for them if they find it out by themselves, if it comes out of their passion for each other. But they come and see it for the first time in a motion picture and say, "Oh, let's try that." For me, the whole thing is a crime against youth.

Because it deprives them of the discovery they would make themselves?

It is a crime against youth, just as *The Getaway* is.

But assuming that people will imitate the action on the screen, which is really more harmful, The Getaway *or* Deep Throat?

---

* *The Getaway* (1972) was directed by Sam Peckinpah.

Probably in the wrong way, *The Getaway*. But it's very possible that the whole sex life of two young people can be gone to hell. I'm thinking about what I did in motion pictures and what other people did in motion pictures. I stopped making films here in 1956 or '57 because I foresaw the downfall of the motion picture industry. It's something very peculiar. We hear so much about the spy business of Mr. Nixon, right? When you made a film for an independent producer or a major company, did you know there were always spies around you, which reported every step you did?

I'll give you an example. I came to the conclusion actually in the last three or four films which I made here that the average citizen breaks the law as often as criminals do but they do it in such a way that it is not an official crime. Do you know what I mean? I wanted to make a serious film showing how average bourgeois did certain things. The last film I made was called *Beyond a Reasonable Doubt*. When Dana Andrews in desperation killed the girl who made his life unhappy, it was a crime of despair. When the woman he loves, who was played by Joan Fontaine, in the end turns him over to the law, she does it out of selfish reasons because she wants to marry another guy. Correct? Now this film started with an execution of a man.

I had been to Sing Sing, to Folsom, to San Quentin. The cage in which Dana Andrews lived, remember, was built absolutely according to how prisoners who were going to the chair lived forty-eight hours or twenty-four hours before their death. So the producer came to me and said, "Fritz, make it really correct and very gruesome." I said, "No, look. You'll have trouble with the main office." He said, "No, no, that's your business." I did not show the death of the man. I showed how he was bound to the chair and how they pulled the switch but I didn't show him doing anything like this [*gestures*], you know? I shot the whole sequence and then I went back to another sequence, which played in Condemned Row, and suddenly the producer came and started to yell, "What are you thinking? What are you doing? That is not the USA 1956. Why do you show such a horrible scene?" A spy had come from the main office. The main office had not called me but had called the producer and given him hell. So the producer comes to me and asks, "What do you think? Do you think we can sell such a picture?"

We had a hell of a fight with each other, and I said, "Look, there's only one possibility. If you want this film to be finished, walk out of here. If you don't walk out, I'll walk out. I don't give a damn anymore." So I finished the film. I had a very close friend, the editor Gene Fowler, Jr., and he knew exactly how I would cut the film, so when the film was over, I said good-bye. The producer says, "But you can't go. You can't leave me alone." I said, "You son of a bitch. I don't want to have anything to do with you anymore or the American motion picture industry," and I walked out and never again made a film in the United States. Same spying business which you have now, if you like, with the government. It's a peculiar business, making motion pictures.

You must have worked with producers who facilitated your work sometime in your career.

Look, a producer can be a great fellow.

If he leaves you alone?

No, if he helps. Zanuck gave me mostly a free hand. I had wanted a discussion with him. He said, "You should have made a close-up here." I said, "I can still make it." "So why didn't you make it immediately?" So I said, "Mr. Zanuck, I want to ask you a question. Sometimes you dictate a letter to your secretary and then she reads it to you. Is it always correct?" He said, "No, sometimes I have to change it." "But from me you want it immediately perfect."

Was it Man Hunt *that he made the comment about?*

No. It was *Western Union.*

How did it happen that you became involved in Westerns?

I left Germany because I couldn't stand the Nazi ideas and the Nazi regime and I went to Paris. I made one film there and then I came here. I was a year at MGM and then I couldn't get a job. And for one year I had nothing to do. I traveled around the country in my car, I spoke to every man, gas station attendant, whatever. I lived with the Navajos and I learned a lot. Then I made *The Return of Frank James.* I had done some research and I had a lot of knowledge. I always thought that Westerns are a certain religion of the American people. The funny thing was, after I finished *Western Union,* I got a letter from old-timers in Flagstaff, who wrote, "Dear Mr. Lang, We saw *Western Union* last night and it's the only film that depicts the West as it really was." How was this for a European director? The old-timers were wrong, naturally, but the film lived up to what they wished the West would have been. I tried to build legends with human beings, that's all.

There were a great many German, Austrian and Hungarian actors and actresses who to the United States came at the same time you did. Why didn't you use more of those European actors?

I can't remember that I ever used a European actor as an American, but when I made *Hangmen Also Die* I used a lot of Germans. I wanted to show an American audience what it means if a country is overrun by foreign powers with absolutely other political ideals. Therefore, as the story plays in Czechoslovakia, I made all the Czechs Americans and all the Germans Germans. I had a fight with Bertolt Brecht, who was responsible for the script. Do you know what a quisling is? A quisling is a man who collaborates with the enemy. There was a quisling among the Czechs, and Bertolt Brecht suggested a very good actor, Oskar Homolka. I said, "I can't use him because he must be an American. If he has a German accent, everybody will say, 'Oh, naturally he's sympathizing because somewhere he has a German mother or grandfather.' Brecht never could understand it, never. I did the same thing in my first anti-Nazi film. It started with an attempted assassination of Hitler.

Are you referring to Man Hunt?

Yes. Afterward, in London, the Nazis are played by Germans.

But what I meant was, if my point is correct, you wanted to make American films.

Naturally.

For instance, when you made Liliom *in Paris, you used French actors; when you came to America, you used American actors.*

Do you know Lotte Eisner?* When she came here, she said, "You know, it's very funny. When I see now the Molnar films which you made in Europe, they are all European characters. Whereas your American films are only American characters." When I came to this country, I stopped speaking German. I didn't speak a word of German.

How did you come to make Man Hunt?

It was very peculiar. I am told that John Ford turned it down for political reasons. Kenneth MacGowan, who was the associate producer, offered it to me; I jumped at the idea because it was the first time that I could try to make the American audience understand the Nazi regime.

Why was the budget so small on Man Hunt? *You had a terrific cast, a terrific crew and a great story.*

I may have a clue to that. When John Ford turned the picture down, and Darryl Zanuck gave it to me, Darryl said, "Don't show too many swastikas. We don't like that." For me, it was the first time that I could really show what the swastika meant, you know, and I showed it as often as I could. Zanuck never said anything, but maybe, because of this, he didn't want to spend.

Of all your films, which is your favorite?

Today I almost like *Liliom* best of all. And *Scarlet Street, M* and *Fury.*

What was your relationship with your crews?

The rule is that you should start your first shot at nine o'clock. I consider the crew very close to me because we are working together. I mean, if someone pushes the cart on which the camera stands, he knows he has to stop exactly on one point for a certain reason. If he doesn't understand why, he may go too far or he may not go far enough. So I was always the first one at the studio at seven o'clock. And do you know why? For a very simple reason. Look, sometimes you have to go into overtime. You usually

*Renowned historian of German cinema (1896–1983).

Joan Bennett with Lang during shooting of *Scarlet Street* (1945).
Edward G. Robinson and Dan Duryea also starred in *Scarlet Street,*
which Lang lists as one of his favorite films.

send your main actress home because if a woman gets up at five or six
o'clock and starts to shoot at nine o'clock, the close-ups made at five or six
o'clock that evening can't be very good anymore. So you send her home
and then you work maybe one hour later. I don't want to hear from the
crew, "Naturally, Mr. Lang, you come at nine o'clock in the morning. It's
very easy for you to work one or two hours longer." But when I come at
seven o'clock and work with my crew and have a cup of coffee, then they
could never say this. I never had trouble with anyone.

Would you comment on how you work with actors?

You have to work with an actor as you would work with yourself. You
have to explain to him how you see the character that he has to put on the
screen. You cannot use him. Maybe he's right, and you have to think it
over. Maybe he is wrong. There's something which you should get from
an actor, something which is under his skin, something which he himself
maybe doesn't know exactly. I never did tell an actor how to play a role. I
don't want to have twenty-five little Fritz Langs running around.

M *is regarded as a classic. How did it come about?*

I had made *Die Nibelungen, Metropolis* and *Girl in the Moon.* Big films, crowds and so on. I got tired of this kind of film and I was thinking of simpler stories. I was talking with Thea von Harbou, my wife. What was the most abominable, the greatest crime which we reject? We decided, let's write some nasty son-of-a-bitch stories. And one day I came to her and said, "Listen, darling, let's make a film about a child murderer who is forced by a power within him to commit a crime which he afterwards resents very much." And then we made *M.*

Those days there were lots of horrible crimes in Germany. There was a mass murderer in the Rhineland, and many reviewers said that was the inspiration, which is not true. *M* was finished long before this mass murderer. At the Berlin Scotland Yard I saw the result of many murders. One case I will never forget—a small shop where a woman was murdered, and the murderer cut her throat and the blood just dripped over the counter into an open sack of white flour. I will never forget that my whole life. Another one was in a big apartment house where they found chopped-off hands on a plate under the bed of the murderer, where he was cooking something. There was a man on the border of Germany and Czechoslovakia who killed travelers and made sausages out of them and sold them, and the people liked them very much. It was really a horrible time.

I first saw Peter Lorre on the stage. He came to Berlin and was in two plays, and my idea was to cast the murderer differently from what Lombroso has said a murderer is: big eyebrows, big shoulders. You know, the famous Lombroso picture of a murderer.* And so I used Peter Lorre, who nobody would think to be a murderer. I had a big fight with Peter. In the kangaroo court scene, which I shot at the Staaken Zeppelinhalle, he didn't want to come because he was playing at night in *Squaring the Circle* and had rehearsals. I had to force him. I said, "Look, I will bring an injunction against you because I have a contract with you." And so he came, and we shot the last scenes and we didn't talk until it brought on a great success, and then we talked again.

The film was Lorre's first great success, wasn't it?

*Cesare Lombroso (1835–1909) was a highly influential Italian criminologist and physician known for his study of the relation between mental and physical characteristics.

Yes. I remember one thing that was very funny. Thea von Harbou and I sat for two hours in front of the room where the censors were looking at the film. We didn't have to be ashamed, and yet you look there like a schoolboy worrying if you got a good note or not. Finally they came out and they said, "Mr. Lang, this film has practically everything about which we disagree and which we cannot accept, but it is done with such integrity that we don't want to make any cuts."

Was M a great success from the beginning?

From the beginning. Contrary to destiny, you know. It's very peculiar because in *M* there's no love story, and I'll tell you what happened. A young man came to me—very elegant. But he had a very peculiar reputation. He asked me if I would like to make a film with him, and I said no. I didn't want to make films anymore. I wanted to become a chemist. And he came again, and I said, "Let me tell you something. I will make a film for you, but you have no rights except to give me the money for what the film costs. You will have no rights to subject, no rights about cutting, no rights about casting." He accepted this. Otherwise *M* would never have been made, because it has no love story, nothing.

You mentioned that Bertolt Brecht worked on one of the films that you did. I understand he had a very difficult time here financially.

Marthe Feutwangler and I and Lillie Latte collected money to help get Brecht over. The European Film Committee brought him here. He worked, I think, on one thing with Leon Feutwangler.

When Heydrich* was assassinated in 1942, I had an idea to make a picture about it, and I asked Brecht if he would like to help. Brecht said, yes, he would like to make this film with me, and we sat together for five days and lined out a story. I was freelancing, and there was a European man here named Arnold Pressburger, who wanted to make a film with me. And I said, "Brecht, how much do you want for this script?" And Brecht said, "Do you think three thousand dollars is too much?"

Because he couldn't speak English, I said, "Let me find out." I knew

---

*Reinhard Heydrich (1904–1942), second only to Himmler in the SS chain of command, was chief of the Reich security head office and protector of Bohemia and Moravia.

what I could do; and I came back, and Brecht said, "How was it?" I said, "Yes, he wants the film. What would you say if I said five thousand dollars?" "Oh," he said, "that would be wonderful, really?" I said, "No, you will get seventy-five hundred," and he was very happy.

We had to search for a man who could work with him, who could speak German very well and be a good writer, and we found John Wexley, who had written *The Last Mile*. We didn't know it, but he was in the Communist Party. After five days Brecht did something which spoiled everything. He came to me and said, "Fritz, I'm not working anymore." I said, "Why not?" He said, "Wexley tells me that Pressburger pays him ten thousand dollars." I said, "Yes, it's correct." He said, "But if he gets ten thousand dollars, I want to have ten thousand dollars, too. I don't work otherwise." I said, "Let me talk to Pressburger. That's blackmail."

I went to Pressburger, and it took me three or four hours, and I said, "Look, twenty-five hundred dollars—what the hell." Finally I convinced him, and then they worked together. In the meantime, I was working with the cameraman, and one day Pressburger called me. He said, "Fritz, something horrible happened." I said, "What happened?" He said, "We have made a mistake. We have to start a month sooner than we expected." Now, I had a script over 220 pages that wasn't finished. So without saying anything to Brecht or Wexley, I started to cut. I cut it down as much as possible, and we started to shoot. Brecht never came to the set. He was hurt. In his diary it says Pressburger and Lang don't want to give him the proper rights of author or some such thing.

To make a long story short, Wexley claimed that much of the film is by him and very little from Brecht, which is stupid and wrong because there are so many scenes that are so typically Brecht that nobody else could have invented them. It came to an arbitration. Pressburger said he would not speak for Brecht because he had blackmailed him for twenty-five hundred dollars, so Eisler and I spoke for Brecht. The arbitration decided to give Brecht the rights of the author of the original idea for the script, but the actual script would be Wexley because Mr. Brecht has always said that he will go back to Europe and he doesn't need the credit whereas Mr. Wexley stays here and he will need it. We couldn't do anything. I said, "Look, the whole idea is from Brecht," and today, if anybody asks, I say the script is from Brecht.

I was the only one who gave Brecht a chance and I am very happy about it. Brecht could probably never understand that you work for an audience. He wanted to push his ideas on an audience. I was always

With Robert Ryan on *Clash by Night* (1952).

opposed to the American line, "An audience has the mentality of a sixteen-year-old chambermaid." If this would be true, I would be ashamed to work for such an audience. I like audiences, but I don't think you should give an audience something fifty steps ahead of them. I asked myself, why is the first work of a writer, of a screenwriter or of a playwright almost always a success? Because he still belongs to an audience. The more he goes away from the audience, the more he loses contact, and what I tried to do my whole life was not to lose contact with the audience.

Films as Director

1919 *Der Herr der Liebe* (*Master of Love*)
Die Spinnen (*The Spiders, Part 1*)
Hara-Kiri
1920 *Das Wandernde Bild* (*The Wandering Image*)
Die Spinnen 2 (*The Spiders, Part 2*)
1921 *Der müde Tod* (*Destiny*)
Dr. Mabuse, der Spieler (*Dr. Mabuse: The Gambler*)
1924 *Die Nibelungen*
1927 *Metropolis*
1928 *Spione* (*Spies*)
1929 *Die Frau im Mond* (*Girl in the Moon*)
1931 *M*
1933 *Das Testament des Dr. Mabuse* (*The Testament of Dr. Mabuse*)
1935 *Liliom*
1936 *Fury* (also co-screenplay)
1937 *You Only Live Once*
1938 *You and Me*
1940 *The Return of Frank James*
1941 *Western Union*
Man Hunt
Confirm or Deny

1942 *Moontide*
1943 *Hangmen Also Die!* (also producer, coadaptation and co-story)
1944 *Ministry of Fear*
The Woman in the Window
1945 *Scarlet Street* (also producer)
1946 *Cloak and Dagger*
1948 *Secret Beyond the Door* (also producer)
1950 *House by the River*
American Guerilla in the Philippines
1952 *Rancho Notorious*
Clash by Night
1953 *The Blue Gardenia*
The Big Heat
1954 *Human Desire*
1955 *Moonfleet*
1956 *While the City Sleeps*
Beyond a Reasonable Doubt
1959 *Der Tiger con Eschnapur* (*Journey to the Lost City*)
1960 *Die Tausend Augen des Dr. Mabuse* (*The Thousand Eyes of Dr. Mabuse*) (also producer and co-screenplay)

The "one man, one film" idea had penetrated bastions of industrial, assembly-line companies just prior to the war. Leo McCarey, George Stevens and I brought all those people to Columbia, all those major directors who came and made their best films there. Everyone loved it because it was one man making a film. It was only Louis B. Mayer who hated all this.

FRANK CAPRA
(Born in Palermo, Italy, 1897—Died 1991)

After four years flying bombers in World War II, Jimmy Stewart returned to Hollywood and found himself disillusioned, with no appetite to resume acting. He recalled how Frank Capra invited him over to his house one day and started telling him an idea for a film. "Now, you're in a small town and things aren't going very well. And you begin to wish you'd never been born. And you decide to commit suicide by jumping off a bridge into the river—but an angel named Clarence comes down from heaven, and Clarence hasn't won his wings yet. He comes down to save you from the river, but Clarence can't swim, so you save him." Stewart thought a moment, then stammered, "Frank, if you want to do a movie about me committin' suicide with an angel with no wings named Clarence, I'm your boy." Such were the beginnings of *It's a Wonderful Life.*

Frank Capra arrived in America from Sicily with parents who couldn't read or write. He worked his way out of poverty to earn a degree in chemical engineering at the California Institute of Technology, joined the army in 1918, but never saw action during the Great War. A series of odd jobs after the war led him to motion pictures.

Capra was small in stature and robust in spirit. "I hated being a peasant, being a scrounging new kid trapped in the Sicilian ghetto of Los Angeles." When he got his first jobs working on two-reelers, Capra recalled, "All I had was cockiness—and let me tell you that gets you a long way."

In the depths of the Depression he signed on at Columbia Pictures, a modest little studio situated in what was called Gower Gulch. There, during the 1930s, he made a string of populist hits, all but one of them written by Robert Riskin, and many of them pitting an idealistic hero against corrupt

Frank Capra (right) with cinematographer Joe Walker at Columbia Studios.
Walker photographed twenty of Capra's films including *It Happened One
Night, Mr. Smith Goes to Washington* and *It's a Wonderful Life.*

institutions. *It Happened One Night, Mr. Deeds Goes to Town, You Can't Take
It with You, Meet John Doe* and *Mr. Smith Goes to Washington* enabled Capra
to become the director with "the name above the title." With Clark Gable,
Gary Cooper and Jimmy Stewart as his leading men, his pictures took home
the lion's share of Oscars, placing Capra on top of the heap and enabling
Columbia to take its place alongside the major studios.

Capra gave up his directing career four days after Pearl Harbor for a commission in the U.S. Army Signal Corps. He spent four years in uniform heading the Army Pictorial Service in Culver City, where he was responsible for

the *Why We Fight* series that oriented soldiers to the reasons for war. I love the story of the cocky little major going to Washington for his first Pentagon meeting. He walked into a conference room and found ten generals. He genially shook hands all around and then asked, "Fellas, are we here to talk about motion pictures?" They nodded. Capra then moved toward a big leather chair and said, "Alright, then I sit at the head of the table."

When World War II was over, he, William Wyler and George Stevens organized Liberty Films. A groundbreaking initiative, Liberty Films was the first independent company of directors, with the goal of making films without interference from studio bosses. The only picture completed by Liberty was *It's a Wonderful Life,* which, though highly popular half a century later, was not a success in its day. With money running short, Capra made a decision he called the worst of his life. He and Wyler voted two to one over Stevens to sell Liberty to Paramount, where Capra soon encountered difficulty launching the stories he wanted to make, demonstrating the importance of the independence the three men had sought. *It's a Wonderful Life* turned out to be Capra's last important film, and though he directed five more films over the next fourteen years, he never regained the spark and the confidence that had kept him on top in the thirties.

Capra lived well into his eighties, speaking at colleges in his later years and paying frequent visits to AFI. He was a relentless optimist and a cheerleader for the importance of film as an art form and for the director's control. His credo was, "One man, one film."

FRANK CAPRA

April 5, 1977*

You've often spoken about retaining control over your films and trying to remain independent even within the studio system. Could you say something about this?

If you have complete control over your films, every film you make will be a chapter in your own autobiography, because your true self will escape into it. If your self doesn't escape into it you'll have a conglomeration of stuff. You'll have too many minds in that one film, and you'll get a committee-made thing, and it's pretty hard to make art with a committee. You've got a chance of making a film that means something if one person guides it from beginning to end. One man, one film. This was very new stuff at the time I was working at Columbia. It was certainly not what was going on at MGM, where the only star was Leo the Lion. They believed that the department heads made the films, and in fact they did. The head of the laboratory was in charge of your cameraman; the head of the sound department was in charge of your soundman, not the director. And how they ever got successful used to bother the hell out of me. If my theory— one man, one film—is right, how the hell can they make successful pictures over there? But they were the biggest and had virtually every star and every top talent tied up. It was pure size and pure money, and whatever they made had that same look about it. Furniture with Grand Rapids polish was what it was to me. They didn't make very many pictures that were of lasting importance because they were a mixture of minds. It is interest-

*This transcript contains segments from seminars Frank Capra gave at the American Film Institute on July 14, 1971, November 6, 1974 and May 23, 1978.

ing to note that the midget major, Columbia—with its one man, one film system—garnered as many Best Picture Oscars as the giant MGM. I still think that is the way to make films. You don't have to agree with it. But if you're thinking of "one man, one film" then you must have courage, which is the most necessary thing to back up an idea or a hunch. Don't ever go with a pencil and try to figure out what happened last week with any film. The businessmen do that. Follow your hunches. Your hunch is creation.

You had an incredible training ground in silent films in the 1920s. Could you talk a little bit about how this affected your career?

From the very beginning my main concern was to be in control of everything: the story, the directing, the cameraman, the sound, the music. I couldn't see how anybody else could insert music I didn't want, or edit one way and photograph another. I thought all these constituents were an integral part of the film and had to come through me. I wanted to control the film even though I didn't write the music or do the actual developing. A battle emerged in Hollywood between individual and assembly-line picture makers. I could only accept art when it was an extension of the individual, not the committee.

Back in the 1930s, if you'd been smart, you wouldn't have done what I did. Anybody could get complete control over his picture from beginning to end if he was stupid enough to want it, because the chances of it being a hit were really pretty low, maybe one out of ten. You can get better odds on a crooked wheel. So if you wanted complete control, everybody was very glad to give it to you because most people didn't want complete control—they wanted alibis. They wanted to say, "They gave me a lousy script. They gave me a lousy cast. They butchered it in the cutting room."

During my first years in film I said, "My God, if they pay me for this crap I'm doing they must be nuts." All I was hoping to get was enough money together so I could go back to Caltech and get a doctorate in physics. Film executives didn't mean much to me. They were just people who were silly enough to pay me for my kind of stuff. I'd say, "It's crazy, a graduate of Caltech who's never seen the inside of a studio, who's never been backstage, is making films." It was probably *It Happened One Night* that changed my mind. When it shook that old Oscar tree, then I finally said, "Wait a minute, maybe I'm pretty good at this. Maybe this is what I should be doing." Boy, they're opposites, science and art, and I chose films. From then on I began to think of cinema seriously, in the sense that maybe I could use it for a purpose besides being entertaining. And so I made my first picture in which I tried to say something that was socially important, *Mr. Deeds Goes to Town,* and from then on I tried to use films to make a social point. But I never forgot that films must be entertaining, that films must be inspiring to an audience, an experience that should be uplifting rather than downbeat. There are a lot of wonderful downbeat films. But we can't all make the same kinds of films. You make the films that come out of you.

Of course when I was making films they were not as well-developed as they are today in style and techniques, so every time you made a picture you would learn something new. I was my own student and my own teacher because I was a complete stranger to this business. All I had was cockiness, and let me tell you that gets you a long way.

What about your years at Columbia?

You've got to believe in yourself and make the other fellow believe that you believe in yourself. And this, of course, I picked up from Harry Cohn.* To deal with Harry Cohn you had to have a lot of brass, otherwise you couldn't get through the door. If he could bully you, out you went, no matter how creative you were. He trusted people who could stand up to his bullying; then he would sleep better at night knowing you were spending his money. If he thought you had enough guts then you might also have enough talent. And by the crude measure of guts he raised that rinky-dink joint he had down on poverty row into a major studio. An awful lot of fine, creative people left his studio simply because they couldn't take his bullying.

Cohn was all kinds of a bastard, but he was also a terrific man to work for because he challenged you every day. He didn't want people around who asked him what he wanted. "How would you like this, Mr. Cohn?" He didn't like that. He knew he didn't know anything about photography or directing. He said, "I know things by the seat of my pants. If my ass squirms, the picture stinks." This is what produced that wonderful crack from Herman Mankiewicz: "Harry, what makes you think the whole world is wired to your ass?" If you weren't cocky, if you didn't think that you knew what you were doing and if you didn't make him think so, then

*Harry Cohn (1891–1958) was founder of Columbia Studios.

you had a rough time of it. You couldn't let him win an argument because if he won an argument with you he'd fire you. He never won an argument with me. Never, and he liked me because of that, so I got complete freedom. How do you think I got him to spend two million dollars on *Lost Horizon?* Because he had confidence in me, because I gave him a good run for his money, that's all. So guts, gall and brass were, and still are, absolutely essential. That's the way it is with personal confidence. It'll get you a long way in a field as fragile and intangible as show business.

Don't be afraid to be confident in yourself and in your own intuitive ideas. Never say, "No." Say, "Yes, I can do that better than anybody else in the world." That's the way you've got to think of yourself, because if you don't, nobody else will, and part of this thing is selling yourself. There's an awful lot of money involved, and these people are not going to put up money for some milquetoast who says, "Gee, may I have that?" If you go in there and say, "Look, I think I've got one hell of an idea and I think it will make a lot of money," then at least you'll be talking with confidence.

I would never have reached where I got to if I didn't have the liberty I had at Columbia to make the films I wanted to make. Why? Because I can't take orders. You tell me to do this and I'll ask you, "Why?" If you haven't got a good answer, I won't do it. I just don't work well under superiors. The army was a tough place for me, but at Columbia I was my own boss. I was making them money and working very cheap, so we had a nice thing going there, and Columbia grew into a major studio, much of it due to the pictures I was allowed to make for them. I never once went over budget. I respected the man who put up the money, and if the budget was twenty-five-thousand dollars I was not going to spend over twenty-five thousand dollars because I wanted his trust.

You have always seemed to respect money.

I think money should be respected wherever it comes from. That's filmmaking—it's a dichotomy of money and art, and you can't make one without the other. It was a hell of a lot of money to gamble on a guy without any collateral. To give you two million dollars to go and spend as you want—that's quite a proposition and it sounds like a great idea. But if you flop, you'll never get it again. I could control the amount of money that was spent. Most stories can be told for fifty thousand, five hundred thousand or five million dollars—the same story. One will look bigger than the other, but it's the same story. So I had little tricks. For instance, I'd put in the script an opera scene which called for a big set. I had no intention of using the goddamn thing, but when we were talking budgets, I'd reluctantly let go of the opera as if I were giving up my life.

Why do you think the kinds of films that you did make are no longer being made?

I don't know. The youth of the country took on another coloration in the 1960s. They weren't interested so much in sentiment; they were interested in changing things, and that's probably why they don't make films like mine. But it could all change overnight.

When you go into the subject of change you get into a subject that's very dear to my heart: trends. It's the dirtiest word in films. Don't follow trends. Start trends. First of all, it's unethical. What you're doing is trying to capitalize on somebody else's creation, and you're starting with two strikes morally against you. Secondly, audiences do not want to see cheap copies of an original. Just because audiences liked a picture about a building on fire once, that doesn't mean they're going to like pictures about buildings on fire all the time. You make automobiles on an assembly line, but it's not how you make pictures. And as for, "What do the people like now?"—the people don't know what they like until they see it. There is no trend. People love good films. So, be individuals, be mavericks, swim upstream. Never float down the tide with the rest of the people.

Could you tell us how you came to make It's a Wonderful Life *just after the war?*

Of course I wasn't the only soldier in the battle for creative independence. People like Sam Goldwyn and David Selznick were part of it. The "one man, one film" idea had penetrated bastions of industrial, assembly-line companies just prior to the war. Leo McCarey, George Stevens and I brought all those people to Columbia, all those major directors who came and made their best films there. Everyone loved it because it was one man making a film. It was only Louis B. Mayer who hated all this. When we had more control over our pictures, even though we were still working in studios, our films got better. We weren't turning out a *product* anymore; we were making individual adventure shows. The audiences liked them and these films became more fruitful financially than the assembly-line product.

But during the war, for some strange reason—maybe because everything else was rationed—absolutely everybody went to the movies. As one manager said, "No matter what crap is playing, all you have to do is open the doors and duck." Quality went out the window to meet the demand of quantity. The assembly line came back into its own because a theater no longer needed to pay more money for an A picture when a B picture could fill it. B pictures were the dominant production of the time. These were the big boom years—everybody got rich, everybody became a star and everybody became a great producer during the four or five years of the war. No matter what was made, it went into theaters and turned to gold.

This is what I returned to after five years in the army, but it didn't last very long. *It's a Wonderful Life* was my first picture after having been in uniform and out of theatrical films for five years. I was scared to death. I had not looked through the eyepiece of a camera at an actor in all that time. I had been in another business entirely. I came back and met people and they'd say, "Frank who?" That is how quickly you're forgotten. Two or three years after the war these assembly-line pictures stopped selling. Audiences got tired of them. Mr. Fan became discriminatory, and the theaters began to lose money. The theater managers no longer opened the doors and ducked. They whistled, but nothing happened. Movies went into a depression in 1947, the same year I made my first film for Liberty Films. In the army I got the idea to form an organization of directors with a few others who were in the army with me. William Wyler, George Stevens and myself, aided by the business ability of Sam Briskin, organized Liberty Films by putting up our own money.

What happened to Liberty Films?

We were going to set up a kind of small United Artists, which we had great hopes for, and many other filmmakers followed on our tracks. We were a bellwether for independents, but we began to make films at the wrong time. Nineteen forty-seven and 1948 were absolutely the most depressing years in theaters. Nothing worked, nothing made any money. As a result I decided we should sell Liberty Films and get out before we all went broke. My two partners were solidly against it, and they were quite right. All we had to do was hang on, to accept much less money and make nothing but quality films, even if we had to make small pictures. That's what my partners wanted to do and what we should have done, but I didn't. I made two pictures for Liberty Films—*It's a Wonderful Life*, which I think is one of my best, and *State of the Union*—before we sold out to

Paramount. All of a sudden we had a million dollars in our pockets, and I became a paper tiger. As the cowardly reigning apostle of the "one man, one film" crusade, I went back on my own idea, having lost my guts and courage. That's the story of Liberty Films. It was my fault.

There were an awful lot of new millionaires when we got back from the army, very pompous guys who had been very successful making films. But they weren't making real films, they were just making product. Let me tell you, I was very worried about what my first film would be about. It certainly wasn't going to be about war. I'd had my belly full of war, and I came out of it a confirmed pacifist. My film wasn't going to be about GIs floating on their belly and that kind of stuff. We were at RKO, and Charles Koerner, the studio head, came in and said he had a script. "My wife said there's only one guy, Frank Capra, who can make this film. You've got to read it." I said, "What is it?" He said, "We've got three scripts on it. One by Marc Connelly, one by Dalton Trumbo and one by Clifford Odets."

Three powerhouse guys had written scripts on it. Man, it must be something very important. He said, "They all missed the idea." I said, "What idea?" "The idea I got when I bought this Christmas card. I paid fifty thousand dollars for it. All you have to do is pay me for the Christmas card, and I'll show you the scripts." I said, "You paid fifty thousand dollars for a Christmas card? Boy, I've got to see that Christmas card." And there it was, in three small pages knitted together with holly and stuff—about nine paragraphs. There was this little Christmas story that this man had written to send to his friends. A man who thought he was a failure was given the opportunity to come back and see the world as it would have been had he not been born. And he finds out that no man is a failure. Well, my goodness, this thing hit me like a ton of bricks.

I finally read the scripts. They headed in all directions. One went political, one commercial, one went some other way, but they didn't go anyplace with the theme. So I envisioned my own version. And finally, although I started out with some fine screenwriters—the Hacketts and Jo Swerling—they weren't hitting what I had in mind. So I wrote my own script. That's the story of *It's a Wonderful Life*. I had never seen the plot used in which a man was allowed to see how his little world would have been had he not been born. That was to me novel, a wonderfully human way of pinning down the idea of the importance of the individual, which had always been the main theme of my films.

Why did you start remaking films like Broadway Bill *and* Lady for a Day *during the period after* Liberty?

I must admit that those were the most painful years of my life. I said I would never work for an assembly-line studio, but finally did. Paramount started telling me what to make. Paramount dictated: You can make this, you can't make that, and you've got to make it for so much money. All my life I had made my own films and wasn't used to that. It was a very sad experience for me, and I knew that I had made a grave mistake in getting my partners to sell Liberty Films. One of the reasons I made remakes was to cut down the costs. Paramount put a ceiling of a million and a half dollars on my pictures. I wanted to get out of Paramount as fast as I could. I made two pictures for them, and then they threw me out because I was becoming too much of a thorn in their side.

In your autobiography, The Name Above the Title, *you mentioned a technique you developed when shooting close-ups. You would play back a recording of the other character's lines instead of having the second actor feed the lines to the person playing the close-up. Did you use it on other movies after* Mr. Smith Goes to Washington?

Yes, every time I had a master scene that was a little complicated. Not for every scene I shot, but for the scenes of importance. And it worked like a charm. Do you all know what we're talking about? You shoot a master shot with four or five people, and then you move in to shoot individual close-ups to cover it. Now, the close-ups have got to match that master shot they will be cut into. They have to match it in tempo, in intensity, in timing, in pitch, in looks, in everything else. It's very difficult to have a highly exciting master shot and then shoot close-ups that match because you put the actress in a position where she can't move. She can't move this way because she'll go out of focus, or she can't move that way because this side of her face is better than the other side. She's surrounded by lights, there's a chalk mark here, where some person she's talking to is supposed to be, a mark there, where somebody else is supposed to be, and she's being fed her lines by the script girl. Now, how can that actress re-create what she did in the master scene? It's practically impossible. Horse-and-buggy days of the worse kind.

I said, "I've got an idea. I'll take the sound track of the master shot, put it on a record quickly at the sound department and have it brought up to me on the stage." I would play that master scene back to the actors, just the sound. I could stop it or start it any time. So then I shot the close-up with the actress hearing herself play the scene, and when we actually shot it I would just clip off her voice every time she had to say something and I let her hear the rest of the scene. So she was reacting to everything just as she was in the master scene. I thought that was the best thing that happened to pictures since Griffith or Garbo. But it evidently wasn't thought so by others because it does take a little time and a little ingenuity.

According to your book there were two reels of Lost Horizon *that you just threw away. How did they affect the story and why did you throw them away?*

It's very simple. It's an example of the value of an audience. We saw the picture with the two reels in it, about twelve of us in a projection room, and we came out of the room raving that it was the greatest picture ever made. We were absolutely riding on cloud nine. Then we took it to a preview at Santa Barbara, and about ten minutes into the film the audience began to snicker, and the laughs begin to get louder. But there were no laughs intended. The film was a complete bust. They left the theater in droves before it was over, and the few who stayed until the end came out in the rain saying that it was the goddamnedest picture. "Did you ever see such a stinking picture?" And why? Why did that picture seem so wonderful to us in a small projection room, and yet a large audience turned it down completely?

It was a new experience for me. It was a two-million-dollar picture, half of Columbia's budget for the year. They made twenty pictures with the other two million dollars. So I walked around the hills trying to figure out—scene by scene—what started these people laughing. I couldn't really figure it out, but I did have one idea I thought might be worth trying. It was to put the main titles at the beginning of the third reel and forget the first two reels. So that's what we did. We went down to San Pedro and showed the picture to an audience there and there was not a titter. Nothing. Everything that was wrong was in those first two reels. Such a simple solution to a complete bust.

Of course, I didn't love those first two reels. I immediately went up to the cutting room and grabbed up the two scenes, found the cut negatives and ran out and threw them into the incinerator. It was nitrate film and the sky lit up with each reel that I threw in. It swooshed up and lit up Hollywood, and I cheered. Now, what was in those two reels? It went right out of my mind. I didn't want to know and I didn't care. All I knew was that those reels made the difference between an unusable film and a very usable film. The real truth was how the audience looked at it. The dividing line between the wonderful and the not so wonderful, between the sublime and the ridiculous, is very thick. We read a book and we're with the author all the time. We don't like one page but like another page, and we read the book through even though we may not like certain parts of it. But as you get more of an audience, after you get to a one-to–five-hundred basis, you've got yourself a different problem. That line between the sublime and the ridiculous becomes very narrow. Any one person can start a titter that will go right through the whole house. That's why you must always preview a film before you let it go out.

You also mentioned in your book about sending someone to the preview with a tape recorder and coming back and listening to the audience laughter, and then tightening the film up where there weren't laughs. Do you think this trick has been used enough?

No, it's not used enough. All the executives go there with one idea: to save the picture. They come back with a thousand ideas and say, "Do this and do that." Also, if you have a subjective interest in the film, you can never look at it objectively with an audience. You can send ten people to see the same preview and they'll all have different opinions.

I was sick in bed the night we previewed *Meet John Doe.* I sent quite a few friends to the preview, and they reported one at a time. No two of them were alike. They just didn't agree as to what the audience thought of it. I didn't give a damn what *they* thought of it, I was interested in what the audience thought of it. So I thought the only thing to do was to put a microphone down over the balcony, to have an editor up there with a tape recorder, and then to listen to the audience and the screen at the same time. And you'd be surprised how you can absolutely tell what the audience is doing by the sound, by the stillness, by the laughs. You can tell by the popcorn, how the paper begins to rattle. And it is completely objective; the truth is there.

From then on I used this method of previewing and studying the tapes the next day. I had them put on records, marking the spots that were too slow, too fast, laughs that overlapped each other, where they missed laughs because they didn't hear the lines. I was tailoring the film to the audience reaction. Once I got two tape recordings that matched, then I thought, "Well, that's as much as I can do." And that would happen about the fourth or fifth time. Up to that time I'd keep making changes, just like a tailor would with a suit. You rip the coat open and sew it up again, rip the coat open and sew it up again. And for me it worked like a charm. Why should the audience lose a laugh because you didn't allow enough time for the previous one? And why should you stay with a scene beyond its climax?

You said that with Mr. Deeds Goes to Town *you started putting your own thoughts and feelings into your films. How did you work with your writer on this?*

I had a very fine relationship with a terrific writer named Robert Riskin. He didn't do *Mr. Smith Goes to Washington* or *It's a Wonderful Life,* but he did maybe eight of the other films. We were very close friends and a very good combination. If two people can be on the same wavelength the situation can be a very symbiotic one. It works because you can bounce ideas off each other, like a tennis ball against the wall.

I had to be in on the writing because I had to understand what the film was about and to understand why I was doing it. I very seldom ever looked at a script once it was finished, but I would type each scene on my own typewriter. Just the mere typing of it and going through the words meant I sort of ingested the scene, and then finally it became mine. I wanted to know that it would fit the scene that came before it, which was shot three weeks ago. And I wanted to know that it would fit the scene that we were going to shoot five weeks from now. That's the thing that makes film a director's medium more than anything else—that you don't shoot a film in sequential order, you shoot it in the order that will match the lowest budget. On a location you shoot everything in the script on that location; you don't go back and forth.

So you have this sticky problem of what happened in this scene we shot three weeks ago now that we're about to shoot the scene following it. How are we going to match the tempo, intensity, timing, the growth of the relationships between the actors? Up here. In your head. The director's head. He's the only guy in the hierarchy who knows where the actors are in space and time. The man upstairs in the office certainly doesn't know. Where would the actors be without somebody to tell them where they were in scenes that were shot in almost random order?

When you wrote the scenes, were they summaries or did you write out all the dialogue?

Dialogue and everything.

Would you write anything about how the scene was to function in the context of the whole drama?

You hear a lot of funny stories about directors going off and walking around smoking a pipe for an hour in back of the stage and then coming back and saying, "Let's shoot it again." That's all he comes back with? Well, what that fellow was doing when wandering around was going through that film scene by scene by scene—the scenes that had been shot and the scenes that hadn't. He's trying to figure out if the scene just shot would fit into that spot. Should he cut it down? Should it be higher in intensity? Lower? Should he speed it up or slow it down? Would it be better if the girl played it silent? All of this is going through that man's mind. He's fitting that scene into the mosaic that he's building with random pieces. So he'll come back and say, "Let's shoot it again." The actors think he's nuts, saying, "But we just shot it." But the toughest part of directing is to keep the story straight.

Based on the fact that your scenes are written out before you shoot, did you ever allow space for a spark to take something in a different direction?

Nothing was ever locked up. You see, you're dealing with human beings when you're dealing with actors, and funny things happen. When you wrote a script, you had no one specifically in mind to play the star parts because our small studio had no contract stars. You'd have a certain kind of person in mind, but then you cast an actor for the part. Okay, now here comes a guy who's six feet tall and he's got a moustache and he talks with a deep voice. All of a sudden the man lives, and he brings his own clout into that part. You're not dealing with fanciful words, you're dealing with flesh and blood. And then you rehearse and you find out that he can't say those words. They don't seem to fit him. So you go back and tailor the stuff to this guy.

You have to leave things wide open. There are many times when an actor comes in and just runs away with a character. And there are many times that an actor comes in and he just can't handle it, so you keep paring his part down. You're dealing with people who breathe and talk and get mad and have a moustache and have pretty legs. Your script becomes just a guideline when you get the real people up there. You've got to make allowances for that, because these people have got to be credible on the screen. They've got to believe what they say. The smallest bit part is just as important as the star's part, because in that mosaic, why should that little part be glass instead of diamond? If the audience believes your so-called little people, they are more liable to accept the credibility of what the stars do.

I walk through the scene once with the actors so the crew and people know exactly what they're going to do, and then I shoot the scene for the first time. And 75 percent of the scenes in the films are that first take because there is quality about that first take, something unsuspecting. The actors actually listen when somebody's talking because they don't quite know yet what he's going to say, and you get a quality of being all mixed up and talking over each other. At the edge it's rough, but it's life, and I'd rather see it happen as it would happen in real life. This is the quality you'll get in that first take. And unless there's something mechanically wrong or you miss a line or forget a line, I use that first scene because as you do more takes the actors know their parts, they know where to stand, they know when to turn, they turn before they should turn. They know too much about it.

The Why We Fight *series was very important in terms of inciting an isolationist, apathetic America into supporting World War II. Could you talk about the series?*

The job was given to me by the Chief of Staff, General George C. Marshall. He selected me because he thought if I could make my own way through Hollywood, I could hack it through the army. Here we were going to put ten million kids in uniform—hot-rodders they were called then—indifferent, apathetic, undisciplined, as they always are and always will be in America when they're young. But what kind of soldiers would these kids make with their zoot suits and their long chains and all that paraphernalia? General Marshall said, "The Germans and Japanese are counting very heavily on these kids running like hell when the first shot is fired." He said, "I don't think so. I don't think free people will run when fired at. But can they take homesickness? Can they take discipline? The dirty, lousy discipline of the desert, the jungles? Can they stand that? Can they stand doing nothing for months upon months upon months? That takes more discipline than the actual shooting."

Then he gave it to me straight. "I've tried it with lectures, but no two lectures are alike. I've got in mind a series of films that will tell these boys why they are fighting. And if we tell them why, and they believe the answers, we may be all right." So that's how the army films got started.

It's interesting that the sort of thing you did would now be considered quite racist, that kind of name-calling. But at the time it was okay.

I don't understand what you mean by "racist." You must understand that these people were kicking the hell out of us. They were enemies. We didn't give a goddamn what their race was. One was yellow, one was white. But they both were out to take us over. They were out to take over *all* free peoples. It had nothing to do with racism. It was war. It had nothing to do with those pretty little things about the color of your skin. We either won it or lost it. You may think we were racist because we called the Japanese "Japs," but you'd be surprised what they called us.

What were the social codes you were playing on to arouse people, to get them interested in what you were trying to say?

To use statements made by their own people. We used Hitler a lot. We used what they were doing. We used their aims, their maps, what they had in mind for the world. Their cry was simply "Today Germany, tomorrow the world." And there was no way you were going to stop it with words. I photographed General Eisenhower at the commencement exercises of the British equivalent of our West Point, Sandhurst, where about two thousand second lieutenants were graduating. It was raining and they were standing at attention, and he began to talk into a microphone. My goose pimples went up and down, hearing what that man had to say. He said, "Gentlemen, I want you to know that you are graduating into the worst profession that man ever created: the archaic, brutal, insensitive profession of being a soldier. It should have been done away with long, long ago. But we have to beat this thing because there are forces loose in the world that are trying to overpower everything that comes along. And until we destroy that feeling of superiority of those who would rule the whole world, we cannot be safe. But remember: Don't be proud of the profession, because it is archaic. And let's hope that we can do away with it this time forever." That was his speech. That was our commanding general. He didn't say to them, "Boys, you're great," and so forth and so on. He wasn't Patton. He laid it out cold: the worst profession the human being ever invented. War.

What kind of people did you work with in the Signal Corps? Were they similar to the studio types you had worked with?

They weren't as talented, nor were they as fervent. I got nothing but stupidity in the army. The army people were entrenched in their uniforms and thought that we had come there to take over their jobs. Now, if there is anything we wanted less, it was to stay in those damned uniforms. We wanted to get our jobs done and take them off as fast as possible. We couldn't convince them that we were professional filmmakers in uniform and not professional soldiers. It created a constant rivalry between our film knowledge and their army entrenchment.

Generally I had a hard time. I made those *Why We* Fight pictures in the alleys, in the sticks, anywhere, without the use of any of the equipment at the command of the great empire of the Signal Corps. I'm glad about it now, because the films turned out better than if the army had helped us out.

Is it true you used to spend your evenings at the Museum of Modern Art Film Library, in Queens, looking at all kinds of documentaries?

I didn't know what a documentary was at the time. I thought only kooks with long hair made documentaries. I soon found out that there was no difference between making a documentary and making a theatrical film. The medium of communication is the same: visual. You have to make your points and dramatic emphasis as entertaining as any other film. The fact that we were professional moviemakers making documentaries for the first time was a plus. We didn't think documentaries had to be dull. The *Why We Fight* films are the great novels of our times. There they were, the great historical heroes and villains of the decade, between 1931 and 1941, between Manchuria and Pearl Harbor, strutting and yelling their way over the world stage. The drama was terrific, it was right there. How the Japanese rose out of nothing, how the Germans rose out of nothing and what they were fighting to get. Nothing could be more powerful than to see these historical figures laid out before you on celluloid. The soldiers had to see them as orientation films before they could go overseas. The films were received very enthusiastically, and I still meet all kinds of people who talk about them. When I was overseas finishing up my tour of duty as the Operations officer of the Signal Corps training film libraries, I saw sixteen-millimeter prints of them in film libraries all over Italy, certainly all over the ETO [European theater of operations]. They were constantly called upon by the Information and Education officers to be shown to people in training camps, replacement depots, hospital installations and so on. They were quite an improvement over pictures about how to clean your M1 rifle.

I came up with the idea of not actually shooting any film for the *Why We Fight* series, but instead to use existing German and Japanese films. I wanted our soldiers to derive their own meanings from them. I think our films had much more of an effect than theirs. This country was full of German and Japanese newsreels that were being shown to German Americans and Japanese Americans. The Treasury Department confiscated all the film, and this is the film I got hold of for my series. We also had the OSS [Office of Strategic Services], who went around photographing new landing places in different countries.

The film you made about Russia was withdrawn in the late 1940s after being blacklisted soon after the House Un-American Activities investigation in 1947. The same thing happened to Michael Curtiz's Mission to Moscow, *a film that was made in the heat of the moment. How did you feel in the late 1940s about that kind of reaction to the* Why We Fight *series?*

I had very mixed feelings about it. After the war, I became soured about the stupidity of war. At first I sincerely believed in going all out to fight the Germans and the Japanese, and I did everything in the world to help that fight. But here we are today, not too long after the war, best friends with the people we fought. It just doesn't fit. I realized the stupidity of the whole damned thing. We lost so many millions in defeating the Germans and the Japanese, and now we are friends with each other. Why? What happens between nations? Somebody's got to come up with some good answers. I became antiwar after those years.

Had you seen propaganda films, like Leni Riefenstahl's Triumph of the Will?

Yes, indeed, I saw *Triumph of the Will,* and it scared the hell out of me. I think that's the powerhouse propaganda film of all time. Nothing but pure propaganda, a film that's simply saying, "Join us, you'll make it.

Fight us, you're gone." And they took over a lot of nations with that film: Austria, Czechoslovakia and others. They'd show them the film and everybody would say, "Okay, I'll sign up."

That's the problem I had. How in hell to undo that film? Fortunately we hit upon an idea. We didn't say, "Look, we're good people, they're bad people." We didn't say how strong we were. We just shot the equivalent of this Riefenstahl film and showed the soldiers what our enemies were saying, what their aims were. Fortunately these strutting people photographed themselves to death. They made a lot of film for us to use. So, in a sense, we were showing pieces of *Triumph of the Will* to the kids, showing them what they were up against if they lost.

The narratives in your feature films seem somehow closely tied to the theater. Do you think that your films are closer to the stage than films being made today?

I was never even backstage. I don't know anything about the stage.

But there's a quality of writing that really seems to be missing today in the majority of films.

We paid a great deal of attention to the writing. Let me give you a day's work to show you. I'd been thinking of a scene all night long, and in the morning I'd be the first one on the set with the scene laid out in my head. Then the actors would come in at nine o'clock, not too well up in their parts, as I had requested. It sounds crazy, but I didn't want them to come in perfectly ready because then they'd have their characters fixed in their own minds. So I'd sit them around a table and ask them to read their parts right out of the script. I just hung around listening so I could feel if the writing fit each person. Then we'd read it again, and usually I'd find some clunkers and change them. Occasionally, if the scene did not come up to what I thought it should come up to—if it was in any way unbelievable to me—I'd just go right in my room and rewrite it just as fast as I could, then come back and try it again. This may sound as if it would take a long time, but it didn't, not when you were in that kind of heat. The main purpose was to see that everybody knew what the scene was about.

I didn't give a damn how they acted it. But I did want them to know who they were, what their relationship was to the others, because if actors are thinking right, then they can't do anything wrong. If they're thinking right, they act it right. In the meantime I had given the crew directions, and they were lighting the set. Once the main actors got the scene fixed in their minds the way I wanted it, then I tried to photograph it as fast and as furiously as possible. I'd use two, three cameras. I would not let them leave the set, I'd keep all the makeup and hair people out entirely because they take up so much time. From then on, my principal aim was to shoot as fast as I could, to maintain the quality of the scene from setup to setup until it was over. The speed part of it was just so they wouldn't lose the intensity, the heat, the understanding. I wouldn't let them go out and tell each other jokes, I wouldn't let them phone their agents. Nothing. I'd keep them right there and get them on film while they were hot. It is a great thing if you can make the actors forget they're actors, make them live that part. This is what directing is all about. The rest is luck.

Every one of you, if you get to be directors, you will find your own way of doing it. There are directors who will want more speed out of a scene. There are people who will play the scene with much slower tempo, and there are people who will play it at a higher pitch. It doesn't matter, as long as that one person is controlling the whole thing. I don't like to tell you these things about directing because they may sound like guidelines to you. Please accept them as just things that I used because they worked for me.

Some critics feel that God is on the side of many of your characters. What's your view?

In *It's a Wonderful Life* I showed a little angel who hadn't won his wings because he was such a lousy angel. But the characters themselves had an idealism within them that eventually won out. They reached for something they had inside, and they came up with a handful of courage and wit, and they proceeded to beat their adversaries with it, not with prayer. The only prayer you'll find is when Jimmy Stewart goes into that saloon and he says, "Show me the way, God. I'm at the end of my rope." He just barely says it. Then he gets punched in the nose and says, "That's what I get for praying." I'm wise enough to know that you can't make a religious tract or a political tract out of a film. People go into a theater to be entertained, titillated, inspired.

You've got to dramatize whatever idea you have. You have to dramatize it with people, not through sermons. Audiences won't buy it. But they will buy a human being who's trying to do the right thing for his fellow man, and they'll cheer for the good guy, for the guy who's got compassion, forgiveness in his heart, for that Good Samaritan. Those kinds of people counteract all the meanness there is in the world. They're idealists. They will go down fighting for a lost cause, and you cheer for them. That's the closest I can get to heaven.

Could you talk about comedy, your technique of speeding up the action to what seems to be an almost unnatural pace?

Again, that was part of my own learning from my own experiences. I'd see my films on a Moviola or in a small projection room, and they'd look fine. But I'd go to the theater, and the audience always seemed to be a little ahead of the film. Those beautiful lap dissolves would come on, and they'd go for the popcorn. All this ego-massaging stuff that we had—we called it fine camera work—it means absolutely nothing. It just interfered with the story. I'd go to other people's films, and they seemed to slow down to me. I said, "I wonder if a large group of people grab the stimuli faster than when you're alone?"

So I went around to baseball parks to see what happened with the crowds. Well, something would happen, and the crowd would get it fast, so I tried to find something on the behavior of crowds and mobs, but there was nothing written about it that really made any sense to me. So I thought, well, if it's slow, I'll speed it up. My film *American Madness* was going to be one of those pictures in which crowds move fast. So I said, "I'll try something and not let anybody know." I would rehearse a scene, and if it felt right at about a minute, I'd ask the actors to speed up the scene so that it would last forty seconds. And that's the way we shot it. In the projection room it looked fast. On theater screens it wasn't fast, but there was an urgency. No heads turned away—they didn't reach for their popcorn, they didn't dare look away because they might miss something. So for once I was ahead of the audience. And forever after that I used that idea of speeded-up tempo, except in mood scenes, where it would have been ridiculous.

Now, the interesting part of it is that other people—George Stevens, for instance, was a man who didn't believe in that at all. We were partners, but he dramatized things by slowing them down. I would no more use a scene that he would use than fly. But he would follow a girl out of a doctor's office, and his camera would stay on her back as she walked down the

Capra, seated below camera, working with Jimmy Stewart and Jean Arthur
on *Mr. Smith Goes to Washington* (1939). Joseph Walker is behind the camera.

street over to another street and got into a bus. By being on her so long
you began to wonder, "What's on her mind?" And she became fascinating. He got his effects by slowing down. So who's right and who's wrong?
Whatever appeals to you.

The actors didn't fight the faster pacing?

You'd be surprised how smart actors are. Actors are wonderful. I once said,
"There are no bad actors, only bad directors." It's almost true. If the stars
don't have confidence in a director, then they begin to lose confidence,
and you have spotty performances. But if they think you know what
you're doing, they're with you.

Jean Arthur plays the girl in Mr. Smith Goes to Washington. *I heard a story
that you built the set so that she was photographed on only one side of her face. Is
that true?*

Yes, that's true. If you photographed one particular side of her face, it would be two different people. As Harry Cohn put it, "She had a face that one side looked like an angel, and the other side like a horse." We built sets so that she entered from the right side, so she didn't have to enter from her wrong side and do an awkward pirouette to get around to the right side.

That's a hell of a job for a director. You had to do it throughout the whole picture, then?

Oh, sure. Directing is a hell of a job. A hell of a wonderful job.

So why don't you make another film?

The real reason is that I had those damn cluster headaches for ten years. They stopped me cold. I stopped having them in 1971, but by that time I was getting a little old and a little tired. Another reason is that you lose the ability to answer questions fast—and that's what you've got to do when you're a director, answer a million questions with bedlam all around you. Worst of all, when you stop and wonder if you've made the right decision, you're on the other side of the hill. Going downhill never interested me; going uphill did. I was a cocky little bastard—I still am—and for me, coming in second is like coming in last. When I felt that I couldn't make a picture exactly as I thought I should make it, then I said, "Well, I'll try something else."

How do you view the editing process as a training ground for aspiring directors?

From what I've seen, the best training ground is where you are: in school. You have a chance to study the styles, traditions and the history. You have the films to see, to analyze. You have the opportunity to find out if you have any talent. You can't teach talent, but you can sharpen it. You've got to be born with it. But many times you don't know that you are born with it. I thought I was a scientist. I didn't know that I had any talent for aesthetics at all, so I would say that your experience here is the best preparation.

One thing I regret is the closing down of the large studios. Studios like MGM made a hundred pictures a year, twenty of which would be A pictures, with lots of money and several stars. Forty would be medium-budget pictures, with perhaps one star, and the other forty would be very low budget, B pictures. Now, into these very low-budget films they would put the beginners—the young starlets, writers, directors, producers—and turn them loose. Here was the trial, and it would be practically unsupervised. You could really experiment. They never threw a picture away, no matter what. If it was really bad, well, they put somebody else on it and spent another ten thousand dollars on it, fixed it up a little bit, shot some more stuff, edited it, put it through the mill. They never could lose money, because no matter how bad a picture they made, MGM could always put it in as a second feature to one of their big pictures, because they owned the theaters. The best part of that system was that the audience got a chance to see these young people, and many young stars were born by the audience picking them out. I hated to see all that go.

To what extent are your films made in the cutting room, as opposed to on the set?

They're made both on the set *and* in the cutting room. If I didn't have the idea to make that shot on the set I wouldn't have had the shot in the cutting room. The original intuition about a scene comes when you're making it. And in many cases you improve it in the cutting room. Film is a funny thing. You take a series of five scenes, and there are perhaps twenty-five different ways you can put them together. But there's probably only one way that makes any sense, and you've got to find that one way. It's almost like music. If you put the notes of a piece of music together you get something wonderful. But if you take those same notes and alter them a little bit, you get dreck. It's the same way with scenes. You do get a chance to compose in the cutting room. If you put scenes together in one way you get a certain power out of them, but if you put them together another way, it's dull and flat. Don't ask me why, it's just part of the whole creative thing about making a film. You don't know why those things happen, because if you did you could get yourself a formula and you could sell it to everybody.

You're kind of a legend now after all these years . . .

Let me tell you, the other night Hal Kanter pulled a crack about me at a banquet that made me fall down in my chair.* He introduced me as "Frank Capra, a legend in his own book . . ."

*Harold Kanter (b. 1918) wrote for Bob Hope and Martin & Lewis in the 1950s, and was executive producer of *All in the Family.*

I was going to ask you about It Happened One Night. *How did you get Clark Gable to do the things you needed him to do in that picture?*

Well, just by being honest with the man. And he fell in love with the picture right off the bat. Really, that's the only picture that Gable ever played himself. He was that character and he loved doing those scenes.

We didn't write the film for Gable. We wrote it for Robert Montgomery, who turned it down. Nobody would play it. No women would play it. Comedies don't read very well in script form, especially light comedies. They're too fluffy. Nobody gets killed, there are no wars, no whores. Five girls turned it down, and finally Claudette Colbert took it because we paid her a lot of money. But we were going to do away with the whole picture when we got a phone call from mister big shot out at MGM, Louis Mayer. He called Harry Cohn and said, "Herschel, I got a man for you to play that megillah in that film you couldn't get off the ground." And Harry Cohn said, "Oh, the hell with it. We're calling it off." Louis Mayer said, "Oh, no, I've got a man here who's been a bad boy, and I'd like to punish him." And Harry Cohn said, "Okay." So the picture was on again because Louis Mayer wanted to punish Clark Gable. We wouldn't have made the picture, you see, without Mr. Mayer wanting to send Gable to Siberia, which was Poverty Row, where we were. They had to triple his salary when he went back to MGM, after the film came out.

When you worked with Harry Langdon, what effects were you after?

First of all we invented a character for him. It was this elfin character, a child-man. Chaplin depended upon wit to get himself out of trouble, Harold Lloyd on speed and Keaton on pure stoicism. But Langdon's character had the mind of a child, and a very slow child at that. You could just see the wheels were going very slowly. He could do a beautiful triple take. He'd see something, a lion or a beautiful dame or whatever. He'd look at it and then come back and look at it again and come back again, and then suddenly see it on his triple take. So the character we had couldn't outsmart anybody. Only God was on his side. If a brick was going to fall on him, why, he'd just pick up something at the right time, and the brick would miss him. God was his ally and took him through life because he was so innocent. Wit, speed, stoicism, innocence—one word each for those four great comedians.

But Harry didn't know his own character. When Harry came to Sennett's, he was a middle-aged little guy who had made a little living for years doing a vaudeville act with his wife. They had a little truck that they took around, and they made enough to live on. They weren't of very high intelligence. Now, when we invented his innocent character, and he became innocence personified, he shot to the top. Then he read in the papers that he was the equivalent to Chaplin. Boy, that was the wrong thing for him to see because right away he wanted to do what Chaplin did. Chaplin wrote, directed and acted. But Chaplin discovered his own character, so he knew more about the character than anybody else in the world. Langdon knew less about his character than anybody in the world. But that poor man decided he would fire me and everyone else because he wanted to play the witty guy like Chaplin. And that's what he did and that's what caused his downfall. It was the only real, honest-to-goodness human tragedy that I have personally seen from start to finish. He was playing extras when he died of a broken heart. This big star who never understood what made him funny.

What do you feel about stylization in film as opposed to the more "naturalistic" approach?

I thought the camera was something that should see life as it was, and I thought the microphone was something that should hear life as it was. That didn't mean you couldn't invent here and there. But I thought you should see people as they would be under the circumstances. Beyond that, I didn't go in for fancy shooting. I stylized only one film, *The Bitter Tea of General Yen,* which is different from anything else I ever made. It's a good film, some fine acting, but there's a kind of sheen over the whole thing. Camera tricks. We used silk stockings over the lens at different places. Where we wanted to see something clearly, we just put a hole in the stockings with a cigarette. But that's the only film in which I ever tried to become arty, because I was trying to win an Academy Award. I had complained once to Harry Cohn that I was making better pictures than the other guys were making. Why shouldn't I win? He said, "They'll never vote for that comedy crap you make. They only vote for that arty crap." So I thought maybe I'd have to try one of these arty things.

Did you always stick with the same crew over the years?

Yes, because if you could work with the same crew, they knew almost what you were thinking and you could work faster, better and easier. With actors? John Ford and I had kind of a mutual arrangement to keep certain pet friends working, the kind of performers you knew would deliver, character actors we could count on. You'd go to sleep at night knowing that if you had Ward Bond and Tommy Mitchell and Beulah Bondi that they were going to get it the first time. That's a very good feeling.

As I say, it's a people-to-people communication. Say you're shooting the actors walking toward the camera on a sidewalk and the forty extras are walking beside them. Well, those forty extras will walk by, but they'll look like sheep. But if you give each one an identity—"You're going to the dentist," "You're going to meet your boyfriend," "You're going to the hospital because your mother is there"—the scene will come alive simply because the extras become human beings.

Are there any people making films today that you particularly like?

Oh yes. I know a lot of young fellas making damned fine films. I don't like Bergman films. I think he's a master at what he does, but I'm just not interested in decomposition and death. I'm more interested in people who are alive and what they do to stay alive. I also don't like stories about old people who are going back to think about what they could have done with their lives. The hell with them. They had their chance.

Were there any projects you always wanted to do but could never get off the ground?

I got quite a few things started and then I'd pull back. Every film that I ever made, except *Lost Horizon,* was about Americans. I thought I knew Americans and that I could direct them knowing how they would react. So every time I got something going that I'd have to make in Europe, or about Asians, or Africans, well, I'd get up to a certain point, but finally back off. Like once when I wanted to make *Cyrano de Bergerac.* I got right up to that and pulled back because I didn't feel at ease with people in costumes. I was afraid I'd laugh at them. I was born in the gutter and I just knew the people that I knew, and I didn't know these people in costumes with lances and swords. I know I'd laugh if a guy pulled a sword on me. Not that I don't like to see that sort of thing when somebody else does it, but my cup of tea is Americans, America, the common people.

Would you share with us your thoughts on why the 1930s were the height of comedy, and its demise in the present day?

Well, comedy is the most difficult of all the genres of film. In the thirties and forties there were people who had been trained in the two main schools of comedy. There was visual comedy and there was verbal comedy, and there were certainly differences between the two. There were two main schools of visual comedy: Mack Sennett and Hal Roach. I started with Hal Roach, making *Our Gang,* then I went to Mack Sennett's. My first directing job was with Harry Langdon, on *The Strongman.* You see, comedy was my forte. I'd been thinking visual comedy and had been trained in it. I think I wrote twenty-six two-reel comedies for Sennett in the year and a half I was there, and I saw these things up on the screen. I was able to evaluate them to see how a gag can be built—toppers and things like that.

It was more talking than writing. There was paper around, but nobody ever used it. Sennett would put you in twos, so one could talk to the other, try something out on each other, find out what's a good idea. He'd call you in, "Now, what you got?" We'd tell him what we had, and if he laughed, the audience was going to laugh. It was a real litmus test. If he liked it, he'd say, "Go tell it to the director." Then you'd go to the director, and the two of you would tell him and you hoped he'd like it. The directors in those days were just miraculous. You gave them a hint and they'd take it from there. You'd say, "A cat drinks some beer." God, that's all. They'd make a five-minute scene out of that. But never a written word. Sennett would not allow a book to come into the studio. "No gags in books," he'd say. He was afraid of intellectuals. He wanted you to be down to his level, where you make him laugh—a funny clown kind of comedy, not witty, wordy, but clownish and visual. It was there that you found out whether you had any talent for comedy. You either are a real comic and can write comedy and feel it right off the bat, or you can't.

I guess I don't actually think that the definitive pictures were made in the thirties and forties. Yes, we made some good films, but hell, that's past. Who the hell's interested in that? I'm surprised you even watch old films. What should interest you is tomorrow. What do you do as young people? What's your stuff about? What's your bag? Where's your ferment? Never mind about how good we were in the thirties and forties, because it's an enormous medium and it's yours. Hell, the Shakespeares of film haven't come out yet. We've been playing around with it, and once in a while we hit one. But really, it is an art form that uses all the other art forms as tools.

You can do anything with film. Film is magic. You can make *Star Wars,* you can make documentaries or the greatest spectacles in the world. Film is the greatest education form ever invented. It educates better than any kind of a book. And this is what has yet to be discovered by the academia of America. And the strange thing, it was invented and created in a little town way out in the West, a little bit of a dusty burg called Hollywood. Three thousand miles west of the Hudson River, where nothing west of the Hudson was any good anyhow. And like the Bible says, "What good could come from Nazareth?" So here was this film being made and sold, being canned and shipped—homegrown, no help from the government, thank God. Nobody knew anything about it. We taught each other, and here it is. We've come to this enormous thing called film that has the power to move and influence.

Your films have aged very well. What do you think keeps them fresh?

That they're probably as humorous now as they were then is due to the fact that they stay away from the temporal, from the one-liners of the day. You stick with things that are humorous at all times, under all occasions—generally visual humor. You stay away from funny lines, because a funny line may stick out so much it will date your film a year later. You use humor more than comedy.

Are you always very aware of your audiences when you make your films?

Without an audience, a film is something in a can, something incomplete, like an unread book. It just lies there, dead. Do not underestimate the power and the ability and the intelligence of an audience. A thousand pairs of eyes and ears seem to react to stimuli much faster and smarter than any one pair of eyes and ears. This is what it's all about—the people-to-people communication, from the people on the screen to the people in the audience. And you can only involve an audience with people. You can't involve them with gimmicks, with sunsets, with handheld cameras, or zoom shots. But give them some person they can worry about, and you've got them.

Optimism is in short supply these days. Do you still believe there are Mr. Smiths and Mr. Deedses in the world?

Certainly they exist today. The Deedses and the Smiths and the George Baileys are to be found in all nations and classes throughout the ages. You can find one on every block. They represent an aristocracy. Not an aristocracy based on power or influence, but an aristocracy based on the compassionate, the plucky and the sensitive. They carry on the human tradition, the one permanent victory of our queer race of cruelty and chaos. And their pluck is not swankiness, but the courage to endure, to stand up and say, "No, I won't go along to get along." Thousands and thousands of them die in obscurity. No headlines, no television. I'd say that we need films that remind us that if good does not have the world to itself, then neither does evil, as many filmmakers would have us believe. History is not made by the high priests of sadism and savagery. History is made by the idealistic rebels, those men and women who think in defiance of the pressures of ignorance, greed and fads. The need today is for courageous artists with ideals, because they have the freedom to lobby for all mankind, to become the paladins who can knock off the dragons of deceit with art.

Today we're governed by cynicism, which is deadly. But you go nowhere with cynicism, where everybody else is a bastard, nobody is honest. It isn't worth living. What can cope with cynicism is idealism, people who will fight for those ideals and lost causes, not because there's something to get out of it but because they care about their fellow human beings. What audiences respond to in *Mr. Smith Goes to Washington* is the

With AFI Director George Stevens, Jr., in May 1971, at an outdoor seminar at the Center for Advanced Film Studies at Greystone in Beverly Hills.

humanity of a man who cares about something and is fighting for it. When they see somebody fight for an ideal, it will always get 'em right here, in the stomach. Whether he wins or loses doesn't matter, so long as he fights and he's not on the take.

All these things are still here. Take all our folk heroes. They're not cynics, they're idealists of some kind. Maybe they have crazy, nutty ideas, but they care for their fellow man. One thing I think I can tell you here—for God's sake, if you believe in idealism, then use it. If my evaluation of what I see in the colleges today is right, I think people are hungry for this idealism again. They want to express themselves, and they can't express themselves in any greater medium than film. No saint, no pope, no general, no sultan, has ever had the power that a filmmaker has, the power to talk to hundreds of millions of people for two hours in the dark. That is a tremendous power, and you have this power as filmmakers. You have the power to say anything you want, so why not say something positive?

———— ◆ ————

Films as Director

1926	*The Strong Man*	1933	*The Bitter Tea of General Yen*
1927	*Long Pants*		*Lady for a Day*
	For the Love of Mike	1934	*It Happened One Night*
1928	*That Certain Thing*		*Broadway Bill*
	So This Is Love	1936	*Mr. Deeds Goes to Town*
	The Matinee Idol	1937	*Lost Horizon*
	The Way of the Strong	1938	*You Can't Take It with You*
	Say It with Sables	1939	*Mr. Smith Goes to Washington*
	Submarine	1941	*Meet John Doe*
	The Power of the Press	1944	*Arsenic and Old Lace*
1929	*The Younger Generation*	1947	*It's a Wonderful Life* (also
	The Donovan Affair		producer and co-screenplay)
	Flight	1948	*State of the Union* (also producer)
1930	*Ladies of Leisure*	1950	*Riding High* (also producer)
	Rain or Shine	1951	*Here Comes the Groom* (also
1931	*Dirigible*		producer)
	The Miracle Woman	1959	*A Hole in the Head* (also
	Platinum Blonde		producer)
1932	*Forbidden* (also story)	1961	*Pocketful of Miracles* (also
	American Madness		producer)

I guarantee you that two directors that are any good can take the same story, change the name of the characters, change the name of the town and make an entirely different picture.

HOWARD HAWKS
(Born in Goshen, Indiana, 1896—Died 1977)

Howard Hawks was born to a wealthy family and enjoyed the advantages of prep school and college, which set him apart from most of the first generation of directors. He was tall and elegant, with eyes that have been described as blue ice cubes. By the time he got into film he had been a race car driver, an army pilot and had earned a degree in mechanical engineering. He learned early in life that he could achieve challenging tasks without great effort, perhaps concluding that making movies couldn't be all that difficult.

The Hawks family moved from Indiana to California, and Howard's first job as a teenager was working in the prop department at Famous Players–Lasky. Years later he came back to Los Angeles and got work as a film editor, story editor and assistant director before writing a screenplay called *The Road to Glory* and selling it to Fox on the condition he be allowed to direct it.

Hawks was at heart a storyteller—in his everyday life as well as for the screen. He had confidence in his skills and throughout his career chose studios that would support his productions without interference, moving on if they did not, thus creating a pattern—never making more than two consecutive films for one company. He also had confidence in his judgment on stories ranging from gangster films and Westerns to comedies and musicals. He gave many actors their first chance on the screen, among them Paul Muni, George Raft, Rita Hayworth, Lauren Bacall, Montgomery Clift and Angie Dickinson, and he used his regulars—John Wayne, Humphrey Bogart and Cary Grant—time after time with great success.

Hawks' films of male camaraderie found special favor with European crit-

John Wayne, Howard Hawks and Joanne Dru on location for *Red River*
(1948), the first of four pictures Hawks made with Wayne.

ics, who crowned him an auteur and placed him high on their lists of great
directors. In *The Grey Fox of Hollywood,* Todd McCarthy describes Hawks'
influence on Brian De Palma, and on John Carpenter and Peter Bogdanovich,
both of whom remade Hawks pictures or excerpted from them. Martin
Scorsese and Quentin Tarantino cite Hawks as a source of inspiration—
highlighting a difference between the first generation, who had no models to
draw on, and succeeding ones who borrow from the masters.

Hawks was a major director for nearly half a century, from the silent era

until 1970, and his screen achievements are sparkling and enduring: *Scarface,*
The Twentieth Century, Bringing Up Baby, Ball of Fire, His Girl Friday,
Sergeant York, The Big Sleep, Red River, Gentlemen Prefer Blondes and *Rio*
Bravo. Hawks was eighty when he came to AFI but still vital and energetic—
still driving fast cars and motorcycles.

HOWARD HAWKS

————

April 23, 1976*

I'd like to introduce you to Howard Hawks, who has apologized for limping slightly as he came in. He told me that he was trying out a new motorcycle in the desert and ran into a bush.

The trouble is that it was a cactus. I would just like to say that I won't make a speech, but I'll be glad to answer any questions. If I make a speech I'll be fifty percent wrong, and if I answer your questions I'll only be a little wrong. So go ahead. Anybody?

I read that you had studied engineering and that immediately after college you came out here and began working in films. Why did you make that switch?

Well, I didn't lose the engineering. I use it a great deal in making stunts and in deciding things for pictures. But actually I started to work as a prop man during vacation while I was at college, and then the war came along, and after the war I got a chance to go back. If you want to hear the whole story, Doug Fairbanks wired from New York that he wanted a modern set, and we only had one set designer and he was in Arizona and they didn't know quite what to do. And I said, "Hell, I can make a modern set." So I made it and Doug liked it and he asked who made it and I met him and he said, "You look like you might be a golfer." I said, "Yes." He said, "What's your handicap?" I said, "Four." He said, "Let's play." So

*This transcript contains segments from seminars Howard Hawks gave at the American Film Institute on February 11, 1970 and November 19, 1970.

we became friends, and he was courting Mary Pickford, and he asked Mary to make me her property man. One day the director got drunk and I said, "Why don't we shoot some scenes?" Mary said, "Can you do it?" I said, "Sure." So I started to direct, and I liked it so much that the only thing I used the engineering for was stunts and building things for pictures and building a car that won Indianapolis and a few things like that. Does that answer the question why I quit? Okay, who else has got one?

How important was all your life experience, do you think, in making pictures?

That would be hard to answer. I drove race cars for two or three years. I did a lot of flying. I made several race car pictures and several flying pictures. I met men who were kind of tough men. Some critics put it that I seem to like professionals, and I do, in anything—people who really are good at their job. You get used to making action pictures. A picture like *Hatari!* was more fun than I ever had before. But in that picture we wanted a net to go over a tree with five hundred monkeys, and it cost forty thousand dollars to do the experimentations to make that net go over the thing. That's engineering. In making *The Dawn Patrol,* I ordered a couple of brand-new airplanes and we dolled them up to look like World War I planes, otherwise we couldn't have made the picture. I like Westerns; I raised horses for about twenty years.

Do you prefer visual or verbal comedy?

I don't think that people study comedy. I made one-reelers, and they were pretty bad, but I learned a lot about making comedies, visual comedies. I don't believe at all in dialogue comedies. The dialogue that you hear that's funny has been tried out for two years in a nightclub, and they finally found something that made the audience laugh. But if you study the older pictures you find out that the things that are funny are the visual things, and if I can find something that is visually funny then I figure, well, we'll get some lines that will fit in it all right. But I don't count on it, because a line that would be good for me might be very bad for somebody else. I was a very good friend of Jack Ford's. We used to meet when he came out to the desert to die. I used to play golf and go in to see him. They'd tell him I was there, and he'd start laughing. I'd say, "What the hell are you laughing about?" He'd say, "I just remembered some things I stole

Hawks shot *Twentieth Century* with John Barrymore (right) and Carole
Lombard in three weeks. "Lombard was so photogenic that it didn't make
any difference how you lit her, and Barrymore didn't care about it,
so we used three cameras."

from you." So the next time I came in I remembered a lot that I stole from
him. And we had a lot of fun because we talked about it. He said, "I can't
do the comedies the way you can." And I said, "I can't do them the way
you can. You do kind of a corny, racial, Irish humor and you get away
with it and it's marvelous, but I wouldn't know how to do it." "Well," he
said, "I wouldn't know how to do yours."

I advise you to find a story that's funny, and then start building and
figuring out the dialogue, because I don't trust any dialogue. In a picture
with John Wayne, somebody had lied to him in a barroom and he hit the

fellow with a gun and his face was bleeding all over, and Dean Martin said, "Hey, take it easy," and Wayne said, "I'm not gonna hurt him." And it turned out to be a very funny line; audiences laugh. Duke says it's so good that he's used it three times since. But it's very hard—what might appeal to you as a comedy might not appeal to somebody else. Capra and McCarey, George Stevens, we all had training making one- and two-reel comedies, and we learned that the best comedies you can make and the funniest situations come out of tragic situations. Study Chaplin. Everything that he made was a tragedy, but he made it funny. The trouble is nobody knows about it. The critics don't know anything about comedies. They don't know what to write so they don't write anything about it. And it's pretty damn hard to get a lesson in making comedies unless you just study and study why a thing is funny.

I started putting more and more comedy into pictures back in the early forties, and I've increased the amount of comedy ever since that time. Some people are very funny, others aren't. Walter Brennan, for instance—every time I look at him, I laugh. I had a very smart assistant director, and he said, "You know that story you were telling us the other day? I know a man who's exactly like the character you told, except he's just an extra." "Well," I said, "if you think he's good enough, get him into a costume and give him these lines so I don't have to see him do any talking, and we'll get right to the root of the thing." And in walked Brennan, and I laughed at him, and I said, "Mr. Brennan, have you got some lines? Are you ready to read them with me?" He said, "Yes. With or without?" I said, "With or without what?" He said, "Teeth." And I was supposed to use him for three days, and I kept him for six weeks and he got nominated for an Academy Award. He won two Academy Awards with me and was nominated for four others. He could do anything. He could make you laugh. So study the old pictures. Study the stuff that McCarey made, study the stuff that Capra made when he was going good, and you'll find that it didn't depend on words; it depended on something that was funny to look at.

What do you think of the state of comedy films today?

I don't know where you're going to find the comics today. There's no training for them. A lot of them came out of burlesque and vaudeville. They were in a great school. Where are they going to come from now? From TV? You don't find a good comedy so easily. There are a lot made that are supposed to be funny but aren't. There's another thing about making comedies—they start out with funny main titles and with ridiculous gags, this attitude of "Look, we're going to be funny and we want you to laugh at it." I try start it as if it's all serious and then all of a sudden surprise them. It's much easier to do it my way than to do it their way. If I go to see a movie and they start off trying to be funny right from the beginning, I get up and walk out.

How do you keep the sense of tempo in a movie when you're shooting it sequence by sequence?

If possible I don't shoot out of sequence, because there's no way of letting a character grow if you do that. If I can't do that, then I rehearse the stuff that we've skipped until I know what's happening. Tempo is a matter of the way you tell a story. You know, Brando is a good actor, but he asked me why he never did a picture with me, and I said, "Because you work five times too slow." When I did a remake of *The Front Page,* I used a trick to make it seem faster. I put in four or five words in front of what I wanted to have heard of a line, and had the actor jump on the line so the only thing that came out clear was the last few words. I used that in many pictures. I had actors jumping on each other's lines. All I did was give them a few words that weren't necessary. One of my favorite lines as a director has always been, "Well now, it took you a minute and ten seconds to do that scene. Do it in sixty, and we'll print it." I think movies are just too damned slow.

I try to make things go fast all the time unless I've got a really good scene that I want to milk. Then I stop and milk it and go on and pick up speed again. I don't think any of the slow stuff is any good. The audience has seen so many more pictures than anybody who makes them has seen, and they've gotten so tired of dawdling over scenes that you've got to have a pretty good scene if you're going to stretch it out. I said an unkind thing the other day. I was asked about Sam Peckinpah. "Oh," I said, "I can't take that slow-motion stuff that he does. I can kill three men, take them to the graveyard and bury them before he gets one to the ground." I love to do scenes of violence fast and hard so that you almost don't appreciate them. You know what I mean?

Then there's another thing I do. When we started *Red River,* John Wayne was very conscious of the fact that this was the first good story he'd ever had, and was trying too hard, so I said, "Duke, you'd better quit trying so hard. If you make two good scenes in this picture and don't annoy the audience the rest of the time, you'll be good." He asked me during a scene, "How's this?" And I'd say, "This is the kind of thing that annoys the audience." And he'd get it over just as quick as he could. Not only that, but when we made three or four pictures after that, if he found an actor was doing something, I would hear him over in a corner saying, "The boss says to get this one over in a hurry." There's nothing worse than an actor trying to put stuff in a scene that isn't in the scene. If he'd just read his lines and get off, then the picture will be a lot better. But when you have a good scene, then really go for it.

In terms of writing, how do you know what's funny?

In *Red River,* I wanted Wayne to get his finger caught between the rope and the saddle horn and come in with it all mangled. Then Walter Brennan would look at it and say, "That finger isn't going to be much good to you." Wayne says, "No, it isn't." Brennan would say, "Get a jug and build the fire up good and get me a chopping block." They'd start feeding him some liquor, and Brennan would say, "I guess he's ready," and he puts Wayne's finger on the block and Brennan sharpens up the knife and cuts it off. Wayne wasn't supposed to even know that it was cut off. But then his line was, "Where's my finger? A man ought to be buried whole." The scene ended with a bunch of fellows looking through the ashes for the finger. Wayne said to me, "You think that's *funny?*" "Yeah," I said, "but we don't have to do it." He said, "I don't think it's funny." I said, "Okay, I'll do it with some actor who's better than you are." And I did it with Kirk Douglas in *The Big Sky,* who isn't nearly as good as Wayne. I think it's the only time they laughed at Douglas. Wayne saw it and came around and said, "Well, I was wrong again. If you tell me a funeral is funny, I'll do it."

You say you don't like dialogue, but the writing in your films is often very sharp. What is the nature of your collaboration with your screenwriters?

I worked a lot with Ben Hecht and Charlie MacArthur, who I thought were the two finest writers of lines in modern times, and when they wrote a script we would sit around and Charlie would play one part and Ben would play one part and I'd play another, and we'd each try to stump one another. We each tried to say things in a different way. For instance, instead of a line "Oh, you're just in love," someone would say, "Oh, you're just all broke out in monkey bites." And we used to get some strange dialogue by doing that. Of course, with them we had funny dialogue and also great situations.

What about Hemingway?

I tried like the devil to get him to write. He and I were good friends. We were fishing, and I said, "Ernest, why don't you do some stories with me?" He said, "Oh, I'm good at what I'm doing. I don't want to go to Hollywood." I said, "You don't have to go to Hollywood. We'll go fishing and write a story while we're fishing. Look, I can make a picture out of your worst story." He said, "What's my worst story?" I said, "That piece of junk called *To Have and Have Not*." "Well," he said, "I need some money." Writers never made any money until paperbacks came in, and he said, "But, you can't make a picture out of that." And for about ten days while we were fishing we sat around and talked, and we decided that the story was no good but the characters of the girl and Morgan, who was played by Bogart, were good, and we started to think about how they met. So I went back and I bought the story for eighty thousand dollars, and he got ten thousand. I did awfully good by the making of the thing; I made close to a million. When I told him how much I got paid he wouldn't talk to me for six months.

Have you people seen *To Have and Have Not*? Well, my secretary made a mistake and sent Lauren Bacall a ticket to come out. All I wanted to do was find out if she'd been to school or anything like that. And out came this kid, and I said, "Well, send her to two or three studios, get a car for her and send her home." She didn't want to go home, she wanted to work, and I had to tell her, "That little high nasal voice that you've got can't read the lines we've written." That didn't bother her. She said, "How do I change my voice?" I said, "I don't know but I can tell you how Walter Huston got his." He had one of the finest voices in the world, and the first song he ever sang in his life he got a gold record on, so he had to have a good voice.* So I told her, and she disappeared for about three weeks, and I asked my secretary, "Where's that girl?" "She phones in but she says she's not ready to come in."

---

*Walter Huston sang the famous "September Song" in the film of the Broadway musical *Knickerbocker Holiday* (1938). His recording of the song became a best-selling hit after his death in 1950.

Then one day she walked in and said [*huskily*], "Hello." So we had a party out at the house Saturday night, and I asked her to come out there. I said, "Can't you get somebody to take you home?" She said, "I don't do too well with the men." I said, "How do you treat them?" She said, "As nice as I can." I said, "Well, try insulting them and see what happens." So she came around the next Saturday and said, "I got a ride home." I said, "What happened? "Well, I insulted a man and he liked it." I said, "What did you do?" She said, "I asked him where he got his tie, and he said, 'What do you want to know for?' and I said, 'So I can tell people not to go there.' " I said, "Who's the man?" She said, "Clark Gable." She was doing pretty good. So on Monday, I went to the writer and told him about this girl who could insult people and make them like her. Insolence, you know—that they liked. I said, "You know, Bogie is the most insolent man on the screen. Do you think we can write a girl that is as insolent as he is?" The writer said, "It would be fun to try."

Bacall was hanging around, and I'd try out a scene and let her read it, and all of a sudden I said, "I'm going to use her in the picture." I told Bogie, "I'm going to try to make this girl as insolent as you are." He said, "Oh Howard, you can't do it." "Well," I said, "I'm the director, and every scene she plays in she's going to walk out and leave you with egg on your face." He said, "I think you've got a chance, then." And, of course, he fell in love with her and that made it all the better. But that was a new character that came out of nowhere. We'd found a girl who could grin and say insolent things and people liked her. All of a sudden we had a girl who was just as insolent as Bogart, who is the most insolent man we've ever had on the screen. From that point of view the film was rather successful—it was entertaining, and it brought a new personality out of Bogart, with him smiling. He had been very dour before, and claimed he had a muscle cut in his lip and couldn't do anything with it.

We had a hell of a time writing it. I wrote a scene to make a test of her that had that line "You know how to whistle, don't you? Just put your lips together and blow." You know that line? Well, we didn't have a scene to put it in, and it made such a good test that Jack Warner said, "Hey, that's really great. Where does that come in the story?" I said, "I don't know," and we had to figure that out. But characters and things like that happen out of nothing.

At the time when the studios were so strong, how did you keep control of your pictures?

I don't know. I just never had trouble, except with Sam Goldwyn. He wanted a say in everything. He wanted everything his way and I wanted everything my way. But I don't think you're right in saying the studios had such control. Today people who don't know anything about it tell you how to make pictures. People like Jack Warner and Harry Cohn and Irving Thalberg and Zanuck—they started you out and let you go. Today they keep trying to tell you how to do things.

I talked to the head of a studio a while ago who said, "I want you to make pictures for us. Have you got a story?" I said, "Yes, I can tell you a story that I think is pretty good." He said, "Wait a minute. I'd like to call in somebody else." And he calls somebody else in, and I tell them the story, and he says, "Oh, that's a great story." And the other fellow that was with him said, "That's a good story. Who were you thinking of using?" I told him, and he said, "We've got that fellow." And the other fellow said, "We could use so-and-so." Then the other fellow spoke up and said, "We could use three or four contract players." The head of the studio asked me where I was going, and I said, "Home. You're wasting my time. I thought you wanted me to make the picture, and here you've just heard an outline of the story and you're casting it. I don't want to work for you." So he waited until the next day to call me up and ask me if I would come back and do that story, and I said, "No, I've already made an agreement to do it for somebody else." So he said, "Well, the next time I won't have a guy in listening." Back then we had far more freedom, and I think the pictures showed it. Too many of them are too stereotyped today.

You made fewer films a year than many of the Hollywood directors during the era of the strong studio system. Were you more deliberate in picking what you wanted to do?

I'd buy three stories and make one. It takes a little work on them to find out if they're good for me. And I've never been under contract, so I didn't have to do things. I've made a couple bad pictures trying to do favors for friends. I'd tell them, "I don't know how to do this picture. I don't know how to tell that story." They'd keep after me until I did it and then they were sorry. I wasn't being cautious, I was looking for a story. I think a director is a storyteller, and I used to wait around for a story that I thought I could tell, one that appealed to me—people that I know, things that I've done, like flying or racing automobiles. I like stories of the West merely because they are so fundamental, basic and honest. It's a question of life and death. The Western is almost surefire if you are any good at it.

How can we find which stories are worth telling before we spend our time actually telling them?

Try it on your friends. If they laugh at it, then you've got something funny.

Have you ever had the opportunity to make films that do not tell a story, something not so linear?

I don't think I've ever made a picture that didn't have a story. I've never seen a picture that I thought was any good that didn't have a story. The director is always working to find out whether or not a scene is telling the story. If not, cut it out. I believe in making entertainment, and I think that you should have a story in mind when you start out, otherwise you get a hodgepodge. I've seen a number of pictures and I can't tell what the devil the picture is about. Nobody can. I asked the fellow who made it, and he couldn't tell me.

I don't want to make pictures for myself or for you. I make them for a whole audience. If you want to do that, you might make one, but they probably won't finance you again. I think the audiences are a lot smarter than we are. I never thought that anything I made was better than they are. Make entertaining pictures, because people don't go to see movies about a bunch of problems. They've got enough problems of their own. Motion pictures are entertainment, and if you're going to preach, if you're going to force your ideas on the audience, you're taking chances. I've never had any desire to do that, and everybody I know who's tried it gets into trouble.

Do you rehearse scenes carefully before shooting them?

It depends on who's in the picture. I made a picture called *Twentieth Century,* with John Barrymore and Carole Lombard. We made it in three weeks and didn't hurry, but it was so easy to do a scene between the two of them because you'd just tell them what you wanted. I would put up three or four cameras, because she was so lovely to look at that you didn't have to worry, and they would start and do strange things. But a picture like

Bringing Up Baby took a long time. You never could tell where the leopard was going to go, and if he came in the set and went one way and it was the wrong way, we had to wait and rebuild the set because the next time he came in he was going to do the same thing.

I don't talk in general terms with actors. I remember talking with Bogart about the private eye he did in *The Big Sleep,* and I said, "Bogie, this is all told from your viewpoint. No scene starts until you come in. I'd like to have a gesture from you that you're thinking." He said, "Go ahead and start the camera." And he started to pull his ear, and he did it all the way through the picture, which is what I wanted. In *Scarface* we had George Raft, who was a pretty lousy actor. I didn't know what to do with him, so I thought if only he could be doing something while he was reading his lines, maybe people wouldn't realize how bad he was. So we gave him half a dollar to flip, and he dropped it a few times, and it was pretty good. With Duke Wayne, before he learns a scene, he comes over and says, "What am I supposed to do here?" "Well, you're supposed to get mad at this fellow first, and then he pops you." I tell him the theory of the scene, then he goes and learns it. With Duke I don't care whether I happen to like a line reading. I don't care how he murders them, as long as he gets the intent.

Once they have that attitude, it's up to them to read the lines. I want the actors to do what I tell them. In England this is rather difficult because if you tell an actor what to do, he says, "Well, I think I'd rather do it this way." "Well," I say, "you just go out the door and we'll get someone else."

Do you ever improvise on set?

In the first place, improvisation is a silly word because when you have a scene to do, you don't really know anything about it until you see the people that are going to act in the picture. I'm more interested in fitting the story around the actors. A script is important as a basis, but it doesn't have to be followed exactly. You can sit in a room and decide what the people are going to do when they get on location, but even a stage play is made by constant changes and alterations during rehearsals. On set you start changing things and fixing it so the stuff that you know the actors can do well is in there, and it becomes fun, especially if it's somebody you haven't worked with before and you don't know exactly what they're good for. I'd get into trouble when the producers would tell me, "Hey, you can't change that." "Why can't I? I wrote it." They seem to think that once it's printed on paper it becomes gospel. But that isn't so, at least not in my way of thinking. A good example was a week before starting a new picture with John Wayne. I was down in Mexico on location and found a Mexican boy who I thought was awfully good. I made a test for him for a small part and gave him the lead opposite Wayne. Well, I had to do some rewriting. His language wasn't the best in the world so I had to keep everything he said simple.

Cary Grant is very good in I Was a Male War Bride.

Yes, he is by far the best comedian we've had, and I've been smart enough not to make any comedies unless I made them with him. We had a scene in *I Was a Male War Bride* where an American sergeant has to ask Cary Grant—a French captain—the questions that would be asked of a little French girl who is going to marry a GI. We thought we had a really funny scene going. He had to ask Cary whether he ever had any female trouble or if he'd ever been pregnant—you know, a lot of things like that—but the scene wasn't funny at all. We didn't know why, and we sat around for about a half an hour. Finally I said, "Cary, you wouldn't be embarrassed by that fellow asking you those questions. You'd say, 'Go ahead, there are some good questions coming.' The sergeant would be embarrassed asking those questions." Cary said, "We can do it. We can do it." And he and the other actor got together and in fifteen minutes had a routine that was really very funny, just completely switched the scene right around. But that's Cary Grant.

It's pretty hard to tell what it is that's funny and what isn't because it surprises you sometimes. I remember shooting a scene with him one time where he asked, "How was that?" And I said, "Pretty dull. You're getting mad like an ordinary person. Let's find some different way of getting mad." And we started trying different ways, and then somebody said, "I know a fellow who when he got mad used to whinny like horse." Cary said, "That's fine, I'll do that." That's what I call an attitude toward a scene.

I wanted to ask you about the character of the psychiatrist in Bringing Up Baby. *How much did the current feeling of that time about psychoanalysis in general inform that picture?*

Hawks with Cary Grant and Katharine Hepburn on the set
of *Bringing Up Baby* (1938).

I haven't any idea because I never paid any attention to that. We just made
up our own character. Katie Hepburn was just a delight to work with.
She'd get all excited and start telling a story, and they'd say that they were
ready to shoot and she would never hear them at all. So one day when she
was talking, gabbing, and the assistant had asked for quiet two or three
times, I just said, "Sit down and just stare at her." All of a sudden in the
middle of this thing she turned around and looked, and everyone was just
sitting there quietly staring at her. She said, "What's happening? What are
you doing?" I said, "We were just wondering how long you could talk."
She said, "I'd like to talk to you for a minute," and she led me around
backstage and said, "Howard, a lot of these people are my friends. They
aren't going to like it with you talking to me that way." I looked up, and
there was an electrician sitting up high—I knew him when I was a prop
man at Paramount—and I said, "Ed, if you had a choice of dropping a
lamp on Miss Hepburn or me, who would you drop it on?" He said, "Get

out of the way, Howard." And Katie started to laugh and said, "I guess I was wrong. I'll never do it again." She was just marvelous.

The Big Sleep is a confusing film. I can't tell what the devil that picture is really about.

Well, there are three or four things in there that I didn't know and the author didn't know. Somebody asked, "Who killed such-and-such?" I said, "I don't know." Somebody else spoke up and said, "I think so-and-so killed him." And we said, "No, he couldn't have done it." So we sent Raymond Chandler a wire asking who killed him, and he sent a wire back: "Joe did it." And I sent him a wire saying, "Joe is out in the ocean—he couldn't have done it." But people still liked the picture, and I thought, why worry about plot and everything? Just worry about making good scenes with interesting characters. That's all we tried to do, hooking it together with something that keeps your interest.

If you're talking to an actor about a part—what kinds of things do you say to him?

I can only answer you in a general way. Actors per se I don't give too much a hoot about, but personalities I do. I can take a personality and make something out of him, though I've worked with a lot of personalities who were both personalities and good actors, like Gary Cooper. In making a scene with Coop, why, you look at it and you wonder, there's nothing happening there. Then you'd look at the film and it was great. I told him, "Keep on doing that." One scene in *Sergeant York* that worked very well—he slept through the whole scene. I said, "You were great in that scene." But you've got to find a new personality, somebody who's got something. Jimmy Cagney had a completely new way of doing everything. You wouldn't say he was a great actor, but he was a hell of a personality. He'd come busting in and do something that was completely out of line and get away with it and do it beautifully. Wayne became, I think, a really good actor. I hate to make a Western without using him. Jack Ford started Wayne in *Stagecoach,* but he didn't have anything to do in it, and when Ford saw *Red River,* he said, "I never knew that big son of a bitch could act." And he put him in two pictures, one after another, and gave him stuff to do in them. But he does a great thing—he does not annoy an audience by trying too much. He just does everything very simply.

You know, Michael Curtiz was supposed to direct *Sergeant York,* and I was supposed to direct *Casablanca*. I had lunch with Curtiz, and he said, "I don't know anything about those hill people." And I said, "I don't know anything about that musical comedy I'm supposed to make. Why don't we switch?" And we were up against each other for the Academy Award. But I couldn't have made *Casablanca*—it was too stagy.

Did you ever get in trouble when you got to the editing room and felt that you wished you had more coverage?

No, not really. If I don't like a scene I protect myself so I can cut it down. If I like the scene I make it so nobody can cut it down, otherwise some stupid jerk will want to cut something out I want to keep. They'll try and make a thing go faster or something. Zanuck was famous for that. He'd say, "Just make this go a little faster." I usually have the cutter come down on the set and I tell him what I'm after. He watches, and we work it out and rehearse it, and quite a number of times we've been able to look at the picture the day after we finish shooting.

Any time you cut, it's much better for the audience if you can cut on an action. There are too many new directors who just cut for no reason at all, and you can't tell who the hell they're cutting to or why and you can't follow it. I'm much more interested in somebody listening than somebody talking. I had a new cutter on one picture, and when I looked at what he'd done I had to fire him and reprint everything. The scenes I had shot were made for reactions, not for somebody talking.

When you shoot a scene with an actor and his timing is off, can it be fixed in the editing?

I'd say it has to work when it's actually done. With a comedy, the only thing I go by is whether it's funny. On *Bringing Up Baby*, both Katie Hepburn and Cary Grant didn't think they could do it. He said, "How will I do this?" I said, "My God, you've seen Harold Lloyd, haven't you?" "Okay," he said, and he was off; he knew what to do. But it was Katie's first comedy, and she tried to be funny, and there's nothing worse than a picture where an actor is trying to be funny. You know? Really trying to be funny. And I didn't want to insult her but I was having an awful time trying to figure out what to do. On the set was Walter Catlett, a great comic actor. I said, "Walter, you've been listening to this. Do you think that you could tell Miss Hepburn what to do, and then I won't insult her?" He said, "I could tell her, but I'm not going to." I said, "What if she asks you?" "Then I'd tell her." So I went over to Katie and said, "Kate, we don't seem to be understanding one another, but there's a fellow on the set here who I think could tell you exactly what you're doing wrong. Do you want to talk to him?" She said, "Sure." So she talked to him for about three-quarters of an hour and came back and said, "Howard, you've got to hire him, you've got to keep him around." All he did was tell her not to try to be funny, and she became funny.

Do you usually shoot with multiple cameras?

Usually with one camera, but it depends on what you're doing in the scene. Sometimes you use two or three cameras. Of course, when you get into a cattle drive, like *Red River,* you get six or seven cameras—you get all the cameras you can afford up there. The picture that was made so quickly with Lombard and Barrymore, it was mostly on a train, and Lombard was so photogenic that it didn't make any difference how you lit her, and Barrymore didn't care about it, so we used three cameras all the time on that one. There's no set way—you're telling a story. If you study Ford's pictures, you'll discover that when he came to a scene he didn't like too much he did it in a long shot, and it was very effective, much better than faces of people saying silly lines. I did the same thing. I stole it from him two or three times. Peter Bogdanovich stole it from both of us. Peter sat on my set for about three pictures, and I'd tell him why I was using a long shot.

There was a German director named Murnau who came over here, and he had the camera move and do the strangest things you've ever seen, really fabulous. I thought I'd try the same thing. They liked the picture so well that they held it up for a year, and by the time it was shown it was old stuff, so I gave it up. Now I just try to shoot from eye height, and the only time I change from that is if I want a shot that the set won't allow, or you need a shot of a man high up in a belfry getting shot and falling down. I don't approve of camera tricks unless they're really good. Of course, every time you make an interesting shot it's a camera trick. In *Red River* we were having a burial, and Wayne was reading. I saw a cloud coming—it was passing and you could see it about a mile away and it was coming pretty fast, and I said, "Duke, get ready. I'll yell when to stop talking but I don't care what lines you say, and then you turn around and come toward the camera." And just as he read the burial service the cloud passed over and turned everything dark behind. It made a great shot. You'd call that a trick shot, but it happened right there.

How did you handle Montgomery Clift and John Wayne?

When I hired Clift he'd never made a picture before, and we took a look at him and Wayne said, "Couldn't you have gotten somebody who could stand up to me a little bit?" I said, "I think he can stand up to you pretty well." We made the very first scene and he came over to me and said, "That kid is going to be good." He said, "He looks like he's just figuring that he can take me apart at any time and isn't worried about it. One thing though—we can't have a fight. It would be silly." Well, I said, "You're a lot bigger and it would be silly, but it wouldn't be silly if you tripped and he kicked you in the face first." "Okay, let him kick me in the face." And we did it that way and it made a perfectly good fight. We had an awful time because Monty Clift couldn't throw a punch. It took us three days.

Clift looked so Western in that picture. How did he get comfortable on horses?

He had something you see rarely today—he really wanted to work. He went out for two weeks with a box lunch and a cowboy and they didn't come back all day. At the end of those two weeks he could ride a horse, he could handle a gun and he could even make a special little mount to get into the saddle. He worked like the devil.

Do you frequently use people who are nonactors?

When Howard Hughes and I made a picture called *Scarface,* every good actor was under contract to a studio. They weren't about to loan us any actors because we were working independently and they didn't like that. I told Howard I'd go to New York to see if I could find anyone back there. I found Paul Muni in the Jewish theater on Thirty-ninth Street playing an old man. I asked him to come out and make a test and he said, "No, I'm a sedentary man. I couldn't play a violent man." Well, I said, "Come on over." And we put him on boards about this tall and we got little people to work with him, had a sweater underneath to make him look big. He became a star. George Raft I saw at a prizefight. He was a dancer, a gigolo and a nightclub bouncer when he wasn't hanging around gangsters. He'd never worked before as an actor.

If you choose unknowns, you have to be pretty good. You have to find out if they photograph, you have to make some tests, things like that. You can't just pick out somebody and throw them in. *The Graduate* was made pretty much with unknowns. When I first saw the picture I couldn't believe they were going to make Dustin Hoffman the leading man, but as I began to see more of the picture you begin to see how good the boy is.

Did you see Midnight Cowboy?

I didn't like it, so I didn't stay.

Why didn't you?

I don't know. Maybe I was tired.

Do you walk out of films often?

Sure. No, what I mean is I've just got something else to do. I've been at it a long time. Every once in a while I see a travelogue I think is better than a feature film.

You work with stars a lot.

All you have to do is utilize the star's value in terms of his providing entertainment. Wayne's proved that. Anthony Quinn has proved that. At Metro it was set up where they had seventy writers writing for the biggest bunch of stars in the business. Gable, Barrymore, Harlow and everyone— and not one of those actors had a damn thing to say about the choice of stories. They did what they were told to do by very smart people. If you went to see Gable you knew that you were going to see a certain type of picture; you knew what he stood for. Then the day came when the stars decided what they were going to do and, holy smoke, what a mess they made. Some awfully good people failed miserably just because they chose bad things, and now there are only two people I know of in the star system who are holding their own.

Lee Marvin got way up there and took a nosedive, all because he has some screwy idea that besides being a good actor he was a God-given producer. They wanted me to make a picture with him. It didn't start too good because they wanted me to go over to his house and talk to him, and I've never been to an actor's house for that reason in my life. So he came by and he was a little hung over. "Well," he said, "I don't want to make a John Wayne Western." I said, "No, that would be awful hard." He said, "What do you mean?" I said, "You're about one-third as good as Wayne." And he kind of laughed and said, "Well, I guess I'll make a Lee Marvin Western." And I said, "I don't know where the hell you'll get a horse that will lean up against a wall." Well, that finished it. As an actor I think Marvin is good, but as a producer and a writer he doesn't know anything. Now it's all changing. Wayne will do any story that Jack Ford or I want to do, but when he asks me, "What do you think of my directing. I mean the stuff I make myself?" Well, the less said the better.

I wonder why things have changed? I don't think the women now are very interesting, nor are the men in a lot of movies that we see.

Well, if you go to cast a something you have an awful time. I made a picture with a woman star, a lovely girl, and she came in and said, "Howard, the left side of my face is so much better." I said, "I've got enough to do without worrying about your face." Eventually I said, "I don't want to work with a woman star," and I started to work with all new people: Carole Lombard, Rita Hayworth, Lauren Bacall. The audience liked to see them, too. And that's the trouble with most of the women today. You see a girl on television that you think is going to be good, and by the time she makes about the third one in the series she's gotten cute and spoiled. I've seen several of them I thought were good, and then all of a sudden they just make you ill.

Howard Hughes started in films and suddenly he disappeared from them. Do you know why?

Oh, Howard is a very odd character. He bought RKO and never had an office over there. He had an office over at Goldwyn. I had a contract with him that said if he ever said no to me the contract was broken. So he would call up and say, "Now, look. I'm not saying no, but why do you want to make it this way for?" I'd tell him and he'd say, "Oh, that's different." He's a strange man. He's got so much money that it doesn't mean anything to him. He'd holler about a penny and throw a million away.

Has there ever been a system in Hollywood where a director will take on a young fellow who he thinks is promising?

Oh sure. Billy Wilder, for example. He wanted to watch me, and I said he could if he would be there when we start every scene and stay until we finish. Don't just come in and look around. He stayed for about two pictures and then he started directing. He was nervous as the devil and called me and said, "Would you come over and help me the first day?" And I said, "Sure. You're getting along all right."

One time Louis B. Mayer had a brilliant idea. He was going to put von Sternberg and me together and get a super picture. Joe and I were quite good friends and we developed a whole story. Then we started to talk about how to treat it. Joe had always taken a little thing and built it up, and I take a big situation and play it down. We both knew this, and I said, "Joe, there is only one thing to do. Let's go into Mr. Mayer's office, and you tell him your way and I'll tell him my way and we'll let him choose, because we're no good to each other." So we did, and unfortunately he chose my way. I told him big things and that seemed fine to him, and Joe told him little teeny things. But that happens all the time. I guarantee you that two directors that are any good can take the same story, change the name of the characters, change the name of the town and make an entirely different picture.

You're one of those American directors lauded by the French critics. How do you feel about that?

You know, I don't go in for analysis. Every time I go to France, I meet with thirty French directors who know most of the dialogue of my pictures and ask me questions. They are very interested in how you make pictures. They go into it and analyze it and read things into it that I had no idea of when I was making the movie. In Europe my name is three times as big as John Wayne's on the posters. I make sure those posters are where everybody can see them.

Films as Director

1926 *The Road to Glory* (also story)
      Fig Leaves (also story)
1927 *The Cradle Snatchers*
      Paid to Love
1928 *A Girl in Every Port* (also story)
      Frazil
      The Air Circus
1929 *Trent's Last Case*
1930 *The Dawn Patrol* (also co-
      screenplay)
1931 *The Criminal Code*
1932 *Tiger Shark*
      Scarface
      The Crowd Roars (also story)
1933 *Today We Live*
1934 *Viva Villa* (offscreen credit)
      Twentieth Century
1935 *Barbary Coast*
1936 *Ceiling Zero* (also producer)
      The Road to Glory
      Come and Get it (codirector
      with William Wyler)
1938 *Bringing Up Baby*
1939 *Only Angels Have Wings*
1940 *His Girl Friday*
1941 *Sergeant York*

1942 *Ball of Fire*
1943 *The Outlaw* (offscreen
      credit)
      Air Force
1945 *To Have and Have Not*
1946 *The Big Sleep*
1948 *Red River* (also producer)
      A Song Is Born
1949 *I Was a Male War Bride*
1951 *The Thing* (also producer for
      fire sequence)
1952 *The Big Sky* (also producer)
      O. Henry's Full House
      Monkey Business
1953 *Gentlemen Prefer Blondes*
1955 *Land of the Pharaohs* (also
      producer)
1959 *Rio Bravo* (also producer)
1962 *Hatari!* (also producer)
1964 *Man's Favorite Sport?* (also
      producer)
1965 *Red Line 7000* (also producer
      and co-screenplay)
1967 *El Dorado* (also producer)
1970 *Rio Lobo* (also producer)

Sometimes it's not how much light you use to get an effect, it's how little you use and still make it work. There are a lot of rules to be broken in photography, and you've got to have courage.

JAMES WONG HOWE
(Born in Kwantung, China, 1899—Died 1976)

James Wong Howe is one of the outstanding cameramen of the Golden Age, and I remember him fondly for telling one of the outstanding Hollywood stories. He had saved some money from working fifty weeks a year on movie sets and decided to open a Chinese restaurant on Ventura Boulevard. On opening day a photographer arrived to shoot a publicity still, and he set up his eight-by-ten camera on a tripod in front of the restaurant. As Howe watched anxiously, the photographer kept moving his camera farther into the street in an effort to get the whole establishment in his picture. The farther he moved out, the more ominous were the speeding cars swerving to miss him. Howe stepped up and said, "Why don't you put on a wide-angle lens and you can shoot it from the curb." The indignant photographer turned to James Wong Howe and said, "Look, Buster, you make the chop suey and I'll take the pictures."

Howe came from China to the United States with his father, who started a business in Oregon. The young Howe was forced to wear his hair with a traditional queue and was subjected to mistreatment by other children. As a young man he worked as a laborer and later as a prizefighter, a trade that gave him a mashed nose. After moving to Los Angeles in hopes of becoming an aviator, he got a job as a darkroom assistant and ran into a former boxer-turned-cameraman on the set of a Mack Sennett comedy. This opened the door to his movie career.

First he worked in laboratories and learned the fundamentals, finally getting his break as a fourth cameraman on Cecil B. DeMille's *Male and Female*, in 1919. He took some flattering still photos of the actress Mary Miles

James Wong Howe, working here as an assistant cameraman on an unidentified picture in the 1920s, went from being a slate boy for Cecil B. DeMille in 1917 to having a distinguished career as an innovative cameraman.

Minter, and she asked if he could make her look that good on the movie screen. Howe assured her he could, and he was off and running, becoming the head cameraman in 1923 on *Drums of Fate* and *The Trail of the Lonesome Pine* with Minter as the star. Soon he was working with major directors and experimenting with deep-focus, wide-angle lenses and sets with ceilings. He developed a realistic style that was shown to advantage in *Walking Down Broadway,* directed by Erich von Stroheim.

The industry was in turmoil when sound came along, so Howe made a long visit to China. Upon his return he had difficulty getting work because studios claimed he didn't understand sound. Howard Hawks broke the ice by hiring him for *The Criminal Code* at Fox, a job that led to *The Power and the Glory* for Preston Sturges. Known as James Howe when he moved to MGM, he acquired the Chinese name Wong when the studio publicity department added it to the credits to lend an exotic aura to Howe's persona. He photographed fifteen pictures in three years at MGM, including *Viva Villa!* and *The Thin Man,* and then shot *The Prisoner of Zenda* and his first color film,

The Adventures of Tom Sawyer, for David O. Selznick. "I tried to subordinate background color," he said, "and confine the major coloring of any scene to the players."

In 1938 Howe signed a contract with Warner Bros. and flourished there with stylish films including *Kings Row, Passage to Marseille, Objective, Burma, Air Force, Yankee Doodle Dandy* and *Body and Soul.* He wanted to join John Ford's navy documentary unit in the Pacific during World War II but, even though he had lived in the United States for thirty-nine years, was forbidden by the Chinese Exclusion Act from becoming an American citizen, so the government would not grant him a commission.

Howe left Warner Bros. in 1948 to work as a freelance cinematographer, choosing assignments one at a time. In the 1950s he photographed *Sweet Smell of Success* in his signature black-and-white style and began experimenting with color in *Bell, Book and Candle* and *Picnic.* But his finest work was in black and white, notably in *Hud,* for Martin Ritt, who called Howe the most committed worker he'd ever known. When Twentieth Century Fox refused to let Ritt make *The Molly Maguires* in black and white, Howe shot it in a muted color that gave it the texture of black and white. "Color gives a certain falseness to me," Howe said. "You see it concentrated and emphasized on the screen, unlike life."

Howe was a hardworking cameraman from his first opportunity in 1919 to his last film in 1974, *Funny Lady,* on which he replaced Vilmos Zigmond to ensure that Barbra Streisand would look good. *Funny Lady* brought him his tenth Academy Award nomination, at age seventy-five. He was one of the most innovative cameramen in Hollywood history, shooting well over 130 films and earning Oscars for *The Rose Tattoo* and *Hud.* Alexander Mackendrick, the director of *Sweet Smell of Success,* admired Howe's single-minded dedication to what was best for the picture and his unwillingness to shoot for the front office. Howe put it this way: "It's the unusual and sometimes even accidental things that are interesting. . . . you're breaking the rules, defying tradition and maybe even taking a chance."

JAMES WONG HOWE

April 7, 1973*

Jimmy's a newcomer to the business. He started in 1912, and became a director of photography in 1917. I remember that when I was a kid, I always wanted to see your pictures with all the great low-key photography.

They call me "Low-key Howe."

In an article from 1968 you said that the photography should always enhance the story rather than exist just to stimulate the viewer. I wonder if you ever found yourself in conflict with a director about this.

The most difficult thing is to find a director who will cooperate with the cameraman, and vice versa. The director thinks of his action with his actor, and the cameraman thinks mostly in terms of lighting. When you're photographing a motion picture, you've got a story to tell, and you can't always keep your actors in the dark. You've got to read their expressions. That's why there are close-ups. Remember this—the eyes convey thought. The top of the head doesn't mean anything, so when you get in close, cut the top of the head. Make the audience look at the eyes.

Now, you find the films of the old-time directors like John Ford and Howard Hawks beautifully photographed and well lit, and with the absence of a lot of movement. Ford never moved a camera unless he had to follow an actor. He didn't move the camera and then say, "Now, actor,

*This transcript includes extracts from the AFI seminar with James Wong Howe held on April 14, 1973.

follow the movement." We're all subservient to the story. I don't say that we do away with camera movement altogether, but it must be done in a way that helps to tell the story. I believe that anything you do technically or mechanically in editing or camera movement to help tell the story is good. If it doesn't work, you throw it out. Take David Selznick, who produced *The Adventures of Tom Sawyer*. I shot a whole sequence that cost $175,000. He thought it would work, but when he put it together, it didn't work. He threw it out.

Could you talk about working with Howard Hawks?

In making films, there are two schools of thought. Howard Hawks is a great director. You can go down the line with his pictures and they're all fine, and he cuts with the camera. You can take his rushes and cut off the slate and put it together and it's cut. Now, you take George Stevens or Willy Wyler, they'll shoot all kinds of angles. They might shoot one scene from six or seven angles. They call it "protection shooting." In other words, they want to play around with it. They're not quite so secure as Hawks, who knows when he comes to the set where he wants to put the camera. I think he does a lot of studying and homework, but you don't notice it. He keeps it in his head. But take *Shane*, by George Stevens. It cost a lot of money, and George put it together and they tested it, and the picture flopped. So he re-edited it. He took nine months. He sat all night until early in the morning. He had two projectors, and would push forward, reverse, stop. After he got through with it, he said, "Send it out again." And it became a big hit that won the Academy Award.*The way Hawks shoots, he can't do anything else with it. He's stuck with it.

Does luck ever play a part when it comes to your camera work?

I was on a film at Warner Bros. called *Air Force*. Howard Hawks was the director. We had nine B-17s for the movie down in Tampa, Florida. They had a shot where they're supposed to be coming in to land. I had to line up all my lights and get the generator. About two or three hours before we were going to make the shot, I asked the electrician to hit the generator and light up all the lights to try it out, and he said, "Jimmy, we're having

---

*Though Stevens was nominated as Best Director and as producer for Best Motion Picture, Fred Zimmerman and *From Here to Eternity* won that year.

problems. The generator doesn't work." I told Mr. Hawks this, and he said, "Don't tell me that. That's not my problem. That's your problem." So I went to the special effects man and said, "Look, do we have any three-minute flares?" He said, "Yes, I got a flock of them." So I took the mirrors off the back of the lights and hung them into the reflector stands and took all the lights down and put these reflectors there in front of the mirrors. I had the electricians wire the flares. So the planes are all lined up, and I tell the electrician to hit the switch, and all these flares came on and flickered. It was wonderful because the landing field was supposed to be on fire, and smoke from the flares drifted across. All the planes were coming down with their headlights on and going through this smoke with their propellers. It created a lot of drama. Hawks saw the rushes and said, "Wonderful effect, shooting this with flares." If the generator hadn't broken, I wouldn't have got this effect. I would've had steady lights with no flickering, and it wouldn't have added to the drama.

What was it like working for the studios?

When you're under contract to the studios, you don't have many choices. You're assigned films. I signed my first three-year contract in 1922 and I worked every week except two. If I wasn't shooting a film, I had to go shoot second unit. I had to shoot inserts. But that was all wonderful because I learned a lot. I could afford to make mistakes on those inserts because it didn't cost much to make them over. I feel sorry for a lot of photographers today. They really aren't given enough time to light their sets. They have a man there with a watch. He keeps looking at it, and then goes to a telephone. You're going to be faced with creating, under pressure, the kind of lighting that will work to express your feelings.

If you really like film—and I think films are becoming much more an art form—you don't really have to go into a motion picture studio to make feature films. There's so many things you can do: documentaries, teaching, science films, television. Maybe they don't have the glamor that you would have with movie stars, but after you see two or three movie stars, they're all the same.

I want you all to understand that there are other things to deal with besides knowing how to use a camera. You have to deal with personalities, especially stars, and it's the stars that can be the ones who make or break you as a cameraman. If they like your work, they put you in their contract. They insist on you being their cameraman. For many years, William

Daniels was Greta Garbo's cameraman. She wouldn't do a film without him. This gives you great security. So when you go to work in the studio you need to know how to deal with the people in front of the camera. It's a family unit. The cameraman has his operators and assistants; the gaffer has his grips.

It was a wonderful relationship in the early days because it gave an opportunity for the assistant and the operator to study the style of the director of photography and learn. If he sees something, he comes up to me and asks, "Jimmy, why did you do that?" I take time to explain, because I remember when I had to learn, I asked the same things. Once I asked a cameraman something, and he said, "Do you think I'm going to tell you in ten minutes what it took me ten years to learn?" I was very embarrassed, and I said, "If I ever become a cameraman, I hope I never say that to anyone."

Did you ever work with Elia Kazan?

Yes, on *On the Waterfront.* Kazan said, "You know I got an ending to this picture, where Brando is fighting. I need more shots of fighting. Would you do that for me?" I said, "Yes." The production manager asked me how many lights I wanted. I said, "No lights." So we went down and shot, and it got later and later and it was getting darker and darker. Finally, I said, "Gee, Gadge [Kazan's nickname], this is about it." He said, "I need a shot of Brando. He's been beaten up so he's dizzy and he's walking into the warehouse. The door opens there." We used a handheld camera. It was an Eyemo that I gave to the operator. I put a piece of chalk down on the cement and said, "Now look through that camera and walk around that chalk mark." He kept walking and walking, and said, "Gee, I'm getting a little dizzy." I said, "Keep walking. Keep walking. Okay. Now point the camera at that door and hit the trigger and walk." He couldn't walk very steady, so it made a wonderful shot from Brando's perspective. If I hadn't spun the operator around and got him really dizzy, it wouldn't have worked.

What are your general feelings about makeup?

The less makeup, the better. We're trying to tell a story and it's supposed to be true. We're trying to make you believe it. When you see a lot of makeup on a person, you start to lose your belief in it. It's like when we used to make war pictures in the early days. They'd get stock shots of

Howe used less light than most camermen, becoming known among
his colleagues as "Low-key Howe."

actual warfare, and they would cut them into our studio shots. It was like
night and day. Right away you'd say, "That's real. This isn't real." Gregg
Toland did a wonderful thing. They had a pre–World War I parade. He
shot it and took the negative and duped it four or five times, and
scratched it, and when it came on the screen, you believed it.

Do you use a light meter?

When I started out we didn't have light meters. We had to judge the exposure by looking through the camera, either through the ground glass or

sometimes through a piece of film. Now, today, say you went over to Africa on a big picture and you slip and break your meter. What would happen? You would really feel insecure. I know I would. But you can learn exposure if you observe light, which is the most important thing in photography. Study light. That's what gives you the mood. You can almost feel the quality and texture of light. At night, walk the streets, or when you're driving, study the lighting.

It's very easy, you know, to buy a light meter. But there's one thing that meter will not tell you, and that's whether you have the right mood or not. That you'll have to decide for yourself.

What was it like working with the old three-strip Technicolor process?

When we had three-strip, cameramen were trained to use eight hundred foot-candles—so much light. There was a reason for it, because it would give a good, strong negative, and with a strong negative they could make many matrices to make their prints. With three-strip you had three strips of black and white run through your camera at the same time, each one with a complementary filter. They would make a matrix; it's like a rubber stamp. They would dye these and print the three strips one on top of the other. With a strong matrix, you could make maybe 150 prints before the matrix wears out. But if you light in low key, you have a weak negative and a weak matrix. That doesn't mean you had bad color or anything, but the studio complains because after ten prints the matrix wears out.

I didn't know this until I worked with David Selznick on *Tom Sawyer.* We're in a cave, there were a lot of lighting effects, and the Technicolor man said, "Jimmy, you haven't got enough light." I think I had 350 or 400 foot-candles. He measured and said, "The least you can go is six hundred." So I bring it up to 600. But it didn't feel right. I didn't think the audience could believe it. So I went back to 350, and opened the lens a little bit more. I didn't care about the background, but Technicolor wanted everything sharp. So David Selznick sees the rushes and he loves it. He says, "Jimmy, that's the kind of effect I want." And finally Technicolor complained to him, saying "You better change cameraman. Jimmy Howe doesn't use enough light." He said, "Look, I love this stuff. I'm not going to change." They said, "But look, he got a weak negative and we can't matrix, and when our prints wear out it'll cost more money." Selznick said, "Look at your contract with me. It doesn't say now many matrices you make. You deliver me some prints and I'll pay for them. But I don't want to change the cameraman."

Is your basic technique different depending on whether you're shooting in color or black and white?

My basic lighting wouldn't change very much. I like color to be a little softer and not give it too much contrast, because if you don't have enough light on it, color changes. Color is very lavish, and I think if you find the right subject for it and put the people in there, it can be very good. But I don't think it's good to use color for color's sake. I think many color films should actually be made in black and white.

The last picture I made was called *The Molly Maguires,* an old mining story set in Pennsylvania. The director, Martin Ritt, said, "Jimmy, I want to make this picture in black and white," but the producer said, "If the film is in black and white, we may not be able to sell it to TV." So Martin Ritt said to the art director and costume designer, "Look, fellows, I wanted to make this in black and white, but we're going to make to it in color, so I want to make it with a black-and-white feeling. Get your noodles together and see what you can do." Somebody had told him about desaturation, when you take the color out of the print. Now, I don't think desaturation accomplishes much. I personally like to do it [create a black-and-white effect] before it's photographed. Sometimes you can do it with gauzes or filters. But most lab men don't have aesthetic feelings. They're not really artists; they're technicians, and you can't expect them to get the kind of emotional feeling out of color that you want. And once they do it, you're stuck with it. You can't change it. So I said, "I don't want to fool around with this. If you're going to make this picture and try to keep the color down, you've got to do it from the very beginning. The art director has to keep the bright paint off the houses."

We went back to Pennsylvania and found the location. The houses were all different colors, and they had to put false woodwork over the houses and paint it a kind of dark, dirty gray green. The branches of the trees looked wonderful against the gray sky. When we started filming there were buds on the trees, and the director said, "What are we going to do?" I said, "Better hire some natives and have them pick the buds off." So we had dozens of guys with ladders, picking the buds off. They thought we were crazy. We also had a helicopter that flew around blowing this black dust all over the countryside.

Sometimes it's not how much light you use to get an effect, it's how little you use and still make it work. There are a lot of rules to be broken in photography, and you've got to have courage. You've got to stick your neck out. You're liable to get some scars, but it's worth it.

Can we talk about The Outrage, *the remake of Kurosawa's* Rashomon, *where you used entirely different techniques in four different versions of the same story?*

I thought *Rashomon* was beautifully done and I asked Martin Ritt, whom I respect as a director, "Why do you want to remake this thing? How are you going to top *Rashomon*?" He said, "I don't think I can. But you know *Rashomon* was released over here and very few people saw the film. I like the subject, and with Paul Newman we might be able to get a good film out of it." We ran *Rashomon* again and again. I said, "Look, I think you're nuts for making it." He said, "Maybe you're right, but I'd like to stick my neck out. You'll still photograph it, won't you?" I said, "Yes, but what are you going to do with the fight scene?" The Japanese choreography was beautiful, you hear that whoosh of the sword go by, the danger of these things and the beauty of it. I asked, "How are you going to stage the fight? With a couple of pistols, and bang, bang, bang at each other like every other Western? You've got to get a good choreographer in there and see what they can do with that fight."

What about your work on Hud?

That was my first film with Mr. Ritt. He said, "This film is set down in Texas, and I don't know if you'll be happy. It's just blank skies and strips of land and nothing much to photograph." I said, "For the film, what kind of clouds do you want?" He said, "I can't tell until I look at them," so for a whole week we looked at stock footage of clouds. He got tired of looking at clouds pretty quickly, and said, "Let's go down and look at the location." I had read the script, and said, "Marty, you're crazy to try and put clouds in." He said, "Why?" I said, "I would shoot it with nothing but blank sky. If there are clouds, put in a blue filter and make the blue go white so the clouds won't show. Wash it out, because it's a black-and-white film. I'd make it as desolate as you can, because that space shows that his nearest neighbor is about ten miles away. Paul Newman's got to graze his cattle under this hot, dusty sky. That's why he wants to get the devil out of there."

Do you plan exact shots and close-ups?

No, I can't go that far, because we have to respect the director. I might plan something, but when the actors are on the stage and the director starts rehearsing, the actor might change the action. When I worked on a film with William Cameron Menzies, the production designer, he made sketches of the entire picture and would mark on the sketch what lens to use. He would say, "A 40 mm here—it fits perfectly. You can't use another lens." It was wonderful. He sketched all the highlights in, and you just take the drawings and say, "That's it."

What would you do if a director asked you to use photographic techniques that you were uncomfortable with?

I can't stand that. As a matter of fact, the last picture I worked on was called *The Horseman,* which I didn't finish. I shot two or three weeks on it and had a disagreement with the director, John Frankenheimer. He had ordered a particular lens and was paying a tremendous rental on that lens, and he had to justify the rental. He asked me to use it. I just said, "No." I told him the reason why, and he disagreed. He said, "Look, you and I just have different ideas. We must come to a separation." I said, "You're correct, because I'm not going to use this lens. I think it's wrong." I packed up and came home.

Films as Cinematographer

1923 *Drums of Fate*
The Trail of the Lonesome Pine
To the Last Man
The Spanish Dancer
The Call of the Canyon
1924 *The Breaking Point*
The Side Show of Life
The Alaskan
Peter Pan
1925 *The Charmer*
Not So Long Ago
The Best People
The King on Main Street

1926 *The Song and Dance Man*
Mantrap
Sea Horses
Padlocked
1927 *The Rough Riders*
Sorrell and Son
1928 *The Perfect Crime*
Four Walls
Laugh, Clown, Laugh
1929 *Desert Nights*
1930 *Chijiku wo Mawasuru Chikara*
(also directed)
Today

1931 *The Criminal Code*
      Transatlantic
      The Spider
      The Yellow Ticket
      Surrender
1932 *Dance Team*
      After Tomorrow
      Amateur Daddy
      Man About Town
      Chandu the Magician
1933 *Hello, Sister!*
      Beauty for Sale
      The Power and the Glory
1934 *The Show-Off*
      Viva Villa
      Manhattan Melodrama
      The Thin Man
      Hollywood Party
      Have a Heart
      Stamboul Quest
1935 *Biography of a Bachelor Girl*
      The Night Is Young
      Mark of the Vampire
      The Flame Within
      O'Shaughnessy's Boy
      Rendezvous
      Whipsaw
1936 *Three Live Ghosts*
1937 *Fire Over England*
      Under the Red Robe
      Troopship
      The Prisoner of Zenda
1938 *The Adventures of Tom Sawyer*
      Algiers
      Comet Over Broadway
1939 *They Made Me a Criminal*
      The Oklahoma Kid
      Daughters Courageous
      Dust Be My Destiny
      On Your Toes
      Four Wives
1940 *Dr. Ehrlich's Magic Bullet*
      Abe Lincoln in Illinois

      Saturday's Children
      Torrid Zone
      My Love Came Back
      City for Conquest
      A Dispatch from Reuters
1941 *The Strawberry Blonde*
      Shining Victory
      Out of the Fog
      Navy Blues
1942 *Kings Row*
1943 *Yankee Doodle Dandy*
      The Hard Way
      Air Force
      Hangmen Also Die!
      The North Star
1944 *Passage to Marseille*
1945 *Objective, Burma!*
      Counter-Attack
      Confidential Agent
      Danger Signal
1946 *My Reputation*
1947 *Nora Prentiss*
      Pursued
      Body and Soul
1948 *Mr. Blandings Build His Dream*
            House
      The Time of Your Life
1950 *The Baron of Arizona*
      The Eagle and the Hawk
      Tripoli
1951 *The Brave Bulls*
      He Ran All the Way
      Behave Yourself!
1952 *The Lady Says No*
      The Fighter
1953 *Come Back, Little Sheba*
      Main Street to Broadway
      Jennifer
1955 *The Rose Tattoo*
1956 *Picnic*
      Death of a Scoundrel
1957 *Drango*
      Sweet Smell of Success

1958 *The Old Man and the Sea*
     Bell, Book and Candle
1959 *The Last Angry Man*
     The Story on Page One
1960 *Tess of the Storm Country*
     Song without End
1962 *Hud*
1964 *The Outrage*

1965 *The Glory Guys*
1966 *This Property Is Condemned*
     Seconds
1967 *Hombre*
1968 *The Heart Is a Lonely Hunter*
1969 *The Last of the Mobile Hot-Shots*
     The Molly Maguires
1974 *Funny Lady*

Films as Director

1930 *Chijiku wo Mawasuru Chikara*
1954 *Go Man Go*

1958 *Invisible Avenger* (co-director)

Don't listen to anybody else when you're on the set. When you're on the set you have to be the boss—you're responsible for it, you're the one that says, "Print it."

MERVYN LEROY
(Born in San Francisco, California, 1900—Died 1987)

Life for the LeRoy family became difficult when the great San Francisco earthquake destroyed Mervyn's father's department store. Young Mervyn got a job as a newsboy, and the ten-year-old was drawn each evening to the street corner in front of San Francisco's Alcazar Theatre, "As though some mighty magnet was pulling me." One day an actor came out of the theater, bought his paper and offered Mervyn a part in a play. Overnight the acting bug bit him hard. My father's parents, Landers Stevens and Georgie Cooper, had a theatrical company and played the Alcazar, and I used to hear stories of Mervyn from my mother and father. He and my father made their first appearances on the stage as boys at the Alcazar.

Mervyn loved performing and entered competitions as "The Boy Tenor of a Generation." He was soon a regular on the vaudeville circuit before heading to Hollywood, where he got a job in a studio wardrobe department, earning the nickname "Mervyn Mothball." This eventually led to parts in silent films and work as a gag writer and assistant cameraman. LeRoy wrote in his autobiography that his experience as a vaudevillian gave him the tools for directing. "I knew the value of the spoken and the sung word; I understood dialogue," he said. "I welcomed the coming of sound and couldn't wait to direct a talking picture."

LeRoy directed silents at First National before breaking through in 1931 with the startling *Little Caesar,* the picture that began the Warner Bros. gangster film era. *Five Star Final, The Heart of New York* and *I Am a Fugitive from a Chain Gang,* a hard-hitting look at southern prisons that introduced Paul Muni to movies, soon put LeRoy in the front rank of directors. *Gold Diggers*

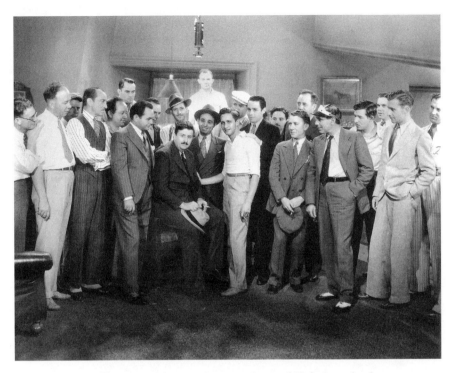

Mervyn LeRoy with cast and crew on the set of *Little Caesar* (1931).

of 1932 and *Tugboat Annie* demonstrated a versatility that in time would take him to MGM.

LeRoy was the ideal studio director at MGM and again, later, at Warner Bros. He was more comfortable with studio authority than the more independent-minded directors and was skilled at making successes of major properties, such as *Random Harvest, Anthony Adverse, Waterloo Bridge, Madame Curie, Thirty Seconds Over Tokyo, Rose Marie* and *Quo Vadis.* In the fifties and sixties he took Broadway hits and brought them to the screen: *The Bad Seed, Mister Roberts* (replacing an ailing John Ford), *Home Before Dark, Mary Mary, A Majority of One* and *Gypsy.* His long string of adaptations was cause for Elia Kazan's jibe about one of LeRoy's acquisitions: "It's got everything. Surprise, great characters, an important theme, fine writing! But I think Mervyn can lick it."

LeRoy's most famous screen credit is for a film he produced but didn't direct. L. Frank Baum's *The Wonderful Wizard of Oz* was a book Mervyn liked, and Louis B. Mayer assigned it to him. LeRoy cast Judy Garland in one of the best-loved films of all time. He wrote in his memoir that he wanted to direct *Oz,* "but L. B. talked me out of it. He thought it would be too much for one man to produce and direct a picture of that magnitude, and he was right." LeRoy made seventy-five films and prided himself on never repeating himself. He wrote, "My films were all so different that there was never a LeRoy trademark."

MERVYN LEROY

———

March 6, 1974*

How did you move from vaudeville to cinema?

I was a lousy vaudeville actor. My partner's father passed away and we had
to break up the act. I was in New York and broke. My cousin was Jesse
Lasky,[†] and I went up and asked him for a job. He didn't want any relations in his studio, so he finally said, "Look, I'll loan you some money." I
wanted to get back to California and I only had about five dollars in my
pocket, so he loaned me train fare. He said, "Go to California, and I'll
give you a note to the studio, but don't tell them you're related to me,
because that will hurt you more than anything else." So I went to the
Lasky studio and I thought I was going to be the head of it right away. I
gave them the letter and they gave me a job folding wardrobe in the
wardrobe department. I couldn't stand the stink of mothballs. It was a
picture about the North and the South, and I was folding Northern uniforms and Southern uniforms all night from the Western Costume Company, stinking of mothballs. The picture was called *Secret Service*. I got out
of that and went into the laboratory. In those days if they had a night
scene they dabbed the film in a blue wash, or with pink if there was a
beautiful flower scene. I would come home with one arm blue and one
arm red. It was really something.

From there I was on a camera. Cecil B. DeMille always said I was the

*This transcript also contains segments from the seminar Mervyn LeRoy gave at the American
Film Institute on July 14, 1983.
†Jesse Lasky (1880–1958) was a producer and one of the founders of Paramount Studios.

one who invented soft focus because I got everything out of focus. And I ended up as an actor. I made a couple of pictures with Wallace Reid, who was a big star in those days, and I played Gloria Swanson's brother in a picture called *Prodigal Daughters*. I couldn't stand it and I went to write gags for comedies at First National, for Colleen Moore and Al Green, who were really the ones who gave me my chance to direct.

Could you talk about what you think made the thirties, forties and fifties the heyday of Hollywood?

Well, of course, I've always said—and Shakespeare will agree with me— "The play's the thing." First, you have to have it on paper, but that's no secret to anyone who knows the value of the story. It's the only thing that counts. You can have the greatest studios, the greatest sets, the greatest camera angles, but if you don't have it on paper first, you don't have it anywhere. And of course there are no stars today; they just don't exist. In the old days they *made* stars, and stars really looked and acted like stars. At Metro they kept Nelson Eddy for five years before he did anything because he was clumsy, he didn't know how to handle his hands.

Were you handed a script by the studio that you directed without question, or did you work with a screenwriter?

I never made a movie that I did without question after being handed a script, believe me, because you have to polish it your way. In the early days they'd hand me a script or they'd hand me a book or something and I'd read it, and then if I liked it, they'd let me do it. In the old days we had Irving Thalberg, who was possibly one of the greatest geniuses ever in the picture business. He was in a class by himself. He was the kindest, sweetest, most unassuming man that I've ever known, outside of Walt Disney. If you met Irving Thalberg right this minute you wouldn't think he knew anything about the picture business. Of course he was tough in a way, but when he told you something it was always worth listening to. I made a lot of pictures for Irving Thalberg, and he would never criticize unless he could improve.

I made a picture called *Tugboat Annie,* with Marie Dressler and Wally Beery, and we had a wonderful preview in San Bernardino. Irving would take three directors to the preview, three writers, three producers, three cameramen, everybody, because he wanted people there who knew the business, that knew about making great pictures. Then we sat around in the MGM dining room and everybody was saying, "Well, fine picture," "You had a wonderful preview," and he said, "Mervyn, I'd like to ask you a question. You know the scene where Marie Dressler is in the school auditorium speaking to the class of kids and grownups?" I said, "Yes." "And when Wally Beery comes down the aisle from the tugboat drunk?" I said, "Yes." And he said, "He tried to sneak in so that his wife wouldn't see him as she's speaking on the platform." And I said, "Yes." "Wouldn't it be funny if he just left the tugboat and he came in and his shoes were soaking wet and as he walked down the aisle the shoes squeaked and squeaked and everybody turned around and laughed, and he was so mad because he was drunk?" It was something like that, and I said, "Yes, Irving, but the set's been torn down. And we'd have to have the same actors to match, it would cost about forty thousand dollars to do it over." Irving looked at me for a second and he said, "Mervyn, I didn't ask how much it would cost. I asked if it would improve the picture." And I said, "Yes, it would." And he said, "Shoot it!" That sums up Irving Thalberg. Nothing was good enough for him.

Have you ever started directing a script and then realized that it wasn't very good?

Before I start a picture I have a reader or a script girl or a script man read it out loud to me maybe three or four times. And if you do this you'll feel the holes and say, "Gee, this is too long; it drags."

What about your work in the silent era? You made quite a few silent films, didn't you?

When I was working in the days of silent pictures, if you made a drama, sometimes it became a comedy when you previewed it. You know, when you wrote titles, all you had to do was open the actor's mouth and then when the titles were put in, the audience would know what happened. They had a man named Ralph Spence. He wrote titles. He would take a comedy and write dramatic titles and make a drama out of it, and if it was a drama he would write funny titles and make something else out of it. A lot of good pictures were made that way.

During your career you've worked with the major superstars of Hollywood. Can you talk a little about your style and how you work with actors?

Well, there are no rules when it comes to style. If you have good actors and they know the story, and I've read the script with them for maybe three or four days before starting the picture, then they will have ideas. No one man makes a motion picture. The guy with the lights is just as important as the man who says "Roll 'em," because if he does the lights wrong, then it's bad. There are maybe two geniuses in our business. The first is Walt Disney, and the second is Irving Thalberg, and I worked with both of them. Sam Goldwyn, Jack Warner—they were great showmen.

Why did you admire Walt Disney so much?

I met Walt Disney when he was making shorts. He was a cartoonist, and we got to be very good friends. He used to invite me out to his studio often. He was a creator. He had a bed in back of his office and he slept there many nights just drawing and working. He was an absolute perfectionist, a genius. There were no secrets with Walt Disney.

What do you look for in an actor?

I could make anyone act who had a heart, I don't care who it is. I don't like mechanical actors. I like people who feel what they're doing, and that means in every branch of filmmaking, from the carpenter up. Intuition tells you that. Let me tell you, I love actors. I love them for one thing— they are trying to do worthwhile things. If they have an idea that I think is good but I think my idea is better than theirs, I'll say, "Look, let's try it your way. Let's shoot it both ways." You have to make an actor feel at home, and the most important thing of all is that the actors want to come to work the next morning.

Are intelligent actors better to work with?

I don't want a cigar store Indian. You take people I've directed, like Ronald Colman—one of the finest actors that ever lived and one of the most beautiful voices that was ever on the screen. He didn't want to direct, he wanted to play the part. Gable was the same way. Tracy, who I made two pictures with, was the same way. He was tough, but he didn't want to direct the picture.

What about improvisation?

If the actor came to me and said, "Mr. LeRoy, these few words here are a little hard for me to say. I don't want to say them," then we'd fool around until we get the few words that will say the same thing but that make him comfortable. If the actor doesn't believe the scene, the audience won't either. I love to have an actor come and say, "I think I can do it better." I may not believe he can and I might print the take that I like, but I will still let him try to do it better. That's when you have a happy company and a happy set, if they know the man in front of them wants them to be as good as possible.

Does this hold true for the crew?

You bet your life. I love to have them feel at home when they come to work. When making a picture, I'll take a suggestion from anybody on the set. I've had carpenters or electricians give me fresh ideas. Always listen to them—they might be good.

I gather that no one wanted to make The Wizard of Oz *at first. What were their complaints?*

That it was for children, and who wants to see it? It was as simple as that. I said, "I want to see it. I've wanted to see it since I was a kid." People thought I was crazy making a fairy story just for kids.

Did you tell them it wasn't picture just for children?

For five years, and then I had Mr. Selznick help me talk to Mr. Mayer. Of course Mr. Selznick didn't know what it was all about. He'd never heard of the *The Wizard of Oz.* What do you think the film cost then?

$750,000? Two million?

It cost $2.3 million. If you made it today it would cost $12 million. About three years ago I took *I Am a Fugitive from a Chain Gang* to the people who make the budgets and told them what it cost, $375,000. I said, "Break it down for me. I'd like to know what this picture would cost today." $2.8 million. With the same sets, the same actor, the same every-thing—from $375,000 to $2.8 million.

How did you cast the lead role of The Wizard of Oz?

Well, this is my favorite subject, naturally, because I had wanted to do it since I was a kid, and it took me a long, long time to sell it. They wanted Shirley Temple. A couple of nights before, I had seen Judy Garland in a picture called *Pigskin Parade* that was made at Twentieth Century Fox, and she was singing as a cheerleader in front of these kids. She was so great that I just couldn't get over her, and I brought her over and made a test and fixed all her teeth, because she had holes in her teeth at the time. They liked her and that was it. I think she was one of the best performers that ever lived. So is Shirley Temple, but she couldn't sing like Judy Garland.

Why didn't you direct The Wizard of Oz?

I wanted to. I was the highest salaried of anyone at Metro in those days, but Mr. Mayer said, "Look, Mervy, it's too tough. Just produce it." So I did, and I had a lot of fun. We had a lot of wrangling and talking about the film because if you didn't understand the characters, then you were dead; you had no chance with it. George Cukor was on it for about ten days. He made tests for it and everything but didn't want to go ahead. Then Dick Thorpe was on it. And finally the studio was lucky enough to get Victor Fleming. I wish I was as good as he was. Victor was a kid at heart. After our first preview in San Bernardino, all of the Metro high echelon came out and one said to me, "You've got to take 'Over the Rainbow' out of there." I asked him why, and he said, "Because she sings it in a farmyard." I had to fight and get on my knees to keep it in.

What special preparations would do you for a musical?

Well, I was in vaudeville for a good many years and I was with a couple of girl acts and I know a lot about musicals, so I guess it came naturally to me.

What exactly was your function as producer? Did you guide Victor Fleming?

I didn't have to guide Victor Fleming. We'd talk things over every night, the rushes and everything. And he had ideas and I had ideas. It was very peaceful. You don't have to fight to make a good picture.

Most of the filmmakers we've had here tell stories of fighting and screaming.

Not with the top boys. Capra didn't have to fight. George Stevens didn't have to fight. Willy Wyler didn't have to fight. I'd argue, but not fight.

How do you deal with screen tests?

I pick a scene out of the script that I think is important to the picture. You rehearse first and then you set the camera down. If you set the camera down first you're dead because you can't move people around the way you want to, so I set the camera down last. To make a successful test, you must have a successful actor in front of you.

Have there been occasions when you have tested an actor you thought would be right for a role and the test turned out otherwise?

Karl Malden and Rosalind Russell work out a dance routine
with Mervyn LeRoy on the set of *Gypsy* (1962). LeRoy started out
in vaudeville in San Francisco.

I made Clark Gable's first test and they said his ears were too big and I wouldn't take him for *Little Caesar.* That's a true story.

What kind of shooting schedules did you have when working at the studio in the early years? Did it take a year to make a film, like it does today?

A year? I made five pictures in a year. But I never worried about the schedule, and I still don't. I do it as fast and as good as I can. I get the script tight enough, then shoot it in the allotted time—unless I'm on location and there is rain for four or five days. But if you know your business, nothing seems to hold you up. That's because you always have a great backfield: a great art director, a great photographer, great everything.

How much time in preproduction would you usually average on a film?

On *Quo Vadis* I took about six or eight months, but on a picture like *The Bad Seed* it may have taken about six weeks after finishing the script. I like to work with the entire staff—the actors and cameraman and art director. I like to bring them in after we have the script finished and I'm satisfied with it, and the producer—if there is a producer—or the head of the studio is satisfied.

Producer David O. Selznick and LeRoy examine a model of Rome of two thousand years ago during the preparation of *Quo Vadis* (1951) which LeRoy directed, with Robert Taylor and Deborah Kerr and ten thousand extras.

Do you prefer producing or directing?

I prefer producing *and* directing because then you're the boss on both sides. But if you have a big movie—like *Quo Vadis*—you can't do it all alone. You have to have a producer no matter how clever you are. There are no rules to making a picture. Everybody thinks that the picture business is a big mystery, but there's really no mystery to it. Do it as you feel it. Don't listen to anybody else when you're on the set. When you're on the set you have to be the boss—you're responsible for it, you're the one that says, "Print it."

There are some spectacular scenes in Quo Vadis. *What was it like handling such huge crowds?*

I used six thousand people for five weeks every day and had eight cameras. For the huge arena scenes I had a gun which I shot off three times. I shot the first bullet; everyone was ready. I shot the second; the cameras turned over and they all yelled "Ready!" I shot the third; the screen opened and the lions all rushed out. They looked up at the sun and went right back in. So I got all the lion tamers, who were dressed as Christians, and asked them what to do. They said, "Starve the lions for two weeks." So I jumped to other scenes and for two weeks all night long you'd hear these lions growling for something to eat. After two weeks we were ready to shoot. The lions rushed out into the sun, looked up and went back in again. I could never get the shot the way I wanted it. I had to break it up into different shots.

Could you tell us about the making of Mister Roberts?

I always wanted to make *Mister Roberts.* Jack Ford started on it and shot about ten days and then he took sick. Jack Warner and Leland Hayward called me up one Saturday about midnight and said, "Mervyn, you have to take over *Mister Roberts* on Monday." I knew the play very well, so I said, "All right. I'll take it over on Monday. Let me see all the rushes Sunday and let me read the script." I didn't sleep for about forty-eight hours and then I jumped in. In looking at the rushes, I didn't like the way Bill Powell was because they played him as a drunk, and I changed him back to the way it was in the play. I'm sure that Jack Ford, whom I love very much, would have made it maybe better than I did, but I made it the best

I could. I stuck to the play as much as possible, except for the soapsuds scene we put in and a few things that were added while we were shooting it. But it was a great play.

Could you discuss some of the strengths and weaknesses of using a play as the basis for a film?

Well, I've done a lot of great plays. I've done *Five Star Final,* I did *Mister Roberts.* I did *Gypsy,* which was a great play, and *Mary, Mary,* which was a great play and a lousy picture. It was cast wrong and that was my fault. You have to open it up a little bit if you can. *Mary, Mary* was almost in one room. *The Bad Seed* was in one room on the stage and I opened that up. But there's no rule to how you should do it.

Why were you disappointed with Mary, Mary?

I wanted to put Barbara Bel Geddes in it, and the studio talked me into Debbie Reynolds, who's a fine performer. But Barbara Bel Geddes would have been much better because she played it for so long on Broadway. She knew the values. I often used all-stage casts in my pictures.

Did you ever decide you wanted to work with an actor and then find a project for them?

The property always came first. I've had actors say they wanted to work with me and I try to find a property that fits them. I do that, sure. But I never worry about the actors until I have the script. If I have a great script I can get any actor if he has brains, or his agent has any brains. If you have a bad script you can't get anybody.

Were you ever handed things that you really didn't want to do?

Yes, and I didn't do them.

Even early in your career?

Even my first picture. I turned down three scripts before I did my first picture. Then I found a little story called *No Place to Go* and I made it with Lloyd Hughes and Mary Astor. That was my first picture.

What do you think of critics?

I don't worry about them. I worry about the audience. There was a laugh at the end of *Quo Vadis*. It almost killed me, after about three hours and twenty minutes, to have somebody come out with a laugh at the wrong time. So we changed it. The audience was right.

You hear a lot of talk today from young filmmakers about the auteur theory and the idea of film as art. When you were making your big films, did you ever sit around and talk about the art that you were making?

I never made anything for art. Nothing. I thought of entertainment. I made a lot of pictures that I thought were artistic, but I never think solely of art. Instead I think of what the audience will enjoy seeing. I love beautiful art in painting, but I don't want too much art on the screen. Ask yourself, what artistic picture have you seen that you would really call art, that had great entertainment to it? I think the business today is full of some great young geniuses, but they have to do it their way. Bill Friedkin is an absolute genius; I think Norman Jewison came up the last few years. But it's tough to make pictures the way I was lucky enough to when I got started, because money is tighter today. You haven't got the men in the studios today that have the vision, like the Selznicks and the Thalbergs and the Goldwyns and the Disneys, men who worried only about making good pictures. They weren't worried about the stock going up.

What do you think is missing?

Creators.

On the directing level or the producing level?

On the writing level and the producing level. In fact, I think on every level. It doesn't seem like a family the way it used to be in the studios. Everybody wanted to help everybody. Now everything seems to be more of a secret. But I feel there should be no secrets. Everybody should want to see a fine picture made because then you have a great business. But there is a lot of jealousy in Hollywood, something we never used to have.

You said that you were always looking at films as entertainment, but it seems that a film like I Am a Fugitive from a Chain Gang *has a very strong social theme to it.*

It sure does, but it was still a very entertaining film. When I say entertainment I don't mean comedy—maybe I should say values. I didn't start out to do it as a message film. I do wish I could find some more stories like that. I'd keep on doing them, believe me.

In that particular film were you consciously trying to say something, to reform something, or to change something?

Well, I would like to have had them take the chains off, which they did, in Georgia, after the picture was shown. They took the chains off the men's ankles and arms, for which I was tickled to death. They had told us not to show it in Georgia, but we straightened that out.

You filmed it in Georgia?

No, I should say not. They would have thrown me in the chain gang.

Was the story based on a real incident?

Absolutely. We had the man who wrote the book—who was really was that character—hidden in the studio for weeks. I talked to him day and night.

Are there any particular problems in bringing a real story to the screen?

If it rings true, I love it. If there's no plausibility to it, then I wouldn't be interested. That's the only way I can say it.

At what point in the script did you have the ending of the film?

You mean the "How do you live?" and "I steal" lines? Well, that was an accident. I was shooting downtown by Chinatown in an alley. And while I was rehearsing—and just as she yelled, "Jim, how do you live?" and he yelled, "I steal!"—the lights went off, really went out. So I said, "Let's shoot it both ways: once when the lights are up, and once let the lights go out." Well, naturally, we let him go off in the dark. But that was a lucky accident. It didn't take any genius to do that—it took an electrician to push the wrong button.

Did you receive any flak from the studio at that time about an ending that black? I mean black in values?

No, you couldn't help that. They had to like it because it was fresh and new.

Some producers urge young filmmakers to know about how much scenes cost because sometimes the producing unit will come to you and say, "You've got to cut ten thousand dollars off the picture."

There's only one thing that the young men have to realize—you don't photograph the money, you photograph the story. There's a lot of geniuses around in our business today who think you photograph the money. Don't worry about camera angles, don't shoot up somebody's nose or through their ears or under their arms because it doesn't mean a thing. I never heard anybody walk out of the theater and say, "Wasn't that a great camera angle?" Never.

How different is it making films today compared to when you worked at the studios?

Well, twenty or thirty years ago you never thought of going anywhere to get money for a picture. The studios and the bank backed the pictures. There was no television then, and the studios had a lot of money to make the pictures—Paramount, Goldwyn, the old Metro studios, the old Lasky studios—they all had the money to make them. What's wrong now with the studios is that you take them a script that you feel is great, and they have twenty people read it to see whether they like it or not. You give a script to twenty people and you might as well forget it. You can't please twenty people; you can't even please five of them. That didn't happen in the old days. You only had Irving Thalberg or Mr. Mayer or Mr. Warner or Mr. Selznick or Mr. Goldwyn. Times change. If I brought in *The Wizard of Oz* today, or *Random Harvest* or *Waterloo Bridge* or *Anthony Adverse*, they would think I was crazy. They'd say, "How could you make a picture like that?" I know they wouldn't like *Madame Curie*, because they don't have the heart for it like they used to.

If someone came to you and wanted to make a film based on the life and times of Mervyn LeRoy, and asked you what the title ought to be, what would you say?

I'd say I'd really rather not do it at all.

———◆———

Films as Director

1927 *No Place to Go*	1935 *Oil for the Lamps of China*
1928 *Flying Romeos*	*Page Miss Glory*
Harold Teen	*I Found Stella Parish*
Oh, Kay	1936 *Anthony Adverse*
1929 *Naughty Baby*	*Three Men on a Horse*
Hot Stuff	1937 *The King and the Chorus Girl*
Broadway Babies	*They Won't Forget*
Little Johnny Jones	1938 *Fools for Scandal*
1930 *Playing Around*	1940 *Waterloo Bridge*
Showgirl in Hollywood	*Escape*
Numbered Men	1941 *Blossoms in the Dust*
Top Speed	*Unholy Partners*
1931 *Little Caesar*	1942 *Johnny Eager*
Gentleman's Fate	*Random Harvest* (also
Too Young to Marry	producer)
Five Star Final	1944 *Madame Curie*
Tonight or Never	1945 *Thirty Seconds Over Tokyo* (also
Broadminded	producer)
Local Boy Makes Good	1946 *Without Reservations*
1932 *High Pressure*	1947 *Desire Me* (codirector)
Heart of New York	1948 *Homecoming* (also producer)
Big City Blues	1949 *Little Women* (also producer)
Three on a Match	*Any Number Can Play* (also
I Am a Fugitive from a Chain	producer)
Gang	1950 *East Side, West Side* (also
1933 *Hard to Handle*	producer)
Elmer the Great	1951 *Quo Vadis*
Gold Diggers of 1933	1952 *Lovely to Look At*
Tugboat Annie	*Million Dollar Mermaid*
The World Changes	1953 *Latin Lovers*
1934 *Hi Nellie!*	1954 *Rose Marie* (also producer)
Happiness Ahead	1955 *Strange Lady in Town* (also
Heat Lightning	producer)
Sweet Adeline	*Mister Roberts* (co-director)

1956 *The Bad Seed* (also producer)
      Toward the Unknown (also
          producer)
1958 *No Time for Sergeants* (also
          producer)
      Home Before Dark (also
          producer)
1959 *The FBI Story* (also producer)
1960 *Wake Me When It's Over* (also
          producer)

1961 *The Devil at Four O'Clock* (also
          producer)
1962 *A Majority of One* (also
          producer)
      Gypsy (also producer)
1963 *Mary, Mary* (also producer)
1966 *Moment to Moment* (also
          producer)

Art and cinema must do something about improving this one little globe that we have, and I wish we would all bear this in mind in our work. This is the great purpose of films: to make life more decent, man more dignified and this earth, the only one we have, more beautiful.

ROUBEN MAMOULIAN
(Born in Tiflis, Georgia, Russia, 1898—Died 1987)

Rouben Mamoulian was a man of the Old World—civilized and articulate, with a European artistic sensibility. He studied at the Moscow Art Theater and worked with Stanislavsky before touring with the Russian Repertory Theater and working in London. In 1923 he made his way to the United States, where he started out directing opera and operettas.

Mamoulian is a prime example of the cultural enrichment that European immigrants brought to the American melting pot in the early twentieth century. Only in this country could a native of Tiflis make his mark directing so distinctively American a play as *Porgy* on Broadway in 1925, and then a decade later stage George Gershwin's landmark opera-musical, *Porgy and Bess.*

Mamoulian's film career began with the advent of sound. He was hired as a director because of his experience working with actors in the theater. His successes in the early thirties included *Applause, City Streets, Dr. Jekyll and Mr. Hyde,* starring Fredric March, and the Rodgers and Hart musical *Love Me Tonight.* He guided two great European actresses to success on the screen—Marlene Dietrich in *The Song of Songs* and Greta Garbo in *Queen Christina*—and directed the first Technicolor film, *Becky Sharp,* in 1935. He was still at the top of his game more than twenty years later when he made *Silk Stockings* at MGM with Fred Astaire and Cyd Charisse.

Mamoulian prided himself on original thinking and searching out innovative techniques in the early days of sound. Even though he had trained in the Russian realist school, he was a student of the arts and evolved into a creator noted for poetic stylization and original uses of color.

Mamoulian lived just a few blocks from the campus at Greystone, and he

Miriam Hopkins (right) played the title role in the first Technicolor feature,
Becky Sharp (1935), which Rouben Mamoulian (seated under camera)
directed. Cinematographer Ray Rennahan, sitting behind Mamoulian,
photographed *Becky Sharp*.

came frequently to AFI. He visited for the first time in 1971, nearly a decade
after his last completed film, having been removed by Sam Goldwyn from
Porgy and Bess in 1959 and from the ill-fated *Cleopatra,* which starred Elizabeth Taylor and Richard Burton, in 1963. Yet he came with undiminished
vitality and a youthful mien. His erudition, his reservoir of experience and
his ready grasp of the full spectrum of artistic endeavor fascinated the aspiring filmmakers who were fifty years his junior.

ROUBEN MAMOULIAN

———

July 8, 1971*

Before we go into the detailed things, I think it would be interesting that we establish a basis for discussion, a bridge where we can meet, either as friends or as enemies. Either one is very good; a mixture is even better. First, I have very bad news for you: I am over thirty. In looking through the roster I noticed that you're not doing as well, that there are just three of you who are over thirty. Let me say this—there's a new cult in our country, which is the cult of youth, physical youth. One treats physical youth now as if it was the most glorious achievement anybody could come to. But remember—we all had it. It isn't as if you have exclusive rights to it. The important thing is spiritual youth. I've talked to a bunch of young people, and a lot of them were, frankly, older than I am right now, spiritually older. Youth after thirty is an achievement. By youth I mean preserving the alertness, the curiosity, the idealism and above all— strange as it may sound—the innocence of youth. That kind of a youth I'm all for, and I think it deserves respect and great consideration.

Now, a couple of words about the so-called Establishment. An artist, or anyone who claims to be creative, is always up against the Establishment. You all know that. I think the world we live in has been completely messed up by the adults, not by the young. Of course there can be no blanket generalization, but I think the hypocrisy, the following of slogans instead of principles, the constant lying that takes place in every medium of advertising and television, is absolutely sickening, and I rebel against

*This transcript contains segments from seminars Rouben Mamoulian gave at the American Film Institute on April 30, 1970 and December 8, 1976.

that just as vehemently as any youth would. But the worst thing about a certain layer of adults, to my mind, is their absolute cowardice. I think they have buckled under the onslaught of the young. I've seen old men, physically old men and spiritually old men, trying to be young by doing rock and roll, contorting themselves on the dance floor until they had to go to the hospital to die. That's their idea of keeping young. Unfortunately I think that young people seem just as able to get ossified into conformity as the older generation.

There are certain clichés that I would like to agree with you on semantically, one of them being "art." You know, man must define everything. If we can't define it we can't progress. If the definition is wrong we change it, but we always have to concretize or articulate whatever principle we believe in. For instance, as a rule, the motion picture industry always contrasts art and entertainment. You'll see an old, wise executive or producer saying, "This script is great box office, commercial stuff" or "This is no good. It's artistic. It won't get anywhere." And of course they're invariably wrong. If they knew what was box office they'd be making nothing but hits, which they're not doing. They're all losing money. So anybody who says, "This is commercial" and "This is not commercial" is an utter fool, because no one can prophesy this. There's only one way to go about it. You're no different from an audience, and if you like it, there's no reason a lot of other human beings aren't going to like it.

But the main thing is that you are in films and theater, the most social of the arts. The artist cannot stand alone; the audience is part of it. In other words, you write a play and you say, "This is a great play," and you put it on, and nobody comes to see it. They don't like it. Well, somehow I suspect it isn't a great play. There are rare exceptions. A great play or a good play or a great film must find an audience, and if it doesn't there's something wrong with it.

Now, you can have at one end something excessively intellectual and esoteric that some exclusive group of people might enjoy, but the great masses of audiences will not. Usually it's on the intellectual side, because the difference between human beings is not in their emotions, because emotions are all the same. We have the same feelings of hunger, sex, envy, love and so on. It's the intellectual difference that counts. Some people are ready to accept certain ideas; others not. On the other end of the spectrum you may have very cheap commercial trash that can be successful, but I think those are the periphery of the film and theatrical art. The great middle section should and does consist of a play or film that is both art and entertainment. Primarily, all good art is entertainment. However, the vice versa doesn't work—not all entertainment is good art.

One more thing about this business of self-expression. It has become a very fashionable cliché. People have said, "I'm doing this because it's me." And with that goes the freedom of self-expression. Well, total freedom is an impossibility in any locality where there is more than just one person. Possibly Robinson Crusoe started out by being free because he was alone. But the minute he got his good man Friday, his freedom became some-what limited. The more people there are, the more freedom has to be lim-ited in order to allow other people to have some kind of freedom. And of course there is no such thing as freedom in art. In art, you find that all great artists have built-in self-censorship, self-discipline and self-control, because art is subject to the tremendous control of a critical mind—which is the heart of the creator.

Therefore, to say, "Well, I just feel like doing this . . ." may be a kind of self-expression, but it belongs to the clinical department. It belongs to a man who goes out and shoots a little film and then sits there with three other people and enjoys it. Again I stress the point—the audience is a vital part of it. Now, does that mean sacrifice for the sake of an audience? No, it doesn't. I think when we are doing a film or a play—which means assuming a tremendous responsibility of influencing, consciously or unconsciously, a lot of people—you have to exercise great discretion and selectivity between what inside you is more suitable for the psychoana-lyst's couch and what in you will appeal universally to another human being. To use the stage or the screen for total self-indulgence or to use it as a psychoanalyst's couch has nothing to do with freedom.

One final thing I want to say—I'm not going to use the patented "It seems to me." I'm sick of hearing in every dialogue, "It seems to me." Hamlet says, "I know not seems. It is." If you have a conviction, if you utterly believe in something, why should you say, "It seems to me"? I'm going to be blunt, and I invite you to be blunt. We're meeting on equal ground. You can alert your suspicions, your skepticisms, and then you can attack and criticize. Let's not mince words. Moviemaking is a very serious business.

At the birth of talkies many theatrical directors came in and started photograph-ing stage plays. Then all of a sudden you arrived and started to open up the medium. What were the tools you used?

I was lucky to have done a series of very successful shows on Broadway, so Paramount came to me—sound had just come in—and wanted me to make some films. They wanted me to sign a seven-year contract and help a silent screen director by directing the dialogue for him for a couple of years. Then, if the studio felt that I had learned the business, they would let me direct a film. And they would have me for seven years. I said, "Why would I want to go into films to direct dialogue? I can do it on the stage and have the whole play."

What attracts me to films is not the dialogue. It's the imagery, the magic of the camera. The dialogue should be subservient to that. My interest in the camera was always in the marvelous things you can do with it—with the angles, the dollying, the dissolves, the props, and with the framing. And I've always believed in stylization and poetry. Even on the stage things are stylized—every movement, every grouping. If you preserve the psychological truth of the emotions and thoughts of the actors—and combine that with physical expression that is utterly stylized and that couldn't happen in real life, the impact upon the audience is one of greater reality. Perhaps that's why they call it surrealism. This becomes more real to the audience than if you had done it in a realistic manner. Done correctly, stylization carries greater reality in its impact on the audience than everyday kitchen naturalism ever can achieve.

Art has to have its roots in the ground, but the tree should be up in the sky. If you are a filmmaker, you have to connect with life but also have your feet on the ground. If you keep that balance, then the audience always accepts it. Stylization is really an extension of feeling and thought, a sharper way of showing that thought. Let me ask you all a question. You probably know *The Thinker,* the great statue of Auguste Rodin. Will you show me how he sits? Let's see. Without exception all of you are wrong. It never fails. His man is sitting, believe it or not, with one elbow on the opposite knee. It's not natural or comfortable, but aesthetically and artistically it has a focus. It has design and rhythm and power. So, what is unnatural becomes true, and you can apply this idea to any kind of a scene. You can put everything upside down or reverse it, provided what it does is sharpen. In your desire to express love or hate or doubt, whatever it is, you ask yourself, "How can I express this more acutely?" Then you'll wind up with a gesture that is not natural, but perfect as an expression of that thought.

You see, I was in a lucky position. I didn't need films; I was going strong on Broadway. So I laughed at the whole thing and said, "Look, I'll tell you exactly what I would like to do. You either say yes or you say no, but there's not going to be any discussion about it. I'd like to do only one film. No seven years. No options." They said, "Well, right there you're dead." I said, "Well, I don't think I'm dead. I'm quite alive." They said, "You're dead for films because we never sign a contract without options." It's one of my few original achievements that I have never signed an option in my life. I've always refused it, and if you refuse it and don't wince an eye, they'll agree. So I said, "No options. There's only one way we can do it. Let me go into the studio in Astoria. Allow me to be on a set and watch the shooting, the projection of the rushes, the cutting and so on. And when I come to you and tell you I am ready to direct, that's when I do a film." I guess they wanted me enough to finally say, "Well, we're dealing with a crazy man, but let's do it." So we signed this contract, and I went to the Astoria Studio.

What I learned there was the way the Latin language puts it: *ad adversus.* In other words, I really learned what I didn't want to do. When I saw a scene done, I said, "That's the last thing I would want to do. It's wrong. I would do it completely differently." Learning the mechanics was one thing, but everything I saw I felt should be done another way. There is no great mystery to the mechanics of motion picture making. I think you can familiarize yourself with all of it in five weeks. I was asking George Folsey, the great cameraman, about lenses, and I asked silly questions in the cutting room. After five weeks I felt that I knew enough about it, so I went to Mr. Jesse Lasky and Mr. Adolph Zukor and said, "I'm ready to direct a film." They laughed at me. "Come on. You have only been here five weeks." I said, "That's enough. Whatever has to do with the mechanics and technology of filmmaking anybody can easily learn in four or five weeks. The point is to initiate the correct use of the tools that you have. Look at the contract. What does it say? When I tell you I'm ready, I'm ready." So there was nothing they could do. They said, "What would you like to do?" I said, "What have you got?" They had some books there and I read this book called *Applause,* by Beth Brown, that I thought was interesting.

In Applause *you used several nonprofessional actors. Did you have that in mind from the start?*

Well, I believe if you are in films that affect a million people, you have to put the truth on the screen—the whole truth, not a fraction of the truth. You hear a lot of things about some of the films being made today, and they say, "This is life." Well, that isn't true; it's a fragment of life. It's part of a truth. It's no wonder that in a courtroom you have to swear to say the whole truth, not part of it. I think partial truth is even more dangerous than an outright lie. The truth in *Applause* that interested me was, first of all, New York as a city. I was fascinated by New York, and I wanted to show it in all its beauty and its ugliness. I wanted to show the burlesque in all its tawdriness and vulgarity. At the same time I wanted to show that even in a garbage dump a beautiful flower can grow, because I believe that nothing is all black or all evil. Therefore I wanted two young, innocent people who should be poisoned by it but yet are not. They win at the end. The reason I had a happy ending with the youngsters was that I believe that the young don't have to succumb to the environment. They can transcend it, and that's what interested me.

For the two young people, I couldn't find actors who I thought would give me the innocence I wanted. There's nothing worse on the screen than a fellow who pretends to be more naïve than he really is. He says something that sounds naïve, but his eyes are wise. I wanted two innocent, young, naïve people, and I got these two out of scores that I auditioned. On the stage you couldn't possibly do this, because in order to keep the curtain up—as we say in our theatrical vernacular—a person must have some experience and background. You can't act for two and half hours just by walking off the street and onto the stage, but you can take somebody off the street and put him in a short scene on film and he can be great. You hypnotize him or browbeat him or convince him or trick him, but he winds up by doing it once excellently.

You know that when there was a festival of my films in New York a few years ago, I received a letter from the Association of Underground Directors that read, "Dear Mr. Mamoulian: Whether you like it or not, we consider you the first underground director on the basis of *Applause*." They asked if I would spend an evening with them and see some of their work, which I subsequently did.

You mention stylization. Do you think that a particular director's style is something conscious?

Style is really your point of view on the world and life—how you see and feel it—so it's not conscious. The worst thing you can do is consciously evolve a style, a method of shooting. You don't want to suddenly become rigid. A scene tells you how it should be shot—you can't have just one way of shooting it. Some people confuse style with mannerism. They say, "Well, let's shoot it all this way and it will give the picture a style." But it doesn't give a style; it gives it a mannerism, and there's nothing more dull and irritating than mannerism.

Symbolic imagery, unrelated and presumably irrelevant sounds, can be a tremendous weapon for dramatic intensification of a scene. I don't know whether you noticed it, but in *Applause,* while Helen Morgan is sitting in the hotel corridor, there are two happy young people saying irrelevant things to each other. And they laugh. Did you notice that? They have no relationship to the scene at all, so you ask, "Why have it then?" Because that happiness of somebody else makes her misery ten times worse. I also wanted the traffic noises to gradually build up so at the end I could bring in a siren—a fire truck or ambulance—going by. There is no more desperate, agonizing sound than the sound of a siren.

How do you begin a film?

Without exception, every film I've made started with a blank page. Now, if it's an adaptation of a play, obviously you have the play as a basis. If it's a novel, you have a novel as a basis. If it's a historical period piece, then you have history as a basis and you have all kinds of research. But, as you know, all the equations in the film world are absolutely personal. There really are no rules. So I start with a blank page and a writer or two. My personal way of working is very simple. I sit and read the script, the basic material, until unconsciously a film is formed, visualized, in my mind. For both stage and screen material, I keep reading the script all the time until I can visualize it. You read it about a hundred times, and each time you see it acted on the screen, you see it cut. The next time, it changes; it gets better, until finally you have the finished script. It's like building a house. You know it needs a solid foundation. It's good to begin at the end. How are you going to get to Washington unless you know that you are going to Washington? You have to know where you are going and then choose the most interesting way of getting there.

A good play sometimes is not going to make a good film. There's a reason why it's a good play—a good play is a succession of words. It's dialogue. It's usually one set, two sets. If you are going to distort it or widen it to fit the film medium, you're going to lose certain advantages and

Mamoulian speaking to AFI fellows, December 1976.

virtues the play had on the stage. If you bring in something that belongs exclusively to the screen that makes up for that loss, then you can make a fine film. I think usually the best films are made from originals or from just the idea of a novel. Then you can start out by structuring the whole edifice of your script in graphic terms. I believe that the main force of the cinema is in imagery, not in words—your main medium of communication, of excitement, is the pictorial one. Therefore you must build your screenplay on a succession of pictorial dynamics rather than words. On the stage you can have a scene that lasts for thirty minutes and it may be the best scene in the play, but on the screen it would bore you to death. On the screen you should achieve the same thing in six minutes. So right there you see how the architecture of the words has to fit the screen. When you cannot do it visually, then you put words in. But the fewer words, the better.

It reminds me of an amusing Ernst Lubitsch story. He was doing a film, and he had a writer, and he explained that the beginning of the film had to show that this man had been married a long time and that he is kind of tired of it. He had gotten used to his wife, and he had got a roving eye. So the writer brought him four pages of introductory exposition of the character. Lubitsch looked at it and said, "You don't need all that." He took all four pages out. "Just put down this—the man walks into the elevator with his wife, and he keeps his hat on. On the seventh floor a pretty blond walks in, and the man takes his hat off."

Did you ever experience any problems working at the studios?

Applause received the most unprecedented critical raves in New York. In fact, they were so good they did me a lot of harm in Hollywood because the studios said, "This young newcomer from the stage who's never done a film has done something which Hollywood will look at and learn from." So they hated me, and I don't blame them.

There is a scene in *Applause* when the young daughter is put to bed by Helen Morgan. She can't sleep, and Helen sings that burlesque song in the manner of a lullaby. I also wanted Joan Peters to take her rosary from under her pillow and whisper her prayers. In those days there was only one microphone, hanging in the middle. You had to rehearse all the time to get the right balance, and we could hear the song but not the prayer. I said, "Let's get another microphone and put it under the pillow for the girl. Record it on two channels." "We've never done that before," they said. "It's impossible." I had resistance on every front. "I don't think it's impossible," I said. "In theory there is no reason it shouldn't work. All dramatic events are foreshadowed by theory. The laws of Einstein were all first theories and crazy dreams."

The sound man said, "I have great respect for Mr. Mamoulian. He's done things on the stage, but I've been in this business a long time and I know what can be done and what can't be done. I'm only trying to save the studio a whole day's money." But I guess the producers had no way out and said, "Well, Mr. Mamoulian is directing this film. Do what he says." We finally shot it, and I went home and was miserable. I thought this was the end of me and films. The next day I drove to the studio, and someone says to me, "I must tell you something before you go on the set. Do you know that you were going to be fired this morning?" "Well, it wouldn't surprise me," I said. "The big bosses gave an order to have the laboratory work on that scene all night"—usually you get the rushes by the evening of the next day—"and to have them in the projection room at eight o'clock this morning. If it hadn't worked out, that was it for you, but it seems they're crazy about it. The order is given to everybody in the studio—give Mamoulian anything he wants."

We are talking about films as an art, aren't we? We aren't discussing the industry or the box office or what makes money or what doesn't make money. Art is individual. A committee cannot paint the ceiling of the Sistine Chapel; it takes one man. A committee cannot make a sculpture or write a novel. The author works with his pen on a piece of paper, all alone;

there's no one to interfere with him. The painter has his canvas and himself. His instruments are mechanical. But the director's instruments are the actors. They are living human beings with their own character, their own ideas, their own aims. And then you have a cameraman who is an artist and a craftsman in his own right. You have the set designer. You have the sound recorder. They're all individuals, and of course the more masterly they are, the more they're inclined to have a point of view. If you start directing a film and allow six points of view, you might as well give up and do something else. You have to fuse the human elements working on the film into a unity. The best way of doing it is to sell them on your idea.

How did you come by the property City Streets, *the Dashiell Hammett story?*

Well, that was the era of gangster films. There was a lot of machine-gunning, throwing bodies out of cars, murders right and left, and there is something perverse in my nature, I suppose. I like to swim against the current, and that's why I thought I would like to make a gangster film, but stylize it a little. I also thought I'd like to make a gangster film with seven murders in it, none of which are shown, except vicariously. Of course, the opinion was that the picture would be a flop because people want to see those things. One time, in Chicago, I was taken to a nightclub and a little fellow came over and sat down and said, "Oh, Mr. Mamoulian, my brother is crazy about *City Streets*. My brother thinks it's the only gangster picture worth looking at. My brother thinks it's got class. It is absolutely great! My brother saw it eight times." I didn't know who the fellow was. When he left, I said, "Who is that guy?" and they said, "He is the brother of Al Capone." Apparently Capone thought the film had class because I never showed the murders. It was all clean. But anyway, that was praise from Caesar. So I wanted to make a gangster film and Dashiell Hammett came up with this five-page synopsis, and then with Oliver Garrett we developed it into a script, which turned out to be *City Streets*.

City Streets *seems to appeal to an unsophisticated mass audience, while* Love Me Tonight *appeals to a sophisticated audience. What sort of public reaction did they receive?*

There's kind of a natural perversity in human nature. While we are unsophisticated and naïve, we want sophistry. We don't like things that are naïve. Once we become very sophisticated, then we can love and enjoy a fairy tale. Of course, these are two completely different films. *Love Me Tonight* is a fairy tale. It's a poem. The whole film is rhythmic. In a great many scenes the dialogue rhymes, and it all comes over naturally. I used all sorts of techniques that are totally unrealistic, and no member of an audience ever raised an objection. *City Streets* was both an artistic and a box-office success. It cost $330,000 and it grossed over $3 million, and it had great reviews. *Love Me Tonight,* curiously enough, went as a musical film in this country. In Germany it played as the *Castle in the Moon,* and it got tremendous reviews. Then, as the years went by, *Love Me Tonight* became a classic musical film. Some things take time. Unfortunately, in films you have to be contemporary to be received by an audience totally. With a book, it can be on a shelf and then ten years later it starts selling. Films exist on the basis of audiences, and rightly so. If you get ahead too much, you lose them. I learned that on *Applause* but not enough to modify *Love Me Tonight.* Anyway, I am quite pleased with it now, and was then.

I read that you like Westerns. Have you ever thought about making one yourself?

I'm crazy about Westerns. When I came to this country, I ended up loving the Western lore. I think that the Western is one of the two or three greatest contributions of America to the world of art. One is music, the other is film, starting with the great D. W. Griffith. The Western is a deathless epic, it's American folklore, it's the great American myth. As a myth it is as important as the *Odyssey* or the *Iliad* or *Robin Hood,* and maybe even more important than that. It is loved in every country of the world. It is the eternal problem which is always with us, that of good versus evil. It is also the problem of one man against many. Only in the Western do you know that the hero is going to conquer. One man on his two feet—or rather on the four feet of his horse—who always won, no matter how many hundreds resisted him. This myth can never die, because of the way our civilization is going. One vote among 215 million people. The Western keeps showing that one man who dedicates himself to something can do miracles. It does happen. The kind of Western I'd like to do would be a poetical Western which would really symbolize the myth. It will not be a modern Western with psychoanalysis or why the villain is a villain. It would be the classical American myth of one man against the world, serving good.

How much say do you give actors and actresses about their characters?

Before I answer you specifically, let me submit the general premise that in films there is no official hierarchy. It's not like in the army or General Motors, nor is it a factory with a foreman at the head of it. It all depends on professional equations. If the producer is very famous and has great prestige, he can overrule the director. If the star has great prestige and the director hasn't, the star will overrule all of them. So when you ask how much say do they have in my films, they have all the say they like, because I like to listen not only to the actors but even to the stagehands. Sometimes an electrician will notice something that all of us miss. They have their say completely, but that doesn't mean that say goes. It is the director's say that goes. If you order a soldier to do something, he has to do it. He hates it, but he does it. You can't do that with actors. That would be silly, so here again we come back to what I first said about exciting the actor, making the challenge a pleasure to him to achieve, and therefore, if he has one opinion and you have another, it is your job as a director to convince him that yours is better than his or hers. Usually this never fails, because actors—most of them—know what's good for them. Once you improve the performance, they get the credit, so they become completely malleable and very enthusiastic, and the stronger the challenge, the better performance you get.

I hear it so frequently, when someone says, "I go on the set and improvise." That's ridiculous. Improvisation is for the birds and for the amateurs. You don't improvise a statue or a painting, and if you do, it isn't much good. Michelangelo put it best when he said that he did not conceive of anything. He would look at a block of marble for long enough until he saw the shape. From then on, he said, "I just take everything superfluous off and disclose what's in that stone." That to me is a marvelous recipe. You see the whole design, a shape. I'm talking about what to me would be the full flowering of a screen work.

The next thing is integration. Let's take a symphony orchestra, where the conductor is there for only one reason—to integrate the hundred men playing, to have each do his part without overdoing it or underdoing it, to tell them also how to do the different sections. If the orchestra is not integrated, you have a cacophony. On the stage, you integrate a group of actors. You only have one movement on the stage, that of the actors. But this is not the case on the screen, where you have three movements—the movement of actors, the movement of the camera, the movement in cutting. These three must be integrated into one harmonious whole so that none of them stick out. Then you get a perfect work with every emotional impact increased a hundredfold, because, as you know, rhythm is the greatest force in nature. Through constant experience I have found that whenever you have a rhythmically directed play or film, its impact on the audience is much stronger than if it's a wobbly and loosely related assemblage.

You seem to have experimented a great deal throughout your career. Were you conscious of this as you were doing it?

Experimentation is a very stupid occupation, unless it has a purpose. You say, "Let's experiment. Ditch this and break free, and we'll see what happens." That's silly. You experiment when you say, "The conventional way isn't strong enough, isn't beautiful enough, isn't elegant enough. How can I do it better? What if I do this? Ah, let's experiment."

The key scene in *Dr. Jekyll and Mr. Hyde*—the one to which everything in the story is geared—is when a young, handsome man is transformed into Hyde. I didn't want to make this just a horror picture. I wanted to make it subjective, I wanted to let the audience feel, at least to the degree possible, the agonizing and fantastic experience. I said, "When I do the first transformation, I'll have the camera be Jekyll." Now, I can't do that in the middle of the scene, out of a clear blue sky. It's never been done before and it has to be established. That's why I did the whole first reel with the camera being Jekyll.

I asked, "What kind of sound can we put with this? The whole thing is fantastic. You put a realistic sound and it will get you nowhere at all." So again, you proceed from imagination and theory and if it makes sense, do it. I said, "We're not going to have a single sound in this transformation that you can hear in life." They said, "What are you going to use?" I said, "We'll light the candle and photograph the light—high frequencies, low frequencies, direct from light into sound. Then we'll hit a gong, cut off the impact, run it backward, things like that." So I had this terrific kind of stew, a mélange of sounds that do not exist in nature or in life. It was eerie but it lacked a beat, and that's where I had to introduce rhythm. So I said, "We need a beat." We tried all sorts of drums, but they all sounded like drums. When you run out of all ideas, something always pops into your head. I said, "I've got it." I ran up and down the stairway for two minutes until my heart was really pounding, took the microphone down and said, "Record me." And that's the rhythm of the big transformation. So when I say my heart was in *Jekyll and Hyde,* it's literally true.

I'm curious why in Dr. Jekyll and Mr. Hyde *you chose a psychological interpretation of the classic Stevenson story rather than using the standard elements of horror.*

Actually, *Jekyll and Hyde* is not a horror story, although every book on horror films mentions it. Hyde is not a monster. What interested me about the story is that it's a tragedy of man. Man with a capital *M.* Man who fights against the Establishment. Man who is a rebel. Man who is adventurous and courageous. Man who goes to the moon and climbs Mount Everest. It's a noble part of human nature to achieve these adventurous things with the idea that they will subsequently benefit mankind. So here is a story of a man who does just that, and what he does ends up controlling him.

When I saw the film the other evening, I felt it had a great deal of connection with today's drug culture. A lot of people use drugs to liberate and expand their consciousness. Unfortunately, many of them wind up being slaves to the drugs and finally are killed off. For Jekyll it's a real tragedy because of the weakness in himself and because he thought he was liberated. Actually, what he did was to imprison himself. So this is not a horror picture. The makeup of Freddie March is deliberately the exact replica of the Neanderthal man, our common ancestor, the animalistic primitive that exists in all of us, which some of us control better than others.

I explained to Freddie that Hyde is not evil to start with, that he is primitive like an animal. To an animal there is no evil. A tiger attacks to eat and sheds blood, and we don't call that evil. But just as Jekyll gets gradually corrupted as he carries on this experiment, so does Hyde. With each stage he becomes worse. To me the most attractive person in the story is the first Mr. Hyde, full of exuberance and joy and freedom. He goes out to celebrate and it's pouring rain. An Englishman always has an umbrella to protect himself, so I had him take his hat off, put his face up and love the rain. Then he goes into this music hall. Everything he does is so wholehearted and vibrant; there's no evil there. He is fulfilling his impulse. Gradually he becomes worse, until the final tragedy.

How closely do you work with your editors? Do you let the editor make the first cut?

Fredric March in full makeup for his role as Mr. Hyde in *Dr. Jekyll
and Mr. Hyde* (1932) on the set with the director and Miriam Hopkins.
Mamoulian said, "The makeup was deliberately the exact replica
of the Neanderthal man, our common ancestor."

There are several methods of shooting a picture, and it varies with the
director. Some directors protect the scene from every angle. They take a
close-up through the whole scene, medium shot through the whole scene,
long shot through the whole scene—so you can pick anything you want
to in the cutting room. MGM was especially famous for that. It also
allowed the executives to indulge in making suggestions and recutting
films. Well, I don't work that way. You see, some directors do a lot of
improvising on the set. But I work the script until I see the whole film in
my head, so when I get on the set I know pretty precisely where I want a
close-up, where I want a medium shot. I shoot that and no more, so the
cutting becomes a very simple thing and the monkeying with the cutting
becomes impossible. It's the best way to protect your film.

I was called in by a producer on *Queen Christina* who said, "Where are
your protection shots?" I said, "What do you mean?" He said, "You know
what I mean. We don't make pictures here. We remake them." That was
the system at MGM. I said, "Well, I don't believe in remaking pictures.
I'm a professional. I never had retakes at Paramount. I'm only shooting

what is needed. Now, do you want me to spend more money, doing it so you can have a little fun by experimenting with a close-up here and a long shot there? I can't do it that way."

So it all depends. Some directors rely a great deal on the editor, but actually a director must be an editor, otherwise how can you direct? I mean, the film is made from cuts, from a certain succession of cuts and angles, and I think the most valid and effective way is to cut while you're shooting, at least approximately. I won't say you may not want two more feet of one shot or the other, but I always protect myself with a little at the end.

Becky Sharp *was the first three-strip Technicolor film. Were there technical prob-lems for you as a director?*

Oh, yes. It was utterly experimental in those days. We had a scene in the film with a beige-colored rug and green draperies, red roses and a yellow table. The film came back and the carpet was red, the roses were green, the hangings were yellow. It can happen with the three-color process, though we corrected it afterward. What seems difficult sometimes isn't, but people believe it's difficult, so they don't do it. Now, in the *Becky Sharp* ballroom scene, I wanted very little light because with little light the chrome is intensified. It has a richness that it loses when more light is thrown on it. Everybody said, "Nothing will be on the screen, it's too dark. This is Technicolor, you have to pump light in it." I said, "Well, let's see what happens," and it was the most beautiful thing you ever saw because of underlighting.

How did you come to direct Greta Garbo in Queen Christina?

I'd never met Garbo. I was working at Paramount and had just finished a picture with Marlene Dietrich called *Song of Songs*. MGM called me and said, "We'd like you to direct the next film of Greta Garbo." They sent me the script of *Queen Christina* and I liked the idea. Then I asked, "First, I would like to meet Miss Garbo. Why don't you ask her if she would like to see a first cut of *Song of Songs*?" She liked the picture and wanted me to direct *Queen Christina*. I said, "I would like to very much, but there is something I have to take up with you. I understand that when you are doing an intimate scene with an actor, everybody has to leave the stage, including the director." She said, "Yes. Clarence Brown used to go have a sandwich." I said, "I can't work that way. I am there every second." She thought about it and agreed.

So we worked on the script. I got S. N. Behrman, a very fine playwright from New York, to work on the dialogue. Garbo never had such extensive dialogue in her films. We came on the set and I said, "Now we rehearse." Garbo said to me, "Oh, I don't rehearse. If I rehearse I become stale. If you do more than one take, I become empty inside." So I said, "Miss Garbo, this is incredible. Let's make a deal. I'll do it your way. If that works out it will be marvelous, because I will earn the reputation of being the fastest-shooting director in Hollywood. I'll get through the picture in four weeks instead of eight. But if it doesn't work out you will try to do it my way."

So I rehearsed the two men for an hour and a half. Then she came in and I told her, "You start here, you do this, you go there, you do this." "Fine." So we made a first take. Afterward, I said, "Well, how do you feel about it?" And she said, "Fine! Fine!" As she was about to walk past me, she stopped and said, "Well, how do *you* feel about it?" I said, "No good. It's all wrong. Let's rehearse." She said, "Believe me. I'll get worse." I rehearsed the three of them for over an hour, and with each rehearsal she said, "I'm getting worse. I am completely empty. There is nothing there at all." Then we shot eight more takes, and I said, "Print take eight, and print take one also. Now, Miss Garbo, tomorrow morning, take one, yours, and take eight, the one I like, will be in the projection room. You go in there alone. You see these two takes and then you tell me which I should use in the picture, and I promise to abide by your judgment." She started walking out and leaned close to my ear, whispering, "Please do not print take one." From then on it was wonderful.

They usually ask me if it was easy or difficult to direct Garbo, and the answer is that it was either easy or impossible. If she respected you as an artist, and if you gave her something that was better than what she had in mind, she was the easiest, the most professional person to work with. In the case of *Queen Christina* she was simply marvelous. It was a sheer pleasure. One of the greatest joys that a director can have is getting an actor to give their best performance, or to take an inexperienced young person and make him or her into somebody. You are helping to create an artist. They have to have something and your intuition must recognize that something in the casting, but after that, when you help them to bring out their possibilities, it's one of the greatest joys.

There are actors who are intuitive and actors who reason. Sometimes

Greta Garbo, John Gilbert and the director on the set of *Queen Christina*
(1932). Of Garbo's enigmatic close-up at the end of the film, Mamoulian said,
"I'm going to have every member of the audience write his own ending."

they are a combination of both, but that's rare. The greatest thing is intuition. For instance with Garbo, I would say to her, "This mood is like the
purple sunset, when the leaves turn their shadows, and now and then a
yellow leaf falls down." She would say, "Oh, I know."

Could you talk about the famous close-up at the end of Queen Christina? *Is it
true you told Garbo to "think of nothing"?*

Yes. I shot it purely visually and rhythmically. Garbo came to me and said,
"What do I do?" Indeed, what? What do you play? Do you cry? Do you
have little glycerin tears? Do you smile for no reason, or do you laugh?
What do you do? Therefore, I said to myself—and this works, if you do it
right it always works—"I'm going to have every member of the audience
write his own ending. I'm going to give him a blank piece of paper, as
John Locke said, a tabula rasa. Let them write it themselves: sadness,
inspiration, courage. Whatever they prefer. We prepare the scene, and
they fill it in." So I said to Garbo, "Nothing. You don't act. Do nothing.
You don't have a thought. In fact, try not to blink your eyes. Just wear a
mask." And she did just that, for ninety feet of film.

Some people say, "Ah, the courage of this woman." Others say, "Oh, the sadness that is beyond tears." "Ah, the serenity." Everybody thought she felt the way they wanted her to feel, so everybody's satisfied. But actually what they're looking at is zero. A very beautiful one, but zero.

I like your musical Silk Stockings, *with Fred Astaire and Cyd Charisse, and I'm wondering how your work on it fits into your general ideas about cinema.*

I told the studio that the only thing that would interest me about the film was being able to use the dancing as a major part of the dramatic development instead of dialogue. It would be like playing a love scene through dance. The best scene in *Silk Stockings* is in a dance where the dancing is dramatic, during which they gradually fall in love. It isn't just exhibition dancing. In this case it was really the major part of the love scene, so they started rehearsing and ten days later called me and asked me to come over to see it. I went over with the producer and we sat there while they did this number, and the producer said, "Well, you're the greatest, as always, Fred. You're the king. Cyd, you're terrific," and so on, and it went on for a very long time and everybody was beaming. I just sat there.

Finally they came to the end of those eulogies and Fred Astaire said, "Well, you haven't said anything. What do you think?" And I told him I didn't like it, and of course his face sank and he got very upset about it. The producer kept nudging me with his elbow, "This is Astaire! This is Astaire!" I said, "I know this is Astaire, but it doesn't fit. It has to be dramatic." So I walk out with the producer, and he said, "Well, you've ruined the whole thing. It's going to be a disaster." I said, "Why do you say that?" He said, "Are you going to tell Fred Astaire how to dance?" "No," I said, "I'm not telling him *how,* I'm telling him *what* to dance. That's different." "Well," he said, "You've lost him." I said, "I think you're wrong. He's too much of a talent not to realize that what I told him is what makes this thing interesting." Sure enough, two days later they called us in and it was perfect, and from then on it was an absolute pleasure.

What directors and films have interested you in the past?

Well, first of all, let's accept the unavoidable premise—what makes directors is their uniqueness. I say that directors are valuable when they are different from other directors, not when they are alike. Now, obviously if I like style and poetry on the screen, then the director who likes that is a little closer to me than the director who likes to shoot everything in a documentary style or in ultrarealistic style. I do appreciate the mastery behind it, but my heart is not in it, because to me naturalism, realism, physical realism is a moribund thing. It has a dead end. So you come as close as you can to life and then what? Life stops you. That's the limit. Realism is good for travelogues and documentaries or the newsreels but not for fiction films. Poetry, imagination, style have no limit and I'd much rather fly in those areas. I feel that any subject—it doesn't have to be a fantasy— should be approached from a poetical point of view. This appeals to me more. There are many directors that I admire. I admire Pudovkin, Eisenstein, René Clair, Carol Reed in his earlier films, Fred Zinnemann, William Wyler.

By the time I was seventeen I had subscribed to the slogan *ars gratia artis*—art for art's sake. To hell with morality, with decency, with truth. Well, by the time I got to be twenty I had outgrown this silly notion. And I firmly believe that art, like everything else, is for life's sake. It's not for art's sake. It should serve life; everything should add to the goodness and the beauty on this earth, to the dignity and the size of man so he can walk proud again. Therefore, the only condition I have when considering a project is that it has to have a seed of value and it is relevant to our time. I feel that the great majority of artists in every field are betraying mankind. To me, the hope of the future is in the arts. It's not in politics. It's not in economics. It's not in religion. It's in the arts, because only the arts are truly universal. Through my life I've been invited as a guest to all sorts of countries, and no matter what the political trend of the country is, other artists receive you as a brother. You sit down and you're one family. That doesn't happen with Catholics and Protestants, it doesn't happen with ambassadors, and it doesn't happen with politicians. But it does happen with artists, whether you're a writer, a sculptor, a painter, a filmmaker. With film we're especially lucky because film is seen by millions all over the world. It's the arts that will make peace.

When the artist begins to wallow in self-indulgence and can only see man as a poor, sick, denigrated, complex-ridden victim, I don't buy it. For one thing, it's much too easy. I don't have to watch films to see how corrupt everything is—you can see that in the newspapers every day. I don't mean that I won't show things like this, but film should serve to remind you that man still has a potential, that he's not just crawling along. He still has wings and he can fly. We need this reminder of faith, of optimism, to reestablish the dignity of a human being. Every other play, every other book, every other film are trampling on this by showing mankind as the worst monsters, lower animals than dogs are. But that's not the whole truth. The greatness of Shakespeare—why he lives today and why he'll live a thousand years from now—is that he knew man. He told the whole truth about man. Not just the bad and not just the good, but all the facets.

Don't you think the reaction today against censorship is going to the other extreme? Almost anything is permitted.

Yes, I do. I think in a democratic society there should be self-censorship. You see, in the old times arts were patronized by nobility—by kings, dukes, aristocracy, popes. The artist lived because of their patronage, so it didn't matter what the people wanted. If somebody wanted the Sistine Chapel, it was going to be built. With films you have a complete reversal of anything that's ever happened in history. Who is the patron of films? The audience, the people, because the money men will go for anything the audience will go for. Therefore, my hope is we can get enough self-censorship and self-criticism from the filmmakers. Many people take the easy and vulgar way out by watching naked people engaging in gymnastics, and the result is deadly boredom. To me it's not interesting. It's dull, and of course dullness is the cardinal sin. It's up to the audience to react to this by not going to this kind of film. When I hear that some of these films are done for the young generation it offends me, and I think it should offend the young generation, too. They should say, "Enough is enough." When they come to the theater they prefer things that stir their mind and their heart a little more than this kind of abundant garbage.

The pendulum does seem to be swinging back a bit.

Yes, I think so. A few months back, the Directors Guild of America arranged an exchange with Russian directors. We had three of them come over here, and I was the official host. One of those directors told this story. He said that in Moscow a fellow gets a four-week vacation on salary, and he would like to get out of Russia and travel, so he comes to this travel agent and asks, "I have never been abroad. Where should I go?" So the man said, "Well, if you want something exotic why don't you go to Africa?" He said, "Africa, eh? Well, isn't that where Biafra and Nigeria and all that slaughter was? No, no, I don't want to go there." So the agent said,

"Well, why don't you go to Ireland, the Emerald Island? It's beautiful there." And the fellow said, "Ireland? Isn't that where the Catholics are murdering Protestants and the Protestants are murdering Catholics? No, I don't want to go there." So the man said, "Well, how about the United States? Great country." "United States?" he said, "Isn't that where they assassinated their president? Then they killed a senator and then they killed a public religious figure and they're throwing bombs and taking drugs? No, I don't want to go there." There's a long queue behind this guy, so the agent says to him, "Look, here is the globe of the world. Go to the corner at the table. Study the globe, and when you make up your mind, come back and tell me where you want to go." So he tends to all the other people. It gets to be closing time. The little man comes back with the globe and the agent says, "Well, did you make up your mind about where you want to go?" The man gives him the globe, looks at him and asks, "Do you have another globe?"

We only have this globe, and we are at a period in time where talk about any of the arts—especially film—as being something exclusive, exotic, purely aesthetic, must be discarded completely. It's not valid. Art and cinema must do something about improving this one little globe that we have, and I wish we would all bear this in mind in our work. This is the great purpose of films: to make life more decent, man more dignified, and this earth, the only one we have, more beautiful.

Films as Director

1930	*Applause*	1936	*The Gay Desperado*
1931	*City Streets*	1937	*High, Wide and Handsome*
1932	*Love Me Tonight*	1939	*Golden Boy*
	Dr. Jekyll and Mr. Hyde	1940	*The Mark of Zorro*
1933	*The Song of Songs*	1941	*Blood and Sand*
1934	*We Live Again*	1942	*Rings on Her Fingers*
	Queen Christina	1948	*Summer Holiday*
1935	*Becky Sharp*	1957	*Silk Stockings*

I would never photograph any woman without diffusion on the lens. Believe me, that's a must. Tallulah Bankhead used to say, "Shoot me through a Navajo blanket."

GEORGE FOLSEY
(Born in New York, New York, 1898—Died 1988)

Looking back on a sixty-year career as a director of photography, George Folsey recalled that his parents warned him that his chosen trade might not provide steady work. "During those early years my family wanted me to quit the film business and go into insurance," he remembered. "The funny thing is I worked consistently since I was fourteen years of age. I was only out of work for a few weeks my whole career." It was a career in which he shot 160 feature films and was nominated for thirteen Academy Awards, but was never recognized with the Oscar itself.

When Folsey finished grammar school in New York in 1914, he needed a job. He was sent to the Famous Players Studio, where he was hired for six dollars a week to work with the pioneer cameraman-director Edwin S. Porter. He learned the technical intricacies as a camera assistant, and when he was nineteen he was promoted to second cameraman, working alongside the main camera shooting a separate negative for foreign distribution. When the first cameraman quit in the middle of a production and the director asked Folsey, "Can you shoot the picture?" Folsey said, "I can move the studio if you want"—and from then on he would be the man in charge.

Until he moved to Hollywood in 1932, Folsey thrived in New York, photographing a range of pictures that included Rouben Mamoulian's first film, *Applause,* with Helen Morgan, and the first two Marx Brothers features, *The Cocoanuts* and *Animal Crackers.*

Folsey was a pathfinder in the early days of motion picture photography, transforming the harsher look of black-and-white pictures to a subtler and more softly lit cinematography. He studied paintings and was one of the first to use "bounced light," erecting huge silk sheets around the sides of the stage

George Folsey on the set of *The Wiser Sex* (1932), at MGM, which starred
Claudette Colbert and Melvyn Douglas. Standing at top of picture (right) is
Fred Zinnemann, the assistant director. Folsey is holding small megaphone;
Joseph Ruttenberg is at the camera. The film was directed by Berthold
Viertel and Victor Viertel.

and reflecting light off them onto the set. Later at MGM he would excel at
color photography. His Academy Award nominations included *The White
Cliffs of Dover, Seven Brides for Seven Brothers, All the Brothers Were Valiant,
Executive Suite, Meet Me in St. Louis, Green Dolphin Street, Million Dollar
Mermaid* and *The Balcony.*

Folsey's seminar at AFI was preceded by a showing of *Seven Brides for
Seven Brothers.* The discussion was conducted by Howard Schwartz, a cinematographer on the faculty who organized a series of meetings among the fellows and leading cinematographers.

GEORGE FOLSEY

———◆———

November 8, 1975

This is George Folsey, one of the most distinguished cameraman in Hollywood and the man who photographed the film you just saw, Seven Brides for Seven Brothers. *When did you start working in pictures?*

I began my life in the motion picture business in 1914. I was Adolph Zukor's office boy before World War I, and became a cameraman when I was nineteen. I shot an awful lot of pictures in my life, black and white, color, sound, silent, cranked by hand, and all that baloney. It's a fascinating and exciting business. I wouldn't change it for anything in the world. I arrived at MGM to do one picture and stayed for twenty-eight years.

What was it like shooting silent films?

I did Mamoulian's first film, *Applause.* Are any of you familiar with what they used to use before we had blimps? We had a thing called an "ice boy." It was huge, and you put the camera inside and you shot through a pane of glass and you hung lights all around. Maybe you could get them on the outside of the thing if you wanted a dolly shot, which was very rare. You put this thing on a big bunch of boards and you pushed it in and out. We had a scene in which Helen Morgan is saying the Lord's Prayer to her little daughter who is asleep, or is supposed to be put to sleep. We had a shot that had to end up with a close-up of her ear and Helen's mouth. We had to shoot it with a four-inch lens because we couldn't get it big enough, and we had to break down the sets behind us and keep pulling back and pulling back to get a long shot. So we shot the long shot with the four-inch lens about four o'clock in the morning and dollied this whole big huge thing in to a close shot of the ear and the mouth. And we were inside this booth all the time, following the focus. It was difficult to judge it; you had to be awfully good because there was no way to mark it. Now you can run it along the side, but back then you couldn't see it very well. So it had to be done very adroitly by the assistant who was changing the focus.

Could you talk about your attitude toward the zoom lens?

I'm an old-time cameraman. I'm not enthusiastic about zoom lenses for their quality and focus. I think I would always want to use a standard lens if I could and dolly it—although the zoom lenses now are certainly awful good, and I'm sure that with use I would change my point of view.

Seven Brides for Seven Brothers *was, I believe, shot in Cinemascope.*

George Stevens said a very interesting thing about Cinemascope. He said that it was very good for photographing snakes, but not good for photographing people. He didn't like it at all, and I don't blame him.

   You might be interested in knowing that almost the whole of *Seven Brides for Seven Brothers* was shot in Cinemascope and normal aspect ratio simultaneously, including the fight in the barn. We did it this way because they couldn't make up their minds which way they wanted to do it. A number of the theaters in the country were not yet equipped to run Cinemascope. There were two cameras on two booms, one Cinemascope and one normal aspect ratio. We set them up side by side so that the same shot would be duplicated, even in close-ups. Two cameras were shooting simultaneously. We didn't have to do the fight over for the other camera; we just did them both at the same time, and it was very effective financially. Stanley Donen, the director, was very pleased.

This was also the period of different color processes.

Yes, the film was shot with Ansco negative, and was printed and released on Eastman stock. Joe Ruttenberg made *Brigadoon* in Ansco. I saw an Ansco print which was absolutely beautiful. I thought the warm tones of the Ansco color system were very appealing, particularly for that picture.

I would have liked to see our picture printed in Ansco, but we never did get to it.

Why was that?

I wouldn't like to get myself involved in legal reasons as to why they did it, but I think it had something to do with the Eastman Kodak company objecting to an Ansco cartel taking over the business in America, and I think they stopped it.

The lighting and color of the barn scene isn't sepia tone, but it does have a different kind of color quality. It's like lantern light.

We just tried to do it the way it would be, with lantern light and lamplight and candlelight. I recall when Howard Keel was out on the porch singing to his brother Gideon, the redheaded brother played by Russ Tamblyn. We tried to make a difference between the color inside and outside. So I had a lot of double fifty-fours and filters on the lights inside—incandescent light, which would actually be like a white light. We would color it with double fifty-fours, sometimes two double fifty-fours, to get a warmer tone. And on the outside, you had regular incandescent lights on Keel and Tamblyn.

When you added color to a scene, you did it by putting color gels over the lights, not bouncing it off of a white card or color gel only?

I just put the color gel on the light. I've found by trial and error that adding double fifty-fours and fifty-sevens to light that would be hitting furniture warms it up and gives a nice tone. I like that warm tone wood has. I didn't like to put blue on the backings. Blue light is supposed to indicate nighttime, which I think is a carryover from the theater. I didn't like to put that blue on there because it looked false to me, so I would put glows on the wall and on the backing and make it dark and have little highlights here and there so that it did look like night. At least it looked like night to me.

Could you tell us more about when you are lighting the backing and the action is in front of it and how to balance it? It's all beautifully matched.

I can only tell you that you just balance it by eye. I don't recall reading it with a meter at all. I think you just look at the backing, and also the blend where the set ends and the backing starts. You have to see to it that there's no definite line of demarcation there, so that it all kind of blends together, and you do it visually. I made a picture called *Forbidden Planet* where we had a very large green sky, and that's the only backing I ever read. I think it was sixty foot-candles, all along that whole backing, and then that low plain of rocks and ground which went into the backing. We had to be very careful to balance that so that it all blended together.

The color on parts of this print seems really garish, and there was even some grain-iness. Why does that happen?

It's very disturbing for a cameraman to go back after some years and look at a picture and see the dreadful things that happen. You wonder if this is what happened when you were shooting, because you just can't remember all of the situations. I do remember *Seven Brides for Seven Brothers* with a great deal of affection because when I saw a print made by Metro, all corrected, it was a rather handsome picture, and I was very pleased with it. As a matter of fact, I was kind of disappointed that I didn't win the award for it that year, and the one that did win it was *Three Coins in a Fountain*. I've lost to a lot of things, but I never lost it to a song before.

Did you rehearse some of those numbers a great deal? They were so intricate.

Oh yes, we rehearsed a great deal. Michael Kidd was the choreographer. He used to teach mathematics, which is unusual. A very fascinating man. They would rehearse for a long time, and we'd have to be there and pick the camera setups and all that business.

There weren't as many cuts in the dance numbers as there often are.

I don't think that dance numbers should be cut up. I remember with the song "I'm a Lonesome Polecat," it had to have a frosty look. We used some venetian blinds, and we had some fifty-fours on the arcs. We'd start out with a broad, which is 6000 Kelvin or 6800 or something, and we'd put double fifty-fours on it to give it a kind of cool, frosty look. At a certain time we gradually opened those blinds and kind of started the light pretty early in the sequence on those faces. I thought it was a beautiful number. I loved that number.

I was wondering if you like to shoot musicals in particular.

It doesn't matter. One job calls for a musical thing and another one calls for something else. I think cameramen should be able to do anything—color, black and white, drama, tragedy, musical comedies. I remember I used to do a lot of pictures with Marion Davies. Now, this is kind of ridiculous, but it got to the point where some people thought I could only photograph blonds. So then I photographed Claudette Colbert, who certainly was not a blond. Such a ridiculous idea; you get stereotyped.

Somebody once asked me, "How do you light the set?" And I thought about it for a minute and I said, "Well, first, you have to find what the story's about. Is it a day scene? Is it a night scene? Is it a tragedy? Is it a comedy?" That dictates how you light the set. Should it be bright? Should it be dark? Do any of you recall Richard Boleslawski? He was a great man, a wonderful director. One time I was doing a light effect with him and he said, "This one's very dark—no light, no light." So I'd say, "Okay." I put a light from way up high and he'd say, "No, no." Now, when you put a light on a wall in a dark set it looks very bright, and he said, "No, no, no—no light, no light." So I killed that light and I put another one someplace else, and every time I did it, he'd say, "No, no, no, no light." So I'd say, "Boley, why don't you take a piece of black leader and put it between the two scenes?" And he says, "Oh no, I have to see something." And I'd say, "That's what I've got that light for—let me alone." Because it was dark in the set and I put the light on, it looked very bright to him. I had found out that a light effect is not no light at all, it is great contrast. Now, just think of that for a minute. You have to have a printing density so that when you make a print, the projection light will not go through it and gray the screen up, which is what it will do if you have it undertimed. So you have to get the light to look very strong and very contrasty. What you really want is something that will print on the normal scale, with the blacks getting deep, rich, velvety and dark. But if you get them thin, with very little light and underexposed, you're going to be dead. It isn't going to look dark, it's going to look flat and gray. So you always see to it that you get enough printing density and increase the contrast.

Do you use a diffuser when photographing women?

I would never photograph any woman without diffusion on the lens. Believe me, that's a must. Tallulah Bankhead used to say, "Shoot me through a Navajo blanket." Are you all acquainted with the chicken coops? Chicken coops are those big lights that have a series of bulbs in them and hang up in the top of a set. The light is thrown back up and it hits into a white surface which is painted a little bit blue to keep the color temperature up, and it throws a soft, scattered light all over the area. It's almost shadowless.

MGM had a fine laboratory, and it gave beautiful halftone, lovely shadow detail—really excellent. We were very comfortable with it. Suddenly we began to get empty blanks—no details in our shadows and a lot of contrast. The halftones were almost like deep shadows instead of that lovely halftone. Everybody was having contrast trouble. It's impossible that every cameraman at Metro was undertiming their shadows at the same time. We were all bewildered, and Robert Surtees and Joe Ruttenberg and myself couldn't find out what was the matter. I began to try, as the others did, to try to find a way to get soft light, to get scattered light in there, to use a bigger source of light from the key and diffuse more, to spread it. It seemed to be the right direction to go, so I continued it, getting bigger and bigger and bigger sources until I was using 10Ks with a lot of diffusion. I began to put big silks up. This is about 1943, so it's a long time ago to be talking about bounce light. I eventually shot almost an entire picture at Metro—*If Winter Comes*—with no key. I used only lights scattered through big silks that I hung up, or I bounced it off hard white walls or reflectors that had white surfaces. I shot the whole picture this way and the empty blacks all disappeared. I got lots of details; inside of people's coats you could see the separation, the difference in the color, the hands of Reginald Owen and Lew Ayres.

We eventually found out that the laboratory had changed its type of development from normal machine development to what you might call agitation. They had installed a system of jet propulsion of the developer onto the film as it went by to increase the speed of the developing time to make it quicker, so that they could get more work through the laboratory and the laboratory could make a good financial report on the amount of film they processed. But it almost killed the product completely. It was an awful thing to do, and Jack Nicholas, the head of the laboratory, was the one who did it.

The Research Council, when it was doing things about inventions in the business, came over to see what we were doing. They said they had heard about this scattered light, and they came on the set and they said to me, "What are you doing?" And I explained it, and they said, "We think we can make a light like that," and a few days later I went into the camera department at Metro at lunchtime, and there on the stage was a light that was about that wide and about that high and it was kind of rounded like this. It was the forerunner of the chicken coop. It had a bar across the center of it and it had some photofloods in there, which were facing in toward this rounded thing.

At the time I was working with Mervyn LeRoy, and I had a shot to do of two people walking down a corridor with the camera close on them and backing away. I don't think there's a harder shot to do because you're stuck with the walls on the side, so you're in a hallway and you can't put any fill light anywhere. You have to project the light to the person, and they are walking to the light so they are getting progressively hotter, and then they have to go out of that light, and then you have to come into a shaded area and then to another light. It takes time, and I knew LeRoy wasn't easy to work with as he's always in a hurry, so I knew that this shot was going to be big trouble. I saw that new light and I said, "Let me have it." I took it right off the camera department stage and brought it over to my stage across the street, and I put it right alongside of the camera. Then we got this shot with the two people in it and moved the thing back with the dolly. We had it on a stand we could roll, so we just rolled it back. This one light took care of the whole thing and we got the shot in ten minutes. So that was my first introduction to that type of thing, which was an off-shoot of the soft, scattered light that I had been using. Incidentally, my electrician, a fellow named Bobby Wherl, saw this light and said, "You know, that looks like a chicken coop." So the name stuck.

In fact, Hal Rosson named the thing the "cockalorus." I don't know if any of you know Hal Rosson. He's a pixie kind of a little guy, and cockalorus is from one of the Grimm fairy tales—the High Cockalorum—and Hal had apparently read this. I was working on a picture called *Lady of the Tropics*. We had Hedy Lamarr in very white costumes, and the usual procedure to take care of the white costume was to put a net in front of the light. But that degraded the quality of it and it didn't look right. I got a door with a grill and found that when I held it up in front of the light, the light would have a toned-down quality to it. And from that, my grip made a thing you could move in and out in front of the lights. Hal and I were working together and I said, "Let's put a grill in front of this thing."

And he liked the idea and he said, "Let's get one of those things—let's get a cockalorus over here." And the name stuck.

It seems to me that there are so many types of diffusion around today.

I really shy away from the nets. I always liked disk diffusion. I always felt that the nets degraded it a little. Disk diffusion is a glass with circles generally ground into it to take the rays of light and distort them. And in proportion to the amount of distortion that it gives you, that's the amount of diffusion you get. It's very slender, you're barely aware of it. Some is a little heavier, and that's why I had that graduation from very light to very heavy which I could use, depending on the closeness that you were to the subject and how much diffusion you felt was needed. There was a time in the picture business—sound changed everything—when we all had gauze which we would burn to insert diffusion to keep the main part of the shot clear. I would pick these things out and take a cigarette and burn it where I thought it was needed. For instance, if this table had some white things on it and you had a little highlight across it, you'd want to diffuse that, throw it down into a shadow, so you'd stick a little gauze in there. It was a

Folsey was nominated for thirteen Academy Awards for cinematography but never took home the Oscar.

way of vignetting. I'm glad it's gone now because it was a hell of a lot of trouble. You couldn't have done it with the moving camera.

Could you talk about Forbidden Planet, *your thinking about how you were going to treat it photographically, and what developed as far as set design?*

Well, at the beginning of the picture, you may recall, there was a huge gray sphere that had a lot of lines and marks and mysterious things on it, which was supposed to indicate the navigation and the orbit about the planets. And I had a hell of a time with that thing because it reflected every light on the set. While there were a series of identifications and marks on it to indicate certain things, I put a hell of a lot more on there because, every time, I'd get a light reflecting in it that I didn't want and there was no way I could get it out of there. So I'd just stick another planet in there, a little blob or something that represented some bit of information.

You remember, there was a scene when they were either going to or coming from the planet Tarius. They were going to go through a time zone and they wanted to make a light change. I wanted to go through the colors of the spectrum, and I wanted to get the set lit the way we normally would light it, and then I wanted to put big wheels of color that would go from ultraviolet to infrared in front of all of the lights and synchronize them together, so that all the changes would come at the same time on all of the lights. Well, the art department was never very enthusiastic about that picture, and they didn't think it was going to be so good, so they discouraged the management from our doing this because it would have been expensive.

Other than that, I thought the picture was very interesting and a lot of fun to do. Did you ever photograph an invisible monster? We had to show the footsteps, so we built some boxes in the shape of a monster foot and we covered all those boxes up with the dirt of the set and had electricity underneath them with trip wires. And as we panned along we would see a footprint appear because the bottom had been pulled away and the dirt fell down and it would make a kind of rough shape of the monster's foot, and it would go from one to the other. It was the same thing when he climbed the stairs. The steps were made of rubber. They were painted to look like steel and they were pulled down by a wired device underneath them. The wires would go up and pull this thing down, and you'd see the steps sag with the tremendous weight of this monster. It was a challenging idea to try and get it over, and I think they did a pretty good job.

When you were given an assignment to light someone, either a man or a woman, as attractively as possible, how would you approach it in terms of creating the shadows on the face?

Let's say we're talking about a woman you want to make look attractive. I think that you must almost always look from a height down at the woman. If you have a big close-up of her, if you get a four-inch lens and get the camera high up, you get her head larger than her chin, because it's the farthest thing away from you and you're using a long lens. Everything drops into place and you throw shadow on it if you want to.

I remember that *Mutiny on the Bounty* ended with Clark Gable going off with a Polynesian maiden who had a face like a pumpkin. She had a big, broad nose. And while she was a very nice girl and had beautiful eyes, she did not look particularly attractive. All of a sudden they realized that this wasn't a good idea. So if they couldn't rephotograph her, they would have to recast her part and do the scenes over. So a number of the cameramen at Metro were asked to make tests of her. I asked them if I could do anything I wanted and they said yes. So I put the camera up in the air on a platform. I had to get a ladder so I could look down into the camera. I put the four-inch lens on, got her head big and her chin far away, and threw shadows on her face to hide these broad cheekbones, and put diffusion on it, with all the necessary highlight in the back of her hair. And they were just enchanted with it. She looked so well because she had great big, luminous eyes. And they said, "Can you do that in the picture?" I said, "Yes, I can." So I did all of the close-ups of her in the picture that way, and they didn't have to reshoot the whole sequence. They inserted these close-ups every now and then and it worked very effectively.

What about using highlights to put a sparkle in the eye?

I think that you have to be very careful about eye lights because it's tough to get an eye light on just the eye. I think it's better if you can get the eye light from the main source, because then it's going to be in the right place and you don't have an additional thing to bother with and worry whether it's going to show on the back wall.

*What was the working environment like at MGM? Did the top office come down
all the time or did they let you be creative?*

We had a lot of that. We had a Tartar who managed the laboratory, a man
named Jack Nicholas, who ran a damn good laboratory, I must say, but he
was a very opinionated man, impossible to argue with, and constantly
after you to get more fill, more fill. And you were limited to some extent.
For instance, I did a picture called *Green Dolphin Street* with Lana Turner
and Donna Reed. We had a big courtyard of a convent and part of a stone
wall, and the director said to me, "George, I'd like this thing to look like
an overcast day with patches of snow. I don't want it to look sunny. I want
overcast and soft shadows." Gee, this is a big set. I mean, a really big set.
So I talked it over with my electrician, and knew if I put opened 10K
lights up high and hit them down there, each one would throw its own
shadow and I wouldn't know how to get rid of them.

So we took great big silk sheets—or sails, I called them—and
stretched them over the top of the set and underneath our light platforms.
We rigged it intentionally to get more lights up there than we normally
would have used. And we lit the whole set through these hanging silks,
and it was all diffused and shadowed. It scattered the light all over the
place. We had warm light on the floor, a back kicker way in the back—we
had a beautiful overall exposure with no shadow. There was a woman in a
black costume and a woman in a white costume and a woman in a gray
silk costume. You could see detail all over the place—in the black and in
the gray and in the white. It was beautiful. And it took us about half an
hour to light the set, which normally would have taken two and a half
hours or more, because it was a big set and you would have had to get this
light in there and balance it. Here, we just threw the light in and the exposure was fine and it worked like a charm.

I took a big gamble, believe me, because if I had been wrong, holy
Moses, the set would have fallen in on me. But I just felt convinced that it
was going to work, and it did. And I have to tell you the sequel to all of
this—when I told you about the scattered light and all that business: I
went down to Jack Nicholas' office one day, after I had seen some of the
results, and I said, "Nick, I think I found the answer to the empty blacks
in the contrast. I've been using reflected light." He said, "Certainly, it's the
only way you can do it." Well, we'd been doing this for two years, fighting
this thing, and I looked at him and I said, "If you knew so much about it,

why the hell didn't you say so two years ago?" We all had been killing ourselves trying to find an answer to it, and now when I come up with the answer, he says, "Certainly, it's the only way you can do it." I was very annoyed at him.

From your experience, is it more common that directors come to you and say, "What are the shots going to be?" Or do they come to you and say, "We're going to put the camera here"?

It's neither one nor the other. You talk it over, and generally the director is the one who makes the decision and has his mind pretty well made up as to how it's supposed to be and how he'd like to have the scene played. He tells you, "This is the way we're going to shoot," and you go ahead and do it. Sometimes, if he's a young or inexperienced director, you can make a suggestion and help him with a thought as to how it could be better. But I would say that it's certainly the director's prerogative to decide, and if he says, "I want the camera here," you put it there, because it's his baby and not yours. I would say that most directors are cooperative, and if you have a better idea, they'll listen to it and use it if they like it.

I'm curious whether you have ever directed, and if not, did you ever have any aspirations to do so?

Once, when I was very young, I thought it would be nice if I could direct a picture, but I fortunately got that silly idea out of my head very quickly. I don't think cameramen make good directors, for a very good reason. Cameramen, at least as far as my experience goes, are so doggone busy keeping up with the technical changes and the complexities of our job that to be proficient with that, and also learn how to be a director, is almost too much to ask. There have been only a few: Victor Fleming, George Stevens, Phil Rosen, Karl Freund, Teddy Tetzlaff. I don't know any others. Ronnie Neame, perhaps.

Sometimes when the director doesn't know what he's doing, you get the feeling the cameraman is, in a sort of way, directing the picture.

I guess there are some instances where you might say that's true. At least you can be a great help. For instance, Cukor is very interested in the quality, the tone. He has great taste and he's a very useful man to work with because he does have good taste. But he wouldn't have any idea how to light a scene. And I don't think he has any inclination to do so. But he is very aware of photography and knows what he would like to have and can explain to you what he wants. But directors don't get into the photography too much. At least none that I know of.

———

Films as Cinematographer

1919 *His Bridal Night*
1920 *The Fear Market*
 Sinners
 The Stolen Kiss
 The Frisky Mrs. Johnson
1921 *The Education of Elizabeth*
 The Price of Possession
 The Sheltered Daughters
 A Heart to Let
 Room and Board
 The Case of Becky
1922 *Nancy from Nowhere*
 The Game Chicken
 Slim Shoulders
 What's Wrong with the Women?
1923 *The Bright Shawl*
 Radio-Mania
 The Fighting Blade
 Twenty-One
1924 *The Enchanted Cottage*
 Born Rich
1925 *The Necessary Evil*
 The Half-Way Girl
 Scarlet Saint
1926 *Too Much Money*
 The Savage
 Ladies At Play
1927 *Orchids and Ermine*
 See You in Jail
 Naughty But Nice
 American Beauty

 No Place to Go
 Her Wild Oat
1928 *Lady Be Good*
 The Butter and Egg Man
1929 *The Hole in the Wall*
 The Letter
 Gentlemen of the Press
 The Cocoanuts
 Glorifying the American Girl
 The Laughing Lady
1930 *The Big Pond*
 Dangerous Nan McGrew
 Applause
 Animal Crackers
 Laughter
1931 *The Royal Family of Broadway*
 Stolen Heaven
 Honor Among Lovers
 The Smiling Lieutenant
 Secrets of a Secretary
 My Sin
 The Cheat
1932 *The Wiser Sex*
 The Misleading Lady
 The Big Broadcast
 The Animal Kingdom
1933 *Men Must Fight*
 Reunion in Vienna
 Storm at Daybreak
 Stage Mother
 Going Hollywood

1934 *Men in White*
    Operator 13
    Chained
    Forsaking All Others
1935 *Reckless*
    Age of Indiscretion
    Page Miss Glory
    I Live My Life
    Kind Lady
1936 *Hearts Divided*
    The Gorgeous Hussy
    The Great Ziegfeld
1937 *The Last of Mrs. Cheyney*
    The Bride Wore Red
1938 *Mannequin*
    Arsène Lupin Returns
    Hold That Kiss
    Marie Antoinette
    The Shining Hour
1939 *Fast and Loose*
    Fast and Furious
    Society Lawyer
    Lady of the Tropics
    Remember?
1940 *Two Girls on Broadway*
    Third Finger, Left Hand
    Gallant Sons
1941 *Come Live with Me*
    The Trial of Mary Dugan
    Free and Easy
    Rage in Heaven
    Dr. Kildare's Wedding Day
    Lady Be Good
    Married Bachelor
1942 *Rio Rita*
    Three Hearts for Julia
    Dr. Gillespie's New Assistant
    Grand Central Murder
    Panama Hattie
    Seven Sweethearts
    Andy Hardy's Double Life
1944 *Meet Me in St. Louis*

    Thousands Cheer
    A Guy Named Joe
    The White Cliffs of Dover
1945 *The Clock*
    The Green Years
1946 *The Harvey Girls*
    Ziegfeld Follies
    The Secret Heart
1947 *Till the Clouds Roll By*
    Green Dolphin Street
1948 *If Winter Comes*
    State of the Union
1949 *Take Me Out to the Ball Game*
    The Great Sinner
    Adam's Rib
1950 *Malaya*
    Vengeance Valley
    The Big Hangover
    Night into Morning
    The Law and the Lady
    A Life of Her Own
    Mr. Imperium
    The Man with a Cloak
1952 *Shadow in the Sky*
    Lovely to Look At
    Million Dollar Mermaid
1953 *The Band Wagon*
    All the Brothers Were Valiant
1954 *Tennessee Champ*
    Executive Suite
    Men of the Fighting Lady
    Seven Brides for Seven Brothers
    Deep in My Heart
1955 *Hit the Deck*
    The Cobweb
1956 *Forbidden Planet*
    The Fastest Gun Alive
    These Wilder Years
    The Power and the Prize
1957 *The Seventh Sin*
    Tip on a Dead Jockey
    House of Numbers

1958 *The High Cost of Loving*
    Saddle the Wind
    Imitation General
    Torpedo Run
1959 *Count Your Blessings*
1960 *Cash McCall*

    I Passed for White
1961 *Anatomy of an Accident*
1972 *Glass Houses*
1976 *That's Entertainment, Part II*
    [new sequences]

Sometimes I'm not very articulate with the actor. If you point out something, it may become too prominent in his thinking and the scene will suffer. I figure that by putting an actor on his own and letting him use all the resourcefulness he has, he won't depend on me. That's when they say I start becoming a sadist, shooting again and again.

WILLIAM WYLER
(Born in Alsace, France, 1902—Died 1981)

One day Charlton Heston approached William Wyler on the set of *Ben-Hur* in Rome to persuade him to take a different tack with a scene. Heston needed a script to explain his idea, so he picked up Wyler's from his chair. He flipped open the weathered leather binder and noticed a list of pictures stamped on the flyleaf. It read: *Dead End, The Heiress, The Little Foxes, Dodsworth, Jezebel, The Westerner, The Best Years of Our Lives, Detective Story, Roman Holiday.* Heston closed the binder, turned to the director and said, "Never mind. Let's do it your way."

Wyler was one of the top five directors in Hollywood for forty years and earned a reputation for having his way on the set. He believed a single point of view was necessary for making a good film. He was famous for demanding thirty takes or more, each one followed by no specific instructions, simply, "Let's do it again." Actors railed and complained but kept coming back to him. Performers in William Wyler films collected a total of thirty-nine Academy Award nominations.

Kirk Douglas starred in *Detective Story.* After weeks and weeks of countless takes, he didn't have the slightest idea whether his performance was acceptable to the director or a total disaster. Wyler would simply say, "Print," and move on to the next setup. Years later Douglas ran into Wyler in Beverly Hills. They greeted one another, then Wyler said, "By the way, Kirk, I saw *Detective Story* on TV last night. You were good. Very good."

David Lean said of Wyler, "He had all the qualities a great director needed. He was both a dreamer and intensely practical—and he had a sense of humor about himself."

Wyler received AFI's Life Achievement Award in 1975, a time when the

William Wyler (left) on the set of *Wuthering Heights* with cinematographer
Gregg Toland in 1939. Toland contributed to Wyler's visual style of capturing
foreground and background action simultaneously with wide-angle lenses.
Toland, who also photographed *Citizen Kane,* died in 1948 when
he was forty-four.

auteur theory was popular among cineasts. In his acceptance speech Wyler,
who was raised in Europe and studied violin at the Paris Conservatory, said,
"When directing scripts by Lillian Hellman or Bob Sherwood, Sidney Kingsley or Jessamyn West, I could hardly call myself an auteur. However, I'm one
of the few directors in town who can pronounce the word correctly."

Wyler was a meticulous craftsman and a powerful storyteller, an artist
who concealed the brushstrokes, never calling attention to himself. He used
wide-angle lenses and pumped light onto his sets to achieve great depth of

focus—playing scenes that used the close foreground and the deep background at the same time. He excelled at comedy, drama, romance, Westerns, musicals, spectacles and even documentaries. At age forty-two he went into the Army Air Corps and flew combat missions in a bomber called *The Memphis Belle,* making a compelling documentary of an American crew flying twenty-five missions over Italy and Germany. On one of these missions Wyler lost all hearing in one ear.

He says in his seminar that there is a fine line between confidence and arrogance. One abiding tension between filmmakers and studio chiefs is the length of films—Wyler made *Ben-Hur,* which ran three and a half hours, and *Dead End,* which was a little over ninety minutes. Strong directors trust their own judgment, but it can be a difficult issue. If a picture is not working perfectly, the studio will want to shorten it, but arbitrary cutting can remove character development or a crucial story point. In 1956, Willy invited my father to see *Friendly Persuasion,* and the three of us had a drink afterward. Willy explained how Allied Artists had begged him to take twenty minutes out of the film, which ran two hours and twenty minutes. The shorter running time would enable theaters to have one more showing each day and sell more tickets. Willy had a dilemma. Allied Artists was a small studio for which this was an expensive make-or-break film, and he felt a personal obligation because they had backed him fully. Yet he had the power of final cut. Dad asked what he did. Willy said that he took twenty minutes out and they had another preview. Dad said, "How did it play?" Willy smiled and said, "It got twenty minutes longer."

Wyler restored the twenty minutes, Allied Artists got one less show a day and six weeks later *Friendly Persuasion* won the Palme d'Or at the Cannes Film Festival. The day Wyler came to speak at AFI, Charlton Heston came along and joined the questioning.

WILLIAM WYLER

December 17, 1975

If you expected any big speeches from me, you will be disappointed. I'm ready to answer questions you have about my pictures, and if I can remember I'll be happy to tell you what went on behind the scenes. Also, I don't hear well, so whoever speaks, speak up. Okay, I'm all tuned in now with my hearing aid.

Your career started in silent films. How did the transition to sound affect you?

To me it was a very welcome thing. I was just starting directing and had made only a few pictures. But I always loved the theater and always felt the restriction of the silent screen. While many people hated the idea of sound, I welcomed it. I knew that to be able to hear what people are saying would be an added value to pictures. In the silents we tried to have as few titles as possible and to get everything over with pantomime. When we could find a way to eliminate a title by gesture, this was supposed to be very ingenious and very good. Of course, there were some subjects that fit into the silent picture era. In a way *The Memphis Belle* is a silent picture because you don't feel the dialogue, though it has spoken words in it.

Did you ever do a silent picture you later remade with sound?

No, not the whole picture. I made *The Shakedown*—a sort of prizefight picture—during the time sound was coming in. The New York office sent the picture back and said, "Put in twenty-five percent sound." This meant that they liked the picture and were willing to spend more money on it.

So I picked out a couple of scenes, and we made those scenes over with dialogue.

You made Hell's Heroes *at the time with Charles Bickford, based on* The Three Godfathers, *which John Ford made later with sound.*

Which he made first and again later. The last time I saw him he said, "It's your turn to make *Three Godfathers* again."

Was your version silent or sound?

Mine was all sound, the first all-talking outdoor picture Universal made. We were in the Mojave Desert and in Panamint Valley, just off Death Valley, in July and August of 1930. It was 120 degrees outside and in the glass booth where the cameraman worked it was 140. Sometimes after a shot we would find that the cameraman had passed out. We had a crew pushing this booth with a microphone hidden in a cactus here and one in the sand over there.

You directed with Sam Goldwyn as producer, and later you became your own producer. Was it easier to work as your own producer?

That all depends on who the producer is. Sometimes it's a burden being your own producer. I never felt I did a good job, because there was too much to do as a producer. The only reason I wanted to be a producer was to be able to do exactly as I wanted. Now, I didn't have much trouble with Sam Goldwyn, except in a few small instances where he overruled me. Of course he had the final word. But in most cases—not all—he seemed to have more confidence in what I thought than in what he thought himself, and he let me have my way.

By and large it was a very harmonious and fruitful relationship, wasn't it?

Fruitful, yes. Harmonious, not always. For instance, he wanted me to do a number of pictures which I refused to do. I didn't have complete freedom of choice in my contract, but if he wanted me to do a film I didn't want to do, I would simply leave town and go to Europe. I had a three-year contract run on for five years because I would be suspended and extended. He'd say, "Here, make a picture called *Woman Chases Man.*

Make a thing called *The Cowboy and the Lady.* Make a picture called *Marco Polo.*" I would say, "No, I won't make them. They're terrible. I don't like the stories." And we'd have fights over that. But when he agreed with me, when he bought stories like *Dodsworth, Dead End* or *The Little Foxes,* or when I got him to buy the script of *Wuthering Heights,* I said, "Great," and we went ahead and worked together in relative harmony.

What always stands out in your films is the intensity and the passion of the performances. Obviously they're of extreme importance to you. How do you work with actors?

When I come to a set, I've studied the scene and I have got a vague idea of how I want to play it. But I haven't mapped it out exactly as some directors do. Before I can make up my mind definitely, I've got to see the actors doing it. Also, I want to see what the actors have to contribute, so I don't tell them very much. If an actor asks me, I say, "You know the scene. Go ahead, show me." And it happens very often that the actor will have a different idea or an even better idea than I have. When we've got it worked out, then comes the technical part of working out the camera moves. Then we start shooting. Sometimes I'm not very articulate with the actor. If you point out something, it may become too prominent in his thinking and the scene will suffer. I figure that by putting an actor on his own and letting him use all the resourcefulness he has, he won't depend on me. That's when they say I start becoming a sadist, shooting again and again. He's got to do and feel it himself. One actor once asked me, "Why don't you tell me when it's good?" I said, "Look, see that camera there? When that camera moves away to another position, then that's a great compliment. When it moves to another shot, that means you were good."

I must confess, though, that sometimes in the cutting room a scene won't look as well as it did when I was shooting it. While something I was looking for was achieved, something else—some spontaneity perhaps—left the scene without my noticing it. Then I'll say, "Let's print up take one or take two, and take a look at those other takes." Sometimes I'll put the early take back into the film. The actor, of course, won't know which take it is.

Your work has been almost exclusively with professional actors. But in The Best Years of Our Lives *you did interesting work with a nonactor—Harold Russell, who plays the war veteran. What problems did you encounter?*

Wyler with Joel McCrea on the set of *Dead End,* 1937. Sylvia Sidney and
Humphrey Bogart also starred in Lillian Hellman's adaptation of the Sidney
Kingsley play. Samuel Goldwyn was the producer.

Well, I've always believed that acting is a business that you have to learn.
It isn't something you can just pick up. Naturally there were problems
with Harold's acting, but I didn't have to explain to him how it feels to
lose your hands; he knew better than I. But there was the problem of
making him feel and react in certain ways at a certain time with a lot of
lights and cameras, which is not conducive to feeling or showing emotions. I had to treat him a little better than I do professional actors, by
putting on my kid gloves. But the result was very gratifying. He finally
knew what was required, and when it came time to feel something—
something he felt a long time before when it really happened—he was
able to do it. All I did was help him. This is all I can do for any actor, professional or nonprofessional. Naturally the professional actors helped him
in every way they could and everybody was very patient. But after a few
days Harold Russell understood what was required. One thing you get
from a nonprofessional actor is that they never ham it up. He never did
too much of anything. In fact, I had to bring things out a bit instead of
toning him down.

In the original story the man was a spastic. It was a little book by
MacKinlay Kantor called *Glory for Me.* It's very easy to act a spastic, and I

guess a lot of actors would have liked the chance to do it. But I felt that it would always look acted. I wanted something real. So I thought about all kinds of permanent injuries that veterans had suffered and we came across the idea of a man who had lost both hands, of which there were several. Then by using a man whom we could undress and show there was absolutely nothing phony about him, it would simply be more real.

The film is one of the most successful films I ever made, and it was also one of the easiest. The reason is that I had been in the service myself. I came back from the war and had a few of the problems veterans have in getting readjusted. I understood these men very well. I had spent four years in research, so to speak, and knew these men better than Ben-Hur or Roman soldiers. I didn't have to think, "Now, what would a man do in that situation?" because I knew the situation. I knew the men. It made me think that very often we do pictures where we don't know our characters well enough. We do a picture because we like the story, or because it's time to make another picture, or we need the money.

The final script of The Best Years of Our Lives *seems very different from the film. Do you leave room for making changes during filming?*

I have to have a script. I need a story that I like and that I think will make a good picture. I don't go out improvising scenes as a rule, though if I can think of something that's better than what was written, of course, I'd do that. But you've got to have a basis for what you're going to do if you don't get a better idea. I think a director is bound to make small changes, contributions to the screenplay, without necessarily being a writer. I'm not a writing director, but that doesn't mean I don't make changes. An example is in *The Best Years,* where we had Dana Andrews walking around the air-field seeing all these obsolete airplanes, which never saw action. All the script said was, "He walks around thinking of how the war had done him in." But it's because I did *The Memphis Belle* and rode in a bombardier's compartment on a few missions that I got the idea that he would climb up into his own plane and have a dream and lose himself in the dream, or rather in hallucination. It was all invented on the spot because the airfield, those obsolete planes, were conducive to the basic idea of the film, of the man feeling lost. It would all come back in his mind, and he would hear in his mind's eye the motors going, even though there were no motors there. It occurred to me that it would be good to hear each motor start, as before takeoff, over shots of the empty nacelles, as part of his hallucination. If I made the picture today, I would end it right there. I think it would be a better ending.

Did you see the remake of Best Years?

Yes. I didn't like it and I most definitely was not involved with it. They seemed to imitate some of the things we did, and it didn't come off. They left out some of the best things in it, and I think it was a big disappointment to everybody. I don't know why they did it. I don't know why they simply didn't show the old picture.

I found your documentary The Memphis Belle *a very strong picture, probably the most emotionally strong of all your films.*

Of course it was the real thing. I had a little crew, only four people. One of them was William Clothier, one of the top cameramen now. You've probably seen his name on some of the great Westerns. We went to a place called Bovington, an RAF training center in England. We all had to go to a school of aircraft recognition and to a gunnery school. We had to learn how to take a machine gun apart and put it back together, because we had to be able to take over the machine gun in case one of the gunners got hurt. We had to go through all that before we were allowed to fly. But the difficulties! We operated sixteen-millimeter cameras at twenty-eight thousand feet, where it was sixty below zero in the cabin. The cameras would freeze. I had another one in my electric suit to try and keep it warm. Besides the electric suit, I had on a Mae West [inflatable life jacket]. If you wanted to move around anywhere you had to plug into what was called a walk-around bottle. And you had thick gloves on. It was all done with these sixteen-millimeter cameras you had to wind. If you wanted to change the film you had to take off your glove, but if you took it off for more than one or two minutes you would lose fingers from frostbite. Being on oxygen, your efficiency was at a minimum. Taking three steps was like walking a mile.

If you filmed out of one side—the windows were open because the machine guns were sticking out—the exposure would be different than from the other side. On one side you'd be shooting into the sun and on the other side away from it. By the time you looked through the camera, any fighter plane coming at you was gone. If you took time to look through, by the time you were ready to shoot you were over a target. We saw some of the other guys, some of the other Flying Fortresses, go down. But you forgot the danger. You didn't even think of the danger. There wasn't time; you thought only of getting it on film.

I think what is most remarkable about the film is that the people really came across. Everything was presented on a very human level.

I guess you could feel it was all done under the conditions of complete reality. The situation was dramatic in itself. You didn't have to dramatize it. You could just show a gunner or a navigator looking around, waving and grinning at the camera, and you'd say, "This is Jim Jones from such-and-such a place in Iowa. He's dead now." You don't need anything else—that's as dramatic as anything you can do. It's the advantage of a documentary. You are the author, you can talk and say things that enhance what you show on the screen, and that can be very dramatic and very emotional.

Incidentally, the film was edited by John Sturges, who was in the air force at the time. An air force sergeant, Lester Koenig, who worked with me on several films after the war, wrote the narration in accordance with my description of the missions. I think both he and Sturges did a first-rate job. This was one place where we had no producer bothering anybody.

Did you feel that with The Memphis Belle *you were doing more than just quoting facts? Were you trying to influence the audience toward a point of view about the men?*

Sure. I was expressing an anti-German point of view. The film was used as propaganda. When the air force and the president saw the picture, they said, "Get it out to everybody." It was run in sixteen thousand theaters all over the country. They all got it free because it was propaganda for the people who were working in the factories. The end of the film in effect said, "You see what these boys are doing, how they're sacrificing their lives? Now all you people who make airplanes, guns and tanks, keep at it. Keep working, and send them the materials."

Ben-Hur *is perhaps the film you're best known for. Could you tell us something about the chariot race scene?*

I should point out that the chariot race was really the work of two men: Yakima Canutt and Andrew Marton. They were the directors of the chariot race, which was a separate unit. They worked about four months doing just nine or ten minutes of film. I couldn't spend that much time on it. It was a fantastic set; I don't think there had been anything like it since *Intolerance,* D. W. Griffith's picture, which I never saw. Originally the chariots were supposed to come out and stand in line, and then the race was supposed to start. I said, "No, my God, we must take advantage of this set." It was my idea to make them go around once in formation. That part of it I shot, showing the set and the chariots parade around. Somebody told me, "They never used to do this in the old Roman days." I said, "To hell with that. That's the way I'm going to do it." It was simply a piece of showmanship. It was like a musical number or an overture. I wanted to take advantage of the production because I knew that once the race started we wanted to stay in the race and be alongside the chariots and the two characters. There would be no time then for long shots. To cut to a long shot at that time would drop the tension. Two hours of the story work up the enmity of these two men and work toward this climax. This is the moment you wait for, so you don't want to cut away from them. After the race, the picture was a letdown for some people because it was no longer as exciting. But you can't have three hours of chariot races.

The race is spectacular, but your camera work in Ben-Hur *and elsewhere doesn't generally draw attention to itself.*

I try to do camera movements that are smooth, unnoticed if possible, and that help to make the scene more interesting. A lot of directors use the camera as a toy. They think it's something to play around with. You see a lamp or post sailing across the foreground for no damn reason. It doesn't help the scene; it means nothing. The movement of camera and the use of camera should be such as to enhance the scene and to give good composition and clarity.

Ben-Hur *took eight months to film, and* The Big Country *took four. The filming schedules today run from sixty to seventy days and no more. Obviously you are someone who won't let himself be hurried.*

It depends on your standing as a director. When I first made pictures, I was simply given a schedule. The first pictures I made were given three days. Two reels, three days, and two thousand dollars to make the whole picture. I got sixty dollars and the cameraman got seventy-five. But later

Charlton Heston, Stephen Boyd and Wyler in the mammoth circus arena
constructed in Rome for the chariot race in *Ben-Hur* (1959).

on I was given a schedule of six or eight weeks. I often went over the
schedule, but within reason. Sometimes I would have to confront the
head of the studio, and he'd say, "What the hell is going on? You're behind
schedule." But it was never serious because they knew I wasn't loafing.
They always knew I was working hard and doing the best I could. I just
tried to make things better, and it took a little more time. Later, when I
received more control, I made my own schedules.

For instance, for a picture like *Detective Story,* the production office at
Paramount made out a schedule for eight weeks. I was also the producer
and I sent it back to them and said, "Make out a six-week schedule." The
production manager came to me and said, "Please, you know we don't
like pictures to go over schedule." It would look bad for him and the production office. I said, "I'm not going to go over schedule. Make it six

weeks." And that's what we did. We made it exactly in six weeks. Of course we had an advantage there because we had a week or two of rehearsals. I've always liked that because, as I've said, I don't rely on improvisation. To be able to see the whole thing rehearsed—now there are very few pictures you can do that with.

Was a picture like Detective Story *all one set?*

Mostly, yes. The original play was all one set. We had the same idea, only more elaborate. We had the police station upstairs, downstairs, the roof, the street out front and café across the street. But still one location. In transferring a play from the stage to the screen, as I did with *Detective Story,* there is the temptation and often the demand to "open up" the play. Nobody likes to be accused of just photographing a stage play. In *Detective Story* we thought it would be nice to see where this man lives, to see his apartment, to find his wife there. We wrote it in the script, but we threw it all out because we found that the play was so constructed that the action was very concentrated, very fast and very good. I said, "I don't want it to look as if I've just photographed a stage play. I want to make it cinematic, give it movement." So I gave it an illusion of movement and of being opened up. In other words, I did not change the construction of the play; I simply changed the set. Instead of having two little rooms as in the play, I have five or six rooms. The construction of the play was not changed, but we did get a feeling that it was not a photographed stage play.

Your films have virtually no spots that drag. The Best Years of Our Lives *is a good example: almost a three-hour film, but it moves rapidly. How do you approach a film's rhythm?*

I have a theory: not to bore the audience. That's a good theory. It sometimes seems that all pictures are too long, mine included, but this is always what I try to avoid. That's why we have previews. If we see the film getting slow or somebody falling asleep or walking out, then you try to correct something to keep the interest up. Some of the directors today don't seem to give a damn about anything except their own feelings. There's a very fine line between self-confidence and arrogance. You make pictures, in a way, for yourself, but you also make them for an audience. I guess some filmmakers don't care about the audience. They only want to

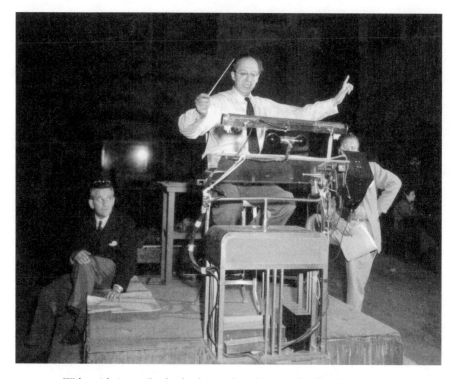

Wyler with Aaron Copland, who conducts his score for *The Heiress* (1949)
with the Paramount Studio Orchestra.

satisfy themselves, and I think this is wrong. To insist on length when it is
not necessary is wrong.

   If you make a film that has something to say, if you want to convey
that thought to a large audience, then you must make it compatible to
them. You must make them accept it and like it. Otherwise, if they don't
come to see your picture, you only reach a handful of people, and you
have not succeeded in getting your message across.

Films as Director

1926	*The Stolen Ranch*		*Desert Dust*
	Lazy Lightning	1928	*Thunder Riders*
1927	*Blazing Days*		*Anybody Here Seen Kelly?*
	The Border Cavalier	1929	*The Shakedown*
	Hard Fists		*The Love Trap*
	Shooting Straight	1930	*The Storm*

1931 *A House Divided*
1932 *Tom Brown of Culver*
1933 *Her First Mate*
      Counsellor at Law
1934 *Glamour*
1935 *The Good Fairy*
      The Gay Deception
1936 *These Three*
      Dodsworth
      Come and Get It (codirector)
1937 *Dead End*
1938 *Jezebel*
1939 *Wuthering Heights*
1940 *The Westerner*
      The Letter
1941 *The Little Foxes*
1942 *Mrs. Miniver*
1944 *The Memphis Belle* (also co-photography)

1946 *The Best Years of Our Lives*
1947 *Thunderbolt*
1949 *The Heiress* (also producer)
1951 *Detective Story* (also producer)
1952 *Carrie* (also producer)
1953 *Roman Holiday* (also producer)
1955 *The Desperate Hours* (also producer)
1956 *Friendly Persuasion* (also producer)
1958 *The Big Country* (also producer)
1959 *Ben-Hur*
1961 *The Children's Hour* (also producer)
1965 *The Collector*
1966 *How to Steal a Million*
1968 *Funny Girl*
1970 *The Liberation of L. B. Jones*

It's all about making sure the film bounces off that sheet and comes to life in the mind of the audience. What is a film outside the audience's mind?

GEORGE STEVENS
(Born in Oakland, California, 1904—Died 1975)

As a boy, George Stevens often did his homework under the stage of the Alcazar Theatre while his parents performed. He remembered the sound of his father's voice as Sidney Carton in *A Tale of Two Cities:* "It is a far, far better thing I do than I have ever done before . . .", and the stillness of the audience as they listened to Dickens' words, the sound of the falling guillotine, the curtain unrolling and thumping onto the stage floor, a breathless silence, then all hands coming together as one in applause. I believe it was in that dark place in a San Francisco theater that my father's keen sense of the audience was born.

He was forced to leave school after the eighth grade when his parents moved south to Los Angeles to find work in films, so he educated himself at the public library, reading the best novels and plays. He broke in as an assistant cameraman for Hal Roach, photographing a wild horse named Rex in Montana, and then, when he was twenty-three, became the head cameraman and a gag writer for Laurel and Hardy, learning from Stan Laurel that "comedy could be graceful and human." He was thirty when Katharine Hepburn asked for him to direct *Alice Adams,* which led to Oscar nominations for her and the picture. Between 1935 and 1940 he directed eight pictures for RKO, among them *Annie Oakley, Damsel in Distress, Vivacious Lady* and *Swing Time,* which the dance critic Arlene Croce called the masterpiece of the Astaire-Rogers canon. By the time he shot his first outdoor picture in Lone Pine, California in 1939—the adventure classic *Gunga Din* with Cary Grant, Douglas Fairbanks, Jr. and Victor McLaglen—he was producing his pictures as well as directing them. Harry Cohn asked him to move to Columbia Pictures, promising him complete control, a condition that marked Stevens'

George Stevens received his Oscars for ambitious dramas, but he also made some of the brightest comedies and musicals. Here with Fred Astaire on the set of *Swing Time* (1935), which dance critic Arlene Croce called "the true miracle" of the Astaire-Rogers canon.

filmmaking from then on. Four romantic comedies in three years would follow: *The Talk of the Town*, with Cary Grant, Jean Arthur and Ronald Colman; *Penny Serenade*, with Grant and Irene Dunne, giving Grant his first Oscar nomination; *Woman of the Year*, the first pairing of Tracy and Hepburn; and *The More the Merrier*, with Jean Arthur, Joel McCrea and Charles Coburn—earning Stevens the Best Director prize from the New York Film Critics.

Stevens joined the U.S. Army Signal Corps in 1942 and embarked on a life-changing experience. As a Lt. Colonel heading a combat motion picture unit under General Eisenhower dubbed the "Stevens Irregulars," he saw men at their best and their worst. He photographed D-Day, the liberation of Paris, the Battle of the Bulge and the discovery of the concentration camps at Nordhausen and Dachau, finally returning to Hollywood in 1946, having seen only one movie in three years (at an outdoor screening for troops somewhere in France). He said that films had become less important to him—and in another way, more important.

He embarked on what is called his American Trilogy—*A Place in the Sun, Shane* and *Giant*—earning two directing Oscars and a reputation for independence and integrity. Of his many qualities, it was his integrity that I admired most, a characteristic also valued by his fellow directors. When Joseph L. Mankiewicz, president of the Directors Guild during the time of the Hollywood blacklist, was subjected to an illegal secret recall by Cecil B. DeMille and his right-wing cohort, it was my father who investigated the conspiracy and confronted DeMille at a full meeting of the Guild membership. Fred Zinneman, who was present that night, said, "To the younger members of the Directors Guild who were idealists and who wanted to make good films, George was a sort of pope, or certainly a cardinal."

He prized the right of final cut, convinced that the integrity of films was important to audience and filmmaker alike. When Paramount and NBC made cuts in *A Place in the Sun* and spliced thirty-eight commercials into the print that was to be broadcast, he took the two corporations to court. "It had to do with this whole matter of selling movies to television," said his friend Warren Beatty, "and the fact that the medium itself was totally polluted by the insertion of commercials and the breaking up of sequences of film. . . . George Stevens took it upon himself, from his position of power among directors, to protect other directors and the medium itself."

In 1958 we worked together on *The Diary of Anne Frank,* a film he referred to as his "war film." Steven Spielberg recently called it a masterwork, noting that Stevens used his clout to make Hollywood's first film dealing with the Holocaust. "We admire Stevens today," Spielberg said, "because he never rushed his images, casting long spells on us, only asking us to be patient with him—and when we were, he would reward us with one indelible moment after the other." He saw *The Greatest Story Ever Told* as an opportunity to take the "mischief" out of the story of Jesus, by which he meant the anti-Semitism that had long been attached to it. The film took five years of his life, was criticized for having so many prominent stars in its cast, and did not recover its cost at the box office. But its pictorial beauty, emotional depth and intelligent rendering of its story have stood up well over time.

"After the actors and the technicians were gone, there was nothing left but George and his film," observed Joe Mankiewicz, who produced *Woman of the Year.* "It always seemed to me that the editing room was where George made his films. I don't know any other director who worked quite that way—and that's why the making of films for George was a very private, personal thing." I joined my father for the final stages of editing *Giant,* which had already taken a year, and being in my early twenties and restless, I became impatient with his meticulousness. We'd had three previews with enthusiastic audience response, but he was still switching one close-up for another to refine performances, trimming frames off shots and sliding soundtracks to sharpen scenes. One afternoon in the projection room I said, "Dad, you have a great picture. Why don't you just lock it up?" After a moment, he said, "When you think about how many man-hours people will spend watching this picture, don't you think it's worth a little more of our time to make it as good as we can?" Forty-seven years later, at a showing of *Giant* at the 2003 Cannes Film Festival, I saw a new generation watch the film on the large screen for the first time—completely engaged for three hours and twenty minutes. I thought, sitting there in the dark—yes, I guess his time was well spent.

Jim Silke, a screenwriter and journalist on the AFI faculty, admired Stevens' work and had a particular affection for *Gunga Din*. It's a film that today would be labeled "action-adventure," but it is distinguished by a blend of graceful comedy and pathos that is rarely achieved. In 1973 Silke ran *Gunga Din* for the AFI fellows and the director, then asked him to look back and answer questions about a picture he had shot in 1938.

GEORGE STEVENS

———

May 23, 1973

Can we start talking about Gunga Din? *Was the film carefully scripted?*

I was doing one thing right after another at RKO with no particular time between pictures. The studio had a script but it was all dialogue. They didn't know what to do with it because it was far from any kind of motion picture. I took one look at it and saw there were no outside scenes—the only thing you saw outside was through the windows of the officers' barracks where some people would ride by occasionally. I was afraid it would be very dreary and just wouldn't have worked as written, so I told the studio that I would take it on but would make a location picture out of it.

The authors were Ben Hecht and Charles MacArthur, two very good playwrights who had written one great play, *The Front Page*—the story of two guys in the newspaper world, one of whom wanted to get married, though his fiancée was the bête noire of the other man. Somebody had the idea to do *The Front Page* in India with the same kind of a relationship, so the studio had engaged two stars—Victor McLaglen and Cary Grant. They had each been in a picture for this company a year before, and it had done very well. I wanted a third character so there would be three men, the reason being a simple matter of arithmetic. It was a slight story having to do with action, cause and effect—action, premise, promise and result. The third character could alternate with the other two, who would be playing against each other, which meant I could be developing the story at the same time. We got Douglas Fairbanks, Jr. for the other man. It's so interesting to see a film like this play itself out. It gives a real sense, for better or for worse, of the adventure of filmmaking—the opportunity of having resources and the disadvantage of having no dramatic concept of a story line that is going to hold it together.

Did the writers do much historical research for the film?

On the screen credit you'll find the name of a delightful fellow and a fine writer named Joel Sayre, who wrote for *The New Yorker* and other magazines. I had worked with him on a couple of things. The other writer, Fred Guiol, was a comedy director for Hal Roach originally. We had a start date in three weeks' time, and got some books and went to Arrowhead Springs. Joel read the books; Freddie and I talked about things. We needed something to glue this whole thing together and Joel came upon it: the cult of Thugee assassins that existed in India. I knew nothing about it and very seldom ran into anyone who did. We worked it into the theme of the story.

What about the locations for the film? Where did you shoot it?

I picked the shooting location from an airplane over the landscape of the Sierra mountains in California. I wanted three locations: the flatland, the midland in the rocks and the higher ground. But the logistics and finances demanded that we do it all in one area, so we put everything in one place, and all three locations were within a few minutes' ride of one another. Our star was Mount Whitney, the highest mountain in the continental United States at 14,497 feet. We changed its aspect by the use of one focal-length lens or another. We'd set it back for the parade ground down below, and bring it up with a longer focal-length lens for the higher ground. It's a rather remarkable area because these are the Sierras at their best. There are these Alabama hills—this strange rugged rock formation that related to places like Persia, Afghanistan and the Khyber Pass in India. They have taken on a very graceful texture because the erosion has been almost like undersea erosion. These Alabama hills are the oldest mountain range in the world. They have a kind of fantasy and character of their own with these nude-limbed trees. As far as I was concerned, that country was very much worth looking at, and lends itself to the composition of every shot.

What was the budget for the film?

The studio didn't bother me because I was doing them a favor by taking on this thing. They had a budget for the film, but I figured we needed another four hundred thousand dollars to take it outside, so that was agreed to. We had to get started on the costumes right away because we would be shooting in three weeks, and the script wasn't finished. I went to the studio and ordered costumes for five hundred Highlander foot soldiers who had to have kilts. And of course we couldn't do it without five hundred Lancers too. We wanted to do it with three men of equal rank, three NCOs; so we had to use a work battalion in which there wouldn't be an officer in command. We found a British unit called the Queen's Own Sappers and Miners, dug up the details on their uniforms and got costumes for twenty-eight soldiers, and three for the sergeants.

Stevens seems pleased with Douglas Fairbanks, Jr. and Joan Fontaine
as they rehearse a scene for *Gunga Din* in Lone Pine, California (1939).
Ben Hecht and Charles MacArthur wrote the screenplay as an interior story
in a British Army barracks. Stevens agreed to produce and direct it if he could
make it an outdoor picture.

You say the script wasn't finished by the time you started shooting?

The horrible day finally arrived when we got onto the location up at Lone Pine but had nothing on paper, so we started with a big parade-ground drill. You'll notice that scene where the parade ground is covered with soldiers and they're all drilling without horses. We didn't have enough horses, and one of the advisors—a sergeant major—told me they used to drill on foot. I knew it would take a good four hours to get this drill organized, so I put this first scene together where Cary Grant meets Gunga Din, who wants to be a soldier like the other chaps—it ends up with Cutter shouting "dismissed" and the colonel is outraged. It gave us time to organize the parade scene and put a little dialogue together. The scene was scribbled out and the script girl passed out the three necessary copies, one for herself and two for the actors. After lunch the drill was ready. It was like that throughout the picture: writing a day ahead, with me organizing the business from a horse using a public-address system, moving around from one shot to another. There was always a script as far as the spoken word was concerned, at least before we started to rehearse a scene.

What about the fight on the roof?

Well, it required an awful lot of shooting—lots of setups and explosives— and it took me longer to shoot than anybody imagined. I know that the studio got terribly anxious, but I didn't need to know anything about what happened in the next reel or the next fade-in to shoot that fight. It took me, I suppose, ten days to shoot it, setup after setup, and it gave Joel Sayre and Freddie Guiol and me time to try to figure a third of our way through the story so we could move ahead.

Could you tell us about how you decided on particular shots, and how many cameras you used?

I'd like to, but the strange thing about it is that I was so busy figuring out what we were going to do the next day that today's work was improvised. And the easiest thing of all, when you have great locations, is working out which direction you want to see. We laid out all the sets within distance of our camp, so shooting it was never a great problem for me. But it was a problem to keep the audience sitting there for two hours and thirty minutes with a tale as fragile as this one. You depend on the energy of the individual scenes.

We tried to give some romance to the country they were moving around in, the village and this force of Thugee religious cultists. One thing that isn't clear is that the Thugees worshipping the goddess Kali were not associated with other tribes and groups in India. They went their own way and were quite belligerent and self-sufficient. We wanted to create an interest in these people who could ride into town in large numbers, occupy a civilized little village and test the strength of the military platoon system. But the boys in the uniforms are going to be the ones with the superior skills, and given the presumed attitudes of the audiences that are going to gather for this film, they're going to root for the boys from their own culture. The concept of the film was a kind of "Rover Boys in India" adventure. It's an insular film aimed at a narrow stratum of audience. Anglo-Saxon Krauts, I'd say.

What about the structure of the film?

All the natural responses and basic prejudices create excitement—the cops and robbers, the cowboys and Indians, the cavalry and the American Indians, and Hindus with neck scarves versus white Nordic Aryans. I hope the film exceeds the audience's anticipation with its alternate sequences of promise, development and conclusion, plus a good story line that keeps the interest going. The film has a kind of ready-made structure as we move from one thing to another. There are occasional changes of tempo where there is a pause and a regrouping before the film takes off on another thing. I suppose this has to do with not giving the audience too much time to think about things.

When producer Pandro Berman was here, he said that you were avoiding him on the set of the film. Was he right?

I would have been there if he was coming up to bring me some help or something like that, but it happened I'd been working for so many nights on the story and days on the shooting that I was looking forward to finishing the day, and then having Sunday off. I needed that Sunday off very badly. I had sent somebody ahead and got a cabin up the road at Big Pine, back in the hills about four miles, where I could go when I finished work—flee from there, pull myself together a little bit and come back

Monday morning. All of a sudden I see a studio car drive in while I'm making the last shot. I'm coming down to go to my cabin, and it's Pandro. I say, "How are you, Pandro?" and get in my car and leave and come back on Monday morning. I thought he'd stay around till Monday if he was interested in talking, but he didn't.

Did you shoot the sequences in the town on location, or is it a set?

It's a set. We built it—actually we designed it before the script was written. The one thing that's continually at work in the film is the landscape, which is fine to look at. It's organized very well for the camera, much better than many films where studio cameramen went out on location with studio lenses. They used a normal lens and wide-angle lens, but I was using long focal-length lenses to bring Mount Whitney into the background. These visuals go beyond the set itself, and give the audience something rewarding.

There are two night sequences. The one at the very end with the colonel and the night bivouac were shot out in the San Fernando Valley with bonfires burning. The final sequence of the picture was break of day—a cloudy sky with daylight rising above the campfires. So it's all night for night. We used a process shot for the shot of the bridge when the solders are crossing it and beneath is a deep gorge. We had about twelve feet of set with a bridge that left room underneath for a solid matte line, and we built a miniature of a canyon to take care of the rest of it.

The Thugee temple near the village was our creation, even though the cult really existed in areas far from the most populous areas. They isolated themselves and ran their own country their own way. This temple, this kind of a dream, has a gold dome on it, which is not too unreasonable— it could have been a jeweled dome in ancient times. For our purposes it was a gold dome that you could see from a greater distance, and its intrinsic value was apparent to Sergeant Cutter and the other boys.

There seem to be many doors and windows in that set.

It was for no reason other than to relate somewhat to architecture of that hill country south of Afghanistan. It related generally to the Khyber Pass.

What do you think of the use of undercranking the camera when you look at the movie today? I noticed it mostly during the fistfights. It bothered me because I haven't seen that kind of thing in such a long time.

Well, you wouldn't be the first to be bothered by it. I wasn't even aware of the scenes where we expedited matters with a slower crank, though I am aware of it in World War I newsreels with our armies marching, in which they're all doing the Hitler rag. Of course it's possible to adjust the camera speed so you expedite things without creating this false choreography of movement. It has to do with the choreography of fistfights, where everything works and the right people are hit and laid unconscious, and the other people stand upright no matter how hard the blows are. That's part of the pageant of the film.

Gunga Din, with all the hazards that existed there, had a tremendous excitement about it to me. It's cavalry-scale improvisation; not knowing just how you're going to do it the next morning really keeps you alive.

You made Gunga Din *just before the war. Do you think you would have made the film differently today?*

I made it just in time. Another year later and I'd have been too smart to do it, because the film is delightfully evil in the fascist sense. It celebrates the rumble of the drums and the waving of the flags. No one in modern times has done that as well or as with as much grace as the British with their uniforms and stiff salutes and all of that. I really got that film done just before it would have been too late. Yet it wasn't a film of any great presumptions. It wasn't after the Adolph Zukor gold bowl or any of those awards, but it did extremely well with the critics.

I know that you started out working with Laurel and Hardy. Could you talk about comedy in film?

With films like Laurel and Hardy, the filmmaker's existence is maintained by the fact that the audience laughs. If they don't laugh, there is a vacuum, a disaster. Laurel and Hardy were marvelous clowns, but also humanists. Although the story was not always immediately present in their films, their humanism gave them validity. You could watch an audience respond to these structured situations and gags that were premised to eventually evoke a laugh. If the scene gives the audience what they expect, they laugh. So the game is to promise them what they expect, and then give them something they wished they had thought of. Then they really laugh. If it's something utterly beyond their imagination, they ask, "Why didn't

I think of that?" By laying out the mechanics of it as grossly as this, it doesn't take anything away from its artfulness.

Why do you think there are so few contemporary comedies?

Maybe we're not in the mood to laugh with pleasure at our infirmities as much as we were at one time. Maybe we're curious about frailty rather than thinking it's particularly amusing.

You've mentioned the length of your films. After Gone with the Wind *and until* Giant, *I can't think of any film that was that long and successful.*

When you do this, the essential thing is to make sure you're telling a story. I watched films that went beyond two hours. I remember being preoccupied with Griffith's *Birth of a Nation* and with *Gone with the Wind,* which was an extraordinarily effective film. I was caught up in it and could have watched even more. What interested me was the similarity between these two milestone pictures. They were both stories based on events in American history, the Civil War and its aftermath. With both films, the second part—the aftermath—would have been far less rich if it had been by itself.

The original script of *Giant* was by Ivan Moffat, myself and Fred Guiol. It was based on Edna Ferber's novel and was 370 pages. I talked with Edna and she liked the script very much, saying "You know, I wrote this book twice already, and wanted to write it a third time and fill it out. But I think you've done it with the screenplay." This was a surprise assessment from a lady whose novel we were massacring. After finishing the script I made a deal with Warner Bros. to make the film there. Then Freddie and I sat down and worked on cutting the script. We cut it from 370 pages to 250 pages. I think we got it down to 240 pages.

The film runs three hours and nineteen minutes and was made to be screened with an intermission. We had worked on the cut to move it along as fast as possible, but I didn't see how we could keep an audience sitting there for that amount of time without an intermission. The end of the first act is when Jett Rink's oil well comes in, and he arrives in his old rickety truck and confronts his rich friends on the porch, salutes Bick Benedict's wife and gets punched on the chin for his trouble and then hits Bick. It was a good act ending: strong and with promise because things were difficult. The next act started with the oil wells coming in. When we first screened it, we found that somehow or other the pace of the picture meant we could get away without an intermission, and we knew we had to run the picture that way. I would have predicted disaster for *Giant*, because when you have an intermission, people go out and talk about it; then they're anxious to go back in and see the rest of it, and it's not such a burden on them. But the picture went straight through, and it's always been run that way. The picture did extremely well; it had far more audience than any Warner Bros. picture ever had.

The structural development, I believe, is what saves it. It has an excellent structure design, which has to do with the audience anticipating and looking some distance ahead all the way to the finish, which is a reversal on how this kind of story would normally end—in which the hero is heroic. Here the hero is beaten, but his gal likes him. It's the first time she's ever really respected him because he's developed a kind of humility—not instinctive, but beaten into him.

On the *Giant* location in Marfa, Texas, in 1955. Left to right, George Stevens, Jr., Elizabeth Taylor, James Dean and George Stevens, Sr.

Stevens on the set with Rock Hudson, later nominated for an Academy
Award for his performance as Bick Benedict in *Giant* (1956). Hudson
said of working with Stevens, "Just make yourself a piece of putty and
put yourself in his hands."

You did some explosive cutting in one scene in Giant, *something I've never seen,
cutting from extreme long shot to extreme close-up. Did that idea come up in the
cutting room?*

Long beforehand. I wanted to see this dowager woman, Mercedes
McCambridge, on a bucking horse from a great distance—beautiful landscape, straight horizon line, blue sky and distant image of this contest
between a woman and a horse—skirts flying and the horse really breaking
it in two. I wanted to go from the extreme long shot to the spur going

right into the horse's flank, which—if you had sympathy for the woman—gave validity for the horse bucking like that. In two cuts there's a story: how we contribute to our own undoing.

In A Place in the Sun *you play one scene with Elizabeth Taylor and Montgomery Clift almost completely in large close-ups, and you seem to keep jumping over the line—at least two or three times they're facing wrong directions.*

You mean the cuts didn't make orthodox cutting sense? I don't mind doing that if it's not disconcerting. There wasn't much use then of those six-inch lenses I used in the close-ups. I went from one side of the face to the other and created a tempo—as fast as the dialogue could be said, it was said. Monty had that kind of emotion that he got steamed up in it. And Liz is so dissolving when she is looking at you.

I wrote that scene the night before—put it into a dictaphone, gave it to the script girl in the morning. It was typed up and they each got a piece of paper, and the little lady says, "Forgive me. 'Tell Mama.' What the hell is this?" I said, "This is what you're going to say." Elizabeth thought it was outrageous that she had to say that. Reasonable too—I am asking her to jump into a sophistication that is beyond her sophistication at the time. And also non sequitur talk because it was spasmodic. I explained I'd like them to get it in their heads, rehearse it offscreen, then I would get them in there and throw them at one another. I tried to create the sense that this was primitive—the excitement of a preordained meeting where they find one another.

In Gunga Din *you use dissolves primarily for transitions, to lead ahead in time. But in* A Place in the Sun *the dissolves seem to have a purpose beyond merely moving the action ahead.*

In *A Place in the Sun* I was interested in the mood and emotional effect of the story. I wanted the audience to relate to a character [Montgomery Clift as George Eastman] whose behavior it might not subscribe to. To bring that about, one must let the audience see his desire. They have to know his need for the thing that, even accidentally, traps him. So how do you do those things? Cinema, at its most effective, is one scene effectively superseded by the next. Isn't that it? The hatchet on the rope and the guillotine falls in the next cut. We have our electricity that creates a current that blows through a film. When I cut the film I became more

Stevens watches as Elizabeth Taylor and Montgomery Clift rehearse a scene
for *A Place in the Sun* (1951). Clift was nominated for an Oscar as best actor
and Stevens won the Oscar for directing.

and more conscious of the value of one scene against another, and how
this spelled something out. I wanted to edit the film together in a way that
meant more than the addition of one scene to another. I wanted a kind of
energy to flow through. What really interested me was the relationship of
images, from this one to that. Shelley Winters busting at the seams with
sloppy melted ice cream in a brass bed, as against Elizabeth Taylor in a
white gown with blue balloons floating from the sky. Automatically that's
an imbalance, and by imbalance you create drama. I'm interested in
knowing—as visually as it can be stated—what's on this boy's mind.

The film uses overlapping images in a different way from anything else
at that time—dissolves of twenty-five feet with another piece coming in
the middle and going out. In planning those dissolves, we used to have to
draw them with a pencil, foot for foot. If I wanted eighteen feet, I'd have
eighteen feet of scene going out, and then six feet down I'd have the other
scene come in. All with a pencil and a piece of paper, and then hand it to
a guy to take to the laboratory and you'd see your dissolve a few days later.
This point of one visual element against another—it's good cinema.
When you see both at the same time in a dissolve, there is a multifold

effect. It's all about making sure the film bounces off that sheet and comes to life in the mind of the audience. What is a film outside the audience's mind?

———————

Films as Director

1933 *The Cohens and Kellys in Trouble*

1934 *Bachelor Bait*
Kentucky Kernels

1935 *Laddie*
The Nitwits
Alice Adams
Annie Oakley

1936 *Swing Time*

1937 *Quality Street*
A Damsel in Distress

1938 *Vivacious Lady* (also producer)

1939 *Gunga Din* (also producer)

1940 *Vigil in the Night* (also producer)

1941 *Penny Serenade* (also producer)

1942 *Woman of the Year* (also producer)

The Talk of the Town (also producer)

1943 *The More the Merrier* (also producer)

1948 *I Remember Mama* (also producer)

1951 *A Place in the Sun* (also producer)

1952 *Something to Live For* (also producer)

1953 *Shane* (also producer)

1956 *Giant* (also producer)

1959 *The Diary of Anne Frank* (also producer)

1965 *The Greatest Story Ever Told* (also producer and co-screenplay)

1970 *The Only Game in Town* (also producer)

One fellow said to me, "Where could I get some books or some-thing to study composition?" And I said, "Go to the comic pages on Sundays. There are some of the greatest artists in the world. Big heads in the foreground, people in the background."

WILLIAM CLOTHIER
(Born in Decatur, Illinois, 1903—Died 1996)

William Clothier was a cameraman of the great outdoors and a specialist in aerial photography. His career and his AFI seminar compensate for a notable omission in this book—the absence of a conversation with John Ford. Ford was the first recipient of the AFI Life Achievement Award but never made it to AFI for a seminar. Clothier's close association with Ford presents an opportunity to consider the latter's work, especially *Cheyenne Autumn,* which Clothier photographed and which was screened before his seminar.

Clothier was born in Decatur, Illinois, and joined the army at age sixteen when World War I started. He landed in Texas after the war, working in con-struction, but soon lost interest and rode the rails to Los Angeles, where he found a job working in the scenery department at Warner Bros. He devel-oped a fascination with photography and in 1926 managed to get hired as one of seventeen assistant cameramen on William Wellman's *Wings,* mainly because he convinced the production manager that he knew every girl in San Antonio, where the picture was to be shot.

In the early days of Hollywood young camera assistants often moved through the ranks to the role of head cameraman in short order, but it took Clothier more time than most. His work as an assistant and camera operator during the twenties and thirties exposed him to leading directors ranging from William Wellman and Ernst Lubitsch, to Wesley Ruggles and Joseph von Sternberg. When he had trouble getting a job in 1933 because of a strike in Hollywood, he found work in Mexico. Then he got a job shooting news-reels in Spain during the Spanish Civil War until he was jailed by the gov-ernment. He returned to the United States in 1939 and was the operator for Joe August on George Stevens' *Gunga Din.* During World War II he was a commissioned officer in the Eighth Air Force, where he flew camera missions in B-17s and photographed *The Memphis Belle,* Lt. Col. William Wyler's documentary about a bomber crew flying over Germany.

Clothier was discharged with the rank of colonel and returned to Hollywood where finally, at age forty-five, he got his first assignment as a director of photography. For the next twenty-five years he held a place in the top rank of Hollywood cameramen. He shot pictures for William Wellman, including *Island in the Sky, The High and the Mighty, Track of the Cat, Darby's Rangers, A Distant Trumpet* and *Lafayette Escadrille.* He worked with John Ford on *The Horse Soldiers, The Man Who Shot Liberty Valance, Donovan's Reef* and *Cheyenne Autumn.* He shot fifteen pictures with John Wayne and was for many years under exclusive contract to Wayne's production company, Batjac. It's the lot of the Hollywood cameraman to serve the director, and Clothier served many of the best: Howard Hawks, Frank Borzage, John Farrow, Sam Fuller, Michael Curtiz, Raoul Walsh, Gene Kelly and Sam Peckinpah. He said that he quickly learned that it was pointless to fight with directors. "If John Ford told me to put the camera upside down," he said, "I'd put the camera upside down. It's the director's prerogative."

William Clothier had a long apprenticeship as an assistant cameraman. It wasn't until after he returned from World War II, where he photographed *The Memphis Belle* for William Wyler, that he received his first assignment as director of photography.

Clothier excelled in both black-and-white and color photography. He did a masterful job in black and white for Ford on *The Man Who Shot Liberty Valance* and was equally adept using color to capture the scope and texture of the West in *Cheyenne Autumn.* "I always felt that black and white is more difficult to shoot than color," he said. "You have to make your own contrast with light and shadows, while color gives you apparent shadows." Clothier was also a colorful raconteur and added to the salty lore of John Ford, remembering the director's reaction when he would see someone pointing at something on the set: "Don't point! You only point at pastry, prostitutes and producers."

Clothier was a student of the Western art of Frederick Remington and Charles Russell, and prided himself on his own skill at composition. He understood that a cameraman's life is one of early-morning calls and long days, and he was known for pushing himself in service to whatever picture he was working on. As he put it, "I never saw the mountain I wouldn't climb if I thought I could make my shot better."

WILLIAM CLOTHIER

———◆———

May 11, 1974

Bill Clothier photographed Cheyenne Autumn, *the picture you have just seen. I was really impressed with Bill's day-for-night. You can learn from this picture that you don't have to use flat lighting exteriors. They were all modeled. Bill didn't use reflectors; he took eight arc lights with him. Most production managers want you to take reflectors and no lights.*

Cheyenne Autumn was, in my opinion, a very fine film by John Ford. Ford is a great director, not only Westerns but all kinds of pictures, so it was a pleasure for me to do this film. I always enjoyed working with Jack Ford. He's a cameraman's director in that he's come to me on many occasions and said, "Bill, why don't you do so and so?" And I found out eighty-five percent of the time that he was right. He had a better idea maybe than I had. Or he was willing to say, "We won't do this shot now. We'll wait, because later on in the afternoon, we're going to get good backlight and we'll make a better job out of it."

Cheyenne Autumn was done in seventy millimeter. It was a bit of a hassle at times, getting big cameras around in the sand. However, at no time did the old man say, "Let's hurry up," or "Let's get this over with." He'd just sit in his chair and let you do your job and never bother you.

Where was the film shot?

A good bit of it was shot in Monument Valley. The river stuff was out of Moab, Utah. And the snow sequences and the old fort, which is an old

museum and was originally an army fort built during the Indian wars—
that was up in Gunnison, Colorado. We were up there around the beginning of December for three or four weeks. And then we shot a lot of stuff
at the Warner Bros. studios. In fact, the last sequence in the picture was
shot the day that John Kennedy was assassinated. We had a couple of
more shots to go and the old man said, "Let's wrap it up and go home."

*There was a shot where they were dragging the Indian chief along with a horse,
and another horse appears in the foreground. Was that your idea or John Ford's?*

I just don't know whether it was my idea or Ford's idea. In many instances,
these things just happen. We were operating with two or three cameras,
and we had a second unit that worked with us. Once in a while, they'd go
out and shoot something, but as a rule, I used their cameras. You have a
trek and you have a lot of people coming toward the cameras and past the
cameras. Actually, you don't know where they're going to go. They're
extras. They're Indians. They're on horses and they're told to walk past the
camera. Some of them go behind the camera, walk on the camera and go
over it.

Did Ford ever shoot things with more than one camera?

We always did in a situation like this. When we're shooting dialogue, we
would use one camera only. But where you have a lot of horses and movement, it's always advantageous to set up several cameras. You save a lot of
time.

You had a lot of footage you didn't use.

I'll tell you one thing—when you make a John Ford picture, you just cut
the slates off and patch it together, because he never shot any superfluous
film. On several occasions, I said to Jack, "Don't you want a close-up?"
And he said, "If I shoot a close-up, they'll use it."

What was the ratio of film that you shot to what you used?

Compared with other directors I've worked with, the old man shoots a
sequence and knows every cut he wants. Sometimes he won't even go all

the way through the master shots. He'll move right in and get a couple of close-ups and that's the sequence. I remember years ago we had John Wayne and Fonda, McLaglen and someone else—George O'Brien, I think. Four people on the set. We shot the sequence in one shot, just a long shot. We never did any close-ups, no cuts of any kind.

Did Ford go in for a lot of second unit work?

The old man shoots almost everything himself. Occasionally, he'll let a second unit director do a shot of the train coming across the railroad bridge. That was a trick shot by a second unit, in Arizona. They had shot the train on location, we built the superstructure in the studio and then they put it together in the trick department.

Were you working five days or six days a week?

We worked six days a week. I must say that working with John Ford was a pleasure because he'd come in at nine o'clock, and about three o'clock the day's work was over. At the studio, the producer, Bernard Smith, came to the old man and said, "Jack Warner thinks you should work until about four-thirty anyway." And the old man said, "He does?" "Yes." "Okay. We'll work until four-thirty." So the next morning I'm waiting at nine o'clock, and the old man doesn't show. And at about ten o'clock, he came into the studio and the producer is sitting around chewing his fingernails and wondering what the devil had happened to the old man. And Ford walks up to Bernie and he says, "You know, this stupid chauffeur of mine got lost on the freeway." And he said, "I wound up way on the other side of town." So that day we worked until four o'clock. The next day, he came in at nine and we worked until three.

In one matte shot, I saw a tearing effect, but I'm sure your average audience will never notice a thing like that.

Any technician, I'm sure, would be able to. You ladies and gentlemen can too, because you're making a study of the motion picture industry. But the public, if they go in there, they don't even look at the photography. They go in and look at the actors. Or they're like my daughter, who said, "Is Pat Wayne in this picture?" She's only interested in seeing Pat Wayne, and wouldn't know anything about matte shots.

I noticed there was a lot of detail in the composition of some shots. Was this strictly your idea, or was it John Ford's?

I couldn't take anything away from Jack Ford, but I've always sort of prided myself on knowing composition, something I don't think you can study. I think it either comes natural to you or you don't have it. Now, in years past I've had a couple of camera operators that just never understood composition. One fellow said to me, "Well, where could I get some books or something to study composition?" And I said, "Go to the comic pages on Sundays. There are some of the greatest artists in the world. Big heads in the foreground, people in the background." I remember one time when I was an operator, working with Joe August, a very fine cinematographer, when we had the cameras down on the floor and we were shooting up and there was a big arch up there. And he got down and looked through the camera. I took it over and he was cutting the top of the arch off. I called Joe over and I said, "Joe, do you mind if I tip up and get the top of the arch?" He said, "No. If it looks good to you, I'm sure it will look good to a lot of other people." And later he said to me, "You know, when I look through the camera, I'm not setting the composition for you. You go ahead and set it the way you want it."

Clothier (far right) worked often with John Ford. Here he stands in black cap
with his hand on Ford's chair as Ford stages a fight between James Stewart
and John Wayne for *The Man Who Shot Liberty Valance* (1962).

I've been working with Ford the same way. Sometimes I called Ford over to the camera—when I was an operator—and said, "Jack, I think this is a better composition." And he'd say, "I think you're right." Or on occasion he'd say, "No, it may be better, but I don't want that." A lot of times you get nothing to photograph. So you roll in a wagon or put a weed in or a bush or a rock in the foreground or frame from a shadow or something of that sort.

I remember when we did *The Alamo,* John Wayne and I went down to look at the Alamo. And Duke said to me, "Jesus, Bill, there's no composition here." I said, "Duke, wait until we dress the set. We'll have cannons, we'll have wagons." Well, he didn't understand that. And when we got the set dressed and we had wagons out in the foreground and horses and people, we had a good frame. I think every time you look through a camera, you should keep in mind that it's got to be an interesting picture. There aren't any rules. It's about what looks good and is pleasing to the eye and what sells the story best. Having a good camera operator helps. If the cameraman has an operator who really has an eye for composition, he tells him the most important things and leaves him alone. It's a matter of communication. He has to know how to tell his operator what he wants. A cameraman can sure watch a scene a heck of a lot better if he isn't having to watch for composition and other problems.

When Ford shot in seventy millimeter, did he compose the shots in more depth?

Monument Valley has always been a favorite location of his. At no time prior to this picture did the old man really have an opportunity to show Monument Valley on a big screen with wide film. I think that sold him on the idea more than anything else. In seventy millimeter, we get things that you can't get in thirty-five millimeter, and I'm sure you can't get in sixteen millimeter.

I remember one scene in The Alamo *that showed the Mexican army coming up, and you showed the whole vista.*

We pulled a trick there too. We had about twelve hundred head of horses. And we had about three thousand extras. We had something like two thousand of them dressed in Mexican uniforms, and we split the screen four ways so when you saw it on the screen, there were sixteen thousand people. And a hell of a lot of horses. We just set the camera up and blocked out a portion of the film. We put all these troops in one quarter of the screen. Then we blocked out that quarter of the screen and opened the second quarter of the screen. We put all of our troops in. We cranked the film back and ran it through the camera again. It took us all day to make this one shot. Then in the lab it was put together. As you recall, it looked like the biggest army in the world.

Is the reason you did it that way because of the huge group of people?

No, money was the reason. You just couldn't get ten thousand horses and fifteen thousand people together to save your life. You couldn't control or feed that many people. The logistics would be out of the question.

I understand that Ford wouldn't let the water wagon onto the set. Why?

The old man said, "Two things make Western pictures: horse manure and dust." And I remember one time, when I was an operator, some camera-man got a water wagon, and Ford blew his top. He was going to fire the guy. The guy said, "We'll have dust." And Ford said, "Hell, that's why I came out here. I want the dust!" And dust, especially in backlight, is ter-rific. It adds to the drama. I rarely use a water wagon. I've had actors scream because they get their eyes full of dust, including John Wayne. He'll say, "I can't see in the dust." I said, "Well, the script said they want dust and wind, so we've got wind machines and we've got dust. Close your eyes or get a double."

With all that dust in the desert on Cheyenne Autumn, *did you have to cover the lens after every shot?*

We always had a camera mechanic. He would come on the set around two o'clock in the afternoon and probably work until midnight. We would shoot through the dust on the lens. You can pile a quarter of an inch of dust on the lens and shoot, and it might soften it a little bit. The amount of dust you get on the lens can't hurt it much. I've had water hit the lens, and actually it might help. Sometimes you get a good effect out of it. You'll never get any dust on the filter if it's in back of the lens. But if you put that filter in front of the lens, then you'll create electricity and static, and the dust will just pull into it and you'll actually pick up more dust than you would on the lens. I've made Westerns all my life, and I've never seen enough dust on a lens to change a situation photographically. I've had horses run over me with the dust so thick it blocks out the picture. But when it was all over with, it never hurt the lens any. You can take a camel's hairbrush and just wipe it off and that's the end of that.

You once said that with Cheyenne Autumn *you had the misfortune of coming out the same year as* My Fair Lady *and Jack Warner put all the publicity behind the Oscar campaign for* My Fair Lady.

Yes, I called the Publicity Department and asked them if they'd get behind my picture. And they said, "No, Mr. Warner is not interested in this picture." He had only five million dollars in *Cheyenne Autumn* and sixteen million in *My Fair Lady*. So he wanted *My Fair Lady*, and I don't blame him. He wanted to get as many awards as he could for that film. I know he figured Ford's picture would make its money back, but when you've got sixteen million dollars in a picture, you have to do everything you can to get your money out of it, so he just told everybody in the studio, "It's *My Fair Lady*—forget *Cheyenne Autumn*."

Is it true that Joe August used to shoot a lot of lights into the lens?

I can tell you something that he did. In the labs they pull film by overexposing and putting the red light on and what have you. Joe August did this thirty years ago on the set. We were making *Gunga Din* and we had the big temple built out in the Alabama hills. And they had a tunnel in this temple which was, I don't know, forty or fifty feet running all the way through this thing. George Stevens wanted a shot inside of it and there was no way to light the thing, because if you got lights back here they were in the way of the camera. So old Joe took a couple of lights. He had a suitcase full of junk that he worked with. It was baling wire and spit and heavy red gauze. He must have had thirty feet of it, rolled up on a spool, like you find in department stores. He took a piece of this and set it up in front of the camera, at about this distance, my eye being the lens. And he set a lamp on the floor and he hit that gauze with the light, keeping the light off of the front of the camera. We shot through that gauze and you saw these two figures come into the foreground. And, by God, he had the light on their faces. And it came from the light that was hitting this gauze.

I remember Joe walked on the set one time with Gregory LaCava. I don't remember what the picture was, but they had a cyclorama, I think, of a village below San Francisco or something, and they wanted to shoot a night sequence. So he went around and cut holes in it and made windows and put lights back there, and it was fantastic. He used to do the damnedest things. He made a picture called *Edith Cavell,* about that nurse the Germans captured and killed. Anyway, the producer was an English producer over at RKO. Before the picture started, the producer called him in and he said, "Now, Mr. August, when the Germans bring this girl out and they're going to execute her, I want a halo around her head." Joe said, "Okay." And later, the producer went to Joe and said, "Joe, you know that scene I was telling you about?" And Joe said, "What scene?" He said, "You know, where they bring Edith Cavell out and they're going to shoot her?" And he said, "Oh, yes. What about it?" He said, "Well, you know, I want a halo around her head." Joe said, "Okay." So a couple of weeks later they're getting ready to shoot and the producer goes to Joe and said, "Have you figured out how to put a halo around her head?" And Joe said, "No." The producer left him and went down to see Sid Rogell, who was running the studio, and said, "I don't know what to think about this man. I've told him about this thing four times." And Sid said, "Well, why don't you wait until you see what he does. He may do something."

So they came on the set, and the producer's there, and he said to Joe, "How are you going to make this shot?" And Joe said, "What? I don't know what you're talking about." The producer says, "The halo around her head." Joe says, "Oh, that," and he walks over and picks up a piece of cellophane and says, "Give me an oil can." And somebody gives him an oil can. He squirts some on the cellophane and says to his assistant, "Put this in the camera." And the producer walks off the set, saying, "This guy is crazy." Naturally, Joe didn't put it in the camera, but he figured out how to do this and when it came on the screen, it was exactly what the English producer had in mind. But this was Joe August. He did stunts like that, and in those days you didn't have all the trick departments we have today. We did a lot of things that cameramen don't have to do today. They've got specialists to do these things.

How about telling us a few things about how you shoot day-for-night, because Cheyenne Autumn *has some of the best day-for-night I've seen.*

I'm normally shooting day-for-night, because I've found, especially in color, it's so difficult to avoid skies and stay away from blue colors. Blue is blue—it doesn't make any difference how much you stop the lens down. If you've got a blue shirt it's going to look blue on the screen, and it won't look like night. I learned that on a picture with Duke Wayne called *The Sea Chase*. So when we got ready to do *Cheyenne Autumn*, I said to Ford, "Look, we're staying at Goulding's in Monument Valley. We can build this set right outside of our quarters and shoot it at night." This is the breakout scene at the beginning of the picture, when the Indians make their escape. He said, "I won't shoot it at night. We're going to do it in the daytime." He said, "Why don't you shoot some tests?" So I shot some tests and sent them over to Giff Chamberlain at Technicolor, and I talked to Leon Shamroy, a great cameraman. He told me, "Bill, I made a mistake on *South Pacific* by putting some colors in. I thought I would like it, and I'm stuck with it. Don't ever try that."

I knew enough about color that if you want something red, you just go to the lab and say, "Let's build the red up and hold down the other colors." But this day-for-night stuff is a little difficult. And I had seen some night stuff that Shamroy shot on *South Pacific*, and Giff told me that they put a lot of green in it and it gave a good effect. Now, out there in the desert, in Monument Valley, everything is red. I had red men and I had red hills. The sand is red, the rocks are red and there's a blue sky. So we fooled around in the lab on two or three occasions and when we were ready to make the picture, we went out to the desert and I said to the old man, "Why don't we do it here?" And he said, "No, I won't do it!" So we started to shoot this sequence and I'm just about ready to make a shot and Wingate Smith, who was John Ford's brother-in-law, came to me and said, "The old man wants to see you." So I went over to see Jack, and he was sitting in his chair chewing on his handkerchief, as he always did, with a patch over his eye. And I squatted down by his chair and he looked at me and said, "I'm worried." I said, "What are you worried about?" He said, "I'm worried about shooting this stuff for night in the daytime." I said "It's a little late, isn't it?" "Well," he said, "what are you going to do about it?" I said, "I think I know how to handle it. And if you'll let me alone, it will be all right."

For three days we worked there and the old man never bothered me. We're out in the middle of the desert where there's absolutely nothing. I talked to Giff Chamberlain and I said, "Now, look, these rocks are red and the people are red. And I've used strong cross lights and backlight and I've got as many shadows as I can. And wherever I had a fire, I put it in a dark corner, so that you could see the flames." And then Giff Chamberlain took it into the lab and he took out a lot of red by printing it on the cold side and using more green than blue, and I saw to it that there wasn't anything blue on the set. If there was an Indian that had a blue jacket, I called the wardrobe people and said, "Give him a black jacket or a gray jacket." And that's the way we did the sequence and it worked out pretty well.

Did you do anything to the sky?

I just stayed away from it as much as I could. I think there was one shot where I had some sky in it, but it wasn't bad. It was a deep blue sky. And I think I got a scrim—a thin black net to use on lights and lamps—and brought the scrim down over the top of that and held it back, and held that sky down.

In the old days, they used to burn holes in the gauze with their cigarettes.

Well, I quit smoking, so I can't tell you.

Did you ever sit down with Ford and have him talk about the kind of feeling he wanted from the picture visually?

He would whistle and say, "Sit down, I want to talk to you." And he'd say, "This is what we're going to do. Bill, this is what I'd like to have." I won't mention the cameraman's name, but Ford made a picture with a cameraman who shot a scene under protest and ended up winning an Academy Award. And I'll tell you another thing about old man Ford. Many years ago I was an operator on *Fort Apache,* and my very dearest friend was the cameraman, Archie Stout. Archie was a rough, tough guy and he'd argue with God. He got into an argument with the old man and he said, "I won't shoot it." It was something with backlighting and he refused to shoot it. So I climbed off the parallel, and old man Ford came over and he put his arm around me and said, "I want you to tell that old s.o.b. never to tell me that he won't shoot something, because if I ask a cameraman to shoot something and it isn't any good, I'll be the first one to take it out of the picture. I won't use it." And I said, "I'll tell him."

Many years later I was doing a picture with Ford called *Donovan's Reef,* and we were in the islands and we had two days' work left, a day-for-night scene, and the old man said, "We're going to shoot tomorrow." We got up the next morning and there was a solid overcast. You're just beating your head against the wall. So we waited until lunchtime. We had lunch and the old man came to me, chewing on his handkerchief, and said, "Bill, I'm not going to wait any longer." I said, "Jack, it won't be any good." He said, "We'll shoot it. It'll be all right." I said, "All right, if you want, I'll shoot it." I learned never to tell a director I wouldn't shoot it. If he wants the camera upside down, I'll say, "Fine. All we've got to waste is the film." So we shot the sequence. It would have been magnificent day-for-night, but this was horrible. So we got up the following morning and the weather hadn't changed and we finished the sequence at about three o'clock in the afternoon.

I did everything I could to make this look halfway decent. So after we left the islands and came back to Paramount, I went to look at the rushes. The old man would never look at the rushes. I went down to the projection room at lunchtime and Otho Lovering was cutting this picture. I said to him, "Did you see this stuff?" I didn't tell him what I thought of it. He said, "Yes." I said, "How was it?" He said, "Terrible. Why the hell did you shoot it?" I said, "The old man asked me to shoot it." So we ran this film and it was just what I expected it to be. It was bad.

Now, the old man never ate lunch. He never left the set—he'd just stay there during lunch. I walked up to him and he said, "How was the stuff?" And I told him, and he said, "You're just prejudiced! It's probably all right!" I said, "Jack, it isn't any good. Talk to Otho Lovering." So he said, "Go ahead and light your set." So I'm lighting the set and I saw Otho come in, and he walked over to the old man and talked to him for a few minutes and then left. I went over to Jack and I said, "What did Otho have to say?" "He said, 'It's not very good, but we can use it.'" And I said, "Jack, I remember a long time ago you telling me that if you asked a cameraman to shoot something and he didn't want to shoot it, you'd be the first one to take it out of the picture. You can't use this in the picture, it's terrible." And the old man looked at me with that one eye, his handkerchief in his mouth, and he said, "Was that *Fort Apache?*" And I said "Yes, it was." He remembered telling me this twenty years ago. And he said, "Bill, I need this sequence like I need a hole in my head. I'll cut it out of the picture, we'll rewrite it and we'll shoot the scene right along this fence here on the stage. That'll take the place of that sequence."

So that's the kind of a gentleman Jack Ford was. When you're on the set, say to the director, "All you've got to lose is the film and the time, but if you want to do it, we'll do it." And old Joe August told me many years ago that he shot something under protest, and it turned out to be great. He said, "I learned a lesson. If I tell my director it isn't going to be any good, I'm going to make damned sure it's no good. If you're a cameraman, you can do that. But in this instance, I tried my best to make it good." In my case I knew it wouldn't be good and that Ford wouldn't use it. But with other directors, I think I would've followed Joe's advice. If you say it's not going to be any good, be damned sure it's not going to be any good.

How did Ford feel about shooting epic films, like Cheyenne Autumn? *Was he comfortable working with big budgets?*

I can assure you of one thing: Mr. Ford wanted to do it or he would never have done it. There's only one way to make a Ford picture and that's Ford's way. When he made *The Man Who Shot Liberty Valance,* they wanted to make it in color and the old man said, "No, I'm not going to do it in color. I'm going to do it in black and white. It won't be right if it's done in color." I wanted to do it in color. But we made it in black and white, and it was great.

What kind of qualities did Ford want in a cameraman?

When I was an operator and we were working in Monument Valley, Ford used to say to me, "Okay, Bill, let's put the camera there." And I'd put the camera there. The director of photography would come over and say, "Bill, I don't like the camera there. Let's move it over here fifteen feet." So we'd move the camera. This went on a couple of times, and each time, when the old man would get ready to go, he would come over and look through the camera, and he'd say, "Is this where I told you to put the camera?" I'd say, "No, I moved it." He said, "Well, bring it back here." So about the third or fourth time this happened, I said to the cameraman, "Look, every time you move the camera six inches, he knows you've moved it. So the next time I'll move it, but by God, you tell him you moved it." So I moved the camera and Ford came over and he said, "What's the camera doing over here?" About this time the director of photography spoke up and said, "I moved it over there." Ford said, "Bill, bring it back. I want it over here!"

I learned working with him that if I wanted to move it, if I saw something that I thought would be better, I'd say to Jack, "I've got an idea. Will you come and look through the camera?" He'd say, "Sure." He'd come over, look through the camera, and I'd say, "I'd like to move it over here because I get a little better composition." He'd say, "All right, go ahead." Or he would say, "No, I want it here. And this is the reason." And he'd have a good reason. So he was pretty set about those things. He would tell you where he wanted the camera and then you could move your people around. You could build roads or anything else that you wanted. But if he wanted a camera here, he wanted the camera there, and that was the end of that.

How do you work with your gaffer on the lighting?

A gaffer knows more about light than I do. I know the camera, but he knows the lights. I would say to a gaffer when I walked on the set, "This is the way I want this set lit. I want some strong lights coming through those windows. I want a soft side on the left-hand side and let them go through some shadows," and I'd sit down and watch him go to work. If he was halfway through and he was doing something I didn't like, I told him so. I only had two gaffers in twenty-five years. I'd say, "Ralph, I don't like this." He'd say, "I get paid coming or going," and he'd start all over again and do it my way. I know some cameramen who will go and move a light, but I don't do that.

How do you deal with the laboratories?

I always look at the first print. Then I say, "This isn't what I was looking for. I want something else." And then they give us another print. At John Wayne's company—I've made all of their films—I have a free hand and I can say, "I don't like this." And Technicolor will take a reel and do it over and over again until it's the way I want it. If it's bad, then it's my fault. There are some times when you can't get the effect you want. Sometimes it's lack of time and sometimes the light changes on you, or you start a sequence and it goes wrong throughout the day. Or maybe you come back the next day and the sky is overcast. Today, it costs forty to fifty thousand dollars a day to operate a picture company. You can't say, "Well, we won't shoot today." That doesn't work too well. So you've got to figure out something. You go inside and work, or you shoot close-ups and hold back your long shots until you get better weather.

On some of those interiors you had on Cheyenne Autumn, *if you had a chance to do it over again, would you do it the same way?*

I'll answer your question this way—in all of the years I've been in the business, I think I've only made one shot in my life that when I see it on the screen I couldn't improve on. I think if you have any imagination, you see your work and think, this would have been better if I'd have done this or that. I think it's like an artist painting a picture. He sits around, he paints a picture, and then he puts it away and he starts on another one. I have a very dear friend who's a very fine Western artist, and around his house he's got twenty pictures on the wall—none of them finished. He just keeps looking at them, figuring them out. He doesn't want to finish them. I think you can improve everything you do.

One last question. How much time did Ford spend with his actors?

Ford spent time with his actors all day long. Between scenes, he'd take his actors and they'd go off in the shade someplace and sit down and he'd tell them what he had in mind, how he thought they should play a scene. He'd spend nearly an hour having tea with the actors. They'd tell jokes, and he'd talk to them about the picture. He loved actors. But if you heard him talking to John Wayne, you'd swear to God he hated him.

━━◆━━

Films as Cinematographer

1927 *Wings*
1931 *Fanny Foley Herself*
    Peach-O-Reno
1932 *Men of Chance*
    Ladies of the Jury
    What Price Hollywood?
1933 *King Kong*
    Flying Devils
    One Man's Journey
1944 *The Memphis Belle*
1946 *The Gay Cavalier*
    Behind the Mask
1947 *High Tide*

1948 *For You I Die*
    Sofia
1950 *Once a Thief*
1951 *Air Cadet*
1952 *Confidence Girl*
    One Minute to Zero
1953 *Phantom from Space*
    Island in the Sky
1954 *Killers from Space*
    The High and the Mighty
    Track of the Cat
1955 *Gang Busters*
    Top of the World

1955 *The Sea Chase*
      Blood Alley
      Sincerely Yours
1956 *Good-Bye, My Lady*
      Seven Men from Now
      Gun the Man Down
      Man in the Vault
1957 *Dragoon Wells Massacre*
      Bombers B-52
1958 *Darby's Rangers*
      Fort Dobbs
      Lafayette Escadrille
      China Doll
1959 *Escort West*
      The Horse Soldiers
1960 *The Alamo*
1961 *Tomboy and the Champ*
      The Deadly Companions
      Ring of Fire
      The Comancheros
1962 *The Man Who Shot Liberty
      Valance*

      Merrill's Marauders
1963 *Donovan's Reef*
      McLintock!
1964 *A Distant Trumpet*
      Cheyenne Autumn
1965 *Shenandoah*
1966 *The Rare Breed*
      Stagecoach
      Way . . . Way Out
1967 *The War Wagon*
      The Way West
1968 *Firecreek*
      The Devil's Brigade
      Bandolero!
      Hellfighters
1969 *The Undefeated*
1970 *The Cheyenne Social Club*
      Chisum
      Rio Lobo
1971 *Big Jake*
1973 *The Train Robbers*

I think students must be taught to visualize, they have to learn there is a rectangle up there and it has to be filled. Personally I never look through the camera. What for? To find out whether the camera is lying?

ALFRED HITCHCOCK
(Born in London, England, 1899—Died 1980)

Though born and bred in England, Alfred Hitchcock became the most famous of Hollywood filmmakers. His trademark cameo appearances not only made him a public figure, they caused many audience members to become aware of the role of the film director for the first time—to be conscious as never before that there was a guiding intelligence behind the movies they were seeing. Hitchcock's on-screen introductions to his long-running *Alfred Hitchcock Presents* television series made him a familiar face in America's living rooms before he extended his brand to magazines and books of suspense stories. Yet, despite this commercialization of his persona and his work, when it came to making motion pictures he remained an artist to the end.

Hitchcock was a student of the medium in its early days, examining the psychology of screen storytelling and developing a precise understanding of the interplay between director and audience. He reduced it to the idea of visualization—the image that would fill the *white rectangle*—and believed his most important work was accomplished before he set foot on the sound stage. "Why, improvising on the set is like a composer composing with a full orchestra in front of him and saying, 'Flute, will you give me a note?'" He wanted an emotional response from the audience, and went so far as to say, "I'm not interested in content at all. I don't give a damn what the film is about."

I met Hitchcock in 1958 when he asked me to direct episodes of *Alfred Hitchcock Presents* at Universal. This was a hugely productive period for him, the era of *Vertigo, Psycho* and *North by Northwest.* His high standards carried over to the television series. While he relied heavily on his capable producer,

Alfred Hitchcock with his wife, Alma Reville, the cowriter of *Notorious* (1946)
and a valued counselor throughout his career.

Joan Harrison, he put his stamp on the series by insisting on careful preparation of scripts, adding his own touch here and there in the editing room and directing episodes from time to time.

I gained two insights in looking back on his career. The first was an observation by Ingmar Bergman, who in discussing his own need for agility and mobility when directing, speculated on how Hitchcock must have suffered from being overweight. He said, "Much of Hitchcock's limitations, I think, but also his greatness within them, are to be found in his heavy body. His way of always working in the studio, using a static camera, not moving about—he has erected it all into a system of using long scenes where he won't have to give himself the trouble of having to move about." Bergman's observation ties in to Hitchcock's declaration that the actual shooting of a film is his least important contribution.

The second was a new sense of Hitchcock as a person. I had seen him as detached, ironic and impersonal, so I was surprised by his remarks when he accepted the Life Achievement Award in 1979. By then Hitch had great difficulty walking, and instead of his going to the stage, I came to his table to present the award. He stood with some difficulty, with his wife seated beside him; listened impassively to a prolonged standing ovation; then took the AFI Silver Star and surreptitiously tucked it under his tuxedo jacket—getting an enormous laugh. He then asked permission to mention by name "only four people" who had given him the most encouragement and constant collaboration.

> The first of the four is a film editor; the second is a scriptwriter; the third is the mother of my daughter, Pat; and the fourth is as fine a cook as ever performed miracles in a domestic kitchen. And their names are Alma Reville. Had the beautiful Miss Reville not accepted a lifetime contract—without options—as Mrs. Alfred Hitchcock some fifty-three years ago, Mr. Alfred Hitchcock might be in this room tonight, not at this table but as one of the slower waiters on the floor. I share my award, as I have my life, with her.

Hitch would die the next year, at the age of eighty, with Alma at his side, leaving behind a legacy of films that bore his unmistakable stamp and that would outlive him to frighten future generations.

ALFRED HITCHCOCK

—▶—

February 3, 1970*

In Sabotage, *when somebody suddenly kills Oscar Homolka, there's a film about a bird called* Who Killed Cock Robin? *being shown. In* Psycho, *Tony Perkins stuffs birds and also his mother, and in* The Birds, *in the crosscut shot of the mother grabbing at the son and also the girlfriend grabbing at the son, he's surrounded by all these birds. I'm wondering if there is a connection you make between birds and women.*

I don't know. I think women are referred to as chicks, aren't they? That's the only connection I can think of at the moment. In *Who Killed Cock Robin?* you see, they ran a small movie house and Sylvia Sidney's little brother had been killed, so it seemed necessary to comment on it by using the cinema. The Disney cartoon *Who Killed Cock Robin?* seemed to lend itself to that association. It's a personal thing with me to utilize the setting and the circumstances, and relate them to the situation.

Could you elaborate on how you use the setting and the circumstance in this way?

It really is a matter of utilizing your material to the fullest dramatic extent. For example, in *Rear Window,* James Stewart is a photographer, so naturally he fends off his attacker with the use of photographic material, such as a flashgun. That's only because it is indigenous to him. As far as I possibly can, I always insist on using those elements that belong to the character and involve them in the actions of the story. In *North by Northwest,*

*This transcript contains segments from the roundtable discussion at the AFI's Center for Advanced Film Studies' University Advisory Committee Seminar on August 18, 1972.

Cary Grant is trapped in an auction room. He can't get out except one way, and that is bidding, crazy bidding, and he gets himself thrown out. But the essential point is that he is in an auction room and you must use the auction room. Now, in that same film there was a final sequence on the faces at Mount Rushmore. Due to the objections of the government, we weren't allowed to have any of the figures over the faces. We were told very definitely that you could only have the figures slide down between the heads. They said this is the shrine of democracy. What I wanted to do, and was prevented from doing, was to have Cary Grant slide down Lincoln's nose and hide in the nostril. Then I wanted Cary Grant to have a sneezing fit. That is a typical example of utilizing your material to the fullest. This is a personal thing with me. As often as I can I incorporate, down to the last detail, the elements of the scene into the film.

This reminds me a little of the opening of I Confess. *In order to get to the window, where we see the murdered man, you have all the street signs. Do you also do this kind of thing with geography?*

Yes, any use you can put it to. What we were doing in that opening was using the street signs which said, "Direction, direction." They point and point, and it was a way of leading the audience right to the dead body.

In The Man Who Knew Too Much *you open in the back of the bus. Could you describe what you were doing in terms of the audience?*

I think that was the introduction of the character. There are moments where you have to use a certain amount of footage to introduce the character. In that particular case you don't just introduce them by small talk. You have a little boy wondering and accidentally pulling the veil off. You need some piece of action that would be interesting to look at rather than just "This is John Smith, this is his wife and this is his son." In other words, it's like all exposition—it's a pill that has to be sugarcoated. You are telling the audience something, giving them some piece of information, but it must appear to be something else.

You indicated in the Truffaut book* that if you don't give the audience the who, what, where and when—the journalistic musts—that it interferes with the sus-

---

*Hitchcock by François Truffaut (Simon and Schuster, 1985).

pense and the emotional process. They will intellectually be trying to figure it out anyway.

Let's say that you set up a suspense scene and you happen to have two characters who look the same. You're going to have the audience say, "Which man is that? No, it's the other man." You are going to distract them from their emotions. Keeping their mind on one thing involves many things, such as clarification, locale, who is who, making sure the characters are not wearing the same suit. There are many elements that you have to clarify so that you leave room only for the emotions.

You open quite a few of your films with an exterior shot that cuts in closer and closer to a window. Examples of this would be Shadow of a Doubt, Psycho *and* I Confess. *I wonder what you think of when you use that opening every once in a while.*

I think the main value of it is that you orient your audience to the locale. If you open on a window then you've got the audience wondering. In my particular genre of work there is a great confusion between the words *mystery* and *suspense*—the two things are miles apart. Mystery is an intellectual process, like in a whodunit, while suspense is essentially an emotional process. You can only get the suspense element going by giving the audience information. I dare say you have seen many films which have mysterious goings-on. You don't know what is going on, why the man is doing this or that. You are about a third of the way through the film before you realize what it is all about. To me that is completely wasted footage because there is no emotion to it.

So on your own terms have you never made a mystery?

No, and I have made only one whodunit, and that was many years ago. Before the five-second revelation at the end of a whodunit there is no emotion from the audience. When you are reading a book you are terribly tempted to turn to the last page all the time, but that is merely an emotion of curiosity. The mystery form has no particular appeal to me because it is merely a fact of mystifying an audience, which I don't think is enough.

I was thinking of Under Capricorn. *At the end it is revealed that Margaret Leighton has been fostering Lady Henrietta's alcoholism all along. We learn things we didn't know before. It's almost as if we have been watching a mystery, but we didn't know it was a mystery.*

Well, you can apply that to *Psycho* as well. There you have a revelation at the end, but that is merely a momentary thing. It doesn't alter the fact that you've been through a lot of suspense wondering when the figure is going to strike.

Are there different kinds of suspense?

Yes. Anxiety, the simplest form of suspense, is being in the taxi on the way to the airport. Will you make it in time? But if you are in a taxi and the police car is chasing you, that is a fear. So the circumstances will change the nature of the suspense.

Could you elaborate on the idea of giving the audience information in a suspense film?

Let's take a very simple, childish example. Four people are sitting around a table, talking about baseball. Five minutes of it, very dull. Suddenly a bomb goes off, blows the people to smithereens. What does the audience have? Ten seconds of shock. Now take the same scene. Tell the audience there is a bomb under the table and it will go off in five minutes. Well, the emotion of the audience is very different. Now the conversation about baseball becomes very vital because the audience is saying: "Don't be ridiculous. Stop talking about baseball, there's a bomb under there." You've got the audience working. You can't expect the audience to go into any kind of emotion without giving them some information. In *Sabotage* I was guilty of making an error, but I've never made it since—the bomb doesn't go off. If you do this, then you've worked that audience into a state and they will be angry if you don't provide them with some relief. Naturally there's a limit. If you stretch it out too long, they start to giggle. They'll relieve the tension themselves. They'll do it for you if you don't do it for them.

Chaplin always said you show the banana peel first, and then you cut to the man approaching it.

Well, in that case, I think you are quite right. If it's the man wearing the top hat who is walking toward the manhole, the nicest shot you could do would be to put the camera on the ground, have the manhole in the foreground, and see the man approaching the hole wearing the top hat. The next cut ought to be the head and shoulders of the man. You dolly with him and he drops out of the picture. You don't have to go back to the manhole anymore. He walks along and suddenly *whoomp,* he goes! To complete this, if you want satisfaction, you should now cut down to the manhole. He is lying there bleeding, the blood is pouring from his head. A policeman looks down and calls an ambulance. He's lifted up and taken to the hospital. The wife is brought to the bedside, and they say, "I'm afraid there is no hope." There is a fine line between comedy and tragedy.

How do you translate the emotion of fear to the screen?

There are many ways of doing it. When I gave the example of the bomb, I was specifically talking about suspense, not so much fear itself. Fear comes after suspense. In other words, the main constituent of suspense is fear. For example, people will go to a fairground and pay money to go into the haunted house because they want to scare themselves. A mother, when she holds a three-month-old baby in her arms, says "Boo!"—though why I really don't know. When the child grows up and goes on the swing it gives itself a different kind of fear. And then later on he has money to go on the roller coaster and pays to be scared, providing, as I explained, the relief—providing they can get off or come out of the haunted house giggling.

You say that you must have that as part of your picture?

If you have the suspense, if you create the fear, you've got to relieve it. In other words, in a picture like *Psycho,* you need a climax after a lot of suspense and fear. Anthony Perkins comes in dressed as a woman with the knife and you have to stop it there. Let's assume you didn't and he came and he stabbed the next girl to death. Where do you stop? You've got to let the people out sometime.

In a scene that is not classically suspenseful but where you must have a certain amount of information and exposition, what do you look for to make that scene play?

Well, the exposition should be dealt with before you start, and set to one side of the picture.

In North by Northwest *there is a scene in the FBI building. It is the first time we see Leo G. Carroll, where you let us on to the fact that George Kaplan doesn't exist and Roger Thornhill is substituting for him. It's a scene of pure exposition that sets up the audience for a good solid hour before any further exposition is required. How do you feel about shooting scenes like that?*

Well, these scenes are a must, but don't forget that it does not come at the opening of the picture. It's when it comes at the opening of the picture that it is difficult. But that scene came at a point when you were accounting for a number of bizarre events that involved an average man.

Is it important that Cary Grant is an advertising man in North by Northwest?

Well, in that he is an average man, yes. As a professional, you see, he is not a detective, not a criminal. He is Everyman. That helps involve the audience much more easily than if he was unique. I have never been interested in making films about professional criminals or detectives. I much prefer to take average men, because I think the audience can get involved more easily.

I wonder if he is an "average man." Just how average is his personality and his relationships with his wives and his mother, for example?

Yes, but he is so preoccupied in getting himself out of the mess he is in that he forgets about his mother for a minute and the wives and anything else. Those particular elements would apply much more to a psychological story than they would a chase story.

In North by Northwest, *why did you select those particular characters, and what was their value?*

First of all, you have available to you a film star by the name of Cary Grant. Don't lose sight of that element. You are actually playing a character, but you are also playing the personality of Cary Grant. The value of having Cary Grant, the film star, is that the audience gets a little more emotion out of Cary Grant than they would from an unknown, because there is identification. There are many members of the audience who like Cary Grant, whether they know about the character he is playing or not.

With Cary Grant on location for *North by Northwest* (1959). Hitchcock:
"The value of having Cary Grant is that the audience gets a little more
emotion out of Cary Grant than they would from an unknown."

*Talking about Cary Grant, I feel that it was a mistake that he was not the mur-
derer in* Suspicion.

I thought so, but I wasn't in charge at that time. I had to more or less conform. I was loaned out to RKO by Selznick and they had the whole thing
set up. The whole subject of the film is the woman's mind—is my husband a murderer or not? The ending, on which I had to compromise, was
that he was not. But the real ending that I had for the film was that he
brings his wife a fatal glass of milk. She knows that she is going to be
killed, so she writes a letter to her mother: "I'm in love with him, I don't

want to live anymore, he's going to kill me, but society should be protected." Folds the letter up, leaves it by the bed. She says, "Would you mind mailing that for me?" She drinks the milk; he watches her die. Last shot of the picture is Cary Grant whistling very cheerfully, going to the mailbox and popping in the letter. But that was heresy, to do that to Cary Grant in those days.

What is your idea about what a heroine should be?

Well, in the first place, I've never been very keen on women who hang their sex around their neck like baubles. I think it should be discovered. It's more interesting to discover the sex in a woman than it is to have it thrown at you, like a Marilyn Monroe or those types. To me they are rather vulgar and obvious. I think it is much more interesting in the course of the storytelling to discover the sex, even though the woman may look like a schoolteacher. Anything could happen to you with a woman like that in a taxi.

You have spoken about the difficulty of finding the right material. How do you know when you've got the right material?

Yes, it is very difficult. It would depend upon which direction you were going. You may be making a psychological murder story or a chase story. I make many, many different kinds of pictures. I have no particular preference, to be quite honest. I am not interested in content at all. I don't give a damn what the film is about. I am more interested in how to handle the material so as to create an emotion in the audience. I find too many people are interested in the content. If you were painting a still life of some apples on a plate, it's like you'd be worrying whether the apples were sweet or sour. Who cares? I don't care myself. But a lot of films, of course, live on content.

But aren't there any general rules about what makes appropriate material? For instance, you've had problems with writers who wouldn't give you what you wanted.

Well, I have had problems with writers because I find that I am teaching them cinematics all the time. You have to remember that with a lot of writers you have to go by what is written on the page. I have no interest in that. As the director, I have that white rectangle to fill with a succession of images, one following the other. That's what makes a film. I have no interest in pictures that I call "photographs of people talking." These have nothing to do with cinema whatsoever. When you stick up a camera and photograph a group of people, and pick up the close-ups and two-shots, I think that is a bore. I'm not saying you've got to make every film without dialogue, because you have to have dialogue. The only thing wrong with silent films is that no sound ever came out of the mouths. But at least it told a story visually and pictorially.

So many films are an extension of the theater. I've made them. But if I pick a subject like *Dial M for Murder*, well hell, I don't even have to come to the studio. I could phone that one in, because there is nothing for me to do. Years ago I made a movie of Sean O'Casey's play *Juno and the Paycock*. I couldn't for the life of me figure out what to do with it, except photograph it in one room with the Irish players. The film was very successful, and I was ashamed to read those laudatory notices for which I had done nothing except photograph the Irish players doing their job.

Are you saying that when you see the material, you can visualize the entire movement of the film?

Yes, definitely.

The whole film?

Beginning to end.

Is this kind of visual response innately within you or is it something that came through being an art director?

I think one of the biggest problems that we have in our business is the inability of people to visualize. What I am about to say is hearsay, but I remember Selznick, the producer, when he was talking about Irving Thalberg, the great name in our business. Selznick used to say, "Thalberg is great with a finished picture." When you examine those words, they mean that the man lacked any visual sense. The visual, to me, is a vital element in the cinema and I don't think it is studied enough. Go back to the early days, back to Chaplin. He once made a short film called *The Pilgrim*. The opening shot was the outside of a prison gate. A guard came out and posted a Wanted notice. Next cut: a very tall, thin man coming out of a river, having had a swim. He finds that his clothes are missing and have been replaced with a convict's uniform. Next cut: a railroad station, and coming toward the camera dressed as a parson with the pants too long is Chaplin. Now there are three pieces of film, and look at the amount of story they told. These are the things that I think are so essential, especially when you send your film into a foreign country—Japan, Italy or wherever. If you send a film which, as I mentioned earlier, is "photographs of people talking" all the way through, and that gets to a foreign country with subtitles underneath, the poor audience will spend the entire evening reading. They won't have time to look at the pictures.

You say you don't like the notion of filming theater, but a lot of your films do fall into acts that peak at certain points.

I think that is true, because in order to sustain an audience's interest you have to give them a series of climaxes. Otherwise you have to have a very powerful yarn to hold them from the beginning to the end. In a sense it's almost like what we used to call the well-made play, which is out of date now. That ran into three acts: proposition, argument and resolution.

Do you have rehearsals with your actors? Do you talk about characters with them?

Yes, privately in the dressing room. Not demonstrably so.

Is that before production?

Before.

You don't rehearse the scene?

No. With dialogue scenes, a duo can be rehearsed, but if you've got very competent actors you can let them go off on their own.

Do you ever use improvisation on the set?

Certainly not. I will improvise in the office. That's the place to improvise, long before you go onto a stage. Why, improvising on the set is like a composer composing with a full orchestra in front of him and saying,

"Flute, will you give me a note?" And he gives him an A, and the composer puts it down. This shows how stupid the process is.

If you previsualize all of your films, what kind of joy do you get out of directing?

I don't, I'd just as soon not do it. The moment the script is finished and the film is visualized, that is the end of the creative part as far as I'm concerned. I'd just as soon not shoot the picture.

Why don't you let someone else shoot the picture after you've got that joy out of it?

They might screw it up.

Do you really feel that most of your creative work is done before the cameras have begun to roll?

All of it. Everything. I don't understand why we have to experiment with film. Everything should be done on paper. A musician has to do it. A composer puts a lot of dots down and beautiful music comes out. I think students must be taught to visualize, they have to learn there is a rectangle up there and it has to be filled. Personally I never look through the camera. What for? To find out whether the camera is lying? I only consider that screen up there, and the whole film to me should be on paper from beginning to end—shot by shot, cut by cut—and each cut should mean something. It's not a matter of just letting the student do it one way or the other. There's only one thing. If you're composing music, you don't have alternatives, you have only one way to do it. And that's what should be taught to these young filmmakers. After all, a litterateur doesn't write three or four sentences and then choose which one is the best later on. He writes the one sentence in his novel; he assembles his words.

What is cinema? The assembly of pieces of film to create an idea. Each cut joined one to the other goes by on the screen and has an emotional impact upon an audience. I remember working at UFA* in 1924, where they were making *The Last Laugh* with Emil Jannings.† This film is to me the prime example of expressing a story even without titles. If you look at *The Last Laugh* today, you'll find the whole story is told visually, from

---

*UFA was one of Germany's most important film production companies throughout the 1920s.
†*Der Letzte Mann,* directed by F. W. Murnau (1924).

beginning to end. The only thing wrong with the silent film is that people open their mouths and no sound comes out. It's the visual that has to be taught, the fundamentals of the medium. It is the only new art of the twentieth century, but it is essentially a visual art. And that's what has to be taught. Not by guessing and wondering how it will come out. Film students ought to be taught to know whatever they put down on paper will come out in a certain way.

Have you storyboarded all your films?

Sometimes, but not always. You can storyboard key scenes. You would storyboard, for example, the shower scene in *Psycho*. Actually, there were seventy-eight setups and it took forty-five seconds on the screen. First of all, the leading lady was a bit squeamish about revealing herself, so I had to get a nude stand-in. It was made up of all those tiny pieces of film because the knife never touched the body at any time. Just an illusionary thing.

So you did the storyboarding beforehand, but it changed in the editing?

Oh, we tightened it up and got the tempo going. Sure.

Once you have this picture visualized, how much do you change, other than casting?

Not too much. You see, it is very essential that you know ahead of time something of the orchestration. In other words, image size. What I mean by orchestration is this. Take the close-up. Sometimes you see films cut such that the close-up comes in early, and by the time you really need it, it has lost its effect because you've already used it. It's like in music—the brass sounding loud before you need it. Now, I'll give you an example where a juxtaposition of the image size is very important. One of the biggest effects in *Psycho* was where the detective enters the house and goes up the stairs. The shots were storyboarded to make sure there was enough contrast of sizes within the cuts. There is a very violent murder to start with, another one less violent—and more frightening.

Then, as the film goes on, there is no more violence. But in the mind of the audience, and in the anticipation of it, it is all there. Here is the shot of the detective, a simple shot going up the stairs. He reaches the top stairs, the next cut is the camera as high as it can go, it was on the ceiling, you see the figure run out, raised knife, it comes down—bang!—the biggest head you can put on the screen. But that big head has no impact unless the previous shot had been so far away. So don't go putting a close-up where you don't need it, because later on you *will* need it. That is where your orchestration comes in, where you design the setup. That's why you can't just guess these things on the set.

Have you ever shot masters and then two-shots followed by close-ups?

No, never. By shooting that way you're bound to the objective, you see, whereas I'm a believer in the subjective—playing a scene from the point of view of an individual. But if you do your master and then you go in close, that's like theater to me. It's like sitting in the orchestra looking at a play, purely objectively, whereas we have the power in film to get right into the mind of a character. I'll give you an example. *Rear Window* is strictly pure cinema. You do a close-up of James Stewart. He looks. You go back to him and he reacts. So you set up a mental process. You can't do that by doing a master shot and these various individual shots.

What you are saying is that you orchestrate every shot in the film, the size of the image, things like that?

As far as possible. Color balance, too. Any element that you've got. Sound definitely plays a part. Mind you, I didn't say you'd get the perfect picture, but you should strive as much as possible.

What work have you left for your editor?

None. This is the point. It seems to me an extraordinary thing—I hope there are no cutters present—that you have, say, six million dollars of film and it might get into the hands of a very indifferent editor. That's a problem.

In Psycho, *I understood why you cut to the close-up of Martin Balsam after he's just been stabbed from the high angle. What intrigues me is why you introduced him in such a strange way. When we first see him in the hardware store he's brought right into the camera. We've never seen him before and therefore I wonder why you used the close-up.*

You bring him in like that because you are bringing in a new possible menace.

I have the feeling I could recognize a shot from your films if I saw it out of context. I wonder if you could comment on the placing of the camera.

Well, I think it is mainly a matter of the interest in the composition. I have a horror of what I call the passport photograph: shooting straight in. It's dull, it's not interesting, and a slight variation on that is not so much the desire to get anything in the way of sharp angles, low or high or what have you, but merely to avoid the standard level shots.

Very often we think of your staging in depth. Does this represent anything thematic in your approach, to use a longer lens even in depth staging?

If you use a wide-angle lens, of course, you naturally change your perspective considerably. As a matter of fact, if you use a short-focus lens, say a one hundred millimeter, you foreshorten. The standard view is about a fifty millimeter—that would give you what the eye sees.

Is your tendency to stage with the formal fifty millimeter?

Yes, sure. Otherwise you make a room look too big and you send the back wall too far away. If you use a wide-angle lens, you make the set much bigger than it really is.

Does this have something to do with the emotional quality, the fact that you would stick with the normal perspective?

No, it would depend. You see, sometimes you get involved with the whole question of the depth of focus. There is a whole group of people who think everything should be sharp in front and equally sharp at a distance, which in actual fact is almost impossible in real life. I remember at Paramount, when they first introduced VistaVision.* They did their first test out in the desert. They were making a film with Martin and Lewis, and when the front office saw the first results they were overwhelmed and

*Paramount used Cecil B. DeMille's 1956 film *The Ten Commandments* to showcase VistaVision. The tagline to the film was "The Greatest Event in Motion Picture History."

ecstatic that a hand in the foreground was sharp as a figure half a mile away. And what the hell that's got to do with picture making, I don't know, but they were delighted. They all thought this was a wonderful system.

Of course, what the camera department failed to tell them was that if you shoot in the desert you have to stop down to a pinhole and it will make everything sharp, including five miles away. But the camera department was afraid to tell them, so they let them think it was VistaVision. I was doing this picture *To Catch a Thief* at the time and I remember the head of the studio, who shall be nameless, comes to me and says, "Look, in these close-ups of yours everything's blurred. That's not VistaVision." I said, "So? The audience is not going to look around Grace Kelly's head, they are going to look at the head we've got on the screen." "Yes, but in VistaVision everything is sharp." So the camera department secretly went around to each cameraman on the lot and told them to pile up more light to make everything sharp, so as to continue to deceive the front office.

In terms of proportions within the image, do you also try to create contrast by using close-ups cut with more distant shots?

I think that comes automatically—the distance of the figures, you see. That's why I think barroom brawls in Westerns are always a bore, because one man hits the other, the table collapses, and he falls back over the bar. If they would only do a few big close-ups here and there, it would be much more exciting, instead of looking at it from a distance. But you see, they make a mistake, they think it creates a greater air of reality by seeing it at a distance, and in fact they are doing the wrong thing.

Could you talk about the problem of getting a set the way you want it?

Yes. One of the biggest problems is the atmosphere of a set. We have a very strange system in this industry, that the man called the art director leaves the set the moment it is painted and finished but not dressed, not even the carpet. And the new man, called the set dresser, walks on, and he is the man who reads the script and then proceeds to dress the set. He goes out and picks furniture and carpets; he goes into the prop room, gets ornaments and paintings. This man is in charge of what is the most vital element of the décor: the atmosphere. Instead of being a set dresser he should be almost a writer because he ought to know the character of the person who lives in that room. But he doesn't, and that is why you see so many films that have an artificial look. It is because they are very badly dressed. And the only way I have ever gotten around it is to hire a photographer with a color still camera. In *Vertigo,* James Stewart was playing a retired detective who had gone to law school and who lived in San Francisco. So I said to the photographer, "Go to San Francisco, find out where a retired detective lives, make sure he went to law school, and go in and photograph his house. Get all the detail and bring it back and dress the set that way."

Very often scripts are written and then the location manager is called in and he tries to find some location that fits the script. I don't believe in that. I think you should go to the location first and then put it in the script. Now, years ago I did a film with Thornton Wilder called *Shadow of a Doubt.* It was set in a small town in Northern California. We went up there and stayed a week before a line was written. But you see, in our business, the way it's run today, a writer is given a book and he's to go off and write it. This writer thinks he's done a wonderful thing when he writes "close-up," but it's ridiculous and stupid. It is a bad system because strictly speaking a writer should be given a treatment written by the director. I usually work with the writer on the treatment. Now, when I say treatment, it is really a description of the film. It describes exactly what is coming on that screen. There are indications of shots in it and so forth. Then you give that to the writer and let him go off.

When you think of the ridiculous things that go on in our business, when you read that a writer has sold his book and has been engaged to write the screenplay, what is he? Is he a screenplay writer or is he a novelist? He can't be both. And I've had that experience. I've said, "Have I got to take this man?" And they've said, "Yes, he's part of the deal."

If you care so much about the authenticity of the sets, in making it look real or feel real on the set, why do you use rear-screen projection that looks fake?

That's a decision that you have to make quite often. It depends. If you are shooting a long dialogue scene and you go outside and shoot it in an open car in the street, you've got to dub the whole scene because of the external sounds. Now, you've got to do that or you can do the best back projection you can get. It can be well done, and it can be badly done. At least then you can let the players have the comfort of being able to play the scene naturally and spontaneously.

With Jimmy Stewart during production of *The Man Who Knew Too Much* in 1956. Hitchcock made an earlier version of the story with the same title in 1935.

Wouldn't they be playing it naturally and spontaneously if they were driving the car?

Yes, but I think they'd be distracted. They'd be distracted by traffic, the guy driving the car. There have been a lot of pictures made that way, with the camera strapped on the front and the windshield taken off, but you do run the risk of having to re-dub the whole thing. When you're dubbing a long dialogue scene, you're not going to get the necessary emotion into it. That's the risk you run.

In Vertigo, *where they're climbing up the stairs in the tower, there is a very strange effect.*

That effect took thirty years to get. It really did. When I was making *Rebecca,* I had a scene where Joan Fontaine is supposed to faint. I explained to Selznick I wanted to get the effect of her looking and everything seeming to go far away. Where I got the idea from was at the Royal Chelsea Arts Ball in London on New Year's Eve. I remembered at a certain time during the evening everything seemed to go far away. And I asked for this effect and they said they couldn't do it. I tried again about five years later. For *Vertigo* they tried different effects, and finally it was arrived at by a combination of a dolly shot and a zoom lens crossing each other. Dollying in and zooming out. When the head of special effects came to me, I said how much was it going to cost. He said fifty thousand dollars to put a camera high and take it up and zoom it, because of the enormous rig. I said, "But there is no one in the set." Why didn't they make a miniature and lay it on its side? "Oh, I hadn't thought of that." So they did it, and it cost nineteen thousand dollars.

Showing pieces of film to create violence as opposed to actually depicting violence is something you've used in Psycho, *the end of* Rear Window, *and* Torn Curtain.

There's no question that for any kind of violence you want to portray on the screen, that's the way it can be done best. Let me see if I can give you a comparison. If you stand in a field and you see a train going by half a mile away, you look at it and it speeds by. Now go within six feet of the train going by—think of the difference in its effect. So what you are doing is you are taking the audience right close up into the scene, and the montage of the various effects gets the audience involved. That's its purpose. It becomes much more powerful than if you sit back and look. Say you are at a boxing match and you are eight to ten rows back. Well, you get a very different effect if you are in the first row, looking up under those ropes. When these two fellows are slugging each other, you get splashed almost. In *Psycho,* once that figure comes in and starts to stab, you're in it. Oh, you're absolutely in it.

Could we return to the discussion of structure? With the last few films you've made, your pictures have seemed to divide up into almost two stories: Topaz, Psycho, The Birds, *through* Torn Curtain *perhaps less so. I wonder if you could explain to us what your fascination is with this device, the double story?*

If you take a picture like *The Birds,* you'll find the personal story is a rather thin one because, traditionally, it's an event story, like the early H. G. Wells stories, like *The War of the Worlds.* In all Wells' famous stories, the personal story is very, very secondary to the events, otherwise you wouldn't get the effect. Whether it is Martians or what have you, they take it over and almost swamp the personal story. So in that type of picture the personal would tend to be on the thin side.

But is there a definite reason, in terms of dealing with the audience, of starting with this kind of story?

Well, the first thing is that you have to remember the audience goes in anticipating something. They've read about it in the ads, so it's a question of how much of the lightweight story you put in the picture in the beginning. I believe it was Fellini who said, "Hitchcock made them wait for the birds to come on. I wouldn't have the nerve to do that." But I think it is a matter of figuring it out and then gradually, one bird just hitting the girl. And the gradual slow buildup.

Did the film The War of the Worlds *influence your thinking?*

No. The film of *The War of the Worlds* is rather vague in my mind. I once had breakfast with H. G. Wells. We were discussing *The War of the Worlds* and I was talking about making it into a picture, and he said in his high, piping voice: "Oh no, you couldn't do that today. I'd have to invent all new devices." So it didn't relate to *The Birds* at all.

Could you tell me about training the birds for The Birds?

Well, we had a bird trainer, and he was able to train a certain number of seagulls, and I think about thirty or forty well-trained ravens and crows. Of course a lot of it was double and triple printing. In fact, the last shot in *The Birds* was composed of sixteen separate pieces of film.

Are any of those birds stuffed?

No. We rented five hundred ducks and sprayed them gray. We started off with chickens, but the neck movement gave them away.

When the seagulls attack at the windows, were you throwing them at the windows?

Oh, yes. We had men on ladders, and the gulls were trained to be thrown and land on the flattable top nearby the camera. And for the little girl with a gull at the birthday party we built a little platform on her shoulder and a gull was put there, but its beak was bound. The girl had a little wire, and as she ran up the dunes she was told to pull her hand up and down so that you got the effect of its pecking.

In the shots where you throw a seagull at a window, why would you use a trained seagull instead of a wild one?

Well, because the wild one may go halfway there and say, "Where the hell am I going?" and turn around and come back. I don't trust them.

Is there a film of yours that you really feel is the best use of music that you've ever had?

I can't think of one offhand.

What about the sort of sweeping lyrical moment in Vertigo, *under the green neon lights?*

You see, here you had a man who was really a necrophile, hence the green light. He was waiting for the girl to complete her hair and everything, and he was in love with a dead woman. So you want to help that, and the music helped it, because he was going to bed with a dead woman.

You would say that the music did more than simply repeat the image.

It, shall we say, intensified his necrophilia.

I notice in Torn Curtain *that you use suspense to discover something which all of a sudden is revealed before the maximum tension has been developed. In other words, we learn that Paul Newman is, in fact, not defecting very early.*

You're forgetting another value. What will the girl say when she finds out? I'll give you a specific example. In *Vertigo,* it was the end of the book before it's revealed that it is one and the same woman. I decided halfway through to blow the whole thing, tell the audience the truth and not wait until the end. People were horrified. "What are you doing? Giving it all away?" I replied that if I didn't, I'm starting another story. Jimmy Stewart has lost one woman. She's dead, she's gone, he was crazy about her, and she even drove him into a nursing home. Now he sees a girl on the street, he sees some resemblance, and he gets hold of her, gets into her room. From that point on in the book, he endeavored to change the girl back into the image of the dead woman he wanted to renew. The reason I gave the whole thing away was to give additional values. First, we know who she is. Added value—what will Stewart do when he finds out? We know something that he doesn't know. Now there is an element of suspense. Second, does the girl resist him? If you haven't told the audience who she really is, you won't understand her behavior—why she doesn't want to wear a gray suit, why she doesn't want her hair made blond.

Do you differentiate between fear and horror?

Well, horror is really an extreme of fear. It's as far as you can go.

Many of your films operate almost like dreams or nightmares.

They are. That's the theory of it. That's why a picture like *North by Northwest* is a nightmare, but it behooves you to be realistic, because when you have a nightmare and you are being led to the electric chair, it is so vivid that you are glad when you wake up.

When you said the theory of it, do you think of it that way?

No, but I think it is very vital that the detail be accurate—however bizarre the situation may be—as part of the nightmare.

And what are your ends in putting nightmares on the screen? What do you want to do to the audience?

Give them pleasure, the same pleasure they have when they wake up from a nightmare.

◄━━►

Films as Director

1929	*Blackmail*	1940	*Foreign Correspondent*
1935	*The Man Who Knew Too Much*		*Rebecca*
	The 39 Steps	1941	*Mr. and Mrs. Smith*
1936	*Secret Agent*		*Suspicion*
	Sabotage	1942	*Saboteur*
1937	*The Woman Alone*	1943	*Shadow of a Doubt*
1938	*The Lady Vanishes*	1944	*Lifeboat*
	The Girl Was Young	1945	*Spellbound*
1939	*Jamaica Inn*	1946	*Notorious* (also producer)

1947 *The Paradine Case*

1948 *Rope* (also producer)

1949 *Under Capricorn* (also producer)

1950 *Stage Fright* (also producer)

1951 *Strangers on a Train* (also producer)

1953 *I Confess* (also producer)

1954 *Dial M for Murder* (also producer)

Rear Window (also producer)

To Catch a Thief (also producer)

1956 *The Trouble with Harry* (also producer)

The Man Who Knew Too Much (also producer)

1957 *The Wrong Man* (also producer)

1958 *Vertigo* (also producer)

1959 *North by Northwest* (also producer)

1960 *Psycho* (also producer)

1963 *The Birds* (also producer)

1964 *Marnie* (also producer)

1966 *Torn Curtain* (also producer)

1969 *Topaz* (also producer)

1972 *Frenzy* (also producer)

1976 *Family Plot* (also producer)

Sometimes when I see a scene, I say, "I don't believe a goddamned word of it. You are acting, and I don't believe it."

GEORGE CUKOR
(Born in New York City, 1899—Died 1983)

George Cukor ended up being talked about in Hollywood in one of two ways—as "a woman's director" or as "the man who was fired from *Gone with the Wind.*" Like all efforts to pigeonhole a life, these labels are much too narrow. While it's true that Cukor directed most of the great female stars of his day to good effect and that he was dumped by David O. Selznick after a year's preparation and several weeks of shooting the most successful motion picture of his time, his career had greater dimensions.

Cukor came to Hollywood from Broadway as a dialogue director, a man engaged to help directors trained in silent films handle the new challenges of spoken text. He quickly moved from a supporting role in directing to a starring role and spent most of his career at MGM, which caused him to become part of the studio system. This seemed to suit him, at a time when other directors such as Capra, Wyler, Hawks and Stevens were staking a claim to control their films, insisting on selecting and shaping stories.

Cukor knew he was not a writer. He considered himself more of a critic than a collaborator when it came to screenplays, and he had an aversion to the physical dimension of film work, relying on his strength with what he called the "human side" of the equation. "There are lots of creative directors," he said, "who can *seize* a script and make it part of their world—like Lubitsch or Ford or Hitchcock. And there are others who try to become part of the script's world. Like me."

MGM was a fiefdom of producers and powerful department heads who were granted authority by Louis B. Mayer. The heads of the art, sound, wardrobe, camera and music departments exerted their authority and were

With Jean Harlow on the MGM set of *Dinner at Eight* in 1934. Cukor liked
working at MGM with its stable of stars.

there to please Mr. Mayer, giving MGM pictures a "look" that made it hard
for directors to put a personal stamp on pictures.

Mayer and Irving Thalberg wanted to maintain control. Cukor was
spending a fortune on a new house, and he recalled Thalberg's reaction to it.
"Go ahead, George, spend a lot of money. I love to have directors in debt, it
forces them to work harder." Cukor responded well to the MGM system.
The studio provided him a continuum of fine properties that enabled him
during the thirties and forties to guide its great stable of stars in such popular
hits as *Dinner at Eight, The Women, Camille, David Copperfield, Holiday, The*

Philadelphia Story and *Adam's Rib.* Two of his most famous efforts, *A Star Is Born* and *My Fair Lady,* came later at Warner Bros. Cukor was, arguably, the best of the "studio" directors.

He said in his AFI seminar that he found studios comforting, and over a career that spanned fifty years and fifty-one films he gave comfort and entertainment to filmgoers across the world. And he met the test of time in a way that few filmmakers have—he was still directing when he was eighty-two years old.

GEORGE CUKOR

———

October 22, 1975*

It is a great pleasure to present to you a master of film, George Cukor, a man who has created one of the most impressive bodies of work. And the nice thing about it is that so much of it is fun.

I'll just say a few words and then let the kids, as you call them, ask me questions. You know, my film *Camille,* which you just saw, when we did it—and I'm not sure in which year we did it—was, even then, something of an old chestnut. It seemed rather archaic. The only point in doing it was the extraordinary meeting of a part and an actress. It's a part which gives an actress a great range, and we felt that Garbo was suited very much for it and so we did it, and I think with great success. But even when we did it, it was old-fashioned and we doubted whether we could get away with certain things: the father's pleading and the bad woman and all that. It must seem very strange to you young people today. However, I think such was Garbo's persuasiveness, the originality of her acting, that we got away with it. And the story and its characters have certain timeless elements.

I found the film very moving. It wasn't really romanticized; rather, it dealt with an issue that I can identify with, that of Armand, the young impassioned man who loves and yet has no understanding of love. And the woman's sense of this, the woman who is giving it up.

*This transcript contains segments from seminars George Cukor gave at the American Film Institute on January 10, 1972, October 5, 1977, February 16, 1978 and May 24, 1979.

I'm glad you like it. It's an extraordinary performance. I'd seen the play done where the actress did a great deal of coughing and panting. Garbo only indicated her illness in the early scenes and just clears her throat occasionally. But such was her persuasion that you knew there was something very wrong with her. You know she is doomed and ill-fated. But I'm glad that you liked it, because many years ago we showed *Little Women* here. The audience was very sweet and respectful, but they really didn't like it. It seemed very strange to them. Maybe they were ill prepared.

How did you bring out the very emotional performance Garbo gave in Camille? *Did you leave it in her own hands?*

No, with Garbo you must create a climate in which she trusts you. While we were doing the picture Irving Thalberg died, but he saw a couple of days' rushes and said, "She's awfully good. She's never been this good." I said, "Irving, she's just sitting there." He said, "But she's relaxed, she's open." Maybe that had a great deal to do with it. She knew she had a very sympathetic, intelligent character and a good audience as well, and I think probably we stimulated each other. There was a kind of gaiety, something unguarded that she didn't give in a great many of her performances.

But how did you draw that emotional performance out of her?

You don't have to—they are actresses, after all. I'm always suspect in these schools where they tell the young actors, "We'll train you how to feel things." Well, if they can't feel anything they should not be goddamned actors, they should stop acting. They may be able to teach you how to do it more expertly, but you cannot teach an actor how to feel. That is absolute nonsense. Garbo is a very imaginative actress. She is also a very original actress. She does things no other actress would do at a certain moment—like how she sank to her knees. You have to know where your actors' strengths and weaknesses are; you have to know what they're likely to do when they're off the beam.

What were your first impressions of David Selznick?

My first impressions were the day that I arrived in Hollywood to be a dialogue director and David was the assistant to a man called Bernie Fineman. It was in the early days of sound. I was going to be a dialogue director because there was a great mystery of what they used to call the titles and how to speak them. They were not trained for that, and it was presumed that because I came from the theater, I know what to do. David was an eager, bustling young man and was very sweet. That first night he said, "Would you come home for dinner with me?" So I did, and there were his mother and father and brother, and it was all rather casual, and he remained that way with me all his life, always very generous and very relaxed. We were friends without interruption until he died.

Could you talk about your experiences working with Selznick on Gone with the Wind?

It's so long ago that I've put it out of my mind, but I have read things about it. I prepared it for a year and made the tests. I certainly did a lot of the casting, though not all. And the sets and everything. Then I shot for a month and I think David was rather nervous about it. I don't know what influence he was under, but he told me he was going to replace me. I'm sure it was very painful for him. Olivia de Havilland, when she did a seminar here, described what happened and she remembers much more than I do. She said that she and Vivien Leigh were both in their widows' costumes and they went in to David and pleaded and stormed and made a great scene, but to no effect. She said that during the picture she would come to me in the evenings or on weekends and I would run her through some scenes, moonlighting. She said that she felt rather guilty about this so finally she told Vivien Leigh, who said, "Oh yes, I do the same thing." I must say that most of the scenes I did, before I left the film, are in the picture. But there was no rupture in my friendship with Selznick. That's the extraordinary thing.

When you were working on Gone with the Wind, *it was said you were giving too much attention to Vivien Leigh and the female characters. Clark Gable is said to have felt quite strongly about this. Is this is why you resigned?*

No, I was fired. It really is a mystery to me. I don't really know why I was removed, and at this moment I don't give a damn. Whatever Gable might have thought, I don't think that a director throws one thing knowingly from one person to another. As a director, I can't determine how it will happen. It is the scene that dictates it. If the man is the interesting thing, if I have any conscience or taste, he will be it. If it is the woman, then the woman will be it. But to knowingly switch that around is a rather stupid, distorting thing.

Weren't the circumstances behind The Philadelphia Story *somewhat unusual? Katharine Hepburn had been branded box-office poison.*

Oh yes, that's right. She'd been a big star, and then things hadn't gone so well and the press said, "Box-office poison." I should think that's libelous. It was a stupid and graceless thing to say. Anyway, *The Philadelphia Story* was a big hit on the stage in New York, and she had control of the film rights. She was very clever about it. MGM wanted to buy the property for this star and that star, but she insisted that it was part of her contract that it be done with two big male stars. I think she wanted Clark Gable and Spencer Tracy. She'd never worked with either of them, but finally we made do with Jimmy Stewart and Cary Grant, which wasn't a bad compromise. She had done the play in New York very successfully and beautifully, and she's been on top, more or less, ever since that film.

When you were casting Adam's Rib, *were Tracy and Hepburn your choices?*

Yes, it was written for them. They were a team at that time and the Kanins—Garson Kanin and his wife, Ruth Gordon—wrote several comedies. We all worked very well together, and it was more or less tailored for Tracy and Hepburn. I think doing it without them would have been incomprehensible. They did something special with it. And if you notice the ensemble playing—the way they played together, there's a lesson in that.

It seems they don't write pictures with dialogue like Adam's Rib *anymore.*

Alas, they don't. Somebody said I was an auteur. Well, I'm not an auteur and I'm not a writer. I'm envious of auteurs, those people able to sit down and dash off a script and then direct it. I'm just dazzled by that. Of course the director does collaborate with the author at all times. I influenced the writing, as every director does. On *Adams' Rib* we were a kind of team. The Kanins would do certain scenes, and we would go to my house and read them and hear how they sounded aloud, then go to the studio where I would stage them kind of roughly with a camera and see how they

With Katharine Hepburn and Jimmy Stewart during filming
of *The Philadelphia Story* (1940).

worked. The Kanins were very prolific and clever, and they knew for
whom they were writing. They would say, "We have an idea that this
might be good." So they would present a script and then we would take it
to the studio, where sometimes it was refined. Certain scenes didn't work
and certain scenes did work. But the script was always extremely well
written to begin with, and a lot of the business that was in it—the "directorial touches"—were right there in the script. We were very lucky that
the Kanins were writing in that vein. I think a director should have his

finger in the pie, should influence what's being done. Writers will do rewrites, and you read the scene and say, "This would be better, don't you think?" On some happy, marvelous occasion you may be given a perfect script. I've yet to come upon that, but hope I do sometime.

When you say that they don't write that kind of dialogue, I don't think life is that witty or funny anymore; it's a different kind of humor. You see, in a way, pictures are a reflection of the times—sometimes distorted, I grant you—but that sort of verbal wit was the style, and they could play it that way. I do urge you all to see those earlier pictures and get a sense of history. I don't think you can understand the present, really, or the future, unless you have a pretty good comprehension of the past. It's very good for you people who are interested in film to see the old ones. I think you can learn a good deal from them.

In Adam's Rib *you have a lot of very tight, crisp dialogue and the camera work is very simple and straightforward. Do you always fit the camera work to the dialogue and the story?*

I believe in that. As a rule of thumb—unless you have to move the camera, unless it does something for you—be quiet. The less you fidget with the camera or the cutting, the better. The audience has got to hear the lines, and if you complicate the action or camera work then the audience will strain to hear every word. I recently did a picture in London for television called *Love Among the Ruins* with Katharine Hepburn and Laurence Olivier. At first I asked, "I've never done something specifically for television before. Do I shoot it any other way?" And they said, "No, just shoot it the way you would an ordinary movie."

I'm curious to know how the script for Two-Faced Woman *was accepted by the studio.*

The script, really, was not very good. At least, that's my excuse. I had agreed to do it. Often, I must confess to you right here, I make mistakes. And it's very easy to make a mistake with Garbo. We coped and so did she. She's a very sensible person and it's a good story. Maybe it wasn't as lousy as it seemed at the time to us. It was difficult to do, but time heals a great many wounds, and some pictures too. Some pictures I did which I cringed at I can now see in a fresh light and say, "Oh, I rather like that."

You have to make a decision when they ask you to do something and you think, "Well, I think I can do this and I think it's good. It entertains me." And that's all one can say.

You say the dialogue is very important and that you try to be very quiet with the camera. It seems to me that in My Fair Lady *you used a moving camera a great deal.*

Well, when I say the camera should be quiet I don't mean that it should be static or that the cutting should be static. I think it should move when necessary—just don't become infatuated with it. If you'll notice in *My Fair Lady*, which was a musical comedy or a comedy with music, when we had the dialogue we did not move around too much. The movement was in the musical numbers. I've had a good deal of experience transferring plays to the screen, and if you just photograph a stage play it's very static. You have to give it a slight movement that might not always be true. On the stage version of *My Fair Lady*, for example, she sang "I Could Have Danced All Night" sitting on a couch. We thought, "Well, the natural movement is that she's going to bed, isn't she?" So we had her sing the song as she went upstairs. You must use a kind of intelligence.

Do you rehearse for scenes like that on the set or beforehand?

I have it just generally planned and then sometimes we rehearse. Rehearsal is only good for big movements, but the actual thing that happens—that spontaneity and immediacy—only happens when the camera is running.

Is there a difference between stage directing and film directing?

Yes, it's quite different. I think you must discover what the movement of a scene is and then do a little more movement on film than you would on the stage. I think if you read the script sympathetically—if you rehearse and try it this way and that, if you have the opportunity—there will always emerge the inevitable place where you should have the camera. Sometimes you try it and it's as though you have a tight collar, the camera is not in the right place. But if your setup is right, it all falls into place.

My experience in the theater proved enormously valuable because I

On the set with Audrey Hepburn at Warner Bros. filming
My Fair Lady (1964).

knew how to cope with dialogue, which, after all, was new to movies when I came to Hollywood. At that time there was this great panic sweeping Hollywood. No one, it seems, knew how to handle dialogue. Many of the studios turned to those of us with experience in the theater, and the result was this great raid on the stage for directors and actors.

How would your approach differ from such films as Holiday *to something like* The Marrying Kind?

Holiday was all verbalized, rather stylish, a comedy of manners, while *The Marrying Kind* was a rather rougher, hurly-burly type of picture.

The reason I bring that up is that in the films I've seen of yours there is always a distinct difference in meaning, people in different classes.

I would call that style—I think with the way it's written. If you're dealing with very grand, stuffy people who live in a very grand house, it's different than if you're dealing with poor people—postal clerks and people like that. It's more hurly-burly. I think you, as the director, must be flexible.

Sometimes I'm asked to read a script and I think, "Well, I could do it. I've been at it a long time and I could do a workmanlike thing, but someone else might do it better than me." And I recommend that thinking. I only try to do things where I know I can fit myself into the style that's needed for the picture. In a way I am *casting* myself.

*Three films you did—*A Star Is Born, The Marrying Kind *and* Bhowani Junction—*are all very diverse.*

There was a different attitude in the scripts. I think it's death for a director to have a knack for doing something special and sticking only to that. I think you stultify yourself. You must always try to do something a little different, even if the penalty is sometimes falling on your face. It's no good when you're just repeating yourself. You have to take a chance on everything you do.

What do you make of the state of American cinema today?

It's changed, everything changes. I deplore that it's limited, I deplore the enormous vulgarity and monotony of it. I think saying four-letter words is not very witty. It doesn't show the range of human experience. It limits the human experience, and that's too bad. If you read anything about the cinema—I've been reading about the very early movies—they did every damned thing in the world. They had quite a range. Today I think we're trying to play it safe. The audience just wants blockbusters, and it's a great pity. Try to make your pictures human, with human disappointment, human laughter.

You worked through the contract system of the big studio heydays. How different are things today?

I was under contract at the studios, but they were not the big, horrible factories that they have been largely written about as. They had some great virtues: you got the best stories, the best scripts, the best actors, the best cameramen. They had all that, and I only realized it after it was gone. You'd ask for something and you'd get it. I never was required to do anything. Maybe the choice of subject, but nobody really interfered. You did it as well as you could, with as much subtlety and believability as possible. You were always encouraged that way.

There were also certain intelligent restraints. People were not allowed to indulge themselves. I worked with these tycoons, and if you had anything at all to give, they encouraged you. Why? Because it was to their advantage. They realized that talent was the coin of the realm, and they were very sympathetic to it. And patient, very patient. Irving Thalberg, if he had any faith in someone, would go with them a long, long way. I find nowadays it's a little too opportunistic. "You're a great director, you're wonderful. You can't do wrong. And you do this and we don't dare come near you." And then, if things don't go well, the dogs throw them out. There used to be much more balance. It had a lot to do with the success of cinema at that time. Back then it was not a heartless factory. I was never a company boy, but I did find the studios comforting. The way I see it today, the studios are production companies who rent their facilities. Today I do a picture and wonder, "Oh God, where is the stage department?" We were spoiled back then. It was no fairyland, but if you wanted to work, you could work, and you could live. Now you have to dig for it yourself.

I was wondering if there is anything in your background or the way you were raised that made you especially good with women and portraying women that are interesting and real?

Well, I don't know. They always say I'm woman's director. In the first place, that was in the days of the movie queens when they had those great personalities and great parts. And I always said, very respectfully, "But there always were men in these pictures—Cary Grant, Jimmy Stewart, Spencer Tracy, John Barrymore." I don't know that there's any difference between the way you direct for a man or a woman. I don't have a different hat, I don't direct them any differently from the men. And sometimes it's been a deterrent because they'll say, "He can't direct this." When it interested me I did a Western, which I liked very much, but the other Westerns I really would not know how to do. Sometimes I admire them and sometimes I don't. I know I couldn't do it and I don't want to.

Have you had any specific problems in working with actresses?

As a matter of fact, women are much more realistic than men. I'd rather handle ten women than ten men because they have less vanity, curiously enough. They're perfectly realistic, and they're tougher, too, in a way.

Could you tell us about working with Garbo? Did you have to direct her a lot?

Well, I instructed her. I coached her absolutely, just like I coached Katharine Hepburn and Laurence Olivier and brought them up from obscurity. No, of course I didn't direct her a lot. A director has to have different attitudes in working with different actors. The director has to know how much to say and when to shut up and what influence he has. The actors have to respect him. Sometimes actors, as great as they are, are stuck, and you have to help them unravel certain things. You have to use different methods when working with an absolutely inexperienced actress. You are, in a sense, coaching. A lot of wonderful directors aren't interested in that and they can't do it, but I rather like working with young people.

As a director, you know in your mind how you hope a performance will be, but you keep your mind open and also know enough not to coach people like Garbo. But that does not mean you abdicate the function of a director because these people are so grand and glorious. You cannot sit by and tremble and be on your knees with "Oh, aren't they great artists?" You have to know how to use them and—if they're very creative—create a climate in which they can work and then influence them in ways that are not obvious. You have to press a different button with everybody, though it's not done deliberately. In *Love Among the Ruins,* which was a very funny, romantic, light comedy, there's Olivier and he was very sympathetic, and I didn't teach him how to be sympathetic. The part itself did that. You've got to know when an actor is good, what he's likely to do when he's off the beam, and how to get him on the beam so he won't be nervous or slow or affected or uptight.

What do you do if you have trouble working with an actor?

You sound as though you've been to a drama school. Sometimes I bully them, sometimes I tell them long sad stories, and I also encourage them. You say, "You can do it" and "Stop it, get on with it." Very often an actor will say, "The one thing I cannot do is a certain kind of scene." Well, I'll say, "Try it and you'll find that's what you can do really very well." They don't really know what they can do, they haven't the reassurance of having done it before. There are all sorts of tricks. I do think directors can influence performances. The director should be interested in acting, in actors, and not in himself. I don't mean to be noble, but you've got to think of what the other person is doing and how you can achieve it together. It's all a collaboration. I think you've got to anticipate. What can they do? What can I give them? What can they get out of me?

You once said that there are certain actors who can't play scenes with women. What did you mean by that?

They're very good at punching someone in the jaw, but they can't play love scenes with women. They don't know how to treat a woman or behave with a woman. Poor women! There are actors who are good but who can't generate eroticism. It is a lost art.

What can you do when you encounter that in an actor?

Well, it's tough. It's too goddamned bad. You do the best you can, but you can't change an actor's personality. And there are some very good actors who are simply not good at this. Shall I talk indiscreetly? Broderick Crawford, who's a very good actor, he played in *Born Yesterday*. His character was played in the stage version by a man called Paul Douglas. Paul Douglas was just as tough as Broderick Crawford, and when he punched Judy Holliday in the face it was terribly painful. But it was erotic in a way. And Crawford punched her like a policeman, you know? He didn't generate that erotic tension.

What do you think has happened to female roles in the last twenty years?

I think they're lousy. They always play whores and cocktail waitresses and dopes. Isn't it odd, since women have been liberated that on the screen they're such dummies? I feel it's more difficult to write a woman's part. You see, when you do bang-up melodramas and shoot-'em-up stories, the woman is always the stooge and she's always dragged along and it's artificially done. But to write a woman's part requires sensibility and a kind of depth and understanding, and that doesn't go these days somehow. I don't know why it doesn't. I think maybe you people know that much better than I do.

What do you do with the actors to bring about the spontaneous reaction you are looking for?

If they're good actors they already have that sense of immediacy. I do not encourage improvisation because I think it's a lot of nonsense. If you have a good text and good actors they should give that sense of freshness. With *My Fair Lady*, Rex Harrison was very nervous because he'd never done anything on the screen that he'd done on the stage. He'd done the play for three years and didn't want to just restage it—he wanted that freshness and it was up to me to see that it came. I've done that on many occasions, like *Born Yesterday* where the actor—Judy Holliday—had done the part before. It's up to the director to help him or her see it in a fresh way. Now, generally, I don't think it's awfully tough to make an actor seem spontaneous. I see it on television all the time. Sometimes I say to actors, "Think of this scene. Think of it, really. You're acting-thinking but you're not really thinking." I see them go through an awful lot of motions. When I see that kind of thing I say, "Stop all that trick stuff. Don't be self-indulgent." There must be some discipline, and this is what you must learn as a director. You also have to learn to detect anything that's phony. You should know when an actor is at his best and then let it go at that. Don't press him. Sometimes it's not exactly what you want but it's the best you'll get out of that actor at that time. You must give an actor the sense that you have faith in him, because it's devastating for them if they look at you and they know you don't have complete faith in them.

They always talk about how a director handles actors. Let me say something about this. Actors can either bore you to death or irritate you with the best intentions. You always do your best, but sometimes they're such bores and they're inflexible and they're opinionated and you get fed up with them, although you're not supposed to. But there must be some kind of interchange—if you're courteous they must return the courtesy.

In a film like Little Women *there is a feeling of real spontaneity with some of the actors. How do you get that kind of feeling?*

In the first place, they didn't improvise it. They didn't make up the words as they went along. It was a very respectable script and they learned the words. They didn't do a lot of that damned nonsense. I can hear it when I see pictures where the actors go, "Eh, oh, yes, well . . ." They are improvising, and it tends to be disorderly and undisciplined. But the job of a talented actor is to make it seem as though he hadn't spoken the lines before. I'll tell you what Helen Hayes said. She said she was absolutely appalled when actors would say, "Well, I don't know, this doesn't feel good," and they would change the words. Helen said when she had difficulty with words she'd just go to her dressing room and do it and do it and do it until she thought it was right. There's no such thing as "No, I can't." That's a lot of crap, and I think there's too much of it.

For *Little Women* there was some rehearsal. I think you can do a certain amount of rehearsal and set things up, but I believe that the actual thing happens when the camera goes because the camera must catch the immediacy and freshness. I find that if you over-rehearse, or if you talk about it too damned much, then the magic goes out of it. We rehearsed some for *My Fair Lady*, but it never really sprang to life until the camera went.

Do you work with the actors ahead of time to develop the motivation for the character or the mannerisms?

No, I don't. Motivation is in the script. You can illuminate it for the actors, but my blood runs cold when I hear the cliché that directors talk to actors to work up motivation. It's in the text—it's in the scenes themselves. You don't have to tell actors or actresses about dramatic conflict, though maybe you can suggest how to achieve it or stimulate it. I think the director sets the tone on the set. In my experience, he sets the tempo of the picture if he has a certain amount of strength and tact. He must be in a sense a commander. Naturally the actors have ideas that are interesting, and you listen. But apparently everybody now thinks that it is their divine right or that they're being denied their civil liberties, if you order them to do this or do that.

Have you gotten more accomplished performances from actors that you've known for some time?

No, not really, except for the first few days when everybody is scared of each other. But after a while it's rather refreshing, and the joke sometimes is to get something from an actor that you're not sure he has. He discovers it in himself. But that comes from experience. These are not great mysteries I'm telling you. When you've had some experience you'll discover these things. There's no special trick.

What is it that annoys you most about the films you see?

Make it believable, make it on the level. That is my greatest criticism. Sometimes when I see a scene, I say, "I don't believe a goddamned word of it. You are acting, and I don't believe it." There was an experience on *It Should Happen to You,* with Judy Holliday and Jack Lemmon that might be a useful tip for you. They did a scene where they had a fight and I said, "It's all well and good, but I don't believe it. You're acting very well but I don't believe it." I said to Jack Lemmon, "What do you do when you're angry?" He said, "I get sick to my stomach. I have cramps when I have a fight." I said, "Do that." And it was terribly funny, because in the midst of this awful row he sat down and indicated that he was feeling very ill. Those are the things you'll find out, the oddities. But don't do things just to be odd.

I think I read somewhere that you liked the Paul Morrissey films.

Oh, yes. I love *Dracula.* Not a word against that, please.

It might be construed as being purposely odd.

Oh, it is. Very odd. He breaks all the rules and it's very diverting. But the style of the pictures is outrageous; they're absolutely unreal and most amusing and fantastic. In their own terms they are believable. But he makes it a whole different ball game. I'm just talking about when you're doing a regular, sincere picture. You can't tell Dracula to be sincere—it's an extravaganza. And I'm sure that in his own terms, in his own phantasmagoric terms, Dracula is believable.

What happens to the trust between the actor and the director if you have to do a large number of takes?

It depends. Garbo, let's say, did six or seven takes and she's kind of finished. Spencer Tracy was that way too. There are others who will do an enormous number of takes and don't mind. Katharine Hepburn was that way, especially when she was inexperienced. She didn't mind it. And Audrey Hepburn never minded—she rather liked it. We are all inclined to do an inordinate amount of takes, but one has to discipline oneself. I did a picture with Connie Bennett—which I hope none of you have seen—and she had just one line of Shakespeare. I believe it was, "Trust me, sir, I shall be more faithful." She couldn't quite get it, and we kept doing it again and again. Those were the golden days of Hollywood when you just kept the cameras rolling, which you weren't really supposed to do. And she'd, say, "Trust me, son of a bitch, trust me, sir." And David Selznick swore that I did eighty-two takes. He also swore that I changed the number and instead of take eighty-two, I selected take number one. It isn't true. But I do it as often as I think necessary, and I don't think I've ever had any trouble with actors saying, "I'm not going to do it again."

Do you always shoot all the takes at the same time, or do you ever realize that an actor is just worn out and you'll have to do it at another time?

Yes, sometimes they've had it, and you'll say, "Let's stop tonight," and you'll pick it up in the morning. On *My Fair Lady*, for example, Rex Harrison had to do some quick-patter numbers and he was just drained, and I'd say, "Let's stop," and we'd do it first thing in the morning, and he'd get it immediately.

You've let a lot of the studios edit your films. I was wondering how you feel about that?

Well, now we have the right to make the first cut. And though in the past we didn't, I always stuck my nose in. I was right in there. At times I've been overridden and I yelled and yelled. But the final cut—the actual cut—is the property of the studio. They own it and have certain rights over it. I never found them to be blatantly against your cut. I'll tell you something about the old tycoons who are supposed to be such terrible villains—they were showmen and perfectly practical men. If you had anything good they wanted it, and they also handled you in a certain way, and I don't think there was all that bullying that people talk about. People say, "Oh, how could you work under that terrible system?" Well, the pictures you see from the 1930s and 1940s were done under that system. So they were smart, they were clever people. You give a little and you take a little. But then you'd come to a point where there was an impasse and you'd have to see how you were going to solve that, and sometimes it was disagreeable.

When you were working for the studios, were you able to suggest an idea that writers would then develop?

You mean the initial idea? No, I don't think I ever did. I don't think I'm inventive enough. I have suggested that I'd like to do a thing in this locale or that. I think the greatest thing of all is the wonderful thing of research. It leads you up these fascinating byroads. Presently I'm interested in doing something about 1875 when there was a lot of fake spiritualism and women's rights. And I've been reading a great deal about this and that, reading biographies. Have you read the brilliant book *Ragtime*? It is such an amusing book because it takes these characters that you know—Houdini and Evelyn Nesbit and Emma Goldman—and blends them together in a new light, sometimes moving and sometimes funny. I'm sure E. L. Doctorow found out all about those people and then said, "This is how I'd treat it." He isn't supposed to be historically accurate. For example, Tom Stoppard, who wrote *Rosencranz and Guildenstern Are Dead,* does somewhat the same thing. He wrote a play that I saw last year in London called *Travesties.* It is a very amusing play. It takes place in Zurich, where there happened to be these characters at that time: Lenin and his wife, preparing the revolution; James Joyce; and Tristan Tzara, the founder of Dada. Stoppard mixed all these people together and set them against a performance of *The Importance of Being Ernest.* It was a very difficult play to do, but one reason it worked was because it was well researched. I urge you all, if you do anything at all, even contemporary things, before you embark on it, just look around and learn. If you are going to do a scene in a hospital, go to a hospital and look at it.

Do you do the same thing with a character—create some back story to give context to the actor?

Yes I do, but I don't go into all that analyzing business. I just tell them what I think. I'll say something like "My mother used to do that." Whatever stimulates them. But that must always be done very lightly; you can't go in and give them a psychoanalysis of the characters because, Christ, it really bogs everything down. I remember a picture we were making in London with Ava Gardner, and she came back from lunch and was absolutely furious. She had given an interview at lunch and she said, "This goddamned woman asked me questions about this and that." This woman was needling her. So we had a scene to do in the afternoon, and there was a man in the scene who was in a very interesting way belittling her. So I said, "He's particularly devilish to you. He's very shrewd and he's getting under your skin, the way that woman did at lunch today." And her face flushed, and I said, "Roll it." She said, "You son of a bitch, I'm never going to tell you anything again." She'd been through it moments earlier and knew what that humiliation was. So you can use things like that. But you must do it lightly. If it's something that happened the day before, let them think it over.

Although Camille *was photographed in black and white, there's a feeling for color in it. Some shots in the opening scenes of dancing girls seem to evoke Degas or Toulouse-Lautrec. Could you talk about the ways you use color in your other films?*

I think color has to be used very discreetly. You have to discipline color the way a painter does. I learned that from a great friend of mine, a wonderful photographer with whom I worked, George Hoyningen-Huene.* He had impeccable taste and enormous knowledge, and I would watch the way he removed the color and used it very originally. In *Les Girls* he did something very interesting. A scene was set in London, and he blew a puff of cigarette smoke and said, "The whole thing should be this color: the background, the set, the girls' clothes. They should be this color." And I said, "Won't that be drab?" He said, "No, no, no." Later I saw that it was a removal of color; color used with discipline the way it should be used. You just can't splash color all over the place.

Do you feel that your style of directing has changed over the years?

I don't think my style of directing has changed. I always tried to make it believable. They showed a number of pictures from the thirties at the Academy recently—the Marx Brothers and Mae West—and then suggested that they show a picture of mine that was done in the thirties. But it was a rather serious picture. And I said, "Do you think that this is the thing to do?" The audience was half serious film students, and half were the members of the Academy. So they set out to show this picture—it was *Sylvia Scarlett,* Katharine Hepburn's first picture—and Robert Wise said, "The director is here and he's going to talk to you about it after we show

---

*George Hoyningen-Huene (1900–1968) was a Russian-born fashion photographer and "color consultant" on several Hollywood productions of the 1950s.

it." And then the picture started and there was a bad laugh here and a bad laugh here and a terrible laugh here, and I thought, "What the hell should I do? Should I go away?" And I said, "No, in for a penny, in for a pound. I'll stick with it." When it was over and they said, "Here's the director," I got a very friendly reception. They weren't aware that they had been rather rude. So I got up and I said, "I was sitting in the back there and I was cringing at times. What you laughed at, what you thought was so absurd, was a more or less romanticized condition of the way a young love affair was carried on." I did the picture in 1930, and I think the play was written in 1920, and it was a more or less accurate, romanticized reproduction of the way people behaved at that time. Look at *Tosca,* for example, which is about the secret police and people being shot. Today we consider it as just romantic melodrama, but at the time it was a representation of what went on. Just because it isn't happening contemporaneously, that doesn't mean it was false when it was done.

What kinds of things do you go through when preparing to direct a film?

One hell of a lot, I can tell you that much. First of all, I am a great believer in research. In a film like *Little Women* you should ask yourself, "What kind of clothes did they wear?" As you know, the clothes were very good in that film. The house is a reproduction of Louisa May Alcott's house; the scale is exactly right. I really submerge myself in the period and the style of the film and learn as much about it as I can. I do that with modern things too. If I do a comedy set in New York, where I was born, I still ask myself questions like "What is a New York apartment like?" If I do a farce in a court, then I will go to a real court and notice how the judge and jury behave. When I have seen something with my own eyes, then I know I am on firm ground.

What did you hope to accomplish with your films?

Well, to explore the possibility of the story and have it acted well. That's all I hope. I don't think I can say that I wanted to solve any great world problems. I think there's an awful lot of pretentiousness, and a lot of crap talked about a lot of these things. I think one should be absolutely honest. I think the great thing about the early movies is that they were on the level. If you see a Mary Pickford picture, she believed in what she was doing. Now I think there's a lot of hocus-pocus going on.

When I watch your films, it seems to me there is definitely a "Cukor style." Do you agree?

I'm not aware of that. I just go into a day's work. I'm not thinking, "Oh, this one's going to knock 'em dead," though I hope it will. But you do whatever you can. It's all filtered through one's sensibilities, what you think is funny, what you think is touching. All of you, when you work, you'll find that out.

I have a feeling that I am not telling you people what you want to know. I wish to Christ that I could tell you how to make films. You could turn me inside out. Experience has taught me many things; we would be here for twenty weeks. It is the knowledge of a lifetime. Don't think that you can learn it that way; life is not that way. You learn out of bitter experience, trial and error. Life teaches you that. As sincere as you all are, you can't learn it all in school. Don't be dopes, that's all I can say. And don't be inflexible. Look around, look and see and learn and try and do it. But be firm. There comes a time when you say, "I've listened, but this is the way I feel it should be done." And that includes working with very powerful and great stars or producers. I don't want to confuse you. There's no mystery. If you work, and work hard, if you're given the opportunity to work, you'll find all the answers for yourselves. I really mean that. Don't be too highbrow. Just get in there and work. If you can get jobs and experience, that is the greatest thing. Stick to it, don't be discouraged. There are an awful lots of kicks in the ass as you go up the hill. It's a happy life, but not an easy one.

Films as Director

1930	*Grumpy*	1934	*Dinner at Eight*
	The Virtuous Sin	1935	*David Copperfield*
1931	*Tarnished Lady*	1936	*Sylvia Scarlett*
	The Royal Family of Broadway		*Romeo and Juliet*
	(codirector)	1937	*Camille*
	Girls About Town	1938	*Holiday*
1932	*Rockabye*	1939	*Zaza*
	A Bill of Divorcement		*The Women*
	What Price Hollywood?	1940	*Susan and God*
1933	*Our Betters*		*Escape*
	Little Women	1941	*A Woman's Face*

1941 *Two-Faced Woman*
      The Philadelphia Story
1942 *Her Cardboard Lover*
      Keeper of the Flame
1944 *Gaslight*
      Winged Victory
1948 *A Double Life*
1949 *Adam's Rib*
      Edward, My Son
1950 *A Life of Her Own*
1951 *Born Yesterday*
1952 *The Model and the Marriage
         Broker*
      The Marrying Kind
      Pat and Mike

1953 *The Actress*
1954 *It Should Happen to You*
      A Star Is Born
1956 *Bhowani Junction*
1957 *Les Girls*
1958 *Wild Is the Wind*
1960 *Heller in Pink Tights*
      Let's Make Love
1962 *Something's Got to Give*
      The Chapman Report
1964 *My Fair Lady*
1969 *Justine*
1976 *The Blue Bird*
1981 *Rich and Famous*

You know, the most important moment—not just in writing, but in the decision of making a picture—is the one split second when you make up your mind and say, "This is the one we're going to do."

BILLY WILDER
(Born in Vienna, 1906—Died 2002)

Billy Wilder spent much of his childhood in a hotel for transients in Austria operated by his father. Particularly fascinated by the resident pool sharks, Billy was beating the regulars at their own game by the time he was nine. "I learned many things about human nature," he remembered of those days. "None of them favorable."

In March of 1986 I picked Billy up at his apartment in Westwood and drove him to the new AFI campus in Hollywood to meet with the fellows. He was wearing a cashmere sport coat and tie and had the zest of a bantamweight fighter ready for a sparring session. The fellows gave him a standing ovation and Billy, his head bowed slightly, received it modestly. "The last standing ovation I had was many years ago crossing the Atlantic on the *Ile de France*," he said. "After dinner they showed *Mrs. Miniver*. They thought I was William Wyler."

Wilder was a screenwriter in the twenties in Germany, left Europe when Hitler came to power, wrote scripts in Hollywood in the thirties, was a star director in the forties and fifties, saw his star fall in the sixties and seventies and had the good fortune to live through the eighties and nineties as the idol of a new generation of filmmakers.

The Wilder wit was evident in the screenplay for Ernst Lubitsch's *Ninotchka*. A man goes into a restaurant: "I'd like a cup of coffee without cream." The waiter says, "We don't have cream. Would you like it without milk?" Billy's pal and partner, I. A. L. Diamond—whom Billy's wife, Audrey, described as the most famous collaborator since Quisling*—noted that the

*Vidkun Quisling was head of Norway's government during the Nazi occupation of the country. He was executed in 1945.

Billy Wilder directing *The Fortune Cookie* (1966), the first pairing of
Jack Lemmon and Walter Matthau. Wilder believed in straightforward
photography. "Let's say I'm old fashioned, or primitive enough
to believe that if somebody grabs your arm and says, 'Jesus, look at that
shot,' then you've lost him."

year *Ninotchka* came out it was competing for the Academy Award against
*Stagecoach, Mr. Smith Goes to Washington, Goodbye, Mr. Chips, Gunga Din,
Wuthering Heights, The Wizard of Oz, Love Affair, Of Mice and Men, Dark
Victory, Only Angels Have Wings, Beau Geste, Young Mr. Lincoln, Intermezzo*
and *Destry Rides Again*. The ever-wry Mr. Diamond observed, "The movie
business has come a long way since then."

Wilder became a director to protect his scripts and rose to the top in collaboration with screenwriter Charles Brackett. They made *Five Graves to*

Cairo, a World War II thriller; *Double Indemnity*, an exercise in suspense; and then scored with Oscars for *The Lost Weekend* and *Sunset Boulevard*. Wilder went on his own as a producer, director and writer, creating—in many cases with co-screenwriter Diamond—a string of successes including *Witness for the Prosecution, Love in the Afternoon, Some Like It Hot, The Apartment* and lesser efforts such as *The Fortune Cookie, Kiss Me, Stupid* and *Buddy Buddy.*

One Monday morning in 1981 I received a call from Swifty Lazar inviting me to a party he was having for the Wilders. *Buddy Buddy* had opened the previous Friday and I asked, "How's Billy's picture doing?" Irving replied crisply, "Billy's picture is dead." Studios were suddenly able to get overnight computerized box-office reports and make instant appraisals of a film's potential, and abandon costly national television ads for weak performers. No longer could a film start slowly and build an audience over time. Studios started placing their bets on costly films designed to be entertainment events for youngsters. Billy Wilder's talent languished when confronted by a new breed of executives serving ever-larger corporations who were convinced that the master's time had passed.

Billy had a sardonic view of the world. His was a European outlook without the underlying American optimism that colored so many of the films of his friends and colleagues in Hollywood. Walter Matthau said that Wilder saw the worst in the best of us and the best in the worst of us. Billy knew that his skeptical view of human nature could be a liability and often quoted George Bernard Shaw: "If you want to tell people the truth, you'd better make them laugh."

Wilder lived to ninety-five and like most of the other great directors he never officially retired. "This here ball game is going into extra innings," he said. "I'm staying in shape. I played winter ball in the Dominican Republic, I changed my stance, I shortened my grip and I got some new contact lenses. There are a few hits left in me, maybe even a triple or a home run." He once told Jack Lemmon, "Remember, you're just as good as the best thing you've ever done," which in Billy's case means a revered place in cinema history. And he might have added, "Nobody's perfect."

BILLY WILDER

—◆—

December 13, 1978*

Thank you for inviting me. We've established some ground rules: no big monologue. I'm not an orator or anything like that. Just questions and answers, and I'm going to ask the questions. No, seriously: questions and answers. Or rather suggestions for answers, because there is really no such thing as an answer to anything. It's only a dilettante, you know, who comes out and makes a picture with a big problem and solves it at the end. But if you have a good problem, then that already is a good picture. It's the question that will make it. So somebody start and I will defend myself.

You wrote many of your films in collaboration with other writers. What are some of the advantages and disadvantages you found in collaborative efforts?

Well, when I started writing in America I couldn't speak any English, so I did need a collaborator. I was lucky to find some very good ones and I found them very helpful. When I became a director, it was always good to have another pair of eyes and ears that could kind of check and double-check as to what I was doing. And for all of you here, for the ones who are writers, you will find out that writing is a very dull and boring, dreary thing. One of the best things about the collaborator is that he stops you from committing suicide, unless you're smart enough to work on the first floor. But then again you can have some cyanide pills in one of your teas,

---

*This transcript contains segments from seminars Wilder gave at the American Film Institute on January 7, 1976 (with his writing partner I. A. L. Diamond) and on March 3, 1986.

like Mr. Goering did. Very often as I walk to the can I say, "Come on, it's not all that bad." But it just depends on what kind of a collaborator you have. I know some marvelous and very successful playwrights, like Moss Hart and George Kaufman. Moss Hart did write one or two plays by himself, but most of the time he worked with somebody. It's fun, you know? You arrive in the morning and you have forty-five minutes of bitching about your wife and how lousy the food was, and you saw a picture and it stunk. It establishes a good atmosphere before you get going on your own crap.

Now, on the subject of collaboration, there are a lot of people who are so egomaniacal that they will absolutely not permit another name on the script. Take the famous story of Chaplin making *Monsieur Verdoux.* Orson Welles came up with the idea. With Chaplin it was not only that he wrote it, not only that he directed it, not only that he acted in it, but he also composed the music, which most of the time he stole. But before I go any further I would like you to know that Mr. Chaplin, up to the moment he started writing dialogue, was an absolutely unique genius. He was a God, just so that you don't think I'm demeaning Mr. Chaplin. I'm just talking about his stinginess of not wanting to share credit. There are a lot of people who would rather do it by themselves than share credit, and there are some very good ones among them, but I just find it more fun to collaborate. It's such an exhausting thing, you know, facing that empty page in the morning. And then you always need help when you're arguing with the front office. You need somebody there, preferably somebody with a machine gun around his shoulder. You have to have specific talent to be a collaborator. It's like a marriage.

Do you actually sit in a room together and pound it out or do you separate and each work on different scenes?

I'm gratified when this question is asked because most people think the actors make up the words. Well, Mr. Diamond and I meet at, say, nine thirty in the morning and open shop, like bank tellers, and we sit there in one room. We read *Hollywood Reporter* and *Variety,* exchange them, and then just stare at each other. Sometimes nothing happens. Sometimes it goes on until twelve thirty, and then I'll ask him, "How about a drink?" And he nods, and then we have a drink and go to lunch. Or sometimes we come full of ideas. This is not the muse coming through the windows and kissing our brows. We just sit together and discuss, having more or less settled on the theme of what we're trying to do and having discussed the three acts in which we divide our pictures. We start to do the dialogue, talking to each other, and we fight it out while we're doing it. If the two of us agree it's no good, we throw it away and try a third version. In other words, it is not one of those things where you kind of get nervous and angry and walk around and say, "That was the best line ever and you rejected it." No, let's find one that we both agree on. So you have to be a born collaborator.

Writing is very hard work, and having done both writing and directing, I tell you that directing is a pleasure and writing is a drag. Directing can become difficult, but it is a pleasure because you have something to work with. You can put the camera here or there, you can interpret the scene this way or that way, the readings can be such or such. But writing is just an empty page—you start with absolutely nothing. I think writers are vastly underrated and underpaid. It's totally impossible to make a great picture out of a lousy script. It's impossible, though, for a mediocre director to completely screw up a great script.

Where did the idea for Sunset Boulevard *come from?*

That came out of our heads. It was an idea that Charlie Brackett and I had long before we tackled it. We wanted to do it, believe it or not, five years before we actually got around to it. We wanted to make a picture with a kind of passé star. We wanted to do it with Mae West. That's all I can tell you. But it didn't come out this way.

There is no such thing as somebody sitting down and saying, "Now, all right, I'm going to make a new picture." Not at all. You have ideas stashed away, dozens of them—good, bad or indifferent. Then you pull them out of your memory, out of your drawer, you combine them. An actor is available, and that's the way it starts. People think when it comes to a screenplay you start with absolutely nothing. But the trouble is that you have a million ideas and you have to condense them into a thousand ideas, and you have to condense those into three hundred ideas to get it under one hat, as it were. In other words, you start with too much, not with nothing, and it can go in every kind of direction. Every possible avenue is open. Then you have to dramatize it—it is as simple as that—by omitting, by simplifying, by finding a clean theme that leads someplace.

Sunset Boulevard was a picture where everything sort of fell into my lap. I needed the Paramount studio, and we got permission to shoot at

Paramount. I needed Cecil B. DeMille to play DeMille, and he played it. I needed somebody to play the part Stroheim played. Stroheim at one time had been a director and had, indeed, directed Gloria Swanson in *Queen Kelly.* We needed old faces and we got Buster Keaton. Everything was just right.

There's a good chance that if Norma Desmond from Sunset Boulevard *were alive today, she'd be working on daytime soaps and not be sheltered away.*

When we made that picture with Gloria Swanson people forget that she herself was considered sort of an "old bag" from silent-picture times. At the time when we shot the picture she was actually fifty years old, that was all. She was then three or four years younger than Audrey Hepburn is today. But it was the split, you know, the divide between sound pictures and silent pictures that made such a difference. She was actually very young for that thing. She was just forgotten because she had stopped making pictures when she was about thirty, when sound came in. But what would she be doing today? As you heard in the picture, she had those oil wells, pumping, pumping, pumping. I guess she would have four or five gigolos. She would now be living somewhere in Santa Barbara with George Hamilton.

What was it like directing Erich von Stroheim in Sunset Boulevard *who himself had been a great director?*

I had admired Stroheim when I was a newspaperman in Berlin and in Vienna; I liked his pictures. When I came here from Vienna we made a picture called *Five Graves to Cairo,* and the idea was to get Stroheim, who at that time lived in Paris, to play General Rommel. We were shooting the tank scenes in the desert in Indio, and he arrived from Paris. When I came back to the studio, they told me that Stroheim was in Western costume trying on his uniform. I had never met him before in my life. So I rushed across and there he is, and I clicked my heels and said, "My name is Wilder." And he says, "How are you?" In order to kind of make him feel good, I said, "Who would have ever thought that little Wilder is going to direct big Stroheim?" And he just sort of barked at me a little bit. Then I said, "You know, Erich, your problem was you were always ten years ahead of your time." And he looks at me and he

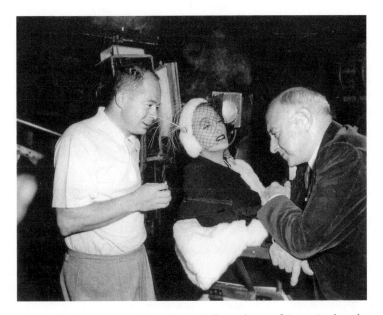

With Gloria Swanson and Cecil B. DeMille on the set of *Sunset Boulevard* (1950). DeMille directed many of Swanson's early films, and Wilder recruited him to play himself in the story of the decline of a silent film star.

Wilder was a great admirer of director Erich von Stroheim (left) and cast him as General Erwin Rommel in *Five Graves to Cairo* (1943). Later von Stroheim played Max von Mayerling in *Sunset Boulevard* for Wilder.

says, "Twenty." That was Stroheim. He was just a unique guy. When you talked to him you felt he was a very close friend of Emperor Francis Joseph.

By the time we made *Sunset Boulevard* we had become great friends. He came to me and said, "Wouldn't it be nice if people find out subsequently that Max von Mayerling was the director who directed Swanson, that I was her husband, and now I'm the butler here? That I am the one who is writing the fan letters to make her feel better?" A wonderful idea, and I took it. Then a few days later he came and said, "Would you do me a favor? I have an idea for a scene." And I said, "What is it?" He says, "I think that we should dramatize the fact that he still loves her." I said, "Well, what did you have in mind?" I'm always listening to what people say, and he says, "I would like to wash and press her panties." I talked him out of that. Then he said he would like to limp. Such a limp! And so I had to calm him down because naturally he was still living in the old Stroheim pictures, which were absolutely remarkable. I don't know whether you run here pictures like *Blind Hostage* or *Foolish Wives*? And *Greed*, of course. You know, this was the beginning of when Hollywood started to be afraid of directors. Somebody told me that he was shooting *Greed* in San Francisco and he stopped shooting for three days because there wasn't enough horse shit in the streets. They had to collect it from San Jose and all over, because that's what he wanted.

What does it mean to you to direct an actor or an actress?

You cannot generalize that. This is like asking a doctor the same kind of question. Well, there are some nice patients, there are some terrifying nudniks, there are hypochondriacs and there are some jolly ones who say, "So I've got a 106-degree fever, I'll be all right, Doc." It all depends. Maybe if there's a kind of a generalization possible, I would say that fifty-five percent are bores. Yes, especially when they start digging deep into the character, because then you spend a week with them saying, "Yes, blah, blah, my father, my grandfather, blah." And then I say, "For Chrissakes, learn those goddamned lines and let's get it over with." Because most of the time the more they ask, the less they project. Some of them bring something, some others just do it because they need rent money. Some are so fatiguing. It's nothing, you know, just a simple line. But with them it's "What is my motivation?" The motivation is that you're going to get forty-five thousand dollars for a small part.

In all your films it seems as if the pacing is very quick. Do you ever tell the actors to deliver their lines faster?

Well, you see there is sort of a misconception that pace and speaking quickly are the same thing. You can have pace by people not speaking quickly. It depends on the cut and the rhythm of the thing, which sometimes I miss completely. I try to get it over with because leisurely moments, silent moments, have much more power. Certain pictures have to be played at a good clip. But don't confuse pace with actors just rattling things off. People in our world confuse poverty with misery. I have known very many poor people and they have not been miserable, and I can tell you about people in the luxury estates next door to here who are really miserable.

You've worked with actors with widely differing temperaments. Can you give us some advice about how to achieve strong performances?

Ah, the advice is that you yourself have to play twenty different parts. You have to be a sycophant, you have to be a sadist, you have to be a nurse, you have to be a cook, you have to be a philosopher, you have to demean yourself, you have to be a screamer. It just depends on the actor. No two actors can be treated the same or they would be bad actors. Everybody has his own little weaknesses, and there are different ways of coaxing it out of them. Sometimes you just have to do it with the whip and they like you for it. Sometimes you just have to beg, or sometimes they don't talk to you for three days because they think you insulted them. But you've got to do it. You know, you're not marrying them, you don't have to live all your life with them. Once it's finished, you can kiss them or you can kick them, or you can avoid them—but the picture must be finished. You go through those things in every movie. It is demeaning. In a play, it's very simple. If the actor doesn't work out—the actor is snotty, or you don't want him— then you just use the understudy for three days and somebody else comes in. Whereas in a picture you've got to finish it because the guy is established, it's going to cost another four million dollars.

Do you tend to have a star in mind when you're writing a script?

With *Some Like It Hot,* we were way into the script when we found out that Marilyn Monroe was available and wanted to do the picture. I think, as a rule, it's bad to tell the actors, "I'm doing something for you and only you can play it." They don't like that. You just say, "I know that you can do it. You can interpret it because you can play anything." They love to hear that.

Could you share with us stories about working with Marilyn Monroe on The Seven Year Itch *and* Some Like It Hot?

You want me to talk about Marilyn? My God, I think there have been more books on Marilyn Monroe than on World War II, and there's a great similarity. It was a very complex thing working with her because she had tremendous problems with herself. She was on the edge of deep depression—whatever you want to call it—at all times. There was always a question which you sweated out: "Is she going to show up? Is she going to show up on time? Is she going to live through the scene? Is she going to finish the picture?" And that is a very nerve-wracking thing if you've got eight million dollars in the enterprise. But when it's all done, it's well worth it. It's that old thing that I said, I don't know, four hundred years ago: "Look, if I wanted somebody to be on time and to know the lines just perfectly, I've got an old aunt in Vienna. She's going to be there at five in the morning and never miss a word. But who wants to look at her?"

You've done a number of films with Jack Lemmon. I'm curious if there's something that draws you to him time and time again?

I'm terribly fond of Jack. We understand each other very well and it's a pleasure to work with him. He is a thinking actor, but not an argumentative one. By that I mean if we start shooting at nine o'clock, he would be there at 8:15 and would come to my office and say, "Hey, I've got a great idea! Look, why don't we do this? Blah, blah, blah, blah." And I just look at him, and he says, "I don't like it either." And he walks out.

I'm interested in whether on the set you are open to spontaneous decisions based on what's happening with the actors and what you see. For example, do you draw storyboards?

You touch on a very good point. I think I should storyboard and will henceforth, if I get another crack at it. I should prepare myself better. But unfortunately the way the industry works is that the actor is just flying in

With Marilyn Monroe on the set of *The Seven Year Itch* (1955). She also starred in *Some Like It Hot* (1959). Asked about the difficulty of working with Monroe, Wilder said, "Look, if I wanted somebody to be on time and to know the lines perfectly, I've got an old aunt in Vienna . . . but who wants to look at her?"

from Yugoslavia, and he arrives on Friday, and on Monday we have to start shooting. And we don't have the time you have when you're working on a play to really rehearse. The script is there, but if something better occurs, I'm the first one to accept it whether it comes from an actor, an electrician, from the script girl, even if it comes from the producer, which is rare. While you're rehearsing it doesn't cost any money. Once you start shooting, it's twenty-five thousand, thirty-five thousand dollars a day. The time to rehearse is before, not once the war has started.

You use the word war. *Do you see filmmaking as a series of events where you have to move through each event to eventual victory?*

Yes, you must go on. There must be something there, you know, because come eleven o'clock the next morning they are going to look at the rushes, and you have to have something. Not that in the front offices they are that observant or discerning. I remember one incident in the old days with the big executives with their enormous salaries, and they would run the rushes of all the pictures that were being shot. Paramount was shooting six, eight pictures at one time, because each studio made something like fifty pictures a year. We made a picture called *A Foreign Affair,* with Jean Arthur, Marlene Dietrich and a guy by the name of John Lund. He played an American captain in the army of occupation in Berlin. We're shooting a scene and as we start to set up the camera, in walks Ray Milland, who is in another picture on another stage. He was in the uniform of a colonel. And I said, "Hey, I'm going to shoot this with you and send it down to the executives when they run the rushes." By this time we had been shooting about six weeks but when I asked how the rushes were, nobody in the front office seemed to have noticed that suddenly there was a new leading man.

There's a book called The Art of Dramatic Writing *by Lajos Egri, and he says you can't write a good screenplay without having a premise such as "Love destroys friendship" or "Greed leads to honesty" or something like that. Did you always have a premise before you started writing a film?*

After you've started shooting, producers come to you and ask, "What is the theme of your picture?" They were very proud, you know, to have a theme. There's kind of a joke among us writers. You tell him, "The theme? Don't you know? The theme of this is 'You can't eat soup with a fork.'" And he says, "That's terrific."

Could you talk about this "three-act" structure in relation to Some Like It Hot?

Let me see. Well, the first act I would think is them getting on the train with the girls. Right? They get away from Chicago; I think that's enough. Then the second-act curtain is the gangsters have a convention at the hotel in Florida. That's suspense, right? Actually, it's four acts. The third act is the guys trying to keep in disguise and they're hiding under the table. Then the fourth act is the chase. It needs that kind of architectural structure, which is completely forgotten once you see the movie. We have to put those pillars in or that beautiful ceiling is going to come crashing down. Another thing, maybe for you guys who are structuring and writing pictures, the most important invention in *Some Like It Hot* was to make the fact of the two male musicians disguising themselves as women a question of life or death. If you don't have death—if you have not seen the St. Valentine's Day murder at the beginning and know that those are ruthless guys who want to bump them off—then these two guys who have hopped into women's clothes could just take their wigs off and say, "Look, I'm a guy."

How and when did you get into comedy?

I guess I was kind of always into comedy. When I was a newspaperman I wrote stories. I guess in high school we were doing comedy, but sometimes I just get bored with comedy. I don't always operate in one field. It's very difficult to do comedy because if they don't laugh when they should laugh you are there with egg on your face, and that's sad. In a serious picture you don't hear them being bored, but in a comedy you can hear them not laughing. You tried so hard and the guy did the pratfall, but nothing—and you wish you were dead.

Timing is the most important thing. You lay in the straight lines, then you have the big laugh, right? But you don't know how big the laugh is going to be, so now you have to kind of feel your way. "When do I start with the next straight line and start a new routine?" You don't want to step on the laughter with the straight line because the laugh is going to be shortened and weakened, and they will not hear the straight line for the next joke. What Irving Thalberg in his infinite wisdom did, when he made the great Marx Brothers pictures, was to have four or five great routines in each picture. He would send the Marx Brothers out on the road and they would play it for live audiences, and they would be timing it in different theaters so they knew exactly how to play it. But it's tough, you know. It's all more or less guesswork.

After being a successful screenwriter, why did you start to direct?

I got very impatient with directors, good directors but people who did not have the proper respect for the script. I was just very incensed. I remember one instance that is very typical. We were doing a script for a very good director by the name of Mitchell Leisen. Arthur Hornblow, Jr., was the producer. We were still working on the third act when they started shooting the picture, *Hold Back the Dawn*. It was about a Romanian gigolo who is trying to get into the country by pretending he loves an American schoolteacher so he can marry her. We had written a scene where he's lying in a hotel in the midst of his misery and he has no way of getting across the border. He was lying there in that dirty bed in that hotel, and there is a cockroach walking up the wall. He would always stop it with a cane, saying, "Where do you think you're going? Have you got a visa? You can't come in here." And bang, that was the scene. So we're going to lunch at old Lucey's on Melrose and we're passing the table of Charles Boyer, who's playing that Romanian gigolo. I say, "Charles, how are you?" He says, "I am very well." Well, sure, he had a big steak, the bottle of red wine, French. And I say, "What are you shooting today?" "Oh, today we're shooting the scene with the cockroach," he says. "Oh, that's a good scene." Then he says, "Except that we have no cockroach." I said, "What do you mean you have no cockroach?" He says, "Well, I came this morning and I talked to the director and I said, 'Mitch, this is stupid. How can I talk to a cockroach if the cockroach cannot answer me?'" "So what did you do?" He says, "We just threw it out. Now I'm just lying there in bed." We left the table and I turned to Brackett and said, "If that son of a bitch doesn't talk to the cockroach, he ain't talking to nobody." And we wrote him out of the third act.

It was this kind of an incident that infuriated me as a writer. They hated writers on the set anyway. You know, once you've finished the script, they grab it and rewrite it. If they're behind schedule, they tear out eight pages and they're on schedule again. It made me so furious I decided to go on and become a director. Not because I had worked in the theater before, not because I went to Strasberg, not because I had theories. I just wanted to have that script on the screen the way we wrote it. That was my beginning as a director, and possibly my end too.

You know, the most important moment—not just in writing, but in the decision of making a picture—is the one split second when you make up your mind and say, "This is the one we're going to do." In the olden days those lucky playwrights would take the play out to Pittsburgh where it does not work, then they take it somewhere in New England and it does not work, then they say, "Well, forget it, no big deal." And they bury it. If we make a lousy picture, we don't bury it—it keeps stinking forever on television. It goes on and on and on. People who are newspapermen or writing for magazines have a kind of a hunch, a feeling. They know what is of interest to the reader. But we have to anticipate that a year and a half or two years in advance, and it can fall as flat as a pancake. There's just suddenly no interest in it. We made a picture, *One, Two, Three,* which had something to do with the division of Berlin. The wall went up while we were shooting and it was funny no more. Now it's funny again and a big hit in Germany. But people were killed trying to escape the very week we were shooting in Berlin. That is the basic difference between comedy and tragedy. Comedy is when somebody falls down and gets up again and does it funnily, and tragedy is somebody falls down and cannot get up anymore. That's the basic difference. One is funny and the other is sad, because he broke his spine or ass or something.

Was it difficult convincing the studios to give you the opportunity to direct?

Picture after picture we made ourselves a reputation as solid, successful writers. The studio was making forty pictures; it was no big deal, so they thought, "What? Crazy Wilder. We're going to give him one picture, he's going to fall on his ass and he's going to come back and be a writer again." And they thought I'm going to do a very arty movie. You know, all very *The Cabinet of Dr. Caligari.* But I just set out and made as commercial a picture as I possibly could. I made it a point. They could not just say, "Well, you had your fun," because the picture made money and now they wanted me to direct. I was once asked, "Is it necessary for a director to know how to write?" And the answer is this—it is not necessary for a director to know how to write. However, it helps if he knows how to read. When you find a director who knows how to read, who asks the proper questions, who is not ashamed to say, "I don't get the meaning of the scene," instead of just going off on location and shooting something contrary to what you wanted to express in that scene, hold on to him. And if you're good I'm sure he will hold on to you, because good writers are rare.

How detailed is your treatment before you start writing the dialogue?

The treatment? There is no treatment. We just start right off. There is no outline, no first treatment, which has to be done very often if you need financing. We just start right off with scene one, and since we are on the film set all the time, there is no "Slow fade-in, camera tiptoes." None of that. Just "Day" or "Night," so that that cameraman knows how to light, not even "Morning" or "Evening." There's a minimum of fancy descriptions. I find with young writers, and some of them with very good ideas, that they get lost in technical descriptions of which they know very little. Nobody will say, "This is a great screenwriter because he always has the camera angles." Just have good characters and good scenes and something that plays. The camera technique is secondary. Writers and directors from the theater in New York are very camera-conscious, and the writers will give you minute descriptions, and directors will get on the dolly and will swish around and up and down. They are afraid that the scene will be too stagy. There's no such thing. Stage directors take a play and say, "Now, we're going to have to open it up." They have a very good scene in a living room that has played six hundred times on Broadway. But for the picture they take the people out and put them on the roof garden, then they take them downstairs, then into the drugstore, and it's still the same scene.

Could you talk about exposition, about how to tell us what has happened prior to whatever wonderful event has opened the story?

Well, this is the artistry of the writer. Usually you can learn about those methods from playwrights, because playwrights create characters like an onion. You peel the layers off. But I think if you are clever at hiding the mechanics, then you can disclose things while entertaining the audience and not give them the whole goddamned big thing they cannot swallow. There really are no rules, though at the end of a masterpiece like *Psycho,* there comes a guy and for seventeen minutes he explains the whole goddamned plot. But it doesn't matter because by this time you are so thrilled by the whole damn thing—by Perkins as a woman and that curious adventure behind the shower. Dialogue has to be integrated. In other words, you have to make the audience swallow the mechanics of what is required to understand the character. It has to be sugarcoated so they don't even know they were fed information.

Are there any particular principles you work with?

There are no mathematics to comedy and how to play a scene. What I usually do is when I start on a scene, I presume everybody has learned his lines. If not then they can just read them. We just sit in a circle and we read the scene. Then read it again, then improve it. Then we get the cameraman in, and I have a kind a feeling this is where we should start the scene, and then we go from this long shot into this two-shot, then that character is going to walk across to that other character and we pan with him. We develop a technique of how we're going to shoot it. Other directors are completely different, for instance my Austrian colleague—he's dead now—a very good director, Fritz Lang. His method was completely Prussian because he came at five in the morning and started making chalk marks on the floor. One, a two, a three, four, and in parentheses "cigarette." That means: you come in, you go from one to two, from two to three, on four you take the cigarette out, on five you extinguish it, then you come back to six. And it suddenly becomes sort of like a guy pulling strings. I rehearse until they feel comfortable with the scene, until it's beginning to happen, until everybody knows what he's going to do and there is no cramp in there, no forced move that is unnatural. Sometimes I add a line, sometimes I cross out the line and sometimes we rehearse from nine in the morning until twelve thirty and don't make a single shot. But then at one thirty when we come back from lunch, suddenly I shoot eight or nine pages because we had rehearsed everything.

I decide where the camera goes in relation to what is the best for the setup and how economical it is for the telling of the story and where it is comfortable for the actor. By that I mean every time you move the camera, you lose time. If you move lights it's half an hour or forty-five minutes, sometimes even longer if it's a complex shot. So I try to accomplish as much as possible with one setup. By that I don't mean I'm going to cement the camera, but I design the shot in such a way that I can eat up two, three, four pages of dialogue. I never set up the camera to astonish. In France they call it *épater les bourgeois,* to astonish the middle classes. "Boy, do I have a setup. I'm going to shoot through the fireplace with the flames in the foreground." I don't do that because I think this is from the point of view of Santa Claus. Who would look there? What is this? Or hang the camera. When I have the camera hanging from up there, in my language of celluloid, I expect somebody watching from there. It has to be logical, where the camera is, not just kind of framed with candles in the foreground. I love to shoot elegantly and I pride myself that it's not whacked together by a dilettante. But I despise doing fancy schmancy shots. I cannot stand it. If anybody in the middle of a picture suddenly grabs his partner's knee and says, "Oooooh, look at that setup!" then the picture is dead to me because he knows that there was a setup. He knows there was a camera, he knows there were people on the dolly pushing backward, forward. I try to involve the audience and make them part of what is happening on that two-dimensional screen.

The key is just make it effective, but don't make it obvious. Make it clear to them, but don't spell it out like the audience are just a bunch of idiots. Just aim it slightly above their station and they're going to get it. This is what I learned from Ernst Lubitsch. He had a real touch, a gift of involving the audience into writing the script with him as it was unfolding on the screen. In other words, he was not the kind of a director who kind of hammered it down and said, "Now listen to me, you idiots. There now, put down the popcorn bag, I'm going to tell you something. Two and two is four." He said, "No, just give them two and two and let them add it up. They're going to do it for you. And they're going to have fun with it. They're going to play the game with you."

I read an interview with Sydney Pollack, who did *Tootsie,* a wonderful picture with Dustin Hoffman. He said, "I suddenly realized the power of the screen is omission. Don't show the in-between because it's boring— the result is what's important. Like when Dustin Hoffman walks down the street—Hoffman the man—and he makes up his mind that he's going to become the actress: I cut, and now you see him walking as a woman." Well, I did that in *Some Like It Hot,* because when Tony Curtis is on the phone talking to that agent, disguising his voice, this means they're going to take the job in the girls' orchestra. Cut, and the two guys are walking down the railroad platform, not their faces, their hairy legs. And the audience started screaming. I'm not saying that we invented it, because Laurel and Hardy invented it. I forget the name of that two-reeler where they are talking about getting rich quick and the guy tells them, "It's Prohibition time. I know people and they take some rubbing alcohol, they put it in the bathtub and they put a little something in it, and suddenly they're rich." "Come on now, for Christ's sake, let's do it." Cut—and you see these two faces, the camera goes back, and they're behind bars in prison. Nobody shows how they got arrested, as we never showed where Lemmon and Curtis borrow the dresses, did they know a makeup woman, did they borrow wigs, nothing. Boom! That's the effect. And it worked.

I wonder if you could elaborate on the "Lubitsch touch"?

The Lubitsch touch, yes. You know, if I knew the formula I would patent it, but nobody quite knows how to arrive at it. But the best illustration is this: if you have a class of students—writers or directors—and you say, "I will now give you a problem, and now you go home and come back with a solution. The problem is very simple. I would like you to dramatize the following situation. There is a king and there is a queen, and there is a lieutenant. The king is played by George Barbier, a very opulent, fat actor in his sixties. The queen is Miriam Hopkins; she was very pretty. And the lieutenant is Maurice Chevalier. Now, dramatize the situation that the queen has an affair with the lieutenant, and the king finds out. Do it any way you want to." And those hundred students—who are very good at comedy, very imaginative—they go out and they come back a week later and they will all have good solutions. Amusing, maybe a little long, maybe they are a little too explicit, maybe it's too censorable, but nobody in the world could have come up with a better solution than Mr. Lubitsch does.

Here's his solution—and now I'm quoting the opening scene in *The Smiling Lieutenant*. We open up in the bedroom of the king and the queen, and he's getting dressed. And there is a little nose-rubbing and it's all very sweet and she is very nice to the king. Now he leaves the bedroom and we see Maurice Chevalier at the door, standing there with a sword and clicking his heels. He is watching the king, who is going down the steps of a long staircase that leads down from the bedroom of that palace. Now we cut back to Mr. Chevalier, who sees the king is leaving, and he enters the bedroom of the queen. The door closes. You don't cut into the bedroom. Now, as the king is descending, he suddenly sees that he forgot his belt and sword. He turns around and he goes up the steps back into the bedroom. Now we have a situation going on. He opens the door, goes in, the door closes. We are still outside; we are never inside. Now the king comes out and he has got the belt with the sword, and he's smiling. Now he's going down the steps, and it's not his belt. It's much too small for him, so he goes back and finds the lieutenant under the bed. So you see how Lubitsch operates that thing. It's all done with a kind of throwing it away. He doesn't want to rub your nose in it. That's Lubitsch.

Or, for instance, his short film in a picture called *If I Had a Million,* a picture that Paramount made with all the stars the studio had. The theme of the picture was that the millionaire was dying and the family is waiting and he hates the family. He says, "Well, screw them," and decides haphazardly to give a million dollars to the people. He takes the telephone book and wherever the medicine dropper drops, that is the person that is going to get a million dollars. George Raft and Cary Grant are in it and we see the adventures of various people who get one million dollars. All kinds of directors, the best directors at Paramount at that time, each made one little segment of the film. This is what Lubitsch did. His was the one with Charles Laughton. Laughton is working in an office, hundreds of desks. He's very meticulous. Now the mail arrives and you see that among the letters is that one letter containing that one-million-dollar check. We know already that the envelope contains the million dollars. And being very methodical, he opens one letter, he opens the second letter, he opens the third letter. Then he opens the letter with the million dollars and he looks at it. No expression on his face. Absolutely nothing. He folds it, he puts it in his pocket. He gets up, he picks up his bowler, he picks up his umbrella, and now he walks past the desks to the president's office. He walks in, opens the door and does this [*makes a mocking sound with his lips*]. That was it, except the sound was a little bit louder. So that is the Lubitsch touch.

How do you see the business as far as opportunities for directors today?

Today it's a big lottery. You're playing not with thirty-six numbers and double zero, but 360 numbers. New ugly words have appeared on the horizon. What they now tell you is the agent got you a date with an executive and you're going to pitch a story. Pitch? The pitch stuff used to be Sandy Koufax. *He* was pitching. Me, I'm no pitcher. Most of the time you sit there and pitch to the executive, and you know his face and you study it, and then finally you figure out where you know the face from. He was the mail boy at William Morris, and now you're pitching a story to him. Then suddenly you're so ashamed of yourself you say, "Forget it. You wouldn't like it anyway," and you walk out.

In the old days, Paramount was not the biggest studio, but that's the first eighteen years of my life here, so I know it best. Paramount made forty pictures a year, and Warner Bros. made around fifty, MGM made sixty, then there was RKO, then there was Universal, blah, blah, blah. Today, if a studio makes six pictures a year, this is a major thing. You do that picture and they are sitting thinking, "Shall we? Shall we not? Shall we put it in turnaround? Shall we go half and half with a group of financiers from Tunisia?" Then when you start shooting they look over your shoulder. Everybody has his own ideas, everybody gives you their criticism, but you want to be left alone. Then, it was only one of forty pictures. Now they make you feel it's life or death for the studio. "If you don't hit with this picture we have to dismiss all the secretaries, all the policemen. Everything is going."

When you were at Paramount, if you brought them a project that they didn't want to do, could you take it to another studio and get it made?

No way. I was under contract then. At the beginning I was collaborating with Charles Brackett, and they made deals. For instance, Paramount wanted Gary Cooper for that Hemingway picture with Ingrid Bergman, *For Whom the Bell Tolls.* He was under contract to Sam Goldwyn, so Goldwyn gave them Gary Cooper for that one picture, because he was not working at the time, and in return Goldwyn got Brackett and myself for a script and Bob Hope for a comedy that he was doing. It was like baseball trading.

Sunset Boulevard *has a real deep cynicism about Hollywood. I wonder what your feelings are about Hollywood at this point in your career.*

Totally different, of course, because in those days there were designated, well-known and advertised enemies or fortresses to take: Warner Bros., Paramount, MGM, Harry Cohn, Louis B. Mayer, Darryl Zanuck. That's all kind of washed out. Now you'd never know which studio is still going to be there next Monday, who is going to be the head of what studio, whose ass you have to lick. It's a whole different game today. How can you wage a war against such huge corporations? People at Paramount never talked, never met, never congregated with people from Warner Bros. Every studio had its own handwriting, its own stable of big stars, of supporting actors. You walked into a movie house and you knew, "This is an RKO picture." They had a style, you know, the art directors. And then of course, the supporting cast at Warner Bros. Then MGM had their people, and Paramount had all their stars and also their secondary people who appeared over and over again in their pictures. They were ensemble companies. And there was a big rivalry that was kind of USC and UCLA, no? But now you want to make a picture, you write it at home, you rent some stages someplace, you shoot and a week after, you walk out of it like leaving the Ramada Inn. You don't live in the studio anymore. You don't even have commissaries. Nothing.

There was a real sense of collaboration back then. If you had a good picture, that was not enough. The other guy had to have a lousy one at the same time. It was a whole different spirit, it was a whole different kind of competition. We talked more about movies. We talked about "What are you doing? What's the picture about? What's the scene? What are you going to have in it?" Now they talk about "What kind of a deal did you get? What kind of percentage? Is it on the gross? Is it in turnaround? Is it a step deal? Is it negative pickup?" All of those things. We never heard of those things before—we just made movies.

I'd like to know about your relationship with your producers over the years, and your thoughts on producers in general.

I'm my own producer, if such a thing exists. The word *producer* encompasses so many things. The producer now is not the kind of producer that Mr. Selznick or Mr. Thalberg or Mr. Goldwyn was. These were creative producers. Nowadays a producer is usually a man who knew a second cousin of a reader who got hold of an unfinished book at Random House about a big fish off Martha's Vineyard, and for some reason or other his brother-in-law gave him ten thousand dollars and he put it down, and now suddenly he has the rights for *Jaws*. He says, "I am the producer," but it's the first time he's ever been in a studio. What I'm trying to say to you is this—if any of you here says, "I would like to become a producer," I say that no such profession really exists. Producers make you feel that if they weren't quite so busy and not quite so involved in six enormous projects which are going to revolutionize the cinema, they could write it better, they could direct it better, they could compose, they could possibly act in it. The truth is they can't write it, they can't direct, they don't know how to write a note of music. If they can't act, if they can't do anything, then they become the overseer of the whole thing.

If you're the head of a studio it's easy to make twenty pictures, because it's just like you're standing around the roulette table and you've got twenty chips and you put them on various numbers. One or two of those chips are going to be winners, right? Then they will talk exhaustingly about the two or three chips that make a lot of money.

Many of your pictures suggest a great deal of forethought as far as the production design and the sets. Does the finished film always look like the image you have in your head?

Well, the direction of the scene happens as you're putting it down on paper. You know where the door is going to be and later you talk to the art director and you say, "Look, I would like to have the following constellation—the desk has to be here and the door to the bedroom has to be there." You do that beforehand. But sometimes a scene that played beautifully in the typewriter doesn't work on film, and I would like to do it again, but this time it's too late because the actor who arrived from Yugoslavia the Friday before we started shooting is now in Bulgaria shooting another picture. I can't get him back. On the stage if you do a play, you know you can fix that very easily. It's just marvelous. You come after one week of previews in Hartford, Connecticut, and say, "Tonight let's do it this way." There's no such thing in film. You commit yourself.

I have great admiration for your attention to detail and objects, like the inhaler in The Apartment *that you took and milked for all it was worth. Do your powers of observation come from your training as a journalist?*

It comes more from me having a lot of colds. Look, you find the prop and you do the best with it you can, you know? And the old school now is rather old-fashioned, where you would plan the gag and then you come back with it again, and then you pay it off. That was the roundness we had at that time. Now it's a little bit looser, now it's a little bit more improvised, but this is not my style. If you find a good prop—let's say in *Witness for the Prosecution,* with the little elevator, the chair that takes the lawyer up and down—then you use it.

When we constructed *The Apartment* we knew we needed a scene in which Jack Lemmon realizes that Shirley MacLaine is the dame his boss, Fred MacMurray, does it to in his apartment. So we go back and plant the little makeup mirror that he finds. When he gets the promotion and buys himself the young executive black bowler hat, she lets him fix his hat in the mirror, and he suddenly realizes she's the girl. But none of those things are improvised; it's all calculated and planned.

Could you tell us where the idea for The Apartment *came from?*

I remember the genesis of the film very vividly. I saw a picture of David Lean's called *Brief Encounter* which was based on a one-act play by Noël Coward. Trevor Howard was the leading man, a married man who has an affair with a married women and who uses the apartment of a chum of his for sexual purposes. I always had it in the back of my mind that the friend of Trevor Howard's—who appears in only one or two tiny little scenes, who comes back home and climbs into the warm bed that the lovers just left—would make a very interesting character. I made some notes, and years later, after we had finished *Some Like It Hot,* we wanted to make another picture with Jack Lemmon. I dug out this notion and we just sat down and started to talk about the characters, the structure of the thing, the three acts and the theme. Then when we had just enough, we suggested it to Mr. Lemmon and Harold Mirisch at United Artists.

You seem to really rely on the flash-forward and voice-over for purposes of exposition.

Yes, it is useful if there is a reason for it, if it is anchored in the story. I think in *Double Indemnity* it was very good because a man is speaking into a Dictaphone in order to help a man who is believed to be a murderer to do the decent thing. There was a reason for telling the story that way. In *Sunset Boulevard* it was a different thing. People were astonished by that thing—a dead man is telling the story. Originally we had a different beginning for the picture with the body of Mr. Holden being taken in a hearse downtown to the morgue where there were about sixteen or eighteen corpses lying around under sheets. I shot this scene where you see through the sheets the faces of the dead people and they begin telling each other the events leading to their deaths. There is a man aged sixty-five who'd had a heart attack, and an eleven-year-old boy who had drowned, and finally Mr. Holden, who says, "Well, you know, I came to Hollywood. I'm a writer. I wanted a pool, I got a pool and I finally died in the pool," and we go from there. But it just didn't work, so we had Holden say, "That's me. Right here, the guy that's drowning."

What is good about narration, if it is properly used, is that it saves you a lot of time and a lot of exposition. If it saves you only, let's say, two or three minutes at the top, that's a lot of time for people to get very restless. But usually I unhappily see narration misused, because they tell you things they are photographing at the same time. You have to say something new, something you do not have in the picture. It has to complement the pictures. Where I think the narration was really bad—and I'm talking about one of my very favorite directors and maybe one of the great ones of all time—is Stanley Kubrick in *Barry Lyndon.* They're telling me there are eighteen horses. Why, I can count eighteen horses; he doesn't have to tell it to me. He went absolutely crazy on that picture. He spent God knows how long experimenting how to shoot a scene by real candle-light. I don't give a damn what that feels like. What's the scene about? Madness has broken out about the goddamn photography. Everybody wants to photograph better than Nykvist* and they are spending six days waiting for the right sunset. A sunset is a sunset. Suddenly it became such a big thing. But what's the story?

With all the lines of voice-over technique of narration, do you think it's important to get a hook into the audience in the opening minutes of the film?

Narration or no narration, you better get a hook into the audience right away. This is all very subtle, you know. The audience is restless. The kid wants to go and pee, the aunt forgot the popcorn, you're worried about the car being stolen—so you've got to find something which makes them forget the popcorn and tell the kids to shut up. "You can pee later or pee in your pants." You need the hook, like when you're at a party and there are like eighteen people around the table and everybody's talking. You want to attract their attention because you want to tell your story, so out of nowhere you say, "Talking about murder, now I had an uncle . . ." and everybody listens. Now it has nothing to do with murder, you never had an uncle, nothing—but they are listening. They say, "Wait a minute, I want to see what's happening."

Do you work closely with your cinematographers before shooting begins?

Very closely, yes. I admire greatly figures like Haskell Wexler—they are just terrific cameramen—but I think it's getting out of hand now. If you tell a good story, which I think our business is about—or let's say I'm old fashioned or primitive enough to believe that if somebody grabs your arm and says, "Jesus, look at that shot," then you've lost him. They should not even know that it's a shot. It should just belong. Everyone is working for the goddamned Academy Award, you know? The only thing that interests me in telling a good story is that it's interesting and it will be good enough for them to go home and call the family, or go to the office and tell their coworkers, "Hey, I saw a terrific movie. I had a great time. It was mar-

*Sven Nykvist (b. 1922), Swedish cinematographer, best known for his collaborations with Ingmar Bergman.

velous. Go and see it." And now it spreads. But that's as high as I want to reach.

You have to have a cameraman who has read the script. You will laugh about it, but believe me you have to ask, "Did you read the script?" and not just, "Which Kodak film are you using?" You make sure that you work with somebody who's as concerned with the outcome of the venture as you are, that he's intelligent, that slowly you begin to speak the same language. With a good cameraman, you yourself have to be clear in what you want.

Let's say you start the movie as a comedy and it becomes a drama, or it starts as a tragedy then it changes into comedy. Can you mix the two styles?

Certainly. I think we did that in *The Apartment* a little bit. But there are rules. I remember I talked to Selznick—who's a very smart man and a marvelous producer, really one of the best—and he asked me what I was working on and I told him a little bit about *Some Like It Hot*. And he said, "The Valentine's Day Murder?" And I said, "Yes. That's in the beginning." He looked at me and said, "You're crazy. You mean real machine guns and blood, in a comedy?" I said, "Why not?" He says, "Total failure." He was wrong. He just thought it's going to be a total failure because you can't mix the two. You just hope that they are in tune with what you try to tell them, that they don't misunderstand you. With an original story the audience doesn't know how to behave. "Am I supposed to laugh at that? Am I supposed to cry? Am I supposed to be touched?" That's the eternal thing. You have to establish very clearly right in the beginning what species of picture it is and what behavior is expected from the onlooker.

Could you discuss the problems you've had with the Hayes office as regards Double Indemnity *and* Sunset Boulevard, *which had a lot of implicit sexuality, and especially* Kiss Me, Stupid, *which I think was one of the movies that helped break down the production code.*

That was not the one that broke it down. We had tremendous problems all the time. There was a man at Paramount in charge of censorship who would constantly be snooping around the set as to whether the décolleté was too deep or not too deep, whether it was permissible. It was not easy, I assure you, because they were very powerful and you had to be very smart. Those days, in order to say, "You son of a bitch," you had to say, "If you had a mother, she'd bark." This kind of a thing. But there would be tremendous fights with censorship. I remember Warner Bros. had a picture I think with Cagney and Pat O'Brien, and they are out on the town and they find a dame and he says, "Hey let's go fifty-fifty on her." And Cagney says, "Yes, I get the half that eats." That you could get away with it because they didn't quite understand it.

You've talked a great deal about the writing process, but I wonder what your thoughts are about editing.

Remember the picture *Rope,* that Hitchcock shot? It had seven or nine setups in the entire picture. It was absolute, total nonsense. He would wind up on the back of somebody's dark suit and the next reel would start. They had to rehearse and rehearse. Every ten days they would get one whole reel and would collapse in exhaustion. But why not cut? This is writing the Lord's Prayer on the head of a pin. What is he trying to prove? I think Hitchcock is a great director, but this film is a joke because the power of movies is the cut. It's the scissors that make the picture so much more powerful than any play—the juxtaposition of the shots. And inserts. Inserts are a tremendous thing unless you blow it right from the beginning and you just waste it—like playing a trump card much too early. You have to know when to use it. Just to demonstrate to you the power of the insert, consider *Battleship Potemkin,* a picture Mr. Eisenstein shot in 1923 or 1924. We are dealing now with some sailors on the battleship *Potemkin* in the harbor of Odessa, 1905, czarist times, and we are telling a story about the revolt. How do you dramatize that? By that I mean, if you see the sailors revolting, big deal. You have to tell the story in such a fashion that the audience wants to revolt too, so they are about to get up and take the chairs on which they're sitting and throw them at the Cossacks or at the uniformed navy people. You must feel with the characters.

Now as you remember, it started with the sailors saying that they don't want to eat that grub because it's rotten. And the captain says, "You're crazy, there's nothing wrong with it." And there's a big unrest there, but the ones with the guns can't do very much about it, and the captain says, "Well, call the doctor, let's see." And the doctor arrives. A small man with a little beard, and he has pince-nez glasses, and the captain says, "Look at that meat. Anything wrong with it?" And the doctor takes the glasses off and doubles the glasses, you know, one over the other, which makes a magnifying glass, and he holds it. And now comes the insert seen through his glasses, and you see thousands of maggots in the meat. Now you've got the audience with you, because the doctor says, "Perfectly all right. There's nothing wrong. Perfectly all right." And from that moment on, Mr. Eisenstein has audiences all over the world; they didn't care it happened in 1905. And they saw the picture in Caracas, Venezuela; they saw it in London; but they all felt, "Jesus, that's unjust. Something must be done." And that's the way he aroused them, just one insert.

Look at the cut, the insert in Hitchcock's *The Thirty-nine Steps,* of four fingers, the power of which is "Ah! That's him. That's the killer!" Or the last of the blood of Janet Leigh gurgling down in that tub in *Psycho.* And talking about famous inserts, you all remember naturally *It Happened One Night.* They would like to hitch a ride, you know—Clark Gable and Claudette Colbert—and he does all kinds of things and nobody pays attention; the cars are passing. Then she lifts the skirt, and now comes the great insert—not her leg, but the insert of the old farmer when he steps on the brake and you just see the wheels. That is the power of the picture and what we should always remember.

What did Some Like It Hot *look like the first time you saw it edited together?*

Any first cut of the picture makes you feel suicidal. It's just the worst moment of your life. Every picture, you say, "Oh my God." Because you've worked, you've slaved, this is a year and a half of your life, and then you look and there it is, an hour and fifty-five minutes, and you say, "Is that all there is? For that, a year and a half? My God." But then you start cutting, and a little music comes in and then you kind of polish it, and it's just like night and day. And it's all worth it. When you preview a picture that really works, you feel that you've got the audience by the throat. It's not very often. That's why I say when you've got them by the throat, don't let go. Just squeeze harder and get them in the gut and stamp on them because they are such bastards. They fight you; they come in and say, "I don't want to like it. I hope that son of a bitch falls on his face." And you don't want to let them go because you suddenly sense "I've got them," whether it's a dramatic scene or the laughter has started. Once you get them into a mood of "Hey, this is funny," then you can say anything.

Have you ever shot more than one ending for a film?

Yes. For *Double Indemnity* I shot an ending which I chopped off, where Fred MacMurray was executed in the gas chamber, and there was a kind of a thing between him and Eddie Robinson, who was watching it. It was all done with minute precision. I had the priest from San Quentin and I had the warden and the doctor. Everything was just absolutely perfect, but as I was proceeding with the picture I wrote a scene where he tries to go to the elevator and get into his car and go to Mexico, and he collapses and can't even light the match anymore the way he always did. And in the distance you hear the police car or the ambulance, so you knew what the outcome is going to be. And I ended it there, because the rest would have been anticlimactic. We knew he was guilty.

What are your feelings about the current new German directors, people like Rainer Fassbinder and Werner Herzog? And I wonder if you would comment about filmmaking in Europe versus filmmaking in Hollywood.

The German film industry is a joke because people don't go to see movies in Germany. They are totally engrossed in television, and it's not that good, I must say—it's government owned. But the film industry, whatever they make is either on the lowest possible level or it is so artsy-craftsy. It's beyond Sartre, you know? It just goes into existentialism that nobody understands. There are some good ones, though. I saw a picture by Herzog, and it was very good. There is a guy, a director by the name of Volker Schlöndorff, who did *The Lost Honor of Katharina Blum,* from the Nobel Prize–winner Heinrich Böll. He is a very good director who was the assistant to Louis Malle. But their subject matters are totally different. When my generation came here we tried to imitate American pictures or to adapt to what is of interest to American audiences. Then it was rather simpler. We cannot tell simple stories anymore because you can see those in any soap opera at ten in the morning.

Isn't it true that many of the German filmmakers who came to Hollywood created a very German feeling that characterized American films of the 1940s?

Not really, not a German spirit. I don't think so. I think they added things. We talk about a man like Murnau, who did *Sunrise* and then *Tabu.* Fritz Lang really never quite took roots here. Lubitsch was never really a German director; he became an international director. But think of René Clair, for instance, and of Renoir. Think of all the Frenchmen

who are giants who came over here and found it very difficult because
they spoke a different language. Or think of a man like Ingmar Bergman
trying to make a picture in English. It's just very tough. But I think, as a
rule—especially if you arrive here after you have found a style and you try
to shift into a new language, into a new philosophy, into a new point of
view—you fail.

*Could you comment on some of the films you've seen recently by American direc-
tors?*

I haven't seen too many, but what I've seen I have got a great deal of
respect for. The craftsmanship is now impeccable. I go back to my pen-
chant for the popular and successful picture. I just think that when people try to belittle *The Exorcist* or *Jaws,* I just think these people are crazy.
Mr. Spielberg knows exactly what he did, and he did it brilliantly. And on
the same level, pictures like *The Turning Point* by Mr. Herbert Ross are
very well made and entertaining. Give me those guys any day, please,
because I can understand it. I don't have to scratch my head. But it doesn't
mean that they have to be cheap, cheesy, too popular. I assure you that a
picture like *The Turning Point* has sent tens of thousands of people to see
a ballet in Tulsa, Oklahoma. They never even knew what ballet was. It's
not that the film explores ballet in any tremendous depth, but it whets
their appetite. They see something new.

Do you have any pet projects that you really wanted to make but never did?

It would be just too crazy to tell you. It's like giving you the key to my
safe. You know when you get to be my age, you just sort of—how shall I
put it?—you hope that the game will go into an extra inning because you
feel that you've still got a few hits left. And if that does not work, I'm just
going to sign up with a Japanese team and sit on the bench and wait for
Kurosawa to break his leg. It's as simple as that.

*I'm wondering whether you've ever seen any pictures and thought, "Damn it, I
wish I'd made that one!"*

Battleship Potemkin, A Place in the Sun, and maybe just for the fun of
shooting it, *Last Tango in Paris.*

Finally, Mr. Wilder, what is the purpose of making films?

Purpose of making films? Well, number one, it's too late for me now to change and to become a gardener. Number two is to get away from the house and the vacuum cleaner. I want to be in my office and think. And number three, it's very exciting. I like to tell stories. Ultimately it's interesting. You meet nice people, it's glamorous, and, if you get lucky, very profitable. You suffer a great deal, but to paraphrase President Truman, if you can't take all that crap, get out of the studio. Believe me, this is not a profession for a dignified human being. I can see the interest in pictures when I talk to you students, especially now that almost every university has something connected with movies. But if I had a son I would beat him with a very large whip trying to make a gardener, a dentist or something else out of him. Don't do it. It's just too tough. It hurts, and the moments of glory are very far between. Well, it's too late for me to turn back, too late for me to become a gardener. I can't bend over the azaleas. Not anymore.

Films as Director

1933 *Mauvaise graine* (Codirector and co-screenplay)

1942 *The Major and Minor* (also co-screenplay)

1943 *Five Graves to Cairo* (also co-screenplay)

1944 *Double Indemnity* (also co-screenplay)

1945 *The Lost Weekend* (also co-screenplay)

1948 *The Emperor Waltz* (also co-screenplay)

1949 *A Foreign Affair* (also co-screenplay)

1950 *Sunset Boulevard* (also co-screenplay)

1951 *Ace in the Hole* (also producer and co-screenplay)

1953 *Stalag 17* (also producer and co-screenplay)

1954 *Sabrina* (also producer and co-screenplay)

1955 *The Seven Year Itch* (also coproducer and co-screenplay)

1957 *The Spirit of St. Louis* (also coproducer and co-screenplay)

Love in the Afternoon (also producer and co-screenplay)

1958 *Witness for the Prosecution* (also co-screenplay)

1959 *Some Like it Hot* (also producer and co-screenplay)

1960 *The Apartment* (also producer
        and co-screenplay)
1961 *One, Two, Three* (also producer
        and co-screenplay)
1963 *Irma La Douce* (also producer
        and co-screenplay)
1964 *Kiss Me, Stupid* (also producer
        and co-screenplay)
1966 *The Fortune Cookie* (also
        producer and
        co-screenplay)

1970 *The Private Life of Sherlock
        Holmes* (also producer and
        co-screenplay)
1972 *Avanti!* (also producer and
        co-screenplay)
1974 *The Front Page* (also producer
        and co-screenplay)
1978 *Fedora* (also producer
        and co-screenplay)
1981 *Buddy Buddy* (also producer
        and co-screenplay)

I think of a script as an organization, like an engine. Ideally everything contributes—nothing is in excess and everything works.

JOHN HUSTON
(Born in Nevada, Missouri, 1906—Died 1987)

If Clark Gable and Cary Grant were symbols of glamour in the movie world, John Huston was the thinking man's version—and most certainly the thinking woman's. Huston combined intellect, charm and physical grace with an effortless camaraderie. He was the most charismatic of the directors I knew, speaking with a soothing, melodic voice that was often mimicked but was unique to him.

John was representative of a certain breed of American moviemakers, men of the outdoors who loved sports and hard liquor, were attractive to women and lived life to its fullest—men who responded before they were called when America went to war. His life seemed a series of adventures, from his days as amateur boxer, reporter, short-story writer, portrait painter in the streets of Paris, to his service in the Mexican cavalry and in combat in World War II, to his cherished position in the Irish hunt country as co-master of the Galway Blazers. "Fox hunting," he noted, "has all of the excitement of battle and twenty-five percent of the risk."

He was a writer at his core and from that gift flowed his success as a director. There are half a dozen of John's films that move me at every viewing: *The Treasure of the Sierra Madre, The Asphalt Jungle, The African Queen, The Red Badge of Courage* and *The Man Who Would Be King.* Each is an expression of his interests and his personality, and each avoids that feeling common to most vintage films that they were made in another time for another audience.

His thirty-seven feature films include a number of misfires and botched efforts that one would not expect from a man who made several masterpieces. One explanation is money trouble that was compounded by five mar-

John Huston (second from right) on the set of *The Treasure of the Sierra Madre* (1948) with his father, Walter Huston (left). With them are Tim Holt and his father, Jack Holt (right). Both Hustons won Oscars for the picture.

riages and an appetite for adventure. He told *Rolling Stone* in 1981, "I've spent it before I made it. Instead of acquiring money, I acquired debts. It was always on the come." This led him to take on projects that were assured paydays but that lacked the potential for excellence. Of these Huston said, "Surgeons operate when they know the patient is going to die."

Many directors shape their work in the editing room, but Huston said, "I don't even know the editor of my films most of the time." This made him exacting on the set. After working with him on *The Man Who Would Be King,* Michael Caine said, "Most directors don't know what they want so they shoot everything they can think of—they use the camera like a machine gun. John uses it like a sniper."

In his 1969 AFI seminar, Houston mentions *The Man Who Would Be King* as a book he remembered from his youth and a picture he wished he'd made. He first thought of it for Bogart and then, after *The Misfits,* for Clark Gable. He finally made it in 1975, at age sixty-nine, with the spot-on casting of Caine and Sean Connery.

I last saw John in 1986, at Swifty Lazar's post–Academy Awards party. John and his daughter had both been nominated for *Prizzi's Honor,* and Anjelica won that night, making her the third Huston to receive an Oscar—

following John and his father, Walter. John was suffering from emphysema and was using a portable oxygen device. That evening, he sat down at our table, ordered a whisky and proceeded to be enchanting—telling stories and listening with concentrated attentiveness. The courage and charm that carried him through life's adventures were still evident. The next year he made *The Dead,* and died before the year was out.

Someone once asked Huston if he had to choose one scene from all his films for a time capsule, which would it be? He thought a moment, smiled and said, "It would have to be my father dancing in *The Treasure of the Sierra Madre.*"

JOHN HUSTON

———◆———

October 23, 1969*

Let's talk about how you begin. What's the starting point of a film for you? An idea? A theme? An actor? I always wondered how you began Beat the Devil.

I did too at the time. I went into that film reluctantly because we had no script at all, or a very poor excuse for a script. We wrote the script on the spot. It wasn't done frivolously, as has been described. We worked very hard to keep ahead of the picture. I remember writing scenes with Truman Capote, and I didn't want the company to know how directly. In fact, on one occasion, I staged the scene that was in the script and made it as complicated as possible in its moves. Then I went upstairs and rewrote the scene while the crew laid out the dolly track. Then I came back with the scene and said, "I've changed it." But we got away with the picture. It was the most fortunate of accidents, and to this day I think it's a good picture.

Are you working on something right now?

I am going to start *Bullet Park,* with John Cheever. I'll probably do it next summer in New York.† I read the novel, liked it very much and saw it as a picture.

What do you mean, "saw" it as a picture?

*This transcript contains short segments from the seminar John Huston gave at the American Film Institute on March 1, 1983.
†This film project never happened. Huston's next film as director was *Fat City* (1972).

Well, I never look for film material. I don't read things unless they're manuscripts sent to me. I don't read books with the idea of making pictures out of them. Very often it's even something I read in my youth that I keep harking back to, and then one day I say, "My word, that could be a film." I suppose, inquiring of myself for the first time, that it's a desire to share an emotional and intellectual experience with a new audience that pushes me to make pictures at all. I started out writing screenplays for other people. I didn't write many original stories, but did write things like *Juarez* and *Dr. Ehrlich's Magic Bullet* and other biographical things, putting them into dramatic form. Time after time I would see something I'd written go on the screen and it wasn't as I had imagined or had hoped it would be. It was a crashing disappointment and I said I didn't want to go on wasting my efforts like that. This is what made me a director. I had it put into my contract at Warner Bros. that after a certain period I would be allowed to direct my own material.

In adapting a novel are you also making a personal statement? What do you bring from the story itself into the film?

It's an adaptation, hardly a conscious interpretation, as I try to bring out the qualities in the story that are distinct to the material. Whenever I make an adaptation I always want to get to the spirit of the material—I don't put it through my own mill. In doing *The Red Badge of Courage,* it was Stephen Crane's story I wanted to see rendered in cinematic terms on the screen. I wanted the same reaction from the film as I got when I read the book.

When you come across these stories, what draws you to them? Is it the mood or a particular character? Is it a view of the world that you relate to?

It's different in each case. There's nothing in common that I am aware of. Of course, there probably is, but certainly not consciously.

It's a cinematic quality you want to see?

Yes. If I see that something can be put on the screen and that the experience I got from the book can even be enhanced, then I set about making a picture.

Do you find any similarity in the range of experiences you have filmed over the years? Can you find your own preoccupations in your films?

No, I can't. They have been pointed out to me on occasion, though. French and Italian critics have described my philosophy to me, but as I say, it's never conscious. It was very interesting what they told me—that I believe in the pursuit rather than the achievement, that it's the game and not the gain. Things like that.

When you have the novel you want to adapt, do you think in terms of acts, scenes, moments, images?

Well, each instance is particular. Take *Moby-Dick*. I must have read that book eight or nine times without ever thinking of making a film. Then I did think about a film version and wrote a script. I put it away and gave up the idea, and it was only several years later that I returned to it. The material fascinated and preoccupied me: how to get it on the screen, how to define it. The book has many faces, and the most difficult problem in writing the screenplay was determining what the point of the story was: a blasphemy. I felt a realization on the part of the crew of the *Pequod* that they were engaged in an unholy undertaking. After all, Ahab shakes his fist at God Almighty and challenges him. The whole script was right except for a scene that would point this up. It was just this one thing that picked at me. I had even started the picture before it suddenly dawned on me what the scene should be—not simply the reaction to the pursuit of the white whale. Starbuck's realization that Ahab was out to kill a whale didn't in itself seem to have a particularly diabolic meaning or significance, but what turned the trick was my realization one day—a ray of light hit me—that they were not doing what they were supposed to do, which is to furnish oil for the lamps of the world. And according to the Quaker mentality, in this they were committing a sin, so we had to see the realization that they were engaged in something devilish.

What was that scene?

The scene in Ahab's cabin when Starbuck confronts him. That was really the heart of the picture, though it was not in the novel. I think that Melville would have approved.

Once you had that philosophy, how did you then communicate to the audience what you wanted?

I sat down and wrote the scene.

But where did you go from there, after you'd written the scene, in terms of communicating it to the people working on the film?

I'd have to go a little further back to answer that question. I think of a script as an organization, like an engine. Ideally everything contributes— nothing is in excess and everything works. In this case that's what was wrong with the script as a whole. It wasn't an inner combustion engine until that scene made it spark and the wheels began to turn on each other. When that happened, the rest was comparatively easy and everything had its function—with, I hope, more or less varying degrees of success.

Do you think it's possible to define what goes into an inner combustion engine in the sense of a script?

Well, I said that everything had a function. I think this is less true in the films that one sees today. In my school of filmmaking—and this not to discredit what I see today, as I think it's fascinating—it's almost a requirement. I feel as though I've cheated in a script unless everything has a function.

Going back to what you said about rendering something "in cinematic terms," just what is cinema?

Cinema is the projection of shadows—to quote from Hitch—on a rectangle. Of course because they are shadows, you can read so much into them. To me the ideal film—which I've never succeeded in making— would be as though the reel were behind one's eyes and you were projecting it yourself, seeing what you wish to see. This has a great deal in common with thought processes. Usually in the first few minutes of a picture—good and bad pictures—you're allowed to see what you want to see, and then usually after about two and half minutes there is a sickening instant when we are brought back to reality and we know we are in a theater looking at trash. Sometimes this happens sooner, rarely a little later, and in extraordinary instances much later or not at all.

Do you make films for yourself or for the audience? Is it defined in your mind?

No, not defined. I am my own audience in a sense. The very idea of trying to manipulate—even to entertain an audience—when you get to the
specifics, is quite beyond me, and so is trying to imagine what an audience would like. My God, I don't know what my best friend or wife or son
or daughter would like. I only know what I like, and I hope that there are
enough like me to feel the way I do about it.

*Do you always want audiences to identify with the hero in your films, even if those
heroes are often morally ambiguous?*

Now that you ask me, I think I would rather audiences identify with the
picture itself than with a particular character. I hope they feel a fascination for the whole material rather than become emotionally involved with
the hero or heroine. Some very fine directors do just the opposite. I suppose that in all my pictures this is more or less true. You're not running
with the boy in *The Red Badge of Courage* as you might do with the hero
of a war picture—you're just watching him. By the same token Stephen
Crane did just that by writing with an austere detachment. In *Moby-Dick*,
Ahab is watched by Melville. Ishmael is the onlooker, the spectator, the
protagonist, the projection of the audience into the frame of the story.

Do you find it difficult to have this onlooker as one of the characters in the frame?

No, not difficult at all.

Are you doing it consciously?

Well, in that instance, certainly. Ishmael is Melville, the author who in
turn becomes the picture maker.

How does this idea of distance affect the way you use the camera?

That really calls for a few words about the camera and film in general.
Again, I didn't start out with these ideas, they occurred to me as I went
about making motion pictures. We touched on how the camera follows
mental processes. I think that even more than this, it also follows physical
processes. I'll give you an example. What is a cut? A little experiment—

look at this man on my right, and then look to George Stevens on my left. I'm going to do the same. Now, in making that shot it can either be a pan or a cut. If I look this way, it's a pan. If I blink, that's a cut. You're used to this room by now, you know what the spatial relationship is, so when you look from there to there, you don't need to keep your eyes open. You can jump back and forth, cut out certain things. You rest your eyes and open them again. That's why I think the camera is an eye as well as a mind.

Everything we do with the camera has physiological and mental significance. I've seen scenes in films where they pan from one thing to another, and it strikes me as rather tedious, unaware of the way we really think and of how our bodies work. It comes out of a novice's first experiences of using the camera. This is just one example of how we're dictated to by the behavior of our bodies and minds. By the same token, we wouldn't be having a conversation of this kind like this [*moves very close to questioner*], even with my bad ear. There are certain things that are said at a certain distance, and I wouldn't be talking this way to George if you—the audience—weren't here. The very size of the figures on the screen is determined by the subject matter and the spirit of the scene, just as the cutting is. Yet very often I see on screen the wrong relationship between people in a dialogue. They are only three feet apart when they should be eight feet apart.

For me the camera is almost a physical presence. It's as though I am the camera, watching what fascinates me. If it is sufficiently interesting I move up to it, or it might be something I want to stand back from and watch with complete detachment. I might say, "This has nothing to do with me" or "I am God watching these people." For example, it would be very hard to make someone amusing or funny if I was shooting up at them. I don't say this couldn't be done, but I think it probably comes from our memories as children, from these things that are bigger, wiser and stronger than us. We look up at these people. It's the same with monumental sculpture. Would you look down at your superior or even God Almighty?

Could you give some examples of the kinds of things that make you want to be either closer or farther away?

I think the material itself always dictates this. I didn't want to be a fool on my first picture, *The Maltese Falcon,* so I made drawings of the setups in each scene. I discovered when I went to shoot the picture that about fifty percent of the time when I'd have the actors rehearse a scene, they would fall into the positions I had drawn out. I direct actors as little as possible, but the other fifty percent of the time I would have to guide them into it. Occasionally something would occur accidentally that was better than my plan, and sometimes the actors themselves would discover something that was better.

But what kind of scene or event makes you want to bring the camera closer, and what makes you stay back?

For instance, I am curious about a thought that you're entertaining, so I lean in.

Yet many times you keep the camera back when characters are thinking about things directly related to the scene.

Perhaps their actions would better convey the thought. Moving in doesn't reveal the thought, it reveals my interest. I move in, which tells me this person is thinking about something that's very important.

Take the Robert Forster character in Reflections in a Golden Eye. *We see him creeping up into that house and just sitting. You cut back and forth between him and Elizabeth Taylor, and move quite close on him. What are you working toward here?*

Obviously his character is a kind of pagan figure that isn't even entertaining thoughts. He's something almost out of pantheism, a wood figure. He's a kind of manifestation rather than an intelligence, and there's something mysterious and primitive about him. He has no desire to violate or attack. I never even saw him as having a physical reaction to the presence of this woman. It was hardly sexual; it was just some strange flow that occurred between her sleeping figure and this remote mind or instinct.

Does he worship her?

A kind of worship.

Do you try to translate that into images?

Peter Lorre, left, with Huston and Humphrey Bogart, right, at work on *The Maltese Falcon* (1941). Huston said, "I didn't want to be a fool on my first picture, so I made drawings of the setups in each scene."

Yes, I tried to. She was beautiful as she lay there. It was a kind of worship of womanhood, of sensuality rather than sexuality.

Did that relationship dictate the decor in any way?

Of course the decor was also part of her, particularly the lighting. I mean the untidiness of this whole feminine world that he sat in. He had never been in an atmosphere like that before.

Earlier you spoke of your "school of filmmaking." Do you feel there is a tension between what you call your school and the best of what is being produced today?

I was speaking of the films that started in France, the Jean-Luc Godard films. I watched them with great interest. I'm a fan of Godard's work, but I couldn't make a film like that any more than a Quattrocento painter could do a Pollock. It's less true even than that. I have great admiration for the well-constructed screenplay, done from the inside out, from an idea, and where every line echoes that idea.

Where Godard would use a pan just to be artificial, you would probably use a cut to be natural. How do you feel about that sort of change in attitude toward technique within the last twenty years?

I think it's entirely a question of subject matter. I don't try to tell the stories that Godard tells. Assuming there is interest in his stories, then he goes about it the right way. Another picture that to some extent utilizes the so-called modern techniques is *Midnight Cowboy,* and I was lost in admiration for it. I thought it was simply a wonderful picture. It came to me as an experience, like the best of literature. I compare the character of Ratso with *The Old Man and the Sea,* for instance. He is a demonstration of human courage, almost exalted.

A question about suspense in film. What do you think permits a director to have these privileged moments where he takes a break and the suspense in the story stops?

Complete interest and absorption. Only when you've gained those things can you afford to have those static moments. There's no rule for it. The best example is the years and years of preparation, the launching of the rocket and the final arrival on the moon. Only then are you privileged to witness a dance.

Your first film, The Maltese Falcon, *was a murder mystery. I gather you're currently finishing up* The Kremlin Letter, *which is also a murder mystery. Compared to how you worked twenty years ago, do you find yourself more eager to show what the film's made of, the constructs of the story? Or are your goals the same: to carry your audience along in terms of character?*

Well, I'd have to answer your question in an entirely different way. The things that interested me in *The Maltese Falcon* have nothing to do with what interested me about *The Kremlin Letter,* a film that holds the mirror up to our political and ethical depravity. It's a portrait of corruption and the deprivation of morality.

Isn't Dashiell Hammett's world of The Maltese Falcon *the same?*

No, no, quite the opposite. Dashiell was highly moral and adhered strictly to the set of rules that his protagonist had laid down for himself. *The Kremlin Letter* is the other side of the coin: there is no morality, individual or otherwise, and that is what the picture is about.

Is the film going to be visually different because of that?

Yes, though every picture is visually different so far as I'm concerned. I try and discover a new way of telling each story according to its own requirements. I try never to impose my own techniques on the material, though I'm not actually even aware of having any.

I'm wondering how you feel about films as statements or socially significant articles of debate.

Hitchcock, a wonderful director, is always on the lookout for material that fits what he likes to talk about, and he never steps out of that circle. I am not that way. I don't do it the way Hitchcock does.

How would you respond to the idea that film is not being properly used unless one really is trying to package a rather vehement social stance within it?

I don't feel that way.

But have you ever been more interested in one theme over another and how it might relate to an important issue of the day?

No. With rare exceptions, when I make a film it's only been because I was completely fascinated by the material itself. I never went out looking for material to express a political faith or anything of that sort. However, one is quite incapable of doing anything other than saying what you believe.

In terms of your own development, where do you think you're breaking new ground in moving from project to project?

Well, I never set out to break new ground. It only occurs because the material requires it, for example the use of color in *Moulin Rouge* or *Moby Dick*. *Moulin Rouge* is actually a picture I don't particularly care for, by the way. I always felt that Toulouse-Lautrec was worth better treatment. The story was sentimentalized. Today one could do a story about the man and tell the real story.

You often try to do something a little different in terms of the conventional use of color. Why did you see the need to do this?

The first feature picture done in color was, I believe, *Becky Sharp,* a very fine picture. I have seen slides of it. Very beautiful. *Moulin Rouge* came along, and I didn't think it would be right to shoot it in straight color, as the color could give another dimension to the picture. So we conceived another approach. It was a wedding between color and black and white, reinforcing the color as it were, giving it a strength. Whereas color was apt to go limp and sentimental, we thought that black and white would give it strength.

With *Moulin Rouge* the idea was to flatten the color and give it a local, almost posterlike look, reminiscent of lithographs and posters of Toulouse-Lautrec. This was, in the way of innovation, the first attempt over a span of years. The film was fought by Technicolor, who I guess didn't want to fool around. They didn't want to do it in the camera, so I showed them the tests we did and what I wanted, and they said they would duplicate it in the laboratory. The examples they furnished were very poor indeed, so we proceeded to shoot the picture our way. Before we ever started, however, Technicolor wrote letters to everyone involved—Warner Bros., Allied Artists and so on—disclaiming any responsibility and advising against us proceeding this way. The others backed us up—they had considerable courage. Of course, the color was certainly the biggest triumph of the picture. I had to fight for color experimentation even as late as *Reflections in a Golden Eye.* I wanted to give a kind of amber, golden look to the whole picture, but the Eastman organization wanted no part of it.

Going into the theory of color and black and white, it seems to me that black and white still has a role in motion pictures. In fact, unless the color is pertinent to the idea, it can come between the beholder and the idea of the picture. One's eye and thoughts can be deflected by the color. For instance, I cannot possibly see doing *Freud* or pictures of a deeply psychological nature in color. Unless the palate and the values of the whole thing coincide and are part of the idea, it better not be color. In the case of *Reflections in a Golden Eye,* they finally let us open the picture in the key cities in that color, but the general release was in the old Technicolor.

*You've worked with a whole range of actors, people in the tradition of the person-
ality actor like Mitchum or Bogart, and also actors like Brando and Clift, who
are more cerebral. Earlier you said you try and direct as little as possible. Do you
find both of these kinds of actors good to work with? Do you have any preferences?*

It depends entirely on the material and the role. I'm not star-minded. I
never start off with an actor—that comes later. I ask myself, "Who is like
this part? Not an actor. Who is actually like this person in the script?"
One goes to an actor because of a facility, but sometimes the individual
himself—his own character and nature—is more important than the
facility that an actor might have. For instance, the English have some
marvelous technical actors for whom I have the greatest admiration. I
remember when Brando played Marc Antony in *Julius Caesar,* one of the
most extraordinary performances I ever witnessed. Here was something
that had nothing to do with technique, and it outraged the British at first
blush, but then they decided it was the best performance of Shakespeare
they'd ever seen. Their own facilities, even in that picture itself, are rather
weak echoes of where Brando hit some vein and passion. But I'm off here
into a description of that natural outpouring that you don't have to be an
actor to have. In *The Red Badge of Courage* I used nonprofessionals and
encouraged them to be themselves. But I encourage an actor to be himself
too. Always try to get the most out of the actor in the way of his own
instinct and spirit.

The reason Bogart was in so many films of mine was not because I
liked Bogart but because that face and voice and figure fitted in with the
kinds of stories that I like to write and make. I relate the actor to the part
and would rather have a personality that fitted than a particular actor I
wanted. I never cast an actor who had to change his personality for the
role.

If you choose a personality or type, in a sense you've already done your directing.

That's right.

*Then who are the actors where you felt as a director that you had to somehow
motivate them? And how did you do it?*

One thing is to put them on track. For instance, Bogart had never played
anything like Charlie Allnut in *The African Queen* before that, though

there was a part of Bogart that I knew was like Charlie. You know, that sneered face, someone quite in control of his own and everyone else's destiny. A little pie-faced runt of a creature. Well, that was in Bogart.

How did you know that?

Because I knew Bogart.

As was the more ruthless and perhaps almost maniacal character of Fred Dobbs in The Treasure of the Sierra Madre?

That's right. That role was easier for Bogart. He had been a gangster in lots of pictures. It was that demoniacal thing that he had in *The Petrified Forest*. All it needed was an element of stupidity which just had to be characterized. That was easier for him than, for instance, *The African Queen*.

How did you interject this element of stupidity?

It was inherent in the lines. Take, for example, what for me is a very beautifully done scene in *The Treasure of the Sierra Madre* when the two men are on the bench in the park speculating about gold. Bogart doesn't see why gold should change a man's soul.

You have acted yourself and are familiar with the kind of functioning that's required of actors in order to play certain roles. I wonder if you actually get into the role yourself to help give direction and guidance to the actors.

Only insofar as it's required. I start out by getting as much as I can from the actor himself. If he goes off the track, then I try to put him back on. If his performance needs to be intensified, I try to help him. I have as few searching conversations as possible. I can tell you a story in this regard. I worked with Katie Hepburn on *The African Queen*. She is a suspicious woman at best, and for the first couple of days she was playing the role as a formidable woman, icy cold and supercilious. She had her own characterization that wasn't very good. It was, actually, banal. She didn't pay much attention to my advice and suggestions, and finally, after a couple of days, I sent a note across to Katie and said I would like to talk to her. We were in the heart of the African jungle and living under very romantic circumstances. I was going to give the occasion all the formality I could to make it impressive. She answered back that she could receive me at her bungalow. I went over there and said to her, "Katie, look. I don't think what you're doing is right and I'm going to talk to you for a few minutes and tell you some things, and when I'm through, don't answer me. Just think about it. The character of Rose should be a lady. I suggest you pattern your performance after what you've seen or know of Mrs. Eleanor Roosevelt." That's all it took, the key. Yes, that's right, the key. And from then on Katie was wonderful and couldn't do anything wrong.

Do you allow your actors the opportunity to deviate from the script at all?

I give a lot of room to the actors, but I don't look to them to make a creative contribution to the dialogue. I think in a sense you're deceiving yourself if you think you can wing it on the set. It has happened, and there are certain directors who have done it with a degree of success, but not me.

How do you tell the actors that you don't want them to be creative with the lines?

Say, "Shut up." I never ran into this trouble, though I'm told it occurs.

What about The Misfits *and your work with the writer, Arthur Miller? It seems almost as if the lives of the actors—Clark Gable, Marilyn Monroe and Montgomery Clift—had something to do with the story and their dialogue.*

I think that's true, but it wasn't immediate at the time. Miller wrote the script for Marilyn. The film was made out of the materials at hand, sure. The things that happened during the course of the picture were almost a counterpoint to the story itself. Marilyn was on her way out. Not only of the picture, but of life.

Could you talk about Freud? *I'm wondering if you did a lot of research before you made the film.*

I first got into that through an experience in a hospital during the war, where I made a documentary about patients suffering from battle neuroses. I was in the army and made the picture *Let There Be Light*. That experience started my interest in psychotherapy, and to this day Freud looms as the single huge figure in that field. The three great figures in human history who have affected the thinking of man about himself are perhaps Copernicus, who told us that the world did not revolve around us, that we were simply part of a system that was infinite; Darwin, who told us that the human race answered to the same laws as other species; and Freud's discovery of the unconscious. It was on this revelation and demonstration of the unconscious that the picture was predicated.

How do you approach the cinematography of your films?

There is an instinctive sense of arrangement that is determined by the material within the scene. It seems to me that in directing a scene, you have to rehearse not according to the requirements of the camera but according to the requirements of the scene itself. Only then you have to discover a way to get into that scene with the camera. Having acted in a few pictures of other directors, I've seen the way they come in and set things up. Pretty soon they'll put chalk marks down. Sometimes the actors aren't even there, but the camera is already located and they're stuck with it. It can become pretty wooden, and they don't know what to do about it. But if they would walk around the scene a bit and ask the actors to do it again, they might more easily find a way to tell the scene with the camera.

And what about editing of the films?

I don't even know the editor of my films most of the time. I am a particular case here because I edit my pictures in the camera. I don't protect myself and take shots other than the ones I need. It's pretty hard to put the film I shoot together in a way I didn't intend. One is almost forced to cut it a certain way. I don't believe that pictures are made in the cutting room. They are sometimes killed there, but not made.

Ray Bradbury was here a week ago and said that the death of Ernest Hemingway had been a crucial point in his life. He suggested it was probably the same in your life too. Do you feel you have ever sought to cope with these kinds of personal problems in your films?

Well, Hemingway was a very close personal friend of mine. I felt a very deep and immediate sense of loss when he died. He had tried to kill himself a couple of times before. Of course, it's a tragic thing to know that a friend has such moments. I've enormous admiration for Hemingway, and to my generation he was a great influence. Apparently there is a kind of swing back toward Hemingway again, though around five years ago the younger intellectuals were decrying him, running him down. Something they hadn't understood was that Hemingway laid down a certain set of standards for my time, standards of behavior. He made some effort to describe tastes and the good things of life and put them down on record, evaluating their importance. I mean, it was important to fish a river well. If you shoot, then it was important you shoot well. It was important for a man to be brave and have valor. It was important to appreciate a good wine or the taste of an oyster. These things in my young manhood and youth hadn't been mentioned for a long time, and I think they influenced my generation to the point of it being, in a funny way, almost a new religion. Is this what you're getting at?

Yes, you express very well the feeling that Hemingway gave you and many of the filmmakers of your generation. Do you feel you have worked that code into your films? Are you aware of consciously bringing it out of your emotional life and into your art?

Not consciously, but I'm sure that the process occurs whenever one's interest is aroused. I don't care to be too subjective or to examine too closely my own motives. One more thing I should note was his great attention to the art of writing. He felt that if you were a writer, you should write well.

A lot of writers, toward the end of their careers, do a "summing up." They want to put down their whole feeling not only about life but also about the art with which they are involved. Not that you're at the end by any means, but do you think this can be done in film too?

I think that the best answer to that is to mention Ring Lardner's collection of short stories, *How to Write Short Stories*. I think you should be best known by your work rather than by your opinions about your work. Hemingway didn't write a great deal about writing. He implied his own great sense of obligation to the written word, and I can tell you a story if you're in the mood for an anecdote. I was with him one time on his boat and we were talking about writing. He was saying how when the words took wing and the writing was going well, then there was no experience to compare with it. I felt that writing had always been torturous for me, and that was the difference between us. A couple of weeks later I was back with him on the boat and we talked about standing up with an orchestra playing, and dancing, doing turns on the dance floor with a woman, and he was saying how one time in his life he had been forced to dance and how he remembered the experience with the horror that he sometimes would experience with writing. "Oh, thank God for that," I said.

How do you feel about the essential difference between the theatrical form and the cinematic form? With the coming of sound, to a certain degree cinema began merely to film theater, and some years ago you adapted Tennessee Williams' play Night of the Iguana *into a film.*

Yes, the adaptation was based on suggestions within the play that would be interesting to put on the screen. The actual operation was done with a collaborator, a very dear friend of mine named Tony Veillers. We worked extremely well together. Our method was that I'd write a scene and Tony would write a scene and I would hand mine over to him, and his to me.

With Humphrey Bogart and Lauren Bacall on the set of *Key Largo* (1945).

One thing I couldn't reconcile in the film was the part Ava Gardner played. She was in Tennessee's original play, and despite a certain charm and humor she had in the original, she turned into a kind of great bloated spider that consumed this man. I didn't change the character out of any desire to sentimentalize the material, but she just defied being put into that role on film. So one day we changed her completely so far as the end of the story and their relationship is concerned. I talked to Tennessee about this and he said it wasn't what he'd intended at all. I accused him of hating women and of twisting her to his own devices and purposes. He said maybe there was that, and agreed my changes were permissible. I wanted his approval, as I have too high a regard for him to have just gone blindly in another direction.

The scene I'm talking about is in Mexico where the girl comes to Richard Burton's room to importune him. She's trying to seduce him, but he's had an unfortunate background so far as the seduction of maidens is concerned and he's doing his level best to avoid this one. But she comes into the room, and this dialogue scene ensues where he tries to explain to her why he chooses not to make love to her. I'd written the scene, Tony [Veillers] had worked on it, but it still wasn't very good. The dialogue was good, but the scene wasn't satisfactory, so I asked Tennessee to look at it and see if he had any ideas. He came back the next morning with the scene he'd written, and if you've seen the picture you'll know what I'm talking about. It opens with Burton standing before a chiffonier and there is a bottle of whisky on the chiffonier, and the girl opens the door and startles him. He's shaving and he cuts himself, and the bottle falls off the chiffonier. The dialogue then continued as he walks on broken glass barefoot. Presently the girl, in the spirit of martyrdom, joins him walking on broken glass, and the scene proceeded in that vein. As these lines bounced back and forth between them they were walking on broken glass, something that served to dramatize the scene. The scene was the same except for broken glass on the floor, and this gave it something extraordinary. It's an example of real dramatic genius, one of the best scenes in the picture.

How did you approach the filming of Williams' long monologue that Deborah Kerr has when Burton is tied up?

There was some rewriting, I guess it was two-thirds as long in the picture as it was on the stage, and I don't believe anything was lost in reducing it.

I shot the whole thing and it wasn't very good, so I did the whole thing over. I made little improvements in Deborah's performance, and there was better use of the camera—more sensitive. Before when I had done the scene, things were *this* big when they should have been *this* big. It was just a matter of distance. I'm not talking about shots or angles—just distance.

I wonder how it felt to direct your father in The Treasure of the Sierra Madre, *and how you feel about being directed as an actor when you appear in other people's films, for example Roman Polanski's* Chinatown.

Well, the director is the father image on the set, so I was my own father's father. As I appeared in the *The Treasure of the Sierra Madre,* I was *my* father also, so that made me my grandfather. When it comes to working for another director, particularly one as good as Polanski, I try to be the most immediate of actors so as to serve as an example to the actors in my own pictures.

Are there any films that you set out to make or wanted to make and never had to the opportunity to?

There were some, yes, that for various reasons went by the wayside. At one time I planned to do the story of the conquest of Mexico, which I think would make a wonderful picture. There is another, a Kipling story, *The Man Who Would Be King.* Also there is a script still floating around, one of the best scripts I ever read. My God, what's the name of the man who wrote it, maybe some of you know? The picture's never been made. I've tried two or three times to get people interested in it. It's called *Harrow Alley,* an examination into death, and it scared the bejesus out of everybody who read it. These are pictures I would have liked to have made and couldn't for one reason or another.

When you made The Red Badge of Courage *there were many complications, apparently because it was felt the film didn't have the necessary ingredients to earn back its money. Could we talk about how a director gets into a position where he is able to maintain control?*

Well, I've never had any difficulty there. In the first place I rarely tried to persuade anyone to make a film. *The Red Badge of Courage* became a cause célèbre before it was ever made. It was a film over which the old and new orders at MGM fought. They were making pictures that cost just as much, but the searchlight was focused on it. I even said to Louis Mayer, "Look, if you're against this, let's not make the picture." And I must say, to my amazement, to his everlasting credit, he said, "If you believe in it, don't you talk like that. You go ahead." So when I do make a picture I assume complete control, even if sometimes the material or situation has got out of control.

How do you feel about studios cutting your pictures after they're made?

With *The Red Badge of Courage* they cut the film and they didn't do really as bad a job as they were supposed to have done. I quite understood at the time why they took the steps they did. I was present at a preview when damn near a third of the audience got up and walked out of the theater. Disheartening experience, by the way. I hope none of you ever go through it.

Do you think if that same uncut print were shown today that audiences would respond differently?

I don't know. I mean, because the situation then was the Korean War, which wasn't as uppermost in the mind of the audience as the Vietnam War is today. I remember when I'd be reading *Life* magazine and I'd look at pictures of the troops in Korea, I didn't want to see what was going on. And I think maybe this had something to do with the reception the picture got. It brought war very close to home. And they cut out one scene that was probably the best scene in the picture, in the way of an anticlimax. Those of you who know the book will remember the rather monumental death of the tall solder. Then the boy and the tattered soldier walk away down the hill, and the tattered fellow says, "I've never seen a feller die like that." He talks along those lines and begins to ramble and begins to walk around in little circles and dies himself. And this moment was the most extraordinary moment in the picture as far as I was concerned. The point of it was that it wouldn't have made any difference so far as the audience was concerned. The picture didn't enjoy any greater success because that scene was cut. They still walked out in the middle of the picture.

Do you think that people left because of a flaw in the writing?

No, they just didn't want to see what was on the screen at the time. Later
the picture was shown on a double bill in London and the critics united in
their belief that the film should be more widely shown, which it eventually was, and still no one went to see it. The climate was simply not right
for that picture then. Today it's being shown almost consistently in some
art house somewhere.

*What about the idea that a film that attempts to hit at too large a segment of the
people will be rejected?*

No, I don't believe that kind of thinking is profitable. I can't do any more
than make a picture I believe in and hope there are enough like me who
want to see it. In this instance, there weren't enough like me. I was in the
minority—only a small minority—who wanted to see *The Red Badge of
Courage.*

Does that happen often?

No, not often. I think that's the outstanding example. I've had failures.
For instance *The Asphalt Jungle* was no great shakes when it first came out,
but it became a success in later releases. I don't really know why it didn't
work on the first release. There were no big names, it wasn't a usual MGM
product. Maybe those were the reasons.

*There is a great suspicion today about "success." It seems that for directors of
integrity, it's difficult to get financing for the kinds of films they really want to
make.*

Of course, but I think a unique film has a better chance today than ever
before.

*Regarding the younger generation of filmmakers, some of them feel that the whole
notion of a story is somewhat passé, that somehow a film can be created without
any dramatic structure.*

You mean the kind of film today that disregards plot, where everything is a demonstration of theme, and the plot itself is of relatively small importance? We've mentioned Godard, and I haven't seen *Easy Rider,* but I gather it moves according to this faith. My own trend—one I can't divorce myself from because it is a part of me—is that there must be a plot. I see plot as a very noble thing. To be abstract about it, plot is about making a formula, a geometric formula. It's reducing a theme down to a formula. Take *The Asphalt Jungle.* The story is built around a crime, and the central character is a man who likes horses. The film is thematic in this sense. He was taken out of his environment and became a hoodlum, and everything he did was dictated by a kind of nostalgia and a desire to go back to his first love. At the end, when he dies in the field, the horses come over and look at him.

The end of The Treasure of the Sierra Madre *is driven by the plot, but also by theme. Do you often seek to find the scene that will be a kind of metaphor of your theme?*

Well, I think if you are faithful to your material it will show itself. You come to the moment of truth in every picture where the bull has to be killed.

Do you break the shooting script down very carefully before you actually go into the picture?

Yes. Not shot by shot, but scene by scene.

You have not picked the camera angles before the scene has been staged and rehearsed?

No. Not any longer.

You used to?

Yes, I used to. But today the drawings are already in my mind. It becomes more exact after the actors come in and try and work out the scene. I give them as little direction as possible. It's a question of orienting themselves to the circumstances, and then when it's been brought down into the form that I see is right, it's usually very easy to find the camera angles. The best scenes I've ever shot, so far as the camera is concerned, are never commented on. I will move the camera a great deal and the actors move. I will try to get three scenes instead of one. One scene goes into another scene, and an entirely new atmosphere and visual circumstance is created. This happens with the camera and the people moving, with a change of environment. You'll move from inside to outside, from a medium shot to a close-up, back to a two-shot of people walking or something else, and they get into a car and the car drives away. Now, these shots are almost ballet—the camera is dancing with the actors and the scene. These are never noticed if they are good. The audience sees them but never realizes what's happening. There are scenes like this in *The Treasure of the Sierra Madre* and *The Maltese Falcon*. I remember one scene that was marked out by the cameraman where there were twenty-six marks. The camera moved, dollied, crabbed and so on. There can be as many as that, and the audience never knew it was happening. No critic has ever commented on this scene.

Do you feel that a film is divided into major movements consisting of scenes or acts in which there are sort of subordinate goals and accomplishments?

Well, this gives me the opportunity to repeat the best piece of advice that was ever given to me, by Henry Blanke* when I was about to make *The Maltese Falcon.* He said each shot you do should be the most important shot. If it's somebody getting out of a car, he must get out of that car perfectly. The camera should be in the right place when he gets out. The car should approach the curb at exactly the right angle. Everything should be perfect. Your entire attention and concentration should be on the shot you are doing at this particular swift instant in time.

Your work incorporates some of the most difficult location pictures ever made, from The Treasure of the Sierra Madre *to* The African Queen. *What do you look for in a producer when you go into difficult circumstances like those?*

Help. To do the onerous things that permit you to give your entire attention to the quality of the picture, rather than to the problems, physical or

---

*Henry Blanke (1901–1981) was the producer of *The Maltese Falcon* and of *The Treasure of the Sierra Madre.*

With Eli Wallach on location for *The Misfits* (1961). Arthur Miller wrote
the screenplay. The film starred Marilyn Monroe, Montgomery Clift
and Clark Gable.

otherwise. A producer must have the ability to bring forth the people that
will help you the most, to understand the requirements of the picture.
Some producers have a false sense of the requirements, or they want to
play a critical role. I don't mean to demean or reduce the producer. It's a
very important role, and I'll probably be a producer myself—when I am
no longer able to navigate.

Films as Director

1941 *The Maltese Falcon* (also
      screenplay)
1942 *In This Our Life*
      Across the Pacific
1943 *Report from the Aleutians* (also
      screenplay and film editing)
1945 *The Battle of San Pietro* (also
      screenplay)
1946 *Let There Be Light* (also
      co-screenplay)
1948 *The Treasure of the Sierra Madre*
      (also screenplay)
      Key Largo (also co-screenplay)
1949 *We Were Strangers* (also
      co-screenplay)
1950 *The Asphalt Jungle* (also
      screenplay)
1951 *The Red Badge of Courage* (also
      screenplay)
1952 *The African Queen* (also
      co-adaptation)
1953 *Moulin Rouge* (also
      co-screenplay)
1954 *Beat the Devil* (also
      co-screenplay)
1956 *Moby Dick* (also producer and
      co-screenplay)
1957 *Heaven Knows, Mr. Allison* (also
      co-screenplay)

1958 *The Roots of Heaven*
      The Barbarian and the Geisha
1960 *The Unforgiven*
1961 *The Misfits*
1962 *Freud*
1963 *The List of Adrian Messenger*
1964 *The Night of the Iguana* (also
      co-screenplay)
1965 *The Bible*
1967 *Reflections in a Golden Eye*
      Casino Royale (codirector of
      several)
1969 *A Walk with Love and Death*
      The Madwoman of Chaillot
      Sinful Davey
1970 *The Kremlin Letter* (also
      co-screenplay)
1972 *Fat City*
1973 *The Macintosh Man*
1975 *The Man Who Would Be King*
      (also co-screenplay)
1976 *Independence*
1979 *Wise Blood*
1980 *Phobia*
1981 *Victory*
1982 *Annie*
1984 *Under the Volcano*
1985 *Prizzi's Honor*
1987 *The Dead*

People come to you and they say, "Boy, we love your work. We love this and we want to buy it." Then, as soon as they buy it, the teeth come out. You become not the father of the work, but the stepfather. All of a sudden, you're an outsider, a villain. I have often said to these people, "Look, I'll do the script free for you if you'll shoot my mistakes instead of yours. My mistakes are better."

RAY BRADBURY
(Born in Waukegan, Illinois, 1920)

Ray Bradbury is a novelist who has had an off-and-on romance with motion pictures for nearly half a century. Many of his film projects were unrealized, but his screenplay for *Moby Dick* was turned into a memorable film by John Huston. Bradbury's visit to AFI stands as one of the more interesting seminars because of his frank exploration of the process of writing the script and working with Huston.

Bradbury was born in Waukegan, Illinois, where his father was out of work for two years during the Depression before taking the family to Los Angeles. The then fourteen-year-old Ray—whose middle name, Douglas, was given to him by his mother in honor of Douglas Fairbanks, Sr., the reigning star at the time of Bradbury's birth—became entranced with the movie world, spending days outside studios to catch sight of the stars. He recalls that the boyhood experience that inspired his creativity was seeing *The Hunchback of Notre Dame.* He could not afford college, so after high school he spent three years selling newspapers and reading voraciously at local libraries. He started writing "to escape the hopelessness and despair of the real world and enter the world of hope, where I could create with my imagination." He was soon selling short stories to magazines.

With *The Martian Chronicles, Dandelion Wine, Fahrenheit 451* and *The Illustrated Man,* all published in the early fifties, Bradbury became a popular and successful novelist, bringing beautiful language and appealing characters to the previously narrow genre of science fiction. Throughout his career he would use fantasy to explore challenging themes in the tradition of Edgar Allan Poe and H. G. Wells.

His writing extends beyond novels to include five hundred short stories,

Ray Bradbury (right) working in Ireland with John Huston on the screenplay
of Herman Melville's *Moby-Dick* (1956).

hundreds of teleplays, a stage play, an opera, essays, nonfiction, a collection of
poetry—and, of course, screenwriting, an activity that can be a frustrating
calling in Hollywood. I have always felt that successful novelists like Bradbury, Gore Vidal and Larry McMurtry are fortified in their forays into
screenwriting by the knowledge that their reputations are secure and not
dependent on the quixotic fortunes of film projects. But as Bradbury makes
clear in his AFI seminar, cinema remained a persistent interest for him no
matter how successful he was as a novelist.

Bradbury is a man of contradictions. He is fascinated by the wonders of
science and space travel but has never driven an automobile, and for many
years refused to fly. He still writes on an old-fashioned typewriter and he told
an interviewer for *Playboy* in 1996 that he opposed the notion that the Inter-
net was a creative tool for writers: "I say, B.S. 'Stay away from that. Stop talking to people around the world and get your work done.'"

Bradbury's love of quality films attracted him to an array of major filmmakers. Though he turned down *War and Peace* for King Vidor, *Friendly Persuasion* for William Wyler and *Les Diaboliques* for Henri-Georges Clouzot, he
did doctor the script of *King of Kings* for Nicholas Ray, wrote a never filmed
adaptation of *And the Rock Cried Out* for Carol Reed and worked with Sam
Peckinpah on a screenplay of his own novel *Something Wicked This Way*

Comes, which never got into production. He wrote the script again for Jack Clayton, and the film was released in 1983. He also worked on an unproduced script of *The Martian Chronicles* for Alan Pakula and Robert Mulligan, and adapted *Fahrenheit 451* for the stage for Charles Laughton.

I remember seeing *Moby Dick* on the big screen when it came out and being enthralled by its poetry and imagery. I think it's a flawed masterpiece that was harmed by the movie-star persona of Gregory Peck, who gave a powerful performance as Ahab that was hindered by his fame.

It seemed a special opportunity, just two months after the conservatory opened, to have a writer of Bradbury's range and stature talk to the AFI fellows. He spoke frankly about the creative process on *Moby Dick,* and offered wide-ranging advice to AFI's young filmmakers.

RAY BRADBURY

———◆———

October 1, 1969*

I'd like to welcome someone who is incredibly unique, the only person I know in the city of Los Angeles who does not drive—Mr. Ray Bradbury.

I guess the secret of being alive and creative in this world is that you can hardly wait to see and do things. I think every day should be that thing of jumping out of bed and saying, "God, another day to do that thing that I love." That's really what it's all about. That is all I ever discuss when I go anywhere, and it's what I'll talk about tonight.

I learned my first valuable lesson when I was nine years old. I collected *Buck Rogers* comic strips. I loved Buck Rogers. I thought he was the greatest thing that ever happened in the world. All my friends made fun of me, and I listened to them and I tore all the strips up. About a month later I burst into tears. I asked myself, "Why am I crying?" The answer was that something was gone from the center of my life. I had allowed other people to use their authority against my taste. The first lesson you have to learn in this world is to go by your own taste. Don't listen to anyone else. Be what you are with all your heart and soul, because that's all you're ever going to have. You have to trust yourself. So I went back to Buck Rogers and said, "I love you madly!" My life was restored, and from then on I never listened to anyone else in the world, because you're the only person who knows anything about your loves.

You can't ever listen to the advice of anyone in this world about the

*This transcript includes segments from AFI seminars with Ray Bradbury held on October 9, 1969, April 15, 1981, and June 2, 1982.

things you need, the things you want, the things that excite you. The only way to explain these things to people is through your work. Those of you who are writers, get it on paper. Become your own critic. You'll be the best critic you will ever have. Seeing yourself grow, you'll look back and say, "Oh, my God. Look at that horrible thing I did a year ago." The same thing is true with making little films, taking primitive steps. You'll look back and say, "Christ, how could I have done that? I experimented and did these things, but now it's over."

When did you become interested in the cinema?

Luckily my mother started taking me to movies when I was three. My first film was *The Hunchback of Notre Dame* in 1923 with Lon Chaney. I have pretty good recall for the early years of my life. I didn't see the film again until I was nineteen. I went to see it with some friends and said I remembered all the scenes, but they didn't believe me. The biggest influence on me in the early twenties was motion pictures—all the Lon Chaney and Douglas Fairbanks films. If you want to work in film, I absolutely demand that you see every important picture ever made. That's a couple of thousand of them. I'd love to join you, because I don't want to see most of the new films.

I think that growing up as I did with comic strips has been very valuable to me when writing screenplays. Screenplays began to borrow things from comic strips thirty to forty years ago. Likewise, comic strips began to imitate things on the cinema screen, and growing up with the two was a very valuable experience. When you look at something like *Prince Valiant,* you see camera angles in every panel. I'm sure that Georges Méliès knew Windsor McKay's *Little Nemo in Slumberland* cartoons* and that McKay knew about Méliès' films. These twin tributaries of creativity grew up at exactly the same time.

How did you meet John Huston?

When I was twenty-nine, I went to a radio broadcast with Norman Krasna, and John Huston came and sat right behind me. I was terrified. I

---

*McKay's cartoon strip, which first appeared in the *New York Herald* in 1905, spawned a Broadway play in 1908 and an animated cartoon in 1911. McKay is perhaps best known for his groundbreaking 1914 animated cartoon *Gertie the Dinosaur.*

wanted to turn around and grab his hand and say, "I love you. I love your films. I want to work for you. You are the greatest thing that ever walked on God's green earth." But I didn't do anything. I just sat on my chair and said to myself, "Ray, you're not going to make an ass out of yourself. You're going to publish two more books first." This was a self-conscious, emotional decision. I had already published one book. I didn't say a word to him. I didn't introduce myself. I missed my chance to meet my beloved hero. Two or three years passed, during which I published *The Martian Chronicles* and *The Illustrated Man.* Then I called my agent and said, "I want to meet John Huston for one hour." When we met, on Valentine's night of 1951, I put my books on the table and I said, "If you love these books as much as I love your work, then we must work together." He took them on the plane with him to Africa, where he went to make *The African Queen,* and wrote me back a letter and said, "You're right. I do love your books. We'll work together someday. I don't know on what, but thank you for the books." I didn't see him again for two years. We corresponded twice a year, admiring one another and circling one another.

He came back in August of 1953, called me up, asked me over for cocktails at the Beverly Hills Hotel. I sat there, and he asked me what I had been doing and what I would be doing during the next year. I said that I had just finished a new book, *Fahrenheit 451,* that had been sent off to the publishers. He said, "How would you like to come live in Ireland and write the screenplay of *Moby Dick?"* Boy, was I being hit in the stomach. I said, "I don't know." He said, "What do you mean?" I said, "I've never been able to read the goddamned book." There was a long pause, and then he said, "Ray, why don't you go home tonight, read as much as you can and come back tomorrow and tell me if you'll help me kill the white whale."

So I went home with the book. I said to my wife, "Pray for me. I've got to read a book tonight and do a book report by tomorrow." How do I read it? Do I start at the beginning? Like hell I do. I just dive in and find the thing about the spirits and the descriptions of panic and terror. I read all about the Versailles fountain, and turned to another section and I found the becalmment. Then I found the section on the whiteness of the whale and read that. The whiteness of polar seas, icebergs, wolves, creatures that live in subterranean caves with no eyes. They never come out into the light in their entire lives. Then I came to the last section where Ahab says, "It's a mild, mild day and a mild-looking sky." I turned back to the opening of the book and I read, "Call me Ishmael." I went back to Huston and I said, "Wow. It's the right time in my life. I'm old enough." If he had come to me three years earlier, I wouldn't have taken the job.

I remember one night in Ireland, sitting around the fire drinking Irish whisky. I turned to Huston and said, "How'd I get this job? Nobody knows me. Nobody reads my books. Why didn't you get James Agee or Robert Sherwood?" He said, "Well, it was that story about the dinosaur falling in love with the lighthouse." He was talking about my story *The Beast from 20,000 Fathoms*. He said, "I thought I smelled the ghost of Melville there." What Huston recognized in my story wasn't Melville, but the Bible and William Shakespeare. I had been raised on the Bible and I'd raised myself on the poetry of Shakespeare. I put all the loneliness that I found in *Hamlet* and *Othello* in my writing. Later in my life, after I finished the screenplay, I discovered how deeply Shakespeare had influenced Melville. It was only later that I realized that Melville's midwives were also my midwives. When I went to work for Huston, I said, "What do you want from me? Do you want the Freudian Melville? The Jungian?" He said, "No, I want Ray Bradbury's *Moby-Dick*. That's why I hired you. Digest the book and bring me what you think is there. That's the only way to do it."

How did you approach adapting such a huge book for the screen?

It's really hard to adapt other people's work. After all, you are not that author. The best you can be is an approximation of that author. When you adapt other people's books, make sure you know the book totally. Do not go at this stuff in a half-assed way. It's got to get into your bloodstream so completely that it can come out on an emotional level. It has to be re-created through your emotions and not rethought. Your emotions will do the rethinking for you. But that is a lot of work, and a lot of people don't want to go to all that trouble. They think you can just chop a thing up and mince it and put it all back together again. That's not true. You have to be expressing real emotions. It takes months to read the book and get it into your bloodstream so you know every word, so finally you can forget that you know it and you're able to begin, to create. Be sure, too, that you love the book. Never take a job you don't love. I've yet to take a single job in Hollywood that I didn't want to take. Starve instead, because you'll do a lousy job and you'll get a bad reputation. One reason why I refuse to adapt anyone else's novel from here on in is that it takes roughly six months of reading somebody else's work before it gets into your bloodstream.

For a ten-year period before I ever met John Huston, people would write to me and ask, "When are you going write a screenplay?" My answer invariably was, "When John Huston asks me to." I knew I wanted to work with him—he was my hero. When Huston gave me the job of writing *Moby Dick,* I went off to Ireland. While I was living in Dublin, I suffered severe depressions. God Almighty, here I was, traveling for the first time in my life. I never had any money in my life, and all of a sudden I had enough money to live in a hotel and eat good food. I could see the sights of the world and I was working on the greatest American novel for my superhero. I was suppressing so much of it I didn't realize what tension I was under. I didn't realize how huge the responsibility was. Probably the weather had a lot to do with it. Probably the responsibility of working for John Huston had a lot to do with it. Probably the presence of Herman Melville had a lot to do with it. Actually, I was going through a process of reading that book nine times over. I was having a hell of a lot of trouble, and Huston wasn't much help because we are both essentially intuitive people and not intellectuals. I'm an emotional intellectual but not an intellectual intellectual. So there was a crippled man helping a wounded man. Huston was a director who didn't know any more about *Moby Dick* than I did, so we had to feel our way.

It was fantastically difficult because it's such a long book. Fortunately you can go through and eliminate about half of the pages because it's fabulous stuff, but it's padding about whaling, so you learn to leapfrog through and get to the basic scenes you need to work with. But it still took me seven months to read that book forty times over—some sections eighty times—until it began to get into my bloodstream. But a beautiful thing happened in about the seventh month. I got out of bed one morning in London. I looked in the mirror and said, "I am Herman Melville." That was the morning that I began to write the really good screenplay of *Moby Dick.* In one day, eight hours, I rewrote the last forty pages. That's a hell of a lot of pages of a screenplay. It all fell into place in those eight hours. That was one glorious day, when I was Herman Melville.

That is what writing screenplays is all about. If you aren't totally prepared on some level, you cannot do the job. It took me six or seven months of getting Melville into my bloodstream so he could finally come out through my fingers. As long as he was just in here [*taps head*], he was self-conscious. "How do I use this ship? Where do I put that captain? What do I do with this lorry?" That's all functioning stuff. It's data collecting and sorting out. But it finally has to be struck with lightning. There are a lot of damn good things in that film, but the last forty minutes of it have a fantastic and inevitable flow. The rhythm is gorgeous because of that one day.

I built the structure of the screenplay slowly. To get the first fifty pages down was the easiest part because all the introductory material was in the book. But from then on, it becomes more complex. I had to realign everything. Every single encounter had to be weighed and I had to see, by the ounce, which weighed the most. The heavier elements had to go at the end of the script, the lighter ones at the beginning. That takes a hell of a lot of thinking and figuring.

I would spend half the day at my typewriter in Dublin, then I would drive out to Huston's estate. We would spend until two in the morning grinding our heads against this thing. One night we came up with a problem so terrific and so terrible that it threatened to destroy the whole screenplay, and I had to start again. I came up against an impasse. I can't even remember what it is now. It is so many years back and it was so traumatic. I was so depressed, and John kept me up until two in the morning when he brought Peter Viertel in to sit with us. Peter was working on another film for John at that time. We kept hitting at it and intellectualizing it. Finally I said, "Stop. Everyone cut it out. We are doing this all wrong. I don't believe in this way of doing things. Let's try an experiment: I'm going to go back to Dublin and put a pad of paper and a pencil by my bed so that when I wake in the morning it will be there. I've got to rethink the thing just before I go to sleep. John, you do the same. Peter, you do the same. One of the three of us will wake up in the morning with a solution to the problem." They laughed at me, they hooted, but I went back to Dublin and put the pad by the telephone. At seven in the morning the telephone rang. I picked it up and it was Huston. He said, "Ray, I've got the solution." And he had it. I said, "You son of a bitch, never argue with me again."

What was the emotion that you felt in Moby Dick?

The emotion is the dedication of saying to Ahab, "What do you want?" Ahab cries, "The whale!" That's the emotion. That's the whole story. Everything is built around that.

John and I spent a lot of time just figuring out the book. It's a long, sprawling novel, and I had to find ways of sewing it together—taking out something from the back and putting it at the front, taking something from the middle and putting it at the end. I was looking intuitively for the images that would tell the story. We needed enough action and images so that when we did get to the talk section you would sit quietly while Ahab describes what the whale means to him. I always tried to find something that was visual. One example was when Queequeg signed in. It was my idea to have him sign with the picture of the whale.

Intuition. Pose the problem and then walk away. You cannot think your way through such a thing. I would much rather have done that screenplay ten times over emotionally and done it wrong so that I would come to it the eleventh time emotionally. Most of the outlines we did got us nowhere. What I am saying here is—depending upon the novel and depending upon the stage play and depending upon the short story, you've got to do a fantastic amount of research, or no research. They may have it all laid out for you in the book. *The Maltese Falcon* is a good example. The screenplay is the book and the book is the screenplay. The next time it's on TV, watch it. And as it plays on the screen, read it off the page. Nobody had to do any research on that. They marked it with a red pencil: "Use this line and that line. Cut this." There will be jumps, but if you keep moving through the book you'll see the whole screenplay laid out for you. There are not too many books like that. Dashiell Hammett was quite a remarkable man, and *The Maltese Falcon* is quite a remarkable book.

Huston was a very smart director. He let me finish the first fifty or sixty pages before he criticized anything. He let me get a real start on the screenplay. Then, after a month, maybe six weeks, I turned in the first sixty pages and very honestly said to him, "Now, look, if this doesn't satisfy you, fire me this afternoon. I don't want to take money under false pretenses. I've known too many screenwriters who are prostitutes, who work ten weeks, turn in a lousy script and run. I can't live that way. I've worked my damndest here to give you what I hope you'll like. If you don't like it, fire me and I'll go home with the kids." Huston said, "Well, kid, go upstairs and lie down and rest up a little bit, and I'll read the script and I'll tell you in an hour." I went upstairs in this big mansion and I lay down. I was a wreck. About two hours later I heard the most beautiful sound I've ever heard in my life—John Huston standing at the foot of the stairs calling up to me saying, "Ray, come down and finish the screenplay." I wept—I was free of the weights.

Were there any important scenes that were in the script that were cut out of the film?

No, I don't recall that there were any. I think this is one of the rare scripts which Huston has shot that was in pretty good shape when they started shooting. I heard that some work was done on the script by another writer who was brought in later, but I gather that none of it was used. I checked over the film and my original script, and there are only very minor variations. The only major change is in the scene with Orson Welles where he had a speech that he wrote himself. He did a brilliant job. I think he was in London for only one or two days. They shot the scene very quickly, and he left. It's a beautiful scene.

Did he write it during that time?

I don't know. I do know that Orson Welles wasn't satisfied with my writing of his scene. I agreed. I never got it quite the way I wanted it. Mr. Welles got it exactly right. This is one thing we have to learn to acknowledge when it occurs. If someone can do something, then bravo!

Were you happy with the script in the end?

I was very pleased with the script. I would change very little at this late date. I think there are things in the performance that don't work, but that's something for you to ask John Huston about. I would be very curious to know what he thought of Gregory Peck's performance. I'd like to know how he got what he got, and where he feels that either Peck failed, or he himself failed in knowing how to work with Peck. I never had a chance to ask John these things.

Is Huston a good screenwriter?

No, he's not. John doesn't know how to write. It's a shame. In the case of *The Maltese Falcon*—which is one of the greatest films ever made—I believe he does have a screen credit. As I recall, the genesis of that screenplay was when another writer at the studio, Allen Rivkin, marked a copy of the book in red pencil and gave it to Huston, who said, "My God, that's the way you could shoot it." He took it to Warner Bros. and got his first directing job. He wound up with the writing credit, too. He did do some screen work years ago, but in the case of *Moby Dick* I did the complete screenplay. Two years after I left Ireland and the film was finished, Huston sent me a letter claiming half the screenplay credit. I fought it and won. Then Huston came back and submitted as proof a mimeographed screenplay that his secretaries had typed and mimeographed with my name on it. He had marked with a red pencil on this copy, and he claimed that those sections he marked were written by him. He didn't write a word of the screenplay. The second time through, he won, and I had to share a screen credit. All but three people on the board that handed down the decision said that if he hadn't been a famous director, they wouldn't have thought about it a second time.

I have found very few directors who are great screenwriters. They may be good at helping the screenwriter at his task, but the number of directors who do their own screenplays is quite small. If I intended going into directing, I might be luckier than some. I have already learned the screen form, as a writer. But you do need inspiration from somewhere. If you can come up with your own idea, then great. Write it, develop it. If you can bring it off, then great. But I think that some of you are going to have to depend on outside material. That seems to be one of the truths of film writing. This has been true over the years in every country. Some of the greatest films have come from novels, short stories and plays. It seems to be the natural thing. There is more of a growth now in individual screenplays that are coming up, but generally they aren't very good. A thing like *Medium Cool* is not a good screenplay. It has some interesting cinematic elements which help it. *Easy Rider* had no screenplay. It's a travelogue with a dime-store philosophy, but it was saved by one performance. I think Jack Nicholson is simply fabulous. Don't kid yourself about being a writer if you're not. A lot of directors kid themselves that they're writers. The two talents don't necessarily come together. In fact, in the history of films, you can't name more than a handful of directors who were good screenwriters. Billy Wilder's the great exception. Coppola's an exception, but the screenplays are not all that brilliant. Huston never had any capacity to write at all. All his credits are shared credits, or controversial credits. On *Moby Dick* it's a shared screenplay, but he didn't write any of it.

What do you think of the kinds of films being made today?

I really don't think it's important that one be avant-garde. That's a dead end. I think that ideas are everything. If you come up with a good idea, if you are thinking for yourself, if you are creating out of your own needs, then your work will automatically be avant-garde, then you are going to be doing something fresh and original.

There are basic things missing from lots of films these days. You have to give us the moments of truth and take enough time with each of the characters so they become ricochet boards off which things happen. A really good production of *Hamlet* sets up the all-important mechanisms in the first scenes for the whole play. The machinery is this—"My father is dead and I hate it, but how can I bring him back?" If you don't convince us of that, if that son is not cracked and distraught because of the death of his father, the whole damned play doesn't work. It's a death play, the darkest play ever written, and the character of Hamlet is written so that if it's played right, you see him destroyed in front of you. And that's what's missing from *2001*. If Kubrick had spent some time with his characters, he would have destroyed all of us. There are no human beings anywhere in Kubrick's films.

A director like David Lean has such ways of engaging you. Next time you see *The Bridge on the River Kwai*, see how he involves you in a very secret, special way. First of all, you don't get to meet anyone at the start. You have these men marching through the jungle and being hit by the sun, and their feet are bloody by the time they arrive at the camp. They're lined up in front of the Japanese soldiers, and Alec Guinness, their commander, stands in front of them and looks at them with this pride and the merest touch of wetness in one eye. He gives you—the audience—permission to feel. What has Lean done? He hasn't marched *them* through the jungle, he's marched *you* through the jungle! He's such a good filmmaker that he's made you suffer with the heat and the mosquitoes. Until such time as he can stop the march and let you know about the characters, he puts you through the mill. Then you feel for yourself that you marched, that Guinness has lined you up, that you're proud, so you weep for yourself.

I go to movies all the time, and I think I have the same experience you do. Halfway through the movie I write my own ending, and then the ending comes and it's not as good as mine. Twice in the last eight years I've written my own endings and sent them to *The New York Times,* and they published them, thereby antagonizing everyone. Once in a while I see a film that's dumb all the way through, but brilliant at the same time, like *2001,* which is one of my favorite films. But it's really a big, dumb idiot of a film. It's like being in love with a gorgeous idiot of a woman. You want to leave because you can't stand the talk, but her legs are so great you can't leave them alone. And the characters are all wrong because there are no characters. When Hal, the computer, finally decides to kill them all off, you're only too glad to see them go because they're bores. You don't know the identity of any of the people killed. Kubrick could have made you care for the film and the characters if he'd spent five minutes on each of them before he froze them, if you found out about their personal lives, you would be hurt when Hal kills them. So Hal is actually the only character in the film you give a damn about. Isn't that strange? *2001* is a film that's irritated me since it came out, but I keep on going back to look at it because it's the gorgeous blond all over again.

The one thing I have noticed most often on the occasions when I have been asked to USC to see student films is the lack of a good screenplay. Without that you don't have anything. Occasionally there was somebody who lucked into something, but it was all kind of derivative and self-consciously avant-garde—it's meaningless. Ideas are everything, they really are. Every time the kids got a story that worked, the whole thing just perked up and came to life and became excellent. One of the students came to me and asked if he could adapt a story of mine called "The Last Night of the World." He wanted to do it as a student project. I think it cost him $325 to shoot it. He made a little film that's ten times better than the same story in the framework of *The Illustrated Man* as done by Jack Smight. That story cost five hundred thousand dollars to shoot out at

Bradbury talking with AFI fellows at the Greystone Mansion in Beverly Hills
on April 15, 1981.

Warner Bros. And do you know why the student's film works? Because he followed the story. If you've got something, then you go with it. Either the story is there or it's not. The instant you finish reading any story or novel, you know whether it's cinematic or not. My advice to students would be to latch onto material that is worth experimenting with. I'm sure there are hundreds of writers all over the world who would be glad to let you experiment with material. I've told people at USC, at UCLA and at Los Angeles City College—if anyone wants any of my material to make as a film, as an amateur experiment, then it's yours. All you've got to do is write me a letter and say that you won't exhibit it as a professional film. Then it's yours to play with. I'll even come up and look at it.

Can we talk about a film that is considered to be avant-garde right now, Jean-Luc Godard's Weekend.

Jean-Luc Godard is such a bore. Jesus Christ, he puts me to sleep. He is not creative. He doesn't know how to use the camera. I think he is a real amateur, in the worst sense of the term. A lovely amateur I would maybe put up with, if he were in love with what he was doing. But Godard is obviously bored himself. He has such second-rate, sophomoric ideas. It's like going to a boring friend's house. You get a little lecture on Sartre and Camus, and think, "Oh, God. Get me a drink fast." The way you judge a Godard film is how often you meet your friends in the lobby during the film. Well, he's an eight–candy bar man. I go out into the lobby eight times and I meet all my friends out there buying popcorn. That's the giveaway. All of a sudden, they've got to piss. Antonioni is the same way most of the time. With *La Notte,* I was in the lobby half the time. Everyone goes because they are bullied into going. That's one hell of a way to go to films. To hell with servicing directors. I don't want to go out of obligation to anyone. I want to go because I want to have a great time. That's the only reason to go to a film. I don't go for a social message, I don't go to be made better. To hell with that.

When did you start reading science fiction?

The first science-fiction magazines began to come out in 1928 or 1929, and this made the biggest change in my life. The great thing about reading science fiction—and then later writing it—is that you have a total education in the arts and all the theologies and all the political schemes. It's a fantastic field, and I think I'm very lucky to have fallen into it. It's been ignored, as all good things are ignored, by intellectuals. Very late in the day people finally say, "Hey, wait a minute. What's been going on?" It turns out that science fiction has been the avant-garde fiction of our times.

We are all science-fictional people, involved with science-fictional machines. Everything in our lives that is suffering a change today is a result of some machine doing something to us. You film students are all involved with the most fantastic of all the "empathy machines," one that is making vast changes in the world. It is changing our customs, our way of looking at everything. Film enables you to be black when you're white, Catholic when you're Protestant, a Jew when you're an Arab, a Russian when you're an American. When you come out of seeing *War and Peace* you say, "My God, they're human beings."

Why in hell shouldn't I be interested in machines and what they do to men? I started becoming interested in them when I was eight. When I was in high school and writing stories, I was the laughingstock of school. I went to Los Angeles High School, and among four thousand students I was the only one who was foolish enough to be writing stories about men who went off and landed on the moon. Of course that was never going to happen, was it? Never ever in our lives was this going to happen. There were no rocket ships visible anywhere in the world. There was no television anywhere in the world. People said to me, "Don't write science fiction. There are never going to be any rocket ships. There is never going to be any of this future that you talk about." I made a decision—out of love and need and desire and high energy—to go on and do these things.

Why do you think science-fiction movies have declined as a genre in the last ten to fifteen years?

I don't think I agree with you. With *2001: A Space Odyssey* it's pretty hard to say that there is no science fiction. It's probably the most titanic film of its type that has ever been released. The impact on American kids has been greater than with almost any other film. They go to see *The Graduate* and *Midnight Cowboy* and they'll have a good evening, but they won't go home out of their minds the way they come out of *2001*. You cannot discuss that film with a young person without endangering your life. It's a religion. Now, in the face of that—regardless of what you think about *2001*—the fact is that a science-fiction film is the biggest event in film history in the last several years.

*I can't remember seeing a science-fiction movie between 1958 and 1968, but before
1958 I would see them every other week.*

It's always been an in-and-out business. Of course, one of the problems
recently has been that even when they make them, they don't make them
very well. *The Illustrated Man* is a good example of this. It's a dreadful
screenplay; it's very poorly directed and isn't very exciting.

Remember, too, that the greatest musical ever made is science fiction.
Stop and think for a minute. Can you guess what it is? *Singin' in the Rain.*
Think about the plot. It's the story of the impact of technology on an aesthetic. In 1926 we had silent motion pictures, then along came sound and
destroyed the whole industry. All ideas in the history of mankind were
once science fiction. Any dream of changing the world through mechanical means is science fiction. If I had written a screenplay in 1920 predict-
ing that sound would be invented someday, you would have thrown me
out of the studio. Any science fiction is the birthing of a scientific idea
before the fact. A good deal of science fiction tells the story of a dream
that turns itself into a fact. For years I'd been searching for a proper definition of science fiction, and I found it in a single line in William Butler
Yeats—"Of what is past, or passing, or to come."

The history of mankind is science fiction becoming science fact. You
write it down as a story or as a blueprint, which you go and build, and it
changes the world. A science-fiction dream of 1920 became a reality—
sound film—in 1928. As a result, from all over the world we had to import
English actors and Bostonian actors to come to Hollywood to articulate
on film soundtracks. All these people moved to Santa Barbara and they're
still there. There's an English colony as a result of science fiction. Cary
Grant, Ronald Colman—they all came here.

I found the film version of your book Fahrenheit 451 *really strange. The first time
I saw it, I thought it was trash. I'm being absolutely honest with you. I've seen it a
couple of times since, and it gets better each time. But I don't think it's ever going
to be a really good film.*

I think *Fahrenheit 451* is quite a nice film. It's certainly a very peculiar film,
but it gets better every year that passes. I'm going to wait another ten
years. After all, I wrote the book many years ago. What is the story? It's a
book about a man who loves books. That's all. And that's all the film is
about—a guy who finds he is falling in love with a book, and who sets out

to save lives. Truffaut's film is strange because there's no romance, apart from a man in love with books. The romance between him and the girl next door is never consummated. Truffaut was brave to do a film without a major romance in it.

It's a brave film in another way. It starts out with the hero being a villain, a Fascist if you want. I think *totalitarianism* is a better term, because *Fascist* and *Communist* are absolutely the same thing. But he is a totalitarian who discovers he's a villain, and then has to grow into becoming a hero. It's really quite a brave thing to do on the screen. I wish I could get Universal to rerelease it in the face of films like *Alice's Restaurant* and *Medium Cool,* which are not brave. It's so easy to do what they are doing. We all hate Mayor Daley, so it's easy to make a film about hating him. With *Medium Cool* it's all out there, raw and naked, and is so obvious that it doesn't work. But to do what Truffaut did—to have the hero creep toward heroism—is far braver.

My wife's mother, who doesn't read many books, went to see Fahrenheit 451 *and said, "You see—that's what happens to people who read books. They end up in the woods somewhere totally disoriented from life, mumbling to themselves."*

This reminds me of a point that I want you all to remember. For Christ's sake, when you make films, make them with brilliant endings, will you? Why do I say this? I've noticed over the years that if you do a mediocre film with a great ending, you have a great film. If you do a brilliant film with a bad ending, then you have no film at all. It's very interesting that it's the last moment that counts for so much. *Citizen Kane* is one of the great films all the way down the line. But it also has that fantastic ending to tie it all together, so it's riveted into your brain and you never forget it. Truffaut, at the end of *Fahrenheit 451,* creates something I feel is commensurate with the one in *Citizen Kane.* It's not my ending; it's pure Truffaut, and it's better than my original ending. I cry every time I see it. The last sequence and the final fade-out is with all the people reciting the books as the snow is falling. It was a happy accident because when they were shooting, it began to snow.

Brilliant openings don't hurt, either.

And if there's meat in the center, so much the better!

Lots of films get better with time.

The Illustrated Man get worse. I've begun to hate it. I didn't work on the script; it was done behind my back. It's a remarkable thing in filmmaking. People come to you and they say, "Boy, we love your work. We love this and we want to buy it and we want to use it." Then, as soon as they buy it, the teeth come out. You become not the father of the work, but the stepfather. All of a sudden, you're an outsider, a villain. I have often said to these people, "Look, I'll do the script free for you if you'll shoot my mistakes instead of yours. My mistakes are better."

This brings me to another point that I discovered a long time ago in writing scripts and novels and short stories: I write emotionally. I never know what I'm going to do from one day to the next or from one hour to the next. I never plan anything. I'm not self-conscious. I don't think my way into things, I feel my way. When you write a script or a novel, there is a certain point when you have to stop. You cannot perfect it. If you try to make something too perfect, you perfect it out of existence. *Something Wicked This Way Comes* is an example. It's a flawed novel of mine. But you tell me a novel that isn't. I decided at a certain point that I had done all that I could to my child. Finally, I had to open the door and shove it out in the snow and say, "Bye-bye. Good luck. Even with all your scars and wounds, you'll make your way." And it has. Melville's *Moby-Dick* is a colossal, fabulous error. It's just full of junk and mistakes and dreadful things, but it's so full of beauty and genius. It's this flawed thing that we're always speaking of. Don't be afraid of the bold enterprise, of the great and foolish idea and concept. Go ahead and do it. Rough it up.

You've often talked about how useful it is for filmmakers to have a good grounding in poetry.

It's taken me thirty years to learn how to write poetry. I've wanted to write poetry all of my life. I've admired poets—Shakespeare has been my constant companion since high school. I carry him around with me. I carry Bernard Shaw around with me. These are old friends who talk to me on trains late at night when I'm going to sleep. During the last year I have begun to write poems that work. This is after thirty years. I read them as they are coming out of the typewriter. Every morning I go to the typewriter when I get up. I begin to write word-association poems, anything that comes into my head. Boom! All of a sudden it begins to take shape. Out of this amorphous thing begins to grow a poem of one page, two pages, three pages. When I'm done and I read it, the hair on the back of my neck stands up. Then I know I'm doing the right thing. I find out what the theme is once I've finished. It might be about my childhood, or I find that I have nailed down a truth.

Starting tonight, every night in your life before you go to sleep, read at least one poem by anyone you choose. Poetry and motion pictures are twins. You'll get more out of reading poetry than you will get out of any other kind of reading. You are people with eyes. You must find ways of extending this vision and putting it on film. The great thing about poetry is its metaphor. Each poet finds a metaphor and expresses it in a few lines or in a few pages. Poetry is the enclosed metaphor, the short form. As an experiment all of you could get out of here and shoot a cinematic haiku. Just go through a book of Japanese haiku and shoot a thirty-second film. They're purely cinematic, very visual. You must read poems every night of your life in order to enable yourself to refresh your images. In forty years you'll thank me for telling you this.

As filmmakers you need to place a lot of this information into your subconscious. At some moment in the future, when you are looking for a solution to a cinematic problem, William Shakespeare, Gerard Manley Hopkins, Robert Frost or Edna St. Vincent Millay is going to come up and tap you on the shoulder and say, "Here it is." Metaphors. Metaphors. Metaphors. The search for the metaphor is everything. When you find that metaphor, then you can speak the truth. So read a poem a night. One year from today you'll have 365 of the best damned poems in your head, in your subconscious. What you're doing is packing your head so full that it begins to explode. You've got a popcorn machine there but no popcorn. You want to fill your head with images, so they'll be there when you need them. You get all these things in your bloodstream, in your mind and soul, so you don't have to think. A good filmmaker is a nonthinker. The best kind of writing is what spills out of your guts impulsively.

This is really what you're up to with motion pictures. You are continually searching for these metaphors. Until you find them, you can't move. That's what poetry is. Of course, in a film like *Moby Dick,* you have so damn many metaphors that you don't know which ones to choose. It's a very rich, big plum pudding with raisins, nuts and bolts, turmoil and everything in it.

Would you ever want to direct?

I do, but I don't know if I have the stamina or patience. I don't know if I can work with people. I'm used to being alone. The gregarious person you see sitting here, that's just part of my day. As soon as I leave here I'll go back to my office and lock myself in and get my writing done. But I've been on the set, and I just don't think I have the patience. I think I'd start yelling at people because of the long waits between shots.

Do you begin your screenplays with character, theme or conceptual structure?

You start with a total cloud of emotion. In an adaptation, you read a book and you run to the edge of the pool and you dive off. You don't even know if there is any water in the pool. On the way down, you yell to someone to put some water in. You hit the bottom and there is six inches there. You're not killed, and then you run back and you dive again. By the time you leap off on the second draft, maybe there is a foot of water.

So you are saying that you work in relation to your emotions?

You have to. It's the only way to create. You can't intellectualize a screenplay.

Do you find it easy to write screenplays compared to novels and short stories?

Screenplays look easy to write, but they're not. Everyone is tempted to try one—"Door opens, in comes so-and-so. He speaks." You can get carried away with the simplicity of a screenplay, but I have read a lot of screenplays and, generally, screenwriters are lazy slobs. They don't put in the things that should be there. When I write a screenplay, I put in everything to help the director and the actor and myself. It's hard to become excellent as a screenwriter because it's such a difficult medium. There are so many things that can go wrong. Let me put it this way: if you want to become a screenwriter without ever doing short stories or novels or adaptations, you've got to start now. If you start now, it will take you roughly ten years of writing one screenplay a month before you start to get excellent. Unless, of course, you happen to be a genius.

It took me from the age of twelve until I was twenty-two, and three million words of utter junk, before I began to write some fairly decent stuff in a short story. It took until I was thirty-three before I felt I was ready for a screenplay. What I am really saying is that you have to be very productive in order to become excellent. You have to go through a poor period and a mediocre period, and then you move into your excellent period. It may very well be that some of you have done quite a bit of writing already. You may be ready to move into your good period and your excellent period. But you shouldn't be surprised if it becomes a very long process. But if you love what you are doing, then it's not really work, is it? Do a hundred screenplays—what the hell? I've done roughly twenty-five, most of which have never been made. I'm doing one right now just for the hell of it.

I got the best advice in my life from Peter Viertel when I started *Moby Dick.* He said, "Write a silent motion picture, and then add dialogue to it." That's what I've always tried to do. *Moby Dick* has more silent moments than talking moments. In my adaptation of my own novel *The Martian Chronicles,* there are only seven pages with dialogue on them in the first fifty pages. If I can find visual metaphors to act out the truths for me, to begin scenes and end them, then I do it. There is usually too much talk in films, unless you are doing a comedy of manners. Tracy and Hepburn did a whole series of films where all you needed was a cameraman and sets. It didn't matter where you shot it. The camerawork could even be lousy, but you didn't care. These two people were just talking and talking. But these are very special things that happen only with very special actors. It's rare that you can find actors who can do this sort of thing, and those kinds of films are the exceptions.

<hr>

Films as Screenwriter

1956 *Moby Dick* (co-screenplay)
1969 *The Picasso Summer*

1983 *Something Wicked This Way Comes*
1998 *The Wonderful Ice Cream Suit*

The key word in art—it's an ugly word but it's a necessary word—is *power,* your own power. Power to say, "I'm going to bend you to my will." However you disguise it, you're gripping someone's throat. You're saying, "My dear, this is the way it's going to be."

ELIA KAZAN

(Born in Constantinople, Ottoman Empire, 1909—Died 2003)

I met Elia Kazan in 1956 in Benoit, Mississippi, where he was shooting *Baby Doll,* starring a young actress named Carroll Baker. I had become friends with Carroll and her husband, the director Jack Garfein, a year earlier in Texas, where she was making her screen debut in *Giant* and they had invited me to visit. Kazan had a muscular, coiled energy, and his style on the set was different from anything I'd seen. He was a man of the theater—the special brand of theater where Method actors created performances by probing their individual psyches. Eli Wallach and Karl Malden were Method actors, as was Carroll Baker. Gadge, as Kazan was known, would talk to Carroll in frank sexual terms to help her find that "river of experience" inside that would spark her performance as the young woman in the white slip who cuckolds her husband, Malden, with the earthy Italian, Wallach. Kazan was after controlled fire and intensity.

Baby Doll came on the heels of *On the Waterfront* and *East of Eden,* two films that changed American moviemaking. Under Kazan's eye, Marlon Brando, Rod Steiger, Lee J. Cobb, Karl Malden and Eva Marie Saint in *Waterfront;* and James Dean, Julie Harris and Jo Van Fleet in *Eden* gave electric performances that opened the door for New York Method actors in Hollywood. Kazan had introduced Brando to the stage as Stanley Kowalski in *A Streetcar Named Desire,* beginning a shift in acting style that resonates today. "You don't deal with actors as dolls," Kazan said, "you deal with them as people who are poets to a certain degree."

Kazan stopped directing before "video assist" came to movie sets—the technology that places the director out of sight of the actors, watching their performances on a distant video monitor. It is hard to imagine Kazan's actors performing the way they did without the director watching intensely beside the camera. The word on the set used to be, "They act for Gadge—to please him."

Kazan was born Elia Kazanjoglou. His parents were Anatolian Greeks, and the influences of his youth come alive in *America, America,* which included the memorable shipboard scene of immigrants passing the Statue of Liberty. As a young man in New York, Kazan joined the Communist Party for a short time, and most of his films were concerned with social issues, starting with *Gentleman's Agreement,* which dealt with anti-Semitism, and *Pinky,* one of the first films to address racial prejudice.

Like so many other great directors he struggled in his later years, abandoning films in 1963 to become a novelist. He returned to filmmaking six years later but could not match his earlier successes. In 1976 he saddled up with Sam Spiegel, his producer from *On the Waterfront,* to direct Harold Pinter's script of *The Last Tycoon,* F. Scott Fitzgerald's novel of Hollywood. His cast included Robert De Niro, Robert Mitchum, Jack Nicholson, Jeanne Moreau and Tony Curtis. Unlike his early films in which he had been involved in crafting the story, he came to *The Last Tycoon,* as he put it, to "realize" Pinter's script. My wife, Elizabeth, and I were invited by Spiegel to see *The Last Tycoon* in a screening room at MGM. Gadge was there with Sam and no more than half a dozen others. In spite of the talent behind it, *The Last Tycoon* simply didn't work. When the lights came up there was a long, quiet moment. Kazan was a shrewd observer, not a man to whom you wanted to dissemble. I said simply, "Wonderful performances, Gadge," and gave him a hug. It was a sad moment in that room with two men whose combined credits included *The African Queen, Bridge on the River Kwai, Lawrence of Arabia, On the Waterfront, Viva Zapata!, A Streetcar Named Desire* and *East of Eden*—films that will live as long as films are shown—and to sense that this was the way it was going to end for each of them.

In 1999 the Academy of Motion Picture Arts and Sciences voted to present Kazan with a special award, which stirred the coals of the still-smoldering controversy over his having named names before the House Un-American Activities Committee in 1954. Kazan's enemies came out of the woodwork and urged Academy members not to applaud when he came onstage. I was at the Oscar ceremony that night because our film *The Thin Red Line* had been nominated for Best Picture. I was sitting in the row behind Warren Beatty. We had discussed the controversy but didn't declare our intentions. Robert De Niro and Martin Scorcese presented a montage of Kazan's work and introduced him. It seemed less than half the audience was applauding as he walked to center stage. Warren and I got to our feet; then

Elia Kazan on the set of *Splendor in the Grass* (1954). Kazan nurtured a new
style of acting in the United States and performers in his films earned
twenty-one Academy nominations and nine Oscars.

gradually others in our section and a fairly good representation throughout
the auditorium rose. It was at best a bittersweet moment. I never discussed it
with Warren, but I believe we were both standing for the same reason—out
of regard for the creativity, the stamina and the many fierce battles and lonely
nights that had gone into the man's twenty motion pictures.

In 1969, Kazan gave the inaugural seminar on the opening day of the
Center for Advanced Film Studies. The meeting took place in an informal
setting on the lawn of the Greystone Mansion and was not recorded. The
discussion that follows took place in 1975, during production of *The Last
Tycoon*.

ELIA KAZAN

———

October 8, 1975

They promised I wouldn't have to make a speech. I didn't have time to prepare one anyway. Speeches really aren't very interesting. What's interesting is if you ask me questions and I'll answer them without planning answers. That makes it more fun. So just fire away.

Fame sometimes affects the work of directors. Do you think it's affected yours?

You'd be amazed how unfamous I feel. I still feel in many ways like a beginner, and part of it is that I've never continued the same thing. I'm writing books, and all my books are put down in America. I've never gotten a really good notice, except once, for *The Arrangement,* and a couple medium-size ones on the other books. I've never really been accepted by the literary fraternity, and that keeps you on your toes. I'm still writing. I've got two more books in first draft. So I've never felt arrived, if that's the word. I don't feel like an expert or a particularly knowledgeable person. I don't think any of my films are completely successful. But taking them all together, I'm proud of them. I think I've done something that is me. But I'm not finished yet. I feel like a young man. I've got good spirits and good energy. I'm still a person in the middle of life, even though I don't look it at times.

You have a reputation for discovering stars and for not being afraid to use untrained actors. What do you look for in a performer?

Very often big stars are barely trained or not very well trained. They also have bad habits. They don't want to look bad and they protect themselves, or they're not pliable anymore. They know what their act is. If I put them in a scene that's a little bit dangerous, their agents come to see me. I get annoyed with all this. And besides, they cost a lot of money. They raise your budget up to a point where it gets silly. I'm now doing a picture that's a circus. It's got everybody in it: Robert De Niro, Jack Nicholson, Robert Mitchum, Tony Curtis, Jeanne Moreau, Donald Pleasance. Like in a circus—first the lions come on, then the tightrope walkers. I don't mind it, though. It's sort of fun.

But if the subject is very real, and you're saying, "This actually happened—not quite as I've shown it perhaps—but real life is reflected here," you'd better get real people all around you. There's a new breed of stars coming up that is a hell of a lot better for my purposes. To take unknowns is a gamble, and I've taken that gamble. Sometimes it has come through, and in a couple of instances it has not. I think the time it hurt me most was in *America, America.* That picture would have been better if I'd run across De Niro or Al Pacino or Dustin Hoffman. I think the lead character of that film has more to it. I took a calculated risk and lost, but I am not afraid to use anyone, because I was an actor and this makes me have less mystique about what an actor can contribute.

You can have damned good actors, and they can louse you up. But I'm not in awe of them, nor am I afraid of them. Now what I try to do is get to know them very well. I take them to dinner. I talk to them. I meet their wives. I find out what the hell the human material is that I'm dealing with, so that by the time I take an unknown he's not an unknown to me.

Where did you find the lead actor Stathis Giallelis, in America, America?

He was from around Athens, a property man for a small Greek filmmaker. He had never acted before. I bundled him on a plane and brought him back to America with some misgivings. And I still have some. I rehearsed him a lot. I did about three weeks of improvisation before we started, and I gave him voice lessons. The damned voice lessons didn't take. He doesn't speak English any better today than he did during the film. It hurt the film, I think, because I was worried about his being understood. The boy has gone back to Greece, which is where he belongs.

Where did you find those evocative faces for the Ellis Island sequence in America, America?

That scene was shot in an abandoned customs warehouse in Athens. We sent trucks up to the border, where there were camps of people who had crossed over into Greece from the Communist countries of Bulgaria or Rumania. By God, their clothing, their looks, their faces—it was perfect. These people's deprivation, their hardship and their continuous anxiety worked for me. How do you direct them? Well, you didn't have to do much. What counts is what they looked like and how they were dressed and the positions I put them in.

Sometimes the face of a real person is far more eloquent than any actor can achieve. There's something about almost all actors that is too well-fed looking. If you have a scene of a working-class person or a person deprived by life or a person who is hard up, it's much better sometimes to get a face. You can't beat a cop in a cop role. They play cops very well, so you go to the police station to get a cop. Fellini says, "I don't give a damn how they talk or whether they talk at all. I'll dub that in later. Give me the face." The face is a piece of statuary, a piece of revelation.

In America, America, *the hero has a tremendous burning desire to get to America, but no real reason was given for these feelings.*

I feel we are given reasons because of everything that's shown nonverbally, the events that are shown, which seem enough to me. The other side of it is that he's just a young boy caught in the situation both at home and in the society where he's declassed as a member of a terrified minority. Seeing his father kissing the hand of that little general is enough to send him to America.

Andy Griffith wasn't exactly an unknown before A Face in the Crowd, *though he wasn't known as an actor. But his performance is probably the best of his career.*

He was not an actor, rather a monologist. He was very eager to be good and had none of the defenses that stars usually have. He didn't want to look a certain way or make a certain impression. There are scenes in that movie that would be difficult for anybody. It's a very hard part. I think the film walks a very tight line, and I'm not sure it bridges satire and tragedy altogether successfully. We were satirizing the whole scene of public communication. The film was made in 1956, and I think we anticipated a lot of what happened in Nixon's time and what's happening today. We tried to satirize it on the one hand and get some sort of human portrait of a man on the other. I would say that considering who Andy was, he gave an excellent performance. I think it would be hard to match.

Was there any relationship between the McCarthy hearings and this film?

No. We started out from a short story by Budd Schulberg about the power and threat of television. We were saying, "Beware of it," but also that it could be a force for good. I believe that television is a terrific force for good. When you see people in close-up behaving off guard, I think you understand them. That was the case in the McCarthy hearings when McCarthy at one point whispered to Roy Cohn. I don't think anyone who saw it will ever forget that whisper.

Like Andy Griffith, James Dean came to you as something of an unknown, a temperamental unknown. How did you work with him on East of Eden?

He did a thing that always attracts me—he wasn't polite to me. He made me feel he wasn't straining to butter me up, that he had a real sense of himself. When I met him he said, "I'll take you for a ride on my motorbike." It was very hard for him to talk while riding me on the back of his motorbike, which I did, like a damn fool, around the streets of New York. It was his way of communicating with me, saying, "I hope you like me" or "Look at my skills." He had his own way, and I thought he was perfect for the part. I thought he was an extreme grotesque of a boy, a twisted boy. As I got to know his father, as I got to know about his family, I learned that he had been, in fact, twisted by the denial of love.

I went to Jack Warner and told him I wanted to use an absolutely unknown boy. Jack was a crapshooter of the first order, and he said, "Go ahead." He wouldn't do that now. Nobody would do that now. He, as they say, bet on the jockey, not the horse. I went back to New York and said to Jimmy, "We're going to California. Be at my house at such and such a time." Jimmy shows up with two packages wrapped in paper. He'd never been on an airplane before. We were heading toward the studio when Jimmy said, "Can we stop here a minute? My father lives in there." We stopped and he went in and got his father. Out came a man who was as tense as Jimmy was, and they hardly could look at each other. It was the goddamndest affirmation of a hunch that I had ever seen. They could hardly talk, they mumbled at each other. I don't know what the hell Jimmy stopped to see him for, because in a few minutes he said, "Let's go."

I got him fixed in a room and took him to the lot to shoot some wardrobe tests. The crew couldn't believe it. They said, "Is that the stand-in?" This was a good sign for me because he looked real. He looked like an actual person. Jimmy bought a palomino horse with his first money. When he got into problems with a girlfriend, I moved him into a dressing room at the studio, and I moved in next door. There was only a thin wall between us so I could hear him. He was nearsighted, which I didn't know when I hired him. He really couldn't see at all, and I was anxious that he was going to do something terrible. One day he was riding in his Porsche at seventy or eighty miles an hour without his glasses and couldn't see what was happening. I had a scene where he had to jump and grab onto a train, and he almost got killed the first day because he missed the handle and the stairs on the freight car. I had lots of adventures with him, but I didn't think he would complete the picture. He was an extremely sick boy at that time. There's a saying that success is harder to take than failure. It's a rather shaky statement, but let's say there's some truth in it. Success was sure hard for him to take.

I know you have a high regard for East of Eden. *Would you call it your best film?*

I don't think I've ever made a film in which I've achieved everything I've wanted. I don't think any of my films are perfect. The nearest one to it, I think, would be *East of Eden,* though it's not my favorite film. That would be *America, America,* because I wrote it and it's about my uncle. I have a great fondness for that film. I love the music and I love the country. But it's far from perfect. *East of Eden* achieves its goals almost without fault. I think all the actors are excellent. Another film that I like a lot is *Viva Zapata!* which is most imperfect. I think some of the sequences are not achieved well at all. There's one sequence I detest, where he says, "I can't read." Every time I look at it I turn away. I wish they'd put a commercial there. But I think other sequences are as good as I've ever done.

Did you run into any problems dealing with a mythical figure like Zapata?

I sure did. John Steinbeck and I did the script. We wanted to shoot it, naturally, in Mexico, and we thought those guys would love it. We were going to make an international film about Zapata, their national hero. But we ran into Gabby Figueroa, the great cameraman, who was the head of the syndicate down there, and he asked for certain controls and script changes. So we said the only thing we could say—"Fuck you." When we said no, he said, "We won't let you shoot it here. Don't you understand? Suppose I took a crew, went up to Illinois, and did a picture about Abraham Lincoln with Mexican actors. How would you feel?" I said, "It would be the most fantastic thing I could imagine."

We told them, "It'll make a really good picture. We have Marlon Brando," and Figueroa said, "No." So we shot it right on the border of Mexico. We used to go over to Mexico for lunch, and we had a lot of Mexicans come over and got a Mexican band. We got as close as we could get, but I think I could have done it better in the state of Morales, which is south of Mexico City. When I saw the city down there with its rocks— it's a little bit like Galway, in Ireland, with its rock walls—I knew I could have been photographing the poverty rather than talking about the poverty. I think Brando and the rest of us would have got a lot from shooting there. It was a loss.

You once said that you regard Zapata *as your first cinematically structured film. That makes* A Streetcar Named Desire *a photographed play.*

Exactly. On *Streetcar* we worked very hard to open it up, and then went back to the play because we'd lost all the compression. In the play, these people were trapped in a room with each other. What I actually did was to make the set smaller. As the story progressed I took out little flats, and the set got smaller and smaller. See, it's not a realistic play at all, and you couldn't photograph it on the streets of New Orleans. There isn't a set in *Panic in the Streets;* it's all the streets and buildings in New Orleans. But you can't do that with *Streetcar.*

The first cinematic picture I ever did was not *Zapata.* I had made up my mind to do *Panic in the Streets* like a silent picture. There is talk in it, but really the story is all told by pictures. Then I did *Zapata.* I learned a lot, as I had from two directors I liked when I first came here: Jean Renoir, who I think is a god, and Jack Ford. I used to hang around Ford and get his goddamned sour answers, which I adored. From him I learned to hold and trust the long shot, not cut into it. A theater-trained person wants to jump in and see the facial expression, when sometimes it should be left a mystery.

*As a theater-trained director, what difference do you find in working with actors
in film?*

In a film what you're trying to do is to lay down the basic behavior patterns of a person. For example, I'm now doing *The Last Tycoon.* Robert De Niro is playing Monroe Stahr, an urban Jew, an intellectual who was born with a rheumatic heart, who dresses up to his role as the head of the studio. Bobby has never played anything but a street-smart kid. Bobby has never played an educated part, an executive who could run a studio. So I've been doing improvisations with him in an office, which is as near to the set as can be, and he's got a secretary and an assistant secretary and four or five people coming in, waiting in his anteroom, each of whom has a different demand on him at the same time. The phone never stops ringing.

I've impressed on Bobby that what he says is never a comment; it's an instruction which someone has to do something about. For several days on the set I've harassed the hell out of De Niro. I've made him feel that his life is at the mercy of his anteroom, that he's a victim of the phone. I've now got him realizing what it means to be an executive, how he has to talk without shouting, showing only the extreme clarity of his mind, the depth of his instructions, and that he has a certain severity in dealing with his problems, and that he's not to be thwarted or challenged or denied. In the improvisations, I've tried to use the actors whom I'm going to use in the movie so he'll begin to get familiar with the world he's going to move in.

I've also tried to get Bobby to *think* like an intellectual, to consider things in ambivalence, to see more than one side of something. Also, I've kept him away from the actress who's playing Kathleen, an ethereal or unearthly figure. If he becomes too familiar with her it'll hurt the scenes when we shoot them. So he's been instructed by me not to chat with her, not to make friends with her, not to go around with her, not to have dinner with her, but to keep her at a distance. However, the other girl, Cecilia, is all over him. She's become a sort of a nuisance to him, so she's pressing at him all the time. He's so familiar with her that he has the basis psychologically for saying, "I never thought of you that way."

So what am I doing? I'm building up behavior patterns. In a play, you have two and a half weeks to prepare. Somewhere in the third week everyone descends on you with the sets and the costumes and their worries. Everyone comes after you, saying this is not working, that is not working. You have to be very strong and very clear about what you want, because one of the first things you have to do is mount the play. I take much longer than most. I don't do it until the end of the second week. A lot of anxious directors do it earlier, and maybe they're right. Garson Kanin has a run-through after two days. I just don't believe in that. No play is perfect, and you're going to make changes in it. You may also go out on the road with it. You're trying out the play, not just the performances.

Sam Spiegel, who's producing *The Last Tycoon,* worked a year and a half with Harold Pinter on the script. Pinter is one of the most ambivalent men I know. His favorite word is *constraint,* and his next-favorite stage direction is "Pause." I made up my mind to do the script as written and not fool around with the dialogue. So here I'm not trying out the play anymore. I'm trying to do what the French call "realize" the play. It's a very apt word. You do realize it. You bring it to life.

De Niro excepted, what atmosphere do you work for among your actors?

A continual effort of getting them to know each other. For example, I take them to dinner. When I see them together, I realize a lot about their relationship that is basic and not even expressed. I see how they relate, how they look together. I have kept people apart. In *The Visitors*—don't repeat this—I stirred up small antagonisms between the actor who played the husband and others. It's uncomfortable, but I think it adds a lot.

How much room is there for the contribution of the actors?

I don't let the actors loose, but I certainly don't nail anything down. I think that if you have good actors—creative actors—even though they might not be experienced, you have to watch them during the rehearsal after you've given them the basic intentions. This is to create the basic pattern of the scene and see what the actors want to get out of it. But once we have that, I try to leave room so that anything they have to contribute can be used. In other words, I say, "Here's the road. Now you can run or do anything down that road you want, but you've got to stay on that road." Somebody once said you're much freer when you know your boundaries. There is truth in that. When I talk to the actors they begin to give me ideas, and I grab them because the ideas they give me turn them on. I want the breath of life from them rather than the mechanical fulfillment of the movement which I asked for.

How do you work with actors on a typical scene?

They say I'm an acting director, which I don't take as a compliment. I don't really agree, but I do deal with actors a lot. I love actors. I used to be an actor for eight years, so I do appreciate their job. One of the most important things in an acting scene, especially a short acting scene, is not to talk about the scene that precedes but to play out the scene that precedes. You play out where the actors have come from psychologically so their ride into a scene is a correct one.

In other words, the actors come in with the experience that they would come in with in life. And none of us comes into any scene in life naked. You go home to your wife after you've had a bad day at the office, and it's a different scene than if you've had an exhilarating day. What precedes a scene is important. Once you've done that, you divide the scene— or I tend to—into sections, into movements. Stanislavsky called them "beats." The point is that there are sections in life. Sometimes even a short scene has a three-act structure. You lay bare the actor, you make him understand and appreciate the structure beneath the lines. That's what's often called the subtext, and dealing with the subtext is one of the critical elements in directing actors. In other words, not what is said, but what happens. Particularly with a writer like Harold Pinter, who is so oblique. What he says is often the opposite of what is happening, or only related indirectly to what is happening.

So your own acting experience helps you communicate with your actors.

It definitely does. I put it in a bad way before when I said that I'm not afraid of actors. I'm not afraid to make demands on them. I believe they can give me more. I reach into them for more. I think it's fascinating to see this on the screen instead of just a face and a piece of behavior. There are directors, very famous ones, who completely disagree: "I don't want you to act. Don't give me any goddamned Actors Studio stuff." But I don't believe in that, even if the Actors Studio people can be awful nuisances. They'll say, "Why do I do that?" Finally you say, "Because I tell you to." Basically, the people I choose to work with are creative people who are sensitive, who want to be good, who have some aspiration in them. You don't deal with actors as dolls. You deal with them as people who are, to a certain degree, poets.

Have years of experience as a strong director made your choices easier on a set?

I find that the more you know the more difficulty you're in, because you know how many different ways something can be done. The terrible thing about film directing is that you wake up at four in the morning after you've shot something and say, "Damn it, why did I do that scene that way? I could have done it differently." The most important thing is to get alone on the set in the morning, when your brain is still fairly clear, and sit there with coffee or a cigar and just think about what you feel and what you're trying to get over and how you can get it over.

Are you ever in conflict when you both produce and direct a film?

Let me give some background first. I wrote books for seven years, and certain personal events made me decide to stop writing books. I'd produced eight films, and there was no conflict because I had my own group of actors, more or less. They were all my friends, most of them in the Actors Studio in New York. I had my own staff—I wouldn't even call them a staff—they were all close friends with whom I made pictures. I had an ideal situation. This ended for me when I started to write books.

Now I want to make films again, and I want, above all, to make the other half of *America, America,* and another film—two films I very much want to make. But it would take me a year to write a script, so I decided to jump in now and do a film. Sam Spiegel I admire. I like him. He's a very bright guy. And Harold Pinter I love. He's one of the nicest men I've met and one of the most interesting. And when they offered *The Last Tycoon* to me, I said, "What the hell? I'll start." Now is there a conflict? There are conflicts when you produce and direct because you're watching two things at once—you're watching the budget and you're watching your own desires. There are conflicts now. I want one thing and Spiegel wants another.

There's no way to take the conflicts out of work. As a matter of fact, conflicts are stimulating. Fights are stimulating. Differences of opinion, if they are between people who basically see the same thing, are much more exhilarating than no conflicts. There's an old corny saying in show business—when everything goes well, the production is going to fail. That doesn't mean you've got to stir up fights, but there are producers who do stir up fights, who do set people against each other. I've heard them say, "When you're in trouble, you're going to think faster and better."

How do you set your priorities if you are both producer and director?

They're always the same, and the obstacles are also the same. If a producer is there, your obstacle is a good one. You try to convince him that your goals are more important. You have constant arguments. There's nothing wrong with it. We're arguing now about how many suits De Niro should have. The producer just left, and he said to me, "Does he need fourteen suits? Doesn't he ever repeat?" So I said, "I'll try to cut out a couple." But I think to myself, well, if he needs fourteen suits, he'd better have them. But it's a tiny point. Does he need this set? Do we need all this? So I cut something. He's blocking you in a way, but he's helping also. Don't try to take the conflict out of anything. Whenever there's a group that makes something, as the Group Theatre used to, as soon as the conflicts go out of it, it means indifference. The number-one enemy of art is indifference. When you say, "What the shit, it's only a picture," don't do it. Go home.

Do you think that the more personal you get in your films, the more you lose your dramatic objectivity?

I guess so. I don't give a damn, though.

For whom do you make your films?

The unwritten premise of every director, in my opinion, is this—if it moves me, it's going to move other people. Sometimes a lot of other people, sometimes a few other people. If you're finally asking, whom do you make them for? Well, you make them for yourself. I think that's the same reason painters paint.

What about the critics? Are you bothered by what they write about your books and films?

I think my books are terrific, though I can see great faults in them. When they're poked fun at, it hurts. I think you've got to have a thick skin and a sensitive soul. You've got to be very tough outside, but if that toughness goes inside and you're no longer able to feel sensitively about other people or sensitively about yourself, then you're in the worst trouble there is.

Kazan at the AFI on October 8, 1975, when he was in
Hollywood directing *The Last Tycoon* for Sam Spiegel.

How do you approach a film like The Last Tycoon? *Do you build a shooting
script, blocking out the scenes before you get in there?*

I never work out all the shots. If you do that there's no use getting good
actors because there are no surprises. If you're going to squeeze them into
a straitjacket, you should get marionettes. I keep a notebook in which I
try to describe every character. I try to get at what the essence of each part
is and how that part serves the whole. And as I make these notes, I begin
to find the moments that are significant, particularly the climax. I don't
want to go into *The Last Tycoon*, but I made a big fat notebook for it
because there are so many characters and it's so involved. I've got to be
very clear about these characters, otherwise they'll run away with me.
Then I take the script and divide it up into scenes, and try to write out
what each character does and feels within each scene. So I don't have a

shooting script, rather a director's book that expresses how each scene serves the whole. And when I begin to direct a scene, I know what I want out of it and what each character is supposed to contribute. If my intention as a director is not clear, I flounder.

Do you work out camera movements with your cameraman?

I arrange a scene with the camera in mind. I sometimes say to the cameraman in the morning, "Take this wall out. I'm going to shoot this way." I'm not a great guy for moving the camera. I nail it down a lot. I never get on a crane, I don't dolly much. I love a set thing because you're not aware of the camera. One thing is to know your final shot, and you work toward that final thing you want to leave with the viewer at the end of the scene. As for close-ups, I think they're most useful when you are recording a change, when you want to see the effect of something on a character.

Do you leave the composition of a close-up to your cameraman?

Hell, no. I don't leave anything to anybody. I don't mean to be mean about it, but I think everything tells a story. Hitchcock's the best example. The way he does close-ups is fantastic. In *The Last Tycoon,* I've tried to make De Niro look like a very sensitive person. You've seen what he usually plays. I used a still camera and I found out that when I got up high, his cheeks sank in a little bit and he looked more drawn, more ascetic. That's something good for me to know. So I try in certain scenes to go up a little bit higher.

Do you keep a journal of your filmmaking?

Yes, I try to. I keep a diary, and every morning when I go in, I write for ten or fifteen minutes, unless somebody grabs me right away. I write on whatever happened the day before and whatever feelings I have. The first entry in my diary of *The Last Tycoon* is a letter I sent to Sam Spiegel in which I'm dubious about doing the picture. When I read the script again I realized there was more in it, that there was a lot I had missed that I'd have to bring out clearly, and I began to like the script better.

What made you take the long trip from Broadway to Hollywood back in 1944?

I was just anxious to make films. For a while I was the fair-haired boy of Broadway, and I got a lot of offers from Warner Bros. and Metro and Fox. I liked the producer at Fox best, and I committed myself. But it was much harder to get into films then than it is now. There is a big road to films now called television. A lot of film directors—Arthur Penn, Marty Ritt, John Frankenheimer—came out of television. Television is sort of a training ground, although it's a monster training ground for a little job. But back then it was very hard to get into film, so I just grabbed that opportunity.

You already had a strong interest in films?

The first artist I admired in my life was Sergei Eisenstein. The second man I admired was Alexander Dovzhenko and a picture called *Air City,* made in 1935. These men were idols, and you are affected by your idols, as I was by Renoir's films. So I became a film director out of admiration, out of wanting to be like that—hero worship. I think it's the most wonderful art in the world.

You did Pinky *while at Fox in the late forties, a fairly bold picture on blacks. Do you have any regard for it these days?*

I'm not too proud of that picture. It's the first time *nigger* was said on the screen, but I think it was a conventional picture. There were a lot of clichés in it. I took it over from Jack Ford and I didn't work on the script. All I think I should do is tell my own story. That's why instead of getting broader and more catholic, I think I'm getting narrower. But *Baby Doll* is the picture in which I think I did the black characters best. They were old retainers on a broken-down plantation, but they laughed at the whites. The laughter was scornful. Affectionate to a certain extent but scornful. But I don't think I've ever done a black person the way a black person can do a black person. I have great sympathy, but I don't think it's possible for me.

You say that television is a training ground for film directors. But there is a big difference between the television I see and your movies. For instance, framing in television is very shallow, while you have action going on three or more different planes.

That's correct. I believe that's the essence of movie composition. In a movie, a long shot is one of the greatest forms of expression. The other great form is a close-up. A medium shot is valuable but often literal. But a long shot often can achieve poetry. In a close shot the camera works more like a microscope; it is a penetrating device. But when you have a long shot on a twenty-five-inch screen it's just a blur back there and it doesn't mean anything. I think the best-directed shows on television are football and baseball games. In a football game you see a play, you see it again in slow motion, you see the coaches looking worried. When someone makes a great play you see a close-up. They alternate between very long shots of action and very close shots of people. It seems to me to be an extremely eloquent thing.

How has filmmaking changed for you since those early days at Fox?

The key word in art—it's an ugly word but it's a necessary word—is *power*, your own power. Power to say, "I'm going to bend you to my will." However you disguise it, you're gripping someone's throat. You're saying, "My dear, this is the way it's going to be." Whenever anybody blocks that, you have less power. So for me I would say that things have gotten better, and they're going to get better yet.

I had trouble with California financially because both *America, America* and *The Arrangement* lost a fortune. I would say most of my films lost money, except *Splendor in the Grass, On the Waterfront* and *East of Eden.* The studios finally said, "If you leave him alone he's liable to lose you a bundle." So power interests me very much. The guy with the greatest power in the world is Ingmar Bergman, because he makes his films with few people and he makes them with few sets. But read *Bergman on Bergman* and see how even he has to practically crawl to someone in Stockholm and say, "What about this project? I want to make this project." It's shocking that probably the most acclaimed director in the world, along with Fellini, has to practically crawl, and the guy says, "No, you can't make it." And Bergman says, "Well, look. I'll make you two comedies after I do that. Will that make it all right?"

You are dealing with power in filmmaking, even with a low budget. I made *The Visitors* for $165,000. *The Last Tycoon* costs $39,000 a day. Nobody would put up money for *The Visitors.* I finally borrowed the money from a bank, hocked some stuff, made an arrangement with

United Artists and did the film with a crew of four. I did the properties, I arranged the sofas and the props. When there was a pancake-eating scene, my son cooked the pancakes. He kept the books. I made the film this way because I did not want to be terrorized by money. I went to see Godard shoot *A Woman Is a Woman* in a room where there was barely space to walk around in. He made that film for very little. When you reduce your costs, you gain some power.

What happened to The Visitors?

You're touching on a very sore spot with me because United Artists killed the picture. They opened it for nine days in New York and it got a wonderful notice in *The New York Times,* but terrible notices everywhere else. They didn't promote it; they just put it away. I'm now trying to buy the picture because it meant a lot to me. It's imperfect but it has value. I'm still very angry. I think United Artists did an inhuman act. It's one of the things that made me say, "Screw it, I'm just going to keep writing books."

The problem with a personal film like The Visitors, *of course, is getting around the distribution system.*

The hope of directors like me is to start our own distribution outfit. Francis Coppola is trying to do that now on a large scale. I own *Baby Doll* and *A Face in the Crowd,* and I have someone who books these in colleges. The rights to *America, America* will revert to me and I'll do the same thing. I'm trying to create another source of distribution rather than the big theaters. The theaters are never going to show *Wild River,* though I think that it's an unusual picture and that the last half of it is wonderful.

Why won't they show it?

Because they don't make any money from it. Minimum advertising in *The New York Times,* the *New York Post* and the *Village Voice* gets up into twenty-five thousand dollars. Nobody's going to risk twenty-five thousand dollars unless they think it's going to come back. The record shows them that they won't get it back.

You said A Face in the Crowd *lost money. What sort of response did it get when it opened?*

I think it received better than average. I think it's a hell of a good film myself, with all its faults. I think it says a lot, anticipates a lot. Nora Sayre said in *The New York Times* last winter that it anticipated a lot of the Watergate hearings. I wish she could have reviewed it at the time. But we didn't do too well with it. A lot of my films didn't. *America, America* started like a house afire in New York City and died everywhere else. Now it's played nine times a year in Paris. In Athens it's constantly playing. In Germany it's played all the time. *Wild River* was an absolute financial disaster. I heard last year that when Twentieth Century Fox cleaned house they burned a lot of negatives, and among them the negative of that picture. Imagine how I feel.

Some of your films have been commercial successes. Have you been able to isolate a common element to explain these successes?

I think so. I think they're films that are recognizable to audiences emphatically. In other words, they say, "There's a piece of me." *Splendor in the Grass* was one of my successful films. It's family life in a small town. Everybody knows people like that, and they respond immediately, simply. But when the message is gritty, when the message is disturbing, I don't know if people want to be disturbed. Then you can have films like *On the Waterfront* where there was the problem of conscience that Brando had. But it was also very exciting, in terms of physical conflict, in terms of danger.

Somebody said that the three things people respond to are death, money and sex. I don't know if any of that is true, but I think people certainly respond to things that worry them in their own lives. I think audiences are much smarter in the intuitive sense than filmmakers in the big studios know. I think they're anxious to see their own lives reflected and to work out their own problems through the behavior of other people. I think if you can get that tie, you will have a film that will be popular. I don't use the word *successful,* I say *popular.* I think people like to be scared—look at *Jaws.* And I think people like to be reassured. It has something to do with the relationship between an audience and a film.

I don't know why anybody should go see *The Last Tycoon,* but don't quote me. I hope to make it so they will. I hope to make it so they'll see a talented guy under the stress of business. They'll watch him and say, "Yes, I have talent, I have feeling and I have known that stress." I'm trying to direct it so it will relate to the experience of the audience.

I remember seeing Wanda, *your wife Barbara Loden's film, quite a few years ago, and I was wondering if she was still making films.*

Well, I think *Wanda* is a wonderful picture. It's completely honest. My wife is now getting ready to make another picture on the same scale. *Wanda* had the setup that *The Visitors* had. There was a crew of four, and it was all small and handmade on real locations. But she makes that picture and gets excellent notices, and it dies everywhere. Nobody goes to see it. Now what does she feel? She feels hurt. She doesn't get any offers. I think she's one of the best actresses within her range in the country today, maybe the best in that range.

Would you say that a successful film, as opposed perhaps to a popular film, hinges to a large extent on structure?

I'm a great believer in structure, though many excellent films are unstructured. I believe in telling a continuous story, in coming to two or three climaxes, each of which changes the relationships in the next section. That doesn't mean that episodic films like *8½* are bad. I thought it was a masterpiece. But I personally believe in storytelling and structure and tension. One of the best laws of structure is "unity from climax" from John Howard Lawson's book on screenwriting, which says that if you know what the climax is going to be, you know you've got to get there, and so everything is determined by the climax you're going to arrive at.

Do you think in movements as opposed to acts?

No, in inner acts that cause behavior as opposed to movements. If you think of people as changing things, as dynamic rather than static, you have to have structure. Godard, for example, shows people in a static state. They are in conflict but in static state. I don't see life that way.

Does your concern for structure mean giving close attention to editing?

I think editing is part of directing. That's why I don't like it when editors get the same credit that directors do. I think a director should do absolutely everything. I think the sets are his. The costumes are his. The editing is his. I'm a believer in the dominance of one person who has a vision.

Your films often contain recurring devices or symbols: the jacket in On the Waterfront, *the gift of shoes at the beginning and end of* America, America.

I'm given to symbols. For example, water is a recurring image in my pictures. I constantly feel something about water. There's always a hydrant
spouting water or a lake or the sea. It happens again in *The Last Tycoon*. I
am aware of repeated symbols. I don't know if it's good or bad. Sometimes
after a film I think I wish I hadn't been so obvious.

You're filming The Last Tycoon *here on the West Coast. As a New Yorker who
loves the streets and the pace, do you find yourself less stimulated here?*

I think the greatest loss you people have out here is that there are fewer
stimuli from the place where you work to the place where you live. In
New York City I live on Sixty-eighth Street and I write in a little office on
Fifty-fourth Street. There are always five, ten, fifteen things I see on the
way down that I can't forget. Recently I was riding on a train to visit my
mother in Rye, New York, and I saw a twelve-year-old girl with a Vivaldi
concerto spread out on her lap. She was moving her hands as if she were
at the piano. Now where could I possibly see that in Los Angeles?

But here, where I'm supposedly successful, I never see a goddamn
thing. I get up in the morning. I ride in the car that the studio provides to
Paramount Studios. On the ride down I'm semiconscious. I don't see anything because I'm thinking about what I'm going to do. I get to the studio
and I'm in an office, which is a protected environment. It's like a hiatus in
my life. I'm a fellow who gets a lot from what he sees around him. But I
feel terribly isolated here. I feel denatured here. When I made pictures in
New York, I always got something. I used to walk around the streets to get
something. I'm not hostile to this neighborhood, but I'm a New Yorker. I
always will be. New York is a battleground, a vicious, dangerous, dirty,
mixed-up but terrific place. I love everything about it.

What led you to switch from filmmaking to novel writing?

It's very personal. My first wife died. We were very, very close, and I
decided I would stop everything and just leave the country for awhile.
Refind myself, whatever the hell the word is. I had been making a film
every year and a play every year for a long time, and it was hard work. I

Kim Hunter (left), Vivien Leigh and Kazan during filming of *A Streetcar Named Desire* (1951) at Warner Bros.

began to write some notes, and they slowly began to develop into a book called *The Arrangement*.

I found myself saying, "I'm not in sympathy with the work of Tennessee Williams, although I love him and I think he's a wonderful writer. And I'm not in sympathy with the point of view of Arthur Miller, although I love him personally and I like his work. And I'm not in sympathy with Bill Inge. I've got to start viewing things as *I* do, and when I go back to films I want to make films that in some way or another express my opinion." The next film I'm going to make, I hope, will be a follow-up on *America, America,* about what happened to my uncle after he got to this country. I want to make more personal films.

What do you look for when you consider doing a film?

I don't move unless I have some empathy with the basic theme. In some way the channel of the film should also be in my own life. I start with an instinct. With *East of Eden* I said, "I don't know why it is but the last ninety pages of Steinbeck's book turn me on." It's really the story of my father and me, and I didn't realize it for a long time. When Paul Osborn and I began to work on the screenplay, I realized that it's just the way I was. I was always the bad boy, but I thought I was the good boy. In some subtle or not-so-subtle way, every film is autobiographical. A thing in my life is expressed by the essence of the film. Then I know it experientially, not just mentally. I've got to feel that it's in some way about me, some way about my struggles, some way about my pain, my hopes.

Films as Director

1945 *A Tree Grows in Brooklyn*	1956 *Baby Doll*
1947 *Boomerang!*	1957 *A Face in the Crowd*
The Sea of Grass	1960 *Wild River* (also producer)
1948 *Gentleman's Agreement*	1961 *Splendor in the Grass* (also
1949 *Pinky*	producer)
1950 *Panic in the Streets*	1963 *America, America* (also
1952 *Viva Zapata!*	producer and screenplay)
A Streetcar Named Desire	1969 *The Arrangement*
1953 *Man on a Tightrope*	1972 *The Visitors*
1954 *On the Waterfront*	1976 *The Last Tycoon*
1955 *East of Eden*	

I just like to do films that are positive in the sense that they deal with the dignity of human beings and have something to say about oppression, not necessarily in a political way but in a human way. I have to feel that what I'm trying to do is worthwhile.

FRED ZINNEMANN
(Born in Vienna, 1907—Died 1997)

Fred Zinnemann was living in London in his later years when his agent urged him to meet some of the new power brokers on his next trip to Hollywood. Zinnemann was a lean and wiry mountain climber who spoke softly with a gentle Viennese accent—you might have taken him for a doctor or a psychiatrist. He and his agent paid a call on the twenty-nine-year-old head of TriStar pictures. After keeping Zinnemann waiting twenty minutes, the studio head welcomed him, saying that he knew of the director's reputation but would he please remind him of some of his credits. Zinnemann quietly replied, "After you."

In the fifties I used to join Zinnemann and my father for lunch at Villa Frascati on Sunset Boulevard, halfway between the Columbia studio where Zinnemann was working and Twentieth Century Fox, where my father and I had offices. Those meetings shaped my view of directors. On the surface both men were modest; they were courteous and soft spoken, enjoyed quiet humor and treated each other with deference and respect. Both carried reputations as men of integrity. A few years earlier, Zinnemann's *From Here to Eternity* and my father's *Shane* had been front-runners in the Oscar race. Zinnemann won Best Director and Best Picture, and I recall my father's genuine pleasure at his colleague's success. (My father didn't go home empty-handed—he was given the Irving Thalberg Award.) Here were two men known for having wills of steel when dealing with studios and difficult actors, yet their manner and conversation during those lunches were warm and lighthearted. If you'd have asked a tourist to go through Villa Frascati and pick out the Hollywood directors there, it's unlikely they would have chosen Zinnemann and my father.

Fred Zinnemann moved to the top rank of directors in Hollywood with *The Search* (1948). Here he directs Ivan Jandl, who played the German refugee whom Montgomery Clift reunites with his mother.

As a young man, Zinnemann, who earned a law degree from the University of Vienna, saw the silent films of Erich von Stroheim, Sergei Eisenstein and King Vidor, awakening him to a new art form full of unexplored possibilities. "I began to see a life of adventure—elbow room, open spaces, expeditions to unheard-of countries known only to Joseph Conrad," he said. "Dimly and excitedly, I sensed that film, like music, offered a direct way to people's emotions." Over the objections of his father, a respected Viennese doctor, Zinnemann went to Paris for an internship in cinematography, then took this training to the United States where he worked with the great documentarian Robert Flaherty. This led to a position directing shorts at MGM. As a young director, Zinnemann chafed under the commercial constraints imposed by Metro. He looked up to what he described as "the handful of nonconformists—John Ford, George Stevens, William Wyler and Frank Capra—who had found it possible to defend their own ideas and beat the factory approach."

Zinnemann developed a talent for handling all kinds of subjects, bringing a high level of craft and good taste to everything he touched. He believed that the greater the personal experience a director had with the four main elements of filmmaking—writing, acting, camerawork and editing—the more fully he would be able to extend the outer limits of the medium. "For me," he said, "the camera, visual imagination and knowledge of what a lens can do were the starting point."

Once he gained a foothold directing small features, he chose his projects with care, delivering pictures that reflected his high standards and exploring how individuals deal with matters of conscience. *High Noon, The Nun's Story, The Sundowners, A Man for All Seasons* and *Julia* earned Zinnemann countless honors and, most important to him, the respect of his peers.

Often the careers of great directors have profound disappointments. This was true in Zinnemann's case. After receiving Oscars for Best Director and Best Picture for *A Man for All Seasons* in 1966, he spent three years preparing *Man's Fate*, André Malraux's acclaimed novel of intrigue and revolution in Shanghai. He was rehearsing with Peter Finch, Liv Ullmann and David Niven on completed sets in London when he received a telegram from MGM's new head, James Aubrey, canceling the picture. Zinnemann later wrote that this marked "the end of an era in picture making and the dawn of a new one, when lawyers and accountants began to replace showmen as heads of the studios and when a handshake no longer meant anything." Aubrey's career in the movies was mercifully short, but long enough to deny the world one more Fred Zinnemann picture.

FRED ZINNEMANN

February 22, 1984

Could you tell us about your start in film and how you got from Vienna to Hollywood?

Actually, I'm a disappointed musician. Very early in life I discovered I had a tin ear, so that was the end of the dream. Yet I did find out later on that there is a good deal of similarity between a conductor and a director, in the sense that you work with a large number of people. What you have to do is persuade them of your own vision so that they form one body working together for one purpose—to the ideal result. But I found all this out much later. In Vienna, shortly after World War I, there was no such thing as a film industry, except for two or three small companies. I studied at a technical school for cinematography in Paris, which proved to be an excellent experience, because one learned all aspects of filmmaking.

I was working in Berlin when sound films came in. Suddenly films like *The Jazz Singer* and *The Singing Fool,* those first Warner Bros. sound films, arrived in Europe, and silent films, regrettably, came to a standstill. So I decided—I thought it a really clever idea—to go to America and find out more about sound and then come back to Europe. Well, when I got here, I was spellbound, so I stayed. My first job was due to an introduction to the head of Universal, Carl Laemmle, who was known as "Quiet Uncle Carl," a very, very nice gentleman who had no idea what to do with me. He turned me over to a casting director who said, "We're just making a war picture here, *All Quiet on the Western Front.* Have you been in the German army?" And I said, "No." And he said, "It doesn't matter." So I became an extra, and I played a German soldier and a French ambulance driver for about six weeks.

But the most important thing in my own view was my meeting Robert Flaherty,* who inspired me not only as a filmmaker but as a man, primarily because he was a person who never made any compromises, no matter what. He probably made no more than about six films. I admired the way he went about it enormously. I worked with him for six months in Berlin, mostly testing cameras for a film he wanted to make about a little-known tribe in Central Asia. The negotiations went on with the Russians for about six months. In the end it came to nothing. By that time, Bob was out of money and so was I. Despite that, just sitting with him and drinking beer by the gallon, by osmosis I got a small part of the spirit of this extraordinary man.

Then I got a job in Hollywood in the shorts department at MGM. This was a very interesting experience because I saw the entire studio system from the worm's-eye view. At the same time, I learned a tremendous amount in terms of self-discipline. The idea was you were hired at an extremely low salary. You were given a script that you could accept or turn down. You could work as long as you wanted on it to prepare it. But you had to prepare it to such a point that you could shoot one reel in three days, or if it was a two-reeler, you could do it in six days—no more. There was also the discipline of not having more than fifteen thousand dollars to a reel, of which five thousand was overhead, and of telling a story concisely in ten and a half minutes, because one had only 950 feet of film to play with, no matter what the story. They would say, "Here's a scene. There's a hospital in an American city and it's burning. It's night, and there's a crowd watching it. For the crowd, you get ten people." What do you do?

So that, more or less, was the way I started. There are two sides to the studio system. A lot of people feel, quite rightly, that it was oppressive, that the bureaucracy was enormous. On the other hand, it did give you a chance to learn your profession in a continuous manner, without having to fight for a job from one film to the next.

Many of your films seem to deal with social issues. Could you elaborate on your philosophy as a filmmaker in terms of the kinds of stories you choose?

*Robert Flaherty (1884–1951) was an American documentary filmmaker. His works include the classic *Nanook of the North* (1921).

I don't have any preconceived ideas except that I know my limitations. I wouldn't try to do high comedy because I don't have the sense of timing, and I don't believe I should try to do musicals. I just like to do films that are positive in the sense that they deal with the dignity of human beings and have something to say about oppression, not necessarily in a political way but in a human way. I have to feel that what I'm trying to do is worthwhile.

If you accept the fact that films are not primarily an intellectual medium, then if you still want to get any intellectual concepts across, it behooves you to put a very nice sugarcoating around it. And the more entertaining you can make it, the better. Otherwise what right do you have to expect the audience to sit and listen to you? Of course, primarily you are there to put a picture in the theater that people will pay five cents to go see. And they should come out and say, "Yes, we were entertained." If they weren't, then you have failed, because then it is some kind of pompous monologue. We are not educators, we're entertainers.

You have to find a discipline that will allow you to get your ideas across. It's not a question of being afraid at all, it's question of organizing the material in such a way that it will project itself to the audience.

Do young filmmakers have an obligation to the audience, or are they simply obligated to express themselves?

This is a very big question, because we were taught that we had the total obligation of pleasing the audience, and never mind how we felt about it. Some of us feel that it is our vocation to entertain the audience, to bring something to them that's worthwhile in terms of an emotional experience. And others would say, "Well, to hell with the audience. I want to put on film what I feel, and if they don't like it, the hell with them." It's probably perfectly valid, this attitude. Now, jumping from the ridiculous to the sublime, we can go back to the great masters of the past, and a lot of them were very humble about things. If you read Mozart's letters, time and again he will be delighted because he has written something he knows the audience is going to enjoy. He knows beforehand that it can't miss, and he writes to his father that he's got some marvelous stuff in his piano concerto, and wait till they hear it! Then he writes about how he played it and there was a terrific ovation. It was so great that he went out and bought himself an ice cream. So nobody can say that all these people were sitting nobly in the garret just expressing themselves. I feel that if I presume to ask people to pay a buck, I've got to have something to sell. It's not just to gratify my ego. It's very good to have a person face himself with this question, and the answer can go both ways. I think it's terribly important to know which side of the fence you're on, because the answers are not the same for both sides.

What are some of the projects that you have turned down?

I've turned things down because either I thought I couldn't do it properly, or because I thought it was worthless for some reason. To make a picture just to make money, at this stage of my life, seems kind of silly. And now I can even afford it.

What were your considerations in choosing Julia?

Several things. One was the story of the friendship of the two women. The other was the fact of conscience—the fact that a woman who is leading a comfortable life is suddenly faced with the question of life or death and decides to go ahead and risk taking the money into Germany. I always find questions of conscience very photogenic. That kind of interior drama is to me very exciting because, among other things, I feel that the fact that somebody shoots a gun is of no interest. What I want to know is why he shoots it and what the consequences are—which means that external action is less important than the inner motive through which you get to know what the person's about.

The performances in Julia *were marvelously modulated, very impressive. What was your experience in working with these actors?*

All I had to do with Vanessa Redgrave—this was the second time I'd worked with her—was to have an hour-long conversation about the character in my office. I like to talk to each actor separately, individually and in depth, so that they understand the whole development of the character, the relationships. And after that we hardly ever talked on the set. She just went ahead and did it and she was so good that I used to forget to say, "Cut," because I felt I was a spectator. Jane Fonda works in a different way. She has a marvelous quality; she can cry at will in quantity. She can give you buckets or drops, and whenever you want it. She is really fantastic, but with a totally different approach, and it was utterly fascinating to see those two women together.

Do you do a lot of research for your films?

It depends very much on what kind of a picture you're dealing with and what sort of story you're telling. Some films don't need it. For *A Man for All Seasons,* the only research you could do was read a few of the historical books. The rest of it came from the marvelous play by Robert Bolt. But on *The Nun's Story* we did a year's research. It was a difficult subject. The Catholic Church was very cautious at first about doing a film where a professed nun left the convent after seventeen years. They said that this was open to being sensationalized and they also worried about an implied love affair with the doctor. It took a lot before they would trust us.

I'll give you a very quick example of the kinds of discussions held on the script. There's a scene when the young girls are first coming into the convent as postulants, and the mother superior explains to them that the life of a nun is a life against nature, and the monsignor who was in charge said, "You can't say that. You have to say, 'The life of a nun is a life *above* nature.'" On that one word they spent about four hours of very learned theological discussion. It went back and forth, and finally a Jesuit came and said, "Well, why don't you say, 'In many ways it's a life against nature.'" The whole thing is that one has to approach it not as a problem but as a challenge and see how you can get around it and what you can do about it. It's surprising how often you succeed.

One of the things I wanted to do on the film was not to have any Catholics, not the writer or the actors, because I was worried about getting an in film, one that would be very meaningful to Catholics but that nobody else would want to look at. So in order to make the actors understand the rhythm and what happens at a convent, we got permission to put each one of them, separately, into various convents in Paris. This was in January when it's very, very cold, and convents are the coldest places in Paris. We stashed out eight of the leading "nuns" in different convents, and I made the rounds every day in a taxi from one place to the other to see how they were getting on. They had to get up at 4:30 a.m. and go through the entire day, and then in the evening they had what was called the "grand silence"—after a certain hour you don't talk anymore until the morning. They had to go through all that, and it helped them enormously in playing the parts.

Your films are generally structured in what might be called a "classical" way, with a beginning, a middle and an end, in that order. Could you talk about this?

I would say that is fairly true of my pictures. I can't say that it is something I would defend as an absolute rule. I think one can make marvelous films that have no beginning, middle or end. In fact, I think the more we get away from that kind of setting-up of general rules, the better off we'll be. I think we have suffered as an art form tremendously from the fact that a lot of arbitrary rules were enforced upon us by a lot of people who had no business doing it, and who only had authority invested in them by various executives who hired us and told us how to make pictures. They filled us full of all kinds of dos and don'ts.

If you go back and examine the kind of rules that were put forth, you find two astonishing things. First of all, you find that they were totally arbitrary, like Louis B. Mayer's famous postulate—there are only two kinds of women, mothers or whores. Or saying that no matter what happens, the star's face must always be very well lit, even if it's in the middle of the night in a railroad town. There was a whole slew of rules of that kind, and no matter how hard one fought against it, I suspect that insidiously some of it stuck. It's very hard to get that out of one's system. But even more surprising, in the 1930s the Hollywood films probably reached their all-time high as far as quality is concerned. That's the extraordinary thing.

The whole medium of film is so young, and it was so abused early on when people saw such financial gain in it, that it never had a chance to develop organically. It was bastardized almost when it was still an embryo. And I think what's happening now, to a large extent, is that certain people are trying to make up for it by trying deliberately to do films without structure. I do believe this is invaluable and it's something that should be paid great attention to. I also believe it has no room, obviously, in what might be called theatrical films—pictures that are made to entertain and that you expect people to pay a nickel to go in and see.

Apparently before he made Citizen Kane, *Orson Welles watched John Ford's* Stagecoach *many times to see how it was structured. Is this something you would ever do?*

I am full of misgivings about that kind of thing because I don't like to present a piece of engineering with my films. I remember Josh Logan and other people saying there must be a scene of revelation in each picture or in each play, where something is revealed to a leading character. I don't buy it. For me there doesn't have to be any revelation of any kind. I can see a guy going through a whole picture and not finding out a thing about himself. Probably much more interesting.

I like to arrive at things by instinct rather than deliberate rationalization. I trust my instinct, but I don't trust my reasoning when it comes to making creative decisions. I am never one for feeling that a film should be subdivided into acts. That's something that we've dragged in from theater. To me, film—if it has to be compared to anything—should be compared much more to a piece of music, because the basis of a film, to me, is to flow. And to arbitrarily chop it into curtains is to deny that very principle. Let's say that a film could be like a symphony—the first movement written in sonata form. There is a main theme, then introduce the second theme, and then introduce the third theme. Then you begin to play one against the other and elaborate on them and modulate. You finally bring it to a conclusion with the reprise. That, to me, would describe the basic structure of a film much more closely than dividing it into acts. Take *From Here to Eternity,* where there are really four or five different stories going on at the same time. They were all written very skillfully by Dan Taradash and woven into a progressive thing that kept going all the time. I would say that I would not be able to detect any structuring into acts for that film, rather that my whole endeavor was to make it flow and build, rather than to present it in segments.

There is a picture that is enormously successful and it illustrates the point that you can make a very successful film without really having much of a story. It's *Bullitt.* First of all, I defy anyone to tell me what it's about, except that there is a crooked politician and a cop, and a key witness has been shot. That's all. The rest of it is a car chase and all kinds of visual excitement, and nobody in the world gives a damn about the story. People flock to see it because of the visual excitement.

Could you talk a little about the structure of A Man for All Seasons?

It was from a play, and we never succeeded entirely in eliminating that feeling of a filmed stage play. The structure of the film consisted simply of introducing each character, very briefly but very poignantly, so that once you had seen him, you remembered him. And the writer, Robert Bolt, is a man who has an enormous interest in dramatic economy, which is something I also like very much. I like to use the minimum to get my point across. In fact, we introduced each character in big close-ups, with one sentence that was in some way memorable in giving a clue to this person's identity. I remember Bolt succeeded in introducing seven major characters in less than two minutes, and it was in such a way that everybody immediately knew where they belonged. You were never under any misapprehension after that. I believe it is enormously helpful if you can introduce the characters in a situation as quickly as possible to "grab the audience," for want of a better term. The sooner you can bring it about, the sooner the audience gets into it.

A Man for All Seasons is a film about an idea. The characters are fascinating only because of the ideas they represent, or their attitude toward ideas. How much are you going to give up for an idea?

Once the structure has been established, how do you then proceed?

I have no fixed rule. It depends entirely on what the subject matter is and what the mood of the thing is, what the style is. How do you want to do it? Do you want to do it as a newsreel, for example? I deliberately wanted to make *High Noon* like a newsreel of the period. Again, talking about music, you subconsciously decide what key it's going to be in. Why does it have to be in F major? Why couldn't it be E flat, or B flat? What is it that makes you do it one way? It's partly feeling and partly a deliberate thing, but there are many things that go into it. A lot of it is subconscious. You get a feel of what it is you want it to be, and you try to approach that basic feeling. You have to find the key as you start working on the script—in fact, long before there is an articulated script, because the script itself is to be shaped toward that key. Will you tell it with a lot of scenes, with a hell of a lot of dialogue?

Take as examples *Doctor Zhivago* and the film I am preparing at the moment based on Malraux's *Man's Fate*. They are both pictures that deal with recent historical events. David Lean's is the Russian Revolution, ours is the early stages of the Chinese revolution. His picture is a romantic one with gorgeous photography, very romantic pastel shades, marvelous sets, great music. Ours is going to be practically the opposite. We are going to deliberately try to make it look as though it had been caught on the spur of the moment, sometimes hiding behind a bush, where it's not important how good the exposure was because we were lucky to get an exposure at all.

Can you pick out some of your films that you've been particularly pleased with?

I feel very happy about *High Noon,* which was a combined effort. The cameraman, Floyd Crosby, and I started with the idea that we wanted to show a film set in 1880 that would look like a newsreel—if there had been newsreels and cameras in those days. And in order to do that we studied photographs, particularly those of Mathew Brady who was in the Civil War, and noticed the flatness, the coarse grain, and the white sky. So we deliberately set out to re-create that. The tradition in Westerns at that time was to have a pretty, filtered gray sky with pretty clouds and be theatrical about it. I wanted to have a newsreel quality to give the thing a reality. No filters. This is also why I didn't want to do it in color.

My whole idea in shaping the drama of the film was to play the threat as statically as possible. But I also wanted to confine the whole thing just to the village itself. And show the menace, the threat, only in a static shot of the railroad tracks, as against the constant motion of the man who is looking for help—Gary Cooper, always dressed in black—against the white sky.

The third part of the visual pattern I used was the clocks, increasing in size as the urgency grew and as time kept slipping by—pendulums moving more slowly, the whole thing finally settling into an unreal sort of suspended animation, familiar to those who had been faced with sudden death. The clocks were of course part of my original pattern indicated on the pages of my shooting script, which is now in the archives of the Academy of Motion Picture Arts and Sciences in Beverly Hills. If you remember, at noon the criminals were going to be back in town and everybody had to get off the fence before that time—in forty minutes, thirty-nine minutes, thirty-eight minutes and so on. The suspense is generated out of that—time is progressively running out.

It's a picture about conscience. It's not a Western, as far as I'm concerned—it just happens to be set in the Old West. It has to do with a man who is about to run away and then stops and says, "I can't do it. I've got to go back." And when he's asked why, he says, "I don't know," and then goes back and takes the consequences, right up to the end.

With Gary Cooper (left) and Grace Kelly on the set of *High Noon* (1952).

Do you get involved with choosing actors? How about Marlon Brando in The Men?

The wonderful thing about that film was that Stanley Kramer, Carl Foreman and I were our own front office. We didn't have to bargain with anybody or persuade anybody. I remember Kramer bringing up three possibilities, and Brando was one of them. We all felt that Brando would be the most interesting. He had just finished *A Streetcar Named Desire* onstage, and it was just a question of how he would work out, not having ever worked in film.

Did he have some of the same problems that many stage actors do when they move to film, of projecting too much?

You know, it's a totally individual thing. Some actors adapt almost immediately without any problems, and others have great difficulty. It was not easy for Brando. On the other hand, once he got the knack he was tremendous.

So he wasn't hard to direct?

No. But one can't really talk in those terms, because its not like being a schoolteacher. I think people with that kind of talent are entitled to have some elbow room, because their instinctive talent is such that one would be really stupid not to take advantage of it and see what they're going to do. If you feel that you need some correction or balancing, then you must discuss it.

Of course the director has the job of getting the right person for the right part, and that usually means not to cast on the nose. In other words, if you succeed in casting against type you usually reveal hidden facets of an actor's character. Take Deborah Kerr in *From Here to Eternity*, who up to that point had played the Virgin Queen of England and was seen as a very cold, remote sort of person. Early in the film one soldier says that she sleeps with everybody on the post. This would have been very flat if we had a very sexy actress playing that part, because people would have said, "Well, okay, so what else is new?" In the case of Deborah, they were really intrigued because they couldn't believe that this very ladylike person would sleep around with a lot of enlisted men, and this created quite a bit of genuine suspense.

You and certain other directors, like George Stevens and Orson Welles, are supposed to be the most rebellious and tough-minded individuals in the business.

I'm just rebellious because I don't want to make shit, and I don't think any of the others do either. I don't like to lower my standards, but that doesn't

Marlon Brando, left, made his film debut with Zinnemann in *The Men* (1950). Brando paid a visit to Zinnemann and Montgomery Clift during the filming of *From Here to Eternity* (1953).

mean I'm being rebellious. It's just that when I am faced with people who don't know their job—people who are mediocre or have no talent—I just think it's a waste of time, whether these people are scriptwriters or producers or actors or cameramen. I think it's wrong to waste one's time with half-baked people.

What's your opinion of the kind of pictures studios are turning out now?

The studios by and large are run by people who don't know anything about show business because they're primarily moneymen, whereas in the old days the studio heads were people who had enormous practical experience and were showmen. That is what's missing to a great extent today in the upper echelons. But more important and more dangerous, I think, is the uniformity of stuff that's coming out. Our only defense is to remember the standards of our forefathers and the kinds of pictures they made.

Films as Director

1942 *Kid Glove Killer*
Eyes in the Night
1944 *The Seventh Cross*
1947 *My Brother Talks to Horses*
Little Mister Jim
1948 *Act of Violence*
The Search
1950 *The Men*
1951 *Teresa*
1952 *High Noon*
1953 *The Member of the Wedding*
From Here to Eternity

1955 *Oklahoma!*
1957 *A Hatful of Rain*
1959 *The Nun's Story* (also producer)
1960 *The Sundowners*
1964 *Behold a Pale Horse* (also
producer)
1966 *A Man for All Seasons* (also
producer)
1973 *The Day of the Jackal*
1977 *Julia*
1982 *Five Days One Summer* (also
producer)

What is directing? It's trying to use a lot of people and some very heavy apparatus, and give it all the lightness of a pen while you are writing.

DAVID LEAN
(Born in Croydon, England, 1908—Died 1991)

When David Lean came to Hollywood in 1990 to receive AFI's Life Achievement Award, Steven Spielberg told the audience that *The Bridge on the River Kwai* and *Lawrence of Arabia* were the films that had most made him want to be a director—"Those two films filled my dreams with unlimited possibilities."

I believe it was Lean's ambition that most set him apart from other directors. I remember reading that he would lie in the bathtub for hours thinking of transitions—conceiving ways to get from one scene to the next that would exceed the expectations of the audience. "I felt in awe of David when I saw *Lawrence*," Fred Zinnemann said. "I went to the opening in New York and I saw the match and the sunrise and the approach of Omar Sharif through the mirage—I had a feeling of awe because that was beyond my reach."

Lean's stunning vistas and breathtaking spectacles are etched in our memories, yet the true power of his work comes from his characters. It is true of the early black-and-white films, *Oliver Twist*, *Great Expectations* and *Brief Encounter*, and true of his later films with gentle characters, *Summertime* and *A Passage to India*. It is also true of the stories with extravagant characters, *The Bridge on the River Kwai*, *Lawrence of Arabia* and *Doctor Zhivago*. He presents us with breathtaking exteriors, yet it is the interior lives of people revealed in intimate moments that engage us and move us.

Lean explained during his AFI seminar that finding a story he wanted to tell was always the hardest part of his job. Over time, he found fifteen stories that he brought to the screen, and a few others, notably *Mutiny on the Bounty*, that self-destructed on the rocky shoals of preproduction—evidence that even the strongest and bravest confront obstacles that can't be surmounted.

When you see a photograph of David Lean in the desert commanding an army of camel riders and technicians, it's hard to picture him as the accountant's son forbidden to see movies who finally wangled a job as a tea boy at Gaumont, a position that opened up the opportunity for him to be an editor, thus giving him his foundation. His success came from his fundamental understanding of how pieces of film come together to tell a story. He believed that making a film was like creating a mosaic—"making each little piece as good as you can possibly get it and then the whole will be that much better."

In his biography *David Lean,* Kevin Brownlow provides a magnificent portrait of the director, revealing the conflicting demands of poet and general, and chronicling the extremes of exhilaration and heartbreak that marked his career. Brownlow tells of Lean's extensive preparations for *Nostromo,* based on the Joseph Conrad novel. Lean's health had deteriorated but he pressed

David Lean (right of camera in trench coat) braces with his crew
against the fierce winds of the Irish coast on location of *Ryan's Daughter*
(1970). After months of weather delays in Ireland, Lean went to
South Africa to finish the film.

on. At the Life Achievement Award dinner in 1990, he announced to the Hollywood audience that financing for *Nostromo* had been confirmed that afternoon, provoking excited applause from a crowd eager for one more David Lean picture.

After Lean returned to London, his illness, an inflammation of the muscles called polymyositis, intensified, and his doctor urged him not to go forward with the film. "Why on earth do you need to do this film?" he asked. "You're wealthy enough. Suppose it goes wrong and you're shot to pieces again?" The eighty-seven-year-old warrior replied, "I have to do it. It's in my blood." Alas, Lean never regained his health, and we were never to see his *Nostromo,* so we must be thankful that the many pictures he did complete will be with us for as long as films are shown.

DAVID LEAN

———

December 12, 1984[*]

We are here with young men and women who have a passion to make films, they have, as one says, caught the fever. When did you catch this fever?

I was brought up in the suburbs of London. I hated them. I was also brought up in a rather strict Quaker family, and wasn't allowed to go to the cinema. We had quite a big house—a kitchen and a basement—and we had what was known in those days as a charwoman, somebody who swept the floors and did the rough work. She was called Mrs. Edgerton. Mrs. Edgerton was absolutely mad about the cinema and, as I wasn't allowed to go, she used to tell me about it. The thing that really first hooked me was when she told me about Charlie Chaplin. She used to imitate Chaplin by running around the kitchen table and skidding and twirling a cane. I used to roll around with laughter. I remember asking her once, "When they talk, what happens?" And she said, "Oh, it comes up on the screen in writing." I said, "Well, that must look ridiculous." She said, "No, it doesn't. It works." That's when I first got the bug.

When I finally was allowed to go to the cinema, one of the first films I saw was Douglas Fairbanks in *The Mark of Zorro.*[†] I'll never forget the sword fights and the villain grasping his head, taking his hand away, and there was a huge *Z* on his forehead. It was magic to me. If you know what

[*]This transcript contains segments from the seminar David Lean gave at the American Film Institute on October 10, 1973.
[†]*The Mark of Zorro,* directed by Fred Niblo (1920).

the London suburbs were like—it was very, very gray—you'll understand that the movies were a journey into another world.

I was absolutely hopeless at school and when I finished—I was just nineteen—my father said, "You better come into the office." I went to this damned office in the city of London with a bowler hat, striped trousers and black coat, as a chartered accountant. Awful. I stayed for about a year. One day I went home—my father had gone some time ago—and my mother said, "Oh, Aunt Edith was here this afternoon. She said, 'I don't see any accountancy magazines here. I only see film magazines. Why doesn't he go into the movies?' "

I was overawed by movies. I thought they were so wonderful, literally a dreamworld. I never thought it was possible to actually work in the industry. I applied to a place that is now a television studio. I said, "I'll do anything—carry tea, anything." They said, "Well, we'll take you on for two weeks. If, at the end of it, you seem to be promising, we'll take you on at five pounds a week." And they did. I remember going into the camera department. I went up to an old Bell and Howell camera asking, "What has that done?" And they said, *Roses of Picardy.* This was a film I'd seen— silent, of course. And I remember touching the camera. I couldn't believe that this was the source of all the magic.

Did you work as an apprentice to a director in your early days?

Yes, I was very lucky. I worked with some good people. Try to sacrifice everything to work with good people. If you're lucky, a bit of it rubs off. I was originally an editor. I never really dared hope I would be a director, and it wasn't until very later on in my editing career when I became a kind of editing director. I remember one film during the war called *49th Parallel.* Over here it was called *The Invaders.* It had a huge cast, with Laurence Olivier, Leslie Howard, God knows who else. They put it together, and it ran for five hours. So they called me in to cut it down. Even though the director was very suspicious, I said, "Look, leave me at it for a bit, will you?" And I took the first half, which ran for two and a half hours, and cut it down to an hour, and asked the director to come and see it. He liked it and said, "Thank you very much. Go ahead and do the rest." Of course, then I started getting ideas.

How did you end up directing such big films?

Well, the one wise thing I think I did was that when I was a cutter, I got offered all sorts of movies to direct but I turned them down because they were what we called "quota quickies." The Americans came in, and because they had to show a percentage of British films in their big theaters, they paid a pound a foot for a film to fill out the program. So the cheaper you did it, the better. I always said no to these films. I was tempted once or twice, but I thought that if it didn't come out good, they would never say, "Oh, well, he did it in a hurry and didn't have decent actors."

But one day, finally, Noël Coward came along. He'd never directed a film before, and he didn't know anything about technique. He asked several people if they knew a good technician and two or three people, I don't know why, said me. And so with fear and trembling, on I went. I remember Noël read the script of *In Which We Serve* to us and asked, "Well, what do you think?" And I said, "Marvelous, but it's six hours long." We'd just seen *Citizen Kane,* and he got the idea of doing the whole thing in flashback so he could get the best scenes out of his six-hour script. I ended up doing the technical side of the film, and Noël, being an actor, did the other side. Noël always rated his acting above his writing and music, above everything else, so when he wasn't in a scene he left me to it. And then he'd say, "My dear, here we have a scene where the guns are firing and the ship has to turn over. You work that out." After the film, he said, "You can do any of my plays you like." So then I went on a sort of Coward jag.

How did you come to work with the playwright Robert Bolt on Lawrence of Arabia, Doctor Zhivago *and* Ryan's Daughter?

With *Lawrence,* we had the rights to Lawrence's book, *Seven Pillars of Wisdom.* We had a very good writer but it just wasn't working out. Sam Spiegel, the producer, said to me, "Baby, you better go see *A Man for all Seasons,*" which was written by Bolt. It was playing in the theater. I went along and thought it was damn good. So Spiegel engaged Bolt for about six weeks to do some polishing of the script, and Robert said, "I'm not a polisher, you know. I'll start from the beginning and write a scene." And so we weren't allowed to meet really, because Sam likes to keep people apart. And finally Robert brought along about twenty pages, and I thought it was marvelous, so Robert found himself on the film for months. I was forced to start shooting with only half a script—the first half. We literally had to stop shooting for eight weeks while we wrote the second half.

How do you collaborate with Bolt?

Well, Robert once said, "By the time we're finished, we don't know who had what idea." When we work together, I don't think there is any competition, and quite honestly, I cannot remember very clearly who thought of what. I'll give you an example. There's a cut I rather like in *Lawrence* where he lights a match and says, "The trick is not minding that it hurts," and blows it out. Robert wrote this scene. And next there was a scene played in the desert at sunrise. I said, "Look, Robert, I don't quite understand what you're at." He said, "Nor do I, really, but I always think when somebody blows out a match, the ember that disappears is somehow the red of the sunrise." And so out of that, I kind of put it in film terms. The trick of that, by the way, was that we just carried the noise of the blowing onto the sunrise. Robert hadn't actually written a film script before. I don't think I'm very good with words, but I feel as if I'm swimming in my own water with pictures. So Robert writes all the dialogue, even though he has a wonderful eye for visuals, even if he doesn't always know quite how to put them into a rectangle.

Could you tell us how you use the camera to achieve those painterly images that tell us what's important in a scene?

Well, you know, it's a terrible job, making a selection on the screen, isn't it? A painter can do all sorts of things to bring up the image he wants people to look at. But we are faced with photography. One of my greatest aids is the focal length of lenses. I start with a fairly wide angle, with everything very much in focus, and gradually bring up the focal length so that I end on a close-up of somebody in which everything is a blur except the eyes. And I use that again and again to choose what the audience looks at, because I try to take an audience by the hand and say, "Come look at this. See that man sitting down at that table? He's being watched by a girl."

Could you tell us about Omar Sharif's entrance in Lawrence of Arabia?

The mirage? I was out there on the mudflat and another jeep was miles behind us. It came over the horizon, and the jeep, I must tell you, looked much better than the camel because the dust went up in the air behind it. Wonderful *V* shape, like an airplane in some wind tunnel. And I thought, "What a wonderful entrance." Then some people said—and I'd heard this before—that you can't photograph a mirage. So I got out my camera and got the jeep to go farther away again and I took a series of pictures. And it did come out. That's all there was to it. Actually, though I knew the scene would be effective, the terrible thing is that I messed it up because I cut about a third out, and it was much better when it was that touch longer. If I had only seen it with an audience from the start, I wouldn't have lost my nerve. I don't know if you've found this, but I'm always losing my nerve. You know, you see the damn thing and you cut it and run it. I always tend to put in too much music. It's a pure loss of nerve. I think, "Well, that's not coming over properly—better bang a drum." It would be much better not to have anything.

I'm curious about how Lawrence *was received in the Middle East.*

They banned it in Jordan, where we shot it, because, as you know, Hussein is the king there, and Faisal, the Alec Guinness character in the film, is portrayed as an unwarlike man who would rather spend his time in his garden. This isn't the history as it's taught over there. And I was told by Omar Sharif that in Egypt the censors appealed to Nasser, who said, "Show it without a cut." At the same time Nasser asked to see the heads of the Egyptian film industry and said, "I want you to see this film because it's disgraceful that you can't photograph the desert like that yourself."

In films such as Lawrence of Arabia *or* Bridge on the River Kwai, *characters like T. E. Lawrence or Colonel Nicholson seem to be almost symbolic of all that may be thought of as the worst in British character. They're very curious people, but they're also very contradictory. Is there any deliberate attempt to do that in your films?*

No. I'm just interested in people who are nuts. I think they make very interesting characters. When we were doing *Bridge on the River Kwai,* Alec Guinness said, "Now, tell me about the character." I said, "Well, Alec, if we were having dinner tonight, he'd be a bit of a bore." He said, "A bore? You are asking me to play a bore?" Never tell actors the truth! And we fought pretty well all the way through that film. Lawrence is a fascinating character. This Oxford don on camelback. I mean, it was absolutely nutty.

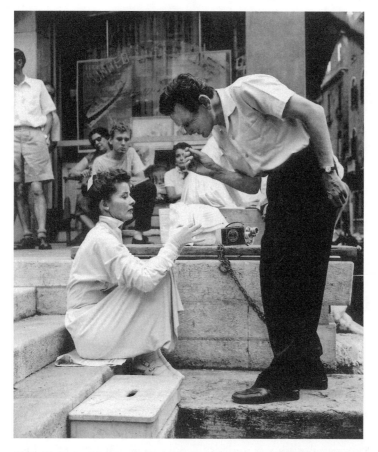

With Katharine Hepburn in Venice, Italy, on location for *Summertime* (1955).

Sort of intellectual, with a gang of Arabs on camels, you know. Peter O'Toole was very young in his career, and he could have done it better later.

I read somewhere that Peter O'Toole was not your first choice for Lawrence.

It was a tough part to cast. The first person we went for was Albert Finney. He was very young. I spent four days doing tests with him before he decided he didn't want the part. And I said, "Why?" He said, "Because I don't want to be a star." I said, "Why don't you want to be a star?" He said, "Because I'm frightened of what it may do to me personally." I said, "I can only talk to you as a director. If you succeed and do become a star, it will give you good parts, the best parts." Anyhow, that may not have been the whole story. Maybe they wanted to put him under contract for Christ knows how long. But he went. I also thought of Brando. In fact, I talked to him about it. I think he would have been wonderful, because he's such a secretive creature. I think he's one of the greatest screen actors in the world.

And then I saw the film called *The Day They Robbed the Bank of England,* and Peter O'Toole was playing a sort of silly ass Englishman fishing. I said to Spiegel, "I think we've got him." He said, "Who is it?" When I told him, he said, "No, baby. He's no good." But we did a test and he was marvelous. And though he is six foot two inches, and Lawrence was only five foot eight, it doesn't really matter, because it's something you can accept after a few minutes.

Could you talk about how you work with your actors?

Dangerous subject. Well, it's intensely personal. I always try not to speak in a loud voice when I'm talking to an actor on the set. I gently take them aside, and I whisper because I don't want to give the impression, for their sake, that they are being told to do this or that by a teacher. I try as hard as I can to make them suggest something that I want them to think of.

The trouble with actors is that it's a very difficult job with this damned glass eye looking at them all the time. It's quite difficult talking to all of you here, but I'd rather talk to all of you than I would have a hundred-millimeter lens pointing at me. It's so concentrated. It's part of a director's job, I think, to get the actor to give as good a performance on the stage as he gave to himself in the bath in the morning. So I try to relieve them of their inhibitions. It doesn't help if you talk from a great height, from a megaphone, as it were. I try to get their confidence. I try to give them confidence.

I can't bear some actors, the rambunctious types who think they know everything. You've got to knock them down and make them realize they don't know everything. If you've really done your homework on the script, you, the director, know the part better than any damned actor because you've been at it for months. I've had lots of actors who want to change dialogue. I see them doing it. I won't have it. They took on the script and they'll stick to it.

I'm terribly tempted to tell you a rather long story about Sessue Hayakawa. You know, I find constantly that actors really are not interested in anything but their own parts. We had a scene in *Bridge on the*

River Kwai where they had all the troops lined up, and Sessue gets up on the soapbox and talks. We went through a rehearsal, and I said, "What's wrong?" Because it was the speech and yet it wasn't the speech. What Sessue had done was to learn all the lines that were only his. He had cut out all the lines that were anybody else's. The main script was about that thick, and his script was only that thick. He marked only the pages in which he spoke. He had thrown out the rest and bound it together. Now, we came to the scene at the end of the picture. Alec Guinness is looking over the edge of the bridge and he thinks he sees some wires. He goes up to Hayakawa and says, "Colonel Saito, there's something rather peculiar going on. I think we better go and have a look." Guinness walked off the bridge, which leads down to the rocks, and Sessue stayed there like a rock. I said, "Go on, Sessue, follow him." He said, "I follow him?" I said, "Sessue, this is where you find the wires and where you get killed." He said, "I get killed?" He had thrown the page away because he had no dialogue.

I'll tell you another story about an actor, though I won't tell you who it was. He was damn good, but I was kind of dissatisfied. I said, "Look, I understand that an actor is projecting ninety percent to the person he's playing with, and ten percent is going out toward the camera. I've only

With Alec Guinness (center) and Sessue Hayakawa in Ceylon, shooting *The Bridge on the River Kwai* (1957). Lean says that Hayakawa discarded all pages of his script except those on which he had dialogue, so he was surprised to learn that his character dies at the end of the film.

just realized that you're putting ninety percent out to the camera, and ten to whom you're playing with." It changed his performance immediately.

Did you ever think of any parts for specific actors, for example, Alec Guinness?

Yes, the part of the priest in *Ryan's Daughter.* It was a heck of a part. I've had various tribulations with Alec. He's a convert to Catholicism and he wrote me two or three pages of things that would have to be altered for him to play the priest. So I said, "Thank you very much for being so frank," and then gave it to Trevor Howard. *Great Expectations* was actually Alec's first film, and he was so riddled with nerves that throughout nearly the whole of his scenes he thought it was a rehearsal and didn't know the cameras were actually going.

How do you keep somebody from being sentimental?

Sentimental? Well, I try to avoid saying to an audience, "Nudge, nudge, isn't this touching?" If the scene is really good, you don't do that, do you? And I try to be very truthful about things in that way. I don't like senti-mentality, but I love big emotional scenes. I think one of the best emo-tional scenes I've ever seen is in Willy Wyler's *The Best Years of Our Lives,* where Fredric March comes back at the end of the war. He goes to his house and the door's opened, I think, first of all, by a girl who's obviously his daughter. And she opens her mouth, and he puts a hand over it, and then a boy appears, and you gradually become aware of a door at the end of the longer passage. And you know that the wife is behind that door because she's the other member of the family, and then she comes out. It makes me choke even now. He's a master at it. I think it's because he has a wonderful heart. He had a wonderful heart, Willy. I loved him.

Have you ever reached a point in the cutting of a film when you hate what you've done, and when you think it doesn't work?

When I *know* it doesn't work. We often sit there, and the terrible thing is that something will look good on the Moviola, and you can't wait to get it into the theater, and you finally sit in the theater all bright-eyed and bushy-tailed and—nothing. Disaster. I'm always doing this. I spend a lot of time on cutting. I love it. But I've never cut anything first time that's anywhere near as good as it ends up. I've never seen a rough cut that doesn't look like a disaster. I'd much rather show people rushes then show them a rough cut. The rushes, because of the clapper board, remind the audience that it's unfinished. As soon as you take those clapper boards out, it looks like a finished article. And of course it isn't.

Have you ever been influenced by a specific audience reaction to one of your films?

In *Ryan's Daughter* we had this idea to show the love affair in the most over-romantic terms, with real bubbles and violins playing, just as one feels when one is right at the height of a love affair. And the audience laughed. Now, the reason they laughed is that we hadn't told them what we were doing. I'm not quite sure how we would have done it, but if we had tipped them off into this over-romantic photography and color and everything else, it would have gone down great. But they thought we were doing it in absolute seriousness and wondered how we could be so corny. So I learned a bitter lesson there.

When you search for a story to tell, what are you looking for?

My dear chap, I wish I could tell you that. You know, once I ended up in one of London's biggest bookstores and found myself next to Carol Reed. We were staring at the shelves and he said, "The bugger of it is that within five yards of us there's a wonderful subject for a film."

Is there a theme that runs through all your pictures?

No. The critics are always doing this. They're always saying, "This is a continuation of that." But it isn't. You fall in love with one, and then with another. Noël Coward gave me good advice. He used to say, "Always come out of a different hole."

Do you plan every shot beforehand?

When I started, I used to spend the evening before shooting a scene drawing diagrams, and I knew exactly where everybody was going to be, and if this person was going to sit or stand or whatever it was. And I rather locked them in. It was nerves, really. Gradually I left all that, and I'd go onto the set and keep it terribly informal. They'd ask, "Where do you want us?" and I'd say, "Well, where would you like to be?" One would say, "I might try the sofa." And we'd go around this a bit, and I'd suggest something else, and we'd start saying some lines, and I tried to ease them in, take rather a long time of it too, because it gives them confidence. If a scene works and is well rehearsed, I've found that it falls automatically into angles, and I can think immediately about how to shoot it. So eventually I chucked away my diagrams.

I heard that the shoot for Ryan's Daughter *was not easy.*

Well, you know that at midday in Ireland, where we shot the film, the sun is very low and lasts for a couple of hours. I remember the production manager coming to me and saying, "Do you realize that for five days we've been sitting on our asses here waiting? We could go anywhere in the world for that money." I said, "Good God, I suppose you're right." So we ended up shooting in South Africa, and shot it very quickly there. I left behind a second unit with a chap who was my assistant, and he filled in with some close-ups.

I'd like you to talk a little about adapting a novel. You have made films out of a number of such significant novels, for example, Great Expectations, *which we saw last night.*

I think the thing is to not try to do a little bit of every scene in a novel, because it's going to end up a mess. Choose what you want to do in the novel and do it proud. If necessary, cut characters. Don't keep every character and just take a sniff of each one. When we were going to do *Great Expectations,* we thought that we were completely incapable of tackling such a master as Dickens, so we looked around and asked, "Who really is an expert at Dickens?" There was a lady novelist called Clemence Dane in London who was sort of a Dickens expert and had also written several plays. She did a script, and it was absolutely awful because she did just what I've said. Every character and scene were there—just nibbled at. We knew it was no good. And I said, "Let's have a go." I got the book and quite blatantly wrote down the scenes that I thought would look wonderful on the screen. What I did was try to join up those scenes and write links between them. Of course, you have to have a narrative, and that chiefly is what I did.

You always have the most interesting characters in your film in the foreground, like Mrs. Moore in A Passage to India. *How did you decide to give her such an important role in the narrative?*

Mrs. Moore is a wonderful part, and I'll tell you the interesting thing. Have you seen Peggy Ashcroft before? No? That's it, you see. She's a great stage actress and very well known in England. And we always said, "I wonder what the Americans will say?" Because here you see an old lady—we're exactly the same age, actually—who is a very accomplished actress. In England, I don't think she would have quite that additional impact that you got. In part this impact is due to this wealth of experience. She can do it off the back of her hand, I assure you.

How do you perceive her character in the film? I didn't quite understand the scene when she was at the caves and you cut to the process shot of the moon and then the fuller shot of the moon. I realized something mythological was going on, but I couldn't pinpoint exactly what it was.

Well, I'll tell you what I was trying to do, because I don't think it succeeded. In the book, Mrs. Moore is a very religious lady. Hence she wears a cross, and in the mosque scene at the beginning she says, "God is here." And when she goes to those caves, author E. M. Forster says, "Those caves were sealed before the coming of the gods, before the coming of man . . . ," and so forth. In other words they were a kind of vacuum when the world was made, I think his expression is "Man grew curious and drilled a hole." And Mrs. Moore loses her faith in those caves, or her faith is badly shaken.

Well, thank you very much—put that on film! So I had her come out, flop back in her chair and look at the moon. I had her put on dark glasses, and from that moment on I was going to have everything seen from her point of view, through a strange color. The special effects failed and I dropped it, so she in fact puts her glasses on for nothing. But I thought the space and the surface of the moon with the line, "Like most old people, I sometimes wonder if we are passing figures in a godless universe," was the best effort I could make at saying that her faith was shaken.

You seemed to take your time in telling the story, yet it keeps our interest. I'm thinking particularly of the scene in the monkey temple. Could you talk about pacing?

You know, I didn't know if I was ever going to make a film again, and we finally managed to get the money together, so I thought I would just obey my instinct. It had to be slow because a mood is slow, isn't it? I always imagined that girl had lived in a sort of vicarage, brought up in very proper surroundings. And I wrote that scene because in the book she's a bit of a stick. And then there was this question of an assault in the cave. I wanted to prepare the way for it. I wanted to have a scene where a rather prudish girl becomes aware of her own sexuality. Now, this has got to be done slowly.

There was a wonderful place in India where I went about thirty years ago. It was discovered by a couple of men who were tiger shooting, and they got into some thickets and realized there were some erotic statues there all overgrown with creepers. Today it's a very nice little park. All the statues have been cleaned. I was there for a week with a camera, just shooting photographs. We reproduced it—it's a complete fake in the film. We found somewhere to build statues in plaster, put fake creepers around them, and the art director, John Box, stuck them up against the background of trees in various places. And then we built a sort of platform for the monkeys. I had the girl go through on a bicycle. We had lots of shots of her, shots of statues, shots of monkeys and so forth. We didn't know how it would look until we cut it together. That temple exists only on film.

This is kind of a gush, but I'd just like to thank you for making A Passage to India. *It sounds like you had to put up with a lot to do it.*

How sweet of you. That's no gush. Yes, well, we did. Nobody wanted it, you see. We came over here because the only people who put money up for films are the Americans. At first, one studio said they'd do it if we put in an explicit rape. And that, thereby, ruined the story, of course. And another person—not American—wrote what he thought was a fascinating memo to me. He wrote words to the effect, "Our audiences are young people. Young people are bored by old people. Cut the old dame."

What advice can you give us in terms of staging large crowd settings? Most of the directors we've talked with have never made the huge spectacles that you have done.

The most important thing, I think, is to get people's enthusiasm. If you say, "When I hold my hand up, you cheer," they'll cheer. Or, "When I put my hand there, fall down on the ground," they'll fall down on the ground. But it's no good. I get on a microphone and try, as simply as I can, to describe what the scene is and explain what I would like them to give the camera. I try to give them a feeling that they're contributing to something. The Indian crowds were simply wonderful. They're the best crowds I've ever worked with. Very emotional. I'd do one take, two takes, probably print take three, which was the end of it. I'd say, "Cut." And I would applaud them. And they would applaud me, and everybody applauded everybody, and that was the end of the shot. And it worked very well because they thought they were part of it.

Brief Encounter *has always been one of my favorite pictures. Do you ever have a desire to do a more intimate, small-canvas picture like that again?*

When I can no longer do a big one, yes. As a matter of fact, I've tried to do it in *Passage to India.* That's very much the play of characters—these wonderful characters of Forster's—and the attempts of people to reach each other and go out across barriers. A lot of that is quite intimate, isn't it? I remember Willy Wyler saying to me once, "I don't see why anything shouldn't be told through a love story." And he could do it. Look at *Roman Holiday.*

Do you feel you've changed as a director from the beginning of your career to now?

I think I have just a little more confidence. I think a little bit of confidence either makes you unbearable or much better. It's a very funny thing about getting old—you don't feel it. You feel exactly the same. So I really don't feel any different than I ever did, but as I say—and I mean it very lightly—I have just a bit more confidence perhaps.

What is your relationship with the cameraman?

One curious thing about cameramen is that they very rarely read scripts, or they read them and then forget them. One of the best cameramen I've ever worked with is Freddie Young. He'd always come up to me and say, "Now, look, this is the scene after they've found the baby's dead, or whatever it is." I'd say, "No, Freddy, that's at the beginning." He always got it wrong. What I generally do with cameramen is remind them of the script and I tell them the mood I'd like to create. I did *Brief Encounter* with a very good cameraman called Bob Cracker. We started *Great Expectations* with him, and it was almost the same as *Brief Encounter*, very real looking. And I said, "Bobby, much more daring. Huge, great black shadows. Great big highlights over the top, because that's Dickens." And he couldn't do it. And I got him this ex-operator of mine who'd only done a bit of a picture before, Guy Green. I remember these shafts of light coming down, and it was simply wonderful. And he got the Oscar for cameraman on that picture. It's rather like casting actors, in a way. You've got to cast people who have a love for the atmosphere.

In *Doctor Zhivago* there was a series of scenes in winter, and I wanted spring, so we wanted some daffodils. We were growing these damned daffodils for weeks. The scene before was the scene of the family in a small room, and I said, "Come on, let's make it absolutely colorless." Freddy said, "It's going to look bloody awful." I said, "Doesn't matter. It's going to look much better in a minute when we go to the next scene." And we took out every bit of color we could. We even got a spray gun and sprayed some of the colors gray. Now, that scene, which was flat and gray, *made* the daffodils because of the contrast. Our game is contrast: fast, slow, close, long, noise, quiet. Look at the scene when we first see Omar Sharif in *Lawrence*. There are two figures coming closer and closer together, but the long shots only look good in contrast to the quick cutting of close-ups.

I often think we are only at the beginning in making movies. I don't know what's going to happen. We've got sort of basic techniques, but I think we've got a long way to go. We haven't begun to use all sorts of things. I think we just photograph what's there, rather than making what's there. That's why I like working on sets as opposed to real streets.

Have you always had final cut of your films?

I have lately. But you know, producers on the whole suddenly become creative when they see a director's cut. They like to nibble, and there's little you can do about it sometimes. On *River Kwai* there are two cuts I could have killed Spiegel for, and I didn't see them until the Los Angeles premiere. It was only a few feet in both instances. One was where the Japanese boy is chasing Geoffrey Horne, the American officer, through the jungle. Suddenly, out of the grass, pops this Japanese boy. I had a close-up of this chap popping up, and a close-up of Horne. There's a moment of hesitation, and in comes Jack Hawkins, who knifes the Japan-

AFI, December 1984. Lean said, "Look at the scene when we first
see Omar Sharif in *Lawrence*. There are two figures coming closer and
closer together, but the long shots only look good in contrast to the
quick cutting of close-ups."

ese boy. Now, I cut it so that when the Japanese stands up, it's clear that he
was a boy. I cut to Geoffrey Horne long enough so he thinks, "My God,
he's a young chap like me." And as he hesitates, two-shot, and boom! He's
cut down. Now Sam, after I'd gone, had the Japanese stand up, but not
for long enough so you see he's a young man. He cut out the pause, so he
stands up, boom, and immediately he's dead. He cut out the beat. He also
buggered up the ending. Everybody asks me, "Did Nicholson intend to
blow up the bridge?" Sam trimmed some shots and cut out another. I
said, "Why on earth did you do that?" And he said, "Baby, it's modern to
be a bit mystifying, to let the audience wonder." But I wanted it to be
quite clear. I meant for him to say, as it were, "My God, what have I done?
There's the plunger, I'm going for it." And as he is quite clearly going for
it—which is not in the finished film—he gets hit, and without him
knowing it, he does succeed. His dead body does it.

I'm fascinated by your use of sound, particularly at the end of The Bridge on the
River Kwai. *Could you talk about how you shoot the scene in terms of sound?*

I try to write sound and music into a script. I try to describe what I hear
in my imagination. I'm always telling the sound people, "Don't be too

realistic with sound. The audience has got to think it's realistic, but use it like an orchestra."

The way you verbally and visually hook scenes together has always been very sophisticated. How do you do it?

Just lying awake at night. You do a scene and you know what the next scene is, and you just ask yourself how to get to it in an interesting way.

What about the collaborative nature of the medium and the way you convey your vision to all these people who have to work together in order to create it?

When I finish a script, I get everybody in the different departments and have endless cups of coffee with them. Just talk, talk. And then they'll start coming up with ideas and bouncing back and forth. I think directing a movie has got to be a very selfish job in a certain way, because the more a movie is one person's point of view, the better. The greatest thing in acting or in a movie is intention. I'm sure of that. Any fool can go on and take long shot, medium shot, over shoulders and close-ups, and then throw it at the cutting room. I could do that. It's an easy way of doing it. I do it sometimes when I'm lost, but only when I'm lost, because I think in doing all these shots and not knowing quite how it's going and then throwing it to the poor editor, you lose intention.

With good actors, you could, if you wanted to, stop them in midstream and say, "What are you thinking about?" He or she would tell you exactly what they were thinking about, because film acting is purely thinking. That's why I hate using doubles, even in long shots. Celia Johnson—my goodness me, what an actress she was—she was wonderful. Unfortunately, dead now. In *Brief Encounter,* we had a scene in which a man had asked her to come to an apartment. She was married, and she said no. And she gets into the train, hears the door slam, and as the whistle blows, she gets out, gets onto the platform, the train starts to move, and she decides to walk toward the exit. And I just had one hell of a great long shot of this small figure walking up the path. And she walked, she half ran, she stopped herself, and I said, "Celia, that was wonderful. How do you do that?" She said, "Well, she would, wouldn't she?" And she was just thinking: I can't wait to meet him, I shouldn't go. And I bet you she could have told every thought passing through her mind. And I think that's the great thing with a script. Try not to get sidetracked. What is this scene actually saying? If you can do that, in my experience, you'll be the stronger for it.

One final question: What is directing?

What is directing? It's trying to use a lot of people and some very heavy apparatus, and give it all the lightness of a pen while you are writing.

———

Films as Director

1942 *In Which We Serve* (co-director and co-film editor)

1944 *This Happy Breed* (also co-screenplay)

1945 *Blithe Spirit* (also co-screenplay) *Brief Encounter*

1946 *Great Expectations* (also co-screenplay)

1948 *Oliver Twist* (also co-screenplay)

1949 *The Passionate Friends*

1950 *Madeleine*

1952 *Breaking the Sound Barrier* (also producer)

1954 *Hobson's Choice* (also producer and co-screenplay)

1955 *Summertime* (also co-screenplay)

1957 *The Bridge on the River Kwai*

1962 *Lawrence of Arabia* (also co-producer)

1965 *Doctor Zhivago*

1970 *Ryan's Daughter*

1984 *A Passage to India* (also screenplay and film editor)

With maturity as a creative artist comes simplicity. To become gimmicky with a camera, with a zoom lens—I don't go for that sort of thing.

STANLEY CORTEZ
(Born in New York, New York, 1908—Died 1997)

Late in his life Stanley Cortez remembered the experience that sparked his interest in movies. He was working in New York as an assistant to the famous portrait photographer Pirie MacDonald, when his brother, the actor Ricardo Cortez, invited him to visit the Paramount Studios on Long Island where D. W. Griffith was shooting *Sorrows of Satan.* "I definitely decided on that day," he said, "that I would become a motion picture cameraman." Sometime later he was watching a parade in New York when he spotted a newsreel cameraman at work. He turned his back on the parade and watched the rhythm and flow of his hand cranking the camera. "It was," he said, "a beautiful thing to see."

Cortez also worked with Edward Steichen in Steichen's portrait studio. This experience grounded him in photographic technique and inspired his artistic sensibility. Cortez went to Hollywood and worked his way through the ranks as an assistant, then a camera operator, learning from cameramen such as Karl Struss, John Seitz, George Barnes and Hal Mohr, on his way to becoming a cinematographer himself on the 1937 film *Four Days' Wonder.* Cortez considered himself fortunate to have apprenticed with some of the great cameramen. "I worked as an operator for George Barnes on some of the Busby Berkeley musicals," he recalled, "and I still get chills when I hear 'The Lullaby of Broadway' and remember how Busby and George encouraged me to design a camera movement."

Cortez had to take the jobs that were assigned to him, and for much of his career these were B pictures of little distinction. But when challenging creative opportunities came his way he rose to the occasion, as when Orson Welles engaged him to photograph *The Magnificent Ambersons. Ambersons* is a beautifully rendered period picture in which Cortez captured the turn-of-the-century mood of a small American town. Welles either abandoned or was taken off the picture, and the task of finishing it was given to Robert Wise, the editor. Today the film survives as a flawed masterpiece, but Cortez's work on it earned him the Film Critics of America award for cinematography.

Other distinguished efforts by Cortez include the extraordinary black-and-white moods of *Night of the Hunter,* directed by Charles Laughton, Samuel Fuller's gritty *Shock Corridor* and the exquisite rendering of Joanne Woodward's split personality in *The Three Faces of Eve.*

During World War II, Cortez served as a U.S. Army Signal Corps photographer and worked with John Huston on the famous documentary about GIs traumatized by combat, *Let There Be Light.*

The AFI fellows watched *The Magnificent Ambersons* with Cortez before the seminar.

Cinematographer Stanley Cortez (right) lines up a shot with director Orson Welles for *The Magnificent Ambersons* at the RKO ranch in 1942.

STANLEY CORTEZ

—————

October 19, 1974

The Magnificent Ambersons *is a great movie. I'd like you to meet Stanley
Cortez, who photographed it. In those days, most cameramen played it safe. They
exposed the negative fully and let the lab print it down. Stanley didn't do that. He
exposed it properly in the camera.*

After seeing this film again I realize more and more that Orson Welles is
one of our great geniuses. You'll find that after doing many films, there are
a few that you are quite proud of, and certainly *Ambersons* is one that I'm
quite proud of. There is a peculiarity about the film. *Ambersons* has
become a controversial film in the sense that there is a difference between
what you saw this morning and what you could have seen. As great as the
film is now, it could have been monumentally greater. The amount that
was cut out was around five thousand feet. If you enjoyed what you saw,
you would have drooled at what was cut out.

I became associated with Orson Welles in a very strange way. Most
of *Ambersons* was made at the RKO-Pathé Studios in Culver City. David
Selznick shared the same studio. I was with Selznick at the time and
I would walk around the different stages and see these sets going up.
And I would often remark to myself, "I pity the poor guy who has to
photograph this goddamn thing." Orson's right-hand man was named
Jack Moss. One day I happened to ask him who was going to photo-
graph *Ambersons.* He said, "Well, we think it's going to be so-and-so at
RKO." I said, "Great." In the meantime, I went to New York to do
some more things for David, and while I was back there I received a tele-

phone call asking when I could head back because Orson wants me to do *Ambersons.*

Well, I had never met Orson. I had tests to shoot in New York for David and George Cukor. To make a long story short, I had to call David Selznick and ask permission to leave New York on Sunday. I arrived in Los Angeles on Monday afternoon, met Orson for the first time on Monday night, and we started shooting the film on Tuesday. That evening I made many changes in the lighting scheme. It was an all-RKO staff, and I was the only outsider. I'd been chosen because Orson, for some reason, didn't quite like the RKO type of work. I'm pretty sure it was Gregg Toland, a dear friend of mind with whom I shared many similar ideas, who recommended me to Orson. Someone who is equally important in this story is a projectionist named Charlie McCloud. A great Irishman and a great human being. I knew Charlie, and Charlie knew that Orson was looking for someone to photograph *Ambersons.* At that time, Hal Kern, who was the film editor for Selznick, had quite a few tests that I had made for David, which Kern had thrown out in the disposal can. It was Charlie McCloud who went to this disposal can, put what Hal Kern threw out onto a reel and called Orson, saying, "I think I have something that you're going to like." And hence, I photographed *Ambersons.*

Going back to my first meeting with Orson, I hadn't read the script, but I had an idea as to what he was trying to do. I had seen *Citizen Kane* many times, and I had marveled at the man's creative talents and his ability to do things with the camera. My respect for him increased enormously because of his profound knowledge of the camera, what it can do and what the potentials are in terms of so-called dramaturgy. The first sequence I shot in *Ambersons* was the sequence where they're all having dinner. It's the exposé of automobile versus carriage. After the first day's work, I went to the laboratory at midnight to get the first test. From what I saw on the negative, I had a good idea that Orson would like the print. The next morning they're all looking at the film. When the film was over, Orson threw his arms around me, and from that moment on we had a relationship which doesn't exist too frequently these days. By that I mean as crazy as he was or might have been, I was doubly crazy. What we shared—and I think this is so important for a director and cameraman to share—were real mental connections. He had many marvelous ideas upon which we built.

Orson is the kind of person who has to be in command. His voice itself is commanding. Not only did he create enthusiasm amongst the actors, but equally important, also among the men behind the camera.

Why was the film cut? And who did it?

What happened was that the studio took out five thousand feet from the film. I doubt very much if Orson Welles saw the same film that we saw today. And the reason is that in those days, Orson had one man to answer to, a man named George Schaeffer, who was head of the studio. Now, you know how this business is. Things happen overnight. And overnight, Schaeffer is out and in came a man named Charles Koerner. Koerner was essentially a theater man. By a theater man, I mean that his interests were not in the creative phase. His interests were in the distribution and exhibition, and it was Koerner who cut five thousand feet from the film.

Where was the snow sequence filmed?

There's an old Union Ice Company house on Eighth and San Pedro. What Orson was trying to do was get a feeling of the cold, so when the actors would speak you saw their breath. The thing that I was trying to create with Orson was a kind of Currier-and-Ives concept of light and shade. I think we captured that to a high degree.

How did you work with Welles on the sets?

On the first Sunday of the picture, Orson and I went out to the RKO ranch where many of the sets were made. The three-story Amberson home had already been built, with car tracks and fences around it. I made an offhand remark to Orson, saying, "Why was that set built here, in this particular section?" I was told the reasons why, because of the light and so forth. And having read the script by this time, I felt that it had been built all wrong. To move this set would cost an enormous amount of money. I didn't want them to move it, but by God they did. The whole house was moved to where I thought it should be. This was the kind of perfectionist Orson Welles was.

Some of the things we did on that film! Do you recall the sequence where Dolores Costello is by herself in the room and she starts at the window in a chair and gets up, and over this is the dialogue from Joe Cotten who had written her a letter? At the time Orson was doing a very important radio show and he couldn't be at the studio this particular day. We were getting tight on our schedule. The day before we rehearsed the whole scene with Orson there and he made a record of his voice directing the scene. The next day we played the record back, and that's how the scene was directed. You may ask, "Why didn't you do it the same day?" The reason is it would have taken too long. It shows how Orson brought in many innovative ideas from the world of radio into the cinema. I think one of the greatest tragedies is that Orson is no longer a director, in the accepted sense. He's become an actor and he's done many films, but this is great and rare talent, and I hope to God that someday Orson will come back as a director and really do the great things he is so capable of doing.

Why do you think Welles never achieved anywhere near the greatness in his later films that he did in The Magnificent Ambersons *and* Citizen Kane?

I don't know the answer to that. Perhaps Orson became fed up with what he had to go through to get financing. I think once a person has talent, he will never lose it. Orson is a born genius.

Never once was I interfered with by Orson with regard to lighting. Never once. One of the nice things about working with him is that he has great sympathy for the photographer and a great feeling for cinematic images. When you're striving for something, he will adjust his people to fit what you're trying to do in terms of light.

Compare directors today with directors of, say, twenty years ago. The directors of twenty years ago came from the silent days. They started out in comedies and knew all about different camera speeds and all of that. They had a very good grasp of the medium. *Grammar* is the word. They knew the potentials of what can be done. So I say to all of you who sit here, get down to the basics of these things and know what can be done, so that as a director or as a cameraman, you know how to work with tools like back projection, front projection, blue screen, traveling mattes.

There is a tremendous shot in The Magnificent Ambersons *that starts in the upper hall, where the family is sitting around the big table, with the punch bowl. Then the camera moves down the hallway on a crane.*

Can I just say something about the opening sequence of the ball, which has been terribly cut, by the way? It's been really chopped up in this version. Orson rehearsed the sequence in about four or five different cuts.

I'm sitting with Bob Wise, who edited the film and who is now a very famous director, and Mark Robson, the assistant cutter. I said to Bob, "If he only did this thing in one cut." Now perhaps Orson overheard me, I don't know. He asked me, "Can we make this thing in one cut?" I said, "Orson, if you're willing, I am more than willing." What this meant was that the camera goes through about seven or eight different rooms, and in each room, which required a different lighting concept entirely, the camera sees all four walls and the ceiling. In some of the rooms there were mirrors. You wonder how we did it. Of course it was all predetermined. Walls would be raised and lowered on a certain cue. Lights would be moved into a predetermined set on the floor marks. Mirrors would be tipped and twisted to accommodate the lens, all in one move. It ends up with a big close-up of Annie Baxter and Tim Holt, which is the opening of the ballroom sequence. It took us about three days to do it, whereas we would have spent perhaps a week on the different cuts. This is where experience comes in and a certain amount of bravery. You've got to be brave. Get out there and do it. Take a gamble.

If you notice, there are many long dialogue sequences without a cut in the film. I kind of like that. It gives a feeling of continuity, where the audience is sort of relaxed. They're not confused by too many cuts; they're ready to drink in and watch the performers. As a cameraman, you depend on instinct much of the time, and that instinct is sometimes based upon what you hear, not what you see. To read something in script form is one thing, but things change when the actors read it.

Take the last sequence, where Agnes Moorehead has five cents for the carfare and he picks her up and they go to the huge room in the back, all in one move. If you notice, at the end of her walk, you suddenly see two beams of light in the eyes. It wasn't accidental. And the reason it was put there is to get inside this person's brain. Using the lighting was one way of doing it. I think any creative cameraman or director of photography really is an interpreter of the drama, so to speak. And all of us who are in our field are basically dramatists to a very high degree, just as a writer is. But we do it with light, with optics, with the camera, with all kinds of gimmicks and things. Who cares? If the result is there, this is what's important. The point I want to make is that thought can be photographed. Think about it. It can be done in many ways—through light, through gauze, call it what you like—but it can be photographed. In pantomime, if an actor thinks, it can come through in the eyes.

I heard that it was Carol Reed and not Orson Welles who completed The Magnificent Ambersons.

It wasn't Carol Reed but Bob Wise, the editor, who did the sequence in the hallway, because I wasn't available. But I've heard the same thing that you're talking about, and was quite surprised to hear that. I don't know where they got that idea. Bob Wise, being as close as he was to the film, was the logical person for it. If Carol Reed had something to do with it, I don't know about it. In fact, even if they had wanted Orson to do the new ending, he wouldn't have done it, because in Orson's thinking, the film was already finished. He was a rugged individualist who had a lot to lose by giving in to what he thought was wrong. If Orson wants certain things, by God he's going to get them.

Do you always take care to read the scripts of the films you shoot?

Of course. It would be wonderful, when a writer presents a script to a producer, or even while the writer is working on it, to have a cameraman there. Many times a script is written by a writer, it goes to a producer who buys it, and he calls in the director and they go into all kinds of conferences. Occasionally they'll call in the art director, but never the cameraman. There are many times when we'll start a film by coming in only a week ahead of time. Or even, as with *Ambersons,* the night before. It's my view that the cameraman doesn't work only with the lighting. He can contribute so many valuable ideas, so many visual shortcuts in terms of telling the story that can be of enormous value.

Could you say something about photographing The Magnificent Ambersons *compared to how Gregg Toland shot* Citizen Kane?

Kane was very difficult, but I can assure you that *Ambersons* was twice as difficult photographically. To be more specific, Gregg and Orson, in *Kane,* would place ceiling pieces around the lights as they went along. In *Ambersons,* the ceilings were already there. We were stuck with them, which presented enormous problems, though it did also add tremendously to the drama of the picture. In *Ambersons,* we had shots where we would start low and go up three or four stories without a cut. How do you light this thing? We were faced with different problems than on

Kane. You can't compare the two films because the problems were so different.

On *Kane,* in order to achieve the feeling of depth in the shots, Gregg used many techniques, like double and even multiple exposures. The end result was that you could see what was going on in the foreground and the background. There were only a few people doing that kind of thing at the time. Gregg was one, Arthur Miller was another, I was the third.

Was that because you wanted a softer quality for Ambersons *than* Kane *had? And also you didn't have any other way to get the lights to build up to that kind of a stop?*

Partly true, yes. Of course, we had no forced film development in those days. We had no flashing. But you can create a feeling of depth by virtue of light. *Kane* was of a more contrasty nature. *Ambersons* did not fit *Kane* in the slightest. The shots in the film had to have depth. They needed a certain amount of contrast, which is what created the depth as against going down to f-11 and f-16.

Each of us have our own different approaches. Many fellows resort to laboratory treatments. That's perfectly all right, but I would rather have the control. I would like to be the one that would get the blame if it's wrong, or the credit if it's right. I don't want the lab to do anything except to give me a darn good negative with the proper color balance. I want to be the one doing the controlling, and nobody else. There are exceptions, of course, where you have a certain amount of flashing these days, or forced exposure. But even that should be under the direct control of the man behind the camera and not in the lab. When it comes to what goes on that screen, we don't care how it gets up there, as long as what comes out of the screen impresses the audience.

What am I talking about? Specifically this: you walk out onto a soundstage. It's black and the sequence calls for so-and-so and so-and-so. You might have a preconceived idea, but how do you actually start? For some people, perhaps, everything that they have experienced in their lives comes to a focal point, and from that point, ideas build upon ideas. I will always spend a great deal of time in museums, studying various paintings. I'll study certain musical compositions because they give me something. I'll go to New York and spend two days in the Metropolitan, or at the Louvre in Paris, or in Florence or Rome and God knows where else, because I'll tell you, it all ties into being exposed to what's happening in

Cortez with Susan Hayward on the set of Universal's *Smash-Up* (1947), produced by Walter Wanger and directed by Stuart Heisler.

the world, so that we, as a creative group, can reflect, in terms of cinematic images, on what the hell this is all about.

Let me give you the example of when I shot *Night of the Hunter* for Charles Laughton. We did many films together with him as an actor before he asked me to do *Hunter*. We were shooting a particular sequence, and Laughton saw me doing a couple of things. "What in hell are you doing, Cortez?" he said. "None of your goddamn business, Laughton," I said—in a very nice, lovable way, don't get me wrong. The respect was there. But he insisted that I tell him what I was doing. "Charles, I'm thinking about a piece of music." And in his particular way, he said to me, "My God, Stan, how right you are. This sequence needs a waltz tempo." And so he immediately sent for the composer Walter Schumann so he could see what I was doing visually, so he could interpret it into a waltz tempo.

Now, some of you may know the story behind *Valse Triste* by Sibelius, which fit perfectly with this whole sequence. The music is based upon a legend, and the legend has to do with New Year's Eve in a cemetery. It's one minute past midnight when these bones that have been buried come to life and do a dance in sheer mockery of life, which was precisely what

Bob Mitchum was doing to Shelley Winters in the scene we were shooting. So what I'm trying to say to you is that people in the creative fields need stimuli. In my world, it's music. Perhaps in yours it's something else.

So go into a museum, talk to a beggar on the street, go to the Sistine Chapel and see how the forced perspective was designed. Go anywhere, but look, see, hear, feel. Let me just finish by saying that I believe that with maturity as a creative artist comes simplicity. To become gimmicky with a camera, with a zoom lens—I don't go for that sort of thing. The most difficult thing in the world is to be simple. And the enthusiasm must always be there, of course. Otherwise you're dead.

◄━►

Films as Cinematographer

1931 *Devotion*

1932 *Panama Flo*
Lady with a Past

1933 *Shanghai Madness*
My Lips Betray

1935 *A Midsummer Night's Dream*

1937 *Four Days' Wonder*
Armored Car
The Wildcatter
I Cover the War

1938 *The Black Doll*
The Lady in the Morgue
Danger on the Air
Personal Secretary
The Last Express
Exposed

1939 *For Love or Money*
Risky Business
They Asked for It
The Forgotten Woman
Hawaiian Nights
Laugh It Off

1940 *It's a Date*
Alias the Deacon
Love, Honor, and Oh-Baby!
The Leatherpushers

Meet the Wildcat
Margie

1941 *Sealed Lips*
The Black Cat
San Antonio Rose
A Dangerous Game
Badlands of Dakota
Moonlight in Hawaii

1942 *Bombay Clipper*
Eagle Squadron
The Magnificent Ambersons

1943 *The Powers Girl*
Flesh and Fantasy

1944 *Since You Went Away*

1947 *Smash-Up—The Story of a Woman*

1948 *Secret Behind the Door*
Smart Woman

1950 *The Man on the Eiffel Tower*
The Underworld Story
The Admiral Was a Lady

1951 *The Basketball Fix*
Fort Defiance

1952 *Stronghold*
Models Inc.

1952 *Abbott and Costello Meet
Captain Kidd*
1953 *The Neanderthal Man
Dragon's Gold
Shark River
The Diamond Queen
Yesterday and Today*
1954 *Riders to the Stars
Apache*
1955 *Night of the Hunter
Black Tuesday*
1956 *Man from Del Rio*
1957 *Top Secret Affair
The Three Faces of Eve*
1958 *South Pacific*
1959 *Thunder in the Sun*
1960 *The Angry Red Planet*

*Vice Raid
Dinosaurus!*
1961 *Back Street*
1963 *Shock Corridor
The Madmen of Mandoras*
1964 *The Naked Kiss
The Candidate
Nightmare in the Sun*
1965 *Young Dillinger*
1966 *The Ghost in the Invisible Bikini
The Navy vs. the Night Monsters*
1968 *Blue*
1969 *The Bridge at Remagen*
1970 *Tell Me That You Love Me, Junie
Moon* (title sequence)
1971 *The Doomsday Machine*
1977 *Another Man, Another Chance*

I broke in with a great editor, Billy Hamilton, who told me when I was a kid, "There's only one real requirement for an editor. You make a scene play. It may not be exactly the way the director shot it, but if it plays, that's it, and he'll like it."

ROBERT WISE
(Born in Winchester, Indiana, 1914—Died 2005)

Robert Wise headed for Los Angeles during the Depression, where his brother, an accountant at RKO, helped him get hired as a porter carrying film cans in the editorial department. His first break came when he was introduced to a young director making his first picture who was unhappy with his editor. Orson Welles hired Wise as his cutter on *Citizen Kane* and *The Magnificent Ambersons,* involving him with two masterpieces of American cinema. During World War II Wise became a director himself—a solid craftsman who took studio assignments as they came and made the best of whatever material he was given. "If you turn them down, they put you on suspension," he recalled. "I was anxious to make more films and learn more, so I made several films that I was not keen about rather than sit it out on suspension." *The Body Snatcher, Mystery in Mexico, The Set-Up, The Captive City, The Day the Earth Stood Still* and *Something for the Birds* were uneven in quality, but Wise's dependability while making them paved the way for *I Want to Live!* and *Somebody Up There Likes Me,* which set him up for two career-changing opportunities.

In 1961 he co-directed *West Side Story,* the Leonard Bernstein–Stephen Sondheim–Jerome Robbins collaboration that had been a hit on Broadway. Three years later, Rodgers and Hammerstein had a huge Broadway success with *The Sound of Music.* Wise took the film assignment. He made it into a blockbuster that further enhanced his standing. In his later years, he gained a reputation as a film industry statesman, serving as a council member for the National Endowment for the Arts, a board member of AFI for more than a decade and a three-term president of the Academy of Motion Picture Arts and Sciences.

Robert Wise (second from left) was the film editor for Orson Welles
(kneeling) on *Citizen Kane* (1941) and *The Magnificent Ambersons* (1942).
Here on the *Ambersons* set with (left to right) camera operator Jimmy Daly,
Welles' assistant Richard Wilson, cinematographer Stanley Cortez
and gaffer Jimmy Almond.

In 1984 I asked Bob to look at a rough cut of *George Stevens: A Filmmaker's Journey*, the film I was making about my father. He reserved a room on the Goldwyn lot, and after the screening we went across the street for lunch. My friend Toni Vellani, a filmmaker who was AFI's dean at the time, joined us. We were hoping for a detailed critique. We ordered a drink and armed with a yellow pad to record his suggestions, I asked Wise for his thoughts. Bob is a quiet man by any measure, but there was a particularly long silence before he muttered, "Take out the plants." I think he would have left it at that, but I pressed. Then he said, "There was an editor at RKO, Billy Hamilton, who taught me everything. We'd come back from a preview and he'd say, 'Okay. Now take out the plants.'" I was afraid I was getting a gardening lesson until Bob explained: "All through a picture you set things up. You plant things because you think you can pay them off later. If you take out all those plants, you'll find the picture really moves." It was priceless advice that helped us sharpen that film, and a piece of wisdom from Robert Wise that I still carry with me in the editing room.

ROBERT WISE

—————

May 21, 1975*

You did a great deal of editing before you directed your first film. What are the advantages of having an editor's point of view?

It's helpful in visualizing how something will look on film—what coverage I feel I can use and under what conditions—but it certainly is not an absolute prerequisite. There always are a lot of people around to help directors who don't know editing. I think the main thing that one gets out of editing is the knowledge of what kind of coverage to get with the camera. I found that you could do a lot of tricks. You can butt words together, cut in the middle of words and make the tempo and the pace go by overlapping dialogue. So I carried that on in my directing. But there's a corollary to that. Most people think that if you've been an editor you shoot less film because you know exactly what you want. Well, the reverse is often true. As an editor you know how marvelous it is to have that coverage, how great it is to have that extra close-up on the shelf in the cutting room three months after the picture's finished shooting, when you need a cutaway to drop a pair of lines. So I found myself knowing how to handle a camera, knowing coverage and angles and setups, and also finding myself wanting to cover scenes more than a director coming from other backgrounds.

---

*This transcript contains segments from seminars Robert Wise gave at the American Film Institute on April 7, 1979, and October 22, 1980.

Some editors say, "I don't want to see the script, I only want to deal with this film after it's already shot."

That is not how I work. I certainly would want to know the script when I started. I broke in with a great editor, Billy Hamilton, who told me when I was a kid, "There's only one real requirement for an editor. You make a scene play. It may not be exactly the way the director shot it, but if it plays, that's it, and he'll like it." I've never gotten another bit of advice that's turned out to be so true. Veteran director Richard Wallace came up to the set on my first day as a director and said, "Bob, I only have one bit of advice. If it seems a little slow on the set, it will be twice as slow in the projection room." And, oh man, have I ever found that to be true.

You edited Citizen Kane. *Would you talk about your work with Orson Welles?*

My experience with Orson was always an up-and-down situation. He is as close to a genius as anyone I've ever come across. A brilliant man, but a maddening man. He was stimulating, fascinating, exciting, aggravating. One minute he could have you so angry at his behavior that you wanted to walk off the picture. But before you could do it, he would come up with a notion so brilliant that it had your mouth gaping, and you'd hang in there. I remember once on *The Magnificent Ambersons* he did something that really pissed me off, and I let it be known. Word got to Orson that I was really upset, and he stopped shooting and went around the lot to find me. So we had a good relationship.

Were you on the set with Welles?

Generally, no, though I would visit and stand by when he wanted. Orson didn't need tremendous help on the soundstages. He had a great instinct for film, for cameras and for composition. I worked with him pretty much as I worked with any other director. He had his own contributions to make about the editing, and I had my own views and suggestions. He had the reputation at the time of being a highfalutin young genius from New York who wouldn't listen to anybody, but I found that not to be true at all. I always felt I could suggest anything to him, though three out of four times he might not accept it, or he might take the idea and change it.

Was there some concern within the industry about the film, as it was a thinly veiled representation of the life of William Randolph Hearst?

My very first trip to New York—I'm from Indiana originally—was in 1940. The purpose of that trip was to take a print of *Citizen Kane,* which we finally had finished—all dubbed, music and everything—to the projection room of Radio City Music Hall and to run it for all the presidents of the film companies. Now, these are the head honchos, not the VPs in charge of production. We had to run *Kane* for them and their lawyers to see whether they felt, as an industry, they would allow RKO to release the picture, or whether they were going to say, "In the interests of our industry, just put this thing on the shelf." That was the whole purpose of the trip.

Orson was there and he gave one of the best performances I've ever seen. I can't give you two words of what he said, but he talked to those gentlemen for at least twenty minutes. It was a marvelous, winning, persuasive performance. We ran the film, and that was it. Nobody said anything. I stayed in New York with the film for six weeks. I had to get some of the actors who were available into a dubbing room and change a few dates, names and lines. We also had to make a few little trims. As soon as I got the work done, I shipped it to the West Coast. They got the changes made and the negative cut, did a dub job, and shipped it back to me. I ran the film again, just for the lawyers this time, and they okayed it, and that's how RKO got the picture into release. But there was a time there when it was up in the air, and we might never have seen it.

Can you think of any specific points in Citizen Kane *on which you and Welles disagreed?*

I really can't say that there were any. The film went very well. You know, it was quite well planned in terms of its continuity, transitions and curtain lines. Some of the special dissolves which are so effective were all planned, so there wasn't much to have a tremendous disagreement about with Orson. I was probably able to bring more to it in some areas than in others. For instance, that remarkable breakfast-table scene. It took weeks of playing around with the film to get a handle on where to start the dialogue and how to achieve the most effective rhythm. It started out as a much straighter sequence than it turned out to be. I think the strongest impression I got from working with Orson was the dynamics and energy he brought to his pictures.

There's a big controversy over who actually wrote Citizen Kane.

I've been asked many times about my evaluation of the Pauline Kael story and I'd simply say, "I don't know."* When I started work on the film, it had already started shooting. Orson had done about three or four scenes. One of them was the scene with the newsreel guys in the projection room, another was the scene coming through the skylight with Dorothy Comingore. These were supposed to be tests that he was making for the film. But after he'd done about four of these, the studio realized that he was actually making the picture. So I guess they just gave him the go-ahead. At that time I had just wound up my work on *My Favorite Wife*. Orson had an old-time editor assigned to those tests and wasn't happy with him, so he asked for somebody else. And I was sent down to interview and ended up on the picture.

During the filming there was never any question about the authorship of the script. There it was, and the names were on it. Herman Mankiewicz was never on the set that I ever saw through the whole picture. So to me the credit question is really pointless because Orson's stamp is so strongly on every frame of that film, and it's academic as to who should get the main credit for the script. I think it's Orson's picture from beginning to end.

How did you move from editing to directing?

I started out working in the film shipping room, working my way up to sound effects editing and music editing for a couple of years. Finally, I got put over on the picture side and became an assistant film editor, and after a couple of years got to be an editor and worked on a number of films at RKO. By this time I had gotten the directing bug. A couple of times I directed added scenes for *The Magnificent Ambersons* and also did new scenes for *Fallen Sparrow,* when Richard Wallace, the director, was unavailable.

*Kael maintains that Herman Mankiewicz wrote the script before Welles was even brought onto the project. See *The Citizen Kane Book* (1971), which includes Kael's essay "Raising Kane."

What do you think the hardest thing was for you to learn coming out of the editing room and becoming a director?

Working with the actors. I learned this just by feel, I guess. Seat of the pants. I took over directing in the middle of a picture, you see. I was editing a little film called *The Curse of the Cat People* for Val Lewton, who was a marvelous producer of small but quality horror films in the 1940s at RKO. It was the director's first feature and he got woefully behind schedule and was told repeatedly by the front office that he had to pick up his shooting pace. There was a really small budget and a very short schedule—a twenty-day shoot—and he couldn't seem to do it. By the time he was halfway through the script, he had used up the whole shooting schedule. So I was called on a Saturday at noon to meet Lewton and was told they wanted me to take over on Monday morning. That was it. So I was thrown right into it. I had no time to sweat or prepare.

I had never had any experience acting myself, but fortunately I knew the actors, as I had been around the set, and found them most cooperative. I did go to some classes. Michael Chekhov, the fine Russian teacher, was giving acting classes at that time, and I spent several evenings before my next film monitoring some of his classes and talking to the actors, and gradually finding my way. When I talk to kids at universities today I say, "If you want to be a director, take some acting classes. Learn how it is on the other side of the camera. You don't have to be an actor, but find out what the process is, what goes on within the actor." It can only do you a lot of good as a director to have had that experience. I didn't have it and I felt the lack of it.

Can you give an example of how your knowledge as an editor helped you when working as a director?

I wanted *Somebody Up There Likes Me* to really move and express the restlessness of Rocky Graziano. I kept pushing Paul Newman to pick his cues up a little faster. Paul never completely grasped what I was getting at. I would say, "Paul, I know the scene feels right to you now, but I'm worried that it's going to lag a little bit. Let's force the tempo just a bit and see if the scene won't be better." I did a very mechanical thing on that picture because I wanted it really to move. I tried not to have a single dissolve or fade-in. I had a whole pattern—when I'd end a sequence, I started the next scene with a close-up of Paul. I also started a technique I have used often since. In order to give that onrushing kind of feeling, I started the dialogue for the incoming scene ten or twelve frames ahead of the actual cut to it to give us a thrust into the scene. I also tried to beat the timing on each sequence by ten percent. It sounds mechanical, I know, but it does work. It's easy to be misled shooting a sequence and then not relate it to the whole picture. In a play you've got a chance to fool around with a sequence, to find the best pacing. But we're down in the cutting room six weeks later and we're stuck with it. Very rarely do we have a chance to go back and reshoot a scene.

As a director, do you find that when you edit sequences together they are very much as you planned them, or do you find yourself eliminating dialogue?

You lose dialogue sometimes, but the sequences generally go together as I planned them. Of course, one of the key people to get my sketches is the editor, so he knows how everything has been planned. But I don't hold him to them. If I feel something comes off particularly well in the rushes—a close-up or a certain reading of a line—I'll mention it to the editor. Other than that, he goes away and makes his own cut, and we work from there.

I saw The Set-Up *a few weeks ago and admired it very much. But I wonder how you would approach it if you were making it today.*

I would probably do one thing you really couldn't think of doing in those days. The original story's leading character was a black fighter, and I'd go back to that. But in those days there wasn't any black movie star with sufficient name value to carry the film. Robert Ryan was under contract to RKO and was dying to do it. He had been the intercollegiate heavyweight champion when he was at Dartmouth. It did quite well critically and it's still thought of highly, but it was not a commercially successful film. Many regard it as the best fight picture; I've been told that many times, anyway. The script, interestingly enough, was based on a long blank-verse poem by Joseph Moncure March. The film had been developed at RKO by producer Richard Goldstone under the reign of Dore Schary. Then Howard Hughes bought the studio and put all productions on the shelf, and Schary left.

I had just been assigned to direct the picture and I was put on layoff, though we were almost ready to start shooting. Sid Rogell, who took over the studio for Hughes, was looking for something to start shooting and he finally pushed Hughes to let us go ahead and make the film. But Rogell never really understood what we were doing. He stopped me one day on the studio street and said, "What in the world do you want to make *The Set-Up* for?" He didn't see the value of it and didn't know what we were getting at. His was a purely hard-nosed viewpoint, and his only interest was to get a picture going under his aegis as head of the studio. He was promoting ours because it was ready to shoot. But he didn't understand it, and I think that was probably a pretty general viewpoint around town.

I would find it very difficult today to get *The Set-Up* going. The smaller film, the film with a strong viewpoint or with a not overly popular subject, is seldom regarded as valid in the market today. You might have a better chance getting something like that on television. As a matter of fact, that's what's happening a lot these days. We read many scripts or properties which we like, but they don't have enough ingredients to sustain a bigger film for the theatrical market. But if you can get something that has a small enough budget—a few hundred thousand dollars—and you manage to scrounge up some independent financing, you take a big fat gamble and go with it. That's still being done, and that may be your best bet. But I think if you went to a studio with *The Set-Up* to try to get money for what it would cost now, you would have trouble getting it made.

What are the major ingredients that a film needs for a major studio to produce it?

You really have to go back to the basics of the story. First, you have to start with something you like yourself that has subject matter and a theme that you want to make. Then you have to look at it to see if potentially it has a wide audience and, hopefully, some strong cinematic possibilities and visual excitement. It doesn't mean that everything has to be big and splashy—like *Hindenburg, Earthquake* or *The Towering Inferno*. There obviously are going to be many fine pictures made that don't have all those ingredients, but these days audiences need something that you can't see on the television set. You have to give an audience something in terms of story, frankness of subject matter and exciting cinematic treatment which will pull them into the movie houses.

West Side Story *had a double directing credit—you and Jerome Robbins. How did you split your duties?*

I'll give you the whole development. Harold Mirisch asked me if I wanted to produce and direct it, and I reacted with great excitement and said, "I'd love it." Robbins, who by contract in the sale of the stage play had the right to do the film choreography, chose not to. He said that he had directed and choreographed the stage show, had done the same for the national company and the English company, and he didn't want to come out to the West Coast just to do the choreography. He wanted to be more deeply involved in the whole production. I said, "Why don't you give it to him, let him direct it." But United Artists thought there was no way they could do that. It was going to be a big, expensive, complex picture, and they were not willing to let a man inexperienced in film direct it.

I thought about it for a while, then put on my producer's hat and said to myself, "What's the very best thing for this picture in terms of the audience?" The answer had to come back, "If you can somehow get Jerry Robbins on this picture, that's the way to go because Jerry is so creative and so inventive." I just knew he would be able to contribute so much more than any of his dance assistants who might come on the film to do the choreography. Jerry would find ways of improving, changing, adapting it for the screen. A period of six months went on with meetings between the two of us, trying to sort out just how we could deal with this.

We finally came to a setup where he would work as codirector and would be involved in all aspects of the film—the script, the production design, the casting, the costumes, the music, the whole thing. When it came to shooting, he would have the deciding voice on the music and dance numbers, and I would have the say on all the "book" aspects of the script. When we had an impasse, I had the final say as the producer of the film. Now Jerry didn't stay on all the way through—he was on over fifty percent of the shooting. We had some rough moments, not too many, but we managed to work them out, though there were a few times when we rather got at each other. But finally we were getting very far behind schedule, and United Artists was very worried. They decided that the tandem arrangement was slowing us down and insisted that I take over the whole show, which I did. However, fortunately for me, Jerry had rehearsed all the dance numbers that remained to be filmed, and his assistants stayed with me to complete the film.

Betty Walberg, who had been on all the rehearsals of *West Side Story,*

also stayed on. Betty was Jerry's rehearsal pianist and general music assistant, and she was an invaluable part of the team he put together to help us
put on the musical numbers. When I finished, I asked Jerry to look at the
first rough cut and he liked much of it, made good suggestions about the
editing on a number of things and wanted to do a little more editing on
some of his numbers. So I think we patched things up fairly successfully.

Did you get the cast that you wanted for the film?

Yes. Any of the criticism that has been thrown at elements of the casting
was my responsibility. Nobody was forced on me, and Jerry was involved
in all the casting decisions.

Would you talk about the difficulty of transposing a stage musical to film?

In *West Side Story* we were taking all the stylized and highly theatrical elements of the stage show and putting them into the realistic medium of
the movie. Those are always the problems you have when you do musicals. The musical form on the stage is a presentation, and you accept that.
Actors break into a dance or break into a song, and nobody in the audience feels uncomfortable because the stage is basically unrealistic. But the
screen is a very realistic medium. Stylized sets just don't work unless your
story is a complete fantasy. So the major problem is to find ways to make
the musical and theatrical parts of the stage show compatible with the
screen, to keep them from being embarrassing.

If you think about *West Side Story*, you realize that from the prologue—with the gang in the playground and their growing dance action
in the streets—through to Tony's song is all daytime. From there on the
balance of the show is at sunset or at night. I felt we needed to open the
film in its milieu, in the real streets, alleys and playgrounds of New York
City. If we could get the whole opening done in real daylight in the real
locations, once we got to the sunset and night sequences, which were all
effect photography, we could accomplish the filming back in the studio or
on the streets of downtown Los Angeles. Jerry agreed with this, but he
said, "You've given me the most difficult task right off the bat: to take my
most stylized dancing in the piece and put it against the most realistic
backgrounds." He struggled with it. We made tests in downtown Los
Angeles streets in daylight. At the Goldwyn Studios we had a rig running
around the studio street, with Betty at a little piano on a trolley with an

Wise (standing left) behind codirector and choreographer Jerome
Robbins (seated), who is discussing a set model for *West Side Story* (1961)
with the production designer Boris Leven (foreground). Standing behind
Leven is associate producer Saul Chaplin.

umbrella over her. She'd be pulled along as she played, and the dancers
would rehearse along the street as Jerry developed and adapted the dance
steps to the outdoors and to the sunlight. He would be changing the
steps, saying, "Try this. Try that."

You wanted a thoroughly realistic setting in New York?

I felt very strong about the New York setting for the opening. We had to
be sure not to do the conventional skyline shot or views from across the
river or from the bridge. That whole helicopter opening of New York—
the delivery, so to speak, of New York—was my idea. And it was done to
show a New York very few people had seen before. We wanted to show
the real New York in a strongly stylized context and eventually to get
down into the playground and to the gang. At that point, Jerry worked
very carefully with the gang. If you recall, one guy would take a step and
then another guy made a dance movement, and gradually they moved
into a dance routine. We felt that by showing the real New York and making it look a little larger, a little different than real life, we would make the

audience accept these dance steps in the streets. We looked for locations that could almost be stage backings. The playground we picked, on East 109th or 110th Street, had a big black wall, and a lot of things were shot against that wall. One key location was where Lincoln Center is now. The block was going to be torn down to make way for the Center, and we got there just before the contractor was to start tearing it down. On one shot in which George Chakiris and three of the Sharks do some dance steps in the foreground, we went very low with the camera and got this big striking background of tenements with their marvelous color and great style. We also used the red front of a fire station on the same street, I think West Sixty-eighth Street. We looked for every opportunity to stage the dance numbers against a real setting that would almost look like a backing on a stage. We wanted to give it that kind of style.

How did you handle the songs?

Ernest Lehman, who did the screenplay, rewrote almost every lead line into the vocals, so that you went into a song as unconsciously as possible. We made some continuity changes that I think were very important. You may not be aware of it, but the "Officer Krupke" number, the comedy routine, was in the second act in the play, and the "Cool" number was in the first act. They did the "Cool" number in Doc's candy store when the kids are getting all revved up, ready to have the talk about the rumble. Ernie Lehman and I said, "Listen, those ought to be reversed. They're in the wrong place. The comedy number ought to be done before we get into the tragedy and heaviness. And that 'Cool' number ought to be later, where the kids have really started to fall apart because of what's happened at the rumble."

I like to start songs in a new and separate camera angle. If I'm doing a dialogue scene and somebody's going into a song, I don't like to have them start the song lyrics in the same angle I've shot my dialogue. I like to cut to a close shot and start the song. I tried to do that every time I could. One of the big problems we had was that great moment in the gym when Tony and Maria discover each other. On the stage, the lights went down on everyone except them. The problem was how to get the quality of being alone in this place in cinematic terms. We fooled with that until we could put them alone in the crowd and make it effective. The treatment that finally ended up in the film was a combination of special lighting on the set and double exposures for vignette effects done on the optical printer by Linwood Dunn.

Are the musical numbers all dubbed? And what is the actual step-by-step sequence after the camera rolls? Is there playback? Is any of the sound recorded live?

Well, there have been whole musicals in recent times when they've done it all live, but that's arduous and expensive. Normally you do it prescored and played back. That goes way back to the beginning of sound. Before I was a film editor I was a sound effects and music editor. I worked on a lot of the Astaire-Rogers films, and those were all prescored, presung and pre-tapped in sessions before you ever get to the set. If it's vocal, it's worked out. If it's a dance number, it's all worked out with a piano, changing and adding on. Only then does the orchestrator come on and work with the piano player and make the lead sheet for the whole number. From that they'll do their orchestrations. A week or two later you'll go on the stage with the forty-piece band or whatever it is.

In the case of *West Side Story,* the music stage was right next to Jerome Robbins' rehearsal stage. He rehearsed all those numbers thoroughly with mock-up sets, and when the orchestra was finally ready to make a take, Jerry would bring his dancers in and they would dance to it. Sometimes he would find the tempo they'd been going at was just a little too fast for his dancers, so he'd ask the musical director to slow it down a little bit or he'd say, "Hey, come on, we can take a little more, make it a little faster." He worked very closely with his dancers to be sure that the tempo was just right. You asked about how it's done. Well, you roll the camera and hit the playback. There are cues and markers for the singers and dancers. One of the tricks to it—something people who have not made musicals are not aware of—is that you can't just mouth the words. The actor has to sing. If you just get up and mouth it and get it nicely in sync, but you're not really singing, it looks like hell.

Would the fact that we aren't hearing Natalie Wood's singing voice in West Side Story *present any special problems?*

Natalie did part of her own singing. She was dying to do the whole thing, and she didn't have a bad voice for the normal range, but she just couldn't handle the higher notes. So the playbacks that she sang back to were partially hers and partially Marni Nixon. Marni is an absolutely sensational talent in terms of really capturing the quality and the expression and the accent of almost anybody. She did Audrey Hepburn in *My Fair Lady.* But then, in the final version we had to replace all of Natalie's voice with Marni's because Natalie just wasn't quite good enough. Marni's a darling lady but she's not very effective on her own. I had occasion to go to a dinner where she sang, and she just doesn't come off. She's got a marvelous voice but the personality doesn't work effectively. However, there's nobody that I've ever known that could do as many variations of her voice as Marni can. Of course the actor or actress is always there when the recording is being dubbed with another voice so they can be sure that it's something that they can handle, that it's the right tempo and the right expression. You don't just take a voice and record it and say to the actor, "Here's what you're going to do."

Were there any camera techniques you used in photographing the dances in West Side Story? *There seems to be a real difference between the dance sequences in that film and those in* Fiddler on the Roof, *which Jerome Robbins also choreographed, where most of the dancers seem to be cut off at their midriff.*

One of the things Jerry always studied in terms of the backgrounds and where the camera was placed was how the dance "read." That's the way he put it—"How does it read? The dance won't be good against that. We've got to do it over here because that background is too busy." So he was always studying angles and background and colors to make his dances read clearly and crisply. If we got a shot without the feet, Jerry went through the roof, so we just didn't do it. He had a very careful and knowing eye. Jerry was like Orson Welles—they both had innate instincts for the camera and for composition. That's part of their artistry. It wasn't like you had a rank amateur coming in. Jerry was an avid still photographer.

I liked your film The Sand Pebbles *very much, though I feel it lost focus in the last part. What are your thoughts on the film today?*

I also liked the film very much. It was a very difficult and complex story to compress, and I worked very hard on that with the screenwriter Robert Anderson, who is a master at construction and in pulling together diverse story lines as well as characters. I think one of the problems with the picture, in retrospect, was that we tried to tell too much of Richard

McKenna's book. I think if I had it to do over again, some of the story lines would probably fall by the wayside. One of my main reasons for making the picture, beyond being fascinated by the China of the period, was a theme which I think was important. I was showing that American military might, displayed around the world, had been unpopular for many years, that the phrase "Yankee, go home" was not just something that came out of post–World War II but had been in existence the whole century. I wanted to remind the American public of this. *Pebbles* came along just at the time when we were starting to get into Vietnam. I was in Vietnam in 1963, looking for locations, and the United States had about twelve thousand "advisers" there. For me, the message of the film was that Vietnam should be seen in this historical context. Maybe that didn't go over strong enough. Maybe that's the lack of focus.

What do you consider the main ingredients in The Sound of Music *that made it such a box-office smash?*

I think they are the obvious ones. The property itself, the score by Rodgers and Hammerstein. The casting of Julie Andrews was very good for us. Our physical production and the locations paid off beautifully. Those were the main, obvious ingredients. But there was one other factor none of us could anticipate that I think was a tremendous plus for us: a matter of timing. *The Sound of Music* just happened to come out when the world was hungry for this kind of warm, emotional family entertainment. It seemed to happen all over the world, with the exception of Germany and Austria, where the film was a bust. I saw the picture play in Japan, I saw it in Hong Kong—and it broke all records. Timing is something you can't write in—it's just there if you're lucky.

On I Want to Live! *you started very far ahead in terms of how music would add to the story.*

Yes. I got into that because Barbara Graham, the lead character, played by Susan Hayward, was known to be terribly fond of music, both jazz and classical. I didn't latch onto how I wanted to do the music until I was in New York on a holiday, before I really started to work on the film. I dropped into a little supper club and there was a lady there named Barbara Carroll, who was a pianist and singer. She was just marvelous. She had a special feeling in her music. I kept finding myself, during the two weeks I was in New York, being drawn back there. I said to my wife, "You know, there's something in that music that relates to Barbara Graham." That was the start of my moving in the direction of doing the pure jazz score with Johnny Mandel.

Normally you don't have your composer work until you finish the picture. But there were several places, one in particular, where I felt that music could help me tell the story. It's when Barbara Graham is in the gambling house, as she tells Emmett Perkins about what she sees in her future, and Perkins builds up a house of cards. I wanted to avoid that obligatory structure of happy marriage, marriage starting to fall apart, and then breakup. I wanted to go from everything being great to everything falling in. So we got the idea of the house of cards. I got Mandel in and I said, "Look, if I move the camera right in on the house of cards as Perkins knocks it over, and I hold on the fallen cards way beyond any normal point and make the audience look and look at it, could you—with your music—tell me about the breakup of the marriage?" He said that he could. And that's what we finally did. Mandel said it was a lovely opportunity. It doesn't often happen that you have a chance to call in a composer and give him such a specific assignment. He helped me tell that story.

I Want to Live! *is about capital punishment. Did you do any particular research before you made the film?*

I think I got more personally involved in that film in many ways than any other I've done. I interviewed a number of people who knew Barbara Graham and got material for the writer. I spoke to the priest who had been at the prison with Barbara. He had quit the prison sometime before and was the parish priest at San Rafael, which is close by. In the course of our conversation, I asked, "How did it happen that you left the prison?" "Well," he said, "Mr. Wise, I don't think you have any idea of the atmosphere that permeates a prison on the day before and the day of an execution. It's just a dreadful atmosphere when you realize that all steps are being taken to end a human life. I just couldn't stand it, and I had to leave." And the lightbulb went on over my head, and I said, "Well, of course this is the clue as to how we dramatize the situation in the film."

I also went to see an execution. I felt like a ghoul when I asked to do it, but I felt if I was going to deal with this subject matter truthfully, I had to know what it was about. I didn't want the critics to be able to say, "Well, that's just some scriptwriter's imagination." So I went to the warden at San Quentin and said, "Listen, I feel a bit strange asking this, but I think if I'm going to treat this the way I want to, and the way it should be done, I have to see an execution." He said, "Listen, I agree with you. I understand your motives. Capital punishment is the law of this state, and I think it's well for the people of this state to see how it works." So I saw the execution of a young black fellow who had been there on death row for a couple of years. Fortunately he was very quiet, and it was unemotional. I didn't know whether I would be able to watch or whether I would get sick. We were inside and there are kind of shutters that you're looking through, and I forced myself to watch it. It took about eight or nine minutes before his body was finally still, and that's what I put up there on the screen.

Could you trace the development of The Hindenburg?

Universal had the property, a book by Michael Mooney, which came out in 1972. A screenplay had been done but the studio wasn't happy with it. They asked me to read the book to see if I was interested, and I got caught up on the totality of the subject: the story about the *Hindenburg,* what might have happened behind the scenes to bring about her tragic end, the whole era of lighter-than-air travel, the experience of flying in a giant zeppelin. But there were two things we would have to tackle right off the bat. Number one, can we reproduce her? How successfully can we bring her back to life and fly her? And number two, can we dramatize the story so it will hold our audience's interest and create suspense for most of a picture that leads toward an end they know is going to happen? Those were the two challenges.

What was your first step?

I talked to the screenwriter, Nelson Gidding, who had done *I Want to Live!* and who is fascinated by airships. He loved the idea, and between us we developed a twenty-five-page approach to the story that we submitted to the studio. They had some questions, but they liked it generally and gave us the word to go ahead. During this time I talked with Al Whitlock, matte artist at Universal and a genius at creating special optical effects— combinations of mattes and miniatures. I said, "Can we do this? Can we successfully have this airship made in Frankfurt, fly her all the way over to Lakehurst and finish her up there?" He felt that it could be done. Then

Nelson prepared a part treatment, part screenplay. The studio liked it, we liked it, and we went into the usual process of one, two, and finally three versions of the screenplay.

Did you settle on a cause for the crash of the Hindenburg?

There has always been a lot of controversy about what caused the accident. Several theories have been advanced—fire, static electricity, sabotage and structural failure. But none of these was proven at the inquiries. Mooney, the author, went to the survivors—the crew and the passengers, here and in Europe. He tracked down everyone he could, got every version, read all the reports of the inquiries and decided that it was an act of sabotage, an anti-Nazi gesture by a young crew member. That provided us with the necessary ingredient to base our dramatization on. It's pretty hard to dramatize something that happens with static electricity.

Are all the characters based on real people?

Some of the characters are real, some are fictionalized. If I had literally told the story of the last flight, with its real people aboard, it would have been pretty humdrum. The captain, Colonel Ritter—the part George C. Scott plays—is based on a real person. The Anne Bancroft part is fictionalized. That was an idea Nelson had. He developed the story of a German countess who was going from Frankfurt to New York and who had known the Scott character sometime in the past. We had no idea that we would have a part for a female star of the stature of Anne Bancroft. But this character, as Nelson wrote it, became so intriguing that people who read the script got fascinated by the relationship between the two characters. We decided to make it more a substantial part without blowing the whole thing up too much.

How did you go about reconstructing the Hindenburg?

I had been going to the Smithsonian and the National Archives, in Washington, getting photographs and everything I could find on the *Hindenburg*. We ended up making a twenty-five-foot miniature, which we shot for most of the flying scenes, and we reproduced endless full-size sections of the actual ship itself as sets: the passenger quarters, the cabins, the lounge, the dining room, the smoking room, the interior of the giant hull, the captain's quarters, the tail, the nose cone, the control car. All the actual drawings and blueprints had been destroyed during the war, but our production designer, Edward Carfagno, found pieces of research here and there—a sketch, a drawing or a detail out of a book. We went to the Berlin Archives, the Deutsches Museum in Munich, and to Friedrich-shafen, where all German dirigibles were built. Nothing's left there these days. Their hangars were all blown up in the war. A little museum at the top of city hall had some pieces of the *Hindenburg*—a large section of the nose cone, a chair, a ladder—and also a lot of photographs that I rephotographed. Carfagno measured some small sections of the shot for detail. A case held a set of the china and the silverware. We photographed them and reproduced those when we got home. Klaus Pruss, son of the captain of the last flight, was most helpful. He gave me a lot of pictures, including small color postcards of the interior of the dining room, the lounge, and the other parts. Before this we had no idea what the colors were. So you see how we had to go around and find bits and pieces in order to get the whole thing together.

How did you handle the explosion?

We used the actual black-and-white newsreel shots of the crash. In spite of the expert technicians we have, there was just no way that we could reproduce the crash to equal the real shots. There had been an attempt before I came on the film to see if they could tint those angles to make them work in color. Though I thought they had done quite a decent job, it wasn't real. You felt the hand of Hollywood had stepped in, and the newsreel shots were so well known that it just seemed wrong. We had already planned to open the picture with a black-and-white newsreel sequence because we found that many of the younger people didn't know what a dirigible was. Then we go into our picture in wide-screen color, up until the time of the explosion and fire.

At that point, my original plan was to slowly, almost imperceptibly, maybe twenty or thirty feet ahead, bleed the color out, down to the moment of the explosion, and then finish the picture in black and white. But it wouldn't work that way. We found, because of the scenes ahead and the cutting involved, that we only had about a six- or seven-foot piece in which to take the color out, and that was no good. It happened too fast and was obvious. We decided the best thing to do was to go in color right up to the explosion and, as Al Whitlock says, "Let the explosion wipe the color out entirely." In other words, the color screen goes white with the explosion and comes back in black and white. The *Hindenburg* actually went down in thirty-four seconds. That's not much of a sequence on the screen, so we had to devise a way of making this into a major sequence. What we did was take a newsreel shot and go so far, stop and hold the frame for maybe three or four feet, but inside, show a certain amount of action with a group of characters, and then come back outside to another newsreel shot, stop at another point, hold frame, and so on. In this fashion we have built the crash into a ten-minute sequence.

How do you work with screenwriters?

We have a thorough session to start with so we know that our thinking is generally in accord. If it's a novel, we make a breakdown of the important scenes and have several weeks of back-and-forth talk. During this time, the writer may develop an outline for me to respond to. But once we have our sights on it, the writer goes off and does his script. I know one producer in town who requires every twenty pages of the script as the writer goes along. But I don't. Once I have the whole first draft, we have script sessions, battle it out, change it, and out of that will come another script.

How do you go about your day-to-day shooting?

I think that beyond a director's artistic and creative abilities, there are two things that he must be very aware of: anticipation and communication. Which is to say, anticipating what you want the next day or the next week, and communicating those needs to your staff and crew. I do preparation for my day-to-day shooting early each morning. I go to bed early and get up early and go through my scheduled day's work, laying out my notes for the day. Some of them have to do with the shooting continuity, others will be for the crew or to the staff.

Is the blocking of the actors and cameras worked out ahead?

The Set-Up was all sketched except for the fights themselves, and they were all choreographed weeks ahead. *The Hindenburg* was the most complex picture I've ever worked on in terms of keeping in mind where I was in the script and in the ship itself. I had to refer to my sketchbook and my script more often than on any picture because of its complexity. But it's another thing when the actors get in there. They might come up with an idea that varies from the set blocking and sketching. You always leave room for those dividends. Usually I'll give the actors a rough blocking for action, tell them where entrances are, explain their movements in relation to the camera and then let them go and build the scene. I don't dictate; I'll bend as much as the idea helps to improve the scene. I'm open to all suggestions. You don't really know the full texture of a scene until the actors are in there doing it. As they do it, they find things that we could never find when writing in an office.

Working with Paul Newman on *Somebody Up There Likes Me* was interesting. Paul would get an idea for something—a little switch or change, something he wanted to do—and on the surface I would say, "No, I don't think that's right, Paul. Forget it," and we'd go on. But I learned very quickly that he couldn't forget it—it was stuck in his craw. So I found it was simpler with him to let him try it and then prove to himself that it was not good. Sometimes I was wrong and it would be good, and it got so I would say, "Well, okay, I don't think it's very good, but who knows? Let's give it a whirl."

How did you develop the fight choreography in Somebody Up There Likes Me?

Paul and Rocky [Graziano] and I spent days and a lot of evenings together in New York. We studied Rocky and his speech patterns, his movements, his restlessness. We would have the fight described in the script, and I brought in a very fine ex-fighter called Johnny Indrisano, who started a profession for himself of staging prizefights. He would break down the fights as written in the script and give me a little outline of what the round would be, and we would talk it over. I would suggest maybe he had too much of this or that, and then he would go off with the actors and rehearse and choreograph. I was shooting *The Set-Up* at the time, but after shooting I would drop by and comment on Johnny's work, and tell him what I thought, whether I liked this or didn't like that. We would change and build up the rounds.

I had a funny experience on *Somebody Up There Likes Me*. Tony Zale had fought Graziano in those three famous fights. He was in Chicago with the Catholic Youth Center, and somebody said, "I know it's been a number of years, but Tony has kept himself in marvelous shape, and I think he'll be able to play a part." So on a trip from New York, I stopped off in Chicago and saw Tony to talk about the possibility of him working with us. So he came out and played himself in the film. Paul had never done a fight picture before, and he as far as I know he hadn't done any boxing at all. So I was shooting some other stuff on the picture, and Johnny was working with Paul and Zale on one of the stages at MGM. After they had worked a couple of sessions, one of my associates came and said, "Listen, I think you ought to drop down there and take a look, because I think you've got some problems." It turned out that Paul was a little gun-shy of this guy Tony. He didn't quite know what to do. Paul was afraid that if he accidentally clipped Tony, a fighter's reflex reaction would be to coldcock him. I could understand Paul's point. Who wants to be belted by Tony Zale? Fortunately there was a club fighter around town, a guy that looked very much like Tony, so eventually we had to go to Tony and say, "Thank you very much." He was very upset.

Do you rehearse before starting to shoot a picture?

Rehearsals are fine, and I've had a few chances to have really good rehearsals three, four or five days before I started to shoot. One of the problems with rehearsing for films is that very often you have a large cast with actors starting on the picture at different times in the schedule. I do try, at least, to sit down with the main cast and read through the script to hear the words and get a sense of the characters. I have the writer there to listen to the actors read the lines and make suggestions for changes. I did that with *The Andromeda Strain*. On *Somebody Up There Likes Me* we were able to do actual rehearsals. We had a group of actors starting at the beginning, including Paul Newman, and we rehearsed about three days and then shot for a period. Then we picked up a new group of actors and repeated. We did that about three times on the show. But it's luxury, in my experience, to have a preshooting rehearsal period. *Executive Suite* has a big three- or four-reel sequence in the boardroom of a big corporation. We stopped shooting, rehearsed that whole boardroom sequence for a day and then started shooting it the next day. Occasionally you do that if you have a big chunk of the picture in one place and you have all of your actors there.

Do you get different results than you expected from the rehearsals?

Some actors like to rehearse, others don't. With some, you really never find out what you're going to get from them until you start rolling your camera.

How do you deal with actors and actresses who prefer not to rehearse?

Sometimes I end up shooting eight or ten takes to get to the point where I think the scene is right. But if I'd had good, full rehearsals, I might have done it in two or three takes.

How much improvisation do you like from your actors?

A moderate amount. I don't say, "Well, let's forget the script and the sketches and let's see what we can play around with." I don't approach it that way. But if an actor feels comfortable saying his lines in a little different fashion, as long as it is not out of context with the theme or character or will not change the plot, that's perfectly fine with me.

What's the main advantage to being your own producer?

When you are director only, most times the first draft of the script is done when you come on. Some of the casting may already be done, and you have to accept that when you come on. But if you are also the producer, you're involved in who the screenwriter's going to be and in working with him on the first draft. You have that chance to be in on the ground floor. You have to see the film finished all the way. You get involved in the very important aspects of the release, the distribution and promotion. So you have continuity from the very beginning to the very end, right into the theaters.

I found the pacing of the movie Star Trek *very slow, especially the long shots of the model ships. What was your intention with those long, slow shots?*

Well, that's an example of how over close you can get to a film when you don't have enough perspective on it. That was my thirty-eighth film, and the first I didn't have a sneak preview on. If we'd had previews and seen it with an audience, we would have gotten some much-needed perspective and then come back and edited those shots down. They were very overextended, but we fell in love with them. We thought they held attention, and it wasn't until opening night in Washington that we realized they just went on too long. As a matter of fact, the editor and I had more than three minutes we could have removed very simply—the introduction going up to the *Enterprise*. But the studio wouldn't let us do it because we had a thousand prints already made and they were afraid it would get out that we were nervous about the picture. That's as specific an example as I can give you on the value of the sneak preview. You get a whole new look at the film when you take it out with an audience.

Some of your films carry political themes, for example, The Sand Pebbles *and* The Sound of Music. *How do you dramatize them?*

They work their way in. I call it a by-product to your basic story. But I've been taken apart by some people who say it's not a by-product but an added product. I think they're right. Out of the book of *The Sand Pebbles* I got a strong antimilitary theme. I liked the fact that *The Sound of Music*, in some ways a sentimental story, did have its point to make about the Nazis. I think you're better off to let your points come out as part of the story development and the characters rather than getting on a soapbox. To me, *I Want to Live!* is a case in point. It's a pretty heavy piece, but we didn't say, in so many words, "Capital punishment is wrong and we should end it!" We felt that if the picture itself didn't say it, we had failed. As a matter of fact, I had an argument with Joe Mankiewicz, whose company we made it for. Just before we started to shoot, he attended the last script session and at the end he said, "I think in that scene at the finish between the lawyer and the newspapermen, you really have to make your point about capital punishment." "Joe," I said, "that's crazy. If this picture itself doesn't indict capital punishment, I don't think anything we say at the end of the film is going to do it." He insisted, and we cooked up something that we shot but never put in the picture.

The main thing is not to pump away heavily at the theme. Let that come out through your characters and the development of the story. That would be my principle. I hope I have never violated it too much. I make these films for myself, but I also make them for audiences. If you have something you feel it is important for your film to say, it's only as valuable as the number of people who see your film. If you make a film that's so

Wise shot much of *The Sound of Music* (1965) at outdoor locations in Austria.
On the set with Julie Andrews.

special and so lacking in general audience interest that only two hundred thousand people see it rather than twenty million, then you haven't really gotten your message over. The thing that's most important about films, the aspect that has really caught me up as much as anything, is the universality of the language of film. If you have made films and then see them in another country and witness the audience's responses, they react so much the same as they do here. I went to a couple of showings of *The Sound of Music* in Japan and it was wonderful to sit there and see the same kind of response from those Japanese audiences toward the things of the heart. It's one of the pluses of the motion picture, and of television too—getting the message over, getting it all around the world. It doesn't seem to be helping a helluva lot, but we must keep trying to get more understanding between peoples, between nations.

———◀▶———

Films as Director

1944 *The Curse of the Cat People*
      Mademoiselle Fifi
1945 *The Body Snatcher*
      A Game of Death
1946 *Criminal Court*
1947 *Born to Kill*
1948 *Mystery in Mexico*
      Blood on the Moon
1949 *The Set-Up*
1950 *Three Secrets*
      Two Flags West
1951 *The House on Telegraph Hill*
      The Day the Earth Stood Still
1952 *The Captive City*
      Something for the Birds
1953 *Destination Gobi*
      The Desert Rats
      So Big
1954 *Executive Suite*
1956 *Helen of Troy*
      Tribute to a Bad Man
      Somebody Up There Likes Me
1957 *This Could Be the Night*

      Until They Sail
1958 *I Want to Live!*
      Run Silent, Run Deep
1959 *Odds Against Tomorrow* (also producer)
1961 *West Side Story* (co-director and producer)
1962 *Two for the Seesaw* (also co-producer)
1963 *The Haunting* (also producer)
1965 *The Sound of Music* (also producer)
1966 *The Sand Pebbles* (also producer)
1968 *Star!*
1971 *The Andromeda Strain* (also producer)
1973 *Two People*
1975 *The Hindenburg* (also producer)
1977 *Audrey Rose*
1979 *Star Trek: The Motion Picture*
1989 *Rooftops*

It would be unthinkable for a writer to tell a director how to direct or a producer how to produce or an actor how to act or a cinematographer how to light a scene. But it is not at all unthinkable for anyone to tell a writer how to write. It comes with the territory.

ERNEST LEHMAN
(Born in New York, New York, 1915—Died 2005)

Ernest Lehman is a man well suited to represent screenwriters in this volume. He had a distinguished career crafting screenplays and was an ardent advocate of the importance of the screenwriter. He was a persistent voice condemning auteur-theory critics who mentioned the director but not the writer in reviews, stating, "I disclaim the authorship to a film for anyone who has not also written it." He was known to telephone reviewers at home and demand to know why the screenwriter's name had been omitted in their articles.

Lehman was born in New York City and raised in the luxurious suburb of Woodmere, Long Island. When the Depression hit, the family was forced to move to an apartment in New York, where Lehman studied writing at City College and worked as a copy editor and Broadway publicist. He wrote eighty short stories and novelettes that were published in *Collier's, Cosmopolitan* and other magazines.

When one of his stories was sold to *Playhouse 90*, Lehman was invited to join Paramount as a contract screenwriter in 1952. Almost immediately he was lent out to MGM to write *Executive Suite*. While he was working at MGM, Paramount failed to renew his option, but he was soon back at the studio to write *Sabrina* for Billy Wilder. He then moved on to Twentieth Century Fox to adapt *The King and I* for the screen.

In 1957 the independent company run by Harold Hecht and Burt Lancaster bought the film rights to *Sweet Smell of Success*, a novelette Lehman had written based on his experiences behind the scenes in the New York theater world. Lehman was hired to write the screenplay. It was originally intended that he direct the film, but the studio had second thoughts and

Ernest Lehman in front of the set built at Twentieth Century Fox for *Hello,
Dolly!* (1969). Lehman wrote the screenplay based on the Broadway musical
and served as producer.

brought in Alexander Mackendrick to direct and Clifford Odets to rewrite
Lehman's script. This was Lehman's baptism in the hard knocks of the system
where the writer has little control and may be subjected to a range of indigni-
ties. Lehman told of one such event when Humphrey Bogart took exception
to his presence on the set of *Sabrina.* The actor snarled, "Get the City College
writer out of here and send him back to Monogram where he belongs."

Lehman's credits include major successes such as *Executive Suite, Somebody Up There Likes Me* and *From the Terrace,* all adapted from books; *The
King and I, West Side Story, The Sound of Music* and *Hello, Dolly!,* adapted
from Broadway musicals; and *Who's Afraid of Virginia Woolf?,* from the
Edward Albee play. His only original screenplay proved to be his most mem-

orable *North by Northwest,* directed by Alfred Hitchcock. Even though he was active as a screenwriter for several decades, he ended up with only fifteen screen credits. There is no way to know how many of his scripts were abandoned, rejected or passed on to other writers.

Lehman finally got his opportunity to direct with *Portnoy's Complaint.* The film, based on his screenplay of the Philip Roth novel, proved unsuccessful and ended Lehman's directorial aspirations. "I'm sure there were some scenes that were poorly directed, but that wasn't why it didn't work," he explained. "It didn't work because as a screenwriter, I never found the right way, if there was one, to dramatize the novel into a film."

The screenwriter's life in Hollywood can be frustrating because writers rarely have control, except for those who become directors and gain greater authority, such as John Huston, Billy Wilder and Richard Brooks. Lehman fought the good fight for fairer recognition of the writer's contribution, but in the end he himself summed up the emotional hardships faced by the screenwriter—"He lives with the constant knowledge that somebody can say, 'I don't like this. Screw it. We're getting another writer.'"

ERNEST LEHMAN

———

March 31, 1976*

How did you become a screenwriter?

I was a short-story writer in New York. A couple of my novelettes, including *Sweet Smell of Success,* brought me to the attention of Paramount Pictures. Their New York office contacted my agent and asked if I was
interested in writing for film. I was very interested, and Paramount
brought me and my family out to California. I've been out here ever since.

*You've written screenplays for some highly regarded directors: Mike Nichols, Alfred
Hitchcock, Robert Wise. They're also very demanding directors. How well have
you survived these encounters?*

There is a long pause here before I answer this question. You've hit a sore
spot in the life of any screenwriter, including this one. My most easygoing
relationship was with Robert Wise, with whom I did four pictures,
though even with him I had my moments here and there. The screenwriter winds up for the most part in an antagonistically cooperative or
cooperatively antagonistic relationship with everyone he's working with:
the producer, the director—even the actors, if they're intellectual types
like Paul Newman or Burt Lancaster. Almost everyone unconsciously
feels he knows as much about writing as a writer. It would be unthinkable
for a writer to tell a director how to direct or a producer how to produce

*This transcript includes extracts from the AFI seminar with Ernest Lehman held on October
22, 1985.

or an actor how to act or a cinematographer how to light a scene. But it is not at all unthinkable for anyone to tell a writer how to write. It comes with the territory.

Now that is bound to produce problems, unless you have a superlatively integrated psyche so that you can take anything and always remember that it's the picture that counts. But your ego, your sense of professionalism, come into play, and you often notice a glaze coming into the eyes of the director and the producer when the script is finished. You get the subtle feeling that they would not weep if you got hit by a truck. I'm not exaggerating. Somehow the mere fact that the director didn't write the picture—he's only directing it—is very difficult for him to take, and some of them have never learned to take it. It's equally difficult for the producer. I've been a writer-producer on three pictures. After you've struggled with the script, done some of the casting, and somehow it has been your picture, in comes the director. Once that picture starts shooting he's the captain of the 747, and it's pretty tough to move to the back of the plane and just sit there, particularly if you see things you don't like in the dailies. Sometimes it gets to be an antagonistic relationship, to put it mildly.

Can a writer ever have the upper hand in these confrontations?

The only way that a writer can have the upper hand is to write something that is so unfailingly, unarguably perfect that there's just no way that anybody can take any objection to it. The problem is, who the hell knows whether it's that good, including the writer? It's a very inexact science. Everybody has an opinion. My advice is to be smart enough or lucky enough in all these creative battles to lose the right battles. I have been very lucky. I have fought for things that would have been awful if I had won, and I have fought for things which other people didn't want and was lucky enough to win. But I don't know what the rules are.

You have to understand that people feel threatened by a writer. It's very curious. He knows something they don't know. He knows how to write, and that's a subtle, disturbing quality that he has. Some directors, without even knowing it, resent the writer in the same way that Bob Hope might resent the fact that he ain't funny without twelve guys writing the jokes. The director knows that the script he is carrying around on the set every day was written by someone, and that's just not something that all directors easily digest.

You've adapted a number of stage works, particularly musicals, like The Sound of Music *and* West Side Story. *What difference do you find between what works on stage and what works on the screen?*

I would say that sometimes a play that is nondramatic, without conflict, without any narrative drive, can work in the theater because it will have other things going for it which somehow engage the audience. Particularly musicals. They can be nothing but fluff, pure fluff—like *Hello, Dolly!*—and if they're dazzlingly directed and choreographed, they can be a great evening in the theater.

The film medium is a little more demanding. *Who's Afraid of Virginia Woolf?* had certain sections on the stage that were marvelous because of the language and the ideas that were being expressed. But somehow or other, even as I saw the play and was knocked out by it, I felt there was a digression from the direction of the story line. I felt that on the screen these things were not permissible.

In the case of *West Side Story*, it was a highly dramatic story on the stage, and it lent itself admirably to film adaptation. But I rearranged it quite a bit to keep the dramatic line very clean, and I moved around musical numbers. If you study the stage version, you'll find there are some significant changes in the placement of the numbers. For example, "Cool" worked beautifully in the film, I think, because it took place after the rumble, when the Jets were distraught as a result of the death of Riff. In the play, "Cool" was done before they met with the Sharks to arrange the rumble, and "I Feel Pretty" was the first musical number after the rumble. I made those changes to create and sustain a dramatic mood. I felt "I Feel Pretty" was a happy number that would take the audience completely out of the mood after two bodies are seen lying on the ground. I felt it was much more appropriate for that number to take place in the film when Maria was happy at the thought of meeting Tony that afternoon in the bridal shop.

You were trying to keep a certain realism even within the confines of a musical?

Right. When you're writing a musical for the screen, one of the big tricks is to find out, first of all, how to lead into the numbers in a way that catches an audience by surprise so it doesn't suspect it's hearing a lead-in to a musical number. And second, the biggest feat of all, if you can get away with it, is to make it seem natural that there is dancing or singing in something as realistic or dramatic as, let's say, *West Side Story.* I'm sure you've heard about all the agonizing that Robert Wise and Jerome Robbins went through before finally deciding that the best way to approach the prologue was to shoot it out on the streets realistically. The gang gradually goes from just strolling along and finger snapping to slight dance movements and then to a full number. That set up a lot of belief on the part of the audience in all the musical elements that followed. But each musical has its own problems in being brought to the screen.

Do you have a general pattern you follow in adapting a musical? For example, do you concentrate on the story and weave in the numbers?

I don't think I go at it too formally. I've adapted *The King and I, The Sound of Music, West Side Story, Hello, Dolly!* Usually I see the show three or four or five times and I begin to get ideas as I'm watching. I think, why the hell did they put that number *there?* I know it's working, and this is a famous Broadway musical, but I wonder if they ever realized that it would have been so much more effective *there!* For example, "Gee, Officer Krupke," in *West Side Story.* That's a hilarious number. But on the stage, "Gee, Officer Krupke" took place in the second act, after the rumble had happened. To me that was totally out of dramatic context.

Apparently it was perfectly all right for a Broadway audience to break into laughter at this funny number, even though the audience was supposed to be caught up in the terrible drama. But I don't think it would have worked in a movie. It may be immodest of me to say so, but I think "Gee, Officer Krupke" fit perfectly where it was placed in the movie. The Jets were quite nervous, they were going to meet the Sharks in the candy store, and all it took was a policeman coming along and telling them to get off the street to get them into a bitter, defiant, funny number.

Another example: the number "America" on the stage was purely about conditions in Puerto Rico. These were Puerto Ricans, transplanted to New York, singing about conditions in Puerto Rico. I thought it would be much more appropriate if the number were about the conditions the Puerto Ricans encountered in America. So Saul Chaplin and I wrote a letter to Steve Sondheim. We sent him some dummy lyrics suggesting what we thought the song ought to be. The music remained the same, the dancing was pretty much the same, although it was filled out more by putting it up on a rooftop, but the lyrics now made a statement that was much more pertinent. In approaching a film musical you have certain guideposts. You know you've got to somehow get to the well-known numbers, unless they happen to be something that you're going to throw out of the movie. In fact, we did throw a few things out of *West Side Story*.

In *The Sound of Music* I did a lot of changing around of musical numbers. There, again, it seemed somehow inappropriate for the mother abbess to be singing "My Favorite Things." I felt how much more appropriate it was for Maria to try to pacify the children, who were frightened by the thunderstorm, and to tell them what she does when she gets upset. She thinks about some other favorite things, and before you know it you're into the number. Much more appropriate. But musical numbers are what you must get to, and they shape your work in that way.

Most of your screenplays have been adaptations. North by Northwest, *instead, was an original. What problems did that pose?*

It was fun in a way but it was extremely difficult. I recall having tried to quit that picture at least a dozen times, unknown to Mr. Hitchcock, who was off shooting *Vertigo* while I was writing the first seventy-odd pages. I never knew what the hell I was going to write next. I used to go to my office and be scared to death because I just didn't know what came next. I would write an opening scene and then the next scene. Some days I wouldn't write anything. It was a lonesome and scary experience because I didn't have anyone to talk to. Occasionally I would talk to Hitch, who was very helpful as we would bounce ideas off each other. Then I would go back to my office at MGM and call my agent and tell him, "I quit."

One day Hitchcock said, "I've always wanted to do a chase across the face of Mount Rushmore." Terrific, I thought, and wrote it down. He told me all the ideas he wanted to do, and I wrote them down. Lots and lots of ideas. He wanted to do a sequence with the longest dolly shot in history, taking place at the assembly line of the Ford Motor Company. It would start at the beginning of the assembly line. The camera follows a car being put together before it's driven off the assembly line and they discover there's a body in the backseat. He always wanted to do a scene in the General Assembly of the United Nations. Somebody is giving a speech to the Assembly and refuses to continue until the delegate from Peru wakes up. So someone taps the delegate from Peru, and he falls over dead. I wrote all these ideas down, but the only idea that is actually in the picture is the chase across Mount Rushmore. I also wrote out a list of possible protagonists, like a Frank Sinatra–type singer, or a famous sports announcer, or a newspaper man or a Madison Avenue advertising executive. I decided the easiest thing for me to write was the Madison Avenue advertising executive, not because I knew any, but because I know how to stereotype him.

Then we moved over to Hitchcock's office at Paramount where he was working on *Vertigo*. We wasted a lot of time talking about the pleasantries of life. One day he told me something rather crucial, that a newspaperman in New York had told him that something like the CIA had once invented a decoy, a nonexistent agent, to throw the scent off a real agent. I thought that sounded good. Our hero, whoever he is, could be mistaken for this decoy. That I liked. I wrote the script page by page, scene by scene, never knowing what was coming next. The only thing I knew for sure was that we wanted to end up on Mount Rushmore, which is my least favorite part of the film, though most people remember it for that. I got only about one-tenth of the way through the story when Hitch gathered all the MGM executives together and told them everything we had. At the point where he ran out of story outline, he told them he had to go and that he'd see them at the preview. That was it.

Then Hitchcock arrived at MGM and he signed Cary Grant and fixed a starting date. Here I am, sweating my way through a first draft, and I still didn't know what the whole third act would be. I was so desperate I called Hitch and said I needed to see him. I think he could sense how things were because he didn't say, "Come down to my office." He said, "I'll come down to your office." We met and I told him the truth. I said, "I'm totally stuck. I haven't written a word in two weeks. It's a disaster. What do we do?" He said, "We'll call in a novelist to sit with us and kick around some ideas." I said, "What will MGM say? I'm supposed to be writing this movie." He said, "I'll tell them it's my fault." I felt very guilty. We went down to his office and he talked about which novelist to get. It was a very gloomy scene.

But I'm sitting there, and it's not as if I wasn't listening to him, but in the middle of this gloomy conversation I said, "Suppose he pulls out a gun and shoots him. Fake bullets. In a minute I'll figure out why." My brain must have been working for months on this without my knowing it, because suddenly it became clear to me what the third act would be. Eva Marie is forced to shoot Cary Grant to draw suspicions away from herself because James Mason was beginning to wonder about her, then Marty Landau would discover the gun and the fake bullets, and only Cary Grant would know that her life was in danger. And it sort of got easy. I left the office and never again was there any mention of bringing anyone else in. I continued writing through the shooting of the film up until Chicago. Then I went back to California and continued working on the final script. Then I went up to Bakersfield where the crop-dusting sequence took place.

North by Northwest *has a field day in the variety of locations. Did you choose all the locations first?*

No. There was a lot of discussion between Hitch and myself, months and months of talk, and a vague idea as to where the story was moving, up to a certain point. At that point he went off to make *Vertigo,* and I went off on a research trip. In fact, I went through quite a few of the adventures that Cary Grant eventually went through. I hadn't written the screenplay yet, so I didn't know some of the locations.

I went to the United Nations and spent five days there just getting the feel of the place and trying to figure out what would be a good place for a murder. I finally decided that the Delegates' Lounge, which I call the Public Lounge in the screenplay, was a great place. Then I went out to Glen Cove on Long Island, because I knew the Russian delegation to the United Nations lived in a mansion there. I hung around Glen Cove, got introduced to a local judge and said that I wanted him to put me through the whole routine of being picked up for drunken driving. He did it, and it was fun. Then I hung around Grand Central Station a bit, got on the Twentieth Century Limited and went to Chicago. I also looked around the train and picked up ideas, though I didn't run into Eva Marie Saint. From there I went to Rapid City, South Dakota, hired a forest ranger on his day off and said, "I want to climb to the top of Mount Rushmore to see what's up there." I got halfway to the top. It's really perilous and steep. I looked down and I thought, What the hell am I doing here? One slip and you're finished. I'm a writer. I told him, "I'm not going another step."

I bought the ranger a Polaroid camera, and he went up the next day and photographed the top because I wanted to see what was up there. There is nothing up there, nothing. In fact, you can't even stand up on the top. That was bad news. I also spent time in the park and the cafeteria and thought it would be a great place for a sequence. Eventually, we just constructed the top of Mount Rushmore at MGM. The U.S. Department of Parks kicked us out before we could begin shooting, so everything but one long shot of Mount Rushmore was built on a soundstage.

Did you have any censorship problems with the film?

The Production Code office, which was in control of censorship, made us dub a word into the dining car scene with Eva Marie. I had written, "I never make love on an empty stomach." That was the line. Big deal. When the picture was released, the word "discuss" had to be put in—"I never discuss love on an empty stomach." That's the way the picture is. You can hear her mouth say "make," but she actually says "discuss."

You've said that you feel the plot of North by Northwest *is full of holes.*

Once I decided Cary Grant had been mistaken for a nonexistent man called George Kaplan, my first problem was how to do this. It's a very hairy thing in this film. I once showed the film to a class at Dartmouth College. After we ran it, I asked them how many understood how he had been mistaken for George Kaplan, and only half of the students said they understood. It wasn't really done properly in the film, either by me or Hitch. It was a little too subtle.

Was the crop-dusting sequence your idea?

Hitch and I acted out the entire crop-dusting sequence in his living room. Then I incorporated every move into the script, and that was the way he shot it.

It's such a visual scene that it doesn't seem the kind of scene a writer would choose.

It seems visual, therefore, the writer has nothing to do with it. Is that what you're trying to say? That is utter nonsense. Let me tell you something, as long as I'm sitting up here on this high horse. Read the first page of the screenplay of *The Sound of Music,* which describes the opening of the film. It was the first time I used the first person singular in a screenplay. I just said, "Here's what I want to see on the screen. Here's the effect I want." *I* want. And you know what? I got it.

Hitchcock is famous for planning all his shots ahead of time, for preparing story-boards. In North by Northwest *and in* Family Plot, *how much did you partici-pate in this kind of detailed planning?*

Storyboarding is really an illustrator's work for the director. A motion picture illustrator puts pictures on paper and puts them on boards. In storyboarding a script for a Hitchcock film, the illustrator is told what pictures to put on the boards by the script, which has benefited from my conferences with the director. Of course, I participate in what is going to appear on that storyboard, because even without the storyboard the script describes exactly what is going to be on the screen. Hitch would have it no other way. The script even describes the size of the shot, whether it's a medium or a tight close-up, whether the camera pulls back and pans to the right as the character walks toward the door, whether it tilts slightly down and shoots through the open doorway, getting the helicopter as the lights go on outside. That's why Hitch says it's a bore for him to get the picture on the screen, because it has all been done already in his office.

In constructing characters, for Hitchcock or others, are you partly guided by what actors are available to play them?

Not usually. But two things come to mind. *North by Northwest* was written more or less with Cary Grant in mind. Jimmy Stewart thought he was going to play the role, and he kept calling up to ask, "How are you fellows coming?" But we really wanted Cary Grant. Halfway through writing the first draft, I knew that the picture was for Cary Grant, and so I tailored the role to suit him, though he complained to me all through the film that it wasn't a Cary Grant film, it was a David Niven film. Jimmy Stewart would have taken too long to deliver that dialogue. But I was actually tailoring the whole thing for the real star—Alfred Hitchcock. There are twenty different ways of doing a movie, but if you know you're doing a film for Hitchcock, the villains should all be suave, there's very little violence, there should be some wit, even when you're killing somebody.

The other thing that comes to mind is the new Hollywood. While I was writing the script of *Black Sunday*, Bob Evans, the producer, kept saying, "You'll have to do something with this role or we'll never get one of the superstars to play it." In other words, the role had to be juicy enough or have enough passion in it to appeal to certain stars, because Bob wanted big stars. He showed one of my drafts to Dustin Hoffman, knowing that Hoffman would not be available for the picture. Bob came to me and said, "Dusty thinks that you have to do so-and-so and so-and-so with that character." I said, "What the hell does Dusty have to say about what I do with that character?" He said, "Well, he's an actor, and he knows what will appeal to other actors, and we want an important actor." Now, Bob was being a good producer from his point of view. It irritated me a little bit, but I could see his point of view. It's hard to get a good actor if there isn't a good role. If you're looking for Jack Nicholson, you'd better have a pretty powerful role, because everybody is looking for Nicholson.

Is it possible to say what qualities you look for in a novel when you go about making the decision whether or not to adapt it to the screen?

The first thing I do is put on the hat of a studio head or the head of a distribution company and say to myself, Is there something about this that might grab audiences? Motion pictures are an art form but also a business. Then the second thing that comes to mind is whether there is something about this that appeals to me as a writer? The third thing I think of is, Do I believe I have the ability to do this? Can I bring this one off? Do I have what it takes? You know, I can't do everything. *Portnoy's Complaint* is a perfect example of biting off more than I could chew. I had no idea how I intended to do it. All I knew was that I wanted to do it. I felt that it would be an enormous hit if it were done well. But, as it turned out, I didn't know how to do it.

So I look for these things first of all, because many projects from prominent producers or producer-directors or heads of studios come into my hands. I read the material and think, What the hell do they want to make that for? It doesn't have a chance. Either it can't be dramatized and they don't know it because they're not writers, or no one is going to see the movie. I don't tell them that. I just say that it doesn't seem to be right for me. But I'm always astonished at the decisions nonwriters make. Some of them don't realize that the projects they have fallen in love with are probably unlickable.

You mentioned Portnoy's Complaint. *What mistake do you think you made in adapting Philip Roth's novel?*

My mistake was in thinking that I had the ability to find a screen drama in that novel. Without being all that formal, a film should have a first, second and third act. I think the beauty of that novel is not in its dramatic potentialities. The novel was first-person singular, somebody lying on a couch talking to his analyst. Some of the very best of it was interior. Some of it could be dramatized, some of it couldn't. I would say a novel which is very, very interior probably is not going to make it as a film. There may be exceptions.

In other words, Portnoy's Complaint *was an impossible job?*

Let's say it was impossible for *me* to do. Charles Champlin, the critic of the *Los Angeles Times,* wrote that he felt that nobody could have done it successfully. But I don't see how anybody could say that. Everyone thought the screenplay was excellent. It read very well. There are those who think perhaps the film might have been better if someone else had directed it instead of me. We'll never know.

Portnoy's Complaint was the wrong kind of picture for me to have chosen to direct for the first time. If I had chosen something which was more visual and less impossible, I might have, let's say, gotten by and been thought of as a potential director. In fact, it was a great personal experience until the picture opened, and I don't mean that as a joke. It really was a very heady experience. I don't seem to have any burning desire to go back to the problems of directing. Believe me, film directing is a hell of a lot more than it seems to be, including incredible physical endurance. Not all writers can be directors, not by a long shot.

Did the problems in directing Portnoy's Complaint *have to do with technical matters or with the actors?*

No, I had none of those problems, really. I shot the whole film on paper first. I took nine months and shot every master shot, every two-shot, every over-the-shoulder, every close-up, every tricky transition shot—everything, with a sketch artist. I had three sketch artists at one time, and I shot the whole film on paper. When we went out location hunting we would take the sketchbooks along and say, "Well, we've got to find a place that's like this. Oh, Nazareth. That would be great for that shot." Or when art director Robert Boyle was designing the sets he would look at how I was going to shoot the scene and say, "Let's see now. No, the door can't be over there. It's got to be over here. Ernie wants to come down in a dolly shot starting in her bedroom and taking her through a corridor and down the steps and over to the table, to have her lean down, open a ciga-rette box and then walk left to right over to the bar. And he wants the camera to be able to dolly over to the bar and hold her and Dick Benjamin in a two-shot." They had to build a set that would permit that, so I never really had to do any homework at night because it was all done. I never had to walk out on a set and have people look at me and say, "Well, what do we do now?" I never had any technical problems, though I had some problems dealing with actors.

Getting them to give the results you were after?

Either that, or my trying to understand what was good and what wasn't. I had never worked with actors before, except as a writer. I can tell a poorly directed scene on the screen when I see one, particularly if it's something I've written and I know what's supposed to be there and isn't there. I know that the director didn't get the point or he went past the point and missed it. But directing is really something else. I wonder why directors aren't satisfied to be directors, why they have to be the auteurs, as though being a film director isn't a fantastic art in itself.

How do you set about adapting a work—a novel or a play—to the screen?

I read it a lot and start getting feelings about it and then start making notes. I usually try to figure out, Where's the movie in this? Where's the screenplay? If the novel is 850 pages and you know a screenplay is anywhere from 115 to 160 pages, what aspect is dramatizable? What aspect of this novel will be the drama that's going to be up there on the screen? For example, for *Portnoy's Complaint* I made the decision that the drama is really Portnoy finally meeting the Monkey and what happens with the ill-fated love affair, with enough up front to show how Portnoy gets to be the way he is at thirty-three or thirty-four. But that was really not the way the novel was constructed.

Each particular film project is different. In *From the Terrace,* for example, the gargantuan task there was to decide which part of the protagonist's life to dramatize. The novel starts with his antecedents and covers them for a few hundred pages. Then he's born, he grows up, becomes successful and he goes on to late middle age at the end of the novel. I made the decision to start with him coming home from the war as a young man and took him up through his leaving his wife. But there was much more up front and in the rear in the novel.

For *The Prize,* I just horsed around with the novel completely. I decided not to do a serious picture and wound up with a sort of road-company, not-first-rate *North by Northwest* kind of film. My first picture, *Executive Suite,* was based on a multicharacter novel. I combined some of the characters into one person. I threw out some of the characters and I invented other characters.

How do you start on paper?

Usually I do some sort of outline for myself. Sometimes I write a long treatment before going into the screenplay. Quite often I take filing cards and I write out a scene on each one. I tack them up on a wall and step back and sort of look at the movie. I may notice that I've got twenty-four cards in act one and six cards in act two and fifteen in act three, and I realize that something is a little out of balance. Sometimes I take a card and say, "Wait a minute, this scene would be better over here." I just move the cards around. It's a way of getting a visual look at a film when I don't even have a film. It has always helped me to use these cards.

Do you think good screenwriting is about good craftsmanship?

I think that much of good screenwriting is about carpentry. It's a juggling of beginnings, middles and endings so that they all inevitably seem to be moving correctly together. Your first draft is dangerously important. Don't ever kid yourself into thinking, "It's okay, it's just the first draft." Beware of that thought, because it's ten times more difficult to go in a certain direction once you've already gone in another direction. The longer you can hold off putting a word down on paper, the better you are. Think about it for another day before you start writing. Rewriting is largely cleaning up things that aren't clear to you, or trying to shorten a scene that's too long, or realizing now that you've written scenes at the end of the story, maybe the scenes at the beginning should be a little different to help set up a scene that comes at the end.

How do you know when you've finished a script?

There's no such thing. It's when there's no way of stalling anymore, when they say, "Where is it? We've got to have it." I remember watching a preview of *Sabrina* with Billy Wilder—we'd never seen the picture with an audience. He jabs me with his elbow and says, "Now I know how we should have done that scene." So a script is never actually finished. It's not a mathematical equation. It never comes out either correct or incorrect. It's completely inexact, where Pauline Kael knows it's wrong and Vincent Canby knows it's right, and I privately know that the director missed this or that moment that I intended, and that this or that scene is much too long, and why did I ever write it that way?

Is your tendency in screenwriting to give a lot of camera directions?

Most directors don't like anyone to tell them how to shoot a picture. Some writers, particularly writers who have written a lot of movies and maybe directed a few, can't help but put down certain things that come to mind because the ideas feel so right. It would be so great to suddenly shock-cut to a close-up of a knife, say, so they put it in. The director can ignore it or he can say, "Hey, that's a hell of an idea. I'll use it." Robert Wise has shown considerable openness of mind toward suggestions written into the screenplay by this screenwriter.

What is not stressed often enough is that a lot of people read a screenplay—agents, directors, actors, producers, financiers—and it should, if possible, read well. It should, if possible, give the flavor of what it's trying to do, without really becoming novelistic. It's not good to put in things that can't be photographed—a lot of interior monologue of the character that can never be put on the screen.

Could you talk about the transition from being a writer who dealt with producers and directors to being a writer-producer yourself, dealing with so many other people?

I had been around moviemaking quite a few years—around the set a lot. I remember writing the last scene of *Sabrina* the day it was shot. On *Sabrina*, Billy Wilder said, "What the hell are you doing at the typewriter?" I said, "I want to put that scene in the script." We were writing at night and shooting the next day all through the movie. I was around on that picture all the way. On *North by Northwest*, I was still writing the script during shooting. I remember having terrible script fights with Cary Grant up in Bakersfield while the crop-dusting sequence was being shot. I was around during most of the shooting. I finally decided that I was sick and tired of having somebody else always taking over my baby. So I wound up producing *Virginia Woolf,* and Mike Nichols promptly took over my baby.

Becoming a producer is a false solution to a writer's ego problems. But I did have a lot to do with what I think were important decisions. If I hadn't been the producer of *Virginia Woolf,* I guarantee you that Mike Nichols would not have been the director. I guarantee you that Elizabeth Taylor would not have been in it, nor would Richard Burton have been in it. I guarantee you it would have been done in color. It might still have been a terrific picture and won twelve Oscars instead of five. Who knows? But because I was the producer, I was able to make certain decisions which had an effect on the picture. If you're only the screenwriter, you have no control over who directs it, who's in it, who rewrites it or who doesn't rewrite it.

I was nervous about the whole movie. I knew that it was a very risky venture from the outset, because it is very much talk and very little so-called cinema. Elizabeth Taylor was quite a scary individual to work with. In fact, that whole production was frightening to me. I tend to project myself as a frightened person. Someone once even called me the "iron butterfly." I was very afraid of everyone on that production, including Jack Warner.

Did you want Elizabeth Taylor, Richard Burton, George Segal and Sandy Dennis, or did you have others in mind originally?

The only actress I ever approached for the role of Martha was Taylor—after I had finally come to the decision and went to Jack Warner for his approval. It took a lot of thinking, until I finally went through the same number all over again with Burton. I didn't immediately get them as a team. First, Elizabeth approved a list of actors, so I could have gone to quite a few others. But finally I was lucky enough to realize that Burton was perfect. He was just great in that role. I think it was the best non–Oscar-winning performance I've ever seen. Sandy Dennis was the first and only choice. Mike Nichols and I wanted Bob Redford for the role of Nick, but he turned it down.

It's often forgotten today what a bold picture Virginia Woolf *was for its time. Back then everyone felt that the play could never be made into a film because of the frankness of the language.*

Lehman (standing at right) at a press conference for the film *Who's Afraid of Virginia Woolf?* (1966). (Back row, left to right) Mike Nichols, Richard Burton. (Front row) George Segal, Elizabeth Taylor and Sandy Dennis. Lehman was the producer and adapted Edward Albee's play for the screen.

That's true. I had read it in manuscript form right after it was produced on Broadway and resolved that I would never see it. I didn't want to be caught in a theater exposed to that play, for some reason which it would take a psychiatrist to unravel. I resisted seeing the play for a year and a half. My wife finally induced me to see it when it came out here to California. I saw it and was knocked out by it, but I did not walk out of the theater saying, "I've got to do it as a movie." I didn't even think of it as a movie. No one in Hollywood would go near it.

I was writing *The Sound of Music* at this time, and Abe Lastfogel, president of the William Morris Agency, kept calling me about *Virginia Woolf.* I told him that I loved it as a play but that I was not interested in it as a movie. He said, "Well, for your information, I'm going to New York, and I'm going to talk to Edward Albee and see if he's willing to sell the play outright with no controls, no holds barred." I said, "You do whatever you want. It's your business, Abe, not mine."

A month later he came back from New York and said, "Well, Albee is willing to sell the play." I said, "That's very interesting." He said, "You know, there's only one person in this town who's ever wanted to do this as a picture: Jack Warner." I said, "You've got to be kidding." He said, "Nope. Jack Warner was knocked out by the play. He's never stopped talking about it. I'm going to him after getting a waiver from the Dramatists Guild and try to sell him the play outright. Now, do you want me to tell him that you're interested in writing it and producing it?" I said, "No siree. You sell that play to Jack Warner if you want. That's your business. If Jack Warner says that he's interested in having me write and produce it, then I'll be forced to answer these questions."

Warner, of course, had been trying to get you over to Warner Bros. as a writer-producer.

But there had never been any projects I was interested in doing at Warner Bros. Finally, Lastfogel sold it to Warner and immediately called me and said, "Jack Warner wants you to write and produce it." I had put off this moment for many, many months. I said, "Well, it looks like I'm going to have to make a decision." I went off and agonized for about five days, because I knew why nobody wanted to do it—there was no way to do it. How do you do that as a movie? But it was such a great play. How do you say no to the opportunity to bring that to the screen?

I met with Jack Warner and all his executives and I said, "The only condition on which I'll do it is that I have the right to select the cast and the director and everyone else of importance." Jack agreed to that, provided that he had the right of approval of my selections. That's the way it worked.

But there were many, many battles. Jack wanted me to use George Cukor, who had just won an Oscar for *My Fair Lady*. Patricia Neal told her agent that she'd fire him if he didn't get her the role. Burt Lancaster called me at home and said he insisted on being on my list. Directors wrote to me. Everybody wanted to do *Virginia Woolf*. Meanwhile, I hadn't the faintest idea of how to do it. I started fooling around with it and gradually realized that one of the ways you do it as a movie is that you don't change it too much. Somehow it holds together. Of course, you can't do it all in one living room, as the play was done. But there is so much dramatic power to it that you don't try to bring in the cavalry and have musical numbers and mob scenes. You just do it.

One of the biggest battles that Mike Nichols and I had with the powers that be at Warner Bros. was over our insistence on doing it in black and white. They wanted it in color, of course. I don't know how we ever won that battle, but we did. Also, Mike was insistent on shooting no cover words for the so-called bad language. We didn't have a rating system at the time, and it's hard to believe that in 1966 the picture was sold with the proviso that the manager himself was responsible for not letting anybody under the age of eighteen into the theater. It was the only way we could get a Legion of Decency seal of approval.

Was it your idea to open up Virginia Woolf *to include the outdoor scene and the roadhouse scene?*

You know, it's really hard for me to recall. Gene Kelly once said that I have a very convenient memory, that I like to remember the good things and forget the bad things. I know damn well that when I decided to do *Virginia Woolf,* one of the things that had bothered me in the play was that Nick and Honey hung around there all night. Why don't they go home? What are they taking all this guff for? I was resolved that I would find some way to get Nick to make the decision, "Come on, Honey, let's get the hell out of here." That worked. Yes, I'm sure that that was my idea—I think. The roadhouse, the parking area was a good Fellini scene, with the lights hitting Haskell Wexler's lenses. I didn't like the unnaturalness of the totally deserted roadhouse, but we tried it with some people around and it just didn't work.

For a short while Mike wanted the whole thing to take place during some kind of bonfire celebration at the college. The students would be dancing around a bonfire, and it would be a crazy kind of night, like a panty raid night. It took a lot for me to talk him into the fact that this damn thing doesn't work unless it's happening while the world sleeps. Nobody's up. This is all happening during those terrible hours when most people are asleep. Somewhere I think he publicly thanked me in print for having talked him out of that. But there is a version of the script in which there are people all over the place. We went through all the motions of trying to open it up and make a so-called movie out of it.

Let's take Mike Nichols as a specific example. You both must have had strong ideas about the adaptation of Who's Afraid of Virginia Woolf? *What contributions— say, in dialogue—did he make?*

Mike Nichols did not have any ideas for dialogue. Wisely so, because I think the result on the screen is mighty powerful. The movie knocks me out every time I see it. Nichols managed to get me to give up almost everything I introduced into the screenplay that wasn't in the play—for example, lines of dialogue or the moving about of scenes. At one time I even created other characters. There were many versions of this screenplay—I think I wrote six. I hate to tell you some of the awful ideas I had which I then thought were good. At one time I even wrote in the son as having actually existed and having committed suicide. His suicide was more than his mother could bear, and she had to create a fantasy that he was still alive. Now, if *Virginia Woolf* were an original screenplay, I think it would have been a hell of a dramatic moment when George forces Martha to look into the closet where the boy hung himself. But that would have violated the spirit of a famous play. A screenwriter is caught in a kind of trap when he is working on something so famous that if he dares to tamper with it, he gets hung, and if he doesn't change it sufficiently, he gets hung.

You've said that you insisted on black and white for Virginia Woolf. *Why?*

We felt that the dialogue would read differently in color, that the characters themselves would read differently emotionally in color. We had a chance to see how right we were, because at the time, ABC was shooting a documentary special on Mike Nichols, which was never released. They were shooting it in color while we were shooting in black and white. I got a chance to see Elizabeth Taylor, as Martha, in color, and everything changed completely. We knew that all our efforts with wig and makeup to make her look older than she was—she was thirty-three and we wanted her to look about forty-eight—would go right down the drain in color. Inasmuch as the movie played totally at night, black and white seemed right for the emotional tone.

Was Haskell Wexler your first choice as cinematographer?

There's a little story behind that. Wexler and Harry Stradling, Sr., were strongly considered by Jack Warner and me before Mike came on the picture. Jack assured me that Harry Stradling was great with first-time directors. He had worked with Elia Kazan on his first picture, and I was becoming sold on Harry Stradling, which put Pete Wexler in the number-two spot. When Mike arrived in town I said, "Mike, Jack Warner wants me to use Harry Stradling." He walked right past me to my desk, picked up the phone, called Sam Spiegel in New York and said, "Sam, what do you think of Harry Stradling? He is? Right." He hung up the phone. "Get him. He's the best."

We got Harry Stradling, and Mike and Harry did not get along well. Mike had definite ideas as to how he wanted the film to look. He kept taking Harry to screenings of *8½, A Place in the Sun,* this picture and that picture. Harry was very nice about it, but he was irritated because he knew that Mike had never directed a picture, and Harry had just won an Academy Award for *My Fair Lady.* It came to the point where Mike came to me and said, "You've got to get together with Harry Stradling and see if you can't make him like me."

I had a meeting with Harry Stradling, and he said, "Look, I like you guys. Don't worry. I'm going to make this picture look so lousy you'll love it." Everything seemed all right until Harry did a camera test of the set. Pretty important, because we were going to be on that damn set for a long time. We went to a screening room, and we saw the set on the screen. It was overlit. Immediately, Mike made a few very pertinent comments. Harry Stradling just got to his feet and said, "I'm too rich and too old to have to put up with this kind of shit. Find yourself another cameraman." He walked out of the room.

This was just a few days before shooting was to begin. I called Jack Warner and told him what happened. He said, "It doesn't surprise me. I saw this coming all along." I called Warner's associate, Walter MacEwan, and said, "Walter, we've got to have Pete Wexler." He said, "He's on location with Irv Kershner. They're just getting ready to start shooting *A Fine Madness.*" I said, "We have to have him." He said, "Just go home. Don't worry about a thing." I said, "What do you mean, don't worry about a thing? We start shooting on Monday." He said, "Go home." That night he called me and said, "I think it's okay. Pete wants to read the script."

Pete came in the next morning and he went into the next office and read the script. He was in terrible turmoil, because he wanted to do both pictures. Anyway he wound up doing ours.

And he wound up winning an Academy Award for his work.

Ironically, one of the many problems we had on the picture was night-location shooting. Even as we had our troubles, Mike and I used to say to each other, "The ridiculous thing is that Pete's going to win an Oscar for this." What got on the screen was truly fine, and it did win an Oscar. But we had a lot of trouble, and Pete got into a very angry mood about directors after that film. He resolved he wasn't going through that anymore, and he became a director himself.

I forgot to tell you: long before Harry Stradling came on the scene, I went to Paris to see the Burtons, to get their approval of cinematographers. I presented Pete Wexler's name to them, and Burton flew into a rage. He said, "My face is pockmarked like the craters on the moon, and Wexler will have every one of them on the screen." He would not accept him. But months later, in our crisis, he had to accept him.

What do you think people want to see in a film?

There are so many different kinds of films. That's what's so great about movies. But there aren't many movies that just sock you right in the diaphragm. *Virginia Woolf* moved me to tears. To me, that's the hardest thing to find in a movie theater, something that really hits you hard. If it can make you weep, I would say that that is a miracle. I weep every time I see *Virginia Woolf* on television now.

Could you say something about your collaboration with Clifford Odets on Sweet Smell of Success?

Well, we didn't really collaborate. Clifford, who was one of my heroes as a playwright, was at Hecht-Hill-Lancaster working on something else. I used to drive him home from the studio thinking, "What is Clifford Odets doing in my car? Doesn't he know who he is? What's he doing here in Hollywood?" I felt that way about Edward Albee when I met him. "God, why did he ever sell his play to Jack Warner?"

Anyway, I had written three different versions of *Sweet Smell* based on my novelette. I was going to direct the picture, but United Artists decided they didn't want to take the chance. I was having terrible battles with Harold Hecht and Jim Hill, and I was developing what turned out to be a spastic colon. All that inner conflict. It was my baby. I had lived the story of *Sweet Smell of Success,* I had written the novelette. It was my picture, and I was going to direct and produce. I also couldn't stand the conflict with Burt Lancaster, who decided he wanted to be in it.

About a week before they left for New York to start shooting, they told me that I would have to go to New York and keep working on the script. I said, "I don't know if I can do that. I have to see my doctor first." My doctor examined me and put me in the hospital for the first and only time in my life. He said, "You're not going back to that film. Take a trip someplace and forget the movie." I said, "Well, I'm not going to tell them. You'll have to do it." So he picked up the phone and called the producers. As luck would have it, a good friend of mine, the screenwriter Jim Webb, was sitting in their office when the phone call came through. Jim was about to sign a multipicture deal with Hecht-Hill-Lancaster. Years later, Jim told me that he never signed with them because he heard Jim Hill and Harold Hecht—who had each picked up a phone extension—both say the same thing over the phone, "I hope the son of a bitch dies."

So Clifford Odets was there, and they took him to New York with them, and he rewrote while they were shooting the picture. Our work was sort of intertwined, and we got co-script credit. In our own way we both did a terrific job.

Did you have personal experience of the world depicted in Sweet Smell of Success?

I had been a Broadway press agent and knew that whole world. A lot of it was based on my own experiences. Tony Curtis' apartment was a place I used to haunt. I worked for a man who was so powerful he could tell Walter Winchell* where to go. I knew what it was like to be a press agent whose whole life depended on whether the columnist would print your stuff or not. It was a miserable world, and the columnists were evil. Winchell was an absolute monster, and I took a big chance writing the novelette. He never attacked it when it was just a published work, but did attack it once it became a movie. A lot of people in Hollywood were afraid of the story and didn't go near it. I was afraid to sell it, and it was only after Hecht-Hill-Lancaster made *Marty* that I felt I'd be safe. Nothing terrible ever happened to me.

You've talked elsewhere of the importance of the right environment for a writer. What do you mean?

*Walter Winchell (1897–1972) was a legendary newspaper columnist and radio broadcaster.

John Houseman, my first producer on *Executive Suite,* once told me that as far as he was concerned his sole function as the producer was to create a climate in which I would feel safe and encouraged and enthusiastic. That may be the last time I felt that way, and it was quite a few years ago. Now, what did he do? When he liked something, he was very enthusiastic about it. A nonwriting producer could be helpful by knowing how to be constructively critical without destroying your confidence, without threatening your sense of yourself as a writer. Very difficult. In fact, it's one of the most difficult things in interpersonal relationships.

Creating a feeling that, come hell or high water, this picture is going to be made—that's another important thing to inject into the aura of a writer. You always have that feeling: this thing is never going to be made. I must say Hitchcock is great at creating the right climate. All during *North by Northwest* and *Family Plot* I had the constant feeling that we were just wasting our time, that there was never going to be a movie, and tried to quit quite often. But if the person you're with tolerates your anxiety and makes you feel that what you are doing is really for the screen and not for the shelves, that makes you work all the better.

Are you working on anything now?

I'm on page 690 of a novel. It's a big, global action-suspense type of thing that's very far removed from me personally. I constantly wonder why I want to express all this. I think one of the reasons we're getting so much of this type of subject matter on the bestseller list and on the screen and on television is not necessarily because readers and audiences want it, but because writers seem to be living out their fantasies, dealing with essentially impersonal experiences. This may simply be an expression of what's going on with most neurotic people known as writers.

Or an expression of what's going on in today's world.

That could be. I read synopses of all the novels that are submitted to the studios. It's just incredible how almost every single one of them has nothing to do with ordinary living. It is all action in high places—thrillers, CIA, assassinations—and has nothing to do with interpersonal, human problems of life on earth. I can remember when writers wrote what concerned them personally, as fine novelists like Saul Bellow still do. It must be very difficult for a novelist today to put a year or two of his life into writing something that is true to him but predictably noncommercial in the world of paperbacks, Hollywood and television. The pot of gold is so huge these days. Then, too, maybe writers are having trouble confronting their own lives and therefore look elsewhere into the fantasy world of high-level intrigue. Who's to say that readers and audiences aren't doing the very same thing?

Films as Writer

1949 *The Inside Story* (co-original story)

1954 *Executive Suite*
 Sabrina (co-screenplay)

1956 *Somebody Up There Likes Me*
 The King and I

1957 *Sweet Smell of Success* (co-screenplay)

1959 *North by Northwest*

1960 *From the Terrace*

1961 *West Side Story*

1963 *The Prize*

1965 *The Sound of Music*

1966 *Who's Afraid of Virginia Woolf?* (also producer)

1969 *Hello, Dolly!* (also producer)

1972 *Portnoy's Complaint* (also director and coproducer)

1976 *Family Plot*

1977 *Black Sunday*

You create a dance by sitting down like a writer and thinking about the scene—a beginning, middle and an end. Then you get up and put it on its feet. No choreographer just gets up and starts to wiggle around and then a dance appears, like a genie out of a lamp when you rub it.

GENE KELLY
(Born in Pittsburgh, Pennsylvania, 1912—Died 1996)

Gene Kelly made a series of landmark musicals that earned him a place among the important American film directors. In 1949 he collaborated with Stanley Donen on *On the Town;* then the two worked together on *Singin' in the Rain* and *It's Always Fair Weather.* Kelly went on to direct *Invitation to the Dance* on his own. These are among the most innovative musicals in film history, and his choreography for *Anchors Aweigh, Cover Girl* and *An American in Paris* influenced the next generation of dance.

Kelly was raised in a working-class neighborhood in Pittsburgh and enjoyed telling reporters that his true ambition was to play shortstop for the Pittsburgh Pirates. His flashing Irish smile and joie de vivre won him friends in life just as they did on the screen. He was seen as a regular guy, and much of his dancing has a blue-collar feel to it. Astaire was aristocratic and elegant; Gene was plebian and broad. Fred was born to wear white tie and tails, but Gene felt that when he put on evening clothes he looked like he was dressed up for the Plumbers' Ball. So he carved out his own style with T-shirts, white socks and loafers. Differences in physique and style didn't prevent Kelly and Astaire from collaborating on delightful dance numbers from time to time, but Gene was influenced by Martha Graham and Charles Weidman, pioneers of modern dance in New York, and his work had a muscular and earthy tone that differed from that of his predecessors.

Kelly's journey from Broadway dancer to choreographer, from Hollywood star to director, would make him known not just as one of the movie's two great song-and-dance men, but as an innovator behind the camera as well. Gene brought Pittsburgh toughness with him when he walked through the gates of MGM, a studio run with an iron fist by Louis B. Mayer and a

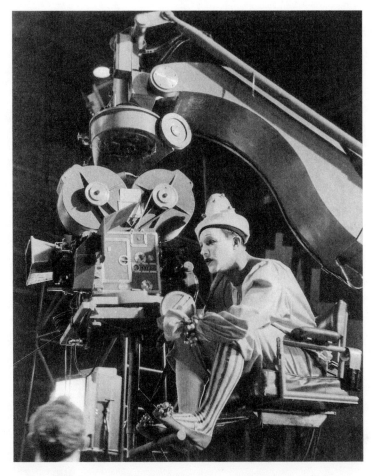

Gene Kelly in costume for the circus sequence in *Invitation to the Dance*
(1956) was co-director with Stanley Donen.

cadre of executives known for keeping directors in their place. Kelly resisted
when he was told that female stars could be photographed only with lenses of
a specified focal length, or that strict rules for scenic design must be followed,
or that Cyd Charisse's skirt could not be cut above her knee. As he said at
AFI, "The creative guys hated the fellows in authority."

I got to know Gene when we asked him to go on a goodwill tour of Africa
for the United States Information Agency during the Kennedy years. He
ended up in half a dozen countries, meeting students, showing excerpts from
his films and talking not just about dance but also the struggle for racial justice in America. The cables to Washington from our embassies were the most
enthusiastic of any I had seen for a goodwill ambassador.

In *The Memory of All That,* Gene's first wife, the actress Betsy Blair, describes him as a man who "believed in freedom of thought, social justice, and racial equality." He never wavered from his democratic principles and wasn't afraid to act on his beliefs. He flew to Washington to support Hollywood's "unfriendly ten" in the forties—a deed not calculated to endear him to his MGM bosses—and we worked together on Robert Kennedy's campaign for the presidency in 1968.

Gene found the dancer's discipline increasingly difficult as the years went by. I remember him saying, ruefully, that he liked to go home and have a couple of beers and a good steak, and how that conflicted with the athletic demands of a dancer's life. He could still get out and do some steps on a television special, but he knew that his days of serious dancing were behind him.

Betsy Blair wrote of their visit to the Vatican and how the Pope blessed Gene, saying, "My son, I understand you are an actor and dancer and you bring happiness to people in your work. For that, heaven awaits you." His Holiness had never actually seen the man kneeling before him stomping through puddles with an umbrella, or dancing with Jerry the Mouse—but if bringing happiness to people was the criterion, Gene very likely found his place upstairs.

GENE KELLY

September 27, 1978

Dance seems to be having a renaissance in the movies and on the stage, for example, The Turning Point *and* Saturday Night Fever. *Do you see a new dance form evolving on the screen?*

One never knows. The social analysts have always tried to predict the forms of popular dance that come in during certain eras. After a war they'll always say, "Well, we're in for an era of violent dances." Witness the end of World War I and the Charleston. Witness the end of World War II and the jitterbug, and after the Korean War, rock-and-roll dance. The only flaw is that all these dance forms—except the Charleston—started before the wars. My own opinion is that dance follows music, and I frankly don't know why we have different music at different times. I only know that if you have a certain style of music, you'll have a certain style of dance, especially popular dance.

Whether the movie industry can make two or three or four more shows like *Saturday Night Fever* because of the disco craze is doubtful. Usually these things come and go pretty quickly. That's what happened historically. In the 1930s, Warner Bros. had a little group that made a different gangster picture every two weeks. It was always the same group: Bogart, Garfield, Cagney, Eddie Robinson. Good actors who would turn out gangster films by the hordes. Then suddenly you couldn't sell a gangster film and the 1940s musicals were popular. There have always been trends in the arts. Musical trends seem to go faster now because everything does.

How did Saturday Night Fever *strike you as a dance film?*

As far as dance goes, it's mild. You can see the same kind of movement at your local disco. There's nothing revolutionary about it. The people who did it, especially John Travolta, did it well. But you can no more call it a breakthrough than if you photographed a hundred-year-old ballet for public television. There hasn't been a real revolution in dance for quite a while. One might make an exception for Twyla Tharp, who a few years ago began to experiment with some flopping-around stuff that's very good. Actually, we tried some of that in the thirties, but nobody bought it. I remember because I was one of the instigators, but I wasn't successful with it, nor were my colleagues. How far Twyla will get with it, I have no way of knowing. The public will decide.

The public has developed a wide interest in dance, and that's a recent phenomenon.

Dance used to be completely an elitist form of entertainment. It wasn't until this century that the masses saw dance. The Church killed dance, at least up until the time of the Renaissance. I can say that with equanimity, being a Roman Catholic myself. But the Renaissance revived dance. It was taken to the courts, Louis XIV brought it to France, and it reached its height in St. Petersburg, under the czars. They treated it as a sort of classical version of the Ziegfeld Follies. The grand dukes had their mistresses in the ballet corps—the prima ballerina might be sleeping with the czar or one of the princes. In this century, people like Fokine, Isadora Duncan, Nijinsky and Mary Wigman had some new ideas—they began to experiment. At first very few people went, but now dance has become a product of the masses. Strangely enough, a lot of the interest is due to the technology of the motion picture and television.

Do you think television is offering any innovations in dance?

No. I am amazed that the fellows who do the choreography in television get it done, because they have so little time. The rule seems to be: don't do it well, do it by Tuesday. There have been no breakthroughs by the great goddess Terpsichore on television, though there have been some optimistic signs. Public television has been photographing some good classical and modern ballets. These are minor but welcome advances. Commercially, there are no breakthroughs that I've seen.

You tried some new things in your own movies. What led you, for example, to take On the Town *out of the studio and put it in the streets of New York?*

I knew it could be done, and I knew it would be different. I had been in the navy and I'd had an experience there with Julius Epstein, a terrific writer who, with his brother Phil, worked on *Casablanca.* Julie and I were officers, and we were assigned to do a picture about an aircraft carrier called the *Ben Franklin,* which had been shot up very badly in the Pacific. A lot of the fellows had managed to escape in miraculous ways. The navy, for publicity, wanted to show how the ship had made its way back to Hampton Roads, Virginia, and from there to the Brooklyn Navy Yard.

The navy thought that if you were in the movie business, you could be a photographer or cutter or anything. I remember the first day I was put in a cutting room. I didn't know how to splice film, but there was a fellow there I had once made a picture with, and he showed me how. I learned a lot of things. For the picture Julie and I were making we had to shoot in New York City, because a lot of the fellows from the ship had come from New York and Connecticut. Nobody ever wanted to shoot in New York, especially the major studios. But I found that you could shoot there without a line of policemen. We would go to a house and ask the landlady if we could shoot out of her window. From the window we'd film two actors, say, walking down the street. We found we could shoot at Grant's Tomb and at the navy yard and at a lot of other sites where we wouldn't be bothered.

I got MGM to buy *On the Town* after seeing it on Broadway. It was written by very old friends of mine, Betty Comden and Adolph Green, and choreographed by a very old friend, Jerry Robbins, with music by another old friend, Lenny Bernstein. After I got out of the navy I explained to the studio that I could shoot a picture on location in New York. The first stumbling block was Frank Sinatra. Those were his famous days, and he was as hard to hide as the Statue of Liberty. He was always being mobbed. To get around that problem we decided not to hire any limousines. Now, that was unheard of. The studios always gave the stars and the directors limousines when they were on location. Instead, we hired Yellow taxis. We would push Sinatra on the floor of the taxi and I'd get on top of him, and Jules Munshin would get on top of me so that the taxi would seem empty. Munshin and I were stronger than Sinatra, and so we always made him the low man in the taxi. No, he didn't like that.

The night before, Stanley Donen and I, who were codirectors, would line up the shot. We hid the camera in a station wagon, and Hal Rossen, the photographer, and the camera operator would lie down inside on their bellies. When I jumped out of the taxi I'd give a loud whistle, the station wagon would start moving and we'd follow it. I had a stopwatch in my pocket. I'd say, "And-a-one, and-a-two, and-a-three and-a-four." Then we'd say, "New York, New York, a hell of a town!" That's the way we shot all that stuff—we stole it. We never had a cop or any protection, and we did the whole thing in five days. We shot on top of the Radio City building, we shot down where the ice rink is with about twenty thousand people around. But we tilted from the top down and if you look at that picture closely you can see thousands of people watching us.

There's a dream sequence in On the Town *that is particularly sensual, with lush colors, characters in silhouette, provocative movements. Did the censors give you problems in these instances?*

There was nothing the censors could put their fingers on. The red color, the girl in black and the sailor in white were very sensuous. The moves were sensuous. Yet I never laid a glove on her. There was nothing the censors could say. If they did, I could have said, "What? Do you have a dirty mind?"

We always had a problem with censors, and it was one of the great good times in making a picture that you'd seethe for a few nights and then find a way to outwit them. Nowadays, everybody who gets together to make a picture loves each other. I hated all those guys who ran the studio, including Louis B. Mayer, and for a while I wasn't too fond of Eddie Mannix.* They were the enemy, the ones who said, "You can only spend this." We'd say, "Yes, but if we spend $5.50 more, this will be better."

To get around them we had to resort to tricks. I would keep cutting the girls' dresses higher and higher. The studio censor finally hired a girl who would come down with a tape and measure poor Cyd Charisse or whoever it was. She'd say, "That's too high. You have to put it there." All dancers know that if your line is truncated, especially on a girl, it makes it

*Edgar J. Mannix (1891–1963) was an MGM studio executive.

much less interesting visually. The minute she left, we'd cheat somehow
and turn the dress up.

It was a constant fight. Mayer, when I was there, didn't have much to
do with the directors and choreographers. He always talked to the writers.
He'd say, "You wouldn't want your mother to hear a toilet flushing or
something vulgar like that." He had an obsession about bathrooms. Others had an obsession about the Catholic Church. They almost created the
Legion of Decency themselves. They happened to be Jewish anti-Semites,
and they wouldn't hire Jewish actors if they looked Jewish. It's like Englishman and Americans who wanted to go into the Russian ballet. We'd
have to change our names. You know, Kelly would have to be Kalinsky,
and so forth. Or the opposite. You'd have to change your name to O'Brien
if you were a Jewish actor. This was a general rule of thumb in Hollywood.

A lot of fellows who worked in the thirties and forties, like Billy
Wilder, had to be very clever at writing because they were not allowed to
show two people in bed. A married couple always had to be in twin beds.
If you had a scene on a bed, one of their legs had to be on the floor, as if
they were playing in a pool tournament. These were laws. So clever fellows like Wyler, Wilder, Stevens and the rest would show two people
walking into a room, and then they'd cut to a messed-up bed.

Wasn't there a sequence from The Pirate *that was cut?*

Yes. That was with Judy Garland and myself, and we were doing a little
bit of over-groping. It was a sensual and sensuous sequence—both words
are applicable—but I think it was too long and said too much. I didn't
mind that they cut a piece of that out. What hurt the picture was that
Vincente Minnelli and I really outsmarted ourselves. *The Pirate* had been
the only flop the Lunts had.* We'd both seen it on Broadway and we
knew something had to be changed. S. N. Behrman's dialogue was brilliant, but we wanted to get in a lot of action and a lot of dash. So we said,
"Let's make it obvious that the pirate is being played like Douglas Fairbanks, Sr., and the actor is being played like John Barrymore. Not too
obvious, just enough to let everybody in on it." Gee, we were being so
clever. Then all the reviews hit us. "This cheap actor tried to imitate the

---

*Alfred Lunt (1892–1977) and Lynne Fontaine (1887–1983) were a preeminent Broadway acting
couple who appeared together in more than two dozen productions.

great . . ." and so forth—the reviews were all of that ilk. Minnelli and I had to skulk behind bushes.

You say the censors worried about the length of dresses. Did they worry about political matters too?

I think that depended on the studio. Where I was, they didn't want to touch anything that had any kind of serious political or social connotations. It was a rule at the studio. Warner Bros. did a lot of such pictures, like *I Am a Fugitive from a Chain Gang,* just a few years after talkies began, but Columbia and MGM just didn't want to bother. They didn't want to take any chances with offending any groups.

Codirecting movies is fairly rare. How did you and Stanley Donen work together?

There are no auteurs in musical pictures. It's impossible. You have to have music and arrangements, a choreographer, a director and so forth. Stanley Donen had worked in the chorus of *Pal Joey,* when I did it on Broadway, and then I put him in *Best Foot Forward,* a show I did the choreography for. He came out here to work at MGM, I think as a chorus boy. But he wanted to come and assist me at Columbia, and after we made *Cover Girl,* I got him a job there. Unfortunately he lost it because he didn't get along with his first producer—fortunately for me.

I was then at MGM, and I told MGM to rehire him because I couldn't do without him. I said. "He must get co-credit with me because I'm helpless without him." He learned so much so fast that by the time I got to *On the Town,* he was not just an assistant and a co-choreographer, he was behind the camera. The dance was always worked out for the camera beforehand, and I used to do one take and use that take. But the camera operator, unless he was a dance-knowledgeable man—and I never met one who was—couldn't do that. So I needed someone behind the camera, and Stanley was that someone at that time. If I was in a scene, I didn't have to look at the camera or glance at the other actors. At the end I would just look at Stanley and he'd say okay. So I always felt he should get credit as codirector. As a choreographer, Stanley actually did not make up any steps, or *enchaînements,* a dancer's word for a dance phrase. But his value was just as great as if he had made up half the steps.

I thought we were a good team. I thought we complemented each other very well. On the last picture we made, *It's Always Fair Weather,* we were so together, we were so used to each other, that we didn't need each other. It was almost dull doing it together. We could have phoned the shots in. It wasn't a bad picture, though it was a little behind its time. That's the only picture we didn't have a lot of fun on. But on the other pictures we did—*On the Town, Singin' in the Rain*—we were a good team. We were one mind working toward an end. It was advantageous for both of us: advantageous for Stanley because it actually gave him a leg up on his career; advantageous for me because I knew when he said the shot was in the can, I wouldn't have to retake it the next day.

Did your collaboration involve the planning of each shot?

Yes, so we would each know exactly what was in a shot, when that person has to walk from here to there, whether the camera will pan with him or let him go out of the field, whether the camera will move in to a close-up of this person and then cut to that person. I wasn't crazy about close-ups, and, happily, Stanley followed along with me. I thought they were way overdone by the time I got to films. I'd done so much studying of von Sternberg and fellows like him that I wished I'd never see another close-up. We did very few of them. A couple of times, if we got an inspiration on the set, we'd just say, "Time," and kill the lights and go off and talk about it.

How did you go about creating dance numbers, for example, the big finale in the studio in Singin' in the Rain?

You create a dance by sitting down like a writer and thinking about the scene—a beginning, middle and an end. Then you get up and put it on its feet. No choreographer just gets up and starts to wiggle around and then a dance appears, like a genie out of a lamp when you rub it. You sit down just like a writer doing a story. Some of the scenes, like the one you mentioned in *Singin' in the Rain,* came about because we'd painted ourselves into a corner. Donald O'Connor and I needed a third duet together, and the studio wanted it. But we found out that Donald had another contract and had to go on *The Colgate Comedy Hour* at a certain date. We had already shot a scene where Donald and I tell the producer, modeled after Arthur Freed, how great the dance scene is going to be, and then the camera moves toward a blank screen. We had that but no Donald O'Connor, and Debbie Reynolds wasn't a strong enough dancer to carry a pure dance scene alone. So we got Cyd Charisse and just wrote a whole new ballet and stuck it in. That's how that came about. We had to have a number there. We never meant it to be that long, but since we were introducing a new character into the show, we had to keep adding to it and adding to it. It went on for hours, it seems.

One of the most memorable numbers in film musicals is "Make 'Em Laugh," with Donald O'Connor. How did that come about?

Donald O'Connor was always making us laugh, and so I said, "Let's do a number called 'Make 'Em Laugh.'" It was all improvisation. It was unbelievable. We had twenty minutes of it that we threw out. The difficulty of doing choreography for it was that Donald was a spontaneous artist and comedian, and he never could do anything the same way twice. We didn't want to place ourselves in the hands of the music department because that would have meant giving away our control. And so to put it on the same beat, my assistants, Carol Haney and Jeannie Coyne, and I would sit there with a notepad, and he would just do tricks, and we'd put them on one beat. We'd say, "Do it again" or "No, you did that on the first beat," and he would adjust for the first beat.

He was so funny that we couldn't contain ourselves. There was no way a director or choreographer could say, "Do it this way and it will be funnier." There's no way you can write that stuff. The dummy he uses in the dance, for example, was lying on a rehearsal stage next door to us. We walked in there one day, and Donald started to fool around with it. For half an hour we just roared with laughter. Finally we said, "Well, let's put that in the number." To get the beats where he'd slap his head on the musical counts was most difficult. All of that number came right out of Donald. None of it was imposed on him, except for the finish. I wanted him to do the trick that he had done as a little boy in vaudeville. So we got his brother over to rehearse him with a rope to get his confidence back and then to break through the wall at the end. The rest was all his, and it was unbelievable.

Was creating a number while making a film a common experience for you?

Very seldom. As I said, there was usually a long period of thought given to the formation and the creation of a number. For the actual choreography, I always liked to get the beginning and the end, because I knew the middle—the actual physical working out of a number—would take care of itself. The best thing was to get help from the script, if it said a certain kind of number belonged there. Usually scriptwriters would only say, Gene Kelly stops the show with a number here or Fred Astaire does a scintillating number there.

But Comden and Green, who did *Singin' in the Rain,* didn't write that way. They liked to be in on everything because they were also songwriters and composers on their own. The trouble with Comden and Green was that they were always busy on Broadway. Hollywood was their avocation and Broadway was their vocation. We would keep trying to nail them down here. They were like most of us who worked in New York. When we first came out here, we hated the movies. We came out to make some money and go back to do a play. When I came out here, I thought of the famous Fred Allen line, "Who wants to make love to an orange?" Every time we'd finish a picture, we'd go back to New York and look for a play.

When they left *Singin' in the Rain* they had no idea that that number of Donald O'Connor's would ever be in. They were doctoring a show in Philadelphia, and I remember being on the phone with them and saying, "We're doing this now. What do you think of this line? Give me a new line." "Oh, call us back tomorrow. We're very busy now." A lot of it was done that way. But quite a few of the numbers came as surprises, though they tried to stay as long as they could with the picture. It was a big advantage working with them, because they not only wrote they also composed, so they could help you meld the things together.

The hardest picture we ever had to do that way was *An American in Paris* because we had a choice of every song the Gershwins ever wrote. You might say, "Oh boy, what riches." But we didn't know what to select. We spent more time trying to fit the songs in. Luckily we had Alan Jay Lerner doing the script. He was criticized by a few people for having a very lightweight and an overly romantic script on *An American in Paris.* But I don't think we could have ever done the film if we hadn't had someone like Alan Jay Lerner, who could adapt every time Minnelli and I changed a song and put it in another place. He'd write into it. He was really a marvel.

Singin' in the Rain is partly a satire on the transition between the silent and the sound eras in Hollywood. What approach were you after?

There had been real satires done on it, of which we were blissfully unaware. There was one movie called *Once in a Lifetime,* based on the play by Kaufman and Hart, which was a biting satire about Hollywood. None of us, including Comden and Green, had ever seen it. I guess it was locked in somebody's vault. We felt it had to be a loving kind of satire. All those things actually happened in Hollywood, and everything that was kidded in it was the truth. We had many more incidents we didn't use. There was a famous incident when the head office at MGM, not knowing what to do about sound, called out the engineers of one of the knowledgeable scientific firms in the East. They were asked, "How can we get better sound?" The engineers walked around the soundstage, but they didn't know any more than anyone else. They said, "Well, you've got metal tacks on all the floors. That kills the microwaves or whatever." So the studio had thousands of carpenters take out the metal tacks and put in wooden pegs. They're now all covered up with Masonite, by the way, because the wood finally got worn away.

We wanted to fit that story in, but it was so expensive to show thousands of carpenters for just one or two shots. It wasn't worth it. There were a lot of stories. I understand that Lionel Barrymore got angry about the microphone one day. The microphone then was huge and had to be hidden somewhere, and you had to be near it when you talked. Barrymore swore like a trooper and he said, "Bring the mike to me." He was told, "Mr. Barrymore, these engineers here say that it is impossible." So he said, "Put it on a pole and carry it over." The microphone was hung on a pole and someone would walk over with it to Mr. Barrymore. They tell me that's how the term "fish pole" started. These are true stories, and that's why Comden and Green had such funny scenes to work with. Now, what other lies can I tell you?

In some of your films there are scenes in one continuous take. What problems did that give the photographers?

They never liked it much because it was very difficult, especially at MGM, which laid down blanket rules that the stars could never look bad. The poor photographers would work hours getting little inky-dinks and spotlights in, especially on the women. I remember I broke a rule once when I shot "Slaughter on Tenth Avenue" with Vera-Ellen for *Words and Music.* I dug a pit below the stage, and at the point where she fell down the stairs, I put on a twenty-eight-millimeter lens. There was a rule at MGM that you could not shoot a woman star with less than a forty-millimeter lens. A close-up had to be with a fifty-millimeter, a seventy-five-millimeter or a one-hundred-millimeter. It was a good rule—MGM was thinking commercially. The executives raised a little hell about it, and then they forgot about it.

Shooting the title number of *Singin' in the Rain,* by the way, was just terrible for the photographer, Hal Rossen. He had to backlight all the rain and then put front light on the performer. Luckily there was only me. The few people who were in the scene, except the policeman, were covered up so he didn't have to get light on their faces. That was as tough a job as I've ever seen, because you can't photograph in the rain and see it. If you notice, a football game played in the rain will look dry on your television set until the camera pans up and you see the lights in back. Then you see waves of water falling. So you have to backlight rain, or you can't see it. It was an easy dance, but very tough on the photographer.

Did you have a preference for static or fluid camerawork for your dance sequences?

I always moved the camera for the numbers. I can't remember one where I didn't. The reason is that in constructing a dance, I know there's a certain angle you can look at that is the most advantageous angle. You can't always be turning and facing one way if you want to get variety in your choreography. It's true that in some pictures the camera moves less than in others. If I'm doing a dance in this much space, I wouldn't have to move the camera. But if I'm going all around this room, I would certainly move it. And certainly if I'm coming down the street, as in the "Singin' in the Rain" number, I would have to move it. Again, that's where having Stanley Donen behind the camera was very important.

Were the tap-dancing sequences in your films dubbed?

Yes, you had to dub them, and it was the worst chore in motion pictures. Tap dance was in vogue, and the reason that we did a lot of tap dancing— we put a little bit of it into most numbers—was to show that it was an American form of dance. We'd pretty much always have it somewhere in a picture, unless it was something like *The Pirate,* where it didn't belong at all. But to dub the taps you looked at yourself up on the screen and added the taps afterward. It was a pain in the neck and we all hated it.

Some moments in your dance sequences are so physical they look dangerous. Did you consider using stuntmen?

Some were dangerous, and I wasn't that brave. But you can tell a dancer's body from a stuntman's when it's hanging in the air. The minute you spot that it's somebody else in the middle of a dance, the phoniness ruins it. But a lot of stunts I wouldn't touch. I wouldn't ride a horse, I just wouldn't do it. There would be dialogue scenes in which, of course, I *had* to ride, so I would go to the wrangler and say, "Look, I can't ride a horse very well. I'm a city boy. I worked on a farm, but it was with plow horses. Can you get me a horse that will make me look good?" He'd say, "Sure." I'd get a horse that bounced well. But most actors would say, "Give me your wildest stallion. I can ride." They all broke their legs. I can tell you about a dozen stars who broke their legs, arms and backs riding horses.

You see, the horse is the dumbest animal in the world, and you don't know what he's going to do. He can be standing still and a fly will go by and he'll go *bl-eh-le-eh* and you'll be on your derriere. The horse may be on his too, on top of you. There are shots of me in *The Three Musketeers* galloping down the sand. But three stuntmen—good horsemen too—broke their backs in that picture.

A frequent problem in musicals is the sometimes jarring transition from speaking to singing or dancing. How did you approach it?

I had seen Nelson Eddy and Jeanette MacDonald and a lot of other people just burst into song and let their glorious voices carry the scene, which was accepted back then in the way we accept grand opera. In opera we accept two mature people as Romeo and Juliet who come out in front of a sixty-piece orchestra and four thousand people, and he sings, "Now we're alone. Speak softly," and you can hear him in the fourth balcony. In a ballet, a fellow comes out as a prince. You know he's a prince because the program says he's a prince and he's got a little hat on that's different from the other fellows' hats. He has a bow and arrow and he's hunting swans. Why is he hunting swans? Why would anyone want to hunt a swan? But he's hunting swans, and then one of the swans turns into a girl. In ballet you accept that.

If a fellow is on a thirty-five-foot stage with a proscenium arch and you want the feeling of aloneness, you kill the footlights and all the backlights slowly. You bring them down until there's just a little spotlight on him and you feel that he's alone. You feel almost claustrophobic with him. The nature of the song and the nature of the music will give you that. In

Kelly and Stanley Donen, codirectors of *It's Always Fair Weather* (1955),
watch Dolores Gray rehearse a scene with Michael Kidd, Cyd Charisse and
Dan Dailey.

motion pictures, if you brought down the lights everybody would say,
"What happened? A power shortage?" In my first picture I knew I was
doing everything wrong. The stuff I had done on the stage didn't work in
the movies.

In analyzing the problem, I said, "The song should take you from the
dialogue into the dance." So for *Singin' in the Rain,* when the producer
said to me, "What are you going to do with the song 'Singin' in the
Rain'?" I could easily say to him, "It's going to be raining and I'm going to
be singing." We had to think up a way to do that. I had to be in love, so
much in love that I could walk out in the rain and let it splash on me, and
singing in the rain seemed very natural to do. But people usually don't go
out and splash in puddles—they often want to, but usually they don't.

To make those transitions is the hardest thing in any musical, even on
the stage where it's much easier than in motion pictures. But I found that

singing a song helped me. I never had a good voice, but the song was just a means to an end, to getting from the dialogue into the dance. I think it's just as bastardized a form to go from dialogue saying, "You're the one, kid," and then jumping into dance. I think you need some transition, whether it's stepping in mud or falling down or whatever. The good song-writers will give you that transition without making it a slap in the face.

Is the performer who can act, sing and dance any more difficult to find today than when you were doing your musicals?

The song-and-dance man or woman has always been the rarest bird to discover because they have to do three functions well. They have to sing, dance and act. That problem will always exist. In some schools, like the High School of Performing Arts in New York City, young people are taught those three skills. There are some young people coming up who can do all three things quite well. But you usually find only one or two in a whole generation. A person may have all this training but not have a personality that appeals to the public.

We can be as serious as we want about musical comedy, but it's a light-hearted and a light-headed thing to do. You do it to bring joy. You do it to bring entertainment. Most classic ballets, the ones that are liked by the people, are the ones that entertain. A few somber ones get by, but they don't last very long. So musical comedy rarely has depth. When I say depth, I'm talking about the writing. If you take *Romeo and Juliet* and make *West Side Story*, or if you take *Pygmalion* by George Bernard Shaw and make *My Fair Lady*, then there's a certain depth to the writing. But usually it's "Hiya kid, howya doin'? *Ya-m-da, ya-m-da.*" It's usually to entertain—that's its function. I hate to say it, but people who see a variety show on television are often just as happy as if they saw *My Fair Lady*.

Television variety shows have taken over some of the functions of musical films. What do you think led to that?

Economics had a great deal to do with it. We were never haunted in the old days by the specter of television. We were haunted by other things. But television has become the prime factor of all the mass media. It's put magazines and newspapers out of business. It's practically put the movies out of business. It's made it very hard in days of rising costs to put on a musical that is any different or any better than something you see on the television screen. If people can see a performer do a song or a dance on television they usually won't leave their home to pay money down at the local cinema.

At first none of us believed that television would ever be the first of the mass media. We never thought it would supplant motion pictures. We thought it was just a very interesting thing that would be used for news-reels and documentaries. It never really hit us that people all over America and all over the world would have it in their homes and look at it as enter-tainment. It never hit the studios. I think the introduction of quick, instant communication is the basis of all our woes. Sometimes it's benefi-cent, but often it's the other way around. Educationally, television has been proved to be bad. My married daughter grew up without television in the house, but my youngest daughter, who's now fourteen, sees televi-sion every night. She also does her homework and she's bright. But I know a lot of her peers who watch too much television, and they can't read.

Performers like Buster Keaton and Charles Chaplin had a number of talents when they started out, but weren't they essentially considered only actors?

Yes, although there was a lot of pantomime, because they were silent actors, and a lot of dance in their form. Keaton had a great influence on me. A lot of his moves I intuitively copied in doing some numbers. I know I was thinking of him when I did a dance with a squeaky board and a newspaper. I didn't look like him, but I often wish I did. He was a com-plete genius, and there was a lot of dance inherent in his movements. I thought some actors in the silent pictures, like Douglas Fairbanks and Lon Chaney, were complete dancers. They were balletic and moved like dancers. There was no talking in those days. They weren't dance trained either. Where they got their training, I just don't know.

Would you say Donald O'Connor was the strongest male partner you ever had?

Well, that's a matter of opinion. I worked with some very good dancers. Mr. Astaire wasn't bad now, was he? Of course, Donald carried comedy with him, and that's a marvelous asset. As I said, I wish I could have been more like Buster Keaton. I wish I carried some dances more comedically.

Donald would come in and do a step and then make it funny. So he was a great partner for me. Whether or not he was the best is not for me to say. We'll leave that to the critics.

How would you compare your work with Fred Astaire's?

Fred and I always disliked the fact that we were often thought of as dancing similarly. We danced completely differently. His style is intimate, mine is broad. When we worked together we always had to accommodate each other. No, our styles aren't alike at all.

You've been quoted as saying that you thought yours was an American dance style.

I think what I said was that mine was a plebian style and Astaire's was an aristocratic one. I always kid Fred, and I kidded him before he got his award at the American National Theatre and Academy. I said, "Well, you're playing the rich fellow again. Helen Hayes is going to come out and give you the award. If it were me, it would probably be Bette Midler." It's true that in the midst of the Depression, he and Ginger Rogers were always playing rich characters touring Europe. Nobody in America had any money—we were all digging ditches—but we all went to movies.

When I came to the movies, I wanted to dance in T-shirts and blue jeans. Some critics claim that's my only contribution, and maybe it is. But if I put on an evening suit I look like someone from *The Iceman Cometh*. I look like I'm dressed up for the Plumbers' Ball. There are some men— like Clifton Webb, Fred Astaire, Jack Buchanan—who look so good in evening clothes you'd think they had invented them.

A lot of this is due to the era in which you're brought up. I know Fred and Adele Astaire came from the twenties, actually at the end of an era. When I came to Broadway, it was the beginning of a dance revolution. It was Martha Graham and Charles Weidman. The only thing I regret is that I wasn't in motion pictures in the thirties, when all the great songwriters were at their height and living in Hollywood. Even Rodgers and Hart—and I worked with them on Broadway—deigned to come out here then.

But the New York theater in the thirties was a completely new kind of theater, and I had the good luck to go through that. I had the good luck to be cast in *Pal Joey* and *The Time of Your Life* and other things. Those were depression times too, but not the worst. It is amusing to look back and to see that the successful pictures practically flaunt big homes and riches. I don't just mean Astaire and Rogers—that's a little in-joke we have.

What are you involved in these days?

I've been involved in a lot of projects. But I've kept them to things I could do in Hollywood, which during the past five or six years has meant television, because I've had two little children to raise. The few pictures I've badly wanted to do were done abroad, like *Cabaret,* which I really wanted to do. I've started work on a picture we hope we'll shoot this year. It's a very nice picture. It's what my sixteen-year-old would sneeringly call "a family picture." We don't know whether to make it a musical or not, strangely enough. I'm still doing a few television appearances just to pay the rent.

I'm not breaking any new ground, just singing and doing a little dance—all that's left of old dad. I never really dance anymore. You know, it's too much trouble keeping in shape. I'd rather have a drink and a hearty meal. Dancing is like any kind of athletics. As you get older, you have to keep narrowing it down and narrowing it down until you become coach or manager—in this case, a director or choreographer. As far as dancing goes, you narrow it down until the little dancing you're able to do is so boring that you say the hell with it. So you keep in shape for nothing. I go on television, but I just horse around. Everybody thinks I'm dancing, but I'm not. I do a few steps. No, I don't dance anymore.

Films as Director

1949 *On the Town* (codirector)	1958 *The Tunnel of Love*
1952 *Singin' in the Rain* (codirector)	1962 *Gigot*
1955 *It's Always Fair Weather* (codirector)	1967 *A Guide for the Married Man*
	1969 *Hello, Dolly!*
1956 *Invitation to the Dance*	1970 *The Cheyenne Social Club* (also
1957 *The Happy Road* (also producer)	coproducer)

When somebody says, "I've been in the business twenty-five years—
let me see the dailies," be wary. My father drove for twenty-seven
years and was a lousy driver till he died.

RICHARD BROOKS
(Born in Philadelphia, Pennsylvania, 1912—Died 1992)

Richard Brooks did not dream of becoming a film director as a young boy.
After his schooling in New York City he hit the road, traveling through
Kansas, Texas and Louisiana during the Depression, working odd jobs and
forming an underdog's view of the world. He got a job as a sports reporter for
The Philadelphia Record and then an opportunity in radio as a writer and
commentator for NBC in New York. His radio work took him to Los Angeles, where he started collaborating with Hollywood screenwriters on the side.
Three years in the marines during World War II interrupted his writing, but
gave him a chance to learn editing with Frank Capra on the *Why We Fight*
series. His service experience inspired a novel, *The Brick Foxhole,* which was
made into the film *Crossfire* in 1947.

Working as a writer of B pictures after the war, Brooks seized the opportunity to collaborate with John Huston on the script of *Key Largo.* By now
the young writer saw that directing was where the action was, and he asked
Huston how you become a director. "If you've got a script," Huston said,
"don't give it to the studio unless they let you direct it." Brooks did exactly
that in 1950 with *Crisis,* starring Cary Grant. This was at MGM, where they
kept directors in the bullpen who could come in on a moment's notice and
replace directors who fell behind schedule. Brooks had his eyes fixed on the
actors' performances one day when a heavy camera dolly ran over his foot. He
called for a second take, and his leading man said, "Take two? You've got a
shoe full of blood!" "Cary," Brooks said, "if I leave this stage, there'll be
another director here in five minutes to finish the picture—they didn't want
me to direct it in the first place." "Really?" Grant said. "Then I'll go to the
hospital with you."

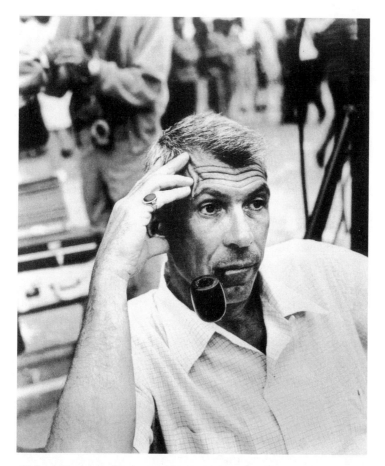

Richard Brooks on the set of *Lord Jim* (1965). He wrote the screenplay which was based on the Joseph Conrad novel. The picture starred Peter O'Toole and James Mason and was filmed in Cambodia and Hong Kong.

Thus Brooks survived his first picture. He claimed that Louis B. Mayer told him that he never liked any movie Brooks made but figured that something new was coming and Brooks might be it. His first big success didn't come until 1955 with *The Blackboard Jungle,* a gritty story of violent life in New York schools informed by Brooks' own boyhood experience. With its theme song—"Rock Around the Clock" by Bill Haley and the Comets—the film introduced rock music to movies. Brooks soon became his own producer. His films were eclectic and wide ranging, adapted from the work of such authors as Fyodor Dostoyevski, Joseph Conrad, Sinclair Lewis, Robert Ruark, Tennessee Williams, Truman Capote and Judith Rossner. The resulting string of solid studio pictures earned Brooks eight Oscar nominations for screenwriting: *The Brothers Karamazov, Lord Jim, Elmer Gantry, Something of Value, Cat on a Hot Tin Roof, Sweet Bird of Youth, In Cold Blood* and *Looking for Mr. Goodbar.*

Brooks was cantankerous and irascible. Peter O'Toole, who worked with Brooks on *Lord Jim,* called him "the man who lived at the top of his voice." When Columbia Pictures was canceling directors' contracts and his name came up, a studio executive was said to have proclaimed, "We can't drop Brooks. You never know what this guy might do—he might burn down the studio."

He was famously secretive about his scripts, refusing to hand over complete screenplays even to his actors and crew. I would see Brooks around Hollywood and enjoyed his company, but I can't recall a conversation where, with haunted dark eyes and a conspiratorial tone, he failed to announce his suspicion that plagiarists were plotting to get their hands on his current screenplay.

Brooks came to the AFI shortly after finishing shooting *Mr. Goodbar.* He was with his wife and frequent starring actress, Jean Simmons, whom he met when she appeared in *Elmer Gantry.*

RICHARD BROOKS

———◆———

May 25, 1977

You started out as a screenwriter. How did you move into directing?

The way it happened with me was that I was at Warner Bros. and Jerry Wald was one of the big producers there. He had a lot of pictures under way, though that doesn't mean he was going to make them all. One day he said that he had a great idea to make a movie called *Key Largo,* based on a play—I think with Paul Muni—which was about the Spanish Civil War. John Huston wanted to direct it and Humphrey Bogart wanted to be in it. Jerry Wald asked me if I would write the script. I said, "I'd be delighted." We all met for lunch across the street at Lakeside Golf Club. We ate for forty-five minutes. John never mentioned *Key Largo.* Bogart never mentioned *Key Largo.* Wald never mentioned *Key Largo.* And I was afraid to mention it.

Finally Bogie said, "Well, I've got to get back to the set," and he left. John said, "You got a car?" I said, "Yes, I have an MG." He said, "Well, can you give me a ride?" He lived way out in Tarzana. He had some kind of a ranch out there. As we were driving out, I said, "John, about *Key Largo.* Are you going to make it?" He said, "I've never read it. Do you have any ideas about it?" I said, "No. I've read the play. I thought since you were going to do it, maybe you knew how to do it." He said, "I hate this kind of play. I don't like free verse. I don't like Maxwell Anderson's work. I don't like *him.*"

Then he said, "I've got a pool table. Why don't we talk about it while we shoot some pool?" So we shot some pool. He said, "How can you do something about the Spanish Civil War now? Maybe if *you* come up with something we'll do it. I don't know." So I'd go over once a week or so, and we'd shoot some pool, and he'd say, "Did you think of anything?" And I'd say, "Well, no, not yet."

Finally I came up with a few things. He was going to Washington for the Hollywood Ten hearings and he said, "Why don't you go down to Key West and I'll meet you there. We'll get a car and go to Key Largo and look it over. Maybe there is no place like Key Largo." So we went down to Key Largo, and every day we would talk about it. He would go out on a pier and fish and I would write. We finally got a script and started to make a movie. He asked me to stay with it while he was shooting, and that was the first time I was ever allowed on a stage or a location to watch a picture being made. In those days if you were a writer you were never allowed to be near where they were shooting, and if you were a director they rarely allowed you anywhere near a cutting room. Everyone was departmentalized. The studios thought it was better if you didn't know how something else was done. Huston always said that a writer should direct his own script, that it's the only way to protect yourself.

There was a cameraman on that picture by the name of Karl Freund, and he said, "I hear you are going to be a director." I said, "I hope so." He said, "I am going to give you the first lesson on how to direct a movie." I said, "That's great. What is it?" He said, "Tomorrow." The next day I came to the set, and he had two little brown bags with sixteen-millimeter film on four-hundred-foot rolls. He said, "You look at these pictures. Lesson number one." I took them home and ran them. I ran them twice. They were pornographic movies, the kind where they wore the socks and the long sideburns. I came back the next day with them in a brown paper bag, and I said, "Karl, they're terrific." He said, "I produced both of them. I write, I direct, I don't act, but everything else I do. My pictures. 1922." I said, "That's terrific. But what's it got to do with directing?" He said, "Lesson number one. Many times you will be wondering, do you put the camera here or up down here? Do you make the scene a little bigger, a little smaller?" Then he said. "Did you watch these pictures closely?" I said, "Yes." He said. "Okay. Lesson number one: Get to the fucking point." And I must say, many times I've wondered, "What do I do now?" Well, just get to the point.

That was my first lesson, and that's how I got into directing. I wrote a script at MGM, and they finally said, "Okay, we'll let you direct one." In some ways back then it was more difficult than I think it is now, and easier in other ways. Once they gave you a chance, even if you failed, they gave you another chance. And they owned their own theaters. Today you'll make your first film and maybe you'll be lucky. Maybe it will be an *Easy Rider* or a *Jaws* or whatever, and the press will praise you very highly. But don't take it too seriously because on the next one they may knock your brains out. You're not as good as they said when they saw your first picture, and you're not as bad as they say you are on your second one.

But the script always has to come first.

Yet movies are different from the written word. When you read something or you go to the theater and the dialogue comes from the proscenium, you have to translate those words. You may do it quickly as you read or as you hear, but it is an intellectual reaction. Now if all the words are put together and structured properly, your secondary reaction may be emotional—or it ought to be. But film, like music—they are very closely related—is almost exactly the opposite. Your primary reaction is emotional. If the scenes are structured properly, you may have a secondary impulse which is intellectual. But the first reaction is emotional. For example, think of any picture you have seen recently. If I asked you to repeat the dialogue of any given sequence, you'd be hard put to do it. But if I asked you about the images, you could tell me a hundred images. You may not remember the words but you remember how he felt, how she wept, how she struggled, how they loved, how they broke up.

You mentioned film and music.

I find it very difficult to judge certain sequences after they've been assembled until I hear them with music. I'll run them with a piece of music that I believe to be conducive to those scenes, or I may have the orchestration or the instrumentation that I believe ought to be with them. Then I can judge them much better, because movies are sound and sight. Take the Academy's best picture of the year, *Rocky*. Do you realize that it's the first fight picture—at least the first fight picture I remember—in which the major battle was scored? The main fight in *Rocky* was scored from beginning to end with an eighty-piece orchestra. Take the score away, and you've got a fight. You put the score in and you've got *Rocky*. That's the difference. People were cheering that fight, but they were cheering the music as much as the fight.

Your new film is Looking for Mr. Goodbar?

Yes. I don't know what that title means. I interviewed about six hundred women who had read the book. I said. "Tell me the story." I don't think three or four people told me the story of the book. They were all different stories, their own stories. Something in the book triggered their own stories. I asked them what the title meant, and they didn't quite know. As a matter of fact Judith Rossner, the author, wasn't sure either. But it doesn't matter. The main character in the novel was a teacher. What does she teach? You can't tell me because it doesn't say. What's more, there is not a moment in the novel when she is teaching. It turns out that the girl upon whom the story was really based taught in a school for the deaf.

What do you see as the key difference between Rossner's novel and your movie?

In the book the young woman has a recurring sense of guilt and depression about her life. On the other hand, at least from talking with a number of women, I felt that she is full of the joy of life. The girl is a Catholic, and interestingly enough, a group of Catholics recently published the results of a survey that found a massive drift among U.S. Catholics away from the Church's ban on contraception and toward a greater tolerance of extramarital intercourse. The study said that some theologians are offering flexible pastoral guidelines by which no behavior, including masturbation, adultery and homosexuality can be regarded as intrinsically evil. The morality of sexual conduct should be measured, they suggest, by whether it is self-liberating, other-enriching, honest, faithful, socially responsible, life-serving and joyous. Well, that's what I was talking and thinking about two years ago, and that's what our story is about. The point of the story—what happens to the girl—is that it could have happened on any day, at any hour and to any of a number of other people.

You're not moralizing about her life.

That's right. The girl had had a congenital disease, and after that she couldn't wait to enjoy life. At the same time she didn't want to make a commitment. I interviewed a number of people—men and women—and put their responses on tape. They all had a different point of view about the actual girl, and that freed me to create a story that is her own. I'm sure, though, that most people who see the picture will say, "Yes, that's the book." But, in fact, it's another kind of girl on the screen, because the novel has been ripped off a half dozen times already on television.

Diane Keaton is probably best known for her work in Woody Allen's films. Did you take into account her talent for comedy in Mr. Goodbar?

We made use of it, very much so. When American movies deal with sexuality, they're very serious, almost tragic. It's rarely with a sense of humor. But most of the time there is an element of humor to sex. Diane is an extremely talented woman with a great range, something I was never aware of. But I suppose she didn't have the opportunity to use it before. She's one of the best pros I've ever worked with. She fractured a rib during shooting but she kept working. She got a cold and she kept working. There wasn't a day she missed. Essentially, she's an extremely shy person, and there were things she was called on to do in this picture that frightened her. But she knew she would have to do them. She knew we were taking care of her, and she felt free enough to express herself.

Do you regard the movie version of Looking for Mr. Goodbar *as offering any answers about the singles culture?*

I'm giving no answers. I'm merely saying that this is one girl's life. I'm not trying to say, "This is the story of womanhood today." If others see in themselves something that applies, fine. I would like for people who come to see the picture, sitting in the dark theater, to feel as if they are looking across the street through a window at something that fascinates them. They can do nothing about it, but they are witnesses to it. What is happening there can be beautiful and joyous and exciting, and they may remember it was that way for them. "I wish it would be that way again with me." If I say to you right now, "What words do you use, what do you see when you are at the apex of lovemaking?" you might find it rather difficult to explain. Those are the things that we're trying to put on the screen.

What techniques did you use to convey those things?

One was lighting. What do you actually see when you're with someone? Do you really see the whole person or do you see just a small piece of him? Is it a cheekbone, a curve? The lighting became very, very important, and

William Fraker, the photographer, did a marvelous job. We were shooting some scenes by candlepower. The lab people didn't know what was going on. They were saying, "What the hell is this? We don't have an image." They said, "What about the drive-ins?" I said, "Well, I don't give a damn about the drive-ins. It's got nothing to do with drive-ins."

The other thing is that this girl has many fantasies, and the technique used is a structural one. The audience rarely knows when a fantasy begins—whether it's real or it's not real—until it's over. Somebody will say, "My God, that didn't happen at all." We do that deliberately, almost all the way through. The structuring of the story is another. There is not a scene in the entire picture, with the exception of one very close to the end, in which she does not lead us in and out of each incident. In other words, nothing happens unless she is there, or a party to it.

With these changes you've made, would you say that you have brought the novel up to date?

I tried to project the story into the future, which is now, and to show that changes have taken place, changes in the thinking of young people. The novel is fine, but I had to make a movie. It was the same with *In Cold Blood.* Truman Capote—quite a character—wanted to know if he could read the script. I said, "No, I don't think it's going to work that way. The studio is not going to see the script. The actors are not going to see the script. I think it would be wrong if you saw it. I'm going to do the best I can in keeping to the intention of the book, and I hope it's going to turn out all right." He never did see the script. You know, he seems like a mild little fellow, but as Muhammad Ali says, "Float like a butterfly, sting like a bee." And he really can sting like a hornet. He never saw the picture until we had it put together. We're still friends. He liked the movie. He said. "It's not exactly my book, but it's a hell of a movie." I was pleased about that because if he had disliked it, he could have murdered us.

You certainly haven't avoided difficult material. But can anything—even the presence of Truman Capote—compare with Elmer Gantry?

Elmer Gantry was very difficult to make. I had written a book during the war called *The Brick Foxhole.* When the book came out in 1945, Sinclair Lewis, who wrote reviews for *Esquire* magazine, wrote a very complimentary review, and I wrote him a letter thanking him. He wrote back and asked me, if I got into New York, to give him a call. I did, and we met at the Astor Bar. I told him how much I liked his books and how I was influenced by him, and I said, "One of your books I'd like to do as a movie someday." He said, "What title?" I said "*Elmer Gantry.*" He said, "Hmmm. If you're going to do it, read all the book reviews that were written about it and you will find that some of them are pretty good, especially some of those that criticize the book. If you compile all of those and think about them, maybe you will find a way to do it that will make a movie." Then he said, "I like movies but they get too diverse, and they get frightened of the book. Don't be frightened of the book."

I finally took an option on the book, but no studio would make it. They said it wasn't about a guy who sang and wanted to get baseball uniforms for the church team. It also wasn't about a Protestant minister and a leaking roof, and if he could raise enough money, everything would turn out all right. It was about everyday religion, and movies didn't make stories about that. Not American movies. So nobody would make it. Besides, the Masons said they would have the picture blacklisted throughout the world because of *Babbitt* and because Gantry was a Protestant. The Catholics wanted the picture made. The Protestants didn't want it made.

Frank Freeman, who was executive vice president of Paramount, wrote a letter to the head of Columbia and said, "Why don't you give him the money he put up for the book and tell him not to make the movie? First of all, it won't make any money. It's going to be a disaster. Second of all, they're going to ban it." But we had Jean Simmons and Burt Lancaster who wanted to make the picture, and we decided to go ahead anyway. That we kept the shooting going for the seventy-six or seventy-eight days is a tribute to the people who worked on the picture, because it was very difficult to do.

What were the problems?

For example, we needed extra money to do the interior fire sequence. I looked at all the films I could find dealing with fires, trying to learn. How do you make a fire? How do you shoot a fire scene? I found out something interesting. No pictures had been made up till then, 1959, with mass scene interior fires. Either it was an outside fire or the camera was outside. In *Rebecca,* as I remember, a woman ran by the window and that was that,

Brooks watches Burt Lancaster and Jean Simmons in a scene from *Elmer Gantry* (1960). Brooks and Lancaster both won Oscars for *Elmer Gantry.*

but the camera was outside. I couldn't find out how the hell you shoot a fire sequence. And how do you shoot nine hundred people in a riot? The budget for the fire was for six days. Thank God Burt Lancaster was one of the stars. He went to United Artists and said, "Brooks says he can't do it in six days." They said, "How long would it take?" "He doesn't know." They said, "How much money do you think it's going to take?" "It might take an extra two hundred thousand." They said, "Two hundred thousand dollars for a fire?" "Yes, maybe more." They said, "Well, will you and he take it out of your fees?" We agreed to do that, so they advanced the money. It took us five to six weeks to shoot that fire.

We shot partly on the studio back lot, where we had to have forty Los Angeles firemen and the sprinklers and everything else, and partly out at the Santa Monica Pier. Furthermore, we had to stop and start the fire over and over again. It was supposed to be a flash fire. Somebody throws a cigar or something into an oilcan and all the bunting and all of the banners— GOD IS LOVE and WE'LL BE SAVED—were supposed to go whoosh, and the fire was on.

We had a thousand people and two cameras and Miss Simmons out there in a white robe. I said, "Roll 'em. Action." Everybody started acting.

The cameras were going. No fire. Nothing. Which, of course, didn't leave me pacified. When they scraped me off the ceiling, I said, "What's going on here? Where's the fire?" The special effects guy came around and said, "I don't know. I pressed the button." I said, "It's not good that you don't know; it could be dangerous. Do you know what you're doing?" Somebody said, "Oh yes, he's been around a long time." That's scary right away. When somebody says, "I've been in the business twenty-five years—let me see the dailies," be wary. My father drove for twenty-seven years and was a lousy driver till he died.

So we got ready again, and with great trepidation I said, "Action." Everyone started to act, we rolled, and nothing happened. The special effects man came around again and said, "I talked to the firemen. They soaked the bunting and the drapes and all the paper. They can't burn." I went to a fireman and said, "Did you do that?" He said, "Yes, we have to do that. Suppose the building burns down?" I said, "Let it burn! The studio would love to see it burn down. It's insured." He said, "Well, we're paid to see that there are no fires, not by the studio but by the insurance company." I said, "Let's call a halt for a while. Miss Simmons, go to your dressing room. Mr. Lancaster, go eat."

I called one of the firemen and said, "Let's go for a walk." I said, "How do you start a fire?" He said, "I'm a fireman. How the hell would I know how to start a fire?" I said, "Why aren't you a policeman? You don't become a fireman just because you decide to be a fireman. You're a fireman because you're attracted to fire. So how do you do it?" He said, "Only one way. You get yourself some old nitrate film and lay it in that stuff there. That'll go." So we went to Columbia and bought fifty or sixty cans of film. They went down into the vault where all the rats are—you know, they never took care of their pictures. They had their negatives and prints down there, but you'd open a can and most of it would be dust. It wasn't even film anymore. So we laid the film along the streamers, everywhere. After lunch we called out Miss Simmons, Mr. Lancaster and the nine hundred people. She came onstage and everybody was ready. The cameras started going, the button was hit and that fucking fire went whoosh across the room. It burned like a bastard—it was really terrific. The stunt people were marvelous. I really don't know why they trusted us. It's about four and a half minutes of film on the screen. It was worth it.

Is it true that your ending for Elmer Gantry *was changed?*

Yes, there were four or five words we had to throw out. There was no rating board at that time, but there was the Legion of Decency, which operated out of New York. It could give you a rating that would ban the picture for Catholics. The Legion of Decency loved the picture, but they said, "We have a problem. Can you come to New York?" I went to New York. "You have to take out these last few words." "Why?" "Well, we think that it would be perhaps irreligious for you to say that." I said, "I don't see how." Three days we talked about it. They asked, "What is your intention? What do you really mean by it?" It was almost like a school of the Talmud and the Jesuits put together, and that's quite a combination. The discussions went on endlessly.

Finally, United Artists settled it. They said, "We've got to get the picture out. Fuck these three words. Take them out. What difference does it make?" I said to Burt Lancaster, "What about it?" He said, "Does it make that much difference?" I said. "If it didn't make that much difference why are they arguing so long?" Well, we lost the few words. The few words were these. At the end of the picture Gantry is leaving. Jean's character has died in the fire, and the people feel guilty. They say, "We hope that Sister Sharon will forgive us." He says, "I'm sure she will forgive you," and he begins to sing, and everybody joins in. He walks off to go back to being a salesman where he can drink and not have to hide it. The reporter looks at him and says, "See you around, brother." That's the end now. What's missing is that Gantry stopped, looked back and said, "I'll see you in hell, brother." He knew where he was going. The Legion would not accept the words. They said, "That means that he knows that he did wrong, and if he knows that he did wrong there's no lesson." I couldn't convince them and they couldn't convince me. But United Artists convinced both of us.

The Masons tried to have the film banned, and I'd say that in half the world the picture has yet to play and probably never will play. Jean Simmons and I went to Jakarta—I was looking for locations—and there was a mob waiting for us there. From the plane it looked like a couple of thousand people, and I thought, "I'd better have a speech ready." So I tried to think of what I was going to say, and how to address the people and so forth, and we got off the plane and I hear a chant that goes up from these thousands of people, "Miss Simmons, Miss Simmons." They didn't know who the fuck I was. They'd never heard of me, didn't even know I was on the plane. As a matter of fact, most of my pictures are banned there. Sukarno the president of Indonesia asked, "You made a picture that got some Academy Awards?" I said, "Yes." Then he talked to a woman who was on his censor board and asked, "Why have we not seen this picture?" She said something so him, and he said, "Ahhh! Religious questions. Very serious. Not show it in this country." I said, "Why not? You've got a hundred million people here. Ninety-seven million of them are Muslims. What's it got to do with you if the film's about Catholics or Protestants?" He said both groups would protest, so the film never played there.

Could you talk a little about Jean Simmons' role in the film?

Jean had a difficult time because she had the most thankless role in the film. She was the only straight line in the story, the only one who actually believed. She knew exactly where she stood, and I had to balance the other characters off her. Gantry was on one side, Arthur Kennedy—who played the reporter—was on the other; and the church was on another side still. Because of this, all the other characters seemed to be much more colorful than her, and audiences remember the other roles more. In one scene, she had to address an assembly where the students were rioting and poking fun at her, and she had to come out and try to stop them because Gantry couldn't do it. They were pretty rough, and she would begin by paraphrasing a segment of Ecclesiastes. I think the beginning was "Dearest God," and she had a little problem saying that. I said, "You're starting this thing off in the wrong way. It sounds like you're writing a letter. You're probably the only person here who actually believes. Is there anything that you, Jean, really believe in? Do you go to church? Do you believe in God? Is there anyone you really feel in the form of God, or close to it?" She said, "Well, my father. He was a wonderful man." I said, "Do you see him? Do you talk to him?" She said, "No, he's dead. He died when I was about sixteen." "And you loved him very much?" "Yes, I still do." I said, "Well, when you go out there, why don't you address yourself to him?" That's all she needed, and she was just fine.

At what point do you begin thinking about casting when you're in the process of preparing a movie?

I usually try not to think about casting at all until I have a script. You have two enemies when it comes to casting. One is the studio, the other is the agents. The agents have a lot of control, and they're related not by blood, not by marriage, but I guess by money. The fact that they all have money or they all want money is their common bond. They are all related to the studios and distribution organizations and are trying to get packages in there. You may think an actor is right for the role, but if you take him you've got to take her, and if you take her there's also that one. Now the studio will say, "All right. You don't want to show us the script. Okay. We know the idea. We'll go along. You're not going to show us the dailies. Well, that's hard to take because we're really good at that. Okay. But we have to approve the two main parts." If you're looking for casting rights, if you're looking for final cut, if you're looking for the right to make your movie your way, it's going to depend on whether or not you've made money for the studio heads. If you make money for them, you can have almost anything, even their wives. Especially their wives. Anything they've got you can have, if you make money for them. If you don't, then it's very tough.

When casting, you'll have to contend with the studio. They begin with this: "Why don't you get Newman and Redford? That's a good combination, don't you think?" You say, "Yes, I'd say that's pretty good." Because if you can get Paul Newman and Robert Redford, the guy in Munich picks up the phone and says, "I'll buy the picture." They'll even say, "The woman's part in this script is very good. Have you ever thought that maybe it ought to be a man, so you've got two men? You know, buddies? *Butch Cassidy and the Sundance Kid* worked out pretty well." And now they have *The Sting* to work with. They'll always come up with that sort of brilliance. Casting against type doesn't attract them.

But you don't cast in your mind while you're working on a script?

I think then you'll bend your story toward someone who has already established a character on the screen. It would be better if you didn't. I think it's better if you write the character, and if the actor is good enough, he will try to play that role. It's the reason I don't give most of the cast the script. It's not because I don't like them. As a matter of fact, I feel very tender and in awe of my cast. They're doing something I can't do. I can't act. They can, and it's the toughest kind of acting there is in the world. It's much more difficult than on the stage, because on the stage you have a chance to build a character from beginning to end in three hours. You can hear the audience. You've had a chance to rehearse for four or five weeks. You know where all the jokes are. You know where the silences are. You can build in an emotional rise. But in film you shoot for twenty seconds, thirty seconds, maybe a minute, maybe two minutes.

The reason I don't give most of the cast the script is this: if they know the entire story, if they know where their character is going, they're likely to play one thing when they're supposed to be playing something else. They're playing the end before the beginning, and the middle before the end. You never shoot in continuity because the cost is prohibitive. So very often the actor doesn't know where the beginning or the end is. But if he's read it all, he's liable to play the whole thing all the time. There's no progression to his character. You and I didn't meet until tonight. If we met again after tonight we'd have a different relationship, but it wouldn't be the relationship we had just now. And so it is in a movie. The actors should know only a certain amount. Not all actors—Paul Newman, for example—can act that way. He has to know what he's going to do from beginning till the end. Then we have to break it down so that he doesn't repeat. Fortunately, he has now directed a movie. I wish everybody I have ever worked with—from the grips and makeup to everyone in the cast— had directed at least one movie. Then they would know my problems.

Your emphasis is always on the actor.

You shouldn't be aware of the director. If anybody at any time says, "Wow, what a shot," then you've lost the audience. They should never know there's a director in it. They should never know where the music starts or ends. They should never see the camera move. They should never have to say, "Isn't that interesting?" They should be lost in the story. That's all you're telling them. That's where the camera is. Christ, I can make a very interesting shot between the legs of that chair, or from the ceiling, or from the balcony. You can pump in a shot from here, and you knock them in with a close shot there, and you get one eye here, and you get something else there, and pretty soon you're saying, "That's terrific."

Well, that's one way of making a movie, and I'm not denigrating it. But *I* say, "The camera is here because that's where the story point is." All I'm trying to do is tell a story. Shooting through a lot of bushes and the wheel of a car makes it more interesting, perhaps, but then there's something missing from your story. You can't get to the characters for the ferns and the latticework and the curtains. I'm shooting for story and I cast for story. All you're going to see up there on the screen are the actors who are up there.

Are you concerned about critics?

You're damned right—concerned and scared. Most of the time the critics are reviewing one another. They write about another critic's review and you're caught somewhere in the middle, and you don't know what they mean. The critics have broken my heart more times than the women I've loved. And when you've finished a picture and the studio sees it for the first time, they'll break your heart too. They'll say that four minutes and thirty-one seconds ought to be taken out. You'll say, "Why four minutes and thirty-one seconds?" Well, it's a good, round number, I guess. I don't know how the hell they decide. "Take six minutes out, and it'll be terrific." "How about seven? How about three and a half?" They'll say, "I just have a feel." Well, they're full of shit. They don't have a feel about anything. They'd just like to get in one more running a day. Instead of five, they'd rather have six.

It's going to be rough on you, but if you love it and your real reward is in the making of the picture—not in getting in that big, fucking black limousine and going out there for opening night—your reward will be when that picture is finished. Your reward for a picture is in the making of it—from the very beginning to the end. But I don't go back to see any of my own movies. I'm afraid to see them on television. I don't want to sit through *In Cold Blood* again because then I might want to do the picture over again. I'm doing something else now. I've gone on from there. I hope to do something better each time. But I love it, and I love my failures.

Which especially?

I like especially *The Happy Ending*. We were maybe four or five years too soon with that. It was a disaster financially. I made the picture because I wanted to do a story about what was happening in this country to women, about the fact that marriage maybe doesn't work. Now, that's a pretty big idea to swallow. I didn't have any bad guys in the picture. We started with the romantic American notion that you marry and live happily every after. In the first four or five minutes of the picture a woman is romanced, quits college because she's in love and marries the guy. As she marries the guy, she sees Gable and Tracy and all those characters that she's grown up with. She's been influenced by the ads, influenced by the movies, by the fairy tales of romantic marriage. Then in less than fifteen feet of film—I think it was a six-foot dissolve, which is pretty long as a dissolve—it's sixteen years later. By the way that woman comes out and picks up the morning paper, you know that something has changed.

The picture was a few years ahead of its time. Afterward four or five others were very successful, along the same idea. But at the time people asked, "The woman is going back to school at the end? She's not going to go back to her husband? What happened? It wasn't infidelity that broke them up. They weren't too rich. They weren't too poor. They didn't have too many children. What was wrong?" One of the things that was wrong is time. Time destroys romance, as can the very act of marriage. Marriage may be—and I tried to say this in the film—antipathetic to love. Love, when you meet someone and have a love relationship, can be changed by marriage. Conditions change, duties change. Time changes, and you're required to perform in a certain way. You don't want to make a phone call, but you make it anyway because you're supposed to. You begin to write down dates. When is the birthday? When is the anniversary? That's not love anymore. Well, Christ, that's not love anymore—that's something else entirely.

Then there's the problem of the woman giving herself up to become a wife. Well, these are not the pioneer days, when the woman did just as much as the man did in crossing the country in a covered wagon. She's got too much time on her hands. What does she do with her time? I was trying to say that the love relationship takes three personalities. The man has his personality, the woman has her personality, and together they make a third personality. If either one of them gives up his or her personality, then you don't have a third personality. That's what I was trying to say in the movie. Nobody wanted to see it. But I'm glad I made it.

When did you begin the practice of not showing the script to the studio or the actors?

It first came about when I found out that the studios were mimeographing my scripts and giving them to the television companies. They were taking sections of the scripts and using them on television before I got a chance to shoot them. Not only the plots and story lines but dialogue. The first thing I had to do was stop the studios from seeing the scripts. That was the beginning. Then I found that actors and actresses sometimes have a tendency to take their scripts home and show them to their wives or their mistresses or their husbands. Or worse, to their agents. The agent is a real danger. As soon as he reads a script he starts talking about it, and he's talking to four other writers, and they've got the same story that you have. It finally got to the point where I said, "I think it might be better if fewer people saw it."

The cameraman is always saying, "If I could read the script, I'd know what we were doing." Well, I've worked with some very good cameramen, and I think when you find one you can trust it's probably a good idea for him to read it—once, in your office, where he can't get out, which is where I allow the cast to read it. Jean Simmons said, "I've got to read the script. I'd like to do the picture, but I don't know what I'm supposed to do." "Sit down and read it. Then leave it. And if you talk about it, you will not be in the picture." I went through that with Diane Keaton for *Mr. Goodbar.* She had to read the script because she was going to do it for less money, because I had to make it for no money. I told the studio I thought it was a very dicey story. If it was going to be told honestly and cast honestly, it shouldn't be made for more than the smallest amount of money possible. Diane was willing to defer a lot of her money if she could read the script. It wasn't an easy decision to make, especially when I found out she was going to an analyst. I thought, if she's going to an analyst she's going to discuss it with the analyst. Suppose she reads it and then decides she doesn't want to do it. I'm altogether dead.

So after threatening her with all sorts of things—like I'd wait for her outside a building and clobber her or something—I let her read the script in the office, and she said, "Yes." I said, "If I ever hear you talked about it, terrible things will happen to you, besides which we'll have to cut parts of the movie." That was the worst threat of all. I said, "If you talk about it, it's going to be seen somewhere else, and if I see it someplace else I'm going to tear it out." That's happened to me a few times. I had to take a few pieces out of this picture. I don't think somebody talked. I think it may have been coincidence. That's why it started.

Speaking of scripts, reading and properly understanding a script is something of a special talent in itself, don't you think?

Do you know how few people know how to read a script? Many studio executives see first how many pages there are. Then they want to know, "Well, is it that long?" What does that mean? Then they read the dialogue, usually just the dialogue. But even if they read the dialogue and the narrative it doesn't mean they can visualize the script. Very few people can see the script the way you have prepared it and the way you're going to make it.

You insist you've created nothing but pictures people don't go see, but that's not really true. What about Cat on a Hot Tin Roof?

George Cukor was going to do that movie. The script was ready when I got a call from Benny Thau, who asked if I was doing anything. I said, "I'm kind of preparing something." He said, "Well, how about *Cat on a Hot Tin Roof*?" I said, "I thought George Cukor was doing that?" But George had decided that he was not going to make it. See, in those days you couldn't mention the word homosexual. You couldn't ever say the word on screen, let alone deal with the subject, so George decided not to do it. Benny Thau said, "We've got one picture left with Elizabeth Taylor, and we've got to start by February first." This was around November. Elizabeth and Mike Todd—who was a terrific character—were in Russia on his private plane at the time, on a honeymoon. "So, if you want to do it— as a matter of fact, you've got to do it." I read the script and said, "Well, I can't do this script." He said, "I know. Neither can we. There are things in here we can't do." I called Elia Kazan—I didn't know Tennessee Williams; I still haven't met him, by the way—and asked, "What did you do about the third act?" Kazan said, "Well, we had two third acts. Would you like to read the other third act? I think it's a little better, but it still didn't solve all the problems." So I finally got a script that I thought I could do, and I told Benny Thau I would try.

How did you cast the male lead?

I had trouble casting the fellow. Onstage he was played by Ben Gazzara, but the studio didn't want Ben Gazzara because he looked Italian. They suggested Robert Taylor, and they had a lot of people under contract. I said, "That won't do. None of these people is right." "Who do you want?" I said, "Well, I saw a guy in New York who was pretty good, in the play *The Desperate Hours.* I think he might be able to do it. He's a good actor. Something happens in this fellow's eyes when you look at him. In the first forty-five minutes of *Cat on a Hot Tin Roof* the character says very little, so something's got to happen." I was talking about Paul Newman. They didn't want Paul Newman because he made a picture called *The Silver*

Chalice which didn't make money. Finally Mike Todd, who had returned with Elizabeth, said, "For Christ's sake, we're going to blow this thing because Elizabeth is going to walk out on the picture. You want Paul Newman?" He went in and talked to the studio heads. That afternoon they said, "Okay, we'll go with Paul Newman." They got him for twenty-five thousand dollars, of which he only got seventeen thousand, and Warners got the other eight thousand.

Two weeks after we started shooting, Mike Todd said, "How about flying into Chicago?" Elizabeth had not been working for two days because she had a cold. He said, "We'll go to Chicago and from there into New York. Just for a day. We'll fly in and come right back and be ready to shoot Monday." I said, "You're insane. If she has a cold and can't work for two days, how in the hell is she going to get on a plane and be back and healthy enough to work on Monday? She shouldn't go." He said, "Well, how about you? We'll have a hell of a time." I said, "What are you talking about? Sunday I'm rewriting for Monday." He got some poor newspaper-man, a sportswriter, to go with him. The plane crashed, and they were killed.

Saturday they were going to take the body and Elizabeth Taylor to Chicago because they were going to bury him on Sunday. I got a call from Elizabeth's secretary who said, "I think you ought to get up here because this girl is hysterical. She's about to go off the deep end." So I went up to the house, and I no sooner had walked in than the secretary said, "She's in there. Bedroom." I walked into the bedroom, and she took one look at me and started screaming, "You son of a bitch! I guess you're here like all the rest of these bastards who have been here all day long! 'When am I going to go back to work?'" And she named them all, the executive staff from the studio, including the producers of the movie. They had gone there with flowers and doleful voices and all that crap, but what they finally got around to asking each time was, "So, how soon do you think you'll be back, honey?" Well, she saw me and figured it was the same deal. I said, "Elizabeth, if you don't want to come back to this movie, don't come back. It's a movie—that's all it is. If you don't do it, they'll start over and find somebody else to do it. If you never want to come back, that's fine." She said, "Well, I'm not. I'm never coming back. Fuck you and the movie and everybody else."

Anyway, on Monday morning I was called to the studio, and the executive said, "I guess we'll close down the company." I said, "You can't do that." He said, "Well, this girl is not going to come back." I said, "Maybe she won't come back, and if any of you calls her again, I won't come back either." He said, "What do you mean? You're going to shoot?" I said, "We'll shoot as much as we can without Elizabeth Taylor. If you close the company now, you're dead. You might as well forget this movie." "How long can you shoot?" I said, "I don't know. I think we may have a week's work, maybe ten days. Perhaps two weeks if we stretch it. With my rewriting, it might be a little more. She only has two outfits—a white dress and a slip. I'll stage the scenes in such a way that somebody in a white dress is going to come by a foot and a half from the camera, and you'll see a white something going by. If it's not Elizabeth Taylor, it'll be somebody else." We shot that way for almost three weeks. I even shot things over.

One day I got a call from Elizabeth Taylor's secretary who said, "Miss Taylor would like to come and see you. Is the set closed?" I said, "Yes, it's always closed." So she arrived in a car with the window shades down, and she said, "I think I'd like to come back to work." I said, "It's up to you." "I don't want to see that producer down here. If he comes on, I'm leaving. I don't know how long I'll be able to work. Maybe I'll start and something will happen." The next day she showed up. I think she worked an hour. The day after that, for a couple of hours. By the end of the week she was working four or five hours. Never missed a day and was never late. People talk about stars who are tardy and are temperamental, but I've never had that problem. Especially with stars. I've been very lucky. So that's the story. She finished the picture, and we finished on time. Everything was fine, and the picture made a lot of money.

Did the element of homosexuality in Cat on a Hot Tin Roof *have to be removed to placate the times?*

We had to find a substitute for homosexuality. I got a call recently from someone who wanted to make a movie of my novel, *The Brick Foxhole,* which was once made into a movie called *Crossfire.* In the novel, a bunch of marines go out on a weekend pass and kill a homosexual because they don't like homosexuals. In my outfit, marines didn't like black people, didn't like Jews, didn't like homosexuals, didn't like Catholics. They didn't like anybody except marines, Protestant marines, especially if they came from Texas or Atlanta. I also had in the novel a Jewish fellow and a black fellow. When it was made into a movie, the Jew and the homosexual were combined—it was the first picture about anti-Semitism. Now I get a call from someone, and he says, "Hey, let's do *The Brick Foxhole* the way it was written, bring it up to date, put it in the Vietnam War or something." I said, "I've written the book, and that's enough."

The times have changed.

Yes. Look at *Blackboard Jungle.* That picture cost about $380,000. We had to use records for music. The studio wouldn't even give us a composer for that picture because they thought that it was Communist propaganda, and they hated the picture anyway. The only one who didn't hate the picture was Dore Schary.* Nicholas Schenck† didn't like it. The MGM executive Edgar Mannix thought it was a little red, and Mr. Mayer didn't like any picture. As a matter of fact he told me in the hallway, "I don't like the pictures you make. *You're* all right, but I don't like the pictures you make. You don't make MGM movies. Always with the dirty fingerprints on the wall. I hate that stuff. And now you're making a picture about a black fellow, and he's so arrogant, a smart-ass. They're not nice people." I said, "Well, Mr. Mayer, maybe you ought to let me go." "No," he said, "they say things are changing. You seem like a nice fellow, but if you could only make our kind of movies it would be much better." When we finally finished *Blackboard Jungle,* the studio said, "That music, that terrible music. It's awful. You've got to do something about that." They were talking about "Rock Around the Clock," which was the first time rock had been introduced into movies. I had heard it on a black station, driving home from a poker game one night two years before. I remembered the record, used it when I was writing the script and finally used it in the picture.

One day, before I had finished the picture, Pandro Berman, the producer, said, "Listen, we've got a problem. We've got to shoot an extra scene." I said, "What extra scene?" He said, "Well, a scene arrived from New York that was written by Schenck or somebody. Read it." It was a page and a half, and the scene took place in Moscow. A teacher in a Moscow elementary school is saying to another teacher, "These rebels, these terrible radicals we've got here, look at what they're doing, tearing up things. We've got the same problems they have in the States, don't we?" I said, "What the hell has that got to do with our story? The school in *Blackboard Jungle* is the kind of grade school I went to when I was a kid." He said, "Well, what does it matter if we shoot it? Shoot it and we won't

*Dore Schary (1905–1980) was head of MGM in the 1950s.
†Nicholas Schenck (1881–1969) was one of the founders of MGM.

use it." "Oh no," I said. "I've heard this before." He said, "Well, maybe you should go see Dore." I went to see Dore Schary. Every time he got a call from New York he went into traction. Half the time he was running the studio he was in traction. He said, "You're here about the scene." I said, "Yes, it's terrible. I can't do it." He said, "I give you my word: do it and we'll throw it away. They'll be satisfied. At least they'll be happy." I said, "Dore, anybody can shoot that. When we're finished, get somebody else, get a classroom, put up a red flag with a hammer and sickle and get two of your character actors. But I'm not going to shoot it."

When the picture was ready, we took it out to Encino and they started to tear up the seats. It was tried in New York. The same thing happened there. So it opened, and people went to see it. A lot of people. Later, when I was coming back from Europe, I was asked to come in to see Mr. Schenck. The Loews building was above the Loews Theater at that time. I went up, and he took me to the window and we looked down. There was a line forming outside Loews Theater, waiting to get in to see the movie. This was about two o'clock in the afternoon. He said, "My boy, you knew something." I said, "Mr. Schenck, I didn't know a goddamned thing." "Oh yes, you knew that the people were going to like it." I said, "No, sir. What did you have to lose? $380,000? That's what the picture cost." "But you knew that they would like it." I said, "No. You hated it. Everybody else hated it. I have no idea why they come and I have no idea why they stay away. It's just something that I believed in. It's a true story. Why they come to see it I have no idea. You didn't even advertise it." He said, "I don't understand you people. You won't tell me the truth. When the people come to see a picture there's a reason." I said, "Yes, there probably is a reason, but I don't know what the reason is." He said, "You'll make a lot of pictures that will fail." I said, "Yes, I probably will." And he was right. I have. But that was a picture that made them a lot of money.

Studios are strange. The day before we started shooting *In Cold Blood,* the studio was still trying to get me to use Paul Newman and Steve McQueen in the two parts—so help me God—and shoot it in color. "Please shoot it in color, because they won't show it on television." Even when they make money, they don't know quite why they made the money. What picture made more than *Jaws?* No picture in the world. They think it's because of the advertising of the shark's head. They think maybe because it was a best seller. Or the advertising campaign. Nonsense. It made a great deal of money because it was very well done. It was an extremely entertaining picture. It had a good score, like the one for the fight in *Rocky*. You knew the shark was coming before you ever saw the shark. People will pay today $3.50 or $4.00 to be scared without being in danger themselves. You can be scared by the shark, which is a common denominator for people, because in the water we're out of our element—water for humans is strange. It's the same with *The Exorcist*, except with *The Exorcist* you have an additional advantage. It's not even a shark. It's something called the Devil, whom nobody has ever seen. Half the kids who ran to wait in line didn't believe in God but they believed in the Devil. I don't know how that's possible. You can't have one without the other.

The basic essential of a movie is a thin line. Here's a railroad track. Here's a train coming. A girl is tied to the track. Here's the hero coming on the horse. The train might run her over first. The hero might get there and untie her while the villain twirls his mustache. That kind of movie used to cost about six cents when I was very small. It was a silent picture, and the piano was playing Beethoven. Why don't you jump up from your seat if your heart is really beating that way and you're so deeply emotionally involved? Run up there and untie her! Because you know you're in the theater. But if you know you're in a theater and it's not happening, why is your heart accelerating that way? Because you can do both. The effect of film can walk that thin line where you can be so excited and so involved that you will weep for someone on the screen. Your heart tempo will pick up, your blood pressure will become higher, and yet you will not run up there and do something. You're playing both roles as a moviegoer. If a writer or director can do that to an audience, he's got a big hit. I must write that down for myself.

Do you have any advice for our students here?

You're going to make mistakes. You're going to make them every time. Now, I hope you won't make the same ones every time. Once you try to repeat your previous success—if you're lucky enough to have one—you're going to have trouble. If you're worried about failing, you ought to get into a different business, because statistics will tell you that sixty or seventy percent of the time you're going to fail. By *fail* I mean that it won't make money. Just do the best you can every time. And if you're going to stay in movies, and you like movies—and I love them—you'd better love them a lot, because it's going to take all your time. If you want to be in movies, it's going to break your heart.

Films as Director

1950 *Crisis* (also screenplay)

1951 *The Light Touch* (also screenplay)

1952 *Deadline—U.S.A.* (also screenplay)

1953 *Battle Circus* (also screenplay)
Take the High Ground!

1954 *Flame and the Flesh*
The Last Time I Saw Paris (also co-screenplay)

1955 *Blackboard Jungle* (also screenplay)

1956 *The Last Hunt* (also screenplay)
The Catered Affair

1957 *Something of Value* (also screenplay)

1958 *The Brothers Karamazov* (also co-screenplay)
Cat on a Hot Tin Roof (also co-screenplay)

1960 *Elmer Gantry* (also screenplay)

1962 *Sweet Bird of Youth* (also screenplay)

1965 *Lord Jim* (also producer and screenplay)

1966 *The Professionals* (also producer and screenplay)

1967 *In Cold Blood* (also producer and screenplay)

1969 *Happy Ending* (also producer and screenplay)

1971 *$* (also screenplay)

1975 *Bite the Bullet* (also producer and screenplay)

1977 *Looking for Mr. Goodbar* (also screenplay)

1982 *Wrong is Right* (also producer and screenplay)

1985 *Fever Pitch* (also screenplay)

In the work you and I are doing, controlled arrogance is a necessity. It's a mixture of drive and the feeling that your imagination is enough to make it cross borders. You have to have a dream—every picture is a dream, and some of them turn out to be bad dreams.

STANLEY KRAMER
(Born in New York City, 1913—Died 2001)

Stanley Kramer is the only director in this volume who started out as a producer. He worked in Hollywood in the thirties as a researcher, editor and writer, then served in the Army Signal Corps in New York during the war. Afterward, he discovered he'd lost his civilian job at the studio. "I decided that the best way to make films," he told biographer Donald Spoto, "was to form an independent company and be the boss. That way, in due time, I could appoint myself the director." His approach was to make small films with controversial themes, a thrust that was to become his hallmark as a producer, and later as a director.

Kramer's first film as producer was *Champion* in 1949, introducing Kirk Douglas as a boxer in the seamy world of prizefighting. Then came *Home of the Brave*, a Broadway play about anti-Semitism that Kramer made into a film about racism. And in 1950 he cast Marlon Brando in his first screen role in *The Men*, a story of paraplegic GIs trying to find their way after the war. He found a way to make socially conscious films—*High Noon, The Defiant Ones, Inherit the Wind, Judgment at Nuremberg* and *Guess Who's Coming to Dinner*. His method was to enlist important stars who provided box-office credibility to pictures with serious themes. He also made conventional Hollywood epics, such as *The Pride and the Passion, Ship of Fools* and *It's A Mad Mad Mad Mad World*.

In 1963 Kramer was invited to the Moscow Film Festival. I was at USIA and had been named chairman of the U.S. delegation. I proposed a small Kramer retrospective that would show the seriousness in American film production to the Russian cinema community, which had few opportunities to see work from the West during the cold war. The State Department objected,

Tony Curtis, Sidney Poitier and Stanley Kramer work out a scene for *The Defiant Ones* (1958). Kramer planned the film for Marlon Brando and Poitier, but when Brando withdrew, he gave the role to Curtis.

citing reasons why each of the proposed films would work against U.S. interests: *The Defiant Ones,* because the Tony Curtis chain-gang prisoner was a racist; *Judgment at Nuremburg,* because the film had a negative portrayal of the Germans, who were our allies in the struggle against international Communism; and *On the Beach,* because it dealt with the specter of nuclear war. The dispute rose to the highest levels of the department, with Averell Harriman, our wartime ambassador to Russia, and Llewellyn Thompson, the most recent past ambassador, taking opposing sides. The Kramer retrospective finally gained approval because the films were to be shown primarily to members of the Soviet film unions.

Kramer was a great success in Moscow. Filmmakers applauded his films, often chanting "Kraaaamer, Kraaaamer, Kraaaamer" at their conclusion. On each occasion, Stanley spoke directly and compellingly to the film community, making a fine impression for his country. Deputy Minister of Culture Vladimir Baskakov, perhaps sharing the State Department view, unexpectedly scheduled a Sunday evening showing of *The Defiant Ones* for festivalgoers and the public in the Palace of Congresses, the elaborate seven-thousand-seat chamber inside the Kremlin, a setting very different from what the State Department expected. Finding myself in an awkward position, I decided that if Sidney Poitier attended the showing, the positive aspect of the film would outweigh any negative impression—it would be evident that in America, artists were free to explore difficult issues. I reached Sidney in London and he agreed to fly to Moscow.

No sooner had he landed on Saturday afternoon than the Soviets, believing we had turned the showing into an advantage for the United States, canceled the screening. Instead, there would be a showing at the Sports Palace, on the outskirts of Moscow, at ten o'clock Sunday morning. We dutifully got up at dawn, and when we arrived at the old wooden facility an hour from our hotel we saw, to our amazement, fifteen thousand people standing in line. We wondered how word had traveled so fast. It was clearly a sign of the appetite of the Russian people to see Western films behind the iron curtain.

The New York Times reported from Moscow that Poitier received a "tumultuous" personal ovation, and that "upon hearing the Negro actor speak the line, 'You live all your life and you never utter a word till you die,' the audience of ten thousand persons, mostly Russians, responded with a roar of applause." The screening was one of the most emotional I have experienced. After the film, the crowd stood—many with tears in their eyes—and gave Poitier and Kramer an ovation that subsided only when we had left the auditorium. Stanley's visit to Moscow marked a high point in the cultural exchange between the two countries during those long years of estrangement.

Kramer saw himself not as a messenger but as a storyteller with a point of view. He was one of the only Hollywood filmmakers to sustain a career making pictures with controversial themes. "I'm trying to determine my own sense of values," he once said, "And sometimes I've done that searching in my films—which hasn't always been *good*, but it's always been *me*."

STANLEY KRAMER

—◆—

March 14, 1973*

Selfishly, I'm a little pooped. I have been working hard and this date crept up on me, so my spirit is willing but not necessarily my morale.

I've traveled through the film circuits of the world, both at a university and a professional level, and the best thing that I can say to you is this: I'm willing to stand still for any amount of discussion—either provocative, controversial, personal, embarrassing or emotional—for as long as you want. On that basis it may be that because you either challenge me or I challenge you, we'll both get the values we seek. I'll get as much value out of what you're thinking as I want you to get out of my thoughts. There is nothing about which I'm not prepared to deal. I've been dealing with it for such a long time, on levels where I smelled the blood of sweet combat—what I call the deliciousness of head-on conflict of ideas. I feel no compulsion that you agree with me about anything. I'm not sure your approbation is necessary, and if that's arrogant it's because in the work you and I are doing, controlled arrogance is a necessity. It's a mixture of drive and the feeling that your imagination is enough to make it cross borders. You have to have a dream—every picture is a dream, and some of them turn out to be bad dreams.

When I started in film I was nineteen—I didn't listen to anybody. I was dealing with film which was elastic and I quickly found that my viewpoint and my ideas were almost as good as anybody else's. So I went ahead

*This transcript contains segments from seminars Stanley Kramer gave at the American Film Institute on September 29, 1976, January 6, 13, and 25, 1977 and February 1, 1977.

and tried to *do,* and sometimes *did* and sometimes *didn't.* By being bold when you're younger you intrude your personality into situations with far greater force. And by ignoring the viewpoints of so many other people, you're more likely to achieve things on your own. I was what my era called a revolutionary. I don't really know what that means, but I did feel the sharp edge of my revolutionary being in relationship to the cinema establishment.

You have a reputation for making a particular kind of film, those that deal with what we might call "social concerns." Why have you concentrated on these kinds of films?

As an artist you need to hold onto something, find an excuse for existence. Am I, as Pauline Kael said, "Someone who if he hadn't been born would have had to be created?" I talk in social terms, and you'll have to forgive me. I was spawned into film out of the Franklin Roosevelt era, the time of the "liberal approach" that promised a good deal and didn't make it. I have been a kind of flag-bearer of that viewpoint and therefore somewhat viciously attacked along the way. After World War II, the things that impressed me and that I became interested in turned out to be issues which I thought could be dramatized. I found out early in my life that nobody really objected to "message" films. They object to messages which didn't make money, which was something very different.

The day in 1939 that Eleanor Roosevelt refused to speak at Constitution Hall under the sponsorship of the Daughters of the American Revolution because Marian Anderson had been barred from singing there—that changed the course of my life. It was provocation, to a certain extent. I was a college student at the time Roosevelt came into office, and it was a time of the greatest social change in the history of America. I was terribly affected by it, and so the things that appealed to me when I became a filmmaker were the things which were the social objectives as laid down during that administration. My work reflected these concerns not because I thought I could change anything or anybody, but because those were the things that interested me. My arrogance told me I might occasionally be able to make them sufficiently entertaining so I could hold an audience. When you do things that have something of a provocative and challenging quality, you find yourself drawn into the political arena. But when I made films I had no coherent political philosophy and never tried to tell anybody anything.

A film like *The Defiant Ones,* for example, was merely an inadequate attempt by a white filmmaker to deal with a contemporary problem. James Baldwin has been very critical of me, and though it hurt, what he said is true. He said I captured all the intellectual and moral viewpoints of my age but didn't capture the soul of the black man. Well, who the hell does he think I am? I'm *not* black. The fact is that I am a white man who made films about human beings who happened to be black. I understood the problems of black men and women morally, socially and intellectually, but the damn soul kept slipping between my fingers. It had to be spoon-fed to me secondhand because I didn't feel it or know it enough. There are so many areas into which I've stepped under the umbrella of what is sometimes amusingly called the Establishment, Hollywood style. The reason I'm defensive about my films is that sometimes—just to get the job done—not enough of the artist and too much of the political tactician and social worker prevailed. That's where my area of sensitivity is. It's just like undressing in front of you and saying, "Well, look, this is where I'm vulnerable. Stab me there."

Where did you get the idea for Home of the Brave?

From the play by Arthur Laurents about a Jewish soldier who was assigned to a unit and became paralyzed because somebody—his best friend—made a racial slur. The Jewish soldier kept saying, "I am different. They make me feel different." But he didn't look that different, so what was all the excitement about? The play was interesting, but the film caught fire when we made the character a black soldier. Don't forget this was an age—it was the early years of World War II—during which black troops were segregated.

I was watching Judgment at Nuremberg *the other day and wondered how it's managed to hold up today given all that's happened. Did you feel you were making a statement that had to be made?*

No, I didn't. I can't ever be accused of mock humility, or even real humility. Let me try to explain something. I've never had that much pride in anything I've been associated with, and I can tell you why. When I began work as a filmmaker, I wanted desperately to be an artist. From my standpoint—and you have to accept this without any mock humility—I never came close. The reason was that I was born into film at a time when to make my mark and to do what I wanted to do, I took on the establishment within the Hollywood firmament. The subjects I tackled and the things I did were all within this establishment. Within it, not without it.

To get them made in the first place as I wanted to make them, I did not sacrifice my integrity in terms of the material I was dealing with. But I certainly surer than hell sacrificed many of the means and conveyances which I had to use to make the films. I prefer to reach the bigger audiences. The most satisfying thing in the world is to sit and watch and listen to an audience in a theater responding the way you wanted them to respond. To get *On the Beach* made, I made a deal with United Artists that I would use two stars and UA would finance the picture. This had happened to me twenty times in my career. I always had to work on such large canvases to get the film made at all. Do you think United Artists wanted to make *Judgment at Nuremberg,* the story of a trial? They weren't at all interested in those people in the ovens and the crooked judges. "Where are the protagonists?" they asked. I studded it with stars to get it made as a film so that I would reach out to a mass audience.

I didn't want Gregory Peck and Ava Gardner in *On the Beach* because that made it much less realistic for me. The presence of the stars made the film less powerful, less to the point, less living at the moment for me, because I felt the challenge to say, "I'm making a picture about the total extinction of the world." For me, a film like *Hiroshima Mon Amour,* which was about being able to sustain life on a planet that is faced with atomic warfare, was ultimately more powerful than *On the Beach.* The difficulty is that I'm an American. I made *On the Beach* and it was seen by millions of people. *Hiroshima Mon Amour* got a limited release and was seen by a select audience.

How did you get someone like Burt Lancaster to play a Nazi in Judgment at Nuremberg?

By appealing to his ego, of course. Burt Lancaster wasn't the first choice. Olivier was supposed to play the Nazi because the British have a way of doing Germans; I don't know—it's fantastic. But Olivier chose to marry Joan Plowright at that moment and he dropped out, and I had to make a quick substitution. I would have liked a German to play it, but I just couldn't get one.

I thought that Lancaster's physical presence gave that particular character more than you could have gotten from the script alone.

With no reflection on Burt Lancaster—you've seen his magnificent work in films like *Elmer Gantry*—I thought it was the least believable piece of casting I had in the picture. That's absolutely a difference of opinion there.

Did other people agree with you or did they think he did a more than adequate job?

I can't remember. At the time the picture was released, it was submerged by so many other pressures that I can't remember any discussion about Burt Lancaster. The film had a world premiere in Germany, sponsored by Willy Brandt,* who forever I shall remember for his speech at the opening in a theater in Berlin that the Americans built after the war. All of Berlin came, all the people who were ex-officials in that other administration, people from Nuremberg, from Munich, from everywhere in Germany, as well as foreign diplomats. And Willy Brandt got up and said "Look, you may not find this film pleasant, but it is necessary if Berlin is ever to regard itself as a capital ever again." The film went on, and much as I should like to say that the total silence which greeted its finish was like the tribute to Lincoln's Gettysburg Address, a perfect tribute, I must say that it was not. It was the most frightening night I ever spent in my life. The film has never done three cents in Germany. It played so many empty houses it finally just stopped. We got into some disagreement because they asked how could I—an American—maybe parenthetically of a minority group, make the film to rekindle this idea of German guilt.

I think that the answers we gave were right. I said that it would have been better had the Germans made it, but they didn't. The German film industry is the most commercial industry in the world today. It's owned by businessmen and operated by businessmen. The old German film industry has quite a heritage, but if anyone of talent pops up his head today, that talent goes down the drain, just like in the old Soviet film industry where there was too much control. In Germany, there is no desire to do anything other than nudie films.

*Willy Brandt (1913–1992) was mayor of Berlin during the construction of the Berlin Wall, and in 1969 became chancellor of West Germany.

With Judy Garland on the set of *Judgment at Nuremberg* (1961); Burt
Lancaster looks on. The film also starred Spencer Tracy, Montgomery Clift,
Maximillian Schell, Marlene Dietrich and Richard Widmark.

You produced The Wild One *in 1953. How did that film come about?*

The Wild One was based on an actual incident which was dramatized in
Harper's magazine. You've got to consider the year and the age in which a
group of motorcyclists go up to Northern California and dismantle a
town. I talk in social terms, so I thought I could get all the motorcyclists
who actually did it and talk with them and find out why they did it.
Right? Well, you know people who do things are the least likely people to
tell you why. But I got all the motorcyclists, and one of them told me
what Marlon Brando says in the film. The girl says to him, "Why do you
do this?" and he said, "What do you mean, why do we do it? You work all
week and the weekend comes and *you got to go, man!*" That's why they did
it. Now, that's a tough thing to make a picture about, but that's how we
got hooked. Brando had on the back of his jacket "Black Rebels Motorcycle Club." She asks him, "What are you rebelling against?" and he says,
"What do you got?" And that's the way all these kids talked. That's where
the dialogue came from.

What was the reaction at that time to the film?

The reaction was a great shock. I was pretty hard hit editorially by the usual journals. The film was banned in England. Banned completely. You know that only the year before last did it get any release in England? They said it was incitation to riot or whatever. You have to realize that the film was not some purposeful idea to try to speculate on what was about to happen. It was just an accidental stumbling upon something shocking which hadn't really taken form but which is quite ordinary today.

In those days, film censors were a little different than they are now. They censored the theme. It used to be that we could do certain things on film if there were parallel benefits. In other words, if crime doesn't pay, you could show the criminal and his work. We always had that compensating virtue for every ill. Actually, the people in Hollister all wanted the motorcyclists back because they brought a lot of business. So I realized that the heavies in the film were the people in Hollister, and that's the way we wrote the script. When the censors got to the script, they murdered us. László Benedek was the director, and he was two weeks away from starting. We had to rewrite the entire ending of the film. The cyclists broke all the windows, pulled out all the bottles from the bar and smashed them. But the people still wanted them back.

Would you talk a little bit about how you work with actors?

I have gotten along wonderfully with some of the most difficult actors, theoretically, in the history of the cinema. But I am not particularly fond of actors. I say that because many nights I go home and I hold my stomach or my head from what I've experienced all day. Yet one of the people I loved most in the world was Spencer Tracy. He gave a lot of trouble to a lot of people in his time, but he remains to me probably the world's greatest moving picture actor. No one was more talented—it was the chemistry of his roles that made him so good.

But generally you don't work a certain way with actors. There are no "rules." Every actor is a personality unto himself. I feel I can make contact with the actor because I come to the set fully enough prepared to say to him, "Let's see how you feel it." Sometimes he feels it better than I do, and I have to give him range. Actors must have a chance, no matter how well prepared the director is, to express what they have to give. If they don't get that off their chests, it's not going to work. The actors are going to have to respect you, and you're going to have to create enough warmth

and mutuality of aim to let them feel that if you say something isn't working, then it isn't working. In working with the actor you've got to
inspire—and I'm careful to use this word—love. It is a love affair, and not
only with the girls. It's with the men too. Because you've got Method
actors; you've got actors who are afraid and insecure who need to be told
three times a day, "You are good."

The young actor who comes from a certain school might say, "I
haven't the proper motivation to come in that door and cross to the
table." That can drive you right out of your mind. One day we were
rehearsing a scene and I had a young actor, and I was being very patient
and nice and let him work out his motivations. We cleared the set so he
could sit alone on the set and figure it out. All he had to do was come in
and cross to a table and wait for the entrance of another actor. He said, "I
don't dig it. Why the hell do I come in the room that way?" Finally
Spencer Tracy said, "You come in the friggin' room because it's the only
way to get into the room and you go to the friggin' table because that's the
place in the middle of the room and that's where the director wants you to
go." When asked what advice he had for young actors—this may seem
apocryphal but isn't—he said the best thing for them was to learn their
lines and try not to bump into the furniture. It isn't a bad definition.

Preparation means that when I come in to shoot the scene, I have in
my mind—reviewed for months previously and also the night before—
what I would like the actor to do. I know the coverage—this in a master
shot, this close-up, a pan over or a zoom in. Then the actor comes in, and
I talk to him as though I have done not one bit of work. Now, George
Scott is an actor who may have had a hell of a night before, but when he's
on set he's there at nine o'clock, he knows the lines and he wants to know
whether I know them. Scott comes in and wants to know what the levels
of demands are upon him. He will do anything to try to satisfy them and
go beyond them. He's very easy to work with—a real joy. There are other
actors who want it all laid out. Spencer Tracy, particularly in his latter
years, wanted to be told, "You come in, sit at this table and play it. You
can get up during the middle. You've got that lane to work in. You can go
back to the desk. You can come forward to the camera. Whatever. But
those are your lines and your limits for the camera." That's what he
wanted, to operate within that frame.

What was it like working with Tracy on his last film, Guess Who's Coming to
Dinner?

In *Guess Who's Coming to Dinner,* the audience was able to identify with Tracy sufficiently to turn their views. He expressed all the things the arm-chair liberals were thinking: "You don't know what you're getting into" and "What about your children?" And then he said to himself, "Son of a bitch. He loves her, and she loves him." So when he said, "If you love each other, screw all those people," the audience believed, just as he believed. But you needed a great actor.

I remember the first day I worked with Tracy. It was on *Inherit the Wind.* I did a scene with him, and the soundman said, "I didn't get the last phrase because it was kind of muttered." So I said, "All right. I thought it was pretty good, but let's do another take." So Tracy waited about ten seconds. I said, "Let's do it again." And he said. "Why?" So I said. "Well, the soundman had a little trouble with it." And he looked at me again, waited—that's where the term "pregnant pause" was born—and then he said, "*Mister* Kramer. It has taken me forty-five years to learn to read a line that way. Now, if you want somebody to come over here from UCLA or someplace, all you got to do is say so." He put me down real bad in front of the crew, and it was the first day of shooting. I took it as best I could, and then said, "Well, can we do another take anyhow?" He said, "Okay." The reason he did all that was because he wanted me to know in no uncertain terms that he did not like to do a lot of takes.

Everybody identified with Tracy from the time he started, when he was a redheaded tough guy—drunk, breaking the windows of cafés and being picked up by the police. Even in those early days nobody could really explain why it was that up against Mr. Movies—Clark Gable—everybody always wanted Tracy to get the girl. He was stocky and he underplayed it. He was kind of the good guy, full of sacrifice, the clichéd character. But, by gosh, he gave it so much more, and somehow you never wanted to see him go. Then, as his stature grew and he became the premiere character actor of his day, he had what a lot of fellows just dream about. He could do it because he listened so well. It was a beautiful thing to behold.

How do you handle difficult actors?

You don't. There is no resolution. Someone like Frank Sinatra had problems; he always did. I made a couple of pictures with him which will go unmentioned. Once he said to me, in the middle of Europe, "Hot or cold, Thursday I'm leaving." I had seven weeks left to shoot. So he left.

That's a problem. It was solved by two days' work back in a studio with potted palms.

Monty Clift was a really wonderful actor. In his youth he was the most beautiful-looking actor on the New York stage. He was a true matinee idol. He was the juvenile of all time. But Monty was drinking and had big problems, and had a very bad automobile accident which scarred him. He needed somebody to be terribly kind, somebody who would say, "You're wonderful and I know that you're having a little problem and you don't remember the lines, but what difference? Do it how you feel it and we'll manage. Monty, you're wonderful. I really wanted you for the part," and so on. This was just to bolster his confidence. If you knew in advance about Monty's condition at that time, and you didn't have enough sympathy for him, you didn't use him.

I made a couple of pictures with Judy Garland, and that was difficult in the end years. How do you handle it? Along with Al Jolson and one or two others, she was the greatest single person before an audience in the history of entertainment. I once saw her at the Hollywood Bowl when it was pouring rain. It was sick, but nobody moved for three hours because she had them so enraptured. It was like watching a snake come out of a basket. It's wasn't necessarily a good thing, but you couldn't take your eyes off it. She murdered people around her. She would keep people up all night, calling them in the middle of the night. I was only making a film with her, but she'd call me in the middle of the night about the damnedest of things, and have her agent there and her business manager and a publicity man. And everybody would be sick the next day, but Judy would go on like firecrackers, as though nothing had happened at all.

What happened to Judy Garland?

Even as the camera slowly pans upward over the headstone, one must admit Louis B. Mayer is the villain. He was the father and she was the child. She was Frances Gumm who was eleven years old, and he was Father Christmas who put her in four pictures a year—dieting, singing, dancing, personal appearances, everything. She had a nervous breakdown at fifteen. I was at MGM during some of those years and I know about it.

How is it working with some of the great stage actors, like Julie Harris and Ethel Waters?

Ethel Waters was a large, stout woman. She played in *Member of the Wedding* for four years in New York and on the road, and now we're making a film with the same cast. It was hot and in the middle of summer, and Fred Zinnemann was directing. He was rehearsing and rehearsing, and finally this poor woman with the perspiration running off her suddenly stops and says, "Mistah Zinnemann"—when she got angry she reverted to the accent of her forebears, which she never used in ordinary conversation. Zinnemann stopped for a minute, as he wasn't too acquainted with the vernacular of this kind of humor. So he was a little bit embarrassed and everybody in the crew just froze. And she says, "Mistah Zinnemann, you ever hear the story of the participating mules?" And he said, "No." So she said, "I'm going to tell it to you. It seems as though there was this picnic with the participating mules and the nonparticipating mules. And the president of the nonparticipating mules was sittin' under a tree in the shade, and the president of the participating mules come over to the president of the nonparticipating mules and said, 'Mr. Nonparticipating Mule, how come you ain't participating?' And the nonparticipating mule said to the participating mule, 'Mr. Participating Mule, in the cool of the evening when the fucking begins, I'll be participating.'" And then Ms. Waters added, "When you're ready to make this scene, I'll be perfectly happy to participate."

How did you cast The Defiant Ones?

I've always been what is laughingly called an independent. I say "laughingly" because latitude is comparative. I have usually had some latitude when casting, something I enjoy doing, but sometimes the distributor screams that you have to do something. *The Defiant Ones* was written for Brando and Poitier. But Brando got tied up in *Mutiny on the Bounty.* I wanted to go with Poitier and a new actor, but United Artists said, "You're chaining two guys together and one of them is black. You've got to give us some stars." At the time I approached Lancaster, Douglas, Mitchum. You know, I went down a lot of the guys. It needed to be a pretty big guy opposite Poitier. Time went by and we just couldn't wait, so I ended up with Tony Curtis. Now, that didn't seem to be a particularly brilliant piece of casting to anyone, including me, but I couldn't get anybody else to play the role. I cut Tony's hair, we straightened his nose. I think he did very well with the role, but it certainly wasn't written for him.

But in the face of all this frustration, you keep on directing. Why?

Because I'm arrogant and I have an ego and I enjoy it. Somebody asked me about handling problems. How about the moments of delicious glory in failure and success? You keep directing because you once heard Spencer Tracy read before your eyes, "This then is what we stand for—truth, justice and the value of a single human being." That was worth a lot of these kinds of difficulties. To have been with Sidney Poitier in his early years and to have seen Mississippi and seen him teach people how to lie on the ground inert so that they could be lifted into a paddy wagon without any opposition whatsoever so as not to excite the people who were lifting them, that was an exciting phase of life brought about by an actor. Poitier is a man of stature who has carried the ball a long time. He's a man who's had his own personal problems but who's a great actor and a great man.

So that's why you keep directing, because you meet people on a level which under ordinary circumstances you would never be operating at. When you make a film people confide and become very personal. You're talking about a scene, and suddenly Vivien Leigh is telling you what there was about Olivier that at one and the same time irritated her and made her weep. An actress will tell you these things because she is going to weep in the scene that's coming up and you get a feeling she is readying herself for something. It's not pertinent, but it's just interesting: Vivien Leigh and Katharine Hepburn are the only two women I have known who could for seven, eight, nine successive takes of a scene, make the teardrop drop on the same line each time. Fantastic! I used to watch Hepburn. She was just fantastic the way she could do that.

Sometimes you seem to use people's faces as landscapes.

I happen to think a person's face—their eyes and what they are thinking—is the most dramatic thing the camera can see. There aren't many actors who can move you in heroic proportions. Spencer Tracy was one. Brando is another. I think at times among the women are Vivien Leigh, sometimes Simone Signoret, Hepburn. Sidney Poitier could do it. When you deal with people with this kind of power, who have that kind of personality, just showing their face has a certain validity.

You were talking about making American films within the Establishment. But for your first few films you had to take a kind of leap of faith that some of us may someday have to make. Would you tell us how you raised the money for Champion?

The old American dream was you go to work at MGM when you're twenty-one years old, and if you keep your nose clean for twenty years you become whatever you want to become. A director, a producer or writer, whatever. Well, of course, that's not the way it happens, and it really never was. It's a lot easier today to find a couple of hundred thousand dollars to make a film than it is to get a job at MGM. I am absolutely convinced of it. And not only that, since there doesn't seem to be any relationship between the total experience of filmmaking and the ability to express oneself in this unusual medium, one might just as well, with some basic knowledge, go out and spend all the time trying to gather the money to make the film.

I speak out of experience from another age. Not quite Neolithic or Paleolithic but another age, which was after World War II. I didn't have a penny but I had a lot of desire and ambition about film. I found that I had been in banks before but never in the rooms where they give substantial loans. What I did was go to the Bank of America one day—and this is the truth—and told the vice president in charge of motion picture loans that I wanted to make a picture called *Champion* and that I owned the story by Ring Lardner. Well, I didn't own the story. Lardner's estate owned it, and I had an option for a very tiny amount of money for something like thirty days only. I told the bank I had Kirk Douglas as the actor, and the banker said to me, "You mean Melvyn Douglas," and I said, "No, Kirk Douglas. This is a wonderful young actor who's been in the New York theater and he's done some parts out here and this part just fits him." The vice president said, "Well, all right." I also said I had a United Artists release for the film, which I didn't have. I didn't have Kirk Douglas either, incidentally.

What it turned out to be was an advanced game of footsy based on what I was supposed to say or what *might* interest them. You're really asking the bank, "If I had these things, would you be interested in putting up money for the film?" And the banker replies, "If you had those things, it would be a good proposition for the bank." Then you go to United Artists and say, "I've got a bank loan, Kirk Douglas and a script." And they say, "Well, if you've got that we're interested, sure." Then you go to Kirk Douglas and tell him you've got the bank loan and United Artists. Eventually I was vouching for everybody, and they wound up asking who I was. You end up in an office one day with all these balloon strings hanging down, and you give a yank and hope that they all come down together. They never do. Instead of Kirk Douglas, you might have to try Burt Lancaster. Instead of United Artists, maybe Columbia. But you create the atmosphere and the climate to try to get them on board.

The bank did not give me the financing. They said that if I could get somebody to guarantee the completion bond, then they would advance the money in exchange for guarantees, which in those days they needed. So I went down to see a retired dry goods manufacturer in Miami Beach. He was sixty-four years old and had just married a University of Miami coed who was nineteen. She was there, and we had a lot of red wine for dinner. He smoked a big cigar after dinner, and we sat down on this great patio that looked out on the lagoon where the yacht was tied up, and he said, "All right, my boy, tell me the story. Before you start, I like lots of fights and action." So I told him a two-hour story which never appeared on film, except for one piece of business which happened quite accidentally. While I told the story I bumped into a wooden partition, and it occurred to me that it would be a good dramatic scene. I hit the partition with my fists and looked at it very dramatically. The scene is in the film— Kirk Douglas does it with a locker. But I look at my hand, and this dry goods guy was transfixed. He said, "That's it. You've got the dough." And that's how I got the money. He got a chunk of the profits. I don't know anything about dry goods manufacturers, but they're out there, and money being what it is today and inflation what it is and people trying to lay off money and take tax deductions and losses and whatever, I tell you the money is out there for a project if you really want it. That's part of the art too—part of it has to do with the relationship with these financiers.

Let me tell you another story. I was out of the army and I was sitting in my uncle's office. He was in the agency business, a tiny agency. He handled a lot of character actors. A fellow named Willie Schenker came there looking for me. This fellow remembered that my mother, who was a widow, had some money. Well, she didn't have that money anymore, and as luck would have it, I was in the office when Schenker came up looking for me. His father was in the dress business in New York, and Schenker wanted one thing only. He wanted to be the owner of a Chinese restaurant. You know already this is beginning to take on comedic proportions. So I am sitting there, and his story is that his father has given him $7,500 and said to him, "Willie, you're a bum, you've always been a bum, and here's $7,500. I'll give you a year, and after this year is up and you have wasted the $7,500, come back and you'll go into the dress business." Willie's got the $7,500 and he's got a potential lease on a restaurant. He had this spot on La Cienega Boulevard and had hired a Chinese chef, whom he cut in on the thing, and a bartender from downtown Chinatown. What he needs is another $7,500 to promote the deal. He needs $15,000 to make the deal go. To make a long story short, and without my appearing in too unfavorable a light, I persuaded him to use his $7,500 to take an option on two Ring Lardner stories. I mean this was real charlatan talk. With his money I proceeded to put into operation a company which made a film based on the Ring Lardner story called *The Big Town,* which we had to call *So This Is New York* because Eddie Robinson had a radio show at the time called *Big Town.*

Now, the film was about the biggest bomb made in the history of the film industry. It was so bad that it never got a New York engagement, which is pretty bad because "New York" was in the title. They opened it in Brooklyn and let it go. So Willie Schenker was wiped out and lost that $7,500. Since I still insist I am a man of conscience, this bothered me a great deal. I had lost everything I had, and all the people who participated in this project got nothing for all of their time and work. But Willie Schenker was wiped out of a Chinese restaurant. So I went to Willie, who by now was really in tears, and I said, "Willie, look, they'll never let me make another movie, I'm sure, but I tell you this: from the next two films, you'll get the same percentage you had on this one, if I ever make them." So Willie Schenker had 9.8 percent of the next two films, and they turned out to be *Champion* and *Home of the Brave.* Willie drew down $411,000 as his share, opened a restaurant in the Valley called The China Trader and drank all the profits.

How do you go about collaborating with a screenwriter?

Wouldn't it be nice if all these relationships with actors and writers could be defined and you could say how you go about it? I really don't know how to answer your question because a writer is as much of a personality as an actor. I have worked with a great many writers. I was a writer myself many years ago, but I always felt that since I took on two functions—producer and director—I should not take on a third.

Abby Mann, who wrote *Judgment at Nuremberg,* is a very solid writer who likes to collaborate on all of the initial stages of the writing. You can spend months with Abby Mann in total collaboration on an outline. He is a powerful writer. I enjoyed working with him, and I think he enjoyed working with me. We did quite a few things together—some good, some ordinary. He is somebody who does a lot of writing by himself but who likes to write in sections so that you can mull it over and work it over as he goes. I think Bill Rose, who wrote *Genevieve,* is the best constructionist with whom I ever worked, even though he needed to work alone on Jersey, which is an island off the coast of England, with the waves beating against the rocks. He was a very inside-of-himself kind of man with the greatest sense of humor in the entire world. But once the pattern was set, he needed to go to Jersey and sweat it out. With many writers, you should depend upon them as they have to depend upon you. If Bill Rose said, "Don't give me pressure. Let me have six months," I always made it nine or ten because I knew what he needed.

I sat in on a press conference with a gentleman who just recently completed a picture on which he served as both writer and producer. He made the statement that the writer and the producer were ninety-five percent and the director was five percent. Can you figure that?

He's an idiot, whoever he was. There are some writers who deserve a great deal more credit than they get for a job, and there are a lot of writers who don't deserve anywhere near the credit that they get for the job. There are so many people who make contributions. The power of the creative project is centered on our being able to create an atmosphere in which the writer and the actor and the director and the musician can come together—all of those people—and give of their talent. Now, sometimes it ends up like cottage cheese, but sometimes you get a glow. We've always had arguments about certain pictures. Some people say, "The director's responsible. God Almighty, the things he did!" But one day the writer might suggest, "When he comes in why don't you have him fold the napkin?" I do it and I think it's mine.

Collaborative effort requires sharing that tiny little space which we reserve for ourselves. We've got to bring it out and share it for a while, even if we put it back afterward. The best material for a film, to my way of thinking, has always been from an original story in which the director and the writer start together and make up what it is they want to do and say in a film.

Stanley Kramer talking at AFI on March 14, 1973. He participated in
seminars with AFI fellows on five other occasions.

*When you set out to make a picture and serve as writer-director-producer, are you
a "community" filmmaker who accepts opinions from others?*

The term I resent most is "director's medium." There is no such thing and
never has been. I started as a producer because the only way to make films
was to be the boss. But I always wanted to be a director, so I made myself
my own director as quickly as I could. Of course one man's thumbprint
has to be on a film because somebody has to make the basic decisions:
"We will do this story. This script is now ready to be shot. We will use this
actor." Somebody has to okay all that. Today it's the director, though it
used to be the producer. The reason I don't like the term "director's

medium" is because when you're running a film, what do you do? You cast it with the best cast that you can. You get the best photographer, the best composer, the best of all crafts. Now, if you have hired these men and women, all of whom are artists in their own right, to work on your baby, you have to create a climate for them to give you their best; otherwise you'll never disturb the norm.

Film is different from anything else in terms of an art form, because the result will never be exactly as you saw it in your mind's eye. In creating this climate where people feel they can trust you, the director has to give something in return. What he gives up is the perfect synchronization and identification of what he dreams his film could be. Reality is sometimes better, and very often worse, but it's never exactly what you dream. In the end there will always be the line the actor doesn't want to read, or the four violins too many on the soundtrack. Or the cameraman says he will diffuse the light, but it's never as diffused as you thought it should be. What I am saying is that it is frustrating. If a painter paints a picture, he can scrape it off and do it again if he doesn't like it. In a film, it will cost you forty thousand dollars to do that again, just for that one scene that didn't come out the way you wanted. All the time I hear young filmmakers say, "But I'll never make a compromise" Baloney! All of life is a compromise. It's one succession of compromises after another.

I've never seen anyone yet with whom I was ever impressed in terms of doing the whole thing, with the exception of Charles Chaplin. He wrote the music and starred in the films and wrote the script three-quarters of the way, improvising the rest of the way, and then did the dances and directed them. But Chaplin is the authentic genius of our age.

You've often spoken about the clash between writers and directors.

Generally what we're talking about here is a credit fight. Personally I don't think even the most naïve writer expects that they can operate under the same rulings as the Dramatists Guild in the New York theater, where not a line can be changed without the playwright's consent. I can be on a set and the studio expects that if I'm on the deck of this ship, and it's pouring rain, that I'm not going to spend twenty-five thousand dollars to wait for the rain to stop. I'll probably play the scene in the cabin, even though it's not written that way. Let's face it, I've changed it and I'm going to change a lot of things along the way because sixty days is the schedule, and if I'm going to make it on or near schedule I'm going to have to run things. Each day is a fortune—we're talking high finance and high art.

What do you look for in an editor?

Someone who is technically proficient and able to carry out yesterday what he wants today. I have worked with a couple of editors who could do it all on their own. It may not be the way I wanted it. It may be better. But with all the respect in the world for the editor, I cannot imagine releasing a film before I have looked at every frame.

When I was very young I worked in MGM's editorial department for four years as an assistant. And I knew then that I didn't want to be an editor because I wasn't making enough of the decisions. Part of the fun of creative filmmaking is to be able to make the decisions. That's why directors all try to be producers, or writers try to be producers, or producers and directors try to combine so that they can make the decisions. The editor today doesn't get enough of a chance to make the decisions unless he's working with people who don't know as much as he knows, in which case they are totally dependent upon him. It seems to me that any director who doesn't stay with it frame for frame isn't worth his salt. You can move scenes out of order, you can cheat close-ups from other sequences, you can snip off part of a scene—everything. A lot of direction is in the cutting room.

I'm working now with one of the best film editors I've encountered in all my years, Folmar Blangsted. He's fantastically creative and a superior technician because he has thirty years' experience at Warner Bros. and is able to adapt to my vacillations and idiosyncrasies. I'll ask him to take off one more frame or add three more because he is cutting away from that close-up too fast. I hang over his back. I need someone who will make allowances for me because I really know what I am trying to do even though I may not achieve it sometimes.

Was the editing of High Noon *problematic?*

The whole concept of playing the movie in real time was in the script from the very beginning. A lot of the script was set outside of the town. The cutting patterns of putting it all in the town and using the clocks came later. I had a very good film editor, Elmo Williams. The clocks were his idea. It was something that came together, that's all.

Let me tell you a little story. Dimitri Tiomkin did the score for the film. Dimitri is of course a very shy, retiring fellow who never makes any fusses or noise. He wrote a ballad, and I thought it wasn't any good. And it wasn't. So he wrote another one. To show him what kind of ballad I thought it should be, I took an old Burl Ives recording of some folk thing and I put it on the picture and ran it for Tiomkin for mood. He got it, and the next thing he came up with was "Do Not Forsake Me, Oh My Darling." Everybody felt it to be a wonderful thing, and I used it in the film as bridges. Everybody now knows that every time Gary Cooper took a walk, the song came on—which, for those days, was very much out of line partly because this was a Western in black and white. Using singing in this thing is crazy, people said. So the film went to preview in Inglewood, California, and I had eleven bridges of this song through the film. On the fifth bridge the entire audience broke into giggles. Now, I am sitting there knowing six more are coming. You can imagine what a preview that was. They wrote on the preview cards, "Get that lousy song out of there." So in stages I finally took out seven of those renditions, not including what was at the beginning and the end. The beginning had the whole song, and at the end it reprised.

Did you use only four bridges because at number five the audience laughed?

Can you think of a better reason? In the final analysis, the four were scattered in different spots than the eleven had been placed. There's a certain chemistry with every film. It's an overused word, but anyone who has worked with film knows this. A film might be perfectly tooled and engineered. Scene by scene it's beautifully done, but the sum total is something nobody really cares for. There is a missing factor—I think it's chemistry, the fizz. You look for it all the time. It's something I get on some nights when I'm sitting there looking at the finished film and am saying to myself, "That's it." If the audience doesn't agree with you when you have satisfied yourself, then you just have to steal quietly away in the night and never be heard from again. Occasionally you've got to satisfy the audience with your tastes, but you have to satisfy yourself first or you won't be worth anything as an artist in my opinion.

What kind of working relationship do you like to have with your cinematographers?

I look for somebody who doesn't come to work in the morning and say, "Where do you want the camera and what do we do? Do we do a close-up shot or a master shot or what?" You look for somebody who says, "Why don't we let him just go out of the shot and we'll hold on this and it will tell the whole thing?"—somebody who is making a real contribution beyond just the lighting. This is very important, and it's unusual except, for the most part, in the younger men. The younger men are coming up creatively because there are no shibboleths. They destroyed them all. It's wonderful when a cameraman is creative conceptually because then, together with the production designer, you say, "All right, we're going to do this set with nothing. If the room is bare and there's a single low couch in the back, suppose that we just use it as a light source, one window, and it's very gray. And when the door opens, we hit it with sharp lights and leave it ajar so there's one beam that can work for us, separating the two people." In sketching the production design and planning a set and lighting in advance, a cameraman can make a contribution which is unbelievable.

Do you purposefully make films for certain audiences?

I spoke earlier of arrogance. You must start with the arrogance of trying to please yourself and not think about trying to please an audience or somebody else. You must please yourself in the hope that often enough you will please others.

Was Inherit the Wind *a success?*

It wasn't a successful picture, which doesn't bother me because I've gotten some of my greatest joy out of the deliciousness of my failures. I have certainly learned more from them and felt more closely aligned to many of them than some of my more successful films. Maybe the bitterness of a failure, or the lack of receptivity from people for whom I had respect, or from the mass public, made them dearer to me. I must say that after all this time, having had both failures and successes, there is nothing to compare to the heady feeling of having dreamed of something and having people in the millions reacting to it in exactly the way you thought they should react to it. I have no supercilious viewpoint about the mass. When the audience cheers and weeps together, it is a magnificent thing. It transcends reviews and awards. Making that bridge to an audience is a source of tremendous satisfaction. Let me tell you, there is no satisfaction at all in something being, as people will say to be kind, "ahead of its time" or "made for a very small, select audience."

Do you feel that your films have a uniformity of form to them?

I don't think the style of *It's a Mad Mad Mad Mad World* is the same as *Judgment at Nuremberg.* I don't know how to explain this except that each thing seems to stand on its own. Both films have flaws, and if I had them to do over, I might do them differently, stylistically or otherwise.

For example, there is too much camera movement in *Judgment at Nuremberg.* The courtroom—and this was an authentic situation—was very long and wide, and the spacing between the attorney's box and the witness box was at least forty feet. Also, the attorney—and certainly not the witness—was never allowed to depart from the box. Unless you want to play a Ping-Pong game with the cutting, what other solution than to move the camera? If I had it to do over I wouldn't do it quite as much.

Is there a problem making films about very contemporary issues in that by the time you get it to theaters your film might be stale? I'm thinking about R.P.M.

I discuss *R.P.M.* freely, at the drop of a hat. It's the most unsuccessful film I ever made—unsuccessful by any standard. The times and events have a way of moving so fast these days they zip past the back of your head before you can turn around. That usually doesn't trap me. If you look at what I've done historically, I haven't generally sought to reflect the times in which I live. But in *R.P.M.* I did this, and got caught very badly. None of the films about the student revolution were really successful in my opinion. The trouble with *R.P.M.* was that I was trapped because I was looking for myself. I was looking for something in which to believe. The film didn't come off because it was attempting to join into the confusion of the times rather than take a step back and speculate on that confusion.

I am past the point where I want to reflect the times. I find it far more interesting to speculate in my own imagery about what might be.

What are the qualities you most admire in a producer?

You see, you are talking about two different generations. Rex Reed or somebody said that I sometimes took credit for films which I shouldn't take credit for because I didn't direct them, I only produced them. Well, that shows an abysmal lack of knowledge of the art form of our time.

In the 1940s and '50s, cinema was the producer's medium. It was the day of Selznick and Thalberg and Goldwyn. They were the powers incarnate because the producer was the boss. In those days the director who was under contract to a studio had in his guild regulations only one week to edit the film after it was finished. In other words they allowed him to string it together, and then the producer took it over. The director went from picture to picture that way. It was an accepted practice, although it eventually created the situation which led to the Directors Guild demanding that the director have certain basic rights.

The producer of today is a different kind of individual entirely. First of all, he's got to be able to work in a team. Younger people didn't become producers before; you had to be in the business a long time. The Producers Guild used to be full of men going back to the second coming of Christ. Now the young producers are putting together packages, and they have to be creative because usually they have to do the selling of the whole package. There are many men today for whom I have great respect, young and old. I've never met Hal Wallis, but I think he must be a very, very good producer.

When you look back at your films today, are you happy with them?

When I think about my films, there's something wrong with every one. I'm very self-conscious about this, so I always hurry over the question about my favorite film because I'm always figuring some wiseass is going to get up in the back and say, "How about this scene in the film?" If you're a perfectionist you can be limited by your own sense of perfectionism. By giving yourself a standard, you have a feeling of falling short. I've never satisfied myself. I've never come close.

You've been in the industry a long time and you've witnessed a lot of changes in Hollywood. Where is the industry heading?

When I went to college, everybody wanted to write the great American novel. I can assure you today everybody wants to make the great American film. I go on the average of every three years to at least twenty colleges on a tour. What is happening is that everybody is in film. My son is graduating from a university this year. Right up until yesterday he wanted to be a child psychologist, but he spent a year with a film bug and now he's in film. Is this healthy? I wonder. We're limited only by our imagination. How much do you have to know to make a film?

I don't know where the film business is heading. Is it heading for a hotel room? Sometimes I think so. Columbia seems so involved with getting films into hotel rooms. I do think that the person who is on the creative side of the film is going to have to produce cinema for whatever his outlets might be. I pray that it still can be in the theater that goes dark and in which the people can be transported. But maybe it won't be.

<hr>

Films as Director

1955 *Not As a Stranger* (also producer)

1957 *The Pride and the Passion* (also producer)

1958 *The Defiant Ones* (also producer)

1959 *On the Beach* (also producer)

1960 *Inherit the Wind* (also producer)

1961 *Judgment at Nuremberg* (also producer)

1963 *It's a Mad Mad Mad Mad World* (also producer)

1965 *Ship of Fools* (also producer)

1967 *Guess Who's Coming to Dinner* (also producer)

1969 *The Secret of Santa Vittoria* (also producer)

1970 *R.P.M.* (also producer)

1971 *Bless the Beasts and Children* (also producer)

1973 *Oklahoma Crude* (also producer)

1977 *The Domino Principle* (also producer)

1979 *The Runner Stumbles* (also producer)

If a director is sympathetic to working with a producer, he accepts his help in all phases on a project. The concept of the film becomes theirs. They are a two-man team working together toward a single goal.

HAL WALLIS
(Born in Chicago, Illinois, 1899—Died 1986)

Hal Wallis was one of the Golden Age producers who served as both a studio head and an independent producer in the tradition of Samuel Goldwyn, Darryl Zanuck and David Selznick. From the time he became head of production at Warner Bros. in the thirties, to his days as an independent producer at Paramount and Universal, Wallis was an exemplar of the Hollywood studio tradition. His pictures earned thirty-two Academy Awards and he twice received the Irving G. Thalberg Award for excellence in production.

Harold Brent Wallis was raised in Chicago where he became fascinated by the nickelodeons in which the new medium of motion pictures was emerging. He left high school when he was fifteen to help support his mother and two sisters, working as an office boy in a real estate company and a salesman for a heating company. Wallis read and studied at night, as his work took him through Nebraska, Kansas and Missouri. In 1921 the Wallis family moved to Los Angeles, where Hal found a job managing the Garrick Cinema. He met Sam Warner, the brother in charge of theater operations for Warner Bros., who gave him a job as assistant to the head of publicity for the Warners' studio, then located on Sunset Boulevard. In time, Wallis became head of publicity and was credited with crafting the phrase "the Lubitsch touch" to promote that director's pictures.

When the brothers Warner acquired the First National Studio in Burbank, Wallis was promoted to studio manager and soon to executive in charge of production just at the time when sound was coming in. He was displaced for three years by Darryl Zanuck, during which time Wallis produced such successes for Warners as *I Am a Fugitive from a Chain Gang*, *The Mystery of the Wax Museum*, *Gold Diggers of 1933* and *Footlight Parade*. When

Hal Wallis at different times in his career served as studio chief and producer.
Seen here in 1930 in his office at Warner Bros.

Zanuck left Warner Bros. to form Twentieth Century Fox in 1934, Wallis returned to the post of head of production.

Hal Wallis was responsible for more than a hundred films over the next ten years. Warner Bros. flourished during this period, with an eclectic list of successes as diverse as *Anthony Adverse, The Charge of the Light Brigade, Green Pastures, Jezebel, Brother Rat, Dark Victory, Juarez, The Private Lives of Elizabeth and Essex, The Roaring Twenties, Knute Rockne-All American, High Sierra, Sergeant York, The Maltese Falcon, Kings Row, Yankee Doodle Dandy* and *Casablanca.*

There has been controversy over the years because some studio heads claimed producer credit for the entire slate of films made during their reign. This reached a bizarre level in the fifties, when Fox referred to Zanuck as "personally" producing certain films. Nonetheless, it's clear that Wallis presided over a flourishing production program in his years as head of production at Warners.

In 1944 he started his own independent company at Paramount and began a mode of production that would continue for the next thirty years in which he selected properties, chose directors and supervised the entire production and marketing of his projects. His pictures again were varied, ranging through high-toned adaptations of plays—*Watch on the Rhine, The Rose Tattoo, Becket;* Westerns—*Gunfight at the OK Corral, Last Train from Gun Hill* and *True Grit;* Jerry Lewis comedies—*Jumping Jacks, The Stooge, Artists and Models, That's My Boy* and *The Sad Sack;* and Elvis Presley pictures—*King Creole* and *Blue Hawaii.*

Wallis once said that a producer must be many things—"a diplomat, organizer, strategist, promoter, planner, businessman, psychiatrist, juggler, midwife and massager of egos—and above all a decision maker." When asked which one of his films is his favorite, he answered, "the next one."

The Wallis seminar is interesting in that it presents a very different perspective from the seminars with directors. Each of the directors to varying degrees placed a premium on controlling his pictures and not being put upon by producers or studio heads. Wallis makes the case for a producer who considered his role to be primary.

HAL WALLIS

———◆———

April 10, 1974

Would you describe a recent project from beginning to end: how you obtained the property, how you found the director, the casting and editing and finally the distribution.

Yes, I might tie two pictures together, *Becket* and *Anne of the Thousand Days*. I saw *Becket* in the theater in New York and liked it very much. It wasn't picked up quickly by anybody else, so I went back to see it again. I went into negotiations and bought the property hoping to get Burton and Peter O'Toole to play Henry and Becket. I went to Europe to see Burton. He knew about the property and was interested. When he asked who was going to play Henry, I told him Peter O'Toole, and he said if that were so he would do the film, as he admired O'Toole greatly. Then I went to London and had a meeting with O'Toole. When he asked who was going to play Becket, I told him Richard Burton. He said if that were so he would do the film, as he admired Burton greatly. So I made a deal with the two of them on that basis and made the picture.

During the production, I asked Burton if there was another English history project he would like to do, and he said he had always liked the Maxwell Anderson play *Anne of the Thousand Days*. I said, "If I buy it, will you do it?" He said yes, but he wanted approval of the actress who would play Anne Boleyn. I started negotiations for the play, which were difficult because we had to contact all the heirs of Maxwell Anderson. I finally made the deal, put a writer on it, developed the script and began looking for a girl to play Anne Boleyn. I saw a Canadian film with a brilliant young actress who impressed me very much, Geneviève Bujold. I took the film to England, showed it to Burton, he approved her and we went ahead with the project. Now, from that point on, I was involved in everything to do with the production—working on the script with the writer, Edward Anhalt; engaging and working with the art director; doing research; approving and selecting the costumes with Margaret Furse; casting and scouting for the locations. I went down to Hever Castle in Kent, saw Lord Astor and got permission to shoot there—which, incidentally, was where Henry actually met Anne Boleyn. Looking for a director, I saw a film I liked made for Canadian Broadcasting called *The Young Elizabeth,* directed by Charles Jarrott, who had never done a feature film. I contacted Jarrott in London, had him come up to the hotel and discussed his directing *Anne.* I liked him and his ideas very much. The next day I called his agent and hired him.

In shooting that film—as in all of my films—I followed through on all phases of production. I am at the studio and on the set every day. I oversee the entire operation. After viewing the dailies, I discuss the previous day's work with the director, approve or suggest improvements and plan any pickup shots necessary. I am in close contact with the company throughout the day's shooting. If there is any problem, I know it immediately. I work with the production manager, planning the call sheets—the logistics of the next day's shooting, which are extremely complicated on a large-scale period picture such as *Becket* or *Anne.* I work with the editor each day as the picture is shot, and we have close to a first cut within a week or two after the film is finished. I have frequent runnings of assembled footage with the director at night or on weekends so that we are in close contact throughout the shooting and in agreement on everything that is being done. I believe in assembling and cutting as you go because you get a very good feel on the picture—how it is progressing, whether there is anything to be corrected in the performances, the photography, story content, anything. When we go into the final editing, the director, of course, has the first cut. We usually see the picture together through the various cuts and into the final cut, then we run with the composer, spot the music, score, dub and finally send the print over to Technicolor. When we get the first answer print back, we look at that to judge the color balance. So, as you see, I follow the picture through from the time of the purchase of the material until the print is delivered to the distributing company with whom I am working.

When you bought the rights to a play, did you buy an option first and then go to a studio and say, "Look, I'm interested in doing this"?

I have always had a continuing arrangement with the distributing company. First it was Warner Bros., then it was Paramount and now it's Universal. Those are the only three companies with which I've been associated. Whenever I find a property and want it, I go out and buy it, knowing the studio will accept it because I have the right to make what I want. I have complete autonomy on my projects.

How is the picture actually financed?

By the distributing company.

So what really happens is that they come in as the producing and distributing company.

That's right.

Your pictures have been exceptionally economical, haven't they, considering that they are costume pictures?

I have always believed in doing as much work as possible on paper, in the preparation. Based on my shooting script, I get a budget. I have always, fortunately, come out pretty close to my budget figures. In other words, I don't like to shoot three hours of film and then cut an hour of it. That is very costly and wasteful—and, incidentally, damaging to the overall picture because there may be gaps in the continuity. I get a good, tight shooting script, time it, budget it, watch the budget and usually come in pretty much under it.

How much are you personally involved in developing the story structure in that first stage?

I work very closely with the writer. If I buy an original story, I devote a lot of time to conferences for developing the screen treatment. If I buy a play or a book, I hire a writer and let him prepare a treatment—if I think a treatment is necessary—a step outline, a continuity outline and a sequence outline. If the material is close enough to screenplay form—like a play—I have him go ahead with a first draft. Then the director and I meet with him with our notes. We begin a series of conferences, rewrites, second and third drafts and so on, until we come out with our final shooting script.

Do you find that a block outline, a breakdown treatment, helps you?

I like the sequence outline so that you see exactly the direction the story is going to take. I think it's very helpful. In a play, of course, like in *Becket*, the scenes are pretty well laid out. We followed continuity in *Becket* except for the gap between the first and second acts, when things took place which were much talked about in the second act. We dramatized, for example, the excommunication, one of the great scenes of the picture which wasn't seen on the stage.

Do you think it's difficult today for someone interested in producing to go through the steps to get a picture produced, if they already have the property?

No, I don't. I think the business is open as never before to new talent and new ideas. Good material is becoming increasingly hard to find, and if you have a property that appeals to a company or a producer, I would say it would be given every consideration.

Do you think it might be very difficult to go to Warner Bros. today and say, "Hey, I have a property and I want to produce it, and yet I don't have any background or track record?"

If you have a good property you could go to Warner Bros. or any studio and say, "I haven't had any experience but I have this very exciting property. Now, if you're interested, I'll do it with you or I'll sell it to you, but I want to be a part of it. I want to be an associate on the picture with a chance to learn and observe." That is done quite frequently.

How did you start as a producer?

I was lucky. I came into the business at the time of its greatest growth. Warner Bros. was expanding and there were many job opportunities. I got a job in the Publicity Department at the Sunset Boulevard Warner Studios. We made seven pictures a year. There was a closely knit organization, including Jack Warner, Darryl Zanuck, a man named Bill Koenig and several others. We were all in on everything—the running of pictures, the cutting of pictures and the previewing of pictures. We just absorbed the knowledge of picture making and then gradually learned all phases of it. I think a knowledge of editing is very important for a would-be producer. It teaches you construction and how a film goes together. Knowing something about all the technical aspects of filming is an advantage. One of the best ways to learn directing is to work as a cinematographer. He works closely with the director, helps him compose his shots, sees how he dramatizes them.

How different is working as a studio producer and working as an independent producer?

As a studio producer, I was in overall charge of Warner Bros. production for a number of years and responsible for their entire program, which was considerable. We would be shooting five pictures, editing five and preparing five or ten at the same time. There was a great deal of work, so we assigned associate producers to individual projects. The load got so heavy, however, that I didn't want to continue carrying it. I became an independent producer at Warners', producing four pictures a year. During that period, I did *Casablanca, Saratoga Trunk, Air Force, Now, Voyager, Yankee Doodle Dandy, Desperate Journey* and others. I concentrated on one picture at a time, taking a project from the beginning to the end, then began another and saw it through to completion. When I left there and went to Paramount in my own independent setup, I did the same thing. I had no fixed number of pictures to deliver, no deadlines. When I found a property I wanted to make, I prepared it and shot it. My advice to those of you wanting to become a producer is to learn all phases of the business, get experience, observe, become affiliated with an editor, an associate producer, a screenwriter or a cinematographer. I think what you're learning here at the American Film Institute is wonderful training for creative producing.

You said before that good material was increasingly hard to find. Why do you think that is?

Perhaps audiences are more selective now, more sophisticated. Pictures have to be something exceptional today, something different, something important.

Has one of the changes been because the studios don't have contract writers and actors?

Possibly. In the early days at Warner Bros. we had a staff of writers, a staff of directors and a contract list of players. Writers wrote for specific stars. They were always busy, and it was a stimulating, exciting era. Sound had just been developed, so all the old silent stories and plots seemed new. There was such a market and need for product that writers worked overtime. Directors, producers and writers worked together in collaboration inspiring, prodding, stimulating. It was a very productive arrangement. We had under contract actors like James Cagney, Eddie Robinson, Humphrey Bogart, Bette Davis, Olivia de Havilland, George Raft and Errol Flynn, so that when we made a picture, we could cast it from our stock company. You can't do that anymore. Today an actor comes from nowhere, has a success and immediately acquires a business manager, a lawyer, a tax man, a publicity man—and the man who discovered him can't get him for a picture. He only works for his own company. So it's not simple anymore.

So it's increasingly difficult to get everything you want to make a good picture?

Difficult, but not impossible. In the early days it seemed simpler.

It seems like a lot of producers these days are not creative producers. They're people who put together the package, like agents.

Yes, that's true. An agent or a business manager or someone on the fringes of the business will sell a star or a property or both to a company on the condition that he be the producer of the project involved. But he isn't actually a producer. He's a packager, a promoter.

Do you think that weakens the film? Doesn't it leave too much up to the director and not enough up to the producer?

Well, that kind of a producer better have a strong director on the picture, because the producer isn't going to be much help. Actually, packagers—promoters—are not producers. They make deals, not pictures. When you find a property, acquire it, work on it from beginning to end and deliver the finished product as you conceived it, then you're producing.

Perhaps one of the differences today is that the idea of being a producer doesn't trip off people's imagination as much as the idea of being a director or a writer. They don't see the producer as a creative person.

Yes, many people still think the producer is the man who goes out and raises the money. But that isn't the fact at all. A producer, to be worthy of the name, must be a creator.

Did you make the choice when you began to be a producer and not a director? I mean, did you have an option to be a director?

Many times I've thought of directing, particularly when I sit in a projection room, watch the rushes and say to myself, "If I had been on the set, I would have done it another way." But I like what I've done. I like being a producer. I like being involved in all phases of production. And it is creative. When I work with a director who is talented and knows his craft, I let him alone far more than I would with a lesser man. As it is, I'm on the set a good deal. I usually go down on the set and see a rehearsal of a sequence, and I do that several times a day. But when I get a director I have confidence in, I'm glad to let him alone. I do my job to back him up and give him as much help as I can away from the camera.

What happens if you're on the set and you see a scene going in a direction that you don't think it should go?

I take the director aside and tell him quietly what I think. If there are scenes in the dailies I don't like, if I think they're definitely wrong, I have them done over. If I think there's something off in the performance or we're going wrong in some way, I discuss it with the director. If I feel we need an added shot—a close-up or a two-shot or a movement of the camera—I'll discuss it with him and get what I want.

Have you ever had an unresolved situation with a director or worked with someone who didn't see your point of view or thought?

No, I can't say that I have. I might have had differences of opinion with many directors but nothing that couldn't be resolved by discussion or persuasion. I don't come down on the set with a whip.

Doesn't the studio or someone higher up have more to say than a producer on a studio picture?

Well, luckily, I've always been the one higher up. I think that used to be true much more so than today. Young filmmakers today have much more freedom of expression once a studio has accepted and approved a project.

When you were at the studio, would you work on a percentage or would you work on a straight salary?

When I was in charge of production, I was on a straight contract deal. When I made my independent deal, which was for Warners, I made a percentage deal.

Would you make more money if you were able to bring in financing from sources other than the distributor?

Even if it cost more, I would rather go through a distributor and be relieved of negotiations and interest charges involved in outside financing. When the distributor has a stake in the picture, he distributes it to the best advantage. I've worked this way throughout my whole career. I've never tried to make an independent production with outside financing.

Do you have your own independent setup at Universal?

I have my offices there. So I can call on any of their departments: their legal department, props department, electrical department, camera, editing, anything. I use all of their facilities. That's part of the arrangement.

You used to make deals with up-and-coming actors for more than one picture. I'm thinking particularly of the Paramount period when you brought Shirley MacLaine, Tony Franciosa and a number of other people to their first starring roles. Do you still try to do that?

It's very difficult to do that now because of the changes in the business. In those days, actors wanted to sign contracts. I signed Burt Lancaster to his first contract, and made deals with Kirk Douglas, Shirley MacLaine, Martin and Lewis and Elvis Presley for so many weeks a year or so many pictures a year with options for several more years. Today it's almost impossible to do that because a newcomer who has registered in a film will seldom make a deal for more than one picture and rarely give options. Actors don't want the restrictions of a contract, even though that was the system that made the great stars.

You've done a very wide scope of films, from Becket *to Martin and Lewis to gangster films. What qualities do you look for in a project?*

I look for projects I feel will make good entertainment. Many of my films contain a message, but I try to see that the message is delivered entertainingly. When I had a list of stars under contract, I looked for properties tailored to their special talents. With Elvis Presley, I looked for original stories with colorful backgrounds and situations which lent themselves to musical numbers, like *Blue Hawaii* and *Hawaiian Paradise*—that sort of thing. I then engaged a team of songwriters who prepared fifteen or twenty songs, of which about five were selected for the picture. For Martin and Lewis, we naturally looked for comedy material suitable for the team. The first one was *My Friend Irma,* which was a radio and television show. I see plays, employ people to read galleys of all current books, read a great deal myself and am constantly searching for interesting and provocative film material. I like to have a varied program. I used to say that I made the Martin and Lewis pictures and Elvis Presley pictures to finance the prestige pictures. But, fortunately, these turned out well too—pictures like *The Rose Tatto, Come Back, Little Sheba, Becket* and others. I have done so many historical dramas lately that I'm looking forward to doing a Western again. My next picture is the sequel to *True Grit,* called *Rooster Cogburn,* starring John Wayne and Katharine Hepburn.

How did you come up with the idea for a sequel to True Grit?

My decision was based on a combination of things. I think the public is ready for a breath of fresh air and a little more *True Grit,* which was a very successful picture and, incidentally, won an Oscar for John Wayne. A sequel to it seems like a natural, and the combination of Hepburn and Wayne—dynamite! They are giants in our industry, and casting them opposite one another is a great coup that is causing much excitement.

So, then, you look at the talents of the people you want to use and find a project for them. Did the project come with Mary, Queen of Scots, *or did you say, "I want to find a property for Vanessa Redgrave"?*

The project came first. In the last scene of *Anne of the Thousand Days,* Anne Boleyn is beheaded because she could not produce a male heir to the throne. We see her daughter, Elizabeth—later to be queen, ironically—toddling down a garden path and into her place in history. Charles Jarrott and I discussed the possibilities of continuing her story, but because *The Young Elizabeth* was such a successful television special, we decided to pick her up as a grown woman during that episode in history when Mary and Elizabeth were mortal enemies. The scheming and melodrama that went on in that period is more exciting than fiction. I hired a well-known British writer to do an original screenplay, and then signed Glenda Jackson to play Elizabeth and Vanessa Redgrave to play Mary, Queen of Scots.

We've been told that there's a golden list of only ten or so actors who are bankable—stars with whom one can get projects going. Is this true?

Sometimes, of course. But if we all waited to cast our films with just the golden ten, there would be only ten films made each year. I think an independent producer who has to go to the bank to get money for a picture runs into a problem more often than I do. He is subject to the bank's evaluation of an individual's box-office draw or box-office poison. I don't go by any such list. If I feel an actor is right for a part, I'll use him. Of course, if his record shows he keeps people out of the theater, I might be influenced by that.

There are many strong producer-directors now. Do you feel that movies are suffering from this or do you think this is a good development?

My own opinion is that with a very few rare exceptions, most directors would be better off having a strong producer.

Does it take such a burden off him?

Yes, it takes a great burden off the director. It lets him concentrate on the story, on the actors, on getting the picture on film without being concerned with the endless details that crop up every day in the making of a picture.

Wallis reviewing the model of the set for *Anne of the Thousand Days* (1969).
Some of the scenes were shot at Hever Castle in England, where Henry VIII
first met Anne Boleyn.

Well, why is it, then, that there are so few strong producers left?

I don't know. It's hard to answer that. Maybe they're all trying to be
directors.

How do you settle the issue of the final cut?

Well, there is no issue. If the director wants to exercise his prerogative, it's
his by contract with the Screen Directors Guild to put the picture in
shape the way he sees it, no argument. He does it. And I look at it, and I
may agree with him and I may not. Then I have the final cut.

*Do you rely on previews of your films to gauge audience reaction before they are
released?*

When we have previews, we don't pass out cards. We sit in the audience
and try to get a gut feel, a reaction from the audience. We listen to their
comments when they come out. I find that in passing out cards, we are
asking for criticism. So we've eliminated that.

Have you ever learned from a preview something that everyone had missed in a screening room?

Yes. A preview can tell you things. You'll sit with an audience and see a cut that you should have made or something in the picture which gets a laugh that you didn't think would get a laugh and shouldn't get a laugh.

What do you want to see a director doing during production?

I like to get a director in on the project as early as possible. For example, *Rooster Cogburn* won't start shooting until September. For me to take on a director five months before production and then hire him for ten or twelve weeks of shooting becomes almost financially impossible. So what I try to do is give the director the script, get his general ideas, have meetings with him, let the work progress, have him go up and look at the locations and then have him come in sufficient time before production to concentrate on casting and so on.

When he comes in, say, just before production, what have you already accomplished by then?

By then the script is usually in pretty good shape. We have lists of actors—possibilities for all parts, which we talk about. We'll have interviews and quite a bit of preparation to do. For example, I have my production manager out now looking for locations. He was in Arkansas last week and is in Georgia today. He's coming back here and then he's going up to Oregon and Washington. He's photographing locations that should fit the action throughout the script. I will go over all of those with him and then I will probably go see the ones that are the best possibilities. I'll see those with the director within the next few weeks.

Have you already decided how much Rooster Cogburn *will cost?*

Yes, four and a half million. When I plan a picture, I know from experience approximately what it will cost. I break the script down into scenes and have it budgeted. If the cost is too high, I make cuts, change locations, whittle down until the price is right and reasonable for a profitable return.

Do you figure this film can probably make so much money, so it shouldn't cost over a certain figure?

Yes, that's exactly the way I figure it. I try to evaluate the potential and combine a business approach with the artistic. When you know how much the picture should do, you spend accordingly. If you know you're going to lose money on it, there's no point in making it.

How do you decide whether to shoot on location or in a studio?

If it's an outdoor picture, it has to be shot on location. For *Rooster,* we need rapids, rushing rivers and mountains, and we'll probably be shooting in Oregon or Washington. As a general rule, it's far better to always use actual locations because they give a sense of reality to a picture. In some cases, it isn't possible. Certain sequences have to be shot on a stage or on a studio back lot. If you're blowing up a building or a car, then you do it on the back lot where the explosions and fire can be controlled.

And isn't it cheaper?

No, it's expensive. You travel with an army. You have any number of trucks, station wagons, cars, eighty to one hundred people on a crew. You have to travel and house them. It's a very expensive operation.

Do you get into the design and the advertising?

Yes. When a film nears completion, the advertising and publicity departments of the studio come up with designs and suggestions for selling it to the public. They submit campaigns. I go over them, discuss logo, artwork, billing—all of the elements involved. If the ads aren't right, they try another angle. In some cases, they engage another agency to come in with a new campaign.

And how about the amount of money that the distributor spends on advertising?

That's pretty standard, unless you have a special picture like *Gatsby,* on which a fortune was spent on exploitation and tie-ins. For the average picture, advertising runs within the prescribed limit.

In the over forty years that you've been in the business, is there any project that you harbor a special fondness for?

Casablanca *is probably my top favorite.* Yankee Doodle Dandy, Kings Row, The Maltese Falcon, True Grit, GI Blues, Barefoot in the Park, Red Sky at Morning—*all were fun to make and memorable. Actually, the next one is always my favorite.*

I recently read a book on Casablanca *which was very interesting. Apparently it was being written as it was being shot. Is that true?*

We started out to make a good picture. We never dreamed it would become a classic. I wanted Ingrid Bergman to play opposite Bogart. I had to borrow her from Selznick, and it was very difficult at that time to borrow anybody from him. I chased him from Malibu to New York and back and made a two-picture deal for her—*Casablanca* and *Saratoga Trunk.* She and Bogie were so great together. We did have writing and story problems on *Casablanca,* and we did make changes in that script all the way through the production.

Wasn't it a stage play first?

It was a stage play, but I don't think it was ever produced. It was called *Everybody Comes to Rick's.* It was an inconsequential play about a saloon keeper in Casablanca. All of the intrigue in the area took place at Rick's. We started with just that.

At what point was Howard Koch, the screenwriter, brought in?

Howard Koch was one of the writers on it, along with Julius and Philip Epstein and Casey Robinson. The three or four writers used to meet in my office after the day's shooting, and we kicked the script around until it finally worked.

Was that done because you had to start by a certain date?

We started with a shooting script, but as we worked on it, we made improvements. There was a long discussion about how to end it, whether Bergman should go away with Henreid or whether she should stay with

Bogart. We could see it ending either way, but finally decided to have her do the decent thing and go with her freedom-fighter husband.

Were other directors considered for Casablanca *besides Michael Curtiz?*

No. And, incidentally, he was one of the great ones. He was a marvelous director doing things twenty years ago that a lot of new directors think they invented. He was a master with a camera, way ahead of his time. He could do anything. He would do a picture like *Casablanca,* then do *Charge of the Light Brigade, The Sea Hawk,* musicals, comedies.

Is that why he isn't a legendary director, because he did so many types of pictures and not just one style?

I think he is legendary. He did some marvelous pictures. He was never happy unless he was working. On the last day of shooting a film, he'd ask when he could start the next one. He was tireless.

Do you prefer finding a period novel or buying a finished play or screenplay?

It's a lot simpler to make a picture from a finished piece of material such as a book or a play. You start with more than just an idea. If it's a play, you've seen it produced on the stage. A book has description, dialogue, situations—everything worked out in black and white. When you start with an original piece of material, all that has to be created. For example, *Gunfight at the OK Corral,* though based on history, was inspired by a nonfiction article in *Holiday* magazine. It was about the strange relation-ship between the leading lawman, Wyatt Earp, and the leading gunslinger, Doc Holliday, and the admiration they had for one another. I bought the article and hired Leon Uris to do the screenplay as an original. We went into research, found what happened with Wyatt and the Clantons and embellished what I had bought. But it was a thin piece of material to start with. I like working that way sometimes.

Are your readers reading a great deal of material?

Yes, and I do a lot of reading. I get synopses on all material that is pub-lished, forecasts from publishers of what they expect to bring out soon, with brief outlines of what the stories are about. If I'm interested, I send

Throughout his career Wallis acquired rights to highly regarded novels and
plays and produced them for the screen. He is seen here with playwright
Tennessee Williams on the set of *The Rose Tattoo* (1955), which starred Burt
Lancaster and Anna Magnani.

for the complete material. Occasionally I get galleys directly from the
publisher, and the competition for material is very keen because everybody is looking for properties. If you do find something, you have to act
very quickly. I had a strange situation on *True Grit*. When the book came
out, the agent sent seven copies of galleys to seven different people in
Hollywood. I got one. The response was so great that he sent out a wire
stating he would send a telegram on a certain day, giving the price, and if
more than one company met the price, the author reserved the right to
choose whom he wanted to have it. I wired and said I would accept it, as
did about five other companies. The author, Charles Portis, was traveling

in a jeep somewhere down in Central America. His agent didn't hear from him for a week. When the agent finally reached him, Portis said he wanted me to have the property. Very fortunate.

Did you ever find out why he wanted your company as opposed to the others?

I think they had probably seen *Gunfight* and *Last Train from Gun Hill* and some of the other Western pictures I'd made. Duke Wayne's company was one that put in a bid. Wayne tried to raise the bid, as a matter of fact, because he wanted it for himself very much. When I heard that he wanted it, all I did was pick up the telephone and say, "I've got it, do you want to do it?" He did.

In all of your years in the business, have you made any big mistakes in producing?

I'd like to think not, but I have. I've made a few in selection of material. I don't think they were bad pictures, they just didn't catch fire. That's bound to happen. It's the law of averages.

What do directors look for in a producer?

I think possibly a collaborator. If a director is sympathetic to working with a producer, he accepts his help in all phases on a project. The concept of the film becomes theirs. They are a two-man team working together toward a single goal. The film is their joint effort. It becomes a collaboration and a very worthwhile one. I know I have found it so.

———◆———

Films as Producer

1939 *Dodge City*
 They Made Me a Criminal
 Dark Victory
 Juarez
 Daughters Courageous
 Each Dawn I Die
 The Angels Wash Their Faces
 The Old Maid
 Dust Be My Destiny

 Espionage Agent
 On Your Toes
 The Roaring Twenties
 The Private Lives of Elizabeth and Essex
 The Oklahoma Kid
 We Are Not Alone
 Four Wives
 Invisible Strangers

1940 *A Child Is Born*
Brother Rat and a Baby
The Fighting 69th
Castle on the Hudson
Dr. Ehrlich's Magic Bullet
Three Cheers for the Irish
Virginia City
'Til We Meet Again
Saturday's Children
Torrid Zone
Brother Orchid
All This, and Heaven Too
My Love Came Back
They Drive by Night
The Sea Hawk
No Time for Comedy
City for Conquest
Knute Rockne-All American
A Dispatch from Reuters
The Letter
Santa Fe Trail

1941 *Four Mothers*
Honeymoon for Three
High Sierra
The Strawberry Blond
Footsteps in the Dark
The Great Lie
Affectionately Yours
Million Dollar Baby
Shining Victory
Out of the Fog
The Bride Came C.O.D.
Manpower
Dive Bomber
Navy Blues
Sergeant York
The Maltese Falcon
One Foot in Heaven
Blues in the Night

1942 *They Died with Their Boots On*
All Through the Night
The Man Who Came to Dinner

Captains of the Clouds
The Male Animal
Kings Row
Larceny, Inc.
In This Our Life
Juke Girl
Desperate Journey
Now, Voyager

1943 *Yankee Doodle Dandy*
Casablanca
Air Force
This Is the Army
Watch on the Rhine
Princess O'Rourke

1944 *Passage to Marseille*

1945 *The Affairs of Susan*
You Came Along
Love Letters

1946 *Saratoga Trunk*
The Searching Wind
The Strange Love of Martha Ivers

1947 *The Perfect Marriage*
Desert Fury

1948 *The Accused*
I Walk Alone
So Evil My Love
Sorry, Wrong Number

1949 *My Friend Irma*
Rope of Sand

1950 *The File on Thelma Jordan*
Paid in Full
My Friend Irma Goes West
The Furies
Dark City

1951 *September Affair*
Peking Express
That's My Boy

1952 *Sailor Beware*
Red Mountain
Jumping Jacks

1953 *The Stooge*
Come Back, Little Sheba

1953 *Scared Stiff*
1954 *Cease Fire!*
    Money From Home
    About Mrs. Leslie
1955 *3 Ring Circus*
    The Rose Tattoo
1956 *Artists and Models*
    Hollywood or Bust
1957 *The Rainmaker*
    Gunfight at the OK Corral
    Loving You
    The Sad Sack
1958 *Wild Is the Wind*
    Hot Spell
    Kid Creole
1959 *Last Train from Gun Hill*
    Don't Give Up the Ship
    Career
1960 *Visit to a Small Planet*
    GI Blues
1961 *All in a Night's Work*
    Summer and Smoke
    Blue Hawaii

1962 *Girls! Girls! Girls!*
    A Girl Named Tamiko
1963 *Wives and Lovers*
    Fun in Acapulco
1964 *Becket*
    Roustabout
1965 *The Sons of Katie Elder*
    Boeing Boeing
1966 *Paradise, Hawaiian Style*
1967 *Easy Come, Easy Go*
    Barefoot in the Park
1968 *5 Card Stud*
1969 *True Grit*
    Anne of the Thousand Days
1970 *Norwood*
1971 *Red Sky at Morning*
    Shoot Out
1972 *Mary, Queen of Scots*
    Follow Me/The Public Eye
1973 *A Bequest to the Nation/The*
        Nelson Affair
    The Don is Dead
1975 *Rooster Cogburn*

I am not a man of general ideas; I am more an artist of the details. I pride myself on seeing that the details become the thing as a whole. I might start with this cup of coffee . . . from such a cup of coffee you can start a story, a wonderful story.

JEAN RENOIR
(Born in Paris, 1894—Died 1979)

"It happens all too often," Jean Renoir said, "that the post of director consists of little more than a folding chair with his name on it." Renoir would never be accused of such passivity. He was a director intent on influencing every element of each of his films, seeking to establish his identity and proclaim it to an audience.

The son of the master Impressionist painter Auguste Renoir, Jean served as an officer in the French cavalry and was wounded in the trenches in 1914. Later he was an air corps aviator specializing in photo reconnaissance. While aviation provided his first contact and fascination with the motion picture camera, it was his desire to advance the acting career of his first wife that led him into the world of cinema.

Renoir had a brilliant career in the thirties, creating the classics *Nana, Le Crime de Monsieur Lange, La Grande illusion* and *La Règle du jeu*. When the Germans occupied France in 1940, he escaped and made his way through Spain to the United States. Though he later returned to his homeland to work as a director for a time, he made his life and career in California where he remained until his death.

One can only imagine the challenges a refugee director who spoke little English faced taking up his profession anew in the United States. Although Renoir was a famous filmmaker, his intimate concepts of screen storytelling were at odds with the Hollywood system. In 1941 he signed a contract with Twentieth Century Fox. His goal was to start a small company specializing in low-budget, experimental films, with casts of either beginners or actors who were down on their luck. "I was confident," he said, "that I would unearth talents that would more than cover the modest cost of the films." Unfortunately this approach led to a clash with Darryl F. Zanuck, the head of Fox, who remarked, "Renoir has a lot of talent, but he's not one of us."

Renoir wrote in his autobiography, *My Life and My Films,* that the history of cinema could be summarized as the war of the filmmaker against the industry. "I am proud," he proclaimed, "to have had a share in that triumphant struggle." He made six English-language films in the United States, including *The Southerner, The Woman on the Beach* and *This Land Is Mine.* Later, in India, he made *The River,* which provided a first experience in film production for a young Indian named Satyajit Ray. "In spite of the money my films made," Renoir wrote, "I was not commercial. It was worse than a label, it was like a tattoo mark on my forehead."

In AFI's first year, I enlisted James Blue, a young filmmaker of great accomplishment and promise, to join the AFI faculty. Jim, who had studied Renoir's work at film school in Paris, and I went to see Renoir at his small house in Beverly Hills to persuade him to spend some time with our fellows in the belief that he would bring a distinctive and nourishing sensibility to our process. Renoir was seventy-six at the time and greeted us in a colorful sweater and with a beaming smile, exuding a twinkling warmth that disguised the vigor required of his successful military and film careers.

Before Renoir's arrival at AFI, we screened seven of his films. Jim Blue conducted the seminar.

Renoir meeting with AFI fellows in 1970. Seated next to Renoir is James Blue, independent filmmaker and member of AFI faculty.

JEAN RENOIR

——————

April 14, 1970

The first question is simple: How do you start a film?

Well, I start with an idea when I can. That's not so easy. You know, I'm probably not the right person to ask such a question, because in the field of motion pictures I'm a director who has spent his life suggesting stories that nobody wanted. It's still going on. But I'm used to it and I'm not complaining, because the ideas which were forced on me were often better than my own ideas. A little mixture of what was brought to me and what I had in my imagination has provided a happy medium, which perhaps helped to make the picture a little more alive. Of course, even if you have to work on a story you don't like very much, you can always do a personal picture, one which will be the expression of your personality. The ideas inside you don't give up, and in the final result it's your picture and not someone else's. This is why I can't give you any recipe about how to start a picture.

Myself—excuse me if I talk about practical recollections—I was very much helped along in my career. I made about forty films, and an examination of my body of work shows that I owe my films to the most unexpected producers of the world. You know, I am not a man of general ideas, I am more an artist of the details. I pride myself on seeing that the details become the thing as a whole. I might start with this cup of coffee. Is this coffee? It's probably very good. Allow me to try. [*He drinks the coffee.*] No, your coffee is not excellent. But from such a cup of coffee you can start a story, a wonderful story.

Can you describe how this idea affects your general approach to the process of film-making?

For me, everything is one operation. It's like literature—you start a sentence and you don't finish it because you can't find the right word. Perhaps with film you find the right word in the cutting room. A picture is a whole. You cannot say, "This is the beginning, this is the middle and this is the end." No. I believe a picture is a state of mind. A picture, often when it is good, is the result of some inner belief which is so strong that you have to show what you want, in spite of a stupid story or difficulties about the commercial side of the film. Yes, it's a state of mind.

In my imagination I divide directors in two big categories: those who start from the camera, and those who don't. Some put the camera in a certain spot which is carefully chosen. It gives a beautiful background, and with props it gives them a certain idea which can symbolically help the telling of the story. Then they take the actors and put them in front of the lens. This means the role of the director is based on the service of the camera. Wonderful directors work that way, for example, René Clair. I will always remember one day I visited René on the set in the silent days. He was shooting a scene with an actor—not a great actor, but a good actor. In the script—I wanted to see a script, and they showed me the page that he was shooting—the jacket of the actor had to caress lightly an object on the table. René Clair shot the scene something like fifty times, and finally he got it and he was delighted. But I am the opposite: I like to start with the actors. I like to put them in a certain mood.

We directors are, simply, midwives. The actor has something inside himself, but very often he doesn't realize what he has in mind and his heart. I always try to start the work from the actor. You rehearse, and when you are happy about the rehearsal, you decide that you can give the rein to the cameraman. You ask the cameraman and soundman to come with you, and you decide what will be the angle of the shot. But this angle depends on the acting and not on the imagination of the director. That's more my method. Now, to talk about this in our profession is childish, because there is no method. You must change your method according to each different shot. The basis of my work is the actors, who make me adopt a different way of cutting the pictures. I always try not to cut the film during the shooting. This is why I use tracking shots and pans so often. It is for no other reason than I hate to cut the acting of someone during his inspiration.

A great director, perhaps the top director of his day, Jean-Luc Godard, is exactly the opposite of me. He starts with the camera. His frames are really a direct expression of his personality but without the in-between worries brought by actors. The actor has a headache and indigestion the day before. His wife left him, but he loves her. When you want to work with the actor, you have to absorb all those things. Now, myself—since I am not Goliath but perhaps a little David—I need all those things. I need the actor who comes to me and says, "Oh, I am so unhappy. I believe my mistress is cheating on me, I cannot stand it." Well, that's my job: to open the door to such confidence and to use that for the film. We directors are midwives using this method. Now, I say "method," but I don't believe in method. I believe that every director must have his *own* method. Does that answer your question?

It was a good start.

May I add a little comment to this question of the importance or the unimportance given to the actors? This is exactly the quarrel going on in every profession, between abstract act and nonabstract act. The director who is searching for an abstract emotion doesn't need forms or faces of actors. He can talk directly from his own chest to the heart of a spectator. Myself, I am more in favor of the other method, which we could compare to what is the figurative art in painting. That doesn't mean you cannot interweave all sorts of methods. I want to have an idea of the scene thanks to the rehearsal with the actors. When I have a clear idea of the scene, all of a sudden I realize everything I was doing was wrong, and I start again. Finally, when the scene shows something that seems to me sufficient, I bring the camera.

I'll tell you a little story. It was during the shooting of my picture *Grande illusion.* Perhaps some of you know the picture? You remember at the end Jean Gabin and Marcel Dalio are walking in the snow, and Dalio is wounded. He'd had a little accident and was limping. He couldn't go any further. Well, I had written two pages of beautiful literature to explain the situation. Gabin was, you know, like a poet, explaining about what's good, what's bad in nature. It was fantastic and I was proud of myself. But I was a little worried because the two actors didn't want to start the scene. They were finding reasons to do something else. Finally Gabin said to me, "Jean, we'd better tell you: your two pages of beautiful poetry are just trash." And it was true. Finally I had an idea, or perhaps it was Gabin. He

was humming a tune I already used in the beginning of the picture—
"The Little Sailor." I took those very innocent words, and they became
the center of the scene, which is, I think, very good.

But without the reluctance of Dalio, without my belief in the help the
actors can give, I would have nothing. Nothing. Oh, I would have a perfectly drawn and conceived scene, but dull. Now, that explains, perhaps
better than what I said before, my point of view with actors. In other
words, you must not ask an actor to do what he cannot do. You know,
there is an old slogan, very popular in our occidental civilization: you
must look to an end higher than normal, and that way you will achieve
something. Your aim must be very, very high. Myself, I am absolutely
convinced that it is mere stupidity. The aim must be easy to reach, and by
reaching it, you achieve more.

The trouble with us human beings is that we are often very stupid.
Things are in front of us but we don't see them. An actress rehearses with
a beautiful face full of emotion, but you don't see it. You're thinking of
your camera angle. I'm not for that. I'm delighted to leave the occasion to
chance and not rely on planning. I'm against planning. I'm in favor of the
art and literature of the Middle Ages, up to the Renaissance. To me, the
Renaissance is a barbarian order which replaced a great civilization. In
the twelfth century—as it is in India and many parts of Asia today—you
have a frame for everything, within which you are free to do what you
want. I believe in this conception of art. The Renaissance brought about
the cult of the individual, but I believe that the individual shows himself
in an interesting way when he doesn't know that he shows himself. It must
be in spite of himself. When you are in the studio and you stand beside
the camera and yell, "I am going to express myself!" then you will express
nothing. But if you are submerged in admiration for the gesture of an
actor or, if it is a documentary picture, the beauty of the piece of nature
you are confronted by, then you have a chance to reveal yourself behind
those images more than if you choose to show yourself directly. Of course,
this is my opinion, and I don't pretend that it is right. As I told you, every
one of us must build up our own grammar, our own method, like the
recipe in a cookbook.

*I'd be interested in knowing when and how you rehearse with your actors. Since
you clearly invite so much collaboration from them, do you rehearse just before you
shoot or do you begin earlier?*

Usually when you work on a picture, the schedule is too short. The money isn't there and you have to hurry. But if I had the time, I would work first in a rehearsal room with no props. This is a very old idea, the name of which is to work *à l'italien*, to rehearse the Italian way. This was very much in favor in the time of the commedia dell'arte in Italy. They brought this method to Paris and London. I tell you what it is—the most important characters and the directors sit down around a table and read the text, without any expression. They read the lines as they would the telephone directory, blah, blah, blah. Monotonous and flat. Let's say we have a little scene which represents a mother confronted suddenly with the death of her son. You are working on this scene and you ask the actress who plays the mother to help you find an expression. The actress might find four or five expressions she and other actors have used a million times before. But the text grows inside her, amongst the actors reciting it flat. The actor must have the feeling that she wrote the part, and you see a little sparkle. Oh, you cannot miss it—it is a baby. The midwife did her job! When you have this sparkle, you start rehearsals. Now, this method is never used because it takes too much time, and time is money in the picture business.

Any great theatrical or film movement must be paced for the slow digestion of situations. That was Stanislavsky's idea. If you want a completely sincere expression of an individual, then that's another question. The individuals who we want to give birth to are to be found partly in the work of the author, the surroundings, the direction and the actor. It's a mixture. Out of this mixture the problem is to have one human being who is real and alive.

Is this not also true when you are creating the story, this slow evolution from an idea?

Exactly, the same thing. After all, in any domain the problems are the same. Slow digestion.

You once said that the writer Marcel Pagnol had told you that ideas came on like an electric lightbulb. Is this true in your case?

Well, I would like this to be my case, as I told you. There are many light-bulbs in filmmaking and in book writing. For instance, one little lightbulb which is quite precious is the voice. One picture that I worked on *à l'italien* was *Boudu*. We didn't know exactly what to do with the Michel Simon character. He seems to be very simple, but he's not. One day Simon got up and started to walk and talk with the voice of Boudu. All of a sudden he said, "I am Boudu. Follow me."

Do you work with the crew—costumes, art direction, cinematographer—in the same way as you do with the actors?

You know, a picture is a little world. Something very important in life is balance. You must balance all the elements. What is very dangerous in pictures is that an actor becomes a star because of repetition of voice and the same gestures. The public becomes used to it, and though the poor soul makes millions, it's nothing to do with talent. To me it's something quite tragic to see a human being always repeating the same gestures that are not even real, not even the expression of reality.

From the start of your career you developed your ideas on camera movement. More and more you began to use tracking and staging in depth.

Well, the reason for my camera work was not to cut in the middle of the acting but to have the camera hanging on the actor, following the story. The camera is just a recording device and not a god. The camera is especially dangerous in this city, in Hollywood. It became so important that in the mind of many people it was the *only* thing that was important. Sometimes I will be on the set working with an actor and everything is wrong. The actor is not satisfied, I am not satisfied. The producer arrives and says, "Please, you are fussy, both of you, looking for the impossible. The shot is sufficient like that, and we must not waste time with such nonsensical tasks." But if the cameraman was looking to remove a little shadow at the tip of the nose of the star, he could take three days if he wanted.

When you shoot tracking shots, do you also attempt to shoot other material which will allow you to shorten the shot in editing if you need to? Or perhaps to change the rhythm?

No. It should be done, but I don't do it, and I'll tell you why. I believe it's a good thing to be committed—to play the game. You have the scene, you believe it's good, so you shoot it. When I can, I shoot my scenes only once. I like to be committed, to be a slave to my decision. If I know that I won't have those shots to cut, my main shot will be better. If I know I have those other shots, I say, "Oh, that's not very good, but we have the others." I don't like that attitude.

I do not have very good eyesight—I mean spiritual eyesight. I don't understand the problems of a shot before it is shot. When we are ready to shoot, when the lights are burning and the cameras are ready, all of a sudden I might think of something which was obvious that I hadn't seen before. The girl should not be wearing a hat, or instead of playing the scene standing and nervous, she should sit and stay still. This is why I cannot decide things in advance, whether the scene will be made up of many shots or with only one main shot. To be very frank, if we're talking of aesthetics, I don't like too many close shots. When I started in this business my first preoccupation was to find lenses which would allow the background to be clear, not out of focus.

I also hate to show people who seem to be just out of an icebox, sterilized. I like a little dirt from the outside to give some life to my shots. That's something else in preparation. I believe the ideal work is to prepare the shot, to be ready to shoot it, to be perfectly satisfied, then to understand the element you are missing, and to add this element. It is exactly like with old buildings. You buy an old farm in the Midwest. You want to fix it for living in. Probably you will get something much more alive than if you were to build a new house.

Story is often considered unnecessary in film today. I wonder if you could talk about that.

Well, as I said, it is the eternal quarrel between abstract art and figurative art. If the author feels he can express himself without the help of a subject, to build a bridge between his own inside and the spectator—good. My own preoccupation is slightly different. You know what my preoccupation is in pictures? It is that I would like the picture to give the feeling to the audience that it is unfinished. I believe that the work of art where the spectator does not collaborate is not a work of art. I like the people who look at the picture, perhaps, to build a different story on the side. Without the collaboration of the public we have nothing except dull art. The artists and the public must be in communion. We must arrive at such and such a point where the public is the maker and the artist becomes the spectator. But you'll notice I'm just dreaming aloud now.

Your films seem to proceed unsteadily, meandering without structure and with a life of their own. Yet when one sees a Renoir film, one says, "My God, look what he did." By the end, it appears to be a structured unit, a clean and clear statement about life.

Well, thank you very much. I believe that even in a nonreligious or non-political story, even in a comedy, which is absolutely flat, or in a Western, if the author is possessed by certain convictions, those convictions will give a kind of meat to the work.

Do you feel it necessary in order for your films to work to get audience sympathy or involvement with the characters?

No, nothing is *necessary.* What you talk about can help, yes. And why not accept any help? Luckily we have it. I believe this question of communication depends on the film, on the author, the people. There is no rule. You talk about the sympathy of the public. Of course we all want it. You are in a preview, your picture is a little dull. The public doesn't follow you, and all of a sudden on the screen some actor cracks a joke which you wrote unwillingly. But you had to have something, you had to fill a space. You hear a little laughter among the audience and you feel like a million dollars. You would like to see who laughed and kiss him. Yes, we depend on the public. What is wrong is to believe the public is inevitably a crowd of ten million people. For some artists, the public is ten people, or one person. The size of the crowd isn't important. What is important is that you are in communication with somebody, with a spirit which is not your spirit but which can influence you for a short time. Now, I repeat—and excuse me if I repeat myself so often—those are my ideas. That doesn't mean they are good. Tomorrow I will perhaps have different ideas. I am not steady.

I would like to know what you look for in writing and directing a scene. You said you looked to see if it did something, but you didn't really explain what this thing is.

I will try to answer your question, which is a very difficult and interesting one. Excuse me if I go back to *Grande illusion.* When writing the screenplay I discovered that the film had another meaning. I discovered that the story was perhaps a little approach to a big problem, that of surrounding and of nations, which is the racist problem. It is also the problem of how people from different religions meet, how they cannot understand each other for some reason. To me the only important thing in the world is how to meet others, and *Grande illusion* was for me the chance to tell everything I had in my heart about such things. But when I wrote the screenplay I didn't know this; it was just an escape story. In certain scenes between Pierre Fresnay and Erich von Stroheim we talk only of questions of surroundings and adaptations, questions of how to get along together. Though I don't ever forget that it was an escape story, the escape part was insignificant. It is by working on the picture that I was pulling out of myself certain ideas more important than I thought in the beginning.

When you have an additional idea—racism, how people meet, so forth—do you then work out how to write a scene based around these things?

Well, let's start with *Grande illusion* again. For instance, I have a scene between Dalio and Gabin. They are preparing a rope to escape. They talk, frankly, about racism. It might appear that it doesn't belong in the picture, but it does. It works. I had entire scenes which were shot only for this expression of origin, nation, race—for example, a scene where half a dozen French prisoners are preparing a show by sewing costumes. They are having a very serious conversation that has nothing to do with the scenery or costumes. It is a question of where you are going, where you come from. I could put fifty situations like this in my pictures.

In introducing ideas such as these into what is essentially an escape film, isn't it difficult to do so without stopping the flow of the picture or losing the interest of the audience?

It is terribly difficult. The problem is the change of style, though in *Grande illusion* it was easy. The setup was ideal for these kinds of discussions, and it was a very easy picture to shoot and write. *The Rules of the Game* was more difficult.

How did Grande illusion *come about?*

I was shooting *Toni* in the south of France. It was a film I made almost entirely on location. Nearby was a big military airfield. Everyone there could see I was shooting a picture—there were reflectors, cameras, trucks.

The planes were above my head the whole day long, and I couldn't record any sound. I decided to pay a visit to the commanding officer of this base, and was confronted by a man with more medals than you could wear. He was a good friend of mine. In fact, during the First War he saved my life several times. He was a fighter in a squadron of fighting planes and I was a photographer. That's the way I became interested in movies—by taking photographs from above. Planes carrying cameras were not very fast and we thought that every time we were confronted by a German fighter, that was the end of us. Several times this man arrived with his little squad and *tak-tak-tak*—the Germans were happy to run away. At the time he was just a noncom, but he became a general. General Pensal was his name. He was shot down by the Germans seven times. He escaped seven times and he went back to his squadron seven times.

We were happy to meet up with each other again, and in the evening took the habit of having dinner together. He told me the story of how he escaped from German jails, and I thought it would make a good suspense story. I asked his permission to use a few of the stories he had told me, and then wrote a screenplay, convinced I had written a very banal escape story. I thought it was very commercial and that I would be able to find financing very easily. That's what I thought. For three years, my dear friends, I visited every office on the Champs-Elysées, in Rome and everywhere else. Everywhere I had the same answer: "No girls in your picture. We're not interested." Finally I met a man who was a—well, I don't want to insult people, but I don't know of any other word but *crook*. He was a brilliant, successful crook. That was his profession. He told me, "Jean, I believe in your picture." I said, "You are not in the film business, but people in the business don't believe in it." "That doesn't matter. How much do you want?" He gave me two million francs, and I shot the picture, and it was successful.

Could you elaborate on the problem of keeping the audience's attention alive, and yet introducing these ideas?

Well, I wrote a first draft of *The Rules of the Game* in which the individual was a little gray and out of focus. I had given too much importance to things like his rich life, his mistress, the château where he's living. I was hoping I could do something light, elegant and amusing with such a background. This happens to me all the time—for instance with *La Chienne*. The head of the studio, a very nice boy who wouldn't kill an elephant, gave me the money to shoot the film with the idea that it was going to be a hilarious farce. Of course I didn't contradict him, being sure that if he knew the truth, I would have to stop shooting. Once everything was shot, he realized I was shooting a somber drama and he told me, "At least I want to try to save the situation. You won't do the cutting." I said, "Okay, I won't do it." We started to fight, with our fists. I was stronger than he was. But the next day when I went to the studio, the policeman wouldn't let me in and said very politely, "Monsieur Renoir, it is forbidden." I was saved by a wonderful man who was making money for the studio—Mr. Monteaux, the president of the most important shoe company in France—and I was restored to my cutting room with only a few shots missing.

What is the origin of Octave, the character you yourself play in The Rules of the Game?

I thought certain situations needed a commentator and that I should add to my story a kind of master of ceremonies, like in a review on the stage. I found out that this master of ceremonies would say everything that I myself, the author, had in mind. I said, "Well, why not say it myself?" He is practically a tramp—the tramp in the tuxedo.

Jean Renoir is perhaps best remembered as the director of two early master-pieces, *Grande illusion* (1937) and *Rules of the Game* (1939). Here he is seen in the documentary *Renoir, The Best* (1985) directed by Jacques Rivette.

We'd like to know how you work with the art director on your films, how much control you exercise over the development of the sets?

May I say that I like to have control over every part of the picture—the art directors, the cameramen, the actors. I like to know intimately what they do, and to suggest and help them decide when there is a choice. But I don't believe in specialists. It can happen that an actor will tell me, "I don't like this part of the set." We have a discussion about it and change it if necessary. In other words, I don't like to make the important decisions alone. I like to feel that around my direction many of the problems are going on, and that I know them and am participating as much as the technicians or the actors are participating in my own worries.

Do you have any rules about casting?

That's where I like to have my friends help me, because I am very bad at casting. Sometimes to be bad helps me, in the way that I am attracted by a certain innocence. I am afraid of clichés and tricks. I am afraid of repeating situations we have already seen on the screen. People with not too much skill sometimes help me to keep a kind of—I use a very ambitious word, excuse me—to keep a kind of innocence.

What happens when you have a difficult actor and you have problems getting him to do what you want him to do? And what happens if you watch the footage and realize he is too hammy and overacting?

I never found an actor in complete opposition with me. Never. I have worked with people with the reputation to be impossible, and I've found them delightful. I believe that everything must come from inside the individual. Again, I use the comparison of the midwife. I don't like to tell the actor to scratch his nose. He must find for himself all those things. An actor must have the feeling that he wrote the part himself. He must reject what doesn't seem to come from him. Of course that brings discussions, but out of those discussions sometimes you find a very big improvement in the scene. I don't believe that an actor can overact. It seems to be a paradox. To me an actor is on the right track when his creation is a real human being. If he is on the wrong track, even if he hardly moves his lips, he is bad. In other words, it's not a question of being loud or exaggerating.

If you are involved in the picture, you cannot go back. What is shot is shot—you can never replace it. What you have to do is try to find a way to match your ideas and the exaggerations of this actor. If you have enough dialogue to allow an actor to play with his words to his discretion, unless he is a perfect idiot—and unless you are a perfect idiot, which may also happen—you always find a way, a kind of happy medium.

If you have a particular tone you're searching for and you want the actors to say a line in a particular way, how do you go about obtaining that?

By starting with no expression and repeating and repeating and repeating. You know, the results are fantastic. Sometimes I did it with actors who were unprepared for that, and they were amazed. It's beautiful the way it works.

Do you ever find yourself reading the line for them?

I hate this kind of work. Too many directors work like this. They tell the actor, "Sit down, my dear friends, and look at me. I am going to act a scene, and you are going to repeat what I just did." He acts a scene and he acts it badly, because if he is a director instead of an actor, it's probably because he's a bad actor.

I have heard that sometimes you will give analogies to people to give them an idea of how to say a line.

No, I am very careful about that. I don't want an actor to imitate me. There is no reason why all of a sudden an actor should be Jean Renoir on the screen. After all, the purpose of art and moviemaking is to find yourself. If you are looking for a character who doesn't exist in life, an ideal character you build in your imagination, well, that's very wrong. If you can prove to the actor that it's false, the actor will be the first to look for something else, and perhaps find it.

I wonder how you feel about the French New Wave directors.

Well, it's difficult for me to judge them because, as we say in French, we are in the same boat. Judging them would be a bit like judging myself. I believe that in this world we proceed by little groups, and you must belong to a little group. That doesn't mean you lose your individuality—not at all. Belonging to a little group helps you to find it. I feel in the bottom of my heart that I am very close to this generation which came after me but who are very much looking for the same thing. We have different ideas on some points. For instance, Godard typically starts from the camera. I end with the camera. Truffaut is in between.

Truffaut seems the closest to you in style among the new directors.

Yes, definitely.

You speak of trying to avoid the staginess of the theater when making films, but in Golden Coach *there is a fascination with the stage and performing. I wonder if you could talk about the way theater relates to the way you view film.*

Well, I cannot answer your question directly because I shot *Golden Coach* probably ten years ago and I have forgotten what my state of mind was in this period. But I can relate your question to one that I am asking myself constantly. Perhaps it is the most important preoccupation regarding filmmaking I've had in my life. It is the question of the outside reality and the inside reality. For instance, you have an actor who is going to play the part of a sailor. Being very conscientious, he buys the real costume of a sailor. He will wear a cap which went through tempests and hurricanes of the sea. He will, perhaps, live in a boat not only to get used to the language of sailors but also to have the bronze skin of a man living constantly outside. He will act the part—and he will look exactly like a ham because he is not a good actor. That's one thing. Now, you suggest to Charlie Chaplin he should play the part of the sailor, and even with a cane and a derby and a tramp's suit he will be a sailor.

You have a reputation of having a hand of iron in a velvet glove. Is it true that on the set you never criticize or never allow yourself to become angry?

I am trying. I don't always succeed, but I try.

I read an article that said on every take—whether or not it seemed successful—you tell the actors that it was in fact good, but that you would rather try another interpretation. Is this a technique that you have used?

Often, yes. I hate to discourage people. The truth is, if you discourage an actor you may never find him again. You'll hide his personality behind a kind of mask of fear. An actor is an animal, extremely fragile. You get a little expression, it is not exactly what you wanted, but it's alive. It's something human. Don't kill it by pushing your own ideas into his imagination. No. Try softly and slowly to help him find what you believe is the truth, because in the picture the truth is the truth of the author. You said a hand of iron in a velvet glove? I am afraid very often I have a velvet hand in a glove of iron.

You spoke of getting the public to collaborate in your work. In writing the script, do you structure the story so that it encourages collaboration from the audience?

I believe it is good to work keeping in mind all aspects of the making of the picture. And since we cannot forget there is a public, and that we work for it, it's better to keep alive the idea of the public at all times during the organization of the picture.

In thinking of how the audience might respond, would you ever change a script in order to engage the audience in a certain way?

Well, of course you have to think of the public. Very often, to think of the public from the beginning leads you to using mechanical devices. My nephew is a cameraman and made a film about Picasso. In the film, Picasso says something repeatedly which to me is a big secret we should all share and use if we can. "Fill it." Those were his words. No empty space. You have a frame, the frame is a scene in a movie or is the frame of a painting. I agree with Picasso. You must fill this frame.

Films as Director

1925 *La Fille de l'eau*
1926 *Nana* (also co-screenplay)
1927 *Catherine*
     Marquitta
1928 *La Petite Marchande*
     d'allumettes (also
     screenplay)

Tire-au-flanc (also
     co-screenplay)
Le Tournoi dans la cité (also
     screenplay)
1929 *Le Bled*
1931 *On purge bébé*
     La Chienne (also screenplay)

1932 *La Nuit du carrefour* (also
    screenplay)
Boudu sauveé des eaux (also
    co-screenplay)
Chotard et cie (also screenplay)

1933 *Madame Bovary* (also
    screenplay)

1935 *Toni* (also screenplay)

1936 *Le Crime de Monsieur Lange*
    (also co-screenplay)
Une Partie de campagne (also
    screenplay)
La Vie est à nous (also
    co-screenplay)
Les Bas-fonds (also
    co-screenplay)

1937 *La Grande illusion* (also
    co-screenplay)

1938 *La Marseillaise*
La Bête humaine (also
    screenplay)

1939 *La Règle du jeu* (also
    co-screenplay)

1941 *La Tosca* (co-director and
    co-screenplay)
Swamp Water

1943 *This Land Is Mine*

1945 *The Southerner* (also
    co-screenplay)

1946 *The Diary of a Chambermaid*

1947 *The Woman on the Beach* (also
    co-screenplay)

1951 *The River* (also co-screenplay)

1953 *Le Carrosse d'or* (also
    co-screenplay)

1955 *French Cancan* (also
    co-screenplay)

1956 *Eléna et les hommes* (also
    co-screenplay)

1959 *Le Testament du Docteur
    Cordelier* (also screenplay)
Le Déjeuner sur l'herbe (also
    screenplay)
Le Caporal épinglé (also
    co-screenplay)

I am not a movie director who consciously plots the movements of the camera, because they are very natural. Imagination is everything. The picture is in my head, and I just try to make it.

FEDERICO FELLINI
(Born in Rome, Italy, 1920—Died 1993)

Federico Fellini was the first of the international star directors. More than any other filmmaker of his time, he had a persona that shared center stage with his films. *Felliniesque* is an adjective used even by people who haven't seen his pictures, and *paparazzi,* coined from the name Fellini gave the sly photographer, Papparazzo, in *La Dolce Vita,* is a word used throughout the world.

In the United States we became acquainted with Fellini when *La Strada* and *Nights of Cabiria* were shown here in the 1950s, earning the director his first two Oscars. These films were the forerunners of what became an American love affair with European films in the sixties and seventies. I was in Rome in 1960 when Fellini arranged a private screening of *La Dolce Vita* for my father. We watched the film in Italian, with an interpreter explaining the dialogue. The film was large, original and bursting with vitality and showmanship. The scene of the statue of Jesus being towed by helicopter over the skyline of Rome, as sunbathing beauties in bikinis watched from rooftops, became an iconic screen image. The Catholic Church would soon condemn the film, making Fellini world-famous.

By the time he came to Los Angeles in 1970 to promote *Fellini Satyricon, The New York Times* had written, "No other director can at this moment quite measure up to his stature." He had won a third Oscar for *8½* and would receive his fourth two years later for *Amarcord. Satyricon* was screened for the AFI fellows and news of his planned appearance at AFI spread. For the first time security was necessary to make certain that the students had seats, because many professionals in the film community wanted to be there as well. The presence of Sidney Poitier, Jack Lemmon, Billy Wilder, Ray Bradbury, Sam Fuller and Haskell Wexler made it a festive night.

Federico Fellini gives the master's touch to the fur hat of Anita Ekberg during
the filming of *La Dolce Vita* (1961).

Fellini walked in smiling and seemed ready for a good time. He was
accompanied by his wife, Giulietta Masina, who had given unforgettable performances in *La Strada* and *Cabiria,* and by Anthony Quinn, who had played
the brutish circus performer, Zampano, in *La Strada.* Though armed with an
interpreter, Fellini understood most questions and answered in English.

We conceived the Center for Advanced Film Studies as a place for a tutorial tradition, where the ideas of accomplished filmmakers would inform the
development of new ones. Most of the fellows had spent the 1960s on college
campuses, and many had anti-establishment views. "Never trust anyone over
thirty" was the rallying cry. This led to tension between some fellows and
those they considered "Hollywood" directors, men who they felt were old-
fashioned and unsympathetic to new techniques, especially improvisation,
which had found favor with the young. To them, Fellini was an idol—an
exemplar of modern filmmaking.

Shortly after the seminar began, a student from New York stood and said,
"I've read that you often come on the set with the actors not knowing what's
going to happen during the day's shooting. Is it true that you do a great deal
of improvisation?" The students and faculty knew this was a moment of truth

for the school—the word was about to come down from the master. Fellini turned to Anthony Quinn for clarification, "Improvistore?" Quinn nodded. Fellini frowned and addressed the fellows, "No, it's absolutely impossible to improvise. Making a movie is a mathematical operation. It is like for you Americans sending a missile to the moon."

I've always felt that this was a crucial passage for this new academy. We were there to advance the principle that creativity was rooted in craftsmanship, and the man who was, arguably, the world's most imaginative director had spoken up for preparation, calculation and structure—ideas that would be the foundation for learning at AFI for decades to come.

Fellini went on to make eight more films after *Satyricon* and continued to amuse or confound people who tried to pin him down or pigeonhole him. In *Fellini: A Life*, Hollis Alpert tells of the director's reply to an American television interviewer who pressed him on what he would like to be if he weren't a director. Fellini sighed and said, "An actor, a singer, a painter, a circus performer, a musician, a writer and a doctor in a mental hospital. I am very fortunate. As a director I can be all of these."

FEDERICO FELLINI

———◆———

January 12, 1970

When we talked about opening the Center for Advanced Film Studies, one of its aims and ideas was to bring together young people who are studying film with the most accomplished and talented practitioners of cinema. What we're concerned with here is the past, present and future of cinema, and Mr. Fellini represents all three. So, Mr. Fellini, we welcome you to Los Angeles.

So let's talk! I have some difficulty with the language, so my friends, I will be aided with the intellectual parts. I thank you for your applause and I am ready to talk with you.

Would you talk briefly about your method of choosing the characters of Satyricon? *Could you also clarify a remark you once made, that the only really systemic thing about your method is never to get an actor to conform to a character, but always vice versa: let the character conform to the actor.*

You want to know what is my system in choosing actors? Well, I do not have a particular system for this. It depends, picture by picture. Certainly the part of choosing faces is very important for me. I think when one is writing the picture, when one is thinking about the picture, it is always a very easy time. I live with a very vague imagination. But when I start to choose the cast, that for me is the hardest moment of the picture because I have to choose, which is always very difficult because you lose one person when you choose some other person in their place. And it is difficult because seeing the other people, talking with them, gives me the feeling that they are all good just because they are alive and make me feel that they can be part of my picture. So I put a little advertisement in the paper saying that I am starting a picture and that I would like to see anyone, any kind of foolish one who wants to come to my office. And I see people, talk with them, look at the ways they are dressed, the shoes that they have, their faces. With *La Strada*, Tony Quinn was just chosen for his shoes! So I start to understand that all those real fragments have some connection with the picture I have in mind.

But are you concerned about acting ability? There are many people in your pictures who have very little acting ability, even complete amateurs.

Sometimes I choose someone for the character I have in mind not only because he is a good actor, but because I see that his eyes, or his voice, that this particular human being has a connection with the character I have in mind.

Did your leading players in Satyricon *have any previous acting experience?*

One, the American boy. I think he has some theatrical experience because he was in the musical *Hair* in New York. The other one, the blond one, is an English actor who has never made movies. He has had some experience on the stage. They were new.

Did they come to you and apply for roles in the picture?

No, no. The blond one, I chose him in London. I went to London because I thought in London it was possible to find some young boy, a beauty, but not heavy. I mean one who did not look sensual.

Would you rather direct actors as puppets—as you have done in Satyricon, *in a sense—or do you really want to feel your soul and their soul becoming entwined during filming?*

It depends. If I choose a friend just because his face is that of a Roman emperor, I have to lose time to explain to him about the emperor and how he thought. If I choose a stranger, I can just use him for what he can give to me physically. I try to help him, if you like, with certain shots. I like it if the actors participate in a very strong way in what we are doing. Or sometimes, when working with someone who is not an actor, I pretend he is doing something deeper than just professional or physical work. I pretend he gives me something from inside. I want him to become the character. In a case like this, the cooperation is much stronger.

I have read that you often come on the sets with the actors not knowing what's going to happen during the day's shooting. Is it true that you do a great deal of improvisation as you're shooting?

No, it's absolutely impossible to improvise. Making a movie is a mathematical operation. It is like you Americans sending a missile to the moon. It isn't improvised. It is too defined to be called improvisational, too mechanical. Art is a scientific operation, and what we usually call improvisation is in my case just having enough of an ear and an eye to use things that sometimes happen during the time we are making the picture. In that sense, I think, to be strictly faithful to what you have written four or five months before is a little bit silly. If you see that the picture is suggesting something new, I think one has to be open to these kinds of suggestions. Sometimes it is the picture that directs you when you work in an open and honest way. This is not improvisation; it is just being humble and faithful to what you are doing.

How were you able to get those huge crowds of people to act so well? They react as if they were living in ancient Rome.

That's my profession. There is nothing mysterious about it, you know. I try to take from each one what they are able to do, even when they don't know exactly what they are doing. For *Satyricon* in particular I tried to suggest gestures, attitudes, looks, grimaces, in a very strange way because I thought that two thousand years ago maybe people talked or moved their hands in ways whose meanings have been lost. So for this reason I obliged the actors to talk as they do and move strangely so as always to give the feeling that we are seeing an unknown society, an unknown world.

I read that you had another ending for 8½, set on a train.

Yes, I shot most of the ending with the train. But before the picture was finished I wanted to shoot a trailer, so I asked the producer if it was possible to call back all the actors and extras who had worked on the picture just to shoot an extravagant trailer. So they came, two hundred people, and I asked for seven cameras—hand cameras—and I told them to go on the staircase and when the music started, to come down, walking and talking. And I said to the second cameraman, "Do what you want. It is a trailer in which I want to use my voice." When the band started to play and all the people came down, I was very moved by this scene and this atmosphere, and I felt this was the right ending for my picture. So I said to the producer, "I have changed my idea. I don't want to use the train. I have a new idea for the ending and I will shoot, more precisely, the cast on the staircase."

Does that happen very often when you make a picture?

I know the young directors want me to say yes, but the answer is no.

That's unusual for you?

In this case I think it was a bit providential. Also, the meaning of the scene I shot was the same as in the original ending with the train, this kind of communication of everybody being together, this kind of anticipation of shade and of light in his life. It was expressed in an intellectual way with the train. When I saw this house of people and of harmony, I felt it was the real ending of the picture.

In Satyricon it seems to me that you have moved further away from a traditional story line than ever before. The film seems more like a series of fragments from the past than a developing story. I wonder if you agree with this analysis, and if you feel this is the way that film will move in the next decade.

Yes, it was certainly done purposely, because the inspiration for the film came from a book called *The Satyricon,* by Petronius. One of the most important aspects of the book for us—for me, I think—is that it is not complete. The author writes in fragments. That's a real stimulus because, if you participate, the book asks your complicity in trying to complete all kinds of obscurities that lie between one fragment and another. It is like seeing some archaeological ruins. They are more suggestive, they are much more fantastic and more beautiful, maybe, than the real thing. So faced with this kind of suggestion, I have tried to give the feeling that it is a picture shot two thousand years ago, and there remains some obscurity between fragments. I try to give the same impression as an ancient fresco in which there are some destroyed figures in one corner. In another corner you see only one hand or one eye.

Do you feel there is a relationship in the kinds of problems you have dealt with in your other pictures, let's say La Dolce Vita *and* Satyricon? *Has there been continuity?*

I don't make pictures just to propose problems, but I think that there is a connection between one picture and another. Sometimes it is very difficult to explain why you made one picture instead of another one. To make some newspaperman happy, I can invent a lot of reasons why I made one picture instead of another. But if I have to be really truthful, I can't say that a director really knows why he makes his pictures. If he knows it, I think he cannot make it. I don't want to appear esoteric, but it's difficult to be very honest in trying to understand what happens.

There are historical coincidences. For *Satyricon* the coincidence was the contract I had signed with the producer, Alberto Grimaldi. I started a little bit anxious and a bit bored with the picture because it's really very difficult to make a picture about ancient Romans. It has a lot to do with extras, with big clothes. It's really a cliché. We have always seen big Italian pictures. So trying to introduce a new virginity to this kind of image, I really was a little bit afraid. And to excite me, to stimulate me in this picture, I said to myself that I had to refuse all the archaeological, cultural and historical perfections. After all, I live in Rome, where we think we know everything about Romans, but that's not true.

So I see right away that to try to survive these adventures was just to say honestly that I don't know. I didn't know anything about what I wanted to talk about. At that moment I felt a bit lost, but I feel that the healthiness of these adventures rests on looking into the complete obscurity in myself. I understood that the real key to making this picture was this unknown dimension, unknown in a psychological way, unknown in a social way, and it is this understanding that gave me a certain kind of courage. For that reason, I said at the beginning something that the press office liked very much. I said it was a science-fiction picture in a sense. Science fiction is something that we don't know because we don't know what has been lost or, at any rate, what is unknown.

Apparently you also told the press that the film was a comment on society today.

I think that would be a little bit too vulgar for me, but certainly this kind of analogy is valid just because I am living today. Now that I have finished the picture, I recognize that it's a picture about our time. After all, you know Petronius is very modern and very touching.

In La Dolce Vita, *you show episodes of a man's life that lead him to an orgiastic experience at the end of the film. The Marcello Mastroianni character understands that the direction he is taking has led him to something—to this orgy— that he cannot accept, and that he turns away from. In* Satyricon *you again show us an orgiastic experience. I'm wondering if in* Satyricon *perhaps you're rethinking the resolution we saw at the end of* La Dolce Vita?

About orgies, I am always very enthusiastic. I hoped in *Satyricon* I created people with a more detached eye, so it was my intention not to suggest any moralistic point of view.

When your main character looks up at the stars in Satyricon, *it's very reminiscent of the scene where Zampano looks up at the sky at the end of* La Strada. *This image, I think, gives a moralistic feeling.*

But what do you see in *Satyricon?*

In Satyricon *there is a scene where we look up at the stars through a roof.*

I don't see that I have done that—it's just a poetic moment. I wanted to suggest that in this garden, where the two people have committed suicide, there are the people inside who go to look around the empty villa. It's a moment of suspension, to show the nature around this villa. I do not recognize any other feeling.

Was much of the picture shot on location?

No, the picture was shot completely in the studio—everything except the ocean scene. I don't think my producers would put the ocean in the studios. I wanted to do everything in the studio, because to shoot on location would have disturbed the atmosphere of what we had re-created in the studio.

Fellini lines up a shot for *Satyricon* (1969). He told reporters
it was a science-fiction picture.

Do you shoot out of sequence?

Sequence shooting is not possible, as any director of movies knows,
because there is a lack of money and time. But I like to start with a
sequence in the middle of the picture because one is obliged, in just
beginning the picture, to give an explanation of a sequence that makes it
richer. I think for myself it's psychologically a good thing not to follow
chronologically in the rhythm. I accept the production schedule.

In what way do you think you are like and unlike Petronius, the author of
Satyricon?

The kind of ambiguity, of complicity and detachment in judgment—and at the same moment, to be the judge and the guilty together—is, I think, one of the components of Petronius. I recognize something of myself in this—to live and write about life.

8½ and Juliet of the Spirits *seem to be derived very strongly from personal material. In* Satyricon *were you purposely trying to move away from that?*

You want to say that *Satyricon* is not autobiographical? But I think it is absolutely impossible not to be autobiographical. I think that *Satyricon* is maybe much more autobiographical than even *8½* because it is not an adapted biography. But maybe the anguish, the fear, the faith, the atmosphere that is in *Satyricon,* maybe that has to do with myself in a more immediate way. I think that the author of *Satyricon* is talking about his book in the same way.

The music in Satyricon *feels quite different from that of the earlier films. Could you tell me a little about the procedure you followed?*

I caused my musician a lot of trouble when I told him we could only have music as atmosphere. So I listened to maybe five hundred records. I was very lucky because a friend of mine has a discotheque—he has folklore, oriental, African records—and I just chose this kind of barbaric and Eastern sound. And I only made some melody in the beginning and the end.

At what stage do you begin to work with the composer?

Sometimes before we start. I like to have some tapes of music because I like music when I work. And it helps because it's another little piece of the body of the picture that you put in your studio so you start to become more familiar. The music is always a big help because it puts you in a strange dimension in which your fantasy stimulates you. Sometimes, as soon as I finish a picture I show it to Nino Rota. We work very strictly and I tell him exactly what I want, and we go to work with the piano and the Moviola.

When did you have the theme for La Strada?

The theme from *La Strada* was created by Nino Rota. He brought it to me. One day he said to me, "Do you want this?"

Did you have it when you were shooting?

No. When I was shooting I had another theme, but it was not original. It was very sad and elegant.

How much editing happens as you film? Is the picture put together week to week by your editor, or do you tend to wait?

For the first picture I was more pretentious. I wanted to cut and do every-thing. I didn't want to miss anything. But going on in years, I prefer to leave the cutter to his work. I don't want to see rushes as I shoot because the picture you make is not entirely the picture you have in mind. So if I see what I'm doing day by day, I start to see that the picture is becoming a little bit different. And the next day, when I am going to shoot, I think of the things I have seen, not of what I am making. So I prefer to separate the work in this way.

You mean you don't ever look at your rushes? Is this the answer to being creative, not being constantly self-conscious about things you are doing, leaving things behind each day and going on with the next day's shooting?

Yes. Watching the rushes is a preoccupation for *producers.* If I go to see what I have done, it distracts me. I prefer to go on like a blind man, fol-lowing the imagination of the picture and perhaps delude myself that I am be going in the right direction.

I read that you felt if a film of yours was in black and white, people could add their own color in their imaginations.

Ah yes, that's true. I did feel like that, you know, but it is very difficult to be faithful for your entire life. I have some idea of stories and the pictures that I have not yet done that I am obliged to see in black and white. You know, it is very difficult now to make a picture in black and white because TV wants pictures in color, so you would be forced to make a picture with a very low budget.

How about the shape of the screen? In La Strada *you used a more normal aspect ratio. I believe* Satyricon *was shot in Panavision?*

Technical things sometimes have to be accepted. I don't need to remain faithful to the old size. I like to change.

I wonder if you could talk about the changes that might occur as you are going through the creative process of making a film.

This is complicated. It is impossible to answer in a schematic way. The history of four or five months of shooting is not only the private story of the director making the picture but also a story of mutual relationships, of love, of enemies, of vanity. Everything has to do with the picture you are making because everything that is happening is happening under this kind of atmosphere. I think I am helped by everything. Everything gives some stimulation to the particular atmosphere of a particular picture. I think the picture is more a lesson of morality—you just try to take the time to acknowledge what is around you and what you are.

Do you have one picture of yours that you consider a favorite or best?

I have never seen my pictures again, so I am not in the condition to have a point of view about them, to judge them from a critical point of view. I can say I like the last one just because it is the last one, and also because the people in it represent the result of many experiences.

I wonder that with an American distributor releasing your new film whether you would compromise the content of any of your films in order to ensure wider distribution and, ultimately, bigger box office.

Until now I have always done exactly what I thought was good for the picture and have tried to work within the dimension and style that the picture asks of me, with my modest capacities. I have always been very faithful to the picture. I try to express things in the way the picture asks to be expressed. I don't think I can make something with a very strong compromise because it makes me unhappy.

Mr. Fellini, your camera moves are quite fantastic. Do you think them out before you get on the set or do you begin on the set?

Yes, you know, when technical things are involved, one has to know technique. One is born with technique. I never think during the night what I am shooting the day after. I mean, I never think consciously. I am not a director who is looking in the camera to find the shot. I have no problem in this sense because the camera is just my eye. It is also very difficult for me to talk when I am outside a picture because there is a particular atmosphere when you are working on a picture. It's difficult to remember what you are doing exactly. Anyway, I can say that I am not a movie director who consciously plots the movements of the camera, because they are very natural. Imagination is everything. The picture is in my head, and I just try to make it.

Films as Director

1950 *Variety Lights* (also co-screenplay)

1952 *The White Sheik* (also co-screenplay)

1953 *I Vitelloni* (also co-screenplay)

1954 *La Strada* (also co-screenplay)

1955 *Il Bidone* (also co-screenplay)

1956 *Nights of Cabiria* (also co-screenplay)

1960 *La Dolce Vita* (also co-screenplay)

1962 *Boccaccio '70* (co-director and co-screenplay)

1963 *8½* (also co-screenplay)

1965 *Juliet of the Spirits* (also co-screenplay)

1969 *Fellini Satyricon* (also co-screenplay)

1970 *The Clowns* (also co-screenplay)

1972 *Fellini's Roma* (also co-screenplay)

1974 *Amarcord* (also co-screenplay)

1976 *Fellini's Casanova* (also co-screenplay)

1980 *City of Women* (also co-screenplay)

1983 *And the Ship Sailed On* (also co-screenplay)

1986 *Ginger and Fred* (also co-screenplay)

1987 *Fellini's Intervista* (also co-screenplay)

1990 *The Voice of the Moon* (also co-screenplay)

I remember the morning after a catastrophic opening of a picture of mine. I was in bed and I was crying, and I said to my girlfriend, "Oh, I think they will never let me make a picture again." The telephone rang, and it was a crazy man who said, "Ingmar, I think you are a little bit more modest now, so perhaps we can work together."

INGMAR BERGMAN
(Born in Uppsala, Sweden, 1918)

When I was in Stockholm in the summer of 1975, Harry Schein, the head of the Swedish Film Institute, arranged a dinner for my wife and me with Ingmar Bergman. It happened to be "midsummer night," when the sun never sets, and I recall a long after-dinner walk with Bergman that seemed timeless and evocative of the Scandinavian mindscapes one associates with his work. His films leave no doubt that there are dark currents in his makeup, but his manner that evening was one of quiet charm and easy warmth. He inquired about the American Film Institute, which gave me an opportunity to ask him if he would visit us if he came to the United States. I didn't hold out much hope because it was widely known that Bergman didn't enjoy public appearances. To my surprise, when he made his first visit to Los Angeles four months later, his agent called to say that Mr. Bergman would come to AFI.

There had been no more eagerly anticipated visitor, because Bergman was not only a master among world filmmakers, he had a reputation for being one of the most elusive and private. He arrived with his wife, Ingrid, and though he said he was nervous and "almost fainting," he engaged enthusiastically with the young filmmakers and offered fascinating insights into the creative process.

No one in cinema history has used the medium for personal expression more fully than Bergman. His twenty-three feature films as writer-director are like pages of an autobiography dealing with spiritual and psychological conflicts. In Stockholm he assembled a creative team and a stock company of actors who were always available to him, and he worked on a small scale that enabled him to maintain tight creative control. He once referred to himself as

Ingmar Bergman setting up a scene with Ewa Froling and Gunner
Bjornstrand for *Fanny and Alexander* (1983).

a radar set: "I pick up one thing or another and reflect it back in mirrored form, all jumbled up with memories, dreams and ideas."

The day Bergman came to AFI, we invited Jeanne Moreau, director James Bridges and the widow of Jean Renoir to the seminar at Bergman's request. He quickly established a rapport with the young filmmakers, sharing the lessons of his life in film and discussing his unique way of working with cast and crew. Aspiring writers and directors at the school were always seeking assurance that spontaneity and improvisation were the keys to moviemaking. Bergman was unwilling to provide much comfort. He said, "I think inspiration and enthusiasm and everything like that is beautiful, but I don't like it. I think when we are in the studio we have to be very strict." At the end of the meeting he volunteered "advice from an old uncle" on what he considered the most crucial decision for a director—whether or not to make a film.

INGMAR BERGMAN

October 31, 1975

I am very nervous. I am almost fainting. I always feel very scared when I have to meet so many people. But you look very friendly, and I will do my best. Somebody told me the first day I was here that I would come to your lecture and I fell into pieces. I said, "Lecture? What's that?" Somebody said, "You go to see the students and say hello to them, and it's all over." I think you will be asking questions, but I don't know what you want from me. I will try to be as honest as possible. It's very difficult because I can't speak in my own language. Sometimes it's absolutely impossible to find the right words. So we will help each other, yes?

Of course. Please tell us how you work with actors—for example, the different steps you use to communicate with them.

This could be a very complicated question; we could talk about it for the whole hour. And it can be a very simple question, because if you want to know exactly how I work together with my actors, I can tell you in one minute—I just use my intuition. My only instrument is my intuition. When I work at the theater or in the studio with my actors I just feel—as I don't really know how to handle the situation or how to collaborate with the actors.

One thing is very important to me, that an actor is always a creative human being. What your intuition has to discover is how to make free the creative power. Do you understand what I mean? I can't explain how it works. It has nothing to do with magic, it has a lot to do with experience. But I think when I work together with the actors I try to be like a radar. I try to be wide open because we have to create something together. I give them some stimulations and suggestions, and they give me a lot of stimulations and suggestions. I know if we try to work without those waves of giving and taking, then it is terrifying. It is the hardest, toughest job that exists, both for me and the actors.

Some directors work with aggression. The director is aggressive, and the actors are aggressive, and they get marvelous results. But to me this is impossible. I have to be in contact with my actors the whole time, because what we first create when we start a work together is an atmosphere of security around us. And it's not only me who creates this atmosphere, we create it together. But for all those very difficult decisions—and you have to make hundreds of them every day—I never think. I have to go straight into it and I have to trust my intuition. If you do this, and train yourself not to start making intellectual discussions with your intuition, you are doing the right thing. Only afterward can you think over every step you have made by asking, "What was this? What was that?"

Do you write in the same way, always using your intuition?

Yes, yes. The best time in the writing, I think, is when I have no ideas about how to do it. I just play the game. I can lie down on the sofa and can look into the fire. I can go to the seaside and just sit down and do nothing. I just play the game and it's wonderful. I make some notes, and I can go on for a year. Then, when I have made a plan the difficult job starts. I have to sit down on my ass every morning at ten o'clock and write the screenplay. Then something very strange happens. Very often the personalities in my scripts don't want the same thing I want. If I try to force them to do what I want them to do, it will always be an artistic catastrophe. But if I let them free to do what they want and what they tell me, it's okay. So I think this is the only way to handle it. All intellectual decisions must come afterward.

You have seen *Cries and Whispers*? For half a year, I went around and just had a picture inside my head of three women walking around in a red room with white clothes. I couldn't understand why these damned women were there. I tried to throw it away. I tried to write it down. I tried to find out what they said to each other, because they whispered. And suddenly it came out that they were watching another woman who was dying in the next room. Then the screenplay started—but it took about a year. It's very strange. The script always starts with a picture with some kind of tension in it, and then slowly it comes out.

After you have developed a script, do you continue to develop the characters through the shooting?

No. I have always worked with actors. I have never worked with amateurs. An amateur can be himself always, and you can put him in situations and give that situation a third dimension, as De Sica did in *The Bicycle Thief.* But if you work with trained actors you must have come to a conclusion, to an idea, about exactly what you are going to do with the characters. We have those discussions before, and then we work in the studio. We just have the freedom of being together and giving each other suggestions. It's very nice. But the whole time we must have in mind what we meant.

It's very dangerous to go away and suddenly start to improvise. You can improvise, of course, in the studio, but you have to be very prepared before you do this, because to improvise on an improvisation is always shit. It always turns into a catastrophe. If you are very prepared and know how to do it, you can go back if your improvisation suddenly fades away, which of course it always does. I think inspiration and enthusiasm and everything like that is beautiful, but I don't like it. I think when we are in the studio we have to be very strict.

What do you say to the actors? Do you do exercises with them?

No, no, no, no. Good heavens, no. I say nothing. Before we start the picture we meet and we talk a lot. We have some sort of discussion. But when we are in the studio I think we say strange things to each other. We make some noises, we tell funny stories, we touch each other. We just find the key words because it's very necessary not to talk too much. Just to hold this intuitive relation is a creative job.

Do you tell them the message of the film?

No. Good heavens, no. No, no, no, no. In a way, I don't know anything about messages or symbols or things like that. I am always surprised when people ask me about the message because I just want to get in touch with other human beings and tell them a story when I make a picture. Or just be together with them or touch them and have them feel things. Sometimes when I have a message, everything goes wrong. So we don't talk about those things. We just talk professionally. "Be careful. Be slower. Don't be in a hurry." You know, the most important thing of all is the ear for the director and the actors—to listen to each other. Very often when I watch a scene I just close my eyes and listen, because if it sounds right it also looks right. It's very strange.

You often fuse reality and dreams in your films. Do you feel that reality and dreams are of equal importance?

Yes. To me, when cinematography is at its best, it is very close to the state of dreaming. You know, in any other art you can't create a situation that is as close to dreaming. Think only of the time gap. You can make things as long as you want, exactly as in a dream. You can make things as short as you want, exactly as in a dream. As a director, a creator of the picture, you are like a dreamer. You can make what you want. You can construct everything. I think that is one of the most fascinating things that exists.

Have you transferred dreams to film exactly as you dreamed them?

Yes. Twice I have written down a dream and filmed it just as I had dreamt it. One is in *Wild Strawberries* with the coffin. Without any translation, it's just as it was. The other picture is *The Naked Night,* the first sequence with the clown and his wife. Writing and filmmaking and the creation of pictures are extremely close to our dreams.

I think also the reception by the audience of a picture is very hypnotic. You sit there in a completely dark room, very anonymous, and you look on a lighted spot in front of you and you don't move. You sit and your eyes are concentrated on that white spot on the wall. I think this is exactly what some hypnotists do. They light a spot on the wall and ask you to follow it with your eyes, and then they talk to you and then they hypnotize you. It's quite different when you watch television. You sit at home, you have light around you. You have people you know around you, the telephone is ringing, you can go out and have a cup of coffee, the children are making noise.

The film medium is some sort of magic where every frame comes and stands still for a fraction of a second and then it darkens. Half of the time when you see a picture you sit in darkness. Isn't that fascinating? That is magic. So we can be as intellectual as we want—we can be as sensible as we want. We are in the position of working with the most fascinating medium that exists in the world because, as with music, we go straight to the feelings. Afterward we can start to work with our intellect. If the picture is good, if the suggestions from the creator of the picture are strong enough, they'll give you thoughts later. You will start to think. They will be intellectually stimulating.

We know you are very fond of music —use music as part of your plan. What do you feel you can do with music on the soundtrack?

I will try to answer your question. It's a bit complicated. I think when the silent picture died and the sound picture came, the silent picture was in a marvelous development. But now we have sound and we have to combine the sound and the picture, and they have to work and live together. I think that is a marvelous medium. I think we can do a lot with the soundtrack. I am a little bit worried about music—electronic and conventional—because I have the feeling that film in a way is rhythm. Music, at the beginning, as Stravinsky said, is also rhythm—they are both unintellectual suggestions. I think it's dangerous to use real music, but to use sounds, different sounds—concrete or synthesized—is very interesting. I think we have just begun to do what we can do with sound and picture together. And that is fascinating.

You have described many of your films as chamber works, and as metaphors for chamber music. What do you mean by that?

It's not my invention. Strindberg, the Swedish writer, had a little theater. It was almost like this room here—I think it was for a hundred people. He arranged, with enormous difficulties, with some friends and some actors, a very primitive theater for which he wrote plays with few actors, with just very simple settings. He called them chamber plays, like chamber music, and I have stolen that from him.

You talk about rhythm. I wonder if you had a problem in making your film of The Magic Flute *so that it followed the rhythm of the opera?*

No, it was wonderful. We had a lengthy production time of fifty-five days. It's a two-and-a-quarter-hour opera. We have not changed anything.

We made a "playback" recording of the score, and it was absolutely wonderful. You had to prepare very much before, because of course every movement, every angle of the camera, everything, must be exactly prepared. But to be in the studio and every day to hear this music—I tell you, it's the best time of my life. We started at nine o'clock. At four o'clock we felt very tired and very bored and very unhappy. But then we had the music, Mozart's music, the whole time, vitalizing us all and carrying us.

How have you gone about financing your films and marketing them outside Sweden?

It has never been a real problem for me. Compared to the American or international productions, my pictures are always low-budget productions. *Cries and Whispers* cost about $450,000. *Scenes from a Marriage* cost us about $200,000. You know, there is always some fool who wants to raise the money. There must be gamblers and optimistic people in the business.

Could you have made the kinds of films you made if you were working in America?

Absolutely not. I think it would have been impossible. No, everything is changing now. I came to the business in 1942, during the war. Sweden was completely isolated, and we could get only German pictures. We didn't want them, so we had to make our pictures ourselves. Because this was before TV, the Swedes were running to the movie theaters. This little country with seven million people made about forty or fifty pictures a year. Suddenly everybody who knew the front and back of a camera was a cameraman, and everybody who had ever spoken to an actor was a director. Of course it was fantastic because in three years I made three pictures. Three catastrophes, three flops, and I was still alive. We could just go on and make films. It was very healthy and unneurotic. It was not a question of making money or having box-office success. But when I made my fifth box-office catastrophe, I was kicked out.

I remember the morning after a catastrophic opening of a picture of mine. I was in bed and I was crying, and I said to my girlfriend, "Oh, I think they will never let me make a picture again." The telephone rang, and it was a crazy man who said, "Ingmar, I think you are a little bit more modest now, so perhaps we can work together." That was the beginning, and I am still grateful to that man. He taught me almost everything about filmmaking because I was a happy amateur, very enthusiastic, and had enormous ideas about making pictures about life and death and everything. Nobody understood my pictures. I don't understand them myself, and when I see one of them I get completely red over my whole body. I think I was a very difficult director. I was very aggressive and I was absolutely terrifying in the studio because I was insecure. If you are insecure you get aggressive, of course.

But this man taught me a lot about filmmaking. Do you all know the most important thing he taught me? What I still use? You know how it is when we see our rushes, our dailies, and we just say, "God help me. Help us all." Isn't it so? And then we say, "This is not so bad." And somebody else says, "No, it's pretty good." And then a third says, "It's wonderful." We try to pep ourselves up to have the courage to continue the next day, because very often when you see the rushes you have the feeling that you want to go under the bed and never come out again, like a dog. He said to me, "I hate this pepping up. Sit. Be objective. Be your own worst critic. Be cold. Don't let yourself fall into a depression or into euphoria. Just sit and see it all quietly. Don't blame your crew. All of you have done your best. The only thing you have to do is to estimate. Is this all right? Or might I have to reshoot it? Just be objective." It's almost impossible, but I think that is one of the best things I have learned in my life, and I still use it. Best of all is to be alone with your God and the projectionist when you see the rushes. To have nobody there, because if someone's there and they are an audience—even if it's a cat—you just sit waiting for something. So it is best just to be completely alone.

What is your relation to the camera? Do you have to buck the technical limitations of the camera?

If intuition is our mental instrument, the camera is our physical instrument. I think the camera is erotic. I think it is the most exciting little machine that exists. To me, just to work together with my cameraman, Sven Nykvist, to see a human face with the camera and with a zoom to come closer, to see the scene, to see the face changing, is the most fascinating thing. I think the choreography of the actors in relation to the camera is very important because every good actor, if he feels he is in a bad position in front of the camera, feels stress and is very unhappy. If he is in a good position, in a logical position—he can be with his back to the camera. It doesn't matter—if he feels this is all right, then intuitively he feels secure and he does his best.

So there is always the question about the relation between the actors and the camera in every scene. The camera has to be the best friend of the actors, and the actors have to be secure with our handling of the camera. They must feel that we're taking care of them, because we who are directors must never forget that we are behind the camera and that the actor is in front of the camera. He is nude, his soul is nude. If he has confidence in us, we have enormous responsibility. We have somebody in our hands, and we can destroy him or we can help him in his creative job. To be behind the camera is never difficult, but to be in front of the camera is always a challenge—to be there with your face and your body and all the limitations you have in your soul and all the limitations you feel of your face and your movements. We cannot lie to the actors—we have to be absolutely true to them. And as better actors, they like the truth more. That is my feeling.

When I read your screenplays they always say only what the actors are saying, like a play. I'm wondering at what point in the planning of a film do you decide on the position of the camera.

The evening before. When I come home in the evening I just sit down with the script and read the next day's schedule very carefully. I make up my mind about it and then I just note the choreography of the actors and the camera. Then in the early morning when I meet Sven Nykvist—you know, we have worked so many years together—in five minutes we go through the scene. I tell him about my ideas for different positions of the camera, for the different positions of the actors and for the atmosphere of the whole scene—and then we can go on the whole day. It is not necessary to have any discussions. Sven is just fantastic. He is a marvelous man, very silent and very shy. Suddenly everything is there, without any complications, and I can look in the camera, and everything I wanted is there.

Do you rehearse with the actors on the set before you plan your shots?

No, never. That's a good question. When the atmosphere is creative, we come to a sort of intuitive understanding of what the scene means to us.

If you rehearse with an actor who is trained to play every evening, something new starts to happen, an intellectual process. That process can be very good, but it's very dangerous for filming because you have something in his eyes suddenly. He's becomes conscious of what he's doing—he must do it intuitively.

Would you talk about some of the similarities and differences in working in the theater and the cinema?

Oh, it's absolutely different because filmmaking is a neurotic job. It's unnormal to every creative process I know. It's some sort of craftsmanship. You must have a lot of physical power to make pictures. Perhaps statistically we make three minutes of the picture a day, while in the theater you will rehearse.

In Sweden we have about ten or twelve weeks of rehearsal. We start slowly, at ten thirty in the morning, and we go on, and if it's lousy you can sit down and relax. "This is not good today, but perhaps next Monday or in the middle of next month we will find out." The creative process is natural, it's unneurotic. In the theater we are a group of artists who just come together in a house that is built for us to work in. It's fantastic. We come

Cinematographer Sven Nykvist (right) with Bergman.
The director says, "I think the camera is erotic. I think
it is the most exciting little machine that exists."

there like very efficient children with our books. At ten thirty a bell rings, and we all go to rehearsal rooms, and then we are there together with Strindberg or Ibsen or Molière or Shakespeare—or any other of those old, marvelous gentlemen—with our thoughts and emotions. We have the opportunity to go into the drama and live with it and try to understand the wisdom of the drama that we are working with. I think that is a fantastic situation.

Filmmaking is always an abnormal process. It's quite another situation. When you are a film director who has written the script yourself, you have to be some sort of Dr. Jekyll and Mr. Hyde, because if Dr. Jekyll had written the script, Mr. Hyde has to direct it. I tell you they don't like each other that well. I think this is a very schizophrenic situation.

If I had to make a choice—God save me from that—if somebody came to me and said, "Now, Ingmar, you have long enough made films and theater, you have to make your decision," I am sure I would choose theater. In the theater if you grow old and stuffy and dusty, you have a lot of experience. If you can just pronounce your experience in some crazy words, the artists will understand you, and you will have a wonderful time with them. My teacher in the theater was a director who was eighty-five years old and he could hardly speak. But still he made wonderful, enormous, incredible performances because his soul was young. He was absolutely a physical wreck. You can't be a wreck when you work in film.

Have your ideas of staging in the theater changed because of film? I remember seeing your production of Hedda Gabler, *and was very impressed by how cinematic the staging was. I was impressed by the marriage of the two mediums.*

No, it's not a marriage. It's a relation, just that. When I was a teacher in the dramatic school in Sweden, we always started the first class with a discussion of what you need to make theater. On the blackboard we wrote down about a hundred things—stage, actors, tickets, clothes, money, spotlights, footlights, makeup, theater—more than a hundred different things that we thought we needed. And then I said to them, "Now we take away everything that you think is not necessary." We went on and went on and went on; we even took away the director. Three things remained. What do you think they were?

Actors?

An actor, yes. That's true.

An empty place. A stage?

It's not necessary.

A script?

A manuscript, yes. We could call it a message, don't you think so? And a third?

An audience?

An audience, yes. The class wasn't sure that the audience was necessary, but I thought it was absolutely necessary. And that is my theology about theater. What we need are actors, a message and an audience. If we have those things we have a performance, because the performance is not here on the stage. It is in the hearts of the audience, and it is very important to know that. In filmmaking we can learn a lot from the theater, because what we need to make a picture is just that little fantastic machine, the camera, and some film. That's all.

I once read of a famous film director who tried to put on a theater production, but he didn't like it because he felt there was only one camera angle. How do you approach a particular film through a camera style?

I have no style. We have no style. We just feel. The director who said that must be a director with an enormous lack of fantasy, because the marvelous thing in the theater is that the theater is absolutely unlimited. Do you know the Shakespearean stage? The performance was always in daylight. When Shakespeare wanted people to understand that it was night, do you know what he did? He let the actors come in with torches, burning torches in the daylight, and the woodwinds played a little thing so the people understood it was night. We have no camera style, Sven and I. What we are interested in is not a style for the camera because the solution of that is in the picture. What we are always interested in is in the light or the shadows, the rhythm in the light and the shadows of the picture. These we discuss a lot and we experiment.

But there is a difference in style in your films. Sometimes it seems the style is more to accommodate the actors. In Persona *and* Cries and Whispers *the style seems to be rigorous and disciplined.*

Yes, but that is no problem because it's a part of the whole decision. It's not an intellectual decision. It comes out from the whole thing. It's just natural. I think it's difficult to talk about it because you can call it a style if you want, but it's not.

Why do you have women as your main characters so often?

I like more to work with women. I have many good friends who are actors, and I like tremendously to work together with them. But in filmmaking it's a job for good nerves, and I think women have much better nerves than men. Women are not, in the first place, women. They are human beings. And God forgive me, but I have the feeling that the prima donnas always are male, and the women aren't like that. It's very difficult to be an actor in our society. It's not so difficult to be an actress.

Now, to conclude this, to me, wonderful meeting, I would like to add something. Perhaps it sounds like it is from an old uncle, but I am so. It doesn't matter. May I give you some advice?

Yes, please.

I think it is a relief to me to know that I have an intention. If I have a passion and an obsession, if I want to tell somebody something and if I want to touch somebody, then film helps me. But if I have nothing to say and I just want to make a film, I don't make the film. The craftsmanship of filmmaking is so terribly stimulating, dangerous and obsessing that you can be very tempted. But if you have nothing to come with—this is the most important of all for me—try to be honest with yourself and don't make the picture. But if you have something to come with, if you have emotion and passion—a picture in your head, a tension—you can know that even if you aren't very technical, even if you don't know where to put the camera, the strange thing is that having worked on the script and having worked with the camera for days and days and the whole time thinking of it, suddenly, when you see the rushes and when you have cut it together, the thing you wanted to tell is there.

I have a very good example and that is Michelangelo Antonioni's *L'Avventura*. The picture is a mess. He had no idea where to put the camera. He had no money. The actors went away. I think he had enormous problems the whole time. But he wanted to tell us something about the loneliness of the human being. I can see this picture time after time, and I don't know what touches me most—how he succeeds without knowing how to do it, or what he wants to say. You have to have something to come with, to give other people. Picture making is some sort of responsibility—that is what I think.

Films as Director and Screenwriter

1946 *Crisis*
    It Rains on Our Love
1947 *A Ship Bound to India*
1948 *Music in Darkness*
1949 *The Devil's Wanton*
    Prison
    To Joy
    Thirst
1950 *Summer Interlude*
1952 *Secrets of Women*
    Summer with Monika
1953 *The Naked Night*
1955 *Journey into Autumn*
    Smiles of a Summer Night
1956 *The Last Couple Out*
    The Seventh Seal
1957 *Wild Strawberries*
    The Brink of Life
1958 *The Magician*

1959 *The Virgin Spring*
1960 *The Devil's Eye*
1961 *Through a Glass Darkly*
    The Pleasure Garden
1962 *Winter Light*
1963 *The Silence*
1966 *Persona*
    Hour of the Wolf
1967 *Shame*
1968 *The Rite*
1969 *Passion of Anna*
1971 *The Touch*
1972 *Cries and Whispers*
1973 *Scenes from a Marriage*
1977 *The Serpent's Egg*
1978 *Autumn Sonata*
1980 *From the Life of Marionettes*
1982 *Fanny and Alexander*

First, it's finding a story which excites you. Second, it's converting it into the terms of a screenplay. Third, it's casting, which I do myself. People just come to my house. There's a knock on the door, and there's somebody waiting outside with acting ambitions.

SATYAJIT RAY
(Born in Calcutta, 1921—Died 1992)

Who would have guessed fifty years ago that a young graphic artist in Calcutta writing scripts in the Bengali language would become one of the world's most admired filmmakers? When Satyajit Ray's films began appearing in the West in the 1950s, they captured a loyal following in American art houses, and Ray himself, a tall, slender man with wavy black hair and striking good looks, became recognized at international film festivals as a director who carried the creative reputation of an entire continent.

Ray came from a family of artists and intellectuals prominent in West Bengal for generations. Assigned to do illustrations for a children's edition of a novel, *Pather Panchali,* he used the story as inspiration for his first film. I saw *Pather Panchali* recently and was struck by the cinematic assurance of the first-time director—handsome compositions, beautifully timed cuts and simple but evocative performances by his players, most of whom were nonprofessionals. From the beginning of his career, Ray wrote his own screenplays and designed his sets, and soon he was even composing music for his films. He pawned his collection of rare recordings and his wife's jewelry to make *Pather Panchali,* and throughout his career, despite working with minuscule budgets, he was always able to capture the truth in the world around him.

In order to recoup the average hundred-thousand-dollar cost of each picture, it was necessary for Ray to aim his films at the relatively unsophisticated Bengali audience. Nevertheless, he was also able to find themes that spoke to moviegoers outside India. His settings, costumes and actors may have appeared somewhat exotic to the Western viewer, but his craftsmanship allowed audiences to see inside the lives of his characters. "I try to pack my films with meaning and psychological inflections and shades," he said, "and

Satyajit Ray was encouraged toward filmmaking by Jean Renoir when Renoir
visited Calcutta to make *The River* (1951).

make a whole which will communicate a lot of things to many people."
"Ray's cinema flows with the serenity and nobility of a big river," said Akira
Kurosowa. "People are born, live out their lives and then accept their deaths.
There is nothing irrelevant or haphazard in his cinematographic technique."

Ray made one of his rare trips to the United States in 1978 for the release
of *The Chess Players*. During that visit, he set aside time to come to AFI. The
fellows, who viewed thirty-five-millimeter prints of half a dozen of Ray's films
before the seminar, understood what a rare opportunity was before them.
This was Ray's last visit to the United States. In the eighties, he developed
heart trouble and had to beg his doctors to let him make his last two films. In
1992 he was honored with a special Academy Award in recognition of his
"rare mastery of the art of motion pictures and for his profound humanitar-
ian outlook." Failing health prevented him from traveling to the United
States for the ceremony, so he accepted the honor on television through a live
hookup from his apartment in Calcutta. He died later that year.

SATYAJIT RAY

———

April 13, 1978

You have been making films for more than twenty years. The subjects have varied widely—the rural poor, commercial urban life, the British presence—but all the films have been set in India. Do you have any interest in directing outside your country?

Not really. I have turned down many offers from here, though I wouldn't mind working with American actors. In fact, I came to Hollywood about ten years ago for a project that would have been filmed in Bengal and that needed an American actor. But I wouldn't want to work outside of India. I feel very deeply rooted there. I know my people better than any other. I certainly know them better than I know the Americans or the British. I react more immediately to things Indian. I would like to narrow it down even further and say, things Bengali, because I think of India as a continent, and every state has its own topography, language and culture. There is an underlying link of Hinduism perhaps, but on the surface the states are very different. You can move from the Himalayas to a desert. I think there is still too much left that I would like to do in my own country. One film takes so much time and energy and money and thought, and now I am getting on in years.

Some moviegoers unfamiliar with Indian films, except for yours, regard you as the pioneer of Indian cinema. What's your response?

We have had a film industry stretching back to the silent period. I think the first feature film was made in 1912, but the first film, a short, was made in 1905. There has been an industry ever since then. You had sound in 1928, and we had it from 1930 onward. Even before *Pather Panchali* got a prize in Cannes, there were other films which got prizes in European festivals. But I think my films were the first to get distribution outside of India.

You've acknowledged Jean Renoir as one of your earliest influences. How did that come about?

In the forties, I saw the American films of Jean Renoir. The first one was *The Southerner.* Eventually I saw *The Diary of a Chambermaid* and a few others. I also read about his French work, and I was familiar with his father's paintings. Then, in 1949, Renoir came to Calcutta to look for locations for *The River.* He put an ad in the paper and was interviewing actors for the various parts. That's how I came to know he was in town. I was an advertising man at that time, and it so happened that the agency where I worked was quite near the hotel where he was staying. I just went and presented myself as a student of the cinema. I got to know him quite well. He was comparatively free in the evenings and I would often just drop in. Later I accompanied him on his location hunts because I knew the countryside quite well. The conversations were extremely enlightening.

Did you talk about films?

Actually, we did not always talk about films. I was also a student of painting, so we talked about his father a great deal, and about people like Vuillard and Cézanne. We used to talk about literature, music. But it was very difficult to talk about his French films, because I had not yet seen them. I remember talking a lot about *The Southerner,* and he talked about the difficulties he had had in Hollywood trying to convince people that the film ought to be shot on location and not in the studio. He dropped occasional remarks which I found very illuminating. For instance, he said that a film doesn't have to show many things, but the few that it shows have to have the right kinds of details. He kept insisting on details and the value of details in films. We would drive through the countryside, and he would say, "Look at that!" and point to a clump of bananas or plantains. "That is Bengal. That little palm, that is quintessential Bengal for me." He was always trying to find in the landscape details that he felt were characteristic of the place and that he was eventually hoping to use in the film. That left an impression, because I myself was very interested in details.

Did you watch him shoot his film?

I'm afraid I was not in a position to watch him work because I had my job. I went on a Sunday, or maybe a couple of Sundays, to watch him. Then I left for England to work for the head office of the British agency where I was employed. It was in England that I first saw Renoir's French films, *Une Partie de campagne* and all of the rest of them. Even before I had seen them I had discussed them with him. I had put questions to him about the various films, such as *La Bête humaine.* The talks I had with him were very, very important for me. By that time, I had already done illustrations for a special edition of the novel *Pather Panchali.* I was already a film buff. We had started our film club in Calcutta. I was toying with the idea of changing my profession, because I was getting a little tired of advertising. I told Renoir what I had in mind for a film. He said, "Well, why don't you make it? It sounds very interesting." After I came back from London, I wrote a treatment and started looking for a producer. And that was that.

What were the Indian influences, particularly on your first work, the Apu trilogy?

The Indian influences do not relate very much to films. But obviously the trilogy was derived from two novels which I admired immensely. The feeling in the first part of the trilogy, and much of the details, came from the book itself. I think I owe a great deal to the author of the novel. Before I started making the film, I had read up on the theory of filmmaking. I was familiar with American films. I thought I had learned a great deal. But when I was actually faced with the problem of handling actors on location, of looking through the camera, I could see that all of this was not of very much use, because my style, my technique, would have to evolve from the material. My knowledge of the Bengali village came from the book. It was a kind of an encyclopedia. Obviously, I was influenced by Indian painting a great deal, though not directly; it's a matter of details. I read some of the Sanskrit dramas and Bengali folk poetry and ballads, and I thought this marvelous visual quality, the imagery of these ballads, were very cinematic.

Your latest films, particularly The Chess Players, *tend to be more openly political than your earlier films. What brought about the change?*

It happened without my being totally aware of it. Obviously, in the Apu trilogy you couldn't make the kind of political statement that is in *The Chess Players.* Back then I was making social statements, which I thought were enough. I was describing the life of a section of my community, of the Bengali people. That was a sufficiently important thing to do. But I made a film fairly early on about decaying feudalism called *The Music Room. The Chess Players* has a similar sort of theme. Then I made a sort of satire called *The Philosopher's Stone.* That is not known in the West at all—it was my first satiric comedy. Then came *Devi*—or *The Goddess*—which was about superstition and religious dogmatism. I went on to make *The Big City,* which was about Calcutta and its problems, about women having to go out to work. Then I wanted to make a classical story, and I took a story by Rabindranath Tagore and made *Charulata.* You see, I don't like to repeat myself. I look for new themes, new styles, new genres, new milieus, new people to work with. It's been an exploration of various social problems, various periods in history.

I finally arrived at a point where I wanted to really concern myself with situations in Calcutta in my own time. I made *Days and Nights in the Forest* which was about Calcutta people cut off from their normal surroundings, with things happening in a remote sort of place. The emotional problems were related to an urban class. Fairly early on I had made a similar film about Calcutta people called *Kanchenjunga,* which was my first original screenplay. It was about a family on holiday up in the Himalayas—their personal psychological problems. *Days and Nights* was a return to the same kind of texture and structure. It was followed by *The Adversary* and by *Company Limited.* The first one about a young man without a job and his problems. The second one about a young man *with* a job and his problems.

Your films sometimes offer pointed commentary on the role of women in India. I'm thinking of the wife in The Chess Players. *She longs for her husband, who is off playing chess, but custom forces her to merely wait for him.*

She waits. Women had to follow certain social customs. So she sends the servant to fetch him. She can't go out and face the husband's friend. It was an early Muslim period, and the women were what is known as purdah—

they were behind. They had to be inside the house; they couldn't come outside. She comes outside once, to throw the chess pieces, but that's an emotional reaction.

How much of that tradition changed for Indian women?

There's a tremendous amount of emancipation. *The Big City,* a film I made in the midsixties, deals entirely with that aspect. A wife who would normally be just a housewife suddenly is faced with a situation where she has to go out and find a job just to make ends meet. She gets a job as a salesgirl. The in-laws are terribly upset at what she is doing. But she becomes a success in her work and begins to earn more than the husband. Then there is psychological conflict between the two.

Has censorship affected your films?

Not to a very serious extent, because I have always been oblique in my statements, even on human relationships. In any case, we can't afford to be too permissive. And I'm not particularly anxious to be too permissive, because I think that there has to be some room left for suggestion and obliqueness. In the cinema there is, I believe, a strong political censorship—there is a censorship of violence. There's a lot of fighting in the new commercial cinema, but there's no blood shown. Apparently you are free to show a lot of bashing about. But if you show catsup, then you are in for it.

How did the government feel about The Chess Players?

The censors didn't object to the film at all. They have just given it the Best Picture of the Year award and the Best Photography award in India. It is known as the President's Gold Medal, and there is some money with it. With *Pather Panchali,* in fact, the government was not particularly anxious to send it out of the country. It was Nehru who eventually intervened, and the picture was sent out. I think they put a stupid little title at the beginning that says, "Such conditions do not exist in India anymore," or something like that.

You seem to cast your actors with special precision. For example, in The Chess Players, *I was struck by how right the faces of the nobility were.*

We were very particular about finding the right faces to suggest that period, that kind of nobility.

Do you mostly use actors?

My method has changed, or, rather, I have used various methods. In the Apu trilogy I used mostly nonactors. Not just nonprofessionals, but non-actors. In *Pather Panchali,* though, the father was a professional actor. The mother had acted on the stage. The old woman had been on the stage in the early twenties and was resurrected for this film, the first film she'd ever made. At that time I used nonprofessionals a great deal—nonactors or amateurs who had never faced a camera before. But with *The Chess Players,* I had to use a different method, because I was dealing here with Hindu, a language which was not my own language. In my Bengali films, when I use nonprofessionals, I have often to do a lot of acting myself to demonstrate what I want. But not being fluent in the language of this particular film, I had to use reliable professional actors with whose work I was familiar and on whom I knew I could depend.

Why did you decide to make The Chess Players *in Hindi?*

There are many answers to that. I liked the story. I had read it a long, long time ago when it was first translated into English. I was a chess addict myself at one time. I wanted to pay a sort of tribute to chess. Also, of late it has become necessary to make films in color, because black-and-white stock is very poor. We are forced to use an East German stock, which the labs are not used to. Awful. I am just not satisfied with the gradations I've been getting, so color has become a necessity. The moment you use color the cost goes up, and you have to think of a larger audience. My Bengali-language films reach a very, very small section of the Indian public. So there you have another reason—a bigger audience and, therefore, a language which is understood more or less all over India, which is Hindi. Well, it's not strictly Hindi; it's Urdu, a classical form of Hindi. And then I was interested in this particular period in Indian history—the Raj period, as we call it—and this particular political event.

The original story is hardly a dozen pages, and it concerns only the two chess-playing friends. The British takeover of the prince's state is just mentioned as an event happening in the background. I decided to expand the story and to have the political event running parallel to the original story. Eventually the film turned out to be bilingual—English and Hindi—because there was an opportunity to use Richard Attenborough. I've given you quite a number of reasons, but there are others as well. I was anxious to work with some of Bombay's professional actors. They're intelligent people, and they're unhappy because they're mostly acting in very stupid kinds of films. I know some of them personally, and they've often expressed a wish to work with me. So I thought this was a good opportunity. There was, for example, Saeed Jaffrey, whom I'd known before, and whom I had seen briefly in a film of James Ivory's called *The Guru*. We had talked about acting a little bit and I said, "Well, perhaps someday we'll work together." I found an opportunity to call him.

What was the budget for The Chess Players?

It's still low by American standards. It was $500,000, but that is five times the budget of my Bengali films, which is a hundred thousand on the average, with color. With black and white, it's even lower.

Unlike conventional films, the two stories in The Chess Players *are never woven together.*

Yes, I knew I was taking a risk there. But I thought that, toward the end of the film, the thematic link would emerge. I was prepared to take the risk.

In The Chess Players *the streets of the city look unnaturally empty. Was the absence of crowds dictated by the budget?*

No. Actually there were very few scenes shot on location. Lucknow, where the locations were done, has too many anachronistic elements, so we couldn't use wide shots there. We had to be very careful to avoid electric poles and things like that. In any case, there are certain crowd scenes, like the cockfight and the kite flying. The other few location shots are all concerned with Saeed Jaffrey walking through lanes which in the daytime are deserted anyway. I haven't shown any main streets because of all the things that would interfere, like wall posters, motorcars, bicycles. It was not possible. Perhaps that's a lack in the film. Perhaps it should have contained more scenes with crowds to suggest there is a big population there.

We had a pretty big crowd around the camera, I can assure you. It's almost impossible to shoot in the streets in Indian cities. There must have been about six hundred people there breathing down my back. They were just right behind me! Of course, one gets used to almost everything. We are getting used to another phenomenon—power failure in Calcutta, which happens about three times a day. It happens often in the middle of shooting. You sit and wait for electrical power to come back. It may take three or four hours. It happens at the time of editing. The worst is when it happens during processing in the lab. It's just because I enjoy filmmaking so much that I can keep going. There's nothing like it. I wouldn't change my profession a second time.

Do you always enjoy shooting?

Yes. Every stage of it. Not just shooting. First, it's finding a story which excites you. Second, it's converting it into the terms of a screenplay. Third, it's casting, which I do myself. People just come to my house. There's a knock on the door, and there's somebody waiting outside with acting ambitions. I usually keep a photograph, name, address and vital statistics. Eventually, I may send for the person. It's happened many times. Then, of course, there is costume design, the set. I'll sit down with my art director to decide on the props. For this particular film, *The Chess Players,* all of the props are period props. All the shawls, the lovely ornamental things that the characters wear, some of them have come from museums. Most of them have come from private collections in Calcutta. Then the shooting is exciting, in spite of all the odds. Most exciting of all is sitting at the Moviola and cutting, when the thing comes to life. I do my music also. That's exciting, again.

You really are, then, not a film director but a filmmaker?

I am a filmmaker. It says on my passport I am a filmmaker. An auteur!

What led you to open The Chess Players *with animation?*

I decided on a prologue when I discovered that not many people were familiar with the political background of this event—the takeover of a prince's state. I'm not talking of foreign audiences, but of Indian audiences. I discussed it with many people, and they were a little vague about what exactly happened. They didn't know the background, the relation-

ship between the British and the Muslims of that period. So I decided
that a prologue was necessary as a device to set the stage for the things that
were going to happen. In order to relate events, I decided on using animation, because I couldn't think of a better way of doing it. There was a
line in a letter which is quoted in the film, a letter written by Lord Dal-
housie: "That's one cherry that's going to drop in our mouth one day." It
seemed to suggest the cartoon form. The decision to use animation arose
from that particular line.

*Is there much opportunity in India to see the works of the new Western filmmak-
ers, for example, German directors like Fassbinder?*

Our equivalent of the American Film Institute in Calcutta has regular
screenings of the new German cinema. I have unfortunately been either
working on a film, or been away, so I have only seen one Fassbinder, *Chinese Roulette.* I find him interesting. Definitely interesting. He's so prolific, I'm amazed at his output. But the new German cinema is quite well
known there. We have an actively thriving film society movement in Calcutta. There are about a dozen film societies composed mainly of students. They've grown over the last ten to fifteen years. We have seasons of
Bulgarian, Czech, Polish, Hungarian films regularly.

Who do you particularly admire among contemporary filmmakers?

It's now more individual films than filmmakers, because the filmmaker
you admire will not always satisfy you. I have great admiration for
Bergman. I like Truffaut. I like some of the American directors like Coppola, who is very talented, and Scorsese—not that I have seen all of their
work, but I'm hoping to catch up with them. I usually do, at film festivals
when I go abroad. I have a great admiration for the Japanese cinema. I
think they have made some of the greatest films ever. Kurosawa, for example. But it's Bergman I continue to be fascinated by. I think he's remarkable. I envy his stock company, because given actors like that one could
do extraordinary things.

Have you written all of the films that you directed?

All of them. I write my own screenplays. But many of them have been
based on other people's stories and novels, considerably adapted.

Would you consider directing someone else's screenplay?

I would probably want to hammer it into some kind of personal shape. After all, it would have to be my personal statement. Maybe there is somebody who feels exactly as I do.

What form do your scripts take?

My scripts are in visual form. They are not written documents which can be duplicated and passed out to the members of the crew. They're just little framed sketches with directions down on the right-hand side, and little notes on dialogue and camera movements. I don't think it's a literary medium anyway, so why waste work? It's only when the question of publication comes that you have to devise a kind of part-novel, part-drama form. But I've never wasted time in being literary.

What led to your approach?

Well, I was trained as a painter; I did illustrations. But I'm not the only one who works this way. I once saw a script by Kurosawa which looks exactly like mine. I know of some other directors who use a visual form.

How do you go about getting a producer and getting funds with such a sketchy script?

The usual method is the conventional Hollywood method of writing a screenplay. Mine is a very special method. That is why I was not able to get any money for my first film, because the sight of my script terrified producers. "What is all of this?" they would say. Producers want to know what the story is about. But it so happened that in *Pather Panchali* much of the impact of the film came from the visuals, certain things which cannot be described in words. When I found that producers were not to be convinced, I produced a book of drawings. While telling the story, I would show them the drawings—"And this is what it's going to look like. This is what is going to happen." It didn't work either. But anyway, the success of the first film helped me. Ever since then I've had my freedom to do just what I like.

Do you tend to plan your films very carefully before shooting them?

Yes, I do. That's been my practice right from the start. The first film had no proper script because the film was made while I still had my advertising job. It was all in my head. It was shot on weekends over a period of two years, because for long stretches we had no money. In fact, the film was shelved several times, and everybody was told, "That's all. We can't work." But later on, realizing that I was making films in the Bengali language, which is a minority language, and that I was aiming at a more sophisticated audience, let us say, I had to be very economical. If you want to be economical, you have to be disciplined. So everything is very carefully planned in my films.

My shooting ratio, incidentally, is four to one. It's been that all of the way through and is rarely exceeded. But there is room left for improvisation, particularly if I'm shooting on location. I get ideas. A certain change of climate, some wind rises, or clouds come and I have to do things which are not in the script. I find new camera angles all of the time. But shooting in the studio, confined within the three or four walls of the set, I have to be very careful.

How many takes do you generally do?

There's hardly any more than two or three takes to a shot. Often the first take is the best, and I keep it.

Before the shooting, do you discuss the film with your actors?

If they want to discuss it, I have no objection to oblige them. I've worked with actors who are very anxious to know all of the motivations and so forth. I wouldn't want to disappoint them. Generally, what happens now is that there is a stage when the screenplay is finished, and the main actors assemble. I read the screenplay aloud. In the process of reading it, I am also doing some acting, being the various actors. They get their cues from that to a certain extent. Of course, later, before shooting, there is a discussion stage, because the director is the only person who has the sweep of the film in his head. Never the actors, never anybody else on the set. So I have to guide them as to emphasis—what comes before, what is going to come after. That is how you achieve a balance and the right sort of rhythm. It is the director, after all, who knows the film from beginning to end while it's being made. But the others are not expected to know the film to the same extent. Therefore, you guide them. You would probably tell them, "The scene that precedes it is this, and this is what is there. So don't overdo it. You have to keep to this level. You have this following. So there you build up." That sort of thing.

The pacing of your films seems invariably slower than Western films.

Yes, that would apply to a great many of my films, but not all. If you see *The Middleman,* or even if you see *Company Limited,* they are much faster paced because they deal with the city, which is technological. The pace arises out of the material anyway. With the trilogy, I dealt with a life where the rhythm itself was slow. In *The Chess Players* I was dealing with indolence and laziness and leisure, in which the pace again had to be slow to be truthful to the times and to the subject. I have made a couple of children's films. One is called *The Golden Fortress,* an adventure-thriller-comedy, which moves fairly fast. It's not that as an Indian I would like to move slow all of the time. You see, the kinds of films that I make deal with certain subtle relationships between human beings. There is no language which is like a telegraphic language for this kind of a film. You have to take your time. You have to make points slowly, surely, because gestures are often taking the place of words, speech or action. It's small, small things. Well, let's call them chamber music films.

Music seems to have special importance in your films. What do you see as its use?

I've been using less and less music in my films of late because I've always had the feeling that background music was one element that was not part of pure cinema. It was an admission of inadequacy on the part of the screenplay writer—or the director, perhaps—to have to use music to underline certain things. Perhaps it was out of a lack of confidence in the audience. Of course, I was quite surprised to see some of the American films of the thirties, for example, *Scarface,* which had no music at all. It's later—late thirties and early forties—that music really came into its own. Then you had the big composers like Max Steiner and Erich Wolfgang Korngold and Alfred Newman writing symphonic scores which run right through the film almost. I find that those are the films which have dated most now.

I personally prefer a slightly drier approach, but I realize that one cannot do without music. In the trilogy I did not write my own music. I used Ravi Shankar, as you probably know. The film without the music would have seemed slower, I'm afraid. I think what music does is to provide the audience with something to react to so that they are kept occupied. At least their ears are kept occupied. With that, there is something happening.

What do you think about using music as counterpoint?

Yes, fine. That's one of the recommended uses, certainly. Kubrick has done that in his films, using "The Blue Danube" for *2001: A Space Odyssey*. I think it's better to do it that way, because the other way would be totally logical. It would be saying the same thing in terms of music as is being expressed in rhetorical terms. In any case, I don't like the Mickey Mouse-ing of music by providing songs with every action. That's very bad.

I watch my films with the audiences. Certainly on the opening night, but I also go just to see how the audience is reacting. I've often found that the audience's reaction in a way changes the film for me. Often, during the passages which have very little dialogue, or just subtle things on the soundtrack, and no music, I felt terrified. I wanted to walk out of the theater. I would think, now why didn't I use music here, which would pacify the public who are being restive and fidgety? It remains a very acute problem, I think, whether to use music or not. I would ideally like not to use music at all. I certainly do not approve of well-known pieces of classical music used in the background. What happens is that the film is rarely able to come up to the level of the music. What really happens is that the music is brought down to the level of the film, which is upsetting.

How did you work with Ravi Shankar on the Apu trilogy?

Shankar was then already a very famous concert virtuoso who was constantly touring, if not outside of India, then inside India. For *Pather Panchali* he was available for just a day. I was able to show him half of the film in rough cut. The music I wouldn't say was composed, because there was nothing written down. He just hummed and whistled, and the musicians just performed. All the music was done in a single session. This is not the best way of doing it, mind you. I got worried, and I had him play three-minute and four-minute pieces and various ragas in various tempos. Either a solo sitar or in combination with the flute, with drums, whatever.

But a lot of the work was done in the cutting room. There was considerable wrestling with the music and the images.

I worked with Ravi Shankar on four films. He's a close friend of mine. He has wonderful ideas. He plays superb musicals. I would love to use his sitar. But the fact remains that he is not a professional film composer. If asked to compose a piece of music which runs for two minutes and seven seconds, he would just throw up his hands and say, "It can't be done." Later, I worked with another great sitar virtuoso called Ustad Vilayat Khan. Then I worked with Ali Akbar Khan. By that time I was getting ideas of my own. Music has always been my first love, right from my school days. I was very fond of Western classical music and also of Indian classical music. There was a period when my favorite bedside reading was a miniature score. I then decided to try my hand at composing. It was very difficult in the beginning, but like everything else, I taught myself.

Have you ever recut your film based on the audience's response?

I don't think that I've ever done that. Once the film goes to the theater, I don't touch it at all. Early in my career, at the first screening, when just the crew and I watched, I made one or two cuts. *Aparajito* was cut, and one or two other films. But what happened in those days was that I would always be faced with a release deadline. The final cutting was always done in a hurry, which is a terribly wrong thing to do, but we were forced to. *Pather Panchali* was cut over a period of ten days because the Museum of Modern Art in New York had announced the world premiere on a certain day in April. Ten days and ten nights my editor and I worked, with no sleep, to do the final cut. When the print came out, I had no chance to see it. Pan American flew it over to New York immediately. When the second print came out, I saw it for myself and made some cuts after that.

How did that screening at the Museum of Modern Art come about?

John Huston had come to Calcutta to set up *The Man Who Would Be King* at that time with Humphrey Bogart. He was staying at the same hotel as Renoir had. I went and said, "I am making a film, Mr. Huston. I know your work." He was quite impressed, because I knew his work very well indeed. He said, "Well, I would like to see what you've done." I think I had about six or seven reels of rough cut at that time. I ran it for him without sound, because there was no soundtrack yet. He happened to be a friend of Monroe Wheeler, who was with the Museum of Modern Art and who was setting up an exhibition of Indian paintings. I got a letter from Monroe saying, "I want your film. If John Huston likes it, his word is good enough for me. But this is the date when you have to have it here in New York."

You operate your own camera?

I've been doing so for the last fifteen years. Not that I have no trust in my cameraman's operational abilities, but the best position to judge the acting from is through the lens. Also I've noticed, working with nonprofessionals, that they are happier if they don't see my face while I'm directing. I'm not staring at them. So they are happier, they feel more relaxed. I have a lighting cameraman, and now I'm using a second cameraman.

I started with one cameraman, Subrata Mitra, who was a beginner. He was twenty-one when he shot the first film—he'd never handled a movie camera in his life. I had to have a new cameraman because all of the professionals said that you can't shoot in rain, and you can't shoot out of doors, that the light keeps changing, that the sun goes down too fast and so forth. I got a new cameraman, and we decided on certain basic things. We believed in available light. We aimed at simulating available light in the studio by using bounced lights. It didn't happen with the first film, but with the second film, when we had to shoot interiors in the studio— supposedly of houses in Benares, where there was a central courtyard with no roof and the light all came from the sky. It was a kind of top lighting, shadowless. We started using bounced lighting, with a cloth stretched over, and the lights bounced back from it.

What kind of cloth?

Just white sheets, what we call longcloths. We also had framed pieces of white cloth, large enormous things, and we bounced backlight from those, which established a source of light. If it's a lantern, if it's electric light, you follow the source. It simplifies things. About seven or eight years later, I read an article in *American Cinematographer* written by Sven Nykvist—at the time of *Through a Glass Darkly,* I think—claiming the invention of bounced light. We had been doing it since 1954. The cameraman and I spend a great deal of time in discussions, but I have already composed my images. Everything is decided beforehand—with the color film, all of the color schemes, every piece of costume. I go out myself to buy the material.

Do you prefer black and white?

No, no. *The Chess Players* I can't imagine in black and white. On *Distant Thunder* I was attacked by some of our critics for using color for a subject that deals with poverty. But one of the points that the author of the original story makes is that this was a famine that was not caused by a lack of harvest or by a drought. Nature remained beautiful, people died and suffered in surroundings of great physical beauty. I was only reflecting what the author had said in the book.

Does the Indian government provide help to young filmmakers?

Many of the state governments are now giving grants to young filmmakers who are not able to obtain money from the usual sources—the usual sources being independent producers. There is no such thing as a bank financing a production. It's just individuals who come forward with more money, and eventually the distributors also advance money. It's been difficult for some of the young people who would like to break new ground to get money from the usual sources. Some of the states in West Bengal are just beginning to provide grants. But some of the southern states are already doing so. There is also something called Film Finance Corporation which advances money to young filmmakers.

Are your films widely distributed within India?

Not very widely. *The Chess Players* opened first in Delhi, not in Calcutta—where I come from—because of the language problem. It was decided to open in areas where the people would be familiar with the language. But my Bengali films play in the major cities in my state, and they play in the other big cities, like Bombay and Delhi and Madras. In Delhi I can get them shown only on Sunday mornings. In Bombay it's very difficult to find a theater in the main city, so they're shown in the small suburban cinemas. There's an exceptional town called Bangalore, in south India, where my films in their original version play for five or six weeks at a stretch in a proper theater. They just have a very sophisticated film audience there.

Why only on Sunday mornings in Delhi?

The exhibitors just won't show a Bengali film otherwise. But I have nothing to do with distribution. I just direct the films. Then the producer takes over and the distributors take over. I'm told that there's great reluctance on the part of the exhibitors in Delhi to take a chance with a Bengali film, even if it's by Satyajit Ray. They want to play safe. They want a film that will play for weeks and weeks. There's no dearth of those in India.

Where are your films most popular?

They are popular in Calcutta. I have an audience there built up over the years. I have a very staunch following, as they say. Whatever I make will play in three cinemas in three parts of the city for at least six weeks. Then, of course, word of mouth takes over. But if word of mouth is weak, then the picture will fold up.

And outside India, like London?

Some of my recent films have had reasonably long runs in London. Some have been bought by Eastern European countries. The Soviet Union has bought a few. Czechoslovakia at one time bought two or three.

Who sees your films in India?

The educated people—not necessarily sophisticated as a film audience, but educated people who are familiar with the literary sources of the films. The films don't reach the really suburban places, where there is a dominance of the commercial cinema. There are no theaters to play our films there, but we have the big cities in Bengal.

How many feature films are produced in India each year?

I believe it's in the neighborhood of six hundred. Out of that, about sixty percent are produced in Bombay, in Hindi. A large number are produced in Madras, in another language and also in Hindi. We in Bengal make, on average, twenty to twenty-five features a year. It's a small industry there.

Do you have a philosophy that you care to articulate?

It's there in my films. I'm afraid I can't be articulate about it. I'm very bad at verbalizations. That's why I'm not a writer; I'm a filmmaker. I'm afraid you will have to draw your own conclusions.

◆

Films as Director

1955 *Pather Panchali* (also screenplay)

1957 *Aparajito* (also producer and screenplay)
Parash Pathar

1958 *The Music Room* (also producer and screenplay)

1960 *Devi*

1961 *Rabindranath Tagore* (also screenplay)
Kanchenjungha (also producer and screenplay)

1962 *Abhijan* (also screenplay)
Teen Kanya (also producer and screenplay)

1963 *Mahanagar* (also screenplay)

1964 *Charulata* (also screenplay)

1965 *Kapurush-o-Mahapurush* (also screenplay)

1966 *Nayak* (also screenplay)

1967 *Chiriakhana* (also screenplay)

1969 *Goopy Gyne Bagha Byne* (also screenplay)

1970 *Days and Nights in the Forest* (also screenplay)

1971 *Seemabaddha*
Sikkim (also screenplay)

1972 *Pratidwandi* (also screenplay)

1973 *Asani Sanket* (also screenplay)

1974 *Sonar Kella* (also screenplay)

1975 *Jana Aranya* (also screenplay)

1977 *The Chess Players* (also screenplay)

1978 *Joi Baba Felunath* (also screenplay)

1984 *Ghare Bahire* (also screenplay)

1989 *Ganashatru* (also screenplay)

1990 *Shakha Proshakha* (also screenplay)

1991 *Agantuk* (also producer and screenplay)

Acknowledgments

The American Film Institute is the mother lode of this book, so all those involved in AFI's creation deserve thanks, especially Gregory Peck, who was with me as chairman when the journey started in 1967, and Charlton Heston, who picked up the baton from Greg and with whom I later served as cochairman. Jean Firstenberg succeeded me as AFI director in 1980 and serves to this day.

The interviews in this book are drawn from transcripts of seminars recorded at AFI beginning in 1969. Several seminars were printed in a different form in AFI's *Dialogue on Film* in the 1970s, and some in our magazine, *American Film*. In instances where an individual gave more than one seminar, the text has been constructed from two or more meetings. The transcripts have been edited for clarity, while care has been taken to retain the intended meaning.

Paul Cronin has been my right hand on this book, assisting me with the editing, and offering knowledge and good advice throughout the entire process. He is talented and tenacious, and I am fortunate that he chose to devote so much of his time to this project.

The AFI staff has been helpful, notably Caroline Cisneros, the AFI librarian who tracked down tapes and transcripts of the seminars. Pat Hanson and the *AFI Catalog* staff were most helpful with the filmographies, as was Nancy Ostertag, who located photos from the seminars. Linda Mehr, Bob Cushman and the staff at the Academy of Motion Picture Arts and Sciences were also helpful. Amy Schireson conducted photo research, and Donna Salmon obtained clearances. Ron Mandelbaum at Photofest also provided photographs. Howell Begle and Christopher Murray sorted out legal matters. Jess Morgan, my business manager for more than thirty years, gave his customary reliable and wise advice.

I want to remember those who took leading roles in the early days of the Center for Advanced Film Studies and conducted many of the seminars. Toni Vellani brought intellect and creative discipline to the conservatory; James Silke provided insight and respect for the filmmakers; James Blue offered his film sense and keen curiosity; James Powers supervised the seminar program. Adrian Borneman, Christine Lamentia and Jane Payne were especially helpful as my assistants over the years.

Dottie McCarthy has worked with me since 1988. Her wisdom, resourcefulness, dedication and attention to detail contributed to this volume and to all my other work as well.

Victoria Wilson of Alfred A. Knopf, a bold and perceptive editor, recognized the potential in these seminars, commissioned the book and nurtured its development. Lynn Nesbit sold this book to Knopf, causing a dream to become a reality.

My wife, Elizabeth, and our children, Caroline, Michael and David, were a source of support, love and encouragement during the taxing years of AFI's creation, as they continue to be to this day.

And, of course, I must state my profound respect for the filmmakers whose ideas grace these pages. Their films have enriched my life beyond measure.

Illustrations

Sources

Alpert, Hollis. *Fellini: A Life.* Atheneum, 1986.

———. *The Life and Times of Porgy and Bess.* Alfred A. Knopf, 1990.

Baer, William, ed. *Elia Kazan Interviews.* University Press of Mississippi, 2000.

Bazin, André. *What Is Cinema?* University of California Press, 1967.

Behlmer, Rudy. *Behind the Scenes.* Samuel French Trade, 1990.

Björkman, Stig, Torsten Manns, and Jonas Sima. *Bergman on Bergman: Interviews with Ingmar Bergman.* Trans. Paul Britten Austin. Simon and Schuster, 1970.

Brownlow, Kevin. *David Lean: A Biography.* Richard Cohen Books, 1996.

Cronin, Paul, ed. *George Stevens Interviews.* University Press of Mississippi, 2004.

Gottlieb, Sidney, ed. *Hitchcock on Hitchcock: Selected Writings and Interviews.* University of California Press, 1995.

Haver, Ronald. *A Star Is Born: The Making of the 1954 Movie and Its 1983 Restoration.* Alfred A. Knopf, 1988.

Kaminsky, Stuart M. *John Huston: Maker of Magic.* Houghton Mifflin Company, 1978.

Katz, Ephraim. *The Film Encyclopedia.* Revised by Fred Klein and Ronald Dean Nolen. Harper Resource, 2001.

LeRoy, Mervyn, and Dick Kleiner. *Mervyn LeRoy: Take One.* Hawthorn Books, 1974.

Levy, Emanuel. *George Cukor, Master of Elegance: Hollywood's Legendary Director and His Stars.* William Morrow and Company, 1994.

Long, Robert Emmet, ed. *George Cukor Interviews.* University Press of Mississippi, 2001.

———. *John Huston Interviews.* University Press of Mississippi, 2001.

Madsen, Axel. *William Wyler: The Authorized Biography.* Thomas Y. Crowell Company, 1973.

McBride, Joseph. *Frank Capra: The Catastrophe of Success.* Simon and Schuster, 1992.

McCarthy, Todd. *Howard Hawks: The Grey Fox of Hollywood.* Grove Press, 1997.

McGilligan, Patrick. *Film Crazy: Interviews with Hollywood Legends.* St. Martin's Press, 2000.

———. *Fritz Lang: The Nature of the Beast.* St. Martin's Press, 1997.

———. *George Cukor: A Double Life.* St. Martin's Press, 1991.

Renoir, Jean. *My Life and My Films.* Atheneum, 1974.

Silvester, Christopher, ed. *The Grove Book of Hollywood.* Grove Press, 1998.

———. *The Art of Alfred Hitchcock: Fifty Years of His Motion Pictures.* Hopkinson and Blake, 1976.

Spoto, Donald. *Stanley Kramer: Film Maker.* Samuel French, 1978.

Vance, Jeffrey, and Suzanne Lloyd. *Harold Lloyd: Master Comedian.* Harry Abrams, 2002.

Vidor, King. *On Film Making.* David McKay Company, 1972.

Walsh, Raoul. *Each Man in His Time: The Life Story of a Director.* Farrar, Straus and Giroux, 1974.

Wanamaker, Marc. "George Folsey." *American Cinematographer,* July 1985.

Zinnemann, Fred. *Fred Zinnemann: A Life in the Movies.* Charles Scribner's Sons, 1992.

Index

Page numbers in *italics* refer to illustrations.

A Note on the Type

This book was set in Adobe Garamond.
Designed for the Adobe Corporation by Robert
Slimbach, the fonts are based on types first cut by Claude
Garamond (c. 1480–1561). Garamond was a pupil of
Geoffrey Tory and is believed to have followed the
Venetian models, although he introduced a number of
important differences, and it is to him that we owe the
letter we now know as "old style." He gave to his letters
a certain elegance and feeling of movement that won
their creator an immediate reputation and the
patronage of Francis I of France.

Composed by North Market Street Graphics,
Lancaster, Pennsylvania
Printed and bound by Berryville Graphics,
Berryville, Virginia